D1548351

Paschal
Beverly
Randolph

R. POOLE.   NASHVILLE, TENN.

SUNY Series in
Western Esoteric Traditions

David Appelbaum, Editor

Paschal Beverly Randolph

A Nineteenth-Century Black American Spiritualist, Rosicrucian, and Sex Magician

John Patrick Deveney

with a Foreword
by
Franklin Rosemont

Unity Library & Archives
1901 NW Blue Parkway
Unity Village, MO 64065

STATE UNIVERSITY OF NEW YORK PRESS

o6\o9

Frontispiece and photo on front cover courtesy of Dr. Gerald E. Poesnecker.

Production by Ruth Fisher
Marketing by Theresa Abad Swierzowski

Published by
State University of New York Press, Albany

©1997 State University of New York

For information, address the State University of New York Press,
State University Plaza, Albany, NY 12246

Library of Congress Cataloging-in-Publication Data
Deveney, John P. (John Patrick)
    Paschal Beverly Randolph : a nineteenth-century Black American
spiritualist, Rosicrucian, and sex magician / John Patrick Deveney.
        p.   cm. — (SUNY series in Western esoteric traditions)
    Includes bibliographical references and index.
    ISBN 0-7914-3119-3 (CH : alk. paper). — ISBN 0-7914-3120-7 (PB :
alk. paper)
    1. Randolph, Paschal Beverly, 1825–1874. 2. Afro-American
occultists—Biography.   I. Title.   II. Series.
    BF1408.2.R364   1997
133'.092—dc20
[B]   95-52244
                                                              CIP

10 9 8 7 6 5 4 3 2 1

To
TK and JJ and PAA
and
to the memory of Mircea Eliade

CONTENTS

*I*LLUSTRATIONS

$\mathcal{F}$OREWORD

All-out war on conventional wisdom is always a duty and a pleasure, not only for poets and hipsters but also for historians and anyone who is not a salaried flatterer of the *status quo*. Not surprisingly, such spiritual guerrillas find much of their best ammunition in the works of those whose wisdom is resolutely *un*conventional: nonconformists so radically outside the "main currents" of their time that they can't help calling all those currents into question.

The problem is, since these recalcitrants by definition don't fit into existing categories, they tend to be left out altogether. They are the homeless of intellectual history. Once their names are scratched from the map, it's hard for later seekers to find them, or even to learn of their existence. Their exclusion from biographical dictionaries is inanely taken as proof of their unimportance; inertia does the rest. The basic ingredient of what E. P. Thompson called "the enormous condescension of posterity" is an overwhelming distractedness, perpetrated nonstop by the official media. Tracers of history's missing persons not only have to cut through the locked steel doors of the ruling ideologies, but also through the massive indifference of a systematically stupefied society.

The way is rough but the rewards (nonmonetary, of course) are great. Recovering lost, ignored and—let's face it—suppressed witnesses of the past does a lot to remoralize the demoralized here and now. And when these rescue missions help topple the dominant models of the past, they make it easier for those who are trying to make the present more liveable. For sheer intellectual excitement, that's hard to beat.

John Patrick Deveney's groundbreaking study of Paschal Beverly Randolph (1825–1875) overflows with this excitement, and he is clearly eager to share it with others. From the remotest corner of oblivion he has retrieved a truly astonishing personage and restored him to a fully merited high place among the most daring against-the-current thinkers of his time. A major contribution to studies of United States culture, this book should do much to dispel long-entrenched misconceptions regarding mid-nineteenth-century nonacademic intellectual life. In the history of American thought, as Deveney convincingly demonstrates, the impact of heterodox undercurrents has been far greater and more enduring than apologists for the "mainstream" have wanted to acknowledge. Moreover, by tracing the involvement of an outspoken occultist in the most vital popular movements of his time, Deveney helps expand the limits of social history, and signals the importance of a heretofore ignored dimension of American radicalism. At the very least this book will drive home the point that there were far more interesting things going on in the life of the mind a hundred and fifty years ago than Arthur Schlesinger, Jr. ever dreamed of.

"The Man With Two Souls," as Paschal Beverly Randolph liked to call himself, was a man of many parts. Like many African–American and working-class visionaries, he was born and raised in the New York slums. A free black, self-taught, always poor, and something of a nomad, he grew up a complete stranger to the ends and means of instrumental rationalism, and came to specialize in the cultivation of nonrational methods of research. His trance experiences started in childhood. A leading, albeit dissident, figure in the Spiritualist movement from its early days, he was later renowned as the best known scryer of his time. Wholly at odds with an acquisitive culture that worshipped common sense and the work ethic, he was incapable of adjusting to the routines of daily life in a rapidly industrializing America. In the Age of the Robber Barons he devoted himself largely to the theory and practice of magic and love, and to the exploration of paranormal psychic states. By trade a practitioner of (to put it mildly) unorthodox medicine, he was a leading confectioner of love potions and a pioneer experimenter with drugs as an aid to philosophical inquiry.

As Deveney shows, Randolph's greatest legacy lies in his writings. He authored over a score of books and numerous pamphlets, all quaint and curious volumes of forgotten lore. Most passed through multiple editions; some were translated into other languages. Like most writers, he had his bad days, and his work is decidedly uneven. Beneath the bombast, however, lies plenty of pure gold. Clearly motivated by impulses that transcended literature, his disquieting novels hover at the crossroads of hermeticism and schizophrenia. He wrote few poems, but authentic poetry flashes through his pages like lightning in a rainforest. His nonfiction, although that hardly seems the right word for much of it, focuses on clairvoyance, time-traveling, wrongs done to women in modern society, sexual disorders, ethnology, erotic elixirs, and magic mirrors. Indomitable theorist of "solar language," he coined such delightful neologisms as Zorvoyance, Tirauclairism, Eulidic, Feminantia, and Sexagyma— all thus far mysteriously overlooked by our leading lexicographers.

He was in touch with many of the best minds of his generation—occultists, poets, revolutionists, and other wayward thinkers, including Frederick Douglass, Thomas Lake Harris, Benjamin Paul Blood, Ethan Allen Hitchcock, Alexander Wilder and Victoria Woodhull. Echoes of his meetings with these and many other remarkable men and women recur in his writings. As Abolitionist, Radical Reconstructionist and, for a time, Black Nationalist, he had important things to say about race discrimination and the future glory of African civilization. An admirer of utopian socialist Charles Fourier, Randolph was himself a sharp critic of what he called our "false civilization."[1] Phrenologist O. S. Fowler pronounced Randolph "an out-and-out Radical in everything."[2] In his early novel,

Ravalette, Randolph joyfully announced "a religious, political, social, moral, emotional and philosophical upheaval, such as the modern world has never yet witnessed or even dreamed of."[3] His *After Death*, arguably the greatest Spiritualist utopia, is a witty *riposte* to its numerous sugar–water antecedents in the genre, and exemplifies Randolph's approach to dechristianization. His version of Rosicrucianism also fits in the radical utopian tradition. Of the esoteric secret societies he organized or inspired, one—the Hermetic Brotherhood of Luxor—exerted considerable international influence.[4]

Randolph was also a champion of women's rights. By today's standards his feminism may appear on the mild side, but he was writing in the 1860s and 1870s when, as Linda Gordon has pointed out, "the prohibition on birth control and on any open discussion of sexual matters had never been more severe."[5] Not only did Randolph make birth control and sexual matters, particularly female sexuality, his central topics, he was also a bold critic of androcentric values. Turning around Pope's old chestnut, he proclaimed that "The proper study of mankind is Woman!"[6]

Above all, Randolph was America's foremost exponent of *magic-inspired erotism*, or as he called it, *Affectional Alchemy*. "People may be proud of their *property*," he wrote, "but the human can have no true, deep joys, save such as spring from Love—pure, strong, earnest, spontaneous and reciprocal."[7] In the sexual love of man and woman he saw the greatest hope for the regeneration of the world, the key to personal fulfillment as well as social transformation, and the basis of a nonrepressive civilization. Nearly all of his books and pamphlets touch on these themes; many are completely devoted to them.

In short, Randolph is such a thoroughly fascinating character that one can hardly believe how thoroughly he was written off the books. Deveney deserves our heartiest thanks for putting a truly outstanding figure into circulation again. Of course, bringing back the dead like this, or otherwise pointing out that our image of the past is full of huge, gaping holes, tends to disturb those who cherish the prevailing illusions of their time. But aren't such disturbances part of the stuff that history is made of? Far from appearing in a vacuum, Deveney's resuscitation of Paschal B. Randolph reinforces and extends the efforts of many other researchers who refuse to regard history as something over and done with. Subversive in the best sense of the term, this liberation of the past is the mirror and echo of desirable days ahead. The way it looks now, the past will never be the same again. Linda Gordon's revelatory history of birth control, Robin D. G. Kelley's inspired studies of African-America's marvelously creative counterculture, and David Roediger's myth-unraveling exploration of American "whiteness"—to cite only three contemporary historians whose work has a direct bearing on Randolph's life and work—are admirable examples of this consciousness–expanding conception of history, a history turned toward the future.[8] Modestly aimed at retrieving the repressed, these works end up overturning age-old obfuscations. More or less incidentally they also reveal that a lot of "common knowledge" is false, and that the expertise of too many historians lies primarily in their ability to withhold vital information.

In the specific field of intellectual history—the history of ideas, books, authors, artists, readers, talkers, listeners, and their interaction in the broader culture—the past has also changed dramatically in recent years. As the "disappeared" figures of yesteryear are discovered anew, patterns begin to emerge. Randolph was in many ways a lone wolf, but there were others roaming at least some of the same terrain.

Consider George Lippard (1822–1854), the most popular United States writer of his day, prolific author of revolutionary Gothic novels, ardent student of Rosicrucian lore, an outspoken radical agitator and editor, with close ties to the extremist wing of the workers' movement. His *Quaker City, or, The Monks of Monk Hall* (1844–1845) was the best-selling United States book before *Uncle Tom's Cabin*, reprinted twenty-seven times in five years. If you haven't heard of him it's probably because he and his works were zapped from the record for well over a hundred years. It is largely thanks to literary historian David S. Reynolds that Lippard's magisterial work is being read again.[9]

Lydia Maria Child (1802–1880) was never as completely lost from sight as Lippard—her pioneering Abolitionist tract, *An Appeal in Favor of That Class of Americans Called Africans* (1833) simply could not be completely ignored, either in her own time, or in ours (at least, not after the Montgomery Bus Boycott). But she, too, was posthumously maneuvered into a position where obscurity was guaranteed. If Lippard was brutally blotted out, Child was disposed of by the old damned-by-faint-praise trick: politely noted in passing as a "one-book author," her other contributions were labeled "minor" (meaning: Don't Read Them), and that was that. Only with the publication of Carolyn Karcher's monumental biography has a wide public become aware of Child's marvelous and many–sided genius.[10] Karcher introduces us to a courageous activist who was not only an inquiring spirit, sensitive to social/cultural tremors commonly overlooked by her contemporaries, but also an original thinker whose increasingly radical vision is as pertinent to our time as her own.

Lippard, Child, and Randolph are among the great *outsiders* in the history of United States thought—rulebreaking free spirits who are only now emerging from a century or more of obliteration. Each differed from the others in many ways, but their agreement on essentials is striking. Politically and otherwise, they ventured far beyond the so-called "vital center" that academic Cold Warriors tried to pass off as the eternal heart and soul of American thought. Not only was their "take" on class, race, and gender more radical than that of most of their contemporaries, and ours—their whole *sensibility* was antithetical to middle-of-the-road caution, and yearned for Something Else. From their various points of view, what was wrong in United States life went much deeper than others seemed willing to admit. For them, the problems exceeded all national limits and involved an entire civilization. They also perceived that the problems involved the physical being of each and every individual; all three affirmed a freer sexuality and defended love against its puritanical and cynical enemies. Challenging what Child called "the great merciless machine of a falsely-constructed society,"[11] they found all ready-made solutions wanting. As partisans of Channing's "moral argument against Calvinism," participants in the post-Hegelian demystification of the "rational" and the "real," and adepts of Fourierist analogy, they readily accepted the imagination as guide, recognized poetry as a source of knowledge, grappled with the questions posed by dreams, and evinced sympathetic curiosity about "animal magnetism" and madness. In a period increasingly dominated by that quintessentially bourgeois form of intellectual tunnel vision known as *positivism*, they not only rejected the world-view of "the men of facts," as Child called them, but went so far as to envision a larger reality, open-ended, multidimensional and full of surprises.

In their writings, nonconformism is paramount. Spontaneous, digressive, hard to classify, genre-defying: Such are the works of Lippard, Child, and Randolph. Their novels diverge sharply from the conventionally novelistic, and their essays ramble heretically every which way. Not one wrote anything like the others, but they all wrote voluminously, in haste and desperation. All showed every sign of being "driven": they let themselves go, even to the point of losing control. All acknowledged their tendency toward incoherence. In a word, they stood at the threshold of *surrealism*, and I mean surrealism not as a journalistic synonym for bizarre, but as André Breton intended it: as the liberation of poetry and therefore as the *liberation of life*.[12] Lippard scholar David Reynolds uses the term again and again to describe and illuminate the many qualities that distinguish Lippard from his "American Renaissance" contemporaries.[13] Although I do not find the word in Carolyn Karcher's biography, her insightful discussion of Child's portrayal of modern urban life in *Letters from New York*—and particularly her comments on the book's "style of free association . . . allowing her unconscious mind to take over"[14]—bring to mind above all such surrealist classics as Louis Aragon's *Paris Peasant* and Gherasim Luca's *Passive Vampire*.

Most surrealist of them all was Paschal B. Randolph. More than any American of his time, he drew the lessons of "pure psychic automatism" and exemplified the quest to determine that "point in the mind" signaled by André Breton in his *Second Surrealist Manifesto* (1929), "where life and death, the real and the imaginary, past and future, the communicable and the incommunicable, the high and the low, cease to be perceived as contradictions."

Wholly in line with surrealism is Randolph's sparkling combination of utopian vision, poetic insight, revolutionary fervor, and black humor; his all-abiding sense of the interconnectedness of all phenomena—an intuitive protoecology, grounded in a love of the Marvelous; his serene confidence that a disenchanted world could be re-enchanted at last, and that the means to this emancipatory transformation are ready at hand.

Randolph embodied what Fourier called *absolute divergence*, a systematic deviation from accepted beliefs and procedures, which is another fundamental surrealist principle (and the title of the 1965–1966 International Surrealist Exhibition). Where others were content to stand pat, Randolph preferred to raise the stakes.

His surrealism was at its deepest and brightest in his Affectional Alchemy. Was there anyone in the United States of his day who delved more deeply into the *experience* of magic and alchemy, anyone who perceived more clearly their sexual basis and implications? Randolph's devotion to love, his passion for the emancipation and exaltation of woman, and for the eroticization of daily life, so radically counterposed to the dominant paradigms of his time (and our own): These are essentials of surrealism's revolution.

To put it simply: no one in the United States during the third quarter of the nineteenth-century exemplified the defining qualities of the surrealist project more than this ardent celebrator of "the seven grades of Love and its forty-nine modifications."[15] And if you think I'm exaggerating, or making this up, I hasten to add that the surrealists themselves, many decades ago, recognized Randolph as a precursor and inspired ally in their struggle to vanquish the forces of miserabilism and to liberate the Marvelous.

Precisely when and how Randolph entered the consciousness of the surrealist movement does not appear to have been recorded, but it is almost certain that this encounter dates back at least to the early 1930s, if not earlier. A group deeply interested in magic and sexuality—impassioned students of Fabre d'Olivet, Eliphas Lévi, Saint-Yves d'Alveydre, Sâr Péladan, R. Schwaller de Lubicz, René Guénon, and Fulcanelli—could not have missed *Magia sexualis*, Maria de Naglowska's charmingly illustrated translation of fragments from Randolph's published and unpublished writings, issued with her introduction in 1931 (*see* Bibliography). Some surrealists, moreover, were personally acquainted with Naglowska; poet/painter Camille Bryen, for example, is cited in a disciple's memoir of Naglowska as one of the latter's close associates in that period.[16] Another of her acquaintances, Ernest de Gengenbach—a former Catholic seminarian who, *circa* 1925–1930, scandalized the Paris public by frequenting the Surrealist Group in his priest's soutane, a beautiful woman on each arm—later became, for a time, an adherent of Naglowska's and her "Sacred Rite of Magic Love."[17] We know that Breton and others found further information on the author of *Eulis* in two books by Pierre Geyraud: *Parmi les sectes et les rites* (1936) and *Les Petites églises de Paris* (1937). It is also more than probable that Pierre Mabille and Kurt Seligmann, surrealists whose knowledge of the history and literature of magic was prodigious, knew something of Randolph.

Like many other esoteric works, *Magia sexualis* circulated among the surrealists for years before any of them mentioned it in print. Not until 1948 do we find Randolph's name in a surrealist publication: an illustrated excerpt from *Magia sexualis* (on magic mirrors) appeared in the second issue of the Paris group's broadsheet, *Néon*.[18] Proving that surrealist interest in his work was no passing fancy, Randolph was profiled in the *Succinct Lexicon of Erotism* published in the catalog of the 1959–1960 International Surrealist Exhibition, which was devoted to the theme of Eros.[19] This unsigned sketch, which also mentions Naglowska, was written at André Breton's request by Gérard Legrand, who had assisted Breton on his last major work, *L'Art magique* (1957).[20] Thirteen years later, the January 1970 issue of the paper *Coupure*, which Legrand coedited, featured an illustration from *Magia sexualis*. A new French edition of the book also appeared that year, prefaced by Gaston Ferdière, a psychoanalyst who, though not a member of the Surrealist Group, had closely followed its trajectory for many years. Finally, it is significant that the only serious study of Maria de Naglowska—an essay in which Randolph is also discussed—is the work of a surrealist: Sarane Alexandrian.[21]

Future research may reveal Randolph's influence on individual surrealists and on particular surrealist texts and images. For our present purposes it suffices to note that his writings on erotic magic were admired by surrealists early on for their imaginative audacity as well as what Alexandrian has called their "moral beauty," and that they remained a source of surrealist thought in later years.

Throughout this book, Deveney rightly focuses on Randolph's sexual magic, "The Mysteries of Eulis," love's "hidden history" and "several sacred rituals"—that is, precisely on the aspects of Randolph's project that mattered most to Randolph himself, and which, significantly, are also most relevant to surrealism. To clarify the development of this doctrine, Deveney devotes much attention to Randolph's multifarious activities in the international subterranean community of scholars, poets, madmen and charlatans known as "the occult," which—and this too is significant—was one of the few milieux in which serious discussion of love was possible at that time. That Deveney has been able to bring so much illumination to this secretive and shadowy domain is a major achievement and helps push back the boundaries of intellectual history.

Few United States historians have been able to discuss any kind of "crank" except tongue-in-cheek and "in passing." Full-blown occultists tend to make them sneer in disgust or, at best, throw up their hands in despair. Rare are those who have attempted to appreciate the views of such people *from within*, or to try to grasp their relation to other expressions of dissidence. Most historians of United States thought have in fact excluded occultists *a priori*. And yet, occultist influence is sometimes so all-pervasive—Madame Blavatsky's impact on the 1890s Bellamyist movement is a well-known example—that to ignore them is to throw the whole picture out of focus. In patiently guiding us down the labyrinthine byways of Randolph's lifelong involvement in the world of the occult, Deveney has provided a useful model for other historians who need to make their way through an intellectual terrain commonly regarded as impenetrable, and a literature derided as gibberish.

Motivated by his zeal to learn the truth about Randolph's life and work, and happily free of "postmodernist" or other neo–obscurantist jargon, Deveney's cool set-the-record-straight approach is exemplary. This book is a solid foundation that researchers in many fields will build on for years to come. I like to think that this first-ever biography will spark a widespread resurgence of interest in Randolph—that it will provoke not only new editions of his works but also special studies of his ideas and their relation to other currents of thought. However important Randolph may be as a historic figure, he was and remains a notable, albeit underground, *force* in the realm of ideas and inspirations, a thinker whose thought responds to many of the most urgent questions of our own time. His own "esoteric" pretensions notwithstanding, Randolph and his work deserve to be better known not only to historians and other scholars, but to any and all who are seriously concerned about the future of humankind and the planet we live on.

And that brings us back to surrealism. The fact that an African-American writer, who never was well known in his homeland and was almost completely forgotten after his death, should be recognized a half-century later as a forerunner, inspiration, and guide by the international "avante-garde" in Paris is a telling circumstance. Surrealism helps us understand those who have been expunged from the historic record because surrealism is above all a method of recovering what has been expunged from the notion of "reality": the subliminal, the unconscious, the repressed, also known as the embarrassing, the unsettling, the subversive. From the beginning, surrealism's revolution in poetry and the arts was accompanied by a sweeping revaluation of values. Such figures as Nicolas Flamel, Sade, Fourier, Flora Tristan, Lautréamont, Jarry, Saint-Pol-Roux, Oskar Panizza, and Jacques Vaché—who were either unknown, ignored, or despised until the surrealists took them up—gradually rose to the status of classics, no less. Only time will tell whether the surrealists' interest in Randolph is to be similarly vindicated. It is already clear, however, that his long-ignored work assumes a new luster—indeed, many heretofore undiscerned facets—*in the light of surrealism.* That he himself had contributed something to that light adds a dash of irony as well as poetic justice. Surely this is a case, to use an expression made famous by Malcolm X, of chickens coming home to roost.

History's great dreamers are never out-of-date. Not only are the grandest of lost causes still having their effects—they are always springing forth anew, reminding us that the problems they addressed are yet to be solved. Listen to Randolph:

> *The table of contents of the human soul may be found under the headline Love.*[22]
> *Our principal life—for we lead several lives at the same time—is the life of Imagination.*[23]
> *Through love man seizes directly on all that is.*[24]
> *All freedom must be self-achieved, else it is not freedom.*[25]
> *Love elevates, ever and always.*[26]
> *Love forever, against the world!*[27]

Isn't *that* the wake-up call this civilization needs?

Franklin Rosemont

$\mathcal{P}_{REFACE}$

Paschal Beverly Randolph was an author, well thought of in his prime in the 1860s. He was also an American black man, with all of the problems associated with that fact in the decades surrounding the Civil War. If this were all, he would be entitled to the obligatory footnote in works of African-American history and little more—though in fact he has been denied even this token recognition and has been totally ignored by all but occult historians, probably because Randolph was first, foremost, and above all a visionary, a man as much at home in the realms of the spiritual world as he was in the world of everyday life, and he was markedly eccentric as a consequence.

In occult circles, where his name and works continue to be known, Randolph has become more of a myth than a man, the subject of much misinformation and vast conspiratorial theories. From the early 1860s on he was "The Rosicrucian," associated in the popular mind with crystal gazing, drugs (especially hashish), secret Oriental brotherhoods, and sex. He was infatuated with women from his earliest years, and also spent most of his mature life trying to improve the lot of women trapped in Victorian marriages by teaching his notions of true sexuality. Beyond this, however, and fundamentally he was a practical occultist and a sexual magician, with a coherent and imaginative view of the universal role of sexuality. His work stands out strongly from the antiquarian compilations of the armchair occult theoreticians of the era and from the secondhand platitudes of the spiritualist movement from which he emerged. He was the forerunner of modern occultism and it was to him more than to anyone else that the transformation of the occult world from the 1870s through the 1890s is due.

René Guénon, the French "traditionalist" who figures in this story both as an exponent of the theory of the "hidden hand" at work beyond the scenes of events and as a historian of sorts of those events, correctly points out that "profane history . . . only permits us to grasp what might be called the outside of things."[1] This, of course, is no small achievement in itself, and profane history, especially in the case of Randolph, at least serves to put the discussion on a firm foundation of fact. But a word still must be said about occult history and occultism itself by way of introduction if only to disabuse the reader of any notion that the subject is necessarily trivial and isolated or that it is a chronicling of the merely eccentric. Most of the people mentioned in this book are indeed eccentric in the true etymological meaning of that term, and contemporary (and present) opinion sets them apart from any mainstream history of ideas, but they and the larger movement to which they are representative are also more than that.

James Webb in his overview of the rise of occultism in the nineteenth century defined the movement as the "flight from reason" and the refuge of outmoded beliefs.[2] This latter comment is certainly true, though incomplete. Occultism in all ages has in fact been the trash heap of outmoded science and beliefs. Mesmerism and animal magnetism in the nineteenth century were pseudo-science, but they would have been regarded as true science in the days of Sir Kenelm Digby's experiments with "weapon salve" and the like in the seventeenth century. Occultism, however, is really much more than that, and the notion that it is merely a collection of dated science and a rejection of reason fails to do justice to what I believe is the real motivation driving it.

Behind the apparent credulity of occultists about the marvelous is really a more positive motivating force, a search for something rather than simply a flight from the everyday world. It is the something sought that really distinguishes the occult mentality and makes the historical study of occultism a study of one of the constants of human nature rather than a catalog of eccentricities. The fundamental notion underlying the congeries of things categorized as "occultism" is the belief that the world of everyday life is only a small part of the real world. The real world is at once vaster and more coherent, hierarchically organized, and meaningful, with intricate patterns of correspondences and relationships, and it unfolds under the dominion of its own occult ("hidden") rules and rulers. It is above all a world in which humans are no mere accident of history, economics or evolution but rather are, at least potentially, central figures in the unfolding of the cosmic drama. Humans, in other words, have within themselves the possibility of transformation, of awakening and taking up their rightful place in the world of true reality.[3]

On one level this conviction is simply an expression of the sociological truism that certain beliefs permit everyday people, the lowly, ignored and powerless, to dress up and pretend that they are secretly great figures in a cosmic drama played out beyond the ken of their neighbors. But again, while this is certainly true to some extent of occultism, it doesn't really do justice to the underlying conviction that there is more to life than meets the eye of the skeptical and that a way exists to experience the greater world and play a part in it.

This belief, of course, is constantly subject to attack and disappointment as events falsify expectation, but disappointment almost never leads to rejection of the underlying belief, which is nonfalsifiable and hence not really the subject of discourse. However, disappointment in expectations does have consequences. Certain mechanisms may be perceived at work in this book and in occultism in general, mainly defense mechanisms having to do with the reluctance of intractable everyday reality to conform to the occultist's expectations. The "guru" is revealed as merely human; the projection of the philosopher's stone fails; the medium's message is discovered to be plagiarized or simply a rehashing of platitudes. Disappointed expectations are a constant of occult life, but, despite this, hope rarely fades for the occultist, though its object frequently changes as the occultist is buffeted by the hard facts of everyday life and his goals recede from his grasp. The Reverend William Alexander Ayton (1816–1909), who figures in these pages in various guises, is exemplary of the type. In the last quarter of the nineteenth century he was a quiet, undistinguished elderly vicar living near Oxford, but in his heart was an unquenchable desire for occult realization and transformation. He spent his entire life wavering between hope for that realization and fear that it would be deferred to the next life. He was vastly learned in the literature of alchemy and had early on become a member of every group promising secret wisdom. When the Hermetic Brotherhood of Luxor (H.B. of L.)—a mail-order organization that taught Randolph's techniques of sexual magic and the use of the magic mirror after his death—appeared, Ayton embraced it heart and soul, precisely because it promised practical means of realizing his dreams. He was devastated in 1886 when one of the leaders of the group proved to be a felon convicted of petty mail fraud. In the face of this crushing blow, however, Ayton did not even consider the possibility that his occult beliefs themselves might be delusions. The blame he felt was his own, the consequence of his (supposedly) dissolute life among the *demi-mondaines* around Drury Lane and Covent Garden during the Regency, and he reconciled himself to the impossibility of occult realization during this life and swore off occult societies altogether. Two years later, however, with unabated enthusiasm he became one of the early members of the Order of the Golden Dawn, giving unquestioned credence to the new revelations and undivided loyalty to yet another set of hidden masters. In the same way, the eighteenth-century alchemist, to take another example, was almost never tempted to renounce his belief in alchemy because of failure. If he failed it was because he himself lacked some crucial bit of technical knowledge, but he never doubted that the knowledge in fact existed somewhere—usually as the closely held secret of mysterious adepts.[4]

One universal defense against or consequence of disappointment is what the Germans felicitously call "Randvölkeridealizierung," the idealization of peripheral peoples. As it becomes inescapably clear to the individual seeker that he or she does not possess the truth or the key to obtain it, the source of the wisdom is made to recede spatially. As the bounds of the known world widened, the search of necessity led ever farther afield. The Greeks had Pythagoras and Plato seek out the wisdom of the East in Egypt; Christian Rosenkreuz, the eponymous ancestor of the Rosicrucians, had to venture to Arabia and Fez; Swedenborg in the eighteenth century and Madame Blavatsky and others in the nineteenth advised that the lost word was to be sought in Tibet and Tartary; and today the search must be made in the hidden realms of Agartha and Shamballa. Randolph appealed to this exoticism in tracing his teachings to the Near East, peopled in the popular mind with wandering dervishes and sufis.

The temporal corollary of this spatial recession of the wisdom of the East is that true wisdom is always primordial wisdom, originating and existing in its purest state in the lost golden age and descending to modern man through the unbroken chain of initiates. Randolph, like the other occultists of all ages, carefully recited the chain of *prisci theologi* (Melchizedek, Zoroaster, Hermes, etc.) reaching back to the beginning whose teachings he embodied and revealed to the nineteenth century—though Randolph like others of his contemporaries had the additional task of trying to reconcile this primordial wisdom with the then-current faith in the march of progress. Coupled with this belief in the secret transmission of wisdom from master to pupil was the idea, especially prevalent in the nineteenth century, that all of the apparently disparate remnants of mythology and antique lore were once, in some lost golden age, coherent and unified, and that their unity could yet be recovered by apprehending the lost key. In the nineteenth century it was generally agreed that this key was cosmic phallicism, the universal concern of practical and bookish occultists alike.

The corollary to this belief that the secret of reality is removed in space and time is the conviction that it is not only distant but is actually hidden—kept pure by secret masters and *supérieurs inconnus*, unknown superiors—and revealed only to the worthy after long testing and travail. The mythology of occultism, alchemy, Rosicrucianism, Theosophy, and the like abounds with apparently chance encounters of earnest seekers with mysterious adepts eager to impart the secret wisdom. Sieur Paul Lucas's meeting in Broussa in 1700 with a dervish, a member of the cabal of seven who lived for centuries and met secretly every twenty years, became a commonplace of later occultism, as did Heinrich Jung-Stilling's unnamed esoteric group that convened "in Egypt, on Mount Sinai, in the Monastery of Canobin, and under the Temple at Jerusalem"—a meeting Randolph claimed he was to attend.[5]

One consequence of all this is a sort of universal occult paranoia. If there are good secret masters, why not bad? Randolph and the other occultists of the time had to grapple with competing Brotherhoods of Light and Darkness, struggling behind the scenes for the realization of their conflicting occult designs.[6] In the late nineteenth century, in the face of the dominant Theosophy expounded by Madame Blavatsky, the expression of this competition was thought to be the struggle between "Western" occultism (embodied in Randolph, which held that the goal of life was individualization and perpetual progress through the celestial spheres, and taught that man should actively pursue that goal through "magic") and Theosophy, or "Eastern" occultism (which taught that the goal was impersonal "nirvana" and that practical occultism and magic were fatal errors). These secret masters revealed themselves to the faithful both "astrally" (or in dreams or visions or the equivalent) and physically, and it is in the latter mode that they present a serious problem for the historian. It is one thing to relate that Randolph encountered Thotmor, "the Imperial Lord of the Imperial Order of Rosicrucia," in the "soul world." This is simply a vision, like Joan of Arc's, and as such it has a recognized place in biography. It is quite another matter to deal historically with the supposed earthly extensions and secret societies presided over by these creatures of vision—by Thotmor or the adepts of the Inner Circle of the H.B. of L. The problem is central to Randolph's work because of his conviction that the Rosicrucian hierarchy "extended on both sides of the grave," but it is historically insoluble, and I cannot pretend to have resolved that enigma here.

The constant background of any study of Randolph and his work is this pervasive occult conspiracy theory that began to be widely accepted at the end of the nineteenth century. The theory denied accident in the growth and development of movements such as spiritualism and occultism and sought (and still seeks) its universal explanation of events in the operation of the "hidden hand," the work of the mysterious brotherhoods and unknown superiors on both sides of the grave that, by hypothesis, direct the revelation of the ancient secret doctrine to modern men.[7] Randolph figures prominently in these theories, and to a large extent he invited the speculation by his efforts to provide a suitably exalted genealogy for his Rosicrucians in obscure Near Eastern secret orders (while at the same time disclaiming such derivation in order to emphasize his own creativity and originality).

The myth of Randolph's work as the opening salvo in the war of the occult brotherhoods against the materialism of the nineteenth century and the inanities of contemporary spiritualism is derived ultimately from the H.B. of L. as it took up his sexual magic after his death.[8] In its version of events, Randolph, Emma Hardinge Britten (a prolific writer of spiritualist works and the "editor" of the teachings of the adept "Louis"), and the mysterious Madame Blavatsky, one of the founders of the Theosophical Society, were all simply stalking horses, originally sent forth by the secret masters behind the H.B. of L. to transform society by showing the poverty of materialism and demonstrating the existence of the invisible world. Behind the facts of Randolph's life and work, then, both in his own view and in that of many of his contemporaries, lies this hidden hand, and its presence must be borne in mind in what follows—always with the caution that, in making Randolph, Britten and Blavatsky the agents or tools of the hidden hand contemporary occult mythographers never lost sight of the fact that all of them were merely tools, and flawed tools at that, of the inaccessible hidden masters. They were "half-initiated" or failed initiates, not masters themselves, chosen *faut de mieux*, and even their faults were convenient for the mythographers as the means of insulating the masters from the apparent errors of the movements they supposedly inspired.

Although the truth or falsity of the claims of the hidden hand conspiracy school is by definition a question that can not be resolved by the historian, the reader will find a surprising consonance in the ideas and practices advocated by those supposed to be the hidden hand's agents in the nineteenth century—

a consonance that the skeptical will more readily explain as simple, unacknowledged borrowing by subsequent occultists.

A second defense or consequence of disappointment and failure in occultism is the retreat to even more nonfalsifiable and indeterminate goals, usually an amorphous mysticism. Disabused of expectations at every turn, frustrated occultists have often turned to the mystical. A good example of this is provided by the life of "Paul Sédir" (Yvon Le Loup) a central figure in the occult revival in France in the 1890s that centered on the teachings of the H.B. of L. Sédir (his occult name) is an anagram of *désir* and is emblematic of his overwhelming desire to realize the marvelous—a desire, however, that was never fulfilled. In a letter to the *Echo du Merveilleux* in 1910, Sédir confessed:

> With my companions I have made the circuit of all the esoterisms and explored all the crypts with the most fervent sincerity, with the strongest hope of success. But none of the certainties thus gained has seemed to me certitude. Rabbis have given me unknown manuscripts; alchemists have admitted me to their laboratories; sufis, Buddhists, Taoists have admitted me into the abodes of their gods; a Brahman allowed me to copy his tables of mantras, and a yogi gave me the secrets of contemplation. But, one evening, everything these admirable men had taught me became in my eyes like the mist that arises at twilight from the over-heated earth.[9]

The new revelation was the Christian mysticism of the "Maître Philippe," a miraculous healer, in whose powers Sédir found comfort for the longings left unsatisfied by occultism.

Another defense of the frustrated or disappointed occultist consisted of a retreat to what might be considered lesser but more achievable or more tangible goals—to "phenomena" and to an arid antiquarianism. As in religion generally, occultism has always had its original visionaries, men and women who have themselves had some compelling vision of reality. Randolph himself clearly was such a person. Dependent upon these visionaries there have always been the *epigoni*, the followers, who believe in the possibilities expounded by the visionary teacher but who do not themselves share the transforming experience. The relationship between Plotinus and his student Porphyry is illustrative. Plotinus, as Porphyry relates, rose to the direct and immediate experience of the one reality four times in his life. Porphyry himself, however, was deprived of the experience, though he was convinced of its reality, and, in despair after years of study with Plotinus, attempted to kill himself. After Plotinus's death, he increasingly turned to the evocations and wonders of Chaldean theurgy for comfort.[10] Similarly, in the nineteenth century, almost all occultists arose originally from the ranks of spiritualism. This movement, in contrast to occultism, was almost entirely an indirect, derivative, and secondhand phenomenon in which the true believer listened passively to revelations of the beauties of the afterlife from the lips of entranced mediums. Occultism promised direct experience, and this promise that lured converts from spiritualism, but in the face of disappointed expectations it was to the tangible wonders of spiritualism (table turning, Ouija boards, and mediumship) and to trivial magic that occultists very often returned for positive reinforcement and comfort.[11] Other occultists retreated in the face of disappoint-ment into antiquarianism and systematization, satisfied of necessity with add-ing learned footnotes and an ordered framework to the experiences of others and with educing hopeful instances of the marvelous through the ages. Such antiquarianism is more a confession of failure than a sign of vitality.

Randolph himself was beyond doubt an original and a visionary, and the strength of that vision sets him apart from his contemporaries—and largely from his followers. Randolph's great contribution to the transformation of passive spiritualism and mesmerism into the active occultism of the last quar-ter of the nineteenth century lay precisely in the fact that he offered his read-ers and followers a variety of practical methods (drugs, sexual magic, and the magic mirror) that would enable them to experience for themselves the truths he taught—or, perhaps more accurately, to elevate themselves to the transcen-dental plane from which they could themselves directly learn those truths. In this respect, Randolph resembles far more closely a "guru" of the 1960s than he does the majority of his bookish contemporaries.

These mechanisms of occult transformation are fairly clear, as is the fact that the world of the occultists seems to provide a home for more than its fair share of charlatanism, crack-pot ideas, and (frequently) outright mercenary frauds—failings which Randolph himself occasionally shared as he struggled to survive in the hard world. However, none of this negates the universality of the drive that impels occultists to seek release from the world of diminished reality or detracts from the creativity (and frequent beauty) of their response to their perceived predicament.[12] Occultism is a very human phenomenon, and Randolph was instrumental in the major transformation that overtook occultism in the second half of the nineteenth century.

A word should be said about my own interest in all of this and about the style of this book. I was introduced to these byways of history when Professor Mircea Eliade of the University of Chicago recommended that I read the works of René Guénon. There I first came across the name of Paschal Beverly Randolph, the mysterious agent of the hidden hand. When I came to look deeper into Randolph's life and works, I was astonished to find that a person who supposedly had such a central role in one of the dominant myths of this subset of the intellectual history of the nineteenth century should be so little known, and in this book I have tried to remedy the lack. With regard to the style of this book, I have favored extensive quotations from Randolph's works in the text and notes both because of the difficulty of obtaining his writings and because I believe that Randolph's own style is itself noteworthy and that his words are a better illustration of his thought than mere paraphrases and summaries. Also, because many of the books and journals discussed are rare, I have tried to include in the notes not only a citation to the source but also some summary description of what the reference actually says. If any real discussion of the transformation of nineteenth-century spiritualism and Randolph's role in it is to come about, as I hope it does, it is important that the discussion proceed on the basis of fact and the texts themselves rather than on the basis of myth.

Finally, I have added three appendices to the text. The first two contain Randolph's principal secret works on sexual magic, *The Ansairetic Mystery* and "The Mysteries of Eulis," which are published here for the first time. The third contains a reasoned bibliography of Randolph's works and their tangled publishing history.

${\mathcal{A}}$CKNOWLEDGMENTS

I would like to thank the following individuals for their assistance, while assuming responsibility for any errors in this book:

David Blackley Board; Geraldine Breskin; Ian Brown; Daniel Caracostea; Jean-Pierre Brach; Maître Christian Chanel; John Cooper; Josef Dvorak; Geoffrey Farthing; Robert A. Gilbert; Joscelyn Godwin; Michael Gomes; Ellic Howe; Dr. Massimo Introvigne; John Hamill; Hon. Hugh C. Humphreys; Jean-Pierre Laurant; C.E. Lindgren; Florine F. Love; R. Russell Maylone; Alwyn Miechel; Justine Mulford; Robert Orme; Roger Parris; Ernest and Rogelle Pelletier; Dr. Gerald E. Poesnecker; Todd Pratum; Leslie Price; Franklin Rosemont; James A. Santucci; David Tse; Anna Maria Turi; Henry O. Wagner; and A. H. Wesencraft.

Thanks especially to R. Russell Maylone, curator of Special Collections, Northwestern University, for permission to publish *The Ansairetic Mystery*, Robert Orme for permission to publish "The Mysteries of Eulis," the Toledo-Lucas County Public Library for permission to reproduce the photograph of Kate Corson Randolph, William D. Moore, Director of the Livingston Masonic Library, New York, New York for the photograph of the Charter of the Triplicate Order, and to Dr. Gerald E. Poesnecker for permission to reproduce the photographs of Paschal Beverly Randolph.

Chapter 1

ЄARLY ЏEARS

On the Streets of New York

Paschal Beverly Randolph was born in New York City on October 8, 1825, the son of Flora Clark and "a gentleman from Virginia." Randolph identified his father as William Beverly Randolph—one of *the* Randolphs of Virginia—but the man's name may have been the more prosaic William Randon.[1] Randolph was illegitimate, though he denied the fact. His mother, he explained, had been "the wife of two husbands"[2] and had apparently "married" Randolph's father when her first husband abandoned the family—only to be confounded when he subsequently reappeared.[3]

Randolph says little of his father, except that the man had not loved him and had abandoned him in the streets of New York.[4] He certainly took no role in raising the child, but Randolph appears to have kept up some contact with him, since he claims to have perceived his father's death clairvoyantly in 1842 and subsequently learned that his vision had been correct.[5] The father was supposed to have been a nephew or other relative of the famous and eccentric John Randolph of Roanoke, and may have been so, though no likely candidate appears in the Randolph genealogies.[6] In his later theories on human generation, Randolph attributed to parents a decisive influence on a child's character and life—an influence amounting almost to the view that the sins of the fathers were visited on their children—and consequently attributed to his father much of his own sufferings and "angularity" (eccentricity) as well as his weakness for beautiful women. He describes his father—in terms that clearly reflect his own vision of himself—as "willful, egotistic, boastful, haughty, vain, proud, conceited, sensual, sensuous, ambitious, dictatorial, intellectual, prodigal, unstable, variable, resentful, imperative."[7]

1

His adult view of his father's sensuality also probably reflects more on his own self-image than on any factual knowledge of the long-absent William Randolph. "I have loved not wisely but too muchly; and my father did so before me! For this inherited bias I have suffered and paid extremely dear."[8] "[I am] not a great sinner myself, yet I have suffered more than fifty malefactors' deaths; whence I conclude three things: that the sins of the fathers *are* visited upon the children; that mine must have been great rascals; and that I have fully paid their debt and my own to boot."[9]

Randolph was born at 70 Canal Street in New York City, a building long since torn down, and he grew up on the streets in the infamous Five Points, the heart of the New York City slums of the era.[10] A contemporary reported that in the Five Points "nearly every house and cellar is a groggery below and a brothel above."[11]

His earliest memories were of the death of his mother in the almshouse of Bellevue Hospital during the worldwide cholera epidemic of 1831 and 1832. The family had been taken there when Flora contracted smallpox, and young Randolph apparently spent a considerable period in the "large, sombre and gloomy old stone house on Manhattan Island."[12] He says of his mother that, unappreciated and unloved, she "fell back into herself, and then, with every tendril of her soul, turned and yearned toward the teeming millions of the dead" and became a seeress.[13] He describes in pathetic tones his life as a little boy in the almshouse, playing with the ghosts in the attic and trying to sleep while the spirits pulled down his sheets and made noises like the sound of cannon balls rolling in the garret.[14]

His half-remembered mother and her early death deeply marked his later life. In his mind his mother and his loss of her made him a medium and a genius and at the same time caused him to be "passional" and "angular"—eccentric and difficult to get along with; they also made him, in his own terms, "love-starved," a man driven by the need to be loved and befriended, and constantly and bitterly disappointed in his quest. Again and again in his writings he harkens back to his lost mother. He describes himself as

a lonely man—one with massive and active brain, but thin, weak and puny body—therefore an unbalanced character. The woman who . . . had given him birth, had imparted her own sensitive nature to her child. . . . The son thus congenitally biased and tainted had grown to man's estate, and from various social and other causes, he being a *sang melée*, had suffered to such a degree that his soul was driven in upon itself to a great extent; which, while rendering him still more sensitive and morbid, also caused his soul to expand knowledge-ward, become wonderfully intuitive and aspiring, yet bound up by the affectional nature within his own personal or individual sphere. But such souls resist this damming up; hence occasionally the banks overflowed, and he became passional; forgot his dignity; was led to believe that whoever *said* love, *meant* love; was beset with temptation, and yielded, until at last his heart was torn to pieces, and his enveloping sphere became so tender and weak, that it could not withstand any determined attack thereon; and thus he, like thousands more whose spheres are thus invalidated and relaxed, became very sensitive to influences of all sorts and characters, and a ready tool and subject for the exploitations and experiments of disembodied inhabitants of the Middle State. He became a Medium![15]

For a few years after his mother's death, he appears to have lived hand-to-mouth on the streets of the Five Points.

When [my mother] went to Heaven, my half-sister Harriet took me to bring up. Out of her hands I passed into those of a ci-devant English actress, of Simpson's Park Theatre, New York, named Harriet Jennings, née Whitehead, and those of her husband—*on the European plan!*—George Jennings, a high-toned sporting character, gambler, and so forth. Here I learned the art of begging, for *I* had to take my basket and solicit cold victuals from door to door to maintain the family larder, while he drove her to the sale of her charms to supply the domestic exchequer. Thus at less than ten years old I had become proficient in knowledge of the shady side of human nature, which had better have been postponed to a riper and steadier period of life. Up to my fifteenth year I was cuffed and kicked about the world; from my fifteenth year to the present time [1872], the pastime has been varied,—that is, I have been kicked and cuffed.[16]

It was under his sister's influence that he passed from atheism (into which his mother's death had cast him) into the Catholic church—a conversion he later repented because of the "Popish doctrine that nature is as God intended it to be."[17] For a time at least he was a bootblack on the New York City streets,[18] and by his early teens, he was in New England, perhaps attracted by some relations of his mother, who was from Vermont.[19] He then shipped as a cabin boy, another common occupation for blacks at the time, on the brig *Phoebe* out of New Bedford, apparently making the circuit from New England to Cuba to England and return.[20] He was miserable as a cabin boy, bullied and brutalized by the older sailors. He even thought of suicide to escape, but finally left the sea after an accident chopping wood.[21] For a time in the early 1840s he settled in Portland, Maine, where he learned the dyer's and barber's trades and also had a little schooling.[22]

Randolph's formal education was minimal and largely obtained the hard way: "Up to my fifth year I had attended school less than a year. In my sixteenth year I was a sailor boy; then I went part of one winter to school to a Mr. Dodge, in Portland, Maine, and *that* completed all the *outside* schooling I ever had,—but then I have had a deal of *under-side*, *top*-side and inside schooling."[23]

In true Horatio Alger fashion, Randolph claimed, probably truthfully, that he had taught himself to read and write on the streets. "One year's schooling only fell to his lot. He taught himself to read—his primers were the posters in the streets, his copybooks the fences, his pen a bit of chalk!"[24]

Despite these handicaps, Randolph became and was recognized as a remarkably literate and even learned man.[25] His writing style is lively and clear and at times humorous, in the manner of Mark Twain or Josh Billings. He mastered the nineteenth-century facility of easy literary allusion, and his writings reveal a better-than-nodding acquaintance with the authors of the Western occult tradition,[26] but his works are always original and never smack of the sterile antiquarianism of most contemporary writers on the occult. Above all else, his writings reveal him to be a seer, a man who was trying to relate what he knew first-hand rather than from merely recapitulating the works of his predecessors. He was also a linguist, acquiring a good knowledge of French and probably more than a smattering of Arabic and Turkish in his travels, and he seems to have been a fair musician.[27] His Rosicrucian novels (*Ravalette* and *The Rosicrucian's Story*) were very well received by critics even in the nonspiritualist press and are still quite readable today.[28] His scholarly abilities are most clearly shown by the quite impressive synthesis of contemporary geology, archeology, and paleontology he presented in his *Pre-Adamite Man* (1863).

The Black Man

A principal impediment to Randolph's advancement—and a constant refrain in his biography—was the color of his skin: he was a black man. New York had taken the first steps to free the children of slaves in 1799, but by 1820, five years before Randolph's birth, less than ten percent of the African-American population of New York City as a whole was free.[29] Even where technically free, African Americans in New York were far from equal and suffered a myriad of indignities. In 1821, a special law applicable only to free blacks, and specifically to those who lived in the city wards where Randolph grew up, effectively reduced to sixteen the number of black voters in Manhattan in the year he was born.[30] African Americans were also, in practice, kept from the professions and even in the mechanics' trades were restricted to a few of the more menial trades, such as barbering and the dyeing trade—both of which Randolph eventually took up.[31] They were even kept off the horse cars in the city until the 1850s.[32] While there was some Quaker-sponsored schooling available, and some public schooling in the 1830s, the "race riots" in Manhattan in 1834 (which occurred in the middle of the Five Points where Randolph was growing up) reduced its availability.[33]

Faced with this uphill battle for recognition, all his life Randolph equivocated on his ancestry, denying any admixture of African ancestry and alternately glorying in and exploiting it when it was to his advantage to do so. In his *Curious Life* (1872) his ancestry becomes a mixture of fiery Caucasian blood and royal blood "fresh from the Queen of Madagascar."

> My peculiar characteristics have usually been attributed to a strain of blood not a drop of which flows in my veins, for I, being tawny of hue, am taken for a half-breed Indian, Lascar, East India man, mulatto, quadroon, octoroon, and I know not what else. The facts are that on one side directly, the blood of THE RANDOLPHS bounds,—a fiery torrent, along my veins; Caucasian, aboriginal, and the darker strain mingling therewith is the royal blood, fresh from the veins of the Queen of Madagascar. Not a drop of continental African, or pure negro blood runs through me. Not that it were a disgrace were it so, but truth *is* truth.[34]

At times he boasted of native-American descent and even, through his father, descent from Pocahontas, and he claimed variously to be a mixture of three races or seven—none of them black African—buttressing the claims with vague references to the College of Heralds.[35] At his death, the local newspaper, undoubtedly relying on the story he was then using, called him "part Spaniard."

Conversely, in his role in the abolitionist movement and as a "red-hot politician" right after the Civil War, he touted his African descent.

In denouncing the plan espoused by the African Colonization Society (and at times by Abraham Lincoln) to ship American blacks to Africa, Randolph slipped easily into the "we" of racial kinship.

We men of color were born here; so were our fathers, and mothers down a long line of ancestry: Our blood, bones, nerves— every material particle of our bodies was and is composed of American soil, air, water, and our souls are American all the way through. . . . What! Are we to go to the lands of our African ancestors because our skins are dark? Are all our sufferings to be rewarded by our removal to African deserts and barbaric climes and places. Ought we colored citizens to even tolerate the idea? No! Never! Here is our home, and here we mean to stay, and on this soil will die, and in it will be buried. . . . We are Americans, and mean to remain such—and Young Americans, too.[36]

Despite this, Randolph never completely made peace with his ancestry, and even when identifying himself with African-Americans, was careful to distinguish himself and his accomplishments from what he saw as the uneducated, passive mass of former slaves (see chapter 7).

Complaints of prejudice and refusal of recognition because of his race are the constant refrains of Randolph's life. Even in his chosen field of spiritualism, he believed with some justification that his faults were attributed to his race while his accomplishments were laid to the door of the spirits:

If then I said anything remarkable or good, above the average intelligence of men of my lineage, why, even then spiritualists refused me the credit, as a general thing, openly taunted me with my natural, ethnological condition, and insulted my soul by denying me common intelligence, but said, by way of salve to the bitter wound, "You are now so extraordinarily developed that the dear angels of the spheral heavens can use you when wide awake!"[37]

You will, no doubt, long since have observed that my cuticular hue is not, in purity and clearness, quite up to the popular standard, and I know that Public Opinion has a thousand times tried me for that crime, found me guilty, and sentenced me to living death time and again. I had some few brains, the possession of which was also a high crime and misdemeanor, and therefore came additional executions and crucifixions without number, all of which made me angry, rebellious, and forever on the defensive. . . . I never had a genuine friend, save one, in all my life, male or female, or of any caste, race, or condition. Those who were cuticularly up to the standard hated me by instinct, because of my brains,—conjoined with the rete mucosum, which, by the way, needed just one-twelfth more of the popular sort to be up to the right figure in the social barometer. If I wrote a book or poem that evinced power or mind, and refused that to admit I either stole it bodily, got it from some one "away over in the Summer Land," or was inspired to its production by rum, gin, or druggery, I was voted an infernal scoundrel, crazy, loony, or an accursed fool.[38]

Emma Hardinge Britten, who was a tireless proselytizer for spiritualism and was later co-opted as a forerunner by the H.B. of L., the magical group that propagated Randolph's sexual magic in the 1880s and 1890s, scorned Randolph, despite her public stance as an abolitionist, and described the manager of the Boston platform where Randolph lectured in 1858 as a desperate man, "glad to accept anything short of negro minstrelsy" to fill his theater.[39] These sorts of small digs and indignities, rather than the larger, more abstract inequalities that began to be remedied after the Civil War, were Randolph's daily fare and must have contributed to the paranoia that is increasingly evident in his life. As we shall see, Randolph was a prodigious traveler at a time when travel was time-consuming and a major inconvenience, even for affluent and well-connected white men. He crossed the Atlantic as an adult at least three times, spent almost a year wandering in the deserts of Egypt, Palestine, Syria, and Turkey and crisscrossed America repeatedly. The list of his travels is impressive for the time, but behind the mere recitation must lie an endless series of rebuffs and insults and a constant background tension as he braced himself against the inevitable challenge and insult. The diaries of Randolph's contemporary, the ex-slave Frederick Douglass, are filled with references to the constant battles he engaged in whenever he stepped onto a train or boat and faced the demand that he remove himself to the baggage car, and Randolph's travels must have been filled with similar abuse.

Although he was rejected because of his race, Randolph's ancestry and his attainments also gave him a recognized place in the turbulent years preceding the Civil War—that of the "educated Negro," dear to the liberal drawing rooms of the North and their habitués—a niche from which Randolph both profited and sought to escape and one in which his eccentricities and contrariety prevented him from attaining permanent recognition. His patrons included Gerrit Smith, William Lloyd Garrison, and Henry Ward Beecher, the first two of whom combined a passion for abolition and patronizing blacks with a taste for spiritualism.[40] Randolph's tours of Europe in the late 1850s and early 1860s promoting spiritualism are part of the established pattern of the educated African American's antislavery *Wanderjahr* through the capitals of Europe, and his spiritualist tours were aimed by and large at the same international liberal and reform audience as that addressed by the American antislavery advocates. It was also his race in part that allowed him briefly to rise to prominence as an educator and politician on the wave of northern benevolence and sentiment that sought to improve the lot of the newly freed slaves in the last years of the Civil War (see chapter 7).

Upstate New York, Spiritualism and Free Love

After leaving the sea about 1845, Randolph turned to the dyeing trade and barbering, and by the late 1840s was living in upstate New York.[41] By 1851 he wrote from Stockbridge, a hamlet in Madison County south of Syracuse, to the educator Horace Mann, seeking his opinion on "the proper course to be pursued by the free Blacks of the North towards Ameliorating their own condition" and on the role of education in the process.[42] In 1852 he was working in Utica as a barber and proclaiming himself the "barber-orator."[43] The next year the transformation was complete and he is listed in the *Utica City Directory* as "Dr. Paschal Beverly Randolph, clairvoyant physician and psycho-phrenologist." What led him to upstate New York may have been the benevolence of Gerrit Smith, his patron a few years later. Smith was one of the richest men in America at the time and was the largest single landowner in New York State. He was also a spiritualist and a reformer and rabid abolitionist—he was justifiably implicated in John Brown's raid. One of his projects was the settling of poor urban blacks on parcels of his land. In the late 1840s he had set aside 120,000 acres for that purpose, and Randolph may have moved originally to take part in this largesse. By 1858 Randolph was living on a parcel of farmland near Smith's home in Peterboro, New York, a farm he had bought with Smith's help, and was finding out that Smith's gifts had onerous strings and conditions attached (see chapter 4).

At some point in the 1850s Randolph married Mary Jane, a woman who is described, in an 1861 advertisement that touted their medicinal formulas, as "an Indian woman, descended from a long line of native

'Medicine Men.'"[44] The claim may have been true, but probably, like Randolph's own claims, it really masks the fact that she was of African-American descent. By the end of the decade they had three children, Jacob, Winnie, and Cora Virginia, only the last of whom appears to have survived childhood.[45] Randolph speaks vaguely of his daughter "Little Winnie" dying of hunger because of the betrayal of a friend, but he also blamed himself and his peripatetic work in spiritualism for her death.[46] By 1860, the family was in Boston,[47] but the next year Mary Jane at least was back in Utica, advertising their perfected chemical treatment for nervous and scrofulous diseases which, she claimed, "put life in hoary age and fire in the veins of ice."[48] In the same notice she claimed that Randolph's system had been transferred to her by deed—a fact which may foreshadow or indicate their separation. Whatever the actual cause of this may have been, Randolph himself attributed the break-up of the marriage to "radicalism"—by which he probably meant his wife's falling into the hands of "free-lovers"[49] —though, as we shall see, his own radicalism undoubtedly played a role as well. Randolph reappears in the *Utica City Directory* for 1863 through 1864, the same period in which Mary Jane Randolph is listed as publisher on the title page of one edition of *The Rosicrucian's Story*, but from 1867 through 1872, she is listed alone and is cryptically described as "Mary Jane Randolph, widow," although Randolph was still alive.

Upstate New York in the late 1840s and early 1850s when Randolph lived there was a hotbed of spiritualism and reform ideas generally. It was the original "burned-over district," exhausted by the excesses of revivalism and primed for novelty—especially spiritual and sexual.[50] The often-quoted remark of socialist prophet John Humphrey Noyes expressed the situation perfectly: "Religious love is a very near neighbor to sexual love. The next thing a man wants, after he has found the salvation of his soul, is to find his Eve and his Paradise."[51] In 1848 the area gave birth to spiritualism when the Fox sisters of Hydesville (near Rochester), New York, began to produce their mysterious rappings.[52] Randolph, as we shall see, was involved in spiritualism almost from the very beginning.

In these early days, Randolph appears to have accepted spiritualism completely and without hesitation. Although the new movement, stripped to its barest essentials, consisted merely in a belief that certain naturally inclined persons could communicate with the "spirits" of the dead, in practice spiritualism carried in its train a congeries of theories and attitudes, both religious and political, that Randolph was later to reject with disgust. Its earliest adherents were largely drawn from the "liberal" as distinguished from the "Evangelical" side of

Protestant Christianity, and they fashioned the new movement in their own image, denying all authority but that of the individual's own experience ("individual sovereignty"), rejecting the uniqueness of biblical revelation, the church and the role of Christ and rejoicing in the fact that death no longer promised judgment and threatened hell but instead was but the gateway to continued life.[53] On the scientific side—and spiritualism prided itself on being "scientific"—it gloried in eternal progress now and the perpetual progression of the soul through higher and more refined (though still earth-like) "spiritual worlds" after death. Spiritualism in its early days also universally rejected as rank superstition the accoutrements of ancient magic and mystery and all reverence for the mysterious East and for a vanished golden age of high, secret wisdom,[54] and the very existence of the new movement itself was seen as the clearest demonstration of progress over such mummeries and outmoded ideas.

On a more mundane, political level, it is fair to say that there was not a single early spiritualist who was not also a reformer and abolitionist and whose views on the spirit world were not intermingled with often radical theories on the abolition of slavery, marriage reform, fringe medicine, feminism, socialism, natural foods, dress reform (the "anticorset" movement, woolen "jaegers," "bloomers"), phrenology, prohibition, the abolition of taxes, universal insurance schemes, the water cure and the like.[55] It appears paradoxical now after the changes wrought later in the nineteenth century by "occultism," but with very few exceptions spiritualism and its related spiritual and religious beliefs in the 1850s really had nothing whatsoever in them of the mystical or transcendental or of individual spiritual development. In spiritualism's early days, the spirits who communicated with their mediums all across America most frequently announced themselves by the names of the great social reformers (Tom Paine, Benjamin Franklin, Thomas Jefferson, and the like) and their messages were messages of social change. The great goal was social reform, here and now, in this world. "From the earliest announcement of modern spiritualism, it has been heralded by its advocates both public and private as a reform movement. The 'Fatherhood of God and the Brotherhood of Man,' 'Free Speech,' 'Free Press,' and Equal Rights under the law, whether the civil or higher law."[56] Individual spiritual development, progress, and attainment were largely unknown or were ignored as irrelevant. Most spiritualists, if they allowed any place at all in their thinking for such things, relegated them to the next world.

Spiritualism also provided a special role for women and had a special attraction for them, perhaps because mediumship provided an acceptable public forum for them in a restrictive world and, in trance speaking, allowed untrammeled freedom, largely without accountability. Radical views on feminism, sex, and marriage reform abounded even before the appearance of spiritualism, but these doctrines were enthusiastically received within the new movement and spiritualists by and large were agreed that marriage as currently understood was merely institutionalized oppression of women.[57] One consequence of this was the common perception in the days before the American Civil War that free love was a necessary corollary of spiritualism. While not all spiritualists were free lovers, it is probably fair to say that most free lovers were spiritualists.[58] The controversy over free love haunted Randolph all his life.

Free love, as the term was thought of in the decades surrounding the Civil War, was a complex phenomenon in which opinions ranged all the way from emphasis on "individual sovereignty" and simple opposition to "marriage-slavery" and the denial of women's rights, through Fourierist theories of "passional attraction," all the way to sublime ideas on eternally paired souls, originally created by God as twins and destined by him only for each other. At the far end of the spectrum were the outright and frank libertines, such as Moses Hull and Steven Pearl Andrews—both of whom, as we shall see, crossed Randolph's path. Most of free love's proponents, who were generally earnest and rather humorless reformers with inherently rigorous New England consciences and senses of morality, emphasized the feminist issues, while its opponents focused upon mate swapping and bacchanals.

To some extent, the free-love wing of spiritualism owed its origins simply to the radical doctrine of unrestrained individual freedom that was shared not only by the partisans of spiritualism but also by other American social and reform groups of the time. For obvious reasons, however, free love within the spiritualist movement gave a greater emphasis to the various theories of the "affinities" of souls which had their modern origin in the ideas of French utopian socialist Charles Fourier and their leading exponent in John Humphrey Noyes, who was himself a Fourierist for a time. All of these rested on the notion (itself based on pseudo-scientific theories of "magnetic" attraction) that feelings of "true love"—and not the mere legal relationship of husband and wife—were the best indicator of a person's God- or Nature-intended partner. Formal marriage, in other words, was irrelevant. At a more thoughtful level, "soul affinity" became enmeshed with variations on the Swedenborgian (and traditional) idea of the androgyne, in which the polar and eternally co-existent halves of the soul must seek each other out in this world or in the next to achieve wholeness and completion before they can, as a unity, proceed back to their divine origin.[39]

In the late 1860s, an old spiritualist described the situation as he had experienced it in the early days of spiritualism:

> Nine-tenths of all the mediums I ever knew were in this unsettled state, either divorced or living with an affinity, or in search of one. The majority of spiritualists teach Swedenborg's doctrine of *one* affinity, appointed by Providence for all eternity, although they do not blame people for consorting when there is an attraction; else, how is the affinity to be found? Another class, of whom Warren Chase is the most noted example, traveled from place to place, finding a great many affinities everywhere.[60]

Randolph (and especially the H.B. of L.) rang out the changes on these themes of affinities, though Randolph perhaps from his own unhappy personal experience with women rejected the "eternal" part of affinityism and opted for a theory of the change of affinities based on the development and progress of the individuals.[61]

An example of the type of milieu in which Randolph moved in the early 1850s is the Modern Times community on Long Island, New York. It was originally founded by Josiah Warren in 1853 on purely individualist-anarchist lines, but shortly thereafter, Stephen Pearl Andrews (the self-styled "Pantarch"), a spiritualist and universal reformer, introduced the community to the notion of absolute sexual freedom. In his "recantation of spiritualism" in 1858, in which he renounced his early errors and excesses, Randolph reserved special venom for Andrews and his doctrines, and he continued to attack him until the end of his life as well as denouncing certain unspecified sexual abominations on Long Island with which he seems to have been suspiciously familiar.[62] He called Andrews the "head-centre of the foul brigade" of free lovers:

> Standing alone in his nasty glory was Andrews, the self-styled "Pantarch" and free-lover general, who, while pretending to be a reformer, really knew as much about social science as a long-eared jackass does of algebraic equations, yet had he brains enough to gather not a few cracked-head, passion-driven fools about him, all of whom considered rape and seduction a fine art and justifiable, and hailed concubinage as lofty gospel. But the theme is too vile for these pages, their creed too horrible and disgusting.[63]

The details are no longer available, but from the vehemence and evident familiarity of his condemnation it seems that Randolph involved himself with Andrews and perhaps with Modern Times as well in the early 1850s. At the same time also he must have met Thomas Lake Harris, another sexual mage, who broke with spiritualism when Randolph did (and for similar reasons) and whose name recurs in Randolph's works over the years.[64]

The brand of free love that Randolph later condemned (and undoubtedly shared early in his career) was that conjured up by its worst enemies, though it is hard to imagine Randolph ever being as cynical as Moses Hull and his followers who advocated the notion that a change of partners was as necessary for mental health as a change of scenery.[65] The practical possibilities and consequences of free-love views were apparent even to the earnest reformers who advocated them. Though their own rigid moral code appears to have restrained them from excess, others were not so high-minded, and spiritualism in the 1850s, with some justification, came close to being identified with libertinism. Andrew Jackson Davis was not the only leading spiritualist who took advantage of the notion of spiritual affinities to acquire a new companion.[66] Emma Hardinge Britten continually went to great lengths to refute a necessary, intrinsic connection between free love and spiritualism, arguing that the physical phenomena of spiritualism were equally convincing to the moral person and to the free-love devotee, and that, if nothing else, the variety of spirit claims on the subject must reveal "a very wide diversity of opinions in the spirit world."[67] In her opinion, no one had more fostered the view of a connection between spiritualism and free love than John Murray Spear, with whom also, as we shall see, Randolph was involved.[68]

Randolph's intimate involvement with this world of free love and shifting affinities was revealed to the world by Benjamin Hatch's *Spiritualists' Iniquities Unmasked and the Hatch Divorce Case* (1858), his diatribe against the debauching of his wife (the child medium Cora Hatch) and the philandering of Judge Edmonds (another leading spiritualist). Randolph appeared prominently, in the company of Andrew Jackson Davis, Moses Hull, Stephen Pearl Andrews, and John Murray Spear:

> P. B. Randolph, a popular Spiritual Lecturer, abandoned his wife and children, married another woman who, in turn soon abandoned him, and he attempted suicide; finally embraced religion, usurped the control of his own mind, confessed his faults and delusions, and like a true and honorable man, returned to the bosom of his family. In this last act he has set a worthy example for others.[69]

All of this radical "ultraism" forms the backdrop of Randolph's condemnation of spiritualism in 1858 (see chapter 4), but in the early 1850s he wholeheartedly gave his allegiance to the new movement.

The principal and continuing lack in spiritualism was a consistent philosophy of what exactly the new movement was dealing with in "spirits" and the "spiritual world." Theories abounded, usually simplistic and as various as the spirits that propounded them through the mouths of the mediums, but a universally accepted philosophical view of the nature of the spirits was lacking. To the extent that there could be said to be a philosophy of spiritualism, however, it was to be found in the voluminous, vision-induced tomes of Andrew Jackson Davis, whose hospitality Randolph shared and from whose early works he first drew many of his ideas.[70]

Davis (1826–1909) began his work before the appearance of spiritualism, and his efforts might have languished as yet another eccentric and isolated production had spiritualism not come along and taken up his harmonial philosophy as the filter through which it attempted to view its experiences.[71] There was really little novel in Davis's work, but his vision is powerfully (though diffusely) expressed. It certainly reflects a deep knowledge of Swedenborg, the eighteenth-century visionary, either—as Davis claimed—because his books were received in visionary trance from the spirit of Swedenborg himself, or—as appears more likely—because Davis had immersed himself in Swedenborg's writings (which began to appear in English in the early 1840s) as a youth. He was clearly a visionary, nonetheless. In the "superior condition," as he called it,

> my previous developments are not only enlarged, but all my mental faculties are set in perfect action. I possess the power of extending my vision throughout all space—can see things past, present, and to come. I have now arrived at the highest degree of knowledge which the human mind is capable of acquiring when in the state that I now am. I am master of the general sciences, can speak all languages—impart instructions upon those deep and hidden things in nature, which the world has not been able to solve—can name the different organs in the human system, point out their offices and functions, as I have often done, tell the nature, cause, symptoms of disease, and prescribe the remedies that will effect a cure.[72]

In his visions he saw a primordial vast globe of central fire, which was either God or in which God was immanent, and which threw off successive series of concentric universes. God was thus immanent in man himself and in nature, and man at death began his progress through ever higher and more refined spheres of the divine.[73] After an early Christian phase, Davis, like many other spiritualists of the time, became increasingly opposed to the Bible and to Christianity, rejecting the unique place of Jesus Christ and discarding the idea of the resurrection of the dead and other Christian doctrines. Davis also, through his own personal marital fickleness, became an embodiment of the worst fears of the nonspiritualist world about "spiritual affinities" and free love.

Davis's writings had an enormous influence on Randolph in his spiritualist career, and Randolph's early views can largely be defined by his acceptance or rejection of Davis's harmonial philosophy. Even to the end of his life, Randolph's cosmology is basically that posited by Davis.[74]

John Murray Spear

John Murray Spear (1804–1887) was another of the molders of early spiritualism who left his mark on Randolph. Even by the somewhat lax standards of normality obtaining in the spiritualist movement in the 1850s, Spear was notably eccentric and, at times, outright bizarre.

Like so many other of the leaders of spiritualism, Spear began life as a New England Universalist minister.[75] Before the advent of spiritualism he had settled down to life as a universal reformer. He was a demon of energy, a temperance advocate, and a leading opponent of capital punishment in the United States, and was active with his friend William Lloyd Garrison in the cause of abolition. All of this changed in 1851 when he became a convert to spiritualism under the influence of Andrew Jackson Davis's writings. He quickly realized that he was a medium himself and could diagnose and heal through the power of the spirits. He concentrated however, on trance writing, and through his agency the spirits initially uttered diatribes (even then commonplace) against slavery, the established church, oppressive society, and traditional marriage (especially men's domination of women), and called for reform in education and all other elements of life. By September 1852 his thinking entered a new phase, when his spirits informed him that a "General Assembly" of prominent spirits (Benjamin Franklin, Thomas Jefferson, John Adams, Seneca, Socrates, Martin Luther, Rousseau, and Swedenborg among others) had made him its chosen instrument to establish the "Patriarchal Order" and usher in the new era in society.[76] The order was to consist of seven groups—called by such colorful names as the Associations of Electrizers, Healthfulizers, Educationizers, Agriculturalizers, Elementizers, Governmentizers and Beneficents.[77] Each of these groups was to receive from the appropriate spirits the fundamental wisdom about the causes of things appropriate to its area of expertise, and in turn each was to impart to society the practical consequences and developments of that wisdom. The overall goal was the general reform of society but that reform was viewed in very particular and specific terms: communism of wealth, women's liberation, and freedom from authority. Spear's spiritualism was "practical" spiritualism, devoted not to individual progress or elevation but to social reform.

In 1853, Spear and like-minded reformers gathered at Kiantone in upstate New York, the location of a spirit-discovered "Spiritualized Magnetic Spring" that Spear believed would revolutionize healing.[78] The next year this gathering began to be formalized as a community under spirit direction, but with clear elements of Fourier and Modern Times. The Kiantone community, as it was called, was to be the nucleus of the universal reform directed by the spirits. As in so many occult and utopian communities before and since, a special architecture was created to reflect the ideals of the new community. A circular city was envisioned, with each building to be modeled on the human body and its organs. As with many similar communities, goods were to be held in common, male dominance was to be abolished, and absolute freedom was to obtain. Authority was deemed unnecessary since as each individual grew under the tutelage of the spirits he or she would inevitably come to realize and strive for the common good rather than any individual advantage.

The same year, the spiritualist literature began to be filled with hints about the first practical result of the intervention of the General Assembly of Spirits in human affairs. Several of Spear's followers, following directions in his revelations (provided, of course, by the Association of Electrizers) began to construct a massive and intricate mechanism near Lynn, Massachusetts, that would provide mankind with limitless free power (the "New Motive Power") which would "revolutionize the whole world"—a perpetual motion machine, in short.[79] The work on the machine went on steadily for a year and a half with tantalizing hints of progress and lifelike movement—"The Thing Moves," announced the *New Era* in a headline—but the experiment came to naught and was finally terminated when the mechanism was destroyed in true Frankenstein fashion by local townspeople.[80]

While the experiment was going on, Andrew Jackson Davis was induced to visit the site and gave it his conditional approval, announcing that "no one can fail to see [in the new machine] the design of some intelligence superior in mechanical contrivances to these faculties in the head of John Murray Spear." He hedged his bets, however, by noting in ponderous jargon that "although the positive and negative, the male and female, laws of nature are very truthfully divulged and prescribed, theoretically, as the 'only rule of faith and practice' in the elaboration of this mechanism, yet, practically, as every student of nature will perceive, the adjustment of the poles, magnets, zinc, and copper plates, etc., are by no means in physical harmony with these laws."[81]

The fascination of the perpetual-motion fiasco lies in Spear's views on sex. He appears to have had from his spirit guides a general view that everything in the universe was sexually polarized, male and female, and that human sexuality and the human sexual union were but limited particularizations of this universal sexuality. With regard to his wonderful machine, Spear was convinced that for it to become "alive" and imbued with the necessary "love element" it would have to be begotten or impregnated and then born in ways analogous to human creation and birth.

> Inherent in the universe, as Spear viewed it, was a dualism in which every part of the universe could be delineated as masculine or feminine, according to observable positive or negative characteristics. Copulative activity involving complementary masculine and feminine phenomena was thought to produce increasingly complex forms, a process which would logically culminate in the perfection of the universe. In constructing his "electric" motor, Spear had paid particular attention to the importance of impregnating the machine with elements representing both masculine and feminine humanity.[82]

Rumors of the machine and the strange method of creating it were rife, making it difficult, as Emma Hardinge Britten remarked, to separate fact and fiction. "The prurient mind, stimulated by the awkward and most injudicious claims of a human parentage for a material machine, indulged in scandalous and even atrocious rumors, whose effect[s] have marked the parties concerned so injuriously that it requires the most unprejudiced consideration of the real facts of the case to disrobe it of its dark and obnoxious features."[83] On one level, at least, it seems clear that the method of impregnating the materials consisted merely in Spear's male and female disciples placing their hands on the machine in order to impart their Odylic, vital fluids to it.[84] When it came to parturition, a female medium from Boston was instructed by her spirits to visit the machine. While there she passed through the trauma of a spiritual and physical gestation and birth that appear to have been consciously patterned on the Virgin Birth. The *New Era* (which was edited by S. Crosby Hewitt, one of Spear's followers), in announcing that "the child is born" hinted that "the history of its inception, its various stages of progress, and its completion, will show the world a most beautiful and significant analogy to the advent of Jesus as the spiritual Saviour of the race."[85]

On another (and more secret) level Spear's spirits appear to have been teaching and Spear appears to have been following a rudimentary form of sexual magic. This is clear from the circumstances surrounding a second machine suggested by the spirits. In 1861, after years of poverty and failed attempts at organizing his reform movement on the spirits' principles—including managing a flotilla of barges that floated down the Ohio and Mississippi rivers toward New Orleans on a treasure hunt—Spear adopted a form of communal capitalism to develop and market a spirit-inspired "magical sewing machine."[86]

Unlike his previous efforts in which the sexual union served to instill life into the perpetual-motion machine, this time Spear taught that the sexual union of male and female would coalesce and heighten the creativity necessary to invent the perfect sewing machine. "Neither the male or female alone can construct a perfect machine. . . . Hence, salvation to man can come in true order by sexual as well as planetary conjunctions."[87] Spear's biographer remarks on the strange mixture in Spear's thoughts at this point, combining the decidedly eccentric underlying notions on sex with very detailed and commonsense instructions for bathing, rest, and privacy that were to accompany the efforts.[88] In a related attempt to generate revenue for his always-strapped organization, Spear, again on the direction of his spirits, later advised his long-time companion, Caroline Hinckley, to think about and if possible handle gold as much as possible, which would increase her "acquisitive" mental power. That power could also be increased by sex. "If the copulation be agreeable, and the mind be . . . upon . . . the accumulation of wealth, the power to get it will be thereby increased."[89] Randolph would later teach the same theory as one of the lesser elements of his sexual magic (see chapter 10).

Veiled hints and allegations of sexual misconduct had haunted Spear's community at Kiantone in upstate New York almost from its beginnings. In 1858, the year that Randolph recanted his adherence to radical spiritualism, especially the brand preached by Spear, the spiritualistic papers were abuzz with claims that Spear's guides had instructed the community, in another reprise of traditional millennialist and utopian thought, that they were to "cease to use clothing for the concealing of their persons."[90] Later the same year, Spear's "amanuensis," Caroline Hinckley, was found to be pregnant, and suspicion attached to Spear, who had abandoned his wife in order to live at the Kiantone community.[91] He denied the charge, but his denial may well have rested on his peculiar notions of paternity rather than on biology. Spear's spirit guides had taught him that it was possible for a pregnant woman to create a superior child by systematically infusing the foetus with the character of chosen spirits and to do so to the point that biological paternity was irrelevant—another idea that Randolph and the H. B. of L. were later to take up.[92]

Like Randolph at the same period, by 1859 Spear was persona non grata to the spiritualists. In late 1859 and early 1860, he attempted to regroup his forces and announced that 147 denizens of the spirit world (including John Hancock, Samuel Adams, Patrick Henry, Ben Franklin, Swedenborg, and Robert Fulton) acting as the General Assembly in the Spirit Life were now directing him to found the Sacred Order of Unionists to replace his earlier Patriarchial Order.[93] On a public level, the only apparent difference between the new group and the old was a tendency to recognize the power and desirability of a modified form of capitalism in the affairs of the group, a change that was to lead to the sewing machine venture. There was considerably more afoot, however, because one of the changes made in the Sacred Order was the institution of an oath of secrecy and the formation of a "secret body within a secret body."[94]

Spear's papers reveal little of the inner workings of the Sacred Order, but some indication is provided by Emma Hardinge Britten. She says that in the spring of 1862 "a rumor went abroad concerning a new movement permeating the ranks of spiritualism which had already enlisted in its interests some of the wealthiest and most distinguished citizens of the New England States."[95] At that point a trance speaker designated as "Mrs. E."—who is obviously Emma Hardinge Britten herself—appeared in Boston. She had learned, she says, of some of "the initiatory features of the new movement," and had been warned in advance by "sources both mundane and supra-mundane" that the movement could work irrevocable mischief on spiritualism. The agents of the new movement sought to enlist her, appealing to prospects of material and spiritual success and buttressing their appeals by angelic authority, but to no avail, and she took to the stage to denounce the veiled secret society with its unannounced principals that lurked behind the public movement. The movement, of course, was the Sacred Order of Unionists.

Emma Hardinge Britten's speech was followed by the defection of "two of the fully initiated, even the hierophants of the most interior mysteries."[96] A quasi-judicial proceeding was then held at Lyceum Hall in Boston in May 1862. Britten masks the names and details as irrelevant for her purposes, but states that Spear's former intimates denounced the "immoral practices, teachings, and tendencies" of the movement and revealed the spirit communications that lay behind the teachings. The upshot was a spiritualist manifesto denouncing "freelovism." Thereafter, the Sacred Order, "affected to drag on an effective existence for some time . . . but in reality it virtually ceased to be, from that hour."[97]

In 1863, a few years after the reorganization of his movement, Spear and Caroline Hinckley departed for England to try to find a market for the sewing machine and an audience for his ideas. Neither purpose was successful, though Spear was well received in the circle of magnetists around John Ashburner in which Randolph had moved a few years earlier.[98] He also met in England the Rev. J.B. Ferguson, who was traveling at the time as stage manager and chaplain for the Davenport brothers (whose biography Randolph was to write), and Ferguson seems to have played a major role in Spear's subsequent efforts to instill life in his Sacred Order. Ferguson also was to cross Randolph's path continually as we shall see.[99] By 1865 Spear was once again back in the United States, and there, except for a few brief appearances and at least one subsequent trip to England where he presented his testimony (along with Emma Hardinge Britten, Frederick Hockley, and a variety of Randolph's English spiritualist friends) to the London Dialectical Society in 1869, Spear and his movement, which by then was in total disarray, largely passed out of the public eye.[100] His last public crusade was in the 1870s, after Randolph's jailing for advocating free love in Boston in 1872, when he became involved in the movement formed to oppose Anthony Comstock's campaign against pornography, immorality, and free love—a movement in which Spear was associated with A. L. Rawson, one of Madame Blavatsky's earliest associates and her traveling companion in Egypt in the 1850s, and with D. M. Bennett, a free thinker who published Randolph's postmortem revelations from the spirit world and who was also singled out for special attention by one of Madame Blavatsky's mahatmas.[101] Although reduced to penury, Spear continued to travel and proselytize until his death, which occurred in Philadelphia in 1887.[102]

At some point in the early 1850s, probably about 1854, Randolph fell under Spear's spell, and it was to Spear's baleful influence that Randolph attributed the insanity and radicalism that characterized his behavior in the late 1850s.

> I met John M. Spear, and he filled my brain with some important mission which he said I had to perform. He made me believe that everything in society was corrupt and wrong. I swallowed those ideas, and believed that I had a great work to do on earth. I discovered that my wife was not my affinity. I went round the country preaching my scandalous impressions. I was crazy; these ideas of radical reform made me mad. This was four or five years ago [1855/1854]. I went to Europe, carrying my insanity with me, and I came in contact with no one who thought as I did; and by meeting so many with sane minds, I was finally magnetized back to sanity and returned home in a normal condition. And I became conscious that radicalism was abnormal, and its tendency was to degrade the race. It was then I said that I would abjure all radicalism, and would flee from the hell into which I had fallen.
>
> I returned to my family again, and since that time my home has been a heaven to me."[103]

Randolph the Spiritualist

All of these radical and reform theories and tendencies, harmonial philosophy and Kiantone came to constitute in Randolph's mind—when he rejected it in 1858—what he called "Pantheistic radical popular Harmonialism"[104] or "Atheistic, Ultra, Radical, Pantheistic, 'whack Moses'" spiritualism.[105] In his early days, however, he could not help being influenced by this potent mixture of ideas and tendencies. He gladly embraced and expounded the prevailing views.

In *The Unveiling: or, What I Think of Spiritualism* (1860), he states his career in the new movement succinctly:

> Everybody knows that P. B. Randolph is a sang melée—a sort of compound of a variety of bloods. It is so; nor is he sorry. With the great disadvantage of an unpopular complexion, and a very meagre education to back it, in the early days of what has since become an extended movement, I embraced Spiritualism; rapidly passed through several stages of mediumship, and finally settled down as a trance speaker.[106]

Although he claimed to have been a seer since the age of four,[107] his involvement with formal spiritualism came very shortly after the movement itself began. In March 1848, the Fox sisters of Hydesville, New York, near Rochester began to experience (or create) the mysterious "knockings" that inaugurated the new movement, and shortly thereafter Randolph says he traveled to Litchfield, Michigan, to see two women who were reputed to have powers similar to those of the Fox sisters.[108] Probably he was already publicly involved in the movement by 1852, when he described himself as a "barber-orator," because the orations he delivered himself of were undoubtedly spirit inspired. Certainly by 1853 in upstate New York he was listing himself as a "clairvoyant physician" and regularly appearing at seances where, fairly typically for the time, he was the entranced mouthpiece for the platitudes of a variety of the famous dead (including Zoroaster, Caesar, Mohammed, Napoleon, and Ben Franklin) and of course for his mother (who chided him on his susceptibility to any passing spirit's whim).[109] His mediumistic abilities, he always claimed, were derived directly from his mother's influence, and she first appeared to comfort him immediately after her death. Thereafter he lived "a strange, double existence" with her presence, a condition that he would eventually condemn as obsession.[110] More significantly for his later development, Randolph also began to be the trance vehicle for other less well-defined entities whom he then thought of as "angels" but who were, in any case, something other than the simple spirits of departed humans.[111]

The trance speaking toward which Randolph gravitated was no novelty in spiritualism at the time but rather was probably the norm. It manifested itself in various forms and was widely accepted by believers as an elevated state of consciousness, though questions were naturally raised about the accuracy of its productions since the spirits tended to contradict each other, and spiritualists contended about the primacy that should be attributed to it.[112] In Randolph's case trance seems to have come on automatically, frequently against his will, and to have manifested itself in a marked, abrupt change in personality and manner as the "spirit" took control—a change that only accentuated his natural angularities.[113] Even this early in his career Randolph was known as an eccentric. S. S. Jones, who later became editor of the *Religio-Philosophical Journal*, recalled his first meeting with Randolph.

We first became acquainted with him in New York City, in the year 1854. Within *thirty seconds* from the moment he stepped into our presence, he was entranced by the spirit of Dr. Benjamin

Franklin, and gave us the most remarkable and deeply impressive dissertation upon the Philosophy of Life we ever listened to from mortal or immortal lips. . . . No sooner had Randolph [shaken hands than his] organism was seized by a spirit who ejaculated in a deep tone of voice, "Bind his eyes," thereupon a handkerchief was bound around Randolph's head, excluding all light from his eyes, when three electrical shocks passed through his system, causing heavy tremors from his head to his feet. . . .

Dr. Randolph . . . was subject to the usual, aye, far more than the usual trials incident to mediumship. He was one of the most sensitive persons we ever met. Hence it followed that he was like a finely polished mirror that reflects the exact image of all that come within the rays of light forming the angle of incidence.

As his surroundings brought spirits exalted in thought within the aura of his being, or spirits all the way along down the line of development, so he reflected their sentiments, diverse and contradictory, almost hourly from day to day.

He told us of his trials and temptations. Suicide with him has been a matter of almost daily cogitation for over twenty years. . . . [B]arometer-like, [he] vibrated from ecstatic bliss to extreme despondency, according to the power and pressure of spirit presence.[114]

This eccentricity and fickleness are lifelong characteristics of Randolph. They amounted at times to what even Randolph admitted was insanity, but at the same time they formed in his mind the hallmarks of genius— in which he gloried. There can be no real understanding of Randolph and his changing opinions and constant friction with his benefactors and followers without taking this angularity into account.

When was real true-born genius otherwise [than angular and eccentric]? Flora, his mother, was said to have been, as is likely, a woman of extraordinary mental activity and physical beauty, nervous, "high strung," and willful. . . . Given: a mother,—herself a composite of conflicting bloods, very nervous, somewhat superstitious, poetical, vain, imaginative, aspiring, deeply religious, confiding, stormy, intuitive, spiritual, imperative, imperious, ambitious, physically and mentally active, quick as lightning, exacting, gay and gloomy by turns; now hopeful, *then* despondent; to-day hilarious, to-morrow plunged in sadness; highly sensitive, refined, passional and passionate, tempestuous; now stubborn and headstrong; cold as ice; full of moods; then Vesuvian, volcanic, loving, yielding, soft, tender, gentle, proud, generous, warm-hearted and voluptuous. And what must the child of such a woman be—but as he is, a genius.[115]

One consequence of this inconstancy is that it is practically impossible to assert dogmatically that any doctrine or idea Randolph ever espoused was in fact his final verdict on the subject.

Driven by the importuning spirits, who announced through him in 1853 that he was to be their voice to the world,[116] Randolph gave himself wholeheartedly to the new movement, traveling, lecturing, and participating in the ephemeral spiritualist organizations of the time. He gloried in his notoriety and labored mightily in the years before 1855, first as an unconscious writing medium and then as a trance medium, completely in thrall to his spirits, to spread the new gospel of reform and "whack Moses" individual sovereignty around New York State.[117] In renouncing spiritualism in 1858 he claimed to have given 3,000 speeches, 2,500 of them in trance as part of his "Spiritual Destiny and Mission" to convert the world.[118] In his "Recantation Speech" Randolph says that he was

a medium about eight years, during which time I made 3,000 speeches, and traveled over several different countries, proclaiming the new Gospel. I now regret that so much excellent breath was wasted, and that my health of mind and body was well-nigh ruined. . . . On the advent of the "New Philosophy," I hailed it with thousands of others, not only as the harbinger true and God-sent of the good time coming, but also as a religion, pure, true, sweet, and elevating; and it was only because I thought it would satisfy the religious needs of my soul that I accepted it as the guide of my life. What was the result? I will tell you. After embracing Harmonial Philosophy . . . I sought to be a medium— made experiments, and obtained my wish. Better had I found my grave! The rapping and other phenomena followed me, produced, as I then thought, by good human spirits. These were soon succeeded by the trance condition, to which I became subject, and the moment I yielded to that seductive influence, I ceased to be a man, and became a mere automaton, at the mercy of a power I believed to be demoniac, but which others accepted as Progressive-Spiritual, but which they cannot prove to be such, try as they may. Mind, I do not say it is not so, but aver that not the faintest proof can be adduced that it is so. As a trance-speaker I became widely known; and now aver that during the entire eight years of my mediumship, I firmly and sacredly confess that I had not the control of my own mind, as I now have, one-twentieth of the time; and before man and high Heaven I most solemnly declare that I do not now believe that during the whole eight years I was sane for thirty-six consecutive hours, in consequence of the trance and susceptibility thereto. I would have lucid intervals, an hour or two at a time, until the next circle. During these rational periods, I would, in words, assert myself, my manhood, and not unfrequently denounce the spirits, and then, in the very next circle, in the trance, retract it all; and for this I obtained the reputation of inconsistency, and having no "balance-wheel."[119]

In the early 1850s, however, the dangers of passive trance and subservience to unknown "spirits" were yet to be recognized.

Randolph's Medical Specialty: Sex

While Randolph continued through most of the 1850s as a trance speaker, his initial specialty in the new movement was as "clairvoyant physician," a role in which he acted as the "subject" for lucid medical diagnosis and clairvoyantly prescribed treatment, a process which usually but not necessarily involved trance.[120] The career was a common one—Andrew Jackson Davis followed it until the end of his life, though he eventually obtained a degree from an Eclectic medical school after the heyday of clairvoyant medicine had passed. By the summer of 1854 Randolph had moved to New York City and was acting for various doctors there, seeing fifty patients a day.[121]

I had a specialty for the occult, and an early friend, whom I loved tenderly, became unhappy by reason of an accident, that for 10 years rendered him utterly wretched and miserable. . . . At that time, 1853, I was a mesmeric subject, and examined for two French physicians in New York,—Drs. Toutain and Bergevin. Here I first saw and prescribed for the man, who afterward became my personal friend. Himself and lady were kind to me, and kindness won my undying affection. I have had so little of it in this world, have so often been robbed, plundered, and traduced, by so-called friends, that when a real one appeared, I hailed it as the Greeks hailed the Sea. I sat one hundred and eighteen times for my friend and his wife, searching for the means to cure, made many costly experiments, and finally was rewarded by the discovery of that which the world knows to-day as Phymylle and its radical, Amylle.[122]

In the more broadminded midnineteenth century, Randolph very easily came to attach "Dr." to his name, defending its use by the thousands of patients he had treated and claimed to have cured.[123] Spiritualism boasted many similar "doctors" at the time, and the pages of the spiritualist press were full of ads for clairvoyant physicians who would consult either in their offices or by mail, and who frequently branched out—as did Randolph—into patent medicines and odd magnetic or electric devices which, it was claimed, would restore vigor and vitality.[124]

In 1854 he cured a sick friend of the problems arising from loss of "vital energy," and curing—especially that of sexual problems—became his lifelong work. He says that the

necessity of conducting our researches in the sphere of causes, gave my mind that turn toward the occult it has ever since retained; hence I had no "gift" in hunting up lost or stolen property, or anything of that sort. I could only philosophize, deliver lectures from the clairvoyant standpoint in the clairvoyant state; nor do I believe that, of the 9,000 speeches I have made, 100 of them were delivered out of that condition. . . . I could only lecture, and cure those complaints that involved the affections, the passions, the nerves and brain, and that spring from disarrangements of the sexual system.[125]

Randolph's own love-starved background and the general reform feminism of the times, together with Randolph's cure of his friend, all combined to turn his attention to the treating of sexual problems, male and female. This sick friend, to whom Randolph returned over and over in his later works, suffered from depletion of the "vital forces"—a code word for the loss of vitality and will caused by masturbation. The fear of this loss was so pronounced in the circles in which Randolph moved and in America generally that one writer on the sexual foibles of the time has called it "the dominant sexual ideology of the nineteenth century."[126] The notion becomes a staple of Randolph's ideas on medicine and later of his sexual magic. In this light, Randolph's medicinal remedies and theories are simply part and parcel of the fringe medicine of the time, which sought to restore depleted energy by replenishing "vital fluids" thought to have been lost especially by sexual excess or abuse. Vital energy under a myriad of names was thought to form the basis for life, intelligence, happiness, and magnetic trance. The theory was simple. Food made blood, and blood made nervous fluid, and this in turn made "Od"—von Reichenbach's mysterious, all pervading "odylic fluid"[127]—which was the basis of all human mental and spiritual life.

In physiological terms, Randolph thought that the nervous fluid was distilled by the sexual glands and secreted as a fluid that he called "Physical Love."[128] In complete mutual sexual union, this fluid becomes part of the body of the future child and, in the sexual partners themselves, it is transformed into an "aeroform" state that transfuses the body and brain, replenishing vigor and giving joy.[129] Both in this world and in the afterlife,

> the love-organs perform the highest office in the spiritual, but not the psychical, economy; for they extract from the system and condense in suitable reservoirs that fluid white fire, which when set open in love's embrace, even here below, rushes like a whirlwind through man, plunges soul and body in a baptism of delight, as it sweeps along the nerves, giving a foretaste of heaven—the most exquisite rapture he is capable of enduring.[130]

In sexual excess and self abuse, the opposite result obtains, and humans are drained of energy. Love—the feeling or sentiment of love—in Randolph's view was thus dependent on this fluidic physical love, and at the same time the production of physical love was dependent upon proper sexual excitement and fulfillment both of the woman and of the man.[131]

Thus, in Randolph's medical views, human vital energy and happiness could be increased by mutual sexual fulfillment. They could also be replenished and increased by supplying the body with potions that directly replaced lost or depleted vital fluids, and the supplying of these elixirs remained a large part of Randolph's work for the rest of his life. He states that in 1854 (or, variously, 1860, which is more probable, given the contents of the elixirs), he discovered "the perfection of the Phosoxygen" of Lavoisiere and Humphry Davy, the "wine" mentioned by Campbell in *Hermippus Redivivus* and by Bulwer-Lytton and Hargrave Jennings, which he called in its various formulations "Phymelle," "Amylle," Phosodyn," "Phosogen," "Lucina Cordial," and "Protozone"—all of which he continued to manufacture and sell throughout his career.[132] The specific contents of these elixirs was a closely guarded secret. Their basic active ingredient, however, is no mystery. It was hashish, a fact that makes more likely the later date for Randolph's discovery, since Randolph was introduced to the drug in France and Egypt only in the late 1850s.

Randolph's general, nonoccult, views on sexual fulfillment and marital happiness were given in a number of books and pamphlets which began to appear in the early 1860s. Most of them, while still readable, are notable now mostly for the evident sincerity he reveals in urging mutual sexual satisfaction and in berating the obtuseness of current views on women's sexuality. Even at this early date, however, the books were really only "teasers," giving only a part of Randolph's complete science of sexual fulfillment, while the rest, the real secrets, had to be written away for—and paid for separately—and the answers returned in manuscript.

Randolph's earliest surviving work on sexual science is *The Grand Secret, or, Physical Love in Health and Disease*, which he published in San Francisco in 1861 just before he began his second trip to the Near East. In addition to the teachings on the replenishment of vital energy, discussed above, and to his usual nostrums on proper sexuality (consideration, cleanliness, affection, etc.) in *The Grand Secret* Randolph also adopted the theory of John Humphrey Noyes and others (which Randolph attributed to the Turks, Arabs, and Hindus as well) that men could be taught to control "the spasmodic ejaculatory muscle" and could engage in sexual intercourse for very extended periods without seminal emission and consequent loss of the vital fluids.[133] For a fee of five dollars he offered to send a pamphlet, "The Golden Letter, or Chart of the Polarities of Physical Love," detailing the technique of sex without male orgasm and without loss of strength.

This technique is what is best known today as "Karezza," the term popularized by Alice B. Stockham later in the century. In Randolph's day it was known as "male continence," after the book of that name published by John Humphrey Noyes in 1866. There can be no doubt that Randolph was familiar with Noyes's ideas, and several of his later theories—notably the "Vampyrism" (or "cannibalism," as Noyes thought of it) of ill-matched lovers who fed off each other's vital energies, the practice of "stirpiculture" (improvement of children by special techniques), and the fundamental doctrine of the exchange and replenishment of "nervous energy" and "vital fluids" through sexual intercourse—echo Noyes's ideas, but at the same time they are simply part of the *koiné* of the reform circles in which both men moved, and it is difficult to trace Randolph's adoption of all of these ideas to Noyes specifically.[134] Randolph's enthusiasm for karezza, however, was short lived and, after his longest trip to the Near East in 1861 and

1862, he came to believe that the moment of *mutual* orgasm was the point of supreme magical power, and he totally rejected Noyes's theory as destructive. "[U]nless both realize what God intended, ruin, sooner or later, is the inevitable result."[135]

All of these medical views on sex were also part of Randolph's larger theories on spiritualism and magic. The vital energy, especially magnetic energy, that flowed in proper sexual intercourse was the support of mediumship and clairvoyance and ultimately, as we shall see, was the energy that connected the human soul with the powers of the celestial spheres.

The two French doctors, Bergevin and Toutain, for whom Randolph clairvoyantly diagnosed in 1853 at the beginning of his medical career also played a very important role in his subsequent development, because Bergevin was associated with Société Magnétique in France and with the leading exponents of continental mesmerism, Baron Dupotet and Louis–Alphonse Cahagnet, and he was undoubtedly one of those who gave Randolph letters of introduction to those circles when Randolph left for Europe in 1855 to carry a spirit message from John Murray Spear to Robert Owen's World Convention in London.[136]

Chapter 2

$\mathcal{R}$ANDOLPH $\mathcal{A}$BROAD:
1855–1858

The World Convention of 1855

In the work of the old social reformer Robert Owen, the American spiritualists found a new and fertile field for their labor. Owen was another universal reformer, and he had been struggling for more than thirty years to refound the social order. In 1852 he had become intrigued with spiritualism, along with Edward Bulwer-Lytton, Earl Stanhope, Dr. John Ashburner, Anna Blackwell and many others of the fringe intelligentsia, due to the seances given in London by Maria Hayden, the first American medium to reach England.[1] When he announced a World Convention to "inaugurate the commencement of the millennium" to be held in London in May 1855, the American spiritualist papers all took note and recognized the opportunity to spread the word of the spirits on the other side of the Atlantic.[2] American spiritualism had as yet made few inroads in England, but the onslaught was about to begin.

John Murray Spear clearly saw an opportunity in Owen's convention. Given his views on reform and the millennium, he must have immediately recognized a congenial co-worker in Owen, and he decided to favor the convention with one of his spirit discourses on the infinite perfectibility of man. The delivery of the message was entrusted to Randolph. In the spring of 1855, accordingly, Randolph traveled to England, bearing Spear's angelic message and credentials from a variety of the leading American spiritualist organizations in Brooklyn, New York and Philadelphia, attesting to his oratorical talents and his desire to spread "reformatory ideas and humanitarian ideals."[3] When he went to present his credentials to Owen, however, he was ignored and was not allowed to deliver the message to the convention. Owen later attributed the slight to the press of business, but he appears to have avoided the subject of spiritualism deliberately in order to concentrate on reform. He later tried to ameliorate the slight by publishing Randolph's laudatory letters of introduction in part 7 of his *New Existence of Man on Earth.*

Sensitive as always, Randolph took the rejection as a personal affront and, frustrated in his immediate goal, he appears to have departed soon after for Paris and the Continent. To some extent on this trip, but certainly on his more extended trip two years later, Randolph was to move familiarly in the highest levels of English spiritualism and animal magnetism and also came to know well what passed for occultism at the time both in England and in France.

English Occultism and Spiritualism in the Mid-1850s

On his first visits to England in 1855 and 1857, Randolph was still a more or less conventional spiritualist and trance speaker, and the traces his travels have left on the record primarily concern his activities in that regard. He was among the very first to take spiritualism to the public stage, unlike his predecessor, Mrs. Hayden, who had largely limited herself to private seances, and he delivered his message both in the middle-class spiritualist groups then coming into being and in more elite circles, where he was feted, much as D. D. Home and others would be in succeeding years. Emma Hardinge Britten proudly lists the distinguished figures who were involved with spiritualism in Great Britain in its early days—mentioning, notably, Dr. George Wyld and Richard F. Burton—and says that Randolph was well received "amongst the *haut ton* of European Spiritualism."[4]

Besides these spiritualist contacts, on his first trips Randolph must also have come to know practically everyone in the small circle of scholars and eccentrics who had an interest in "the occult." There were undoubtedly groups with a serious interest in occult experimentation and magic in England while Randolph was a visitor there. His curiosity would have made him seek them out and his talents would have made him welcome. Leaving aside Randolph's on-again, off-again claims to membership in various secret societies, however, his published comments on the occultists he met in his travels show them in a less than flattering light. He mentions that in one of his sojourns in Paris: "I became acquainted with a few reputed Rosicrucians, and after sounding their depths, found the water very shallow, and very muddy—as had been the case with those I met in London—Bulwer, Jennings, Wilson, Belfedt, Archer, Socher, Corvaja, and other pretended adepts—like the Hitchcocks, Kings, Scotts, and others of that ilk, on American soil."[5]

Most of these London "Rosicrucians" are unknown, or practically so. Hargrave Jennings, that strange proponent of a phallic-Buddhist Rosicrucianism, will be discussed in chapter 6. Randolph certainly met him and learned much from his books, which began to appear at the time of Randolph's second visit to England in 1857, but the influence must have been on a purely literary and theoretical level. Jennings' ideas on the secret tradition were the basis of Randolph's own, and his ideas on the sexual aspects of Rosicrucianism also undoubtedly provided one of the justifications for Randolph's cloaking his system in a Rosicrucian guise, but there the influence appears to have stopped. Other than Jennings's professions of interest in the crystal or magic mirror as the path to the invisible world, he was a mere theorist and antiquarian rather than a practitioner of magic.

The same is probably true of Edward Bulwer-Lytton's influence on Randolph. He was, of course, the author of *Zanoni* and other romantic occult tales, and there is no reason to doubt that the two met as Randolph claimed. Randolph certainly knew Lytton's books, and it would be hard to imagine Randolph's writing his own Rosicrucian novels at all had Lytton not paved the way for the genre. Randolph later equated his elixir with the mysterious "wine" mentioned by Lytton and also borrowed the occasional mystery term from his works (without attribution),[6] but his final judgment on Lytton ("shallow and muddy") probably reflects the reality of their intercourse. Lytton, despite his wide knowledge of medieval and Renaissance magic and his acquaintance with circles that practiced the evocations of the old grimoires,[7] was really a literary magician. His own efforts at practice appear to have been limited to heavy opium smoking and to secondhand crystal scrying through young girls.

The Scryers

Crystal seeing was to become one of the fundamentals of Randolph's later magic. It had never been totally out of vogue in England,[8] and it was the practical supplement to the long and revered English tradition of manuscript copying and grimoire collecting. It was certainly all the rage at the time of Randolph's visits. John Dee's piece of polished cannel coal reposed prominently in the British Museum for all (including Randolph)[9] to see, and the novels of Walter Scott, Kinglake, and George Sand all featured visions in the crystal.[10] Nineteenth-century travelers' tales from the Orient also recounted for European audiences the almost universal use of the crystal.[11] Shaping the direction of inquiry in all of this were the formal directions for the consecration of mirrors and the evocation and dismissal of spirits that Francis Barrett had made available in his *Magus* published in 1801.[12] Mirror visions, accordingly, were everywhere in vogue in England in the 1850s. Christopher Cooke, the occult gossip of the age, in his recounting of the various ill-conceived schemes into which the astrologer "Zadkiel" (Lieutenant R. J. Morrison) had dragged him (and left him holding the bag), mentions successful mirror experiments he had seen in 1856.[13] Morrison himself was later the plaintiff in the "Great Crystal Trial" in June and July 1863 when he sued Admiral Belcher for libel for questioning his good faith in using the magic mirror. (Morrison was awarded twenty shillings in damages; the admiral received costs of one hundred and twenty pounds.)[14]

The most notable of these crystal users was Frederick Hockley (1808–1885), who devoted his life to copying ancient manuscripts on scrying and magic and to recording the voluminous messages received over the years by his young female scryers, primarily from the "Crowned Angel of the Seventh Sphere"—an entity that will figure again later in our story. Hockley appears to have been an earnest man who sincerely believed in the truth of the revelations he received. He also thought that his work was an authentic part of the Rosicrucian tradition and certainly knew and corresponded with all of those who were later to figure prominently in a kaleidoscopic array of secret societies and Rosicrucian revivals—Kenneth Mackenzie (1833–1886), Francis G. Irwin (1828–1893) and his son Herbert Irwin, Benjamin Cox, and the rest. He knew Morrison and Cooke, corresponded for years with the Rev. William Alexander Ayton (later provincial grand master of the north of the H. B. of L.) and, like practically everyone else, he was a friend of Emma Hardinge Britten and gave his testimony on crystal seeing before the London Dialectical Society in 1869. It is tempting to imagine that Randolph moved in Hockley's circle while he was in England and perhaps there first came to call himself a Rosicrucian, but although it is not improbable that the two met—Hockley, like Spear, had sent a spirit message (from the Crowned Angel) to Robert Owen's World Convention—neither mentions the other, and there is no direct evidence of any contact.[15]

Emma J Iardinge Britten's World

The biography and writings of Emma Hardinge Britten (1823–1899) reveal a more serious side of English practical occultism of the times— if they are to be believed. She is herself worthy of a scholarly book, though the research has yet to be done and her papers lie inaccessible in England. Her life abounds in mysteries, and she reappears constantly in any discussion of Randolph, Madame Blavatsky, and the H. B. of L. She was born Emma Floyd in London in 1823, and spent the first thirty years of her life in England. She was a very talented singer, actress, and pianist and came to the United States with her mother in 1855 to perform on the stage.[16] She was introduced to spiritualism soon after her arrival by a fellow boarder at a theatrical rooming house in New York, and was reportedly terrified at first by the results.[17] Spiritualism nonetheless became her true calling, and for the next ten years she traveled the United States as an "inspirational speaker"—a medium who spoke while in a light trance. Typically, she also involved herself with American "reform" and moved in the same abolitionist circles that Randolph was to frequent at the same period. Like Randolph, she also lived in Boston during the 1870s, and the two must have known of each other, though there is no proof that they ever met. Randolph does not mention her by name, and although she does mention him in her histories of spiritualism, it is only in passing, and usually slightingly.[18]

If this were all of her story, Britten would be no more than another obscure medium, long forgotten. She was considerably more than that, however, and was, with Randolph, one of the real forerunners of modern occultism. She also figures prominently in any discussion of the operation of the hidden hand of secret societies and brotherhoods supposedly operating behind the occult revival of the second half of the nineteenth century. By her account, her occult life began long before she left England. In her *Autobiography*, published in 1900 after her death,[19] she tells of her childhood experiences with a magical group in London. She says that from her earliest childhood she could automatically produce various phenomena and that, in the 1840s, because of this talent, she "was called [by] and associated with a secret society of Occultists and attended their sessions in London as one of their clairvoyant and magnetic subjects." This society she later named the "Orphic Circle."

This story of Emma Hardinge Britten's years of functioning as a magnetic subject years before her encounter with spiritualism in

America comports poorly with her reported reaction to her first spiritualist seance and with her other accounts of her life, but, assuming its truth, it gives some insight into the functioning of the magical circles that undoubtedly existed in England in the first half of the nineteenth century. Further information may be gleaned from *Ghost Land*, a wonderful novel she published first in installments in her short-lived magazine *The Western Star* in Boston in 1872[20] and then in book form in 1876.[21] By her account, the mysterious "Chevalier Louis de B." actually wrote most of it from his forty-year experience in occultism, while she only edited the tale for publication and supplemented Louis's story with excerpts from the diary of their mutual English friend "John Cavendish Dudley." It is impossible to answer the questions of authorship and the reality of Louis, which have been debated for more than a century without resolution.[22] The more important point here is Emma Hardinge Britten's view of the world of secret, magical societies, a view which was almost universally shared by contemporary occultists and which probably reflects the real practices of actual groups on a level that is only partially accessible to the historian. Literally true or not, the works of the Chevalier Louis reflect an amazing agreement with Randolph's, and it is no wonder that the founders of the H. B. of L. proclaimed the works of the Chevalier Louis as propaedeutic of their own and contemporaries viewed Emma Hardinge Britten, Randolph, and Madame Blavatsky as the originators of modern occultism.

Ghost Land purports to be the recollections of Louis's life in occultism. He says that his father was a Hungarian noble connected on his mother's side with "the most powerful native princes of India," and that his mother was Italian. Louis was born in Hindustan, where his father was apparently in the military, but at ten was sent to Europe to study. There at about twelve he met the mysterious Professor Felix von Marx, who was to be one of his teachers. Von Marx saw in the boy a perfect subject for the experiments being conducted by "the Berlin Brotherhood" of which he was a member, and for the next six years, the Brotherhood used mesmerism and drugs (nitrous oxide) to free young Louis's consciousness from his body in order to transform him into a "flying soul" that could explore the mysteries of the unseen universe for the Brotherhood. From his travels as a flying soul, Louis comes to know that the Berlin Brotherhood is but one of many similar societies in Arabia, India, Asia Minor, Hungary, Bohemia, Italy, France, Sweden, and Great Britain, all of which used their powers to project the "double goer" and to control the "earthly spirits" of fire, water, and the other elements. All of these secret groups shared the same beliefs in the nature and destiny of man. From their experiments they had determined that man's soul was merely a mortal composite of elemental spirits. While it could act independently of the body during life and acquire wondrous powers, after death the composite dissolved and individuality was lost, even though the various components in turn might be subsumed as unconscious elements of even greater composites, such as the "planetary spirits" who "ruled the fate of nations and from time to time communicated with the soul of man."[23]

Louis begins to have his doubts about this fairly pessimistic view when he meets Constance Miller, the beautiful young ward of one of the members of the Brotherhood. When she had been used as a flying soul, she had "winged through space and pierced into the real soul of the universe, not the mere magnetic envelope which binds spirit and body together."[24] She had entered "the soul world"—precisely Randolph's term[25]—and learned truths unknown to the Brotherhood.

> Man as a perfected organism cannot die. . . . The mould in which he is formed must perish, in order that the soul may go free. The envelope, or magnetic body that binds body and soul together, is formed of force and elementary spirit; hence this stays for a time with the soul after death, and enables it to return to, or linger around the earth for providential purposes until it has become purified from sin; but even this at length drops off, and then the soul lives as pure spirit, in spirit realms, gloriously bright, radiantly happy, strong, powerful, eternal, infinite. That is heaven; that it is to dwell with God; such souls are his angels.[26]

In the best romantic tradition, Constance then dies and her "soul"—not merely her atmospheric spirit—returns to tell Louis that she is an immortal individual.

Professor Marx and Louis next tour Europe and the East (including Arabia, which keeps appearing in the story), and finally arrive in England, where Louis was to enter military school. Their real interest in England, of course, is the kaleidoscopic world of English secret magical societies that Louis says burgeoned in the first half of the nineteenth century, and their reputations gain them easy entry. Here Louis meets John Cavendish Dudley, a distinguished occultist and friend of the professor, and his associate Sir James M——. Both names are obviously intended to conceal real individuals, though it is not possible now to identify them.[27] Magic is everywhere, and Louis says that "nearly all the English gentlemen to whom Professor von Marx had letters of introduction were members of secret societies, and . . . pursued their studies in the direction of magic, deeming they could ultimately resolve the nature and use of all occult powers into a scientific system, analogous to the magical art as practiced in antiquity."[28] In other words, while the English groups, by and large, held the same beliefs as the Berlin Brotherhood, their practice differed considerably because they adhered more closely to the magical tradition of the grimoires and held a more *ex opere operato* theory of the efficacy of magical formulae and operations—a view Louis eventually espoused.

> Next, we found another and still larger class . . . in whom the most wonderful powers of inner light, curative virtue, and prophetic vision could be awakened through artificial means, the most potent of which were the inhalation of mephitic vapors, pungent essences, or narcotics; the action of clamorous noises or soothing music; the process of looking into glittering stones and crystals; excessive and violent action, especially in a circular direction; and lastly, through the exhalations proceeding from the warm blood of animated beings. All these influences, together with an array of forms, rites, and ceremonials which involve mental action and captivate the senses, I now affirm to constitute the art of ancient magic, and I moreover believe that wherever these processes are systematically resorted to, they will, in more or less force, according to the susceptibility of the subject, evoke all those occult powers known as ecstasy, somnambulism, clairvoyance, the gifts of prophecy, healing, etc.[29]

Louis mentions specifically one of these magical societies, the Orphic Circle, whose grand master was Lord Vivian and whose recording secretary was John Cavendish Dudley. These magicians used crystals and mirrors, with young ladies as seers, to commune with planetary spirits. It was in this circle that Emma Hardinge Britten herself later claimed to have been a seer, and presumably the reader is expected to make the connection and realize that this is how she and Louis first met.[30]

At this point, Louis had become increasingly aware of the futility of much that he learned as a flying soul among the elementaries and was obviously ready for the transition to the higher things seen by Constance. The process is initiated by the death of Professor von Marx, who also was apparently in despair over the uselessness of what his experiments had shown him. Before he dies, he writes Louis and promises to transfer his life to him. Louis then has a powerful vision of the soul world reminiscent of Constance's, and collapses in a somber forest. He is cared for by Mr. Dudley, who is horrified to discover that young Louis's personality has been taken over by that of Professor von Marx and the full power of the Orphic Circle and of an unnamed

American spiritualist is necessary to recover his personality and separate the soul of the professor—which is finally seen undergoing purification in a spirit world peopled by the elementaries he so prized in life. Louis and Mr. Dudley then part ways, the former to India to become an adept and take up his military career, and the latter to America to explore the wonders of American spiritualism.

All through his life, Louis had vaguely perceived the guidance of something quite different from the Berlin Brotherhood and other magical groups. This was

> an order that owes nothing of its working or existence to this age or time. Its actual nature is only recognized, spoken, or thought of as a dream, a memory of the past, evoked like a phantom from the realms of tradition or myth; yet as surely as there is a spirit in man, is there in the world a spiritual, though nameless and almost unknown association of men, drawn together by the bonds of soul, associated by those interior links which never fade or perish, belonging to all times, places, and nations alike. Few can attain to the inner light of these spiritually associated brethren, or apprehend the significance of their order.[31]

This nameless, "sublime Brotherhood" had been in England when Louis first arrived there, and he encountered it again in India in the person of Chundra ud Deen, who introduces Louis to what he calls "the Ellora Brotherhood," which meets near the famous caves at Ellora. Chundra–ud–Deen takes Louis into a cavern whose description is an example of romanticism run wild: an amphitheater decorated with Egyptian and Chaldean emblems, mysterious words in Arabic, Sanskrit, and other oriental languages; sphinxes; and Babylonian and Assyrian bas-reliefs. On a central platform before seven smoking tripods sit seven robed figures. Six of these are adepts, whose silver thrones are connected (in the finest mesmerist tradition) to galvanic batteries; the seventh is an angel or other celestial being who focuses his thought on the six adepts while they in turn focus on Louis, the other pole of the giant electrical battery. Louis promptly experiences a spectacular clairvoyant vision of the "univercoelum."

> Then I saw a boundless univercoelum, in which were represented myriads of hemispheres. Above, below, around, stretching away into endless horizons, and ascending from thence beyond every imaginable limitation, were piled up hemisphere upon hemisphere, densely massed yet all separate from one another, and all blazing with systems, every system sparkling with suns, planets,

comets, meteors, moons, rings, belts, and nebulae. Millions and millions of these systems swarmed through the spaces of the universe, yet all differed the one from the other, whilst all moved in the same resplendent order, swinging around some mighty and inconceivable pivotal center. . . . In the Apocalytic vision now presented to my dazzled sight, every sun, star, planet, comet . . . was a living being, a body and soul—a physical form destined to sustain a transitory material existence . . . an immortal spirit moulded and grown through the formative element of matter, destined to survive its dissolution, and live eternally as a perfected soul, carrying with it all the freight of soul atoms which is sustained and unfolded, like the leaves and blossoms of its own parental germ seed. . . . The universe of matter became translucent, and throughout its illimitable spaces I saw that creation was filled with piercing beams from the central sun of being. . . . I might have counted millions upon millions of such beams. . . . The external or visible shaft of every ray was formed of physical light [and] this shaft was lined by a ray of astral light or force, and this again by spiritual light, or the element from which is formed the imperishable soul. Conceive of the whole universe filled with these rays so thickly planted that space becomes annihilated; trace them to their source; and you will resolve them all back to one illimitable realm, into which no worlds, suns, systems, bodies in space, spirits, souls, nor men have ever penetrated; where thought becomes madness, ideality is lost; from which light, life, force, motion, matter, government, order, power go forth, but to which nothing that is returns again, and know then the source from which those rays of living light emanate; know then the central sun the body and soul of the universe, the God, of whom man cannot even think and live.[32]

Under the guidance of his special teacher, a noble Brahmin curiously named Nanak Rai, Louis is taught to understand the secrets of the Brotherhood and eventually becomes an adept, one of the six, though occasionally his soul occupies the seventh throne while his body is far away. The last lesson he learns is the supremacy of the human will in all development and magic. He also learns the true nature of spiritualism. The spiritualist movement, it turns out, is a giant deception practiced to prepare humanity for real, conscious communion with the entire spectrum of "spirits," and the trance messages received by passive mediums supposedly from earth's departed notables are really in large part the result of those spirits magnetizing the mediums.[33]

In the final pages of *Ghost Land*, almost as an afterthought, Louis marries Lady Blanche Dudley (Mr. Dudley had apparently succeeded to the earldom of D——and then died since he and Louis had parted), saves her from the vile clutches of an evil sorceress, and then loses her to death—only to find her again in the soul world.

In Louis's second literary effort, *Art Magic; or, Mundane, Sub-Mundane and Super-Mundane Spiritism*, published in 1876,[34] the adept (or Emma Hardinge Britten) provided the theoretical bases for the events related in *Ghost Land*, and from the exposition it is immediately apparent why contemporaries immediately classed Emma Hardinge Britten with Randolph as one of the forerunners of occultism and why the H. B. of L. essentially made the Chevalier Louis one of its own. It is simplest to list Louis's views by category.

1. "Spirit is the one primordial, uncreated, eternal, infinite Alpha and Omega of Being," and its one attribute is Will.[35]

2. This Spirit is God, and God in his purest form is the Central Sun. "This Spiritual Sun throws off from the centre the elements of new-created worlds by centrifugal force, and draws them back and keeps them in determinate orbits by centripetal force. Its Nature is SPIRIT; its attribute, WILL; its manifestations, LOVE, WISDOM, POWER."[36]

3. Man, before being born on earth, "was already an immortal existence, a spirit; not a perfected, self-conscious, individualized entity, but a bright luminous emanation of the Divine mind. He was the Divine idea in the shape of the man that should be. Angelic in essence, spiritual in substance, he lived in a paradise appropriate to him, pure and innocent, but still wholly lacking in those elements of love, wisdom, and power which can be perfected alone through incarnation in a material body, and progress through probationary states."[37]

4. "Man lives on many earths before he reaches this. Myriads of worlds swarm in space where the soul in rudimental states performs its pilgrimages ere he reaches the . . . earth, the glorious function of which is to confer *self-consciousness*. At this point only is he a man."[38]

5. This process of individualization is not to be confused with reincarnation, which is a delusion.[39]

6. Man is a trinity of body, spirit and soul, and the Soul, having become individualized by incarnation as a human, at death

progressively "gravitates to a fresh series of existences in purely spiritual realms of being." After death men become "God-men— heavenly men—strong and mighty Powers, Thrones, Dominions, World-Builders, glorious hierarchies of Sun-bright Souls . . . Gods in person."[40] This progress is never-ending: "Higher and still higher, ever stretching away where roads are made of star dust, and paths are strewn with glittering Suns; where time is no more, and space is lost in infinity; stretching away into hemispheres where new sidereal heavens form the boundary walls and gateways to new corridors of an Universe wherein, *end there is none.*"[41]

7. The worldview of spiritualism is incomplete in teaching that the only spirits are the spirits of the dead. Man stands at the midpoint between hierarchies of supra-mundane and sub-mundane beings. Far above men stretch vast hierarchies of celestial beings who have never been incarnated and below him are equally vast hierarchies of "Elementaries," more material, semiconscious beings who themselves can progress to individuality. None of these entities was ever incarnated as a human, but both may be communicated with by man and come to his aid.[42] "*As it is above, so it is below—on earth as it is in the skies.* The Universe is an endless chain of worlds in which spiritual spheres above, and semi-spiritual spheres below, stretch away from the lowest tones of being to the highest, in which embryonic life is swarming upwards to manhood, as man himself aspires to spiritual existence beyond."[43]

8. "There are no phenomena produced by disembodied spirits, which may not be effected by the still embodied human spirit, provided a correct knowledge of these powers is directed by a strong and powerful will."[44] Most of such phenomena are in fact the product of the spirits of the dead, but some are caused by men alone or with the aid of elementaries.[45]

9. There is progress in human affairs, but nonetheless the accumulated wisdom of the ages expressed in mythologies and religions (and in the Rosicrucian tradition) has much to teach the modern world, especially about practical methods for communicating with the celestial and elementary hierarchies. "Spiritism" is the communication with these beings and "Art Magic" is the "practical science of Spiritism."[46] Mediumship is essentially passive; magic is active, the science of summoning spirits by method and controlling them by will.[47]

10. The universe is pervaded by an all-encompassing fire or astral fluid or magnetism which is the agent of all magic and which is in turn controlled by the will.[48]

11. Magnetizing is the most powerful means of achieving power and communicating with the hierarchies, and drugs also (especially hashish, opium, and nitrous oxide) are useful. "The use of Hasheesh, Napellus, Opium, the juice of the Indian Soma, or Egyptian Lotus plant, besides many other narcotics of special virtues, constitute a large portion of the preparatory exercises, by which Oriental Ecstatics produce their abnormal conditions; but when we name the last essential for the due performance of magical rites, we may include all lesser means, and are about to disclose the true secret of the Philosopher's Stone, and the mystic Elixir Vitae, . . . the all-omnipotent and resistless power of the Will."[49] The power of the Will itself may be cultivated by exercise.[50]

12. Magic mirrors and crystals are helpful in the process of achieving spiritism and charge the mind with the astral fluid. Louis reprints Alphonse Cahagnet's method of making a coated magnetic mirror, and the directions of Agrippa, Peter d'Abano, and others for calling celestial beings and the spirits of the dead into the mirror.[51]

13. The results of this magical practice include communication with the spirits of the dead and with the beings of the upper and lower hierarchies; spiritual sight independent of the senses—that is, conscious clairvoyance—the projection of the astral fluid; astral travel; the production of the phenomena of spiritualism; the control of elementals; and the power to read minds.[52] "Trance is considered to be the complete liberation of the soul from the chains of materialism, as—except a small portion of the Astral fluid, which inheres to the body, and maintains the action of instinctive life—the fetters of matter now become so loosened, that the soul can go forth, and wander abroad in space. Its spiritual senses have free exercise. It is all eye, all ear, all perception. It can ascent to the 'third heavens,' traverse the spheres, wander over the earth, read the hidden things of the heart, penetrate into all secrets, behold the past, present and future outstretched as in a vast panorama, in short, Atma (the Soul), then becomes the true spark of Divinity, and enjoys unfettered powers and unlimited functions."[53]

To this list there might be added from *Ghost Land* itself the notions that there are competing secret brotherhoods, of similar power but with differing goals and theories; that all that appears in visions and controls mediums is not necessarily good; that magical power (including power over elementaries) can be used for evil purposes; and that the spiritualist movement itself is merely a front, a deception practiced to prepare mankind for real spiritism. All of these, of course, are the elements of the hidden-hand theory that came to haunt occultism at the end of the nineteenth century and envisioned Randolph, Emma Hardinge Britten, and Madame Blavatsky as the more or less conscious agents of secret brotherhoods that competed for the minds and allegiances of men.

Randolph foreshadowed Louis in each of these teachings and would have subscribed to all of them, with the possible exception of the stress on "elementaries" or "elementals," which is present but undeveloped in his writings, and the H. B. of L. would have subscribed to them all. The Chevalier Louis's emphasis varies a bit from that of the H. B. of L. in emphasizing communication specifically but not exclusively with the spirits of the dead, but that emphasis was shared by Randolph also. The one area where Randolph and the H. B. of L. really appear to differ from Emma Hardinge Britten—and, as we shall see in chapter 13, from Madame Blavatsky—is on the role of sexuality, and even there the difference may be more apparent than real.

Emma Hardinge Britten, as we have seen in connection with John Murray Spear, was an ardent opponent of free love in all of its guises and always strove mightily to separate it from spiritualism.[54] Despite this, at various points in her life she appears to have been associated with occult groups in which sexuality played a practical role. The first of these involves the Orphic Circle itself. Rumor always had indicated that she had acquired the name *Hardinge* while a subject for the Orphic Circle, when a member by that name had "married" her while she was magnetized, in a ceremony which she later discovered was bogus. In revenge she took the name *Hardinge*, which she used until she died.[55] It is conceivable that the purpose of this otherwise unknown Hardinge was only to seduce the young Emma, but the context at least allows of a more serious and occult goal. The second incident involves Britten's membership in an obscure occult group in America in the 1850s.

In the very early days of her mediumship, probably in 1856, Emma Hardinge Britten became a "hierophant" in a secret society called the "Order of the Patriarchs," which had been started a few years before by an unnamed man, probably William H. Bayless, in Cincinnati, Ohio, and which (she claimed) had thousands of members throughout the country, "extending as far as Maine and New York, and establishing branch societies even in the remotest portions of the South." As she reports, the man "received directions" to visit a strange house in the city. Once there he was told to return home, where he found a large box in which was a "marble slab, all honey-combed with perforations." He and a friend consulted the spirits on what was to be done and were told that "the perforations of the slab [were] a language destined to be taught to the human family." A key to the language was given, and the men were told to start a secret society in which the secrets of the slab were to be revealed progressively to the initiates as they advanced through the degrees. What the slab taught was free love—though Emma Hardinge Britten is careful to add that "the position of openly-avowed 'free loveism,' if it was read at all on the mysterious slab, was one of the doctrines which happened to have temporarily withdrawn itself, on all such occasions as the author perused its mysterious hieroglyphics." Apparently, the perforations in the slab were

> mysteriously changeable, so that they will admit of infinite variations; hence the mysteries are endless. The moral teachings of the slab-language, as we learn, embrace that of "free love," in its most revolting form. It teaches that the marriage contract should be regarded as a mere rope of sand. Any man or any woman may repudiate it at will; and one of the fundamental principles inculcated by this *holy* stone, is that "all women have a right, under all circumstances, to choose for themselves who shall be the fathers of their children; and that all men without regard to any covenant, engagement, previously entered into, may become such fathers whenever the animal love-passion is reciprocal in its promptings."[56]

It is hard to believe that Britten, who was a hierophant and not a mere novice in the society, was as ignorant of the teachings of the slab as she says she was or that those teachings themselves were the simple excuse for lust she describes, but little more is known about the Order of the Patriarchs or her connection with it.[57]

One person who certainly was involved and who probably brought Britten into the organization was John Shoebridge Williams, a Swedenborgian engineer from Cincinnati who had been converted to spiritualism early on and became one of its first itinerant preachers.[58] As disillusionment with Andrew Jackson Davis's anti-Christian views grew in 1853 and 1854, Williams and others, notably the financier

Horace H. Day, moved to form a dissident group more in line with their views—the Society for the Diffusion of Spiritual Knowledge. Initially Day and Williams attended seances at the office of the *Messenger of Light*, of which Randolph is said to have been an editor, and then bought the paper and turned it into the *Christian Spiritualist*. Randolph contributed to this, and J. H. Toohey, with whom Randolph attempted to set up a Brooklyn branch of the society, was its first editor[59]—until he resigned and the work fell on the shoulders of Emma Hardinge Britten (writing under the pseudonym *Ezra*). With Day's financing, the offices of the new journal at 553 Broadway in New York City became a nucleus for spiritualists. Kate Fox, one of the original Rochester Rappers, was hired (Emma Hardinge Britten says "at a liberal salary"), and Emma herself was given a room. Both young women acted as "test mediums" to demonstrate the wonders of the new movement.[60] The journal and the new organization came to an end in the spring of 1857.

Some support for an occult-sexual side to Emma Hardinge Britten perhaps may also be gleaned from several otherwise inconsequential passages in *Ghost Land*. When John Dudley was first introduced to Louis, he noted that he was distant and abstracted, and thought to himself: "I'll wager that this young fellow has got a spirit bride somewhere off in one of the planets. Perhaps he might deign to chant a sonnet to a Sylph or serenade an Undine but as to his falling in love with any of the pretty butterflies that call me dear papa . . . , pshaw!"[61] Of course, later Louis does precisely that. Before he does, however, he has a long discussion with a friend on love. This, he teaches, is of three kinds. The first is "magnetic affinity"—the attraction of one person to another. The second is simple friendship. The third is what is relevant here.

> It is soul affinity, . . . the realization that man and woman have no actual existence apart from each other; that they are, in fact, counterparts, without which their separate lives are imperfect and informed. Life is dual . . . and love, true soul-love, is the bond of union which reunites the severed parts. It exists independent of personal charms or mental acquirements. It annihilates self and selfishness; prefers the beloved object beyond all adventitious acquirements; subsists through sickness or in health, through good or evil report, lives for the one beloved, dies and realizes heaven only in the union which death may interrupt but cannot sever. Divine spiritual affinity survives death and the grave, unites the two halves of the one soul, and in eternity perfects the dual nature of man and woman into one angel.[62]

This is the spiritual affinity theory in its purest form. The partners' souls are complements of each other, halves of an original whole, and eventually reunite to form but one angel. The H. B. of L. taught exactly the same idea. Randolph, while he believed in the creation of soul monads in pairs and the progress of the soul through the soul worlds in company with a partner of the opposite sex, rejected—perhaps because of his own unhappy experiences with marriage—any notion that this affinity was always for the same partner (chapter 1).

It is a very short step from these ideas to the logical consequence, the notion that the sexual union of the eternal affinities itself plays a role in the progress of the soul. It is impossible to say that Emma Hardinge Britten ever took that step as a practical matter, but it is utterly improbable that the idea would have been foreign to her. She certainly believed, in some sense, that the means (sexual union) whereby the rudimental soul becomes incarnated to begin its ascent were also the means of progress for the soul.[63]

The underworld that Emma Hardinge Britten describes in *Ghost Land* is fascinating and reflects at a minimum the beliefs and hopes of her contemporaries in the action of secret forces on man's history. In its description of innumerable secret circles of practicing occultists and crystal seers, *Ghost Land* probably reflects historical reality to a large extent, but the details of this side of English occultism in the first half of the nineteenth century are largely impervious to us in the present state of research. The issue is further clouded by the free intermixture of fact with fantasy, mythology, and fiction. The imaginary and historical worlds constantly overlap and interact. In *Ghost Land* (26–27, 30), Louis, on his first venture as a flying soul, sees in the mirror the Crowned Angel, the elevated spirit being that governed Frederick Hockley's crystal, and Professor von Marx is said to be a member of the mysterious society described by Goethe's friend Johann Heinrich Jung-Stilling in his *Autobiography*, a group that met "in Egypt, on Mount Sinai, in the monastery of Canobin, and under the temple of Jerusalem." Randolph also had taken up the identification with Jung-Stilling's society in seeking a pedigree for his own Rosicrucians. In *Art Magic* (340), similarly, Professor von Marx again defers to "our ruling spirit, the 'Crowned Angel,'" and the Crowned Angel, in turn, reveals to Frederick Hockley's scryer the existence of the "sacred society of which the Fathers are at Jerusalem," a reference which can only be to Jung-Stilling's mysterious group.[64]

Leaving the miraculous aside, there were undoubtedly groups with the same intent as that of the Orphic Circle operating in England during the period, but by their very nature they were secret, and it is impossible now to gather many details of their operation. Randolph would later claim connection with various European and Oriental secret groups, including Jung-Stilling's as we shall see, but the facts of the connection, if it existed at all, cannot now be separated from the elements of fiction and the supernatural.

On the level that is accessible to us historically, the English influence on Randolph appears slight indeed. Despite the almost universal interest in crystals in Great Britain during the period of his visits in the 1850s, little of English scrying seems to have rubbed off on Randolph—and with good reason. By and large, the effects obtained from the crystal in contemporary English practice either smacked of the doctrinal discourses of contemporary spiritualism or were trivial from Randolph's point of view: mere fortunetelling and visions of absent loved ones. Universally, scrying was a secondhand phenomenon, with the real party in interest reduced to reading or hearing the revelations of the actual seer. Similarly, the English preoccupation with the magical formalities of crystal seeing (the evocations, calls, and dismissals derived from Barrett, Agrippa, and Peter d'Abano) is totally absent from Randolph's work. Randolph also, as we shall see, preferred the French magnetic mirror to the simple crystal favored by the English. Ultimately, what we know of the world in which Hockley, Cooke, Morrison, Mackenzie, the Irwins, and the rest moved—a strange, incestuous Masonic and pseudo-Rosicrucian underworld, devoted to mysterious initiation rituals, secret societies, unknown superiors and antiquarianism—appears to have been foreign to Randolph, and perhaps closed to him by his eccentricities or his race.[65]

Randolph and the British Spiritualists and Mirror Magicians

From Randolph's own point of view, his strongest recollections of his English trips in later years were of the friends he had made in spiritualist circles, and it is probably in those circles that we must look for the path by which his full-blown sexual magic survived in England, ultimately to reappear in the early 1880s in the H. B. of L. In 1870 Randolph gave a seer friend of his (a Dr. Botfield of Illinois, who is otherwise unknown) a letter of introduction to the *Medium and Daybreak* in London, asking that the journal give the good doctor the addresses of Randolph's old English friends. Among these he mentions specifically Hargrave Jennings, Dr. Dixon, Thomas Shorter, Luke

Burke, Luxmore, and Bielfield.[66] Little is known of most of these, but the unifying thread that connected almost all of them was their enthusiasm for spiritualism in its early days in England and their relationship with the *Spiritual Magazine* of London in the 1860s.

Luke Burke was a very well known anthropologist of the time, and Randolph was to draw heavily upon his work in writing his *Pre-Adamite Man* in 1863, but nothing is known about his spiritualist or occult activities.[67] Luxmore (actually John Charles Luxmoore) was a wealthy justice of the peace with a house in Gloucester Square who very early on became involved with spiritualism. In the 1870s he acted as patron for several prominent social mediums, including Florence Cook and Mary Rosina Showers, and moved in the exalted circle of the countess of Caithness. He was also a close friend of Emma Hardinge Britten, and with her attended the deliberations of the London Dialectical Society on spiritualism and went to see D. D. Home perform.[68]

Of these London friends mentioned by Randolph, Thomas Shorter is the best known. He was a very fair scholar, and, as " Thomas Brevior" (the Latinized version of his name), he was the author of one of the standard spiritualist histories of the time. Shorter also arranged Emma Hardinge Britten's appearances in England on her first return there as a spiritualist in 1865. Most important for our purposes, Shorter, with William Wilkinson, edited the *Spiritual Magazine*, a Swedenborgian, pro-Christian spiritualist magazine that ran in England from 1859 to 1877 and provided a sympathetic forum for many of the ideas and persons that recur throughout our history, including many of the men referred to by Randolph in introducing his friend Dr. Bottfield.[69] Emma Hardinge Britten submitted a piece on "The Rosicrucians"[70] and her efforts for the Union cause in the Civil War were sympathetically chronicled in the journal. Shorter wrote a detailed biography of Johann Heinrich Jung-Stilling, giving the often-quoted excerpt from Stilling's *Autobiography* that would become a *locus communis* for later occultists, including Randolph (see chapter 6). Dr. John Ashburner (1793–1878), the old animal magnetist whose contributions on clairvoyance and the supreme power of the human will had been running in the *Yorkshire Spiritual Telegraph* at the same time that Randolph's seances in England in 1857 were being featured,[71] was a frequent contributor.[72] Of the "fringe-Masonic" figures and mirror seers we have discussed, Christopher Cooke and Kenneth Mackenzie both frequently contributed articles.[73] Mackenzie's submissions reveal a little known spiritualist side of the man who was the first to launch the "Brothers of Luxor" upon the world a few years later.[74] Crystal seeing and drugs (hashish) as aids in developing clairvoyance were also frequently and prominently featured in the *Spiritual Magazine*.[75]

Dr. Jacob Dixon, who also was mentioned by Randolph in introducing his friend, was a London homoeopathist. He had been active in investigating animal magnetism in the *Zoist* group in the 1850s and had been converted to spiritualism along with many others by the American medium Mrs. Hayden on her trip to England in the fall of 1852.[76] He was a frequent contributor to the *Yorkshire Spiritual Telegraph* when Randolph's trance visions were appearing there in 1857, and also contributed to Kenneth Mackenzie's short-lived *Biological Review* (1858–59; on trance) and to the *Spiritual Magazine* (on clairvoyance and magnetism).[77] Dixon was very active in organizing early British spiritualism and in July 1857 became the first secretary of the London Spiritualistic Union (later the Spiritualist Union) that was organized by Shorter, Dr. Ashburner, and others out of the Charing Cross Spirit-Power Circle before which Randolph appeared. For our purposes, his main distinction lies in the fact that he advocated drugs to polarize the "vital forces" and emphasized that beyond the usual degrees of clairvoyance familiar to the British animal magnetists there was "a seventh degree—that of *Extasis*, or *Trance* . . . , that degree in which there is interior relation with the individualities and objects of the spiritual world."[78] Dixon also, with Mr. "Bielfield" (who also was mentioned by Randolph in his letter of introduction and who is almost certainly the same as the "Belfedt" that Randolph condemned in his novel *Ravalette* as a shallow and muddy English Rosicrucian) worked with Thomas Welton and his clairvoyant wife, Sarah Welton.[79]

Thomas Welton, a surgical instrument maker, was yet another crystal gazer and spiritualist of the 1850s and 1860s, and his name and that of his wife appear frequently in the pages of the *Spiritual Magazine*.[80] He is also notable for his belief in the efficacy of drugs for stimulating clairvoyance. While he knew Lieutenant Morrison ("Zadkiel") well— he dedicated his book on magic mirrors to him—his own circle appears to have been different.[81] It included Dr. Dixon, Bielfield (described as an artist and avid user of the "planchette," a device Welton claimed to have invented—the forerunner of the Ouija board), and Robert H. Fryar, who eventually published Welton's book on magic mirrors. Fryar was a minor publisher of works on the occult and of mildly pornographic antiquarian books on art and universal phallicism. In the 1880s he was to become the purveyor in England of Randolph's manuscripts on sexual magic, and it was through him that the existence of the H. B. of L. was first revealed to the world in 1884 (see chapter 11).[82] Fryar was also, curiously enough, an acquaintance of John Murray Spear, whom he had met on one of Spear's trips to England. (Spear made a psychometric analysis of Fryar's wife, who was also his scryer, and judged that "her true character would be indicated by the name, 'British Seeress.'")[83]

It is probably among these obscure by-ways of the contributors to the *Spiritual Magazine*, rather than in the circles of the better known occultists and spiritualists of the time (such as Bulwer-Lytton and Hargrave Jennings), that Randolph found a real welcome in England, and it is probably through them that his work remained alive until its revival by Robert H. Fryar and the H. B. of L. in the early 1880s. Randolph's name appeared occasionally in the magazine, but with only passing reference to his visit to England in 1857 and with no reference at all to any continuing influence exercised by him there.[84] He was praised for his conversion to "Christian Spiritualism" and his first major work, *Dealings with the Dead* (1861–1862), was enthusiastically reviewed, but fundamentally he was seen as simply another medium—though a medium with very strong talents and marked eccentricities.[85]

The effect on Randolph of his visits to Paris in the 1850s was of quite a different order.

The French Occult Milieu at Mid-Century

For information on Randolph's first trip to England and the Continent and his later ones there and to the Near East, we are largely dependent on passing references in his books, especially his Rosicrucian novels, which themselves warn of anachronism and deliberate obfuscation.[86] In many cases it is impossible to distinguish the events of one trip from those of another. Concerning his first trip, however, there is no reason to doubt that his earlier psychometric work for Drs. Bergevin and Toutain gave him an entrée in 1855 to the circle of magnetizers around Cahagnet and the Baron Dupotet in Paris. He said that he carried letters of introduction to them, but even without them his psychic abilities alone would certainly have made him welcome there. "In 1853–4–5 I had this power [clairvoyance] to a remarkable degree; used to play cards, chess, and read books blindfold, and this power caused me to be invited to visit Paris, where I exhibited it to the astonishment of the Savans, and my own glorification."[87] Like various other seers of the time, such as Mme Dablin and Alexis Didier in Paris and Alexis's brother Adolph in London—all of whom he came to know—he had a talent that was much in demand.[88]

At the time, Randolph was convinced that his mission in life was to spread the good news of spiritualism, and he undoubtedly spent most of his first European trip doing just that. He later said, on temporarily renouncing spiritualism, that, had God

> not vouchsafed this great mercy, the probability is, that instead of trying to serve Him, and atone for the mistake of a lifetime, I should still be wandering up and down the Capitals of Europe and Asia in the accomplishment of my "Spiritual Destiny and Mission," desperately intent on converting Ferdinand, Louis Napoleon, the King of Delhi, Nasr-oo-deen, and the Grand Turk; for I believed that I was Heaven sent to save humanity in general, and crowned heads in particular.[89]

Though he does not mention the fact, he must have been introduced among the few early French enthusiasts for spiritualism and must have demonstrated to them the full range of America's more developed brand of spiritualism.[90] In those circles, however, he had nothing to learn and much to teach. They were the neophytes and probably looked to him for guidance.

Continental mesmerism was a different matter, and Randolph's encounter with the French mesmerists must have been an eye-opener for him. France at the time provided in mesmerism an atmosphere that was far more congenial to mystery and magic than was the case in common-sense, scientific, progressive America or even in England. Mesmerism had begun to make inroads in America in the late 1830s and early 1840s, but its influence had been largely restricted to fringe medicine, and the full paraphernalia of continental mesmerism were lacking.[91] Spiritualism was a very new phenomenon at the time on the Continent, but animal magnetism and mesmerism had by then a long tradition and were everywhere in vogue. Strange mages—such as Baron Dupotet and Louis-Alphonse Cahagnet—haunted the salons.

The eponymous father of all of this magnetic turmoil was Franz Anton Mesmer. He was a German physician working in Paris in the late eighteenth and early nineteenth century who proposed the existence of a universal magnetic fluid pervading the universe and then harnessed this fluid in glass containers and used the stored "magnetism" to cure disease.[92] In the process he incidentally provoked the first manifestations of what was to become a tidal wave of somnambulists, ecstatics, visionaries, healers, and miracle workers who overran Europe by mid-century. These soon learned that the universal fluid could be accumulated, controlled, and directed by passes of the hand or by the "operator's" will alone and did away with the apparatus of the earlier mesmerists; some even dispensed with the fluid itself and still under the banner of Mesmer, attributed their discoveries to the power of the soul and will alone. The great discovery of these magnetists, as we may call them, was the trance state ("somnambulism"), the radically different state of consciousness, attended by strange powers and visions of the other world, into which their subjects could be cast. To some extent, especially in England and in America, the magnetists tried to continue to toe the line of "scientific" medicine, but everywhere, especially on the Continent, Mesmer's disciples soon mixed his theories with all of the occult and mystical debris of the preceding centuries and discovered in ancient magical agents and practices superior methods of provoking and directing magnetic phenomena.

The chief among these magical magnetists was Baron Denis Jules Dupotet de Sennevoy (1796-1881). Randolph undoubtedly moved in his circle when in Paris and on one of his trips probably was taken by him to perform before Napoleon III.

At length, there came in invitation from Baron D——t, for me to attend and take part in, a Mesmeric Séance. I attended; and from the reputation I gained on that occasion, but a few days elapsed ere I was summoned to the Tuilleries, by command of his majesty, Napoleon III, who for thirty-four years had been a True Rosicrucian, and whom I had before met at the same place, but on a different errand than the present. What then and there transpired, so far as myself was actor, it is not for me to say, further than that certain experiments in clairvoyance were regarded as very successful, even for Paris, which is the centre of the Mesmeric world, and where there are hundreds who will read you a book blindfold.[93]

Dupotet was born in 1796 and, from the time he first heard of mesmerism in 1815 until his death in 1881, he devoted his life to its study. He initially sought out the leading lights of the new work—Deleuze, Puységur, the Abbé Faria. By 1820 he was absolutely convinced of the existence and power of the new science, and by 1826 he had set himself up to give free, public lessons, all the while continuing with his discoveries. These consisted most notably in his confirmation within the realm of mesmerism of the efficaciousness of abstract symbols (lines, circles, triangles) in affecting the behavior of the somnambulist. From this it was an easy step to the equation of that effect with the power attributed in the magical grimoires to sigils, magical circles and the like, and Dupotet easily—if secretly—took that step.[94]

Dupotet's most important discoveries, for present purposes, concerned the operation of the magic mirror. All ancient civilizations had used such things (crystals, pools of water or ink, silver or glass mirrors) and the magical literature abounds in directions for their manufacture and use. Dupotet's mirrors usually consisted simply of a spot drawn with charcoal on a wall or on a metal plate, and he soon realized their power to collect the universal fluid and to entrance the subject.[95]

Dupotet spent a considerable time in England in the late 1830s, where he was well received by Lord Stanhope (whom Emma Hardinge Britten later numbered among the members of the Orphic Circle, as we have seen) and other British magnetists whose brand of mesmerism was by and large more scientific and more exclusively devoted to medical purposes.[96] Dupotet published his discoveries in his *Journal du Magnétisme*, but he reserved his teachings on the real scope of magnetism to an inner group and distributed his ultimate teachings to these adepts only under seal of secrecy.[97] Primary among these ideas was the equation of the light reached by the somnambule at the finest level of the magnetic trance with the light and life of the Gospels and the light or fire described by the entire magical and mystical tradition, including (to name only those also singled out by Randolph) Hermes Trismegistus, Melchizedek, Zoroaster and the Guebres, those mysterious Persian priests of fire so dear to the fantasies of the nineteenth century.[98] Unlike Eliphas Lévi, who was to teach that the mesmeric subject reached only his own mental projections, Dupotet was convinced that "magic is founded on the existence of a mixed world, located outside ourselves, and with which we can enter into communication by the use of certain methods and practices."[99] In the magnetic slumber it was thus possible to contact the dead (or at least some imprint left by them on the magnetic fluid) and also to contact never embodied beings—celestial spirits.[100] Dupotet compared the subject's entering the magnetic light to a person placed "at the entrance to the invisible world, [whose] body is like a lyre whose strings vibrate, exposed to the wind."[101] Entrance to this world was to be gained through the concentration of vital force, usually in a magic mirror. The result could be like an eruption: "It is necessary, if only for a moment, that a fire circles in you, that a sort of erection, which has nothing of the erotic in it, permits you to cause a cerebral emission to leave your being."[102]

The details of Dupotet's practice and accomplishments within his inner circle have not been preserved, but it would appear that special practices were evolved. Music undoubtedly played a role in causing trance,[103] as did hashish. The members clearly believed—as did Randolph—in the possibility of acting upon others at a distance, by the projection of magnetic currents.[104] Also, Dupotet believed in and taught the existence of evil as well as good forces which could be encountered in vision and trance, and he constantly warned of their dangers.[105] Randolph was soon to renounce spiritualism and to do so primarily because he felt obsessed by just such evil forces.

Another prominent magnetist into whose company Randolph undoubtedly fell while in Paris in the mid-1850s was Louis-Alphonse Cahagnet (1809–1885).[106] He was a cabinet maker and furniture restorer, and in general was a far more simple and naive soul than Dupotet. In hundreds of experiments throughout the 1840s he found that his subjects while in trance could give the most astounding descriptions of the heavenly worlds and could converse freely with angels and the glorified spirits of the departed—including the almost omnipresent Swedenborg. These descriptions read now much like those of the early spiritualists a few years later, and the problems he wrestled with were the same as those that later were to haunt spiritualism. Can we really identify a particular "spirit" with a particular dead person? How can we separate the thoughts and impressions of the subject or operator from the true revelations of the spirit? Do we love and marry in the afterlife?[107] (On this last, Cahagnet's spirits assured him that we are eternally united with our husband or wife after death, but that there was no "love" in the sense that a Frenchman might understand the term.)[108] The primary goal of his experiments was to demonstrate that the soul was an entity that existed and could act independently of the body and that survived death. At a very early point his spirits revealed the idea of the pre-existence of souls, but Cahagnet always denied reincarnation.[109] Like Dupotet and indeed all of the contemporary mirror magicians, Cahagnet's experiences with visions in the mirror were second-hand: the entranced subject actually beheld the visions and then related them to him.[110]

Cahagnet's methods of inducing trance in his subjects included, besides the usual mesmeric passes, both magic mirrors and the use of drugs, especially hashish, as aids to clairvoyance. Randolph was familiar with him on both these counts. He speaks knowingly of the forms of hashish used by Adèle Maginot, Cahagnet's most famous seeress,[111] and explicitly attributes his acquaintance with hashish to the writings of Cahagnet.[112] Cahagnet advocated the use of hashish and other drugs in a variety of forms, in a liquor distilled from the flowers of hemp, in a pomade or salve (flowers of hemp and poppy, hashish, lard), and as the magnetic agent in magic mirrors.[113] Cahagnet says he first learned of magic mirrors from the spirit of Swedenborg, who had such a mirror during his life (he says) and who gave Cahagnet directions to make them. Swedenborg's original mirror consisted of a plate of glass, heated almost to melting, which was then covered with a paste of fine powdered lead mixed in oil. When this hardened it provided a pewter-like surface that was a good receptacle for the operator's magnetism.[114]

Over the years, Cahagnet experimented widely with magic mirrors, trying to find one that could maintain a greater reservoir of magnetism that would enable the seer to enter the highest states of consciousness, and eventually he hit upon complex mirrors of the type that Randolph (and the H. B. of L.) later adopted for use. These usually consisted of two pieces of glass or metal, one convex and one concave, that were fitted in a frame either rim to rim (to make a hollow shell) or hollow to hollow, leaving a narrow space which could be filled with various substances—including ink and hashish. In the mid-1880s, the Rev. William Alexander Ayton, of whom we shall have more to say later, had his friend T. H. Pattison make for him one of the former sort out of zinc and copper plates from Cahagnet's description, and Robert H. Fryar of Bath later republished Cahagnet's descriptions in various works.[115]

Yet another mage to be found walking the streets of Paris at the time of Randolph's first visits was Eliphas Lévi (A.-L. Constant). Many have concocted a detailed pseudo-history of Lévi's having initiated the young Randolph into various secret orders and then resigned from their leadership himself to make way for Randolph.[116] It is an enticing tale, but there is no reason whatever to think it true, and many reasons to believe it false.

Lévi (1810–1875) was a walking contradiction: a failed candidate for the priesthood and *quondam* revolutionary who simultaneously touted the authority of the magical tradition and condemned its practice as evil. The publication of his romantic exposition of magic—*Dogme de la Haute Magie* and *Rituel de la Haute Magie*—occurred in 1855 and 1856, coinciding with Randolph's first visit to the Continent.[117] From the mid-1850s until his death, Lévi proclaimed himself the great repository of occult truth and for a fee taught occultism to a small band of disciples.[118] It is thus clearly possible that Randolph might have become acquainted with the reclusive former abbé or his works, and in many ways, indeed, there is a clear parallelism between the thought of the two men. Lévi believed that Mesmer and the mesmerists, in announcing the existence of the subtle, universal magnetic fluid that pervaded the universe, had accidentally stumbled upon the innermost secret of all magical and religious traditions. He named this universal medium the "astral light," a term A. E. Waite says he borrowed from the eighteenth-century Martinists, and proceeded to systematize and interpret the whole of mythology and the magical tradition in its light. Basing himself experimentally on the discoveries that the magnetists, especially the Baron Dupotet, had made about the strange possibilities inherent in man (scrying, necromancy, action at a distance, angelic and celestial communication), Lévi rang out the changes and permutations of the idea throughout classical antiquity, the ancient high civilizations, the medieval grimoires, the Rosicrucians—and especially alchemy, which he taught was the effort to condense the astral light for practical use, especially in the form of the elixir of life, the universal medicine. The key to the control of the astral light, in turn, lay in the human will, whose cultivation and nurture were the essence of the secret tradition.

Lévi's similarities with Randolph are obvious. The astral light is simply Randolph's "Æth" under a different guise; the recitation of a genealogy of forerunners—reaching back to antediluvial times and culminating in the Rosicrucians—who taught the secrets of the æth and its possibilities is found throughout Randolph's work, and Randolph indeed believed he had discovered the elixir vitae and the universal medicine. Finally, the primacy of the will is one of the keys to all of Randolph's magic.

Despite all of this, the possibility of any real influence of Lévi on Randolph is extremely unlikely, and the undoubted similarities are far more easily explained by their common debt to the French mesmerist tradition. Lévi was an antiquarian, perfectly at ease in the by-ways of ancient lore, and he was most at home in the bookish interpretation of obscure symbolism. He did so, moreover, in the style of high romanticism. All of this is foreign to Randolph, who, while he may drop a name occasionally, is never pedantic and never (or rarely, in his novels) descends to the frills and chills of romanticism. Additionally, it is difficult to see how Randolph could really have been influenced by Lévi without adopting the term astral light—which became part of the *koiné* of occultism in the second half of the nineteenth century—and without betraying some interest in the kabbalah or the tarot, Lévi's main interests.[119] The primary difference between the two men, however, is that Randolph is first and foremost a practical, visionary occultist.[120] He relates what he himself has seen and experienced, and it was his goal to bring others to the same experience. Lévi is exactly the opposite. In his earliest works he at times glorifies magic as the key to all science and clearly advocates its use. Indeed, there is the one famous occasion in July 1854—the year before Randolph arrived in Europe—when Lévi was induced to cross the English Channel to evoke the spirit of Apollonius of Tyana, an evocation that left him terrified. Whether because he was fundamentally an orthodox Catholic or because he was terrified of the results of his dip into practical magic, Lévi in his later works condemned magical practice and magic in general (except the speculations of the tarot and the kabbalah) as delusions and evil.[121]

The names of other midcentury French magnetists, spiritualists, and occultists abound as do hints of private groups working out the secrets of animal magnetism, but little serious work, has yet been done in examining their work and most of these searchers are distinguished now only by their eccentricities.[122] Henri Delaage is one, now remembered if at all because he wrote a book collecting magical formulas used through the ages to increase beauty.[123] Eliphas Lévi's low opinion of him was exceeded only by his opinion of yet another mage—the Comte D'Ourches, who in fact had ties to Randolph. Lévi says

> It is owing to his rank as a publicist that we have placed [Delaage] in the first place among the Fantasiasts of Magic, but in all other respects it belongs to the Comte D'Ourches, a man of venerable age who has devoted his life and fortune to mesmeric experiments. Ladies in a state of somnambulism, and any furniture at his house, give themselves up to frenzied dances; the furniture becomes worn out and is broken, but it is said that the ladies are all the better for their gyrations.[124]

In magnetism, Lévi noted, the Comte D'Ourches was the pupil of the Abbé Faria (as was Dupotet originally), and in necromancy he belonged to the "school" of Baron Ludwig de Güldenstubbé, an expatriate Estonian noble who had experimented (in decidedly odd ways) with Allan Kardec's brand of spiritualism from its beginnings. The examples given by Lévi of the sorts of phenomena (knockings, table turnings, automatic writing) produced by these two aristocratic researchers fully justify his judgment on the count. From the phenomena the Comte D'Ourches generated he appears to have been basically a spiritualist of the grosser, table-turning sort.[125] Despite this, Randolph spoke highly of him as one of those who published the teaching of the Rosicrucian Order.[126]

Randolph's admiration indicates that there may have been more to the Comte D'Ourches than Lévi's jibes reveal—though the eccentricities obscure the man. The count also figures in the account of no less a personage than one of Madame Blavatsky's masters, an account that paints a vivid picture of the milieu in which Randolph moved in his visits to Paris.

In November 1875, Madame Blavatsky transcribed (apparently from the narrative of her Master Hilarion) a short piece for the Boston *Spiritual Scientist* entitled "An Unsolved Mystery." This centered on a mysterious figure calling himself "Vic de Lassa" who moved in the occult underworld of Paris in the early 1860s—the time of Randolph's third visit to Europe.[127] De Lassa passed himself off as a Hungarian and claimed a great age. He supposedly astonished fashionable Paris in the fall of 1861 with his predictions and crystal gazing. The truth of these revelations concerning M. de Lassa were in turn vouched for in a later issue of the *Spiritual Scientist* by a certain "Endreinek Agardi of Koloswar," whom Madame Blavatsky in her scrapbook identified as a disciple of Master Hilarion. Agardi in addition told of the amazement of the aged Count D'Ourches who believed that Madame de Lassa was none other than the wife of Count Cagliostro whom he had met in 1786—the implication being, of course, that de Lassa was Cagliostro himself. Madame Blavatsky in her scrapbook comments on the passage that "initiates are as hard to catch as the sun-sparkle which flecks the dancing wave on a summer day. One generation of man may know them under one name in a certain country, and the next, or a succeeding one, see them as some one else in a remote land."[128]

The effect of his French travel on Randolph was marked, and, as we shall see, the knowledge of magic mirrors and drugs to facilitate clairvoyance that he acquired on his trips in 1855 and 1857 was the main impetus for his earliest publications.

Return to America

Randolph's travels on his first trip probably extended only to England, France, and Germany,[129] and before the end of 1855 he was back in America. His European trip revitalized his career in spiritualism in the United States, but his apparent slight at the hands of Robert Owen at the World Convention still rankled. In November the *New England Spiritualist* prominently reprinted part 7 of Owen's *New Existence of Man Upon Earth* in which he explained that it was only the press of business (and a suspicion that spiritualism might distract from the general reform tone of the World convention) that prevented him from allowing Randolph to speak.[130] Randolph replied with a blistering letter to the same journal in December 1855, relating some "spicy criticisms" of the goings on at the convention and on that class of mediums in general who "farm out their services at the best possible price, while his motto is, 'Let the truth be free.'" The *New England Spiritualist* noted the letter but refused to print it, adding: "We think the sensitive nature of our friend has led him to speak with more pungency than his better feelings will justify at a future date."[131]

For the next few months, advertisements of Randolph's trance lectures around New England and New York and reports of his discourses appear frequently in the spiritualist papers—often with disclaimers based on his "sensitivity."

> All who have ever heard him speak, under favorable conditions, will bear testimony to the fact that, although his extreme susceptibility leads him at times to erratic and startling expressions, yet his discourses furnish much food for thought for philosophical minds. We are glad to learn that improving health allows him to undertake an effort of this kind, and trust that it may result in mutual profit to him and his auditors.[132]

His advertisements for performances give some indication both of the state of his finances at the time and of his interests. In December 1855 he announced a series of six lectures for the Music Hall in Boston, at 50 cents for the series. The lectures included "The Human Soul—its Parallelism with Nature, Art, Death! Is Man a Free Agent! with Glances at Model Men—Telegraph Men, Vegetable Men, and Humor Man," "The Spirit of the Age, and Human Genius; Slavery, Freedom, Reform, Civilization," "The Twelve Apostles of the Modern Gospel" (including A. J. Davis, T. L. Harris, James L. Scott, and "the lecturer Randolph"). He also intended to speak, from his observations in England, France, and Germany, on the general progress of humanitarian ideals. In announcing the topics of the lecture series, however, the editors of the journal cautioned tantalizingly: "It is Mr. Randolph's intention to deliver these Lectures in his *normal* state, yet it is *possible* that he may be controlled by superior or *spirit* influences; if so he cannot be held responsible should there be an entire change of subject."[133]

Randolph did not disappoint his audience's expectations.

> I attended the second lecture of Mr. Randolph's course on Thursday evening last. When I entered the lecture room, he was reading from a manuscript, in which he had evidently better arranged and elaborated his ideas than in his extemporaneous discourse of the Sunday evening previous. Soon, however, he suddenly paused in his discourse, abruptly snatched his manuscript from the desk before him, and exclaimed, "I am impressed to throw this all away!" He remained silent for a few moments, in which, I should judge, he became profoundly entranced, when

he commenced speaking as by spirit-influence; the spirit purporting to impress him remarking at the outset, that the medium having no definite and systematic idea of the subject upon which he was attempting to speak, he had volunteered to elucidate it for him; for which condescension and kindness, I most heartily thanked the spirit; and I would advise the lecturer in future, at all times, to invoke that spirit's aid. After this 'prefatory remark, he proceeded to deliver, for the space of about an hour, one of the finest discourses to which I have ever listened. It was consecutive, systematic and logical, replete with profound thought clothed in rare rhetorical beauty, and enunciated in a style of elocution *much superior* to that of the medium in his normal state. The spirit impressing him was evidently versed in the learning of the schools, using scientific technicalities with accomplished precision, and illustrating his subject by figures drawn from the various departments of science. He struck deeper veins of thought, and soared to higher heights than many who are regarded as profound and brilliant lecturer, are accustomed to in their discourses. Some passages were cumulative and climacteric, and would do credit to many mundane rhetoricians and elocutionists who have already achieved enviable reputations, reaped lustrous honors and grasped the "keys of fame!"—Who that should listen to P. B. Randolph in his normal condition, and as influenced upon this occasion, could doubt that he was the recipient of spiritual assistance in the utterance of a discourse of such rare beauty and power.

P.S. Since writing the above, I have heard the third lecture of Mr. Randolph's course, which exceeded in interest and power the second. He commenced by saying he again appeared as an advocate of Spiritualism, a definition of which he attempted to give in a previous discourse—when suddenly he became entranced, and the spirits announced: *"And we come to finish what he so badly began!"* He recapitulated the prominent ideas of his Thursday evening's lecture, and then proceeded to illustrate the soul's progress and development, speaking for about an hour and a half with thrilling effect.[134]

The message on spiritualism that Randolph conveyed in his lectures after his return from his first European trip was that the new movement led "to the development of the intellectual, moral and spiritual perceptions of those who accepted it, lifting them above the fogs of skepticism and materiality into a *certainty* of endless life and a *consciousness* of all-embracing love."[135] In addition to these spiritualist efforts, Randolph also began to speak (probably not intentionally in trance) on such reform topics as "The Negro and His Destiny; the Means to be used to Elevate the Race, and Banish Slavery."[136]

By May 1856, when he was speaking in Cleveland, Randolph began announcing his plans to return to England in the fall—for a year or perhaps for good, "if a sphere of 'usefulness'" were to be opened for him there—at the direction of the "Royal Circle of the Spiritual Heavens."[137]

Second European Trip: 1857

In early January 1857, Randolph was in London and appeared before the "Spirit-Power Circle" at Charing Cross where he presented the views of four spirit members of the Royal Circle.[138] The Spirit-Power Circle was a recently formed body that sponsored seances and exhibitions for the public free of charge, and Randolph's trance speeches, by now somewhat old-hat in America, were very well received by English audiences. Some fifteen to twenty-five persons would attend, and the evenings began with general conversation on spiritualist subjects and "table-turning" by lesser spirits. After several hours came the high point of the evening—Randolph's trance.

> The time for Trance had now arrived, but there seemed a deadness in the room, and it was not till a few minutes before 9 o'clock that Mr. Randolph was under Spirit influence, and after stating that the Spirit who had promised to take up the subject "Sanity and Insanity" could not stay at the circle as we had not, at the time appointed, attended to the conditions as arranged at the previous circle,—but that . . . a "little Spirit" from the 5th sphere would answer a few questions. He stated he was known on earth as a chemist—that his time was occupied in endeavoring to develop the power of the gases &c., and after eloquently speaking and using telling similes, shewing us the necessity of obeying the directions of the spirits in the course of the seance, as they saw the nature of the emanations flowing from each sitter at the circle and had to arrange those emanations so as to produce a result to satisfy the circle. He at the close gave the name of H. D. (Humphry Davy).[139]

In March 1857, the *Yorkshire Spiritual Telegraph* printed the transcription of one of Randolph's trance addresses in which he channeled a spirit calling himself "The Stranger" and replied to the audience's question, "What and where is God?" The discourse painted a vast panorama of God's action in every atom of creation, from the mineral to man, and culminated in the statement that shows that Randolph was moving away from the pure immanentism of Andrew Jackson Davis.

I cannot tell you that this universe is complete in itself, because it is only a particle in a vast creation. God is an immense central sun, throwing out his rays in various directions; some darting to the north, others to the south, to the east, and to the west: incarnating themselves into various universes, but not in all universes alike. The attributes of his power vary according to the intensity of the ray they receive.

God is more in the vegetable than in the mineral kingdom, more in the sentient than in the vegetable, more in man than in the sentient.

There is one man in each world who as a crystal, receives one ray from God: Christ is that man.[140]

Randolph's exhibitions were not limited to public trance speaking. In late January he presided over a "Dark Circle" at a private home in London during which he caused "multitudes of lights" in the shape of "bright starry specks" to be seen by the sitters and made a "column of greyish white light" move about the table. He next produced for an instant "a *human form* about two feet high," and ended with some quite creditable materializations.

The next thing that took place was very singular indeed. Mr. P. the artist, sat opposite Mr. Randolph the medium, and directly between the two appeared several times two rather indistinct and ropery human forms, which floated as it were together, and then mingled into one, and then disappeared in a sort of grey blue mists and as they did so, a bright star, intensely brilliant ascended from Mr. F's. head and seemed to pass through the ceiling. Streaks of light, and half moons now appeared in different parts of the room, and almost instantly thereafter Mr. F. accused Mr. W. junior, of touching him, which accusation was indignantly repelled by the young gentleman. But now came a great wonder, for a Spirit hand took Mr. F's. hand in its grasp and shook it till the house fairly trembled; it was the greeting of a dearly loved one, and affected us all very much indeed by its fond earnestness. It kept this up for at least five minutes, and Mr. F. declared the hand felt as soft as satin.[141]

On other occasions, he acted as the medium for the thoughts of the dead and correctly answered his listeners' questions on the earthly life of the deceased, even when asked in a foreign language.[142] Also on this trip Randolph appears to have spoken publicly on topics of more general interest and to have done so to enthusiastic reviews.[143]

Despite his favorable reception at the time, there are vague rumors in the spiritualist press that hint of conflict between Randolph and British spiritualists, and Emma Hardinge Britten's conclusion appears justified that Randolph's eccentricities prevented him from having a permanent effect on English spiritualism.[144]

After his performances the spiritualist press urged Randolph to stay and spread the good news in England, but, after extending his stay for a few weeks, Randolph let it be known that he had just arrived from Egypt and was in such poor health that he could not be expected to live long and "that he returns to Egypt very soon for that reason, and hopes to visit Persia, India, China and Japan, in order to finish a great philosophical work on which he is engaged."[145]

From this account, it would appear Randolph had visited the Continent and gone on to Egypt in late 1856, immediately before coming to England. There is reason, however, for doubting this chronology.[146] It appears more likely that Randolph's next trip to Paris took place in the spring of 1857 after his successful appearances in London, and that from there he first went on to the mysterious East. His account of the trip, given to a reporter, was garbed in the most mysterious terms:

> During his absence, he informs me, he has visited Spain, and various parts of Europe, Egypt, Asia Minor, Jerusalem, etc.; and his observations and studies have, of course, been more or less in the channel of the occult. In particular he would seem to have cultivated the acquaintance of Egyptian and Persian wonder-workers, and Indian Brahmins.
>
> The Brahmins, he says, deny that the intercourse with invisible beings, claimed by American Spiritualism, is with the spirits of the departed of this earth. They say that our apparently spiritual visitors, are simply the natural inhabitants of refined planets belonging to our system, on tours of discovery, fun and pleasure among us. In proof, they call flitting figures, of a small race of beings, upon a marble table, visible to the naked eye, who, they declare, are not spirits, but inhabitants of those refined material spheres.
>
> The Brahminical theory is this: Our solar system contains twenty-four planets, the one nearest the sun being the most gross; and thence they refine the ratio of distance, to the outermost or last.

The thirteenth of the series is too refined to obstruct rays of light, or to be visible to our organs of sight. And the intangible beings pouring in on this earth so thickly at the present time, according to the Brahmins, are the natural inhabitants of those worlds.[147]

It is impossible now to disentangle any details of this trip from a later one he made in 1861 and 1862 after which he began increasingly to clothe his teachings in Oriental garb and to invoke the name of the mysterious Ansairee or Nusa'iri. However, we can, distinguish at least some of the events of this trip in 1857 and 1858 on the basis of their effects on his later work, more specifically on the "perfection" of his hashish elixirs and his use of the name *Rosicrucian* to describe his thought.

Over twenty years ago [i.e., c. 1852], Mr. Randolph was known to be a Rosicrucian, and in that period he ascended the steps of that mystical brotherhood, outstripping thousands and rushing past hundreds of gray-beards in the mental race, until he attained the chieftainship of the true Rosicrucians in America and the Isles of the Seas, and finally to the supreme High Priesthood of the Order and Grand-Mastership of the combined Lodges of the earth likewise, reaching the double office through his absolute defiance of poverty and wealth, and persistent pursuit of ideas alone!

* * *

Twenty years ago Randolph began his part of the work. Fifteen years ago [i.e., 1857 or 1858] he suddenly disappeared from the American continent. When next heard from he had not only made the tour of Europe, circulating in the highest literary, philosophical, scientific, even royal circles, but among the most secret, mystical societies of England and France (For an account of his astounding experiences in Paris, and with Napoleon III, see his "Ravalette."—Editor.), and had penetrated Greece, Syria, Arabia, Turkey, Egypt, until at length the "London Times" and New York "Herald" correspondents announce him as the favored guest of the Abyssinian king, Theodore, and his black majesty of Dongola; and he passed everywhere unquestioned, unscathed by serpent, climate, beast or man! Not only so, but by some secret means and power, penetrating with impunity the wild fastnesses of savage men, which no other native of a Christian land, not even

Livingstone, Baker, Gould, Cummings, Huc, Bird or Tytler had even ventured to distantly approach. . . . and all this journey bent on discovering the grand secret which the arch-fraternity had been seeking during two hundred—not years—but centuries, this universal medicine, which all men feel really *does* exist somewhere in nature, and that was to heal all disturbances of human, physical love-nature, chemical, organic, and magnetic, nervous and dynamic alike, thus restoring the equilibrium between the natural forces, then, by reaction and reflection, curing those of the immortal part likewise."[148]

If this is not simply more of the conflation of events and anachronism that Randolph warned about in his novels,[149] the reference to the search for the universal medicine—which was *dowam meskh* and which Randolph was selling as "protozone" at least as early as 1860—indicates that Randolph took the occasion of this second trip to improve his familiarity with hashish in the Near East, as did many another Western traveler at the time, notably Madame Blavatsky and Richard F. Burton. He certainly returned from this trip with an unalloyed enthusiasm for hashish as an aid to the development of clairvoyance.[150] He also returned, as we shall see, as "Le Rosicrucien," with a mature view of the nature of the soul and with a full-blown method, based on the use of magic mirrors, of reaching the soul world and higher clairvoyance.

In the present state of research it is really impossible to say anything specific about the denizens of the magical and occult world Randolph found on his Near Eastern trips. The entire region from the Caspian to the Nile and the Bosphorus was teeming with obscure cults and orders, sufis, dervishes, charmers, crystal gazers, magicians, and obscure Masonic and nationalistic currents, and Randolph had both the opportunity and the inclination to investigate all of them.[151] Certainly, as we shall see in discussing his longest trip in 1861 and 1862, he found something there that led him later to call his system of sexual magic "Ansairetic" and to garb his subsequent teachings in Oriental dress. Equally certainly he encountered there something that confirmed for him the reality of what he was to learn in vision—that the Rosicrucians extended on "both sides of the grave."

$\mathcal{T}$HE $\mathcal{F}$RUITS OF $\mathcal{R}$ANDOLPH'S $\mathcal{T}$RAVELS IN THE 1850s

B y March 1858, Randolph was back in the United States where he labored from October 1858 through the spring of 1860 on a work that would embody what he had learned on his travels.[1] By mid-1860 he was advertising his new knowledge for sale in a pamphlet entitled "Clairvoyance; How to Produce It, and Perfect It, with an essay on 'Hashish, Its Benefits and Its Dangers.' Also, 'How to Make the Magic Glass, or Mirror of the Dead, by means of which the Oriental Magi are said to have held intelligent commerce with spirits.'"[2] This was the fruit of Randolph's travels and summarized the ideas on clairvoyance, hashish, and the practice of the magic mirror that he had learned in France, England, and the Near East on his trips in 1855 and 1857. The work, unfortunately, has not survived, but Randolph's *Guide to Clairvoyance*, published in 1867, undoubtedly reproduces its teachings on clairvoyance and on hashish,[3] and the sections on clairvoyance and on magic mirrors were frequently reworked by Randolph under various titles in the late 1860s and early 1870s.[4]

$\mathcal{H}$ashish

As he later explained in the fall of 1858, when he recanted his early commitment to spiritualism, Randolph believed that early in his career he had fallen completely under the control of an evil power, a "vampire," by yielding his will and consciousness to trance, and that for years his speech and his every movement had been controlled.

Once in my career, when for years I have been under the control of a power, strong almost as Fate, wicked as Sin itself, I was made to think, say and do things, against which, in the rare moments, when the good angel was in the ascendant, my soul protested; yet in vain. The vile power was as unrelenting as death, as persevering as the seasons. . . . For a time reason was aberrated, self-destruction attempted, and all the world looked black as night, nor should I now be here to warn others, had not Infinite Wisdom directed my steps to far off lands, in which, thank Him, the lost balance was to a great extent restored. The effects of this original folly—the yielding of the will to an unseen, unknown, unfathomed, invisible influence, are yet, at the end of long years, keenly felt.[5]

While it may have been the infinite wisdom and foreign travel that released Randolph from his possession, the more immediate cause of the cure was a "marvelous drug" called *dowam meskh* (Arabic: "medicine of immortality")—whose principal component was hashish—which he first took in France in 1855 and later studied more carefully on his subsequent trips to the Continent and Egypt.

Hashish had come into prominence in Europe in the beginning of the nineteenth century with the return of Napoleon's soldiers from Egypt and the opening up of the Near East to European travel. Sylvestre de Sacy had written on the drug as early as 1809, and the book of Moreau de Tours on the treatment of hallucinations with hashish (1845) had made it fashionable in France among the poets and literati of the period who attended the Club des Hachichins of Baudelaire and Théophile Gautier.[6] Hashish use was also highly regarded among the French mesmerists—including Cahagnet and Dupotet—in whose circles Randolph first came into contact with it, and it began to make inroads among American and British spiritualists at the end of the 1850s.[7] In the Near East, *dowam meskh* was prepared as an electuary of hashish and other (active or inactive) components, but in France among the mesmerists and later the occultists the term became synonymous with hashish.[8] Randolph, as we shall see, in at least one recipe attributed to him continued the older usage and advocated the use of a salve compounded with opium, henbane, and belladonna.

Randolph says, variously, that he first encountered the drug in 1855 or 1856, "[l]ured by what Cahagnet wrote about the use of narcotic agents, and strengthened in the hope by what Théophile Gautier, Bayard Taylor, Fitz Hugh Ludlow, and various other travelers, wrote regarding the use" of hashish, and that he was led to make two experiments with the drug[9] and later studied it thoroughly in Egypt.[10] He took eighteen grains of the preparation and had "the serenest and most beatific vision" he had ever experienced. "It perfectly illuminated me, but the lucidity infinitely exceeded anything I had ever known before, with no loss of will or self-consciousness."[11] The drug changed him from an atheist into a believer and freed him (at least temporarily) from his feeling of being controlled by the "spirits." It was quite literally a revelation to him.

In his early days of open enthusiasm for the drug, Randolph—as the French mesmerists had before him—found that hashish constituted the perfect food of the soul. Man was a triple being, soul, spirit, and body, and at each level he fed on the corresponding, appropriate level of food. Hashish, or rather its essence, directly fed the soul, man's highest portion.[12] If, as Randolph says, he had been searching for years to find the "wine of life," the elixir that would perfectly restore the depleted vital fluid that served to connect soul and body, he had found it in hashish, the real secret of the wisdom tradition.

There is no doubt that Confucius, Pythagoras, and his disciples, the Alchemists, Hermetists, Illuminati, and mystic brethren of all ages used it to exalt them while making their researches for the Philosopher's Stone (Crystals, rings, and mirrors—means of clairvoyance); Secret of Perpetual Youth (A fluid so fine, as when taken, to be instantly converted into vital magnetism, thus supplying all waste, repairing all effects of excess and exhaustion, reinvigorating the brain, nervous forces, and therefore restoring the vigor of youth); and the Elixir of Life (An universal solvent,—a fluid that will vacate the body of all morbid humors, and thus let the vital forces have free action).[13]

On his return from his European and Near Eastern trip of 1857 and 1858, Randolph was regularly using hashish and experiencing wonderful visions of light, expanded consciousness, and out-of-body travel, but he was at first reluctant to mention his experiences. This changed by mid-1860, when he became an open, avowed, and enthusiastic proponent of hashish use as the royal road to clairvoyance and the replenisher of vital forces.[14] At one point before the Civil War he was probably the largest importer of hashish into the United States. His commitment is revealed in an advertisement he placed in the *Banner of Light* in October 1860:

HASHISH!

In reply to numerous correspondents let me say that nearly all the Hashish I brought with me from Europe, (and none other is fit to use,) is exhausted. The balance I will sell at $ four a bottle, with full directions how to secure the celestial, and avoid the ill fantasies. I have only twenty-five cases left out of three hundred and fifty, so that those who want the genuine Oriental article must send at once to

Dr. P. B. Randolph
17 Bromfield St., Boston, Mass.[15]

Randolph's expressions of enthusiasm for hashish, however, waxed and waned over time. As with almost every other idea he ever took up, Randolph's positions on hashish and its value appear to change from year to year—and often even from edition to edition of his books, where earlier references to "hashish" are later replaced by "Fantasie" or omitted altogether.[16] The drug becomes alternatively a dangerous and "pestilent thing"[17] and a wondrous guide to clairvoyance.[18]

The overwhelming impression received from all of Randolph's accounts is that of a man, already unstable from years of spirit-trance, who had undergone a staggering and pivotal experience, both frightening and enlightening, from his use of hashish, and who then tried to come to grips with it for years after, all the while terrified and tantalized in turns by the drug's power. In other words, Randolph sounds like a man who, has had "a bad trip." His disclaimers of fear of the drug sound hollow, especially when he reveals that twice he fell under the influence of the drug "accidentally." "People often ask me if I use hashish, and I reply, I took it twice on purpose, and twice accidentally, many years ago. I have not used it since, not that I fear its power, but because I need it not."[19] He was certainly familiar with the drug's power, and his descriptions of its powers sound like passages from Moreau de Tours or Fitz Hugh Ludlow. In advising its use for clairvoyance, he says "Look sharp, be steady, for there's a power at work within you, capable of plunging you into thick gloom, elevating you into the bliss of paradise, and of leading your soul through the shadow, into regions of ineffable light, and glorious, illimitable, transcendent beauty."[20] Passivity in the face of the drug would lead to fearful visions. "It will burst upon you like the crash of ten thousand thunders, and for hours you will be the sport of imaginations turned to realities of the queerest, strangest, weirdest, and perhaps terrific kind."[21]

Another—and not unlikely—view is that Randolph's warnings about hashish were simply window dressing, adopted for social reasons, and that fundamentally he never lost his real enthusiasm for the drug.[22] In 1867, he reprinted as part 2 of his *Guide to Clairvoyance* a treatise entitled "Extasia, Fantasia, Hashish and its Uses" that is probably a reworking of the original enthusiastic pamphlet on hashish he had published in 1860. In this, he cautions that he did not as a rule approve of hashish for "extasia, fantasia or clairvoyance" for the simple reason that it was difficult to obtain the pure article. The finer sorts of true Turkish or Egyptian *dowam meskh* were prepared "by adepts" from the unripe capsules of hemp mixed with sugar, glycerine or jelly, and were not widely available in the United States.[23] This disclaimer was really an enticement to his readers rather than a condemnation of hashish use because it was precisely this superior preparation of the drug that Randolph claimed to be selling under a variety of names throughout his career.[24] In one of his last books, *The New Mola* (1873), he advertised that two of his patent medicines, phymylle and amylle, provided pure forms of the drug. He touted the first as especially suited for nervous exhaustion and the second as the panacea for "passional excess, onanism, etc." Together they were the best "aphrodision" in the world. He offered the elixirs for ten to twenty-five dollars a bottle, and also offered to sell physicians the recipe for "Mauret's granules and lozenges" and his phloxine—all concocted with hashish.[25]

Hashish also played a substantial role in Randolph's esoteric teachings that circulated only in manuscript.[26] *Magia Sexualis*, a book which was published in Paris by Maria de Naglowska in 1931 but which is in large part a translation of various of Randolph's public and private works, gives what is claimed to be his formula for an ointment to produce visions in magic mirrors. Among other ingredients, it calls for:

300 grams of hashish
250 grams of opium
50 grams of henbane
20 grams of belladonna.[27]

The recipe, even if it was not derived from Randolph's private lessons to his followers as de Naglowska claimed, is at least consistent with his ideas, and the admixture of hashish with other drugs correctly reflects what Randolph learned about the preparation of the drug on his travels in the Near East.

Clairvoyance

Clairvoyance, as the term had been used in American spiritualism and animal magnetism of the time, usually meant only an elevated sense of visual perception, present in or out of trance, which enabled its possessor to read sealed envelopes, play chess blindfolded, visualize the interior of the body to diagnose and cure disease, and the like. Even where the term had been applied to true "vision"—as, for example, to the "superior condition" enjoyed by Andrew Jackson Davis— it usually meant a state that descended unprovoked on the seer as a gift from heaven. There were no American "schools of clairvoyance" at the time.

Randolph changed all of that. For him, clairvoyance, in its highest manifestations, was always the flight of the conscious soul to the furthest regions of the soul world (as he would come to define the term). Nor was it a third-party, indirect phenomenon in which an "operator" entranced a "seer" and then listened passively to the seer's descriptions of the vision. Rather, it was a state that the aspirant himself could be taught to reach through drugs and by magical practice, especially magic mirrors. It was a science, and Randolph professed himself its teacher.

For Randolph, clairvoyance in its lowest and most natural manifestations, was an almost universal possibility for men. It was "a generic term, employed to express various degrees and modes of perception, whereby one is enabled to cognize and know facts, things, and principles; or to contact certain knowledges, without the use, and independent of, the ordinary avenues of sense."[28]

As such, clairvoyance covered a vast range of phenomena extending from simple sympathy or empathy, through psychometry to "intuition." Sympathy was the (more or less conscious) feeling of knowing that accompanies visual perception. Psychometry was not visual at all, but "magnetic contact" that placed the clairvoyant en rapport with persons or objects, even in their absence. Intuition was "the highest quality of the human mind," and in its ultimate form as "clairvoyance absolute" gave a "magnificent sweep of intellect and vision that leaps the world's barriers, forces the gates of death, and revels in the sublime mysteries of the universe."[29] In the last degrees of this highest stage of clairvoyance,

> [s]pecial cerebral organs become lucid, soon succeeded by an entire illumination of the brain. This is a grand, a sublime, a holy degree, for the subject sees, senses, feels, *knows*, by a royal power; is *en*

rapport with a thousand knowledges. A step further, a step inward, and the subject is in harmony with both the upper and lower universes. He or she thenceforth is a POWER IN THE WORLD.[30]

But, what *is* true clairvoyance? I reply, it is the ability, by self-effort or otherwise, to drop beneath the floors of the outer world, and come up, as it were, upon the other side. We often see what we take to be sparks or flashes or light before us in the night; but they are *not* really what they seem, but are instantaneous penetrations of the veil that, pall-like, hangs between this outer world of Dark and Cold, and the inner realm of Light and Fire, in the midst of which it is embosomed, or, as it were, enshrouded; and true clairvoyance is the lengthened uplifting of that heavy pall. . . . [I]t is a rich and very valuable power, whose growth depends upon the due observance of the normal laws which underlie it. The price of power is obedience to law. . . . "What, then, is clairvoyance?" I reply: It is the LIGHT which the seer reaches sometimes through years of agony; by wading through oceans, as it were, of tears and blood; it is an interior unfoldment of native powers, culminating in somnambulic vision through the mesmeric processes, and the comprehension and application of the principles that underlie and overflow human nature and the physical universe, together with a knowledge of the principia of the vast spirit-sea whereon the worlds of space are cushioned.[31]

The terms in this vivid description are, as we shall see, terms of art with very specific meanings for Randolph. The "inner realm of Light and Fire" is the Æth, the all-encompassing magnetic fluid that unites the soul to the soul world, and the "thousand knowledges" that clairvoyance puts the aspirant *en rapport* with are not mere generalities, but the awful denizens of the celestial hierarchy.

Randolph strongly believed that spiritualism was a temporary measure—a movement deliberately excited for the sole purpose of convincing the modern world of the immortality of the soul. Its own results were questionable at best, but it was really only a preliminary step toward clairvoyance, the next step in the planned development of mankind. This was a superior stage of development, and one that gave firsthand experience rather than mere secondhand, indirect knowledge.

The difference, therefore, between positive seership and mediumship in any form is the difference of a whole species; or that between *hearing* a description of Paris and *seeing* Paris one's self; that is to say, it is the difference between act and experience, and the merest hearsay.[32]

The superiority of Psycho-vision to the so-called mediumism of the day, for all purposes whatever, is too apparent to further need argument. Spiritual manifestations subserve the grand end of demonstrating the sublime fact of post-mortem existence, but, as a revelative power, otherwise is of little use; the quality of mediumship unquestionably injurious, because it is impossible to *know* whether the possessing invisible is good or evil. A "Hearsay" is good; but "I see and know," is a great deal better.[33]

The differences between spiritualism and clairvoyance, for Randolph, were many:

First. Not ten percent of what passes for spiritual intercourse has a higher origin than the "medium's" mind.

Second. What one sees, feels, hears, is positive proof to him or her. All spiritual communications come second-handed, but the clairvoyant sees *directly* and reaches knowledge by the first intention.

Third. If a person is lucid (clairvoyant), he or she has a secret personal positive power, and need not consult any other authority whatever.

Fourth. "Mediumship" is automacy; a medium is a machine played on and worked by others, when it really exists; but the clairvoyant sees, knows, understands, learns and grows in personal magnetic and mental power day by day; and, while embodied, makes the very best preparations for the certain and absolute life beyond the grave, which awaits us all when this "fever called living is over at last."

Fifth. Clairvoyance necessarily subtilizes and refines the mind, body, tastes, passions and tendencies of everyone who possesses and practices it.[34]

Randolph's clairvoyance thus differed not merely from spiritualism but also from the almost universal understanding of clairvoyance that Randolph had encountered in America and on his European travels. It is also the first shot in the battle that was to transform spiritualism into occultism (See chapter 12). For Randolph clairvoyance not only was an exceedingly sublime state of vision, but it was also a conscious phenomenon, rather than a result of trance, and it was a condition that was available, if not to everyone, at least to most.

Randolph boasted that clairvoyance was a science and that, "as far as America was concerned," he was "the only teacher of clairvoyance as a *System* and *Science*."[35] The qualification on America is important because it implies a claim to dependence on foreign sources and authority. He left no doubt that to some extent the methods he taught were his own discovery[36] and that their organization was the result of his efforts, but his debt to what he had seen and learned abroad is clear.

[Clairvoyance] is, in my case, the final reward and guerdon bestowed for faithful service in the great cause of superior truths,— truths, the result of an experience almost without a parallel on earth, and the result of years of research and travel throughout this country, England, France, Scotland, Ireland, Egypt, Syria, Arabia, Palestine, Turkey and other lands—an interior unfoldment of native powers, culminating in somnambulic vision through the Mesmeric Processes, and the comprehension and application of the principles that underlie and overflow human nature and the physical universe, together with a knowledge of the principia of the vast spirit-sea whereon the worlds of space are cushioned. Thus true clairvoyance in my case, is knowledge resulting from experiment, born of agony, and purified by the baptism of fire.[37]

This vague recognition of foreign sources will become for Randolph the chain of succession from the mysterious Ansairee or Nusa'iri of Syria and the Supreme Temple of the Rosicrucians.

Randolph thought that a person desiring to develop clairvoyance should first be tested to determine his or her proclivities. Self-tests were possible and could be performed by looking steadily at a speck on the wall in a darkened room or by hyperventilating. If dizziness or drowsiness resulted, or, in some cases, if flashes of lights or luminous clouds passed before the face, the person was a good candidate for clairvoyance.[38] Randolph offered to perform a more thorough examination and asked the candidate to answer a long list of personal questions (character, physical type, fondness for sweets, type of hair, large or small brain, etc.) and to send a photograph—and, of course, a fee of five dollars plus return postage.[39]

Randolph's general instructions on clairvoyance were fairly pedestrian, common to the mesmerists of the time both in France and

England. Healthful, light food, cleanliness, deep breathing, and temporary sexual abstinence (at least in this version of Randolph's teachings) were preliminary prerequisites—aided, of course, by Randolph's various elixirs for those suffering from depletion of their vital energies. The actual production of clairvoyance could then be brought about in various ways. In Randolph's view the capabilities of the individual determined to some extent the method chosen to develop clairvoyance. The methods he openly acknowledged included "the Mesmeric, Magnetic, 'Circles,' Spiritual and Mesmeric, Self-Mesmerism, Opium, Hashish, and Muust."[40] The simplest method taught was little more than an injunction to try to see with the eyes covered. The aspirant should "set apart the first hour after retiring to bed nightly. Eat a light supper; bind a light silk bandage over the entire forehead and eyes, turn the face toward the darkest corner of the room, and endeavor to see."[41] The results of this would be: "1st, You will see a dim haze. 2d, A spark of light. 3d, A greater light. 4th, Misty forms will float before you. 5th, They will grow distinct. 6th, Answers will flow into your mind. 7th, You will gradually merge into a radiant light; behold the actual dead, converse with them, and realize your soul's desire."[41]

Mesmeric clairvoyance could also be induced magnetically simply by holding a quartz crystal, horseshoe magnet, or suitable magnetized bar of wax (filled with iron filings) or magnetic ring near the head.[42] It was also obtainable through various traditional mesmeric methods, either by joining in a circle of persons joining hands or by holding a circle of twisted iron and copper wires—carefully seeing to it that the chairs were insulated from the ground by glass globes—or by being magnetized by passes from a person of the opposite sex.[43] Randolph also gave a "special" variant of these mesmeric methods that he thought the "most perfect of its kind upon the earth.

> I now give the special method of thorough magnetization, to gain which I went from Paris to Marseilles, and remained there till I learned it of the greatest mesmerizer the world ever saw,—the Italian Count,—mentioned in my book "Ravalette." I consider this single piece of information worth ten times the cost of this little book, because it is the most perfect of its kind upon the earth.[44]

This magnetic method of inducing clairvoyance could be worked either by a subject and operator or in the insulated mesmeric circle already mentioned. First a mirror was to be hung on the north wall of the darkened chamber. The person who sought to develop clairvoyance was then seated with his or her back to the mirror so that the operator's gaze could reflect off the mirror and rest on the back of the subject's neck. "Soft and tender" chords were to be played on a piano, if one was available. Two magnets, suspended from the ceiling, were then to be arranged so that north and south poles rested on either side of the subject's head, and a third, waxen magnetic bar (composed of beeswax and iron filings) was to be held by the operator and also pointed at the subject's bare neck. If all of these requirements were met, Randolph predicted that in nine cases out of ten, a "perfect, magnetic slumber, and frequently the most surprising clairvoyance" would ensue.[45]

Magic Mirrors

Superior to all of these methods in producing clairvoyance was the magic mirror.[46] The mirror was not only an "agent" upon which images of distant objects and persons, the spirits of the dead, and the thoughts and imaginations of others, embodied and disembodied, might be cast, but it was also and primarily a means of achieving the highest clairvoyance—though the details of the method were carefully guarded by Randolph.

> It is equally well established, however fools may sneer, that for ages men of the loftiest mental power have used various physical agents as a means of vision, either to bring themselves in contact with the supernal realms of the Æther, or to afford a sensitive surface upon which the attendant dead could, can, and *do*, temporarily photograph whatever they choose to. Nor is this all: I know that by a mysterious process, whose principles it is needless here to expound, a mirror is the *means* of a better, and far more reliable clairvoyance than nine out of ten would suspect.[47]

This reference to a mysterious process appears in *Guide to Clairvoyance* (1867) and may or may not have been part of Randolph's original (1860) thoughts on magic mirrors. Given the probable nature of the process, however, it is more likely that it is something that he learned in the Near East on his trip in 1861 and 1862. Randolph offered to provide the details of the process to correspondents, presumably for a fee, but they have not survived, and it is impossible now to determine exactly what the mystery was that made a mirror into a superior method of obtaining clairvoyance. It is clear, however, that it was not the glass or mirror box, but rather the fluid or coating within the complex mirror that was essential: "Nothing depends for success upon either the box, the curtain, or the glasses, but all depends upon the peculiar fluid between them [i.e., between the parallel concave and convex plates], which is . . . of a dark brown color, but at a distance quite inky to the eye."[48] The secret process appears to have involved this fluid or coating and the intimations from Randolph's later writings were always to the effect that the process involved sex and was Oriental in origin—something Randolph had learned on his Near Eastern travels. The implication is clear in *Eulis* (1874):

> People of the West (Europe,—America) are not subject to the same extremes of passion (sexive) as are Orientals; and hence know not either its awful intensity, or its terrible penalties, because they dwell far more in the Brain than in the gender, wherefore they have less *verve élan*, and passional power than their brown brethren and sisters of the far-off eastern lands; as a general rule, with occasional exceptions, they are unable to reach the magnificent goals of soul-vision and magic power easily attainable by the sallow devotees of Sachthas and Saiva; and therefore cannot realize the intense passional furore, essential both to the successful invocation of correspondent Ærial Potentialities, and the charging of mirrors with the divine spiritual reflective powers which characterize them. I here alluded to a profound mystery connected with their construction, known only to the initiate . . . —a mystery at which dolts and fools may laugh— provided they sense its nature, but which higher souls must reverence, honor, and adore.
>
> *There is another secret about them which can only be revealed to such as have and use them!*—and not then till they shall have proved worthy of the knowing.[49]

In his published books Randolph always urged a variety of precautions (cleanliness, exposure to moon- and sunlight, and so on) to be taken in maintaining the mirrors.[50] In *Eulis* he adds to these exoteric instructions and gives the clearest (though still obscure) hint about the secret process of consecration:

> Due care is essential that [the "Glyphae Bhattahs" or magic mirrors], like a child, be kept clean; to which end fine soap and warm soft water, applied with silk or soft flannel, is the first step; followed by a similar bath, whereof cologne, fresh beer, or liquor

spurted from the mouth, are the three ingredients: the second [i.e., the bathing of the mirror] for the sake, 1st, of the spirit; 2d, of the individual magnetism; and 3d, the symbolism embodied in the ritual—so palpably as not to need further explanation. *Write for other information* on this delicate point.[31]

A further clue can be found in one of Robert H. Fryar's books. Fryar as we have seen was the authorized agent in Great Britain in the early 1880s for the sale of Randolph's manuscripts on sexual magic—and was at the same time a member of and the publicist for the H. B. of L. and a distributor of "Bhattah Mirrors." In his compendium, *Sexagyma,*[32] he hinted at the nature of the "Ansairetic" mysteries and then coyly dropped into his own variety of French:

Touchant, la secret renvoyée, qui est la redoubtable force, qui est dite redresser la union des sexes, et la rite plus puissante, que les êtres de la terre peuvent employer. Seulement est necessaire, pour l'homme, avoir une femme intelligente et affectionée, avec laquelle il est en rapport ample; et alors à la moment d'orgasm, l'un et l'autre, qu'ill [qu'ils] veuillent absolument et qu'ils desirent la force ou quel conque ils desirent en verité. Serait il pour la clairvoyance; qu'ils veuillent à l'object, qui est en vue, à l'exclusion sans réserve autre entierement. Alors après cette union, le propriétaire, qu'il donne immédiatement la magnétism à sa mirror. Cette est une secret Orientale.

From all of this the conclusion seems inevitable that the secret consecration and magnetic charging of magic mirrors for Randolph (at least in his later years) involved ejaculation on the surface of the mirror, the smearing of the mirror with the commingled sexual fluids of the partners, or even the preserving of those fluids in the magnetic reservoir of the mirror. From the descriptions, the first appears the most likely, but all are possible, and they may have been used together. In a more general sense it is also clear that the sexual act was always considered by him as the means of generating an excess of magnetism that was used in turn to charge the magic mirror. The practice of magnetically charging mirrors (though without the sex) was universal in France and, as we shall see, Continental mirrors for vision were almost universally constructed in such a way as to retain the magnetic fluid. The sexual side of the consecration, however, has no known parallel in Europe or in the Near East where Randolph traveled— though admittedly it is not the sort of thing that curious Europeans might pick up in their casual travels and set down in their travelers' tales. There was a spate of these travel books by midcentury, and Randolph knew many of them,[53] but the descriptions of Oriental mirror use in such books are all superficial, expressions of wonder at quaint curiosities, and the practices related are restricted to simple fortune telling and prediction. Randolph's own observations of Near Eastern sexual magic and of the use of the magic mirror appear to have been more pointed and penetrating, though it is not possible now to identify specifically the magical circles within which he might have learned his techniques.[54]

Whatever the sources of Randolph's sexual techniques in consecrating magic mirrors, his ideas were confirmed by a book that he said was lent to him in August 1873 by William Gifford Palgrave. Palgrave (1826–1888) was a world traveler and orientalist with a wide experience in the Orient, both in India and in the Near East. His knowledge of the mysterious side of the East was comparable to that of Sir Richard Burton. While a young lieutenant in the Indian army Palgrave had turned to missionary work among the Muslims of south India. He later become a Roman Catholic and continued the same work as a Jesuit. He was transferred to Syria in 1853, where he narrowly escaped death in the Druse uprisings against the Maronites in 1860 and 1861. The Christian Maronites offered him command of their troops, but he refused because of his collar. In 1862 and 1863, he crossed Arabia in disguise in the pay of Napoleon III, later publishing his still very readable *Narrative of a Year's Journey Through Central and South Arabia* (1865). He quit the Jesuits and the Catholic church in 1864 and became a diplomat for Great Britain and was widely posted, using the assignments to explore Trebizond, Georgia, Bulgaria, the Philippines, and Uruguay, dabbling in obscure philosophies and Eastern religions, especially Shinto in Japan. He died in 1888 after being reconciled to the Catholic church. Palgrave's Near Eastern sojourns thus coincide with Randolph's travels, and it appears almost inevitable that the two met at some point as Randolph claims. No more is known about their friendship or what may have passed between them, but they apparently kept up contact since Randolph says that Palgrave looked him up again in Toledo, Ohio, in 1873 on his way to the Far East and, in passing, lent him a copy of Colonel Stephen Fraser's book *Twelve Years in India*.[55]

The book gives clear support to the practice of charging magic mirrors that Randolph had been using for years. It contains a truly lurid description of the sexual "Sebeiyah dance" by which the "Muntra-Wallahs, or Magic-working Brahmuns" of Muttra in India charged their sacred mirrors. A special black material ("Parappthaline gum") was first gathered by virgins, and then, after being left to settle for forty-nine days, was carried in pots to the ceremony by two brides and two grooms who placed it near the central "Eternal sacred Fire of the Garoonahs" and the customary Lingam and Yoni. They then proceeded to perform a sensual dance around the pots, and at the end of the ceremony the material was found to have become rose colored. When this was smeared on one side of an oval glass plate and allowed to dry it formed a dark coating, making the plate a mirror. The colonel was invited to look in the glass and saw clearly, in far off England, the death of a relative and his receipt of a large inheritance—both of which visions he subsequently learned were true.

The aged "Sheikh" who presided obligingly informed the colonel in words that sound like a paraphrase of those of Randolph:

Sahib, Ardor begat the Universe! There is no power on earth either for good or ill, but Passion underlies it. *That* alone is the spring of all human actions and the father and mother alike of all the good and evil on the Earth! It is the golden key of the Mystery, the fountain of Weakness and of Strength; and through its halo alone can man sense the ineffable essence of the Godhead![56]

On his return to England to enjoy his inheritance, the colonel's magic mirror was stolen, but—again in words that could have been spoken by Randolph—he found that the loss was not irreparable.

I have since found that these strange Muntra-Wallahs, as they are contemptuously called by their Islamic foes in the Carnatic (but true magi in the opinion of better informed people), have brethren and correspondents in nearly every country on the globe—Brazil, China, Japan, Vienna, and even our own London; while they have a regular Lodge in Paris, of some of whom the initiated, and favored ignorants even, can and do obtain occasionally, not only well-charged and polished Bhatteyeh, but actually, now and then, a gourd full of Moulveh-Bhattah,—the strangely mysterious substance which constitutes the seeing surface.[57]

Leaving aside the unanswerable questions of the truth of the narrative (especially the references to a worldwide organization and a "regular Lodge in Paris"—a recurring theme in nineteenth-century occult circles, as we shall see) and of Palgrave's reasons for sharing the book with Randolph in the first place, Colonel Fraser's tale was custom-made for Randolph's uses. It becomes a *locus communis* for mirror magic and sexual magic patterned on Randolph's work. In December 1883, Peter Davidson, the provincial grand master of the North of the H. B. of L., reprinted Randolph's excerpt from Colonel Fraser verbatim in *The Theosophist*.[58] Madame Blavatsky, in her extended commentary on the tale, vouched for it as factual and cited it as an example of the fact that English officers in India before the mutiny were not afraid of the marvelous. Additionally, from the references to the "Sebeiyeh dance" and the "fire of the Garoonahs," Madame Blavatsky believed she was able to identify the

> Fraternity of true magicians, now disbanded and so widely scattered about the country as to be virtually extinct. They are "left-hand" adepts, Mohammedans belonging nominally to the sect of the Wahabees, who learned throughout centuries their magic at (or rather added to the knowledge brought by their ancestors from Arabia and Central Asia), from the Tantrikas of Eastern Bengal and Assam. . . . But the manufacturers of the "Bhattah Mirrors" are not regular practitioners of Black magic. The knowledge they have acquired by the "left-hand" path is used for good or bad purposes according to the inclination of the practitioner.

Madame Blavatsky's faith in the reality of this method of consecration of bhattah mirrors is also shown by a letter she wrote to the *Banner of Light* in October 1879, describing her visit to the spot at the juncture of the Jumna and the Ganges which the Sakti worshippers ("worshippers of the female power") use "for the performance of their pujas; during which ceremonies the famous black crystals or mirrors mentioned by P. B. Randolph, are fabricated by the hands of young virgins."[59]

It would be interesting indeed if the facts supported some direct historical connection between Randolph's mirror ritual and the Eastern and European groups (assuming they existed) identified by Madame Blavatsky and Fraser. Randolph himself makes no such specific claims, although, as we shall see, he does attribute the source of his mirrors to a "mystic brotherhood" in Paris—a clear intimation of his desire to have the reader identify his sources with the brotherhood mentioned by Fraser. Some additional light is thrown on the issue by Randolph's use of an odd phrase found in Colonel Fraser's book. Fraser had described the trance into which the Indian users of these mirrors fell while telling fortunes as "the Sleep of Sialam." Whether from Palgrave or from an earlier familiarity with Fraser's book or from his own knowledge derived from his Near Eastern trips, Randolph had long before 1873 (when he says he got the book from Palgrave) made the term his own. In *Ravalette* (1863), the "Sleep of Sialam Boaghiee" was used by Randolph to describe the prophetic trance, possible only once in a hundred years, that the mysterious "Ravalette" sought to make the Rosicrucian undergo. In his later writings, the term came to mean the higher sort of clairvoyance generally—the elevated, conscious perception of and intercourse with the aerial and aetherial states and beings of the universal hierarchy—that resulted from the application of his magical laws to mirror use. The sleep of Sialam as he finally expressed it was not the mere vision of a celestial thing, but the "mental crystallic, ascensive, penetrative, and comprehensive grasp" of it.[60]

Here again, Madame Blavatsky follows in the footsteps of Randolph (or at least of Fraser). In *Isis Unveiled* (1877), the "Sleep of * * *" is a drug-induced, prophetic "sublime lethargy" in which the unconscious subject is made the "temporary receptacle of the brightness of the immortal Augoeides"—an interpretation of the sleep of Sialam far closer to Randolph's ideas than to those found in Fraser's book.[61] Later, the sleep of Sialam becomes for Madame Blavatsky the final soma-induced trance during which the new initiate—both in the Orient and in the ancient mysteries—comprehends the ultimate mysteries after undergoing the tests of initiation.[62] In the *Secret Doctrine* (1888), Madame Blavatsky specifically identifies the term as the one in use "to this day among the Initiates in Asia Minor, in Syria and even in higher Egypt."[63]

Randolph provided his readers with fairly specific detail on the types of mirrors suitable for obtaining clairvoyance. In his earliest writings on the subject, he had distinguished different mirrors and their various uses. For some purposes (by which he meant "ordinary" purposes, such as fortune telling or seeing absent friends), he preferred the "Oriental" mirror made by spilling a few drops of ink into a vessel of water.[64] This is the commonest method described by travelers, and Randolph must have seen it frequently in Egypt and Syria.[65] He also described the method of making a "Claude Lorraine" mirror, "every bit as good he says as any described by Lane in his *Modern Egyptians*," by molding two pieces of glass into concaves and then nesting them a little apart and filling the reservoir with ink.[66] Randolph had described such a mirror in *Ravalette* (99), shown him by Miakus. In none of his earliest works, however, did he actually offer these mirrors for sale or claim to import them, and the conclusion seems inescapable that before the Civil War Randolph was without a supplier for mirrors and contented himself with instructing others in a general method of making them.[67]

This situation changed after the Civil War. In 1867, Mrs. Mary P. Crook, the proprietor of the Boston Rosicrucian Rooms where Randolph was employed as a clairvoyant, claimed to be able to "procure SYMPTHETIC RINGS, LOCKETS and STELE, Rosicrucian Mirrors (for seeing the dead, etc.)" for those interested. When Randolph thereafter came to revise his pamphlet on magic mirrors for *Seership* in late 1869, he added new information—supposedly copies of the rules for mirror vision used by Oriental seers—that had not appeared earlier,[68] and distinguished three classes of "Trinue" mirrors: the mule or neuter (small, bifocal, and more of a toy than a serious instrument); the female or well-sexed (a mirror of great power, capable of holding a magnetic film eight inches deep on its surface, but still not capable of the grander "photoramic displays" or of affecting distant persons); and the male (a bifocal ovoid mirror, about seven by five inches, that was adopted for all grades of seeing and could allow the vision of three "distinct vivoramas" at one time).[69] These splendid magic mirrors, at least at the time *Seership* was published, were imported into the United States solely by the mysterious "Armenian" seer, Cuilna Vilmara.[70]

> I have often wished I could make these mirrors; but that is impossible, as three continents furnish the materials composing them. And even the frames and glasses must be imported from beyond the seas; as must also the strangely sensitive material wherewith the sympathetic rings are filled; concerning which rings and their brightening, when the future is well, and their strange darkening, when evil impends, or friends fall off, and lovers betray, the quadroons of Louisiana, as well as the women of Syria, could tell strangely thrilling tales. And in consequence of the importance attached to these rings and mirrors, counterfeits of them have been, in times past, put forward, albeit the parties who obtained them were themselves to blame, seeing that but one person— Vilmara—ever imported either to this country.[71]

This "Cuilna Vilmara" was not only the importer of these mirrors into the United States but was also "one of the first masters of occult science now on the globe," and it was from his deep knowledge of the subject that Randolph says he wrote *Seership* during a visit by Vilmara to the United States, apparently in 1869.[72] Randolph (and probably Vilmara also) was somehow involved with what Randolph calls the "Fraternité de la Rosecroix" at the time, since Randolph adds that those seeking these superior magic mirrors must go to "head-quarters" to obtain them:

I neither import, manufacture, have made, or keep these mirrors and rings for sale. The small ones are of but little value; the next size is almost impossible to procure, although occasionally one can be obtained. The large, professional, but more expensive and immensely better ones, are much easier to get hold of, but must be handled very tenderly. When I want either mirrors or rings, for myself or a friend, I either go to head-quarters and select them personally, or procure the services of an expert. The members of the *Fraternité de la Rosecroix*, are hereby informed that they must procure these things also, at head-quarters, as I have no time to spend for those who know the true points of the compass; and all such must travel straight towards the setting sun, and at the end of the journey the LIGHT will be seen![73]

Who, then, is this mysterious Cuilna Vilmara? In *The Master Passion* (1870)[74] he has become an Italian, the purveyor of elixirs to the jaded: "and this very day the Italian, Cuilna Vilmara, supplies his numerous aristocratic patrons with the old form of [the hashish elixir] Phosgene known as Phloxine" to increase the stamina of those whose energy had been depleted by fast living. This person, in turn, had already made his appearance in Randolph's writings. In *Guide to Clairvoyance* (1867) Randolph had spoken of a mysterious Italian count, the greatest mesmerist on the globe: "I now give the special method of thorough magnetization, to gain which I went from Paris to Marseilles, and remained there till I learned it of the greatest mesmerizer the world ever saw, — the Italian Count, — mentioned in my book 'Ravalette.' "[75]

The implication seems to be that by the late 1860s, after years without a source for superior magic mirrors, Randolph had established (or, as he more likely wants us to conclude, had re-established) contact with a supplier of mirrors who was involved with a Continental Fraternité de la Rosecroix and who, as the mysterious Italian count in *Ravalette* (1863), had taught Randolph the secrets of mesmerism on one of his European trips.

In *Ravalette*, the count is described as a member of the "*Supreme dome* of the Rosie Cross," a wonder-worker who had learned his secrets from the magi of the East. On one occasion when Randolph also was displaying his powers of clairvoyance before Napoleon III, the count astonished the court by mesmerizing the entire audience without the usual mesmeric passes of the hand and without even glancing in their direction. He then caused bolts of lightning to play over the heads of the audience.[76] This description closely fits the exploits of the little-known Antoine Regazzoni, a traveling Italian mesmerist whose powers were praised by Madame Blavatsky, among others, and who passed into the mythology of the hidden hand in the nineteenth century.[77] Regazzoni, like the Italian count, was one of those wonder-workers who demonstrated their powers before Napoleon III, and he did so at the time of Randolph's first visit to France when Randolph too probably performed for the emperor and there met the Italian count.[78] In touting his "extraordinary powers" as a mesmerizer, the *Spiritual Telegraph* described how Regazzoni, at a nod from Napoleon and without any of the passes or paraphernalia of traditional mesmerism, stopped a diva in mid–aria as she performed before a crowd of court dignitaries, and then, equally without effort, restored her voice. This demonstration of mesmeric power is very markedly like the one Randolph ascribed to the mysterious "Italian Count" who "makes no passes, scarcely glances for an instant at his subjects, and invariably looks *away*, not toward, them."[79]

Whether or not Randolph's Italian/Armenian count was based on or intended to evoke Regazzoni, Randolph's relationship with his European source of magic mirrors had its ups and downs, and he appears to have changed his supplier in the years immediately before his death. He continued to sell the "black ovoid" mirrors (those supplied by Cuilna Vilmara) until 1873,[80] but thereafter disparaged them as mere "spirit-seeing" mirrors and touted instead the "perfected spirit-seeing or magic-glass, formed of materials prepared in the Orient, and fitted for use in Paris, France."[81] These, he thought, were the "*ne plus ultra* of mirrors," "of greater sensitiveness, magnetic calibre, focal range, Æthic basin or magnetic reservoir, and of a capacity equal to the solution of almost any subject of demonstration by such means."[82] These mirrors, he said, were acquired from India and mounted by "the Mystic Brotherhood of Paris, France" and then charged by magnetism in the United States before sale.[83] It was one of these, supplied by Randolph to a "Mrs. R." of Brooklyn, about which Colonel Olcott was to wax eloquent in the months before he and Madame Blavatsky founded the Theosophical Society (see chapters 10 and 13).

Randolph was obviously obtaining the mirrors he sold from some source, and there is no reason to doubt that he was getting them from the Continent. Whatever the details of his relationship with the source may have been, the conclusion he wished drawn was that they were supplied by a mysterious, secret brotherhood, with links to the Orient and Paris. In his last years he obviously intended the reader to equate his source with Colonel Fraser's Oriental brotherhood that had a "regular Lodge" in Paris.[84]

By 1860 Randolph had established himself as the foremost advocate of the magic mirror in America and was teaching a systematic method for producing, not merely second sight in the user or trance visions in a mesmerized "subject," but true conscious clairvoyance in which the user him- or herself penetrated the surface clouds and phenomenal visions of the mirror and beheld the "spot of golden light . . . resolved . . . into an *ethereal lane through which magnificent supernal realities [could be] seen.*"[85]

In ordinary use, in Randolph's final version of mirror magic, the mirror was to be leaned against a wall, with a light "thrown full and round upon its glowing face."[86] The would-be scryer sat staring at the mirror "until the gazer shall pass into a transcendentally lofty and most interior state—absolute, unequivocal supra-clairvoyant condition, and *then*, as myriad glories unfold and roll before the Soul's eyes the seer is every inch a king or queen, and can laugh this life and world, and all their trials, troubles, and infinite littleness to utter scorn."[87] The mirror was like a telescope that enabled the seer to penetrate not merely the spirit world but also the "essential" world beyond it. "[W]e Rosicrucians hold that supernatural beings only are possible, visible at that cross-point where the angelic contraction and the magic dilitation intersect. In short, man being himself as the telescope, it is only at the magico-magnetic focus at which the spirit world and the *essential worlds* are to be spied into. . . . Divine and supernatural illumination is the only road to absolute truth."[88]

The mirror, in other words, in this final exposition of its virtues, is the supreme agent of white magic, capable of producing the highest states of clairvoyance:

During my travels through Africa, Egypt, Turkey, Arabia, Syria, and my intercourse with the *Voudeaux* of New Orleans and Long Island, I became thoroughly convinced of the existence of two kinds of magic. One good and beneficent, ruled and governed by the Adonim, the other foul, malevolent, revengeful, lustful, and malignant. They antagonize each other. The one revels in the saturnalia of the passions; the other, the true Rosicrucian, moves in the light producing SHADOW OF THE OVER SOUL. In the one, the adept is surrounded by an innumerable host of viewless powers, who lead him on to great ends and power, but finally sap out his life, and utterly ruin and destroy him or her. And this accounts for much of ill seen and experienced by modern sensitives.

The other leads its votaries through the Glimmer towards the light, and unfolds at length that FINAL and CROWNING CLAIR-VOYANCE, which consists in a clear perception of relations, causes, connecting-links, effects, and uses, by far the noblest and highest attainable while embodied, and this it is that I aim to enable others to reach. . . . It is God's highest gift to man, and cannot be had without a struggle.[89]

Chapter 4

$\mathcal{R}$AN$\mathcal{D}$OLP$\mathcal{H}$'S $\mathcal{R}$ECANTATION OF SPIRITUALISM

R andolph returned from his second trip to the Continent and from his travels in Egypt in March 1858.[1] By May he was living on a farm near Southbridge, New York, and sending pathetic letters to Gerrit Smith to help him find a cause to serve that would provide enough money to feed his family. Smith, as we have seen, was a wealthy reformer whose project of settling poor urban African-Americans on farms in upstate New York probably accounted for Randolph's presence there in the first place—and, as we shall see, certainly contributed to the financial woes Randolph sets out in the letters.

Randolph's fortunes were never good, and they declined markedly throughout 1858 and 1859 as he struggled to make a living while writing his first books on clairvoyance, magic mirrors, and hashish. In a pattern that was to be repeated again and again during the rest of his life, he compounded his problems by alienating his natural benefactors.

The Utica Philanthropic Convention

In the first week of September 1858, Randolph attended and addressed the Philanthropic Convention held at Utica, New York. It had been called by Andrew Jackson Davis to consider "the cause and cure of evil," and was a fairly typical gathering of the time, mixing spiritualism, reform, and abolition—all natural constituencies for Randolph. Ignoring tact and self-interest, however, Randolph proceeded to attack both the spiritualists and the (predominant) radical reformers and succeeded in calling down the wrath of practically everyone on his head.

Taking on the reformers first, Randolph angered the wing of the reformers led by William Lloyd Garrison by rejecting their fundamental principle of "No union with slaveholders," and then stirred up the still more radical reformers by adopting Garrison's principle that slavery was to be abolished by nonviolent means alone.

> Mr. Randolph said that his high Virginian blood would not allow him to remain longer quiet. He must set some of these gray-headed philosophers right. Single handed and alone, and black at that, he would tell these reformers they were wrong. The unwise action of the abolitionists had done more to degrade the slave than all the slave owners in existence. . . . Those who are trying to abolish slavery by means mentioned on the platform, will only rivet the slave's chains. People denounce the union between the North and South, forgetting that this union is the impregnable fortress against despotism, the only home of pure and liberal sentiments.[2]

These eccentricities raised the hackles of the reformers and brought swift retribution. Parker Pillsbury of Boston, a leading abolitionist (and one who always strove to isolate abolition from the cranks of spiritualism), wrote to Garrison's *Liberator* condemning Randolph's speech in the most insulting terms:

> A colored man, a Spiritualist, there was, who rejoiced in the name Randolph, and claimed immediate descent from the sage of Roanoke. John Randolph may have been the father, but would now be ashamed of the son. I never saw a colored man, woman or child, who so nearly proved the oft heard assertion that "*the colored race are fit only for slaves*"! He said "slavery might be an evil, but that radical anti-slavery was a much greater evil"! Such was a sample of him. Of course, the rowdies and reporters cheered him loudly, which he seemed to enjoy.[3]

The mention of Randolph's name in the pages of the *Liberator* in turn served to evoke other comments. In the issue of November 5, 1858, a certain D. S. Grandin of Bethel, Maine, wrote that Randolph

> is to me the most interesting object of thought, a real peripatetic idea. William Wells Brown can perhaps give some account of him as he once did in the Liberator, if he is the man I mean.

If he is a light mulatto, about 30 years old, accusing, impudent, airy and pompous, he is probably the same person (claiming the same name) who introduced himself to our friend WWB on the occasion of one of his lectures in Portland, and showed his interest in the objects of the meeting by officiously assisting in counting the contributions contained in one of the hats, from which it was afterwards learned that at least one dollar-bill, and it was believed more, had mysteriously disappeared; and, upon inquiry, it was likewise ascertained that he was equally unknown to the lecturer and to the audience. It would be characteristic of him to attend the Convention, and speak as represented of him. Pass him around. When a light mulatto quadroon, claiming the name and paternity of Randolph, appears in a Reform or Anti-Slavery Convention, let it be understood among Abolitionists, that there is sufficient moral and logical, although not legal evidence for supposing him to be a thief. True, this may not be the man, but he is one just like him.[4]

On November 12, 1858, Randolph replied to both letters, denying that he was the thief and citing in his defense the fact that he had not even been in Portland, Maine, since he was fourteen years old (i.e., since 1839) and that he had only lectured on slavery once, and that within the last month—neither of which claims appears true, since he had gone to school in Portland in 1842 and had lectured on "The Negro and His Destiny" as far back as January 1856. Randolph also defended his contrariness, citing the proud blood of the Randolphs of Virginia:

Every man seems ready to immolate me, because I have changed my opinions on various subjects. Prostrated on my bed of sickness, I had leisure to review the actions of my former life, and in them I found much to deplore, but no such thing as perfection to guide me. So I asked God for light and truth. I believe the infinite mercy, extended help to my sad and groping soul. A change came over me . . . and now I go thanking God for his goodness, and acting up to my highest religious light. So let the world, Wm. L. Garrison and every man say of me what may seem pleasant to say, but in my loneliness God says, "Thou art right!" and I am comforted even in all this darkness of obloquy. Let me correct a misstatement. I never boasted of the blood that runs in my veins, further than to adopt the maxim taught me by my father—"While the blood of the Randolphs runs in your veins, never forbear to speak the honest convictions of your soul. If subsequently, you find you were wrong, own it, and do better, if you can, next time." I do so.[5]

The editor of the *Liberator* had his hesitations about Randolph's reply, but decided to give him the benefit of the doubt until more could be determined. The letters continued, with Grandin specifying that the theft had occurred in the summer or fall of 1856 and that *his* Randolph (the officious trickster) was tall and slender while he had heard that the Randolph who had written to the *Liberator* was short, stout, and square, with broad features—a description that is squarely at odds with the Randolph shown in his photograph or described in various places.[6] He added that a friend of his knew P. B. Randolph and had been at the Portland convention and could vouch for the fact that there were two separate men involved. Finally, Randolph himself went to the offices of the *Liberator* in Boston and presented glowing references from Gerrit Smith and others on his character and abilities, and the furor died.[7]

Recantation of Spiritualism

As his letter to the *Liberator* shows, for several years Randolph had been re-evaluating his life and his career in spiritualism. As early as 1856, after his first trip to Europe, he had begun to be disillusioned with spiritualism and disgusted with what he saw as its excesses ("Ultra-ism" and "Eolism") and especially with the trance state which he felt made him and his sanity mere playthings of the spirits.[8] Just before his trip to Europe and the Near East in 1857, after months spent in trance trying to restore a sick friend, his physical and mental health had broken and he tried to commit suicide. "In a moment of despair, during that terrible madness, with dreadful intent, I severed the blood vessels of both arms in four places."[9] He attributed his return to sanity as we have seen to foreign travel and hashish, but he also credited his conversion to Christianity.

The result of my illness was, that I became convinced that however scientific Spiritualism . . . might do to live by, it would never do to die by. The anti-Bible, anti-God, anti-Christian Spiritualism I had perfectly demonstrated to be subversive, unrighteous, destructive, disorderly and irreligious; consequently to be shunned by every true follower of God and Holiness. I had not for ten years seen a happy day prior to my conversion. In the extremity of my woe, I called on spirits for aid, but no spirits came to my assistance. Reduced to the verge of horror and despair, I called on that God whom I had, in the insolent pride of intellect, so often derided. I believed my prayer was answered, my understanding opened, my body healed, reason restored, mind comforted, and my trembling feet set, as I believe, on the Eternal Rock of Ages.[10]

From his anguished tones it is apparent that his conversion was sincere, although the spiritualist press generally dismissed it was a mere publicity stunt. By the early fall of 1858 he was ready to publicize his conversion and his break with spiritualism, and he took to the lecture circuits to denounce spiritualism, an endeavor in which he was not alone. He was but one among several prominent mediums (including Lizzie Doten and Thomas Lake Harris) whose recantations and claims of obsession were widely publicized at the time.[11]

In September, he took the occasion of the Utica Philanthropic Convention to denounce spiritualism in general and Andrew Jackson Davis in particular. Jackson had preceded him on the platform, speaking on the "History and Philosophy of Evil" and strongly advocating the current spiritualist and reform position that evil was nothing but "imperfect organization, defective education, and immoral situation"[12]—a position that Randolph had once advocated but which his own tortured experience as a trance medium had led him to reject.[13]

Randolph was especially critical of the practical consequences of Andrew Jackson Davis's philosophy, and it is apparent that he really felt that he had been led astray and betrayed by the Poughkeepsie Seer. Davis, along with most early spiritualists, denied the real existence of evil, especially evil spirits. "Evil spirits" were merely immature souls, progressing more slowly than others, but still basically good.[14] Randolph had learned the error of this belief from his life as a trance medium. He *knew* that there were evil spirits, because they had possessed him for years and driven him to do acts he abhorred in the waking state. If spiritualism was to be judged by its results, no "progress" could be seen, but only "adultery, fornication, suicides, desertions, unjust divorces, prostitution, abortion [and] insanity." Randolph also, as a newly converted Christian, rejected Davis's replacing of a personal God with the impersonal, all-pervading Fire, and vehemently denied Davis's most recent revelation, the so-called "Buffalo Doctrine" that not all souls were immortal.[15] (Randolph in typical fashion, ended his days teaching this latter idea: along with Madame Blavatsky and others he believed that immortality was not a necessary attribute of humanity but rather was conditional, something that could be gained or lost by individual effort.)[16]

Randolph was a very well known medium, and his Utica speech was widely publicized and discussed. When he subsequently delivered his denunciation at the Melodeon in Boston he was much made over by the local (antispiritualist) Christians and baptized into some unknown sect and even claimed to have accepted a call to the Christian ministry.[17] In November, in response to the invitation of Charles Partridge, the editor of the *Spiritual Telegraph*, he gave his fully polished "recantation speech" to large audiences at Clinton Hall in New York City.[18]

To some extent, the recantation speech merely repeated the commonplace antispiritualist rhetoric of the time. Randolph pointed out the humbug and contradictions of the movement—Mirabeau's spirit's forgetting French, and glowing-spirit hands produced with phosphorous—and painted a nice poetic picture of the braggadocio of the typical speaking medium of the era:

> He talks of systems, suns and worlds, and "interplanetary
> spaces."
> Then Ossa upon Pelion hurls, in speech about the human
> races.
> He leads you through a "vasty realm," in sweet discourse
> on "Primal causes,"
> Explains who 'tis that holds the helm, and prates of "Nature,"
> twixt the pauses
> Thro' "Spacial Halls" he roams scot-free, and "Azure
> domes" and "Universes."
> "The gods," he knows them all, and he, "was well acquainted
> with their nurses!"

* * *

> Why I dug up old Adam's bones to count his ribs, I heard
> the groans
> Of Cyclops—but I must be off, I hear I've caught the
> *whooping* cough,
> For I met some Indians on my way: Good bye; I'll call
> another day.

When he described his own plight, as a man trapped and driven insane by trance, however, Randolph's words took on a new force.

> I frequently resolved to break my fetters, but some good-natured miracle-seeker would persuade me to sit in a circle, just

once more, in order that some great defunct Napoleon, Caesar, Franklin, or Mohammed, might, through my lips, give his opinion on the subject, and edify some dozen or so with metaphysical moonshine and transcendental twaddle. I would consent, "just to oblige," and then, good bye reason, sanity adieu, common sense farewell! Like the reformed inebriate, who, so long as he tastes not, is safe from the destroyer, but who is plunged into a deeper misery the instant he yields to the tempting "one glass more," so the medium. Nothing can rescue him or her but the hand of God, who is "mighty to save." It pleased Him to reduce me to the zero of human woe, that I might be snatched as a brand from the burning. Had He not vouchsafed this great mercy, the probability is, that instead of trying to serve Him, and atone for the mistake of a lifetime, I should still be wandering up and down the Capitals of Europe and Asia in the accomplishment of my "Spiritual Destiny and Mission," desperately intent on converting Ferdinand, Louis Napoleon, the King of Delhi, Nasr-oo-deen, and the Grand Turk; for I believed that I was Heaven sent to save humanity in general, and crowned heads in particular.[19]

In his recantation speech and elsewhere, Randolph singled out free love and its votaries for special attack, deploring its consequences (divorce, adultery and the like) and attributing its origins to the same congeries of "Ultra" ideas that animated early spiritualism. This insistence obviously reflects Randolph's own evaluation of his life and of his early guides in spiritualism.[20] Of these, Andrew Jackson Davis and John Murray Spear were widely rumored (with some justification) to practice free love in the worst sense of the term and, on the basis of the evidence at least, probably did; the third, Steven Pearl Andrews, openly gloried in advocating the doctrine. The freedom from stereotyped roles and social constraints permitted by seances, especially to trance mediums such as Randolph, were notorious, and Randolph's excesses in this regard—excesses that he alternately bemoaned and gloried in as the natural consequences of genius, heredity and his "love-starved" nature—were probably typical of the times.[21]

Two more serious points stand out in Randolph's set piece of antispiritualism, both of which are essential to his later development. First of all, he was careful to avoid saying that trance was a mere sham or that it was always necessarily evil.

An eight years' experience has convinced me that the possession and profession of the faculty is fraught with frightful dangers. I now speak of the genuine spiritual trance—for there are two kinds. I have been in trance about 2,500 times. Of these about 150 were involuntary on my part, the balance resulted from self-volition, was spiritual in its nature and results, but spiritual personages had nothing to do with it. I formerly thought they had, but subsequent self-examination and study has corrected that notion entirely. . . . [Nonfraudulent and nondeluded trance speakers] have the power in themselves (although they assign it to the spirit) of inducing at will a dreamy sort of ecstasy or conscious trance, during which they are frequently insensible to physical pain, and possess the extraordinary power of mental concentration, being able to pursue the thread of an argument, trace a principle, and follow an idea almost infinitely beyond their waking capacity. It is this kind of trance that educates the person, and makes philosophers and orators; and not the ghost-induced state. This trance can easily be induced. I can enter it at any time in five minutes, when I choose to do so. It can also be brought on by the use of lozenges made of sugar and the juice of a plant that grows wild by the acre in Central New York. Generally five of these lozenges will produce a kind of waking clairvoyance and mental intensity, fully equal to the solution of any problem that can engage the attention. . . . It is in short the highest state of mesmerism, reached by a shorter, safer and quicker road.[22]

Randolph was thus taking the first step towards redefining "clairvoyance," removing "spirits" from the process entirely, as the French and English among whom he had moved on his travels had already done, and viewing the state as the elevated mental condition in which the soul, freed from the confines of the body and spirit, could traverse the limitless universes of the soul world at will—often with the help of hashish.

Randolph's recantation speech also brought into prominence the idea of "evil spirits" operating in spiritualism and raised more generally the question of the identification of the spirits, insinuating plainly that there were other sorts of beings involved in the manifestations of spiritualism than simply the spirits of the dead.[23] In 1858, when the speech was given, the universe of possibilities of American spiritualism was extraordinarily limited and almost all of the phenomena of spiritualism were attributed to the "spirits of the dead." "Angels," though they appeared, by and large were dismissed as unscientific; "elementals," "elementaries," "planetary spirits," and the like were unheard of in the English-speaking spiritualist world, and with very rare exceptions[24] it had never crossed anyone's mind that living "adepts" or the like might be at the root of the manifestations. Randolph was to develop the role of all these entities, and in so doing he became the forerunner of the rise of occultism in the nineteenth century.

The response of the spiritualist press to Randolph's recantation was not slow in coming. The *Spiritual Telegraph*, in a piece entitled "Spiritual Mountebanks," described him snidely as "one Randolph, who had appended to his name, as is usual with such persons, the title of 'Doctor,'" and continued:

This man has pretended to be a trance-speaking medium, and that when he talked, he did not know what he was talking about. We confess this has generally been our own dilemma while hearing him; and the best evidence (if it can be called evidence) of his entrancement has been that we were hardly willing to attribute to any man in his normal state of mind such incoherent gibberish as he has given utterance to. For want of evidence, we declined his solicitation for indorsement as a medium, and as a representative of Spiritualists when he went to Europe. His prominence as a medium or Spiritualist has been confined chiefly to his own estimation. Spiritualists are tolerant, and have been willing to listen to him, and it was rather amusing to hear such a quantity of good, innocent words dumped in such hodge-podge. Persons who simply listen to words rather than the sentiments of the speaker, may have naturally supposed that the fount of divine wisdom was tapped, but on searching for the *sense* they do not find it. It may have run out long ago. We have often thought he was better adopted to revival enterprises.[25]

Emma Hardinge Britten, writing about Randolph's conversion more than a decade later, in a chapter she entitled "Spiritualism and Spiritual Mountebanks," still reflected the standard spiritualist position that Randolph's recantation was merely a publicity stunt to revive a flagging career.

It was in the year 1858 that a great jubilee was proclaimed in Boston by the societies of Christendom, who make that city their headquarters, on account of the public "recantation" of an individual known as P. B. Randolph, a Spiritualist and a trance speaker. Randolph, it was acknowledged, had not been very well sustained in his career amongst the Spiritualists, and it was suggested that some of their number neither desired to sustain him nor retain his services in connection with the cause; hence, no very great alarm for its future was experienced when he came out in the form of a "recantation," throwing himself at the same time into the arms of a certain sect of Christians in Boston, by whom he was most cordially received, formally baptized, and greatly patronized and prayed over. Even while in the full tide of his popularity amongst his new brethren he was induced, for a "consideration," to appear on the Spiritualists' platform at the Melodeon under the management of Dr. Gardner, for the sake of making his "recantation" more public and proclaiming it in the very heart of the spiritualistic ranks. . . . Some declared that [Dr. Gardner] only desired to fill the hall; others that he was just then destitute of a sensation, and was glad to accept anything short of negro minstrelsy. . . . [Randolph], having made some rambling and utterly inapplicable remarks about Spiritualism, interspersed with evidently sensational attempts to show that he was still "under the influence" and compelled occasionally to break off from his written lecture and return to his old style of improvisation, the whole affair concluded by the said Dr. Randolph's speedy return to the ranks of Spiritualism, in which he has been practicing on and off ever since.[26]

Whatever may have been the intention of his original recantation, after the speech Randolph, whether in response to the criticism or compelled by his spirits and general instability, made it clear that he was still a spiritualist, though now a Christian one. He had "turned a somersault out of Atheism into Scientific Spiritualism; out of that into Philosophic Spiritualism; out of that into Religious Spiritualism, and here I am to-day, and feel decidedly happier for the change." "I now repeat, that my battle is against unproductive, anti-religious Spiritualism. . . . Beyond all question, there are good Spirits in communication with mortals, and evil ones also, communication or association with whom leads to results most deplorable."[27] His real break, he explained, was not with spiritualism as the convincer of immortality, but with the confining doctrines and optimistic ideas of its proponents.

On the wave of this publicity, Randolph proposed a speaking tour featuring his recantation speech and a lecture entitled "Free Love Theories Weighed against Common Sense" and sought bookings in the spiritualist press,[28] though probably without much success because he had become persona non grata on the spiritualist lecture circuit.[29] In January 1859 he announced that he was giving up the spiritualist lecture circuit because of his unhappiness at finding himself classed with the professional debunkers of spiritualism.[30] Of necessity he had to seek new avenues for his talents, and for a time he thought of turning to temperance lecturing. A letter of recommendation written for him in November 1858 states,

[H]e has a laudable ambition to occupy some field of labor which shall be worthy of his capacity, and give fair scope to his intellect; but the slight taint of African blood in his veins has proved to be and is an effectual barrier to the attainment, in almost all directions, of positions of honor, trust and distinction, which few men are better qualified to fill.

He is an original thinker, a logical reasoner, an eloquent speaker—has a memory that forgets nothing; and if he could obtain service in the ranks of the Temperance cause, or other kindred movements of the day, or could be aided to take the field in behalf of his brethren in the Free States (which he desires to do) I have no doubt he would be of great service to the cause he may thus advocate.[31]

However, even these ambitions were to be thwarted by circumstance.

Gerrit Smith

As he alienated the spiritualist community, Randolph turned increasingly for advice and aid to the reformer Gerrit Smith, whose benevolence in settling poor urban blacks on small farms in upstate New York may have brought Randolph there in the first place. Smith (1797–1874) was a radical even among the reformers of the time. He was a fervent abolitionist, temperance advocate, and spiritualist, and Randolph could reasonably have expected his assistance.[32] Early in 1859, Randolph took up temperance lecturing at Smith's suggestion, but he had a hard time making ends meet even with the publicity given him by Henry Ward Beecher and others to whom Smith had introduced him. Randolph was clearly desperate, and he wrote beseechingly to Smith: "Can you not, Sir, suggest something for me to do? If so, please do it and I am ready to travel and labor wherever duty calls."[33] Nothing was forthcoming, however, and Randolph was reduced to attempting to sell his small farm in Southbridge, a town a few miles from Smith's own home in Peterboro, to raise money. He and his wife had acquired the farm at some point in the 1850s, apparently with Smith's help. Randolph actually went so far as to sign the contract to sell the land, only to discover that he held title to the farm, not in his own name, but as agent for Smith. Randolph, who understood nothing about the law, found to his dismay that he was in an impossible situation: by the terms of his contract of sale he either had to sell a piece of land that he did not own or face a lawsuit for a fifty dollar penalty for not conveying the land to the buyer. Worse still, in the expectation of selling the land, he had borrowed money to move his family and to find a new home in the East, money which he now found himself unable to repay. He wrote despairingly to Smith to transfer the deed to him:

> I am reduced to the last extremity, and have not a shilling to go on with my Spring's work with, or purchase a stick of wood to keep my family comfortable. I am forced thus to lose another year of precious life in a field where I can do no good. No one will give me work here, and if they would I am not strong enough to do it. . . . I do not feel strong to battle the world as I once did. I feel that my days on Earth are numbered, and regret that I am thus prevented from taking a path lately opened to me, whereby I might render my family comfortable, and do some good before the final day. I have no property—not an article that I can Sell. You have all. But one thing I ask of you Sir, which is, that if this disease under which I labor should cut me off suddenly, that you will see that my family are not wronged out of what I have saved. Going so much in this wet weather has given me another distressing season of cough and internal bleeding, and my unhappy mental state exacerbates it greatly. My dear sir, I trust that you will not feel that I have for a moment forgotten your and my relative position. I have been [beset] on all sides on account of this Land affair, and even accused of intent to defraud—not openly, but by insinuation. If I am Sued, What must and what can I do? I am sure I do not see or know. My poor wife is still more miserable than I am—plunged back into a pitiless gloom just when hope began to paint a bright and glowing future.[34]

By the end of April 1859, Randolph was at the end of his rope, begging Smith to help him, at least to the extent of removing his lien on the Randolphs' personal property so that he could sell his watch to raise money for the spring planting.

> Spring is here, and owing to the affair with Arthur Leonard, we are unable to go on with the culture of our land. Our liability

to you is one we expect to liquidate this season, for we both intend to do our best, but must have a start. We have 3 children, and no cow, nor have we the means to plow our land. Now sir the lien you have on the land is surely ample security for the sum total that we owe you. Will you not transfer the whole debt to the land, and permit us to sell the watch for a cow, pigs and feed?[35]

It is hard to believe that Randolph's pleas to Gerrit Smith would have fallen on deaf ears, but they must have,[36] and the next time we hear of Randolph he is no longer living on his farm. He was wiped out financially, and it is probably in this desperate period that we must place the obscure incidents surrounding the death of his daughter Winnie. In his later books Randolph harkened back again and again to his undying hatred for two men who betrayed and robbed him. He speaks very movingly of the "starver of little children" and of "little pale hands reaching vainly for food" and of the death by neglect of his daughter while he was on the seas. It is impossible now to identify the villains, though Smith was certainly involved, at least to the extent of allowing the events to occur.[37] In more sober moments Randolph recognized that his own haughtiness in refusing to "ring the dull changes suited to the edification and advancement of so-called 'Philosophers and Reformers'" had taken "many a mouthful of bread from his wife and little ones."[38]

In December 1859 Randolph announced his return to the spiritualist lecture circuit, supplementing his income by advertising his ability to delineate character for a fee from letters submitted to him.[39] All through the latter part of 1860 he spoke regularly at the weekly Boston Spiritual Conferences sponsored by the *Banner of Light*, but his reputation for eccentricity and his continued denunciation of the evils of mediumship must have prevented him from achieving any financial success in spiritualism. In March 1860 he gave up lecturing to become an attache of the "New England Healing Institute" in Boston,[40] advertising his treatments as "the Indian system, combined with that of the higher system for which he is so well known."[41] By November he was practicing medicine on his own.[42]

In June 1860 Randolph attended the New England Anti-Slavery convention and again opposed the dominant (Garrisonian) view of "No union with slaveholders" with an appeal to the power of the ballot box. His appearance, however, which began with a claim to be "a descendant of Pocahontas," was interrupted by a spectator who "wished to state some facts disparaging to the speaker's character." The nature of the attack is not made clear, but Randolph attributed it to the years of near madness brought on by surrendering his will in trance to the spirits before his renunciation of spiritualism in 1858, and his hashish use may have played a role as well. The interruption effectively ended Randolph's speech.[43]

By mid-1860, Randolph had alienated both of his natural audiences—the spiritualists and the reformers—and his survival depended on his pen and on what little he could eke out of the practice of medicine. He made good use of his forced inactivity to begin to write his thoughts on what he had learned in his travels. With the exception of a few months in the winter of 1859 he said that he spent the entire period from October 1858 until October 1860 writing his pamphlet on clairvoyance, magic mirrors, and hashish, and 1860 also saw the appearance of *The Unveiling: or, What I Think of Spiritualism*[44]—Randolph's recapitulation of his recantation of spiritualism—and the next year he completed his most coherent theoretical work, *Dealings With The Dead; The Human Soul, Its Migrations And Its Transmigrations*, which he published early in 1862.[45]

Chapter 5

$\mathcal{D}$EALINGS WITH THE $\mathcal{D}$EAD: $\mathcal{T}$HE $\mathcal{M}$ATURE $\mathcal{V}$ISIONARY

In early 1862, all the elements of Randolph's mature thought, with the exception of his fully developed sexual magic, made their appearance in *Dealings With The Dead; The Human Soul, Its Migrations And Its Transmigrations*.[1] This is the first major shot in the battle that was to transform naive American spiritualism into "occultism," and its echoes resound constantly in H. P. Blavatsky's *Isis Unveiled* (1877), in Emma Hardinge Britten's books, and in the teachings of the H.B. of L. The book is Randolph's masterpiece, and after the passage of more than 130 years the sweep of its vision is still impressive.

Cosmology and Soul Monads

In *Dealings with the Dead*, Randolph's cosmology still bore the imprint of his early reading of Andrew Jackson Davis, but he had now made Davis's ideas his own and expressed them as a visionary in his own right. The origin of the "All" is the radiant, primordial, "Central Sun," "more glorious than a seraph might tell."[2] The "Central Sun" is not itself divine, but God is immanent within it or rather concealed in the shadow beyond its light.[3] Coruscating out eternally from this sun are three forms of fire or light. One of these becomes matter, another is the highest form of the all-pervading and sustaining fluid of the magnetists, and the last is the stream of soul monads—thoughts of God, as it were. "Individual monads—all men and women—are scintillas or parts of this third great thought of the Mighty Thinker, God; they are coruscations from The Over-Soul, while Matter is constituted of ethereal emanations from God's Infinite Body."[4] The monads "are the original soul-germs of immortal beings—they are the sparks which fell, and fall from God himself—particles of the Deific brain, unique, *sui generis*, unparticled, homogeneous; old as Deity, young as the new-born infant; always existed, ever will exist. They are Phay souls (Fay-souls), or Monads."[5]

All of the infinite universes of creation are bathed in the flow of these soul monads, not merely the earth, and at every level of creation these strive for and achieve individuality by something akin to incarnation and thereafter perpetually progress towards their source. These nonterrestrial beings constitute a vast hierarchy, far exceeding the paltry imagination of the spiritualists of Randolph's time. He names them, apologizing for using the "Oriental" terms in default of current names:

1. Spirits—Angels;
2. Seraphs;
3. Arsaphs;
4. Eons;
5. Arsasaphs;
6. Arch-Eons;
7. Antarphim.[6]

The last of these, the antarphim, "ultimate in a Perfection whereof the human mind cannot conceive. They become deions, a supreme order of creative intelligences and energies, whose power, in combination, is only second to that of the Infinite God Himself. These constitute the towering hierarchy of the supernal Heaven. Their number is infinite."[7] All of these entities have their field of activity in the finest form of the subtle all-pervading fluid which Randolph will later call "Æth." In its striving to be "progressive" and "scientific," spiritualism had almost entirely rejected the traditional celestial hierarchies as mere superstition, and had peopled its postmortem universe only with the spirits of dead humans. Randolph's enumeration marks the first reappearance in midnineteenth-century spiritualism of the traditional notion of 'ascending hierarchies' of celestial entities.

The soul monads destined to become man and to bloom into souls become encased in the "outer shells" of matter and over vast ages progress upward through the mineral and vegetable worlds, always toward greater intellectuality and individuality, shedding at each stage an outer coat of materiality, like the outer layers of an onion, until they reach the animal kingdom and, finally, man.

And so I ran the gamut of change through countless ages; every new condition being more and more favorable, brought out new properties from within me, and displayed new beauties to the sun's bright eye. I was still a monad, and will ever be such, in one sense; albeit Time, after reaching my human form, will be of no account,—only states. Something whispered me that I should ever advance toward, but never reach perfection. I felt that, monad though I was, yet at my heart, my core, my center, I was the germ of an immortal soul, and that soul itself was destined to throw off form after form after its material career was ended, just as I had all along the ages. And thus I passed through countless changes, exhibited a million characteristics, until at last, I who had at first worn a body of fire, then of granite, then of moss, now put on a higher and nobler dress, and became for the first time, self-conscious, intelligent, and in a degree, intuitive both as to the past, the present, and the future. And all these infinite changes were effected by throwings off, in regular order, just as material suns throw off ring after ring, which in turn resolve themselves into planet after planet. During all these transmigrations, my monad body was active, my monad soul quiescent, but ripening all the while.[8]

Each monad is a unique thought of God, and the core of each monad is the germ of the "imperial human soul" whose goal it is to progress asymptotically back to its origin.[9] After transmigrating through the lower, more material spheres of earth, these monads swarm through the atmosphere, seeking incarnation, and in the sexual act and procreation they are finally clothed with the various "envelopes" of heredity and are born as man.[10] Once incarnated, the monad as such ceases to be, and in its stead stands an immortal soul, an individualized being, more or less awakened but "self-existent to all future states—not times only."[11]

Soul and Spirit

In *Dealings with the Dead*, Randolph clearly distinguishes the "soul" from the "spirit" and the "soul world" from the "spirit world." As will become commonplace in later occultism, and as had been traditional in the circles inspired by Hermeticism and Neoplatonism in late antiquity and the Renaissance, man for Randolph is a triplicate being: body, spirit, and soul—although Randolph reverses the usual order of the names of the last two principles and makes soul rather than spirit, the highest principle.[12] For Randolph, each monad must become and eventually does become a "soul," an individual, self-conscious, enduring entity. "The soul is really a divine monad, a particle, so to speak, of the Divine brain—a celestial coruscation from the Eternal heart; and, for that reason, an eternal existence—immortality being its very essence, and expansion constituting its majestic nature; and the Soul, this monad, was once an integer of God himself—was sent forth by His fiat— became incarnated and an individual."[13]

The monad/soul is the polished sphere of light over whose surface pass a man's thoughts, memories, and actions,[14] and is, in itself, a little universe. Even if a person were trapped in his own soul,

> there would remain, not only an infinity of duration, but also a universe to move and be in, quite as infinite in both extent and variety beside; for the Soul, I soon discovered, was a Vastitude in and of itself; and should it happen that not one of the moments of its mighty year be spent in the society of others like unto itself, yet there would be but little occasion for ennui; not one lonely minute need be spent, for all its days—if for illustration's sake, I may predicate time of that whereof emotions and states are the minutes and the hours—might be profitably employed in visiting its own treasure houses and in counting the rare jewels there stored away; besides which, it could perform many a pleasant voyage, visiting mighty continents, rare islands, wondrous cities, and marvelous countries of its own tremendous being; . . . nor would its resources be exhausted at the thither end of the rolling wave of Time; *because* time is not to the soul: its duration and successions are of thought, not seconds.[15]

For Randolph, once the monad has transmigrated through the lower, material realms and reached individualization as a soul incarnate in man, it is an immortal entity, an individual, and it never—with minor exceptions—returns to rebirth on earth. "As for the reincarnation dogma, it, like the Oriental transmigration story, is beneath contempt."[16] Randolph occasionally uses the term *reincarnation* for the progress of the monad/ soul, but in so doing he is clearly describing what would more properly be called "transmigration"—the progression of the nonindividualized monad through the material universes toward incarnation.

> After repeated incarnations—for I have already proved that the soul does *not* originate on earth, but pre-existed myriads of ages before the worlds were made, and that it will exist myriads

of ages after the last material globe shall have ceased to be!—I
repeat, after repeated incarnations, has the final life-point, the
primal intelligentsia, the crystalline mystery, called Soul, come
on and upward from the informing spark of a jelly-speck in the
mud of rivers, to the analid or worm, tadpole, fish-frog, dog-fish,
bird, quadruped, to the bimanna in varied form . . . simia,
cynocephalus, monkey, baboon, gibbon, ape, troglodyte, gorilla,
msciego, bushman, Hottentot, and so on, up to and through, the
fifteenth amendment, and away beyond to the highest, loftiest,
noblest specimen of the creature called Man![17]

In itself, Randolph's rejection of reincarnation is not unusual. It in
fact represented the almost universal consensus of American and British spiritualists, while a belief in reincarnation in the sense of the
rebirth of the same individual on earth was limited almost solely to
France, and even there the idea was advocated only by the Kardecist
school of French spiritualists and was rejected by the magnetists, such
as Dupotet.[18] However, Randolph's position and the exceptions he
admitted are especially significant because opposition to the dogma of
reincarnation while admitting certain curious exceptions identical to
Randolph's forms one of the hallmarks of the H. B. of L. school of
occultism—and also of the ideas of Madame Blavatsky when she
published *Isis Unveiled* in 1877. Randolph allowed for a sort of rebirth
on earth only in the case of abortions and congenital idiots who had
never become properly individualized and "ensouled" and whose
frustrated monads returned to earth to try again.[19] He also appears at
times to have thought that "special" souls—among which he included
himself—were occasionally incarnated again on earth to atone for past
crimes—another doctrine with echoes in *Isis Unveiled* (see chapter 12).[20]

One of Randolph's greatest contributions to the development of
nineteenth-century occultism was the notion of the 'soul world', the
natural realm of activity of the soul. It is within the soul itself and
infinite, an ever-receding series of higher and more sublime worlds
through which the soul progresses, asymptotically approaching but
never merging in or being reabsorbed into God, and never losing its
individuality.[21]

Man, throughout the countless eternities of progressive
unfoldings, can never reach the intra-edeonic plane. . . . [M]an's
proclivities, tendencies, and aspirations will be forever,—not to
God, but to the outflowing attributes, powers, and essences which
proceed from God in rays. . . . Edeonic is a word signifying the

inmost essence of Spirit. In man's progressive unfoldings, there are varied and various degrees of excellence, refinement, enjoyment, power and capacity,—human, spiritual, angelic, celestial, seraphic, edeonic,—each a discrete remove above the other. The edeonic plane of being is that point of progression which man reaches on his upward journey, when all his powers, capabilities, qualities, essences, and attributes coalesce, and mind becomes a unitary kingdom, instead of a confederacy of faculties, governed by a master principle, or king faculty; and is that point where man ceases to be moved by material essences, forces, and powers, loses his attractions for matter and the outgrowth of matter, and commences the movement on the other plane of the universe.[22]

Although Randolph speaks of this process in temporal and spatial terms, it is clear that it is really atemporal and a matter of "states" rather than of places.[23] After it is once individualized and immortal, the soul commences this infinite journey, becoming in the process a god or godling, mounting the hierarchy of seraphs, arsaphs and the like in its turn. "Then man is, in very deed, almost a—God?—You have said! He creates worlds, and becomes the deity of his creation?—Man is a godling!"[24]

Randolph described the soul as a "Winged Globe of Celestial Fire" seated in the brain, and this image, undoubtedly both visionary and derived from the universal presence in Egypt of the symbol of the winged globe, became one of his trademarks.[25] Ordinarily the soul sleeps while man (embodied or a denizen of the spirit world) is awake and awakens only in dreams, but Randolph thought—based on his own experiences and visions—that it was possible to awaken the soul to this "intuition" even during life on earth.

Randolph's soul was first awakened and revealed to him at some point between 1848 and 1854, when he had an experience that changed his life forever.[26] He says that while a guest of Andrew Jackson Davis and his wife in Hartford, Connecticut, he found one of Davis's crayon sketches of a "vortical sun, discharging from itself countless hosts of lesser suns—a world rain from the eternal cornucopia."[27] He stared at this for days, pondering the nature of man and the universe, and finally wandered into the countryside and sat under a tree, still trying to resolve his questions.

Long and persistently was this endeavor continued, until, for the first time in my life, I became aware of something very, very strange, and supremely interesting going on within me. This sensation was somewhat analogous to the falling off into a deep sleep, only that it was the body alone which lost its outward sensibility; it was the physical senses only that became slowly and gradually benumbed and sealed, while the mighty senses beneath them appeared to intensify themselves, draw together, and coalesce in one grand All-sense; and this continued going on until it reached a strange and awful degree, and a sensation as of approaching death stole over, and, for a little while, frightened and alarmed me. . . . Slowly . . . came the sense of coldness over my limbs; inch by inch the crafty hand of Mystery gained firmer hold. . . . Soon all sense of organization below the neck was lost, and the words "limb, body, chest," had no meaning. After the first great thrill of terror had passed over, I became comparatively calm, and soon lost all consciousness whatever. . . . Gradually the sense of *lostness*, which for a time possessed me, passed away, and was succeeded by a consciousness altogether distinct from that of either dream or the ordinary wakeful condition. Not a sensation ever previously experienced . . . now swept the nerve-harp within . . . but, instead, there came an indefinable PLEASURE-SENSE—a sort of hyper-sensual ecstasy, by no means organic, but diffused over the entire being. . . . I was not, at first, conscious of possessing a body; not even the ultra-sublimated material one of which we hear so much said in these latter days; but a higher, nobler consciousness was mine—namely, a supremely radiant soul-majesty. . . . My ears did not hear; but Sound . . . seemed to pour in upon my ravished soul. . . . The eye did not see, but I was all sight. There was no organ of locomotion . . . but my spirit seemed to be all motion, and it knew instinctively that by the power of the thought-wish it could reach any point within the boundaries of earth where it longed and willed to be.[28]

In was in this exalted state that Randolph first envisioned his soul as a globe of resplendent white light. In the center of this light existed his consciousness, and on the mirrored walls of the light his thoughts and perceptions were projected.[29] In this state he found that he could pass at will over the earth, visualize the fire life that filled and animated all material objects, and obtain the answer to all questions merely by posing them. He felt himself move naturally toward ubiquity and omniscience.[30]

This vision and the others he experienced over the years[31] are the true source of the powerful sense of conviction that Randolph conveyed to his contemporaries. They are also undoubtedly an added cause of Randolph's frequent changes in doctrine as he strove to give a rational exposition of his overpowering experiences.

The "spirit" stands in sharp contrast to all the sublimities of soul and the soul world. Unlike the individualized soul, which is eternal, man's spirit is a temporary thing, "sempiternal," "a phantasmal projection" and mere material artifact of the soul,[32] although it too has its purpose since, as a triplicate entity itself, it forms the bonds between the soul and the material world and is the locus of man's mental operations and thoughts.[33] The "spirit world" similarly is a lesser place. It is exterior, located like the spiritualists' "Summer Land" in the atmosphere or aura of the earth, and is envisioned in terms analogous to earthly existence. The individual's abode in the spirit world, like his or her antecedent terrestrial existence, is purely temporary.[34] The spirit world, the "middle state," is the transitional abode of most humans after they slough off the body at death. Death, in other words, does not automatically lead to the soul world.

Randolph envisioned this middle state as a vast, labyrinthine series of "worlds" in which the spirits try to work out their passage to the soul world, all the while burdened with the consequences of their earthly lives and habits. These create delusions consonant with the person's earthly beliefs and fears, and Randolph's spirit world is peopled with Buddhist spirits who believe they are in nirvana, tortured spirits who believe they are in hell (and suffer accordingly) and the spirits of insane and evil men.[35] Eventually—at least as Randolph envisioned the matter in *Dealings with the Dead*—all see the error of their ways and pass into the inner soul world. Later on as we shall see, Randolph, like Madame Blavatsky after him, was less optimistic and came to believe that individualized immortality was something to be gained or lost during life on earth, not a birthright, and that the middle state was not only the abode of individualized entities striving to progress but also the realm of the decaying psychic residue of failed entities headed for oblivion.[36]

In Randolph's view in *Dealings with the Dead* it was the spirit world that most mediums reached in trance, and it was the spirits abiding there, with all their faults and delusions, that obsessed mediums and spoke through their mouths—a neat solution to Randolph's own personal problems. The passive medium who gave up his consciousness at seances became the prey of the unknown denizens of the middle state—"demons" and "vampires," beings that had never been embodied and the spirits of disembodied men that roamed the confines of the material world until released.[37] Randolph, while never teaching an absolute dualist theory, very definitely believed in the existence of an evil force, almost an evil center, at work in this world and in the spirit world—though not in the soul world. On one level, this was personified in the spirits and souls of disembodied evil men.

> A man's elevation on the scale depends upon himself—if he loves disorder more than its opposite, hatred than love, the deformed than the lovely—why, the man, in so far forth as he departs from rectitude of his own purposes and will, just so far does he demonize himself. And as there is no limit to advancement or descension, so he may become guileful to an immense degree— be a demon.
>
> There are myriads of such within the compass, and on the confines of the Material Realms, but none beyond them in the Divine City of Pure Spirit. But *within* those limits exists a Badness, so awful, so vast, that the soul shrinks before the terrible reality. These beings cannot injure our souls, save by the voluntary co-operation of our own wills and loves.[38]

In addition to these "demons" there are also "larvae" that "inhabit the spaces between the rolling globes."[39] These are ill-defined, but appear to be the spectres or projections of men, created perhaps by "onanism" or by selfish sexual intercourse.[40] Beyond all of these embodiments of evil are the mysterious Brethren of the Shadow— evil but powerful counterparts of the Brethren of the Light. Both intermingle in human affairs and direct and control them for their own purposes.[41]

All of this, of course, was in marked contrast to the almost universal optimism of spiritualism (exemplified by the early Andrew Jackson Davis and by Randolph's old opponent Dr. A. B. Child) which flatly denied the existence of real evil in the world.[42]

Despite all of the problems and dangers inherent in mediumship, however, Randolph still believed that spiritualism had a purpose and that it had been set in motion deliberately to accomplish that purpose. Over and over, Randolph asserts the idea, later echoed by Emma Hardinge Britten, Madame Blavatsky, the H. B. of L. and others, that spiritualism was a planned, created phenomenon under the control of superior, mysterious beings. Its purpose was to convince us of immortality, nothing more. "The legitimate use of this great spiritual raid was to convince us of immortality."[43] Once that purpose had been accomplished, the time had come to move on to higher things—conscious clairvoyance under the control and direction of the will.

[N]ot only [do] the inhabitants of the Soul-worlds have much to do in moulding the great world's future, but that occasionally they manage things that their thoughts are spoken, and their behests, ends, and purposes fulfilled by us mortals . . . we doubtless are oftentimes merely the proxies of others, and act our allotted roles in a drama whose origin is entirely supernatural, and the whole direction of which is conducted by personages beyond the veil.[44]

Disembodied, or rather ethereal people, of a lofty order, generally, but by no means universally, undoubtedly direct, in all essential respects, the great spiritual movement of the age. . . .
    Yet a demonstration of immortality could never have been had without the aid of mediums. The grand object of the people on the further shore was to convince us of our absolute deathlessness, to do which they were compelled to avail themselves of all such means and agencies as have been in use since the grand movement began; and while mediumship fulfills its office in proving the fact of immortality, there its use is ended, for as a revelative power it is worthless; while just at that point the value of clairvoyance begins."[45]

Beginnings of Practical Occultism

Spiritualism for most people was a passive exercise, equivalent to reading devotional or reform literature. Perhaps the messages of the spirits were more impressively delivered and thus imparted more conviction than mere reading, but basically both forms of communication consisted in the imparting of information to a spectator who himself received words about something rather than experiencing the thing himself. The listener's experience (moral uplift, intellectual conviction or whatever) was the same as that of a reader. The medium and the magnetist's scryer who actually "received" the communication, moreover, were themselves usually no better off, since they performed in trance, unconsciously, and upon waking were as surprised by the content of their messages as the audience had been.
    By its very nature, then, spiritualism and the magnetists' third-party trance revelations were an external and social phenomenon. Nor were they a path or method of self-development or inner progress. The audience listening to a trance speaker deliver the spirits' message basically had to take the revelation on faith; they could agree or disagree with its content but could not replicate the vision itself. As a practical matter this was also true for the unusual seer who consciously

experienced the higher, angelic realms he described. The vision descended upon him like a lightning bolt, without explanation or rationale, and then vanished, and even if the seer himself eventually learned a method for putting himself in a receptive mode to undergo the experience, the practice was never a thing that could be taught to others or consistently repeated.

Randolph's innovation, as we have seen, was precisely here, in his advocacy of the practical means (drugs and magic mirrors) to produce conscious clairvoyance. He was the first person in modern times to introduce a practice which at least claimed the power to enable a person to experience for himself the visions and states described by seers. The difference between Randolph and the spiritualists was the same as that between the "gurus" of the 1960s and the "channelers" of the 1980s. Randolph, in other words, was the first modern Western guru.

While there are hints in *Dealings with the Dead*—how to enter the soul world ("clairvoyance") and how to communicate during life with the hierarchies there—the book is really a work of theory, the summary of Randolph's vision experiences to 1861. The underpinnings of occult practice, however, are clearly present. Randolph is adamant that the foundation of all spiritual and occult development is the will, not the intellect. "Try!" becomes his motto.[46]

> Try! the Soul groweth tall and comely, and waxeth powerful and strong only as it utteth forth its Will! Mankind are of seven great orders: the last and greatest are the Genii of the Earth, the Children of the Star-beam, the Inheritors of the Temple. Weak ones can never enter its vestibules; but only those who Try, and trying for a time, at length, become victors and enter in. Man fails because of feeble, sleeping, idle Will—succeeds, because he wakes it up and ever keeps it wakeful.[47]

Through the will, man could achieve conscious clairvoyance or intuition, which, as Randolph now used the terms, meant the state of soul consciousness with all its consequences. *Dealings with the Dead* also added to this rich mixture the idea of "Blending."

Blending

In *Dealings with the Dead*, Randolph taught that, once "clairvoyant" and in the soul world, communication with the hierarchy of evolved beings was by a process he called "Blending." This was totally different from mediumship, in which the medium gave up his or her will and consciousness and submitted as a passive organ to the control of an unknown "spirit."[48]

> It will be seen, therefore, that this condition is as widely separated from those incident to the "Mediums," as theirs is supposed to be different from the ordinary wakeful mood. *They* reach their state by a sort of retrocession from themselves; they fall, or claim to fall into a peculiar kind of slumber, their own faculties going, as it were, to sleep. On the contrary, *mine* is the direct opposite of this, for, instead of a sleep of any sort, there comes an *intense wakefulness*. Nor is this all in which we differ; as are the processes and states apart, so also are the results different. . . . [B]y slow degrees I felt that my own personality was not lost to me, but completely swallowed up, so to speak, in that of a far more potent mentality. A subtlety of thought, perception and understanding became mine at times, altogether greater than I had ever known before; and occasionally, during these strange blendings of my being with another, I felt that other's feelings, thought that other's thoughts. . . . For a time I attributed these exaltations of Soul to myself alone, and supposed that I was not at all indebted to foreign aid for many of the thoughts to which, at such moments, I frequently gave utterance; but much study of the matter has at length convinced me, not only that the inhabitants of the Soul-worlds have much to do in moulding the great world's future, but that occasionally they manage things that their thoughts are spoken, and their behests, ends, and purposes fulfilled by us mortals . . . [and] we doubtless are oftentimes merely the proxies of others, and act our allotted roles in a drama whose origin is entirely supernatural, and the whole direction of which is conducted by personages beyond the veil.[49]

Randolph had first experienced this state when a friend, "Cynthia Temple," died in 1854 and her soul, at first intermittently and then for longer and longer periods, "blended" with Randolph's:

> This continued for nearly two years, at intervals, and after about eighteen months had passed, one portion of the process seemed to have reached completeness—for in a degree it changed, and instead of momentary, as before, the transmutations became longer, until at last, as now, the changes last sixty, and in one instance has reached two hundred and forty-five minutes.
> It may here be asked: "Where are *you* in the interim?" and the answer is: "We are two in one, yet the stronger rules the hour."[50]

This process of communicating with the entities in the soul world became of major importance in Randolph's later magic and recurs repeatedly under a variety of names and guises throughout the nineteenth century.[51] The goal was to become consciously receptive to the influence of elevated entities of whatever sort—disembodied spirits and souls, the never-embodied beings of the celestial hierarchies, and the still-embodied "adepts." Mere formal, doctrinal exposition after the manner of Andrew Jackson Davis and the like was thus a secondary matter, not a *means* of elevating the soul but a *consequence* of that elevation. Once the clairvoyant soul was in communication with these beings, they themselves would provide the teachings and explanations necessary to understand them and the universe. In "The Mysteries of Eulis," circulated only in manuscript to the members of his Brotherhood of Eulis in the 1870s, Randolph made the point clearly.

> All centers, Spheres, Potencies, Hierarchies, and Brotherhoods, in fact, all things on earth externalized, have their orbits and periods. In like manner all conceivable powers, qualities and energies in the spaces, have the same. There are times when they are, and are not, contactable, and it is very difficult, if not impossible, for any [person] living in domestic turmoil to contact them at all save through the exercise of a resolute, unbending will, and perfect indifference to the surrounding in harmony; but there are orders of beings, invisible to material eyes, who were of earth once, and others who have never been ultimated on, nor incarnated within this external plane of objective life who understand anything and everything which man can conceive; who possess every species of knowledge, and who respond to the desire and invocation of those who follow the same lines of thought and feeling, who belong to the same state of intelligence, or who voluntarily place themselves under the essential conditions of rapport and contact.[52]

While Randolph always continued to teach the central importance of receptive contact with the hierarchies of disembodied and never embodied souls, he later appears to have realized more clearly the dangers of at least one variety of blending. In *The New Mola* (1873), Randolph presented under the guise of "Atrilism" what he called a new revelation: the body of the medium or seer frequently could be taken over and occupied by other entities, both embodied and disembodied, who would use it for their own purposes.

> There is one point of spiritualism almost entirely overlooked by most of the believers in the New Mola, and everybody else.

They seem to be practically ignorant ... of either the facts or possibilities of MIXED IDENTITIES. That a well-attested medium, one with whom spiritual rapport is easy, can readily have his or her individuality, personal consciousness—absolute identity—the real *proprium*—entirely, completely, thoroughly subjugated, subverted, suppressed, to the extent of being, so far as the mental, moral and conscious personality is concerned—*non est*, not merely for the brief duration of an ordinary seance or trance, but for a period of time limited only by the will of the invisible possessor. Nor is this condition one of trance at all, for the party is to all appearance wide awake, performs all the ordinary functions and duties of life, yet the consciousness within is not theirs, nor the guiding intelligence, but wholly, totally ANOTHER'S. This condition may last for days, weeks or months together, during which time the earthly party resume themselves only at brief intervals, like short and vague snatches of wakeful consciousness in the midst of deep sleep. This mergement of identities is the Oriental *Atrilism*, during the continuance of which forced or magnetic abnegations *other* souls than the subject's carry their bodies about, eat, drink, sleep, quarrel, fight, talk, laugh, conspire, get tipsy, make love, and in short do anything which the possessor's fancy, whim, caprice, hatred, love, revenge, remorse, ambition or conceit may prompt, be the actions good or bad; nor can the possessed party, while in that state, help him or herself in the least degree, and are as wholly irresponsible for, and innocent of, what may transpire during that time, as a man would be for the flow or non-flow of the tide.[53]

Despite his statement, however, atrilism was not a new revelation, but it is clear that the perception of the dangers involved had changed over time. In *Ravalette* (1863), he had already pointed out the possibility of such control. "Nor was this all: He taught that the souls of people sometimes vacated their bodies for weeks together, during which they were occupied by other souls, sometimes that of a permanently disembodied man of earth; at others, that of an inhabitant of the aerial spaces, who, thus embodied, roamed the earth at will."[54]

To the uninitiated at any rate—and to Randolph at troubled moments—the practice seems dangerously close to the spirit control Randolph had rejected and thrown off in his recantation of spiritualism in 1858. Only the occupying entity was different, a living adept or celestial entity instead of a "spirit" of the dead. It also appears easily confounded with blending. The two seem merely varieties or extremes of the same phenomenon, intended to be distinguished perhaps by the degree to which consciousness was retained or surrendered, but frequently overlapping or confused in practice.[55]

From an occult point of view, the interesting question that arises from Randolph's description of blending and atrilism and from his conviction that the entities of the celestial hierarchies intermingled in the affairs of men and secretly directed the great spiritual movements of the time is the degree to which the transformation of spiritualism into occultism initiated by Randolph was the work of unknowable "personages beyond the veil," of the omnipresent hidden hand, acting for its own secret purposes. The question is unanswerable historically, but as we shall see it is central to the discussion of Randolph's Rosicrucians, who dwelt "on both sides of the grave," and to his relationships with the work of Madame Blavatsky (see chapter 12).

Practice and Blending

Dealings with the Dead contains the germs of Randolph's grand vision on communication with the celestial hierarchies and even some of the details which, together with his teachings on clairvoyance, magic mirrors, and drugs, will later be elaborated in his fully developed sexual magic.[56] In discussing how to achieve blending, Randolph mentions that the first step is to become receptive. The method, he says, is like the practice attributed to Machiavelli, of trying to read another's thoughts or intentions by placing oneself in mental rapport with him and then trying to assume his features and posture.[57] In Randolph's later system, this principle, which the H. B. of L. was to describe as the "Receptive Principle," came to be called "Posism," the posing of the body in a receptive manner, set to receive what was given by the celestial entities (see chapter 10).

Also sketched out in *Dealings with the Dead* but not fully elaborated is the idea that sex played a central role in the unfoldment of the soul, both in developing clairvoyance or soul sight and in blending, and that it played this role both here, while embodied on earth, and in the spirit and soul worlds. This intuition is the key to all of Randolph's later magical practice.[58]

Sex really means more than people even remotely suspect. In the Soul-world it does not serve the same purposes as on earth. *There*, sex is of the mind—on earth it is of the body mainly. . . . Now let two such meet in the Soul-world, and if they are adapted to each other, their spheres—nay, their very lives—blend together; the result of which is mutual improvement, purification, gratification, enjoyment, and happiness—which state of bliss continues until new unfoldings from within shall unfit them for the further continuance of the union.[39]

In his later Rosicrucian manifesto the Asiatic Mystery (1871), Randolph brings this idea to its full development.

We hold that no power ever comes to man through the intellect. We say that the adage "Knowledge is Power" is false; but that Goodness alone is Power, and that pertains to the heart only, hence that Power comes only to the Soul through LOVE (not lust, mind you), but LOVE, the underlying, Primal FIRE LIFE, subtending the bases of Being,—the formative flowing floor of the worlds,—the true sensing of which is the beginning of the road to personal power. Love lieth at the foundation, and is the synonym of life and strength. . . .

Thus it happens that a loving couple grow youthful in soul, because in their union they strike out this divine spark, replenish themselves with the essence of life, grow stronger and less brutal, and draw down to them the divine fire from the aerial spaces. (This now is by accident. We teach how to do so at pleasure).[60]

Before death, while here on earth, sex is tied up with the mystery of procreation, the embodiment of the eternal monads—a facet of the sexual union that will later be stressed almost to exclusivity by the H. B. of L. After death and in the soul world, procreation is no longer one of the purposes of sex, but, as on earth, the sexual union and blending of souls continues to be the primary means of soul progress.[61]

Sexual differential, for Randolph, was primordial. The soul monads were created eternally in pairs, male and female. In the soul world they "are always together: in couples they come from the Eternal God, in couples they return."[62] Behind this idea is the common spiritualist notion of the affinity of twin souls, of conjugal mates. Randolph's works echo these commonplace ideas on affinity, and he both stresses and downplays them in turn,[63] although, as we have seen, perhaps for reasons having to do with his own personal problems with women, he consistently rejected the idea that these affinities were eternal.[64] The male and female halves of the original divine monad, while they always remained in some sense associated, progressed at different rates, and disembodied man was constantly changing his affinity in the soul and spirit worlds.[65] At one point Randolph appears even to have conceived the extraordinary image of a perpetual accretion of bisexual pairs ascending in ever-greater complexity toward the divine:

> From the positive ray, man derives wisdom; from the negative, woman [derives] love. The spheres blend, and I will elucidate it thus:—
>
> (*Here the fore and middle fingers of the speaker's hands were spread open in the form V, and their ends put together, forming this figure <>.*)
>
> The spheres blend, for the divergences of the female and male souls, perfectly correspond, and the celestial marriage takes place. Now, all men correspond to some principle-ray from God, some attribute and perfection of Deity. A man dies on the earth, he enters the spirit-world, meets his other self, and they two become one; being the completeness of the second sphere. Now, mark you, that *one*, also, corresponds to a positive or negative principle, and it progresses to another sphere, where the duality positive meets the duality negative; and so on, *ad infinitum*, until God, or Death positive, produces a God infinite, negative, and the unitized democracy of humanly developed gods shall be complete, and correspond to and receive direct rays of living light from the God positive of all gods.[66]

These ideas provide the occult background to Randolph's medical views on sexual union as the great purifier and distiller of "Physical Love," the fine fluid that bathes and feeds the soul (chapter 1). In *Dealings with the Dead* he says that "Od" (Baron von Reichenbach's term for the all-pervading ether) is the fluid that mediates between the body and the spirit and that "Ethylle" "connects soul with spirit, and unites all three worlds, body, soul, and spirit together, and constitutes not only the spheres, but the 'Personal Nebulæ,' out of which the immortal spark creates its surrounding sphere or world, when disembodied."[67] Ethylle is what Randolph will call "Æth"—the primal fire at the root of the universe and the medium and fuel of sexual magic.

Chapter 6

THE ROSICRUCIAN

The Rosicrucians of history were the wonder-working fraternity launched upon the world by the publication of the *Fama Fraternitatis* in 1614. The story of the pious, reform-minded secret brotherhood of Christian adepts who possessed unsuspected knowledge derived from the mysterious East fascinated Europe then and over the centuries became the rallying-point around which gathered all the forces of magic, alchemy, Hermeticism, Freemasonry, Paracelsian medicine and occultism generally.[1] In the process it generated an enormous literature—a literature with which Randolph claimed, probably with some truth, an intimate familiarity.[2]

When Randolph published his series of articles on "Dealings with the Dead" in the *Banner of Light* in the fall of 1859, he did so under the pseudonym *Le Rosicrucien*, and it was in the role of Rosicrucian that Randolph worked for the last fifteen years of his life. What he intended by this cloaking of his work in the guise of Rosicrucianism—beyond the genealogy and universal tradition it allowed him to invoke—is a difficult question and one that, despite Randolph's familiarity with the literature, takes us far afield from the Rosicrucians of history. Sylvester Clark Gould, a member of the H. B. of L. and one of the cofounders of the Societas Rosicruciana in America—groups that incorporated versions of Randolph's sexual magic after his death—correctly pointed out that Randolph's system "had scarcely any fundamentals pertaining to those of the sixteenth and seventeenth centuries, nor even [to] the Rosicrucians of modern times."[3] Randolph's work certainly lacks the formal alchemical and Paracelsian elements usually associated with the Rosicrucians, and even his occasional use of alchemical terms to describe his system is largely mere window dressing.[4] The "elementals" also—the "spirits of the elements," the entities below man in the chain of being—played only a slight role in

Randolph's thought—surprisingly, in light of the emphasis given to them by earlier revelations of Rosicrucianism, such as the Comte de Gabalis, and by Randolph's contemporaries, such as Eliphas Lévi. Randolph mentions the elementals and clearly believed in their existence but they played no prominent role in his magic.[5]

Rosicrucianism for Randolph really meant his own system, based on the supremacy of the will: "Rosicrucians never fail! Try!" The field of activity of the will, in turn, was the sexually polarized universe, peopled with the ever more sublime and awful denizens of the ascending celestial hierarchies—reaching back to the divine Central Sun and even beyond—through which man was destined to progress as a godling in this life and after. Communication with these hierarchies of the living (secret adepts) and of the dead and the never embodied through the separation of the soul, "astral travel" and blending was the key element of Randolph's Rosicrucianism,[6] and through this communication the seeker learned the secrets of existence, including (and more in line with the original Rosicrucian movement) the secret key to human health, happiness, and longevity.[7]

Any theory that Randolph simply guised his own thought in the convenient cloak of Rosicrucianism without regard for or belief in the Rosicrucians themselves, however, fails to do justice to the complexities of Randolph's ideas—even though this theory was precisely the explanation put forward by Randolph himself.

Disclaimers

In his later books, goaded probably by the continuing failure of the public to recognize his talents and the tendency of the world to attribute his successes to others (usually spirits; in this case Rosicrucians), he explained his use of the designation *Rosicrucian* as one of convenience and publicity only. In *Eulis* (1874) he emphasized his own creative role in the origins of his Rosicrucianism:

> I became famous, but never popular. I studied Rosicrucianism, found it suggestive, and loved its mysticisms. So I called myself The Rosicrucian, and gave my thought to the world as Rosicrucian thought; and lo! the world greeted with loud applause what it supposed had its origin and birth elsewhere than in the soul of P. B. Randolph.
>
> Very nearly *all* that I have given as Rosicrucianism originated in my soul; and scarce a single thought, only suggestions, have

I borrowed from those who, in ages past, called themselves by that name—one which served me well as a vehicle wherein to take *my* mental treasures to a market, which gladly opened its doors to that name, but would, and did, slam to its portals in the face of the tawny student of Esoterics. . . . In proof of these statements, and of how I had to struggle, the world is challenged to find a line of my thought in the whole 4,000 books on Rosicrucianism; [or] among the brethren of that Fraternity.[8]

Still earlier, in *Soul! The Soul World* published in 1870, he had explicitly disclaimed all connection with the Rosicrucians.

Spiritualism, as popularly understood and advocated by its champions, could, in consequence of the mental states of exaltation and out-sight to which I was subject, no longer feed my soul. Then I fell in with certain men, several of whom had read much that I had written, and listened oft to the strange and weird knowledge that fell from my lips in public speech, when inspired by an august power, not of this earth, or of dead men. These said to me: "You are a Rosicrucian; what you proclaim are the sublime doctrines of the Rosy Cross." Said I: Rose Cross let it be, and thenceforward I wrote as "The Rosicrucian," and as such became noted far and wide. But in other years I visited foreign lands, and learned all the world contains of Rose-cross doctrines, tenets, practices and beliefs,—not every book, but most of them, and all that are really worth reading,—which most of them are *not*, by reason of excessive verbiage, and paucity of ideas,—and Rose-cross was found wanting,—that it was not all that I had hoped it to be. Still, as it came nearer to my ideas than aught yet encountered, I continued to call myself "The Rosicrucian," that name being as good as any other to distinguish my thought from the world's thought.

Presently, as I wrote and spoke, here and there, one encouraged me, and called themselves Rosicrucians, not because they were Rose-cross-ists, but because they liked my writings and modes of thought and expression. . . . The whole train of thought and discovery is my own. I have borrowed nothing from any one; and the system, as I conceive, and originated it, is as far beyond what Rosicrucianism, pure and simple, is, as that system is beyond what it was popularly supposed to be. Of course I disclaim all connection and affiliation with any systems but my own, go by whatsoever names they may. Indeed I have give my own name, "Paschian" from Paschal, as the true title by which, when I am dead, I wish my system of thought to be known.[9]

These disclaimers and Randolph's denigration of various contemporary "Rosicrucians" must be taken seriously, but they should not be viewed as an unqualified repudiation by Randolph of his equally frequent claims to be a *true* Rosicrucian and part of the *real* Rosicrucian order. Quite the contrary is in fact the case. Behind Randolph's transparent attempt to promote his own originality and genius is an unusual vision of the nature of the Brotherhood of the Rosy Cross and an acknowledgment, repeated over and over in his works, of his debt to the Rosicrucians as he conceived them to be. The crux is in the nature of his vision of the Rosicrucians and his free mingling of flesh-and-blood Rosicrucians with the denizens of the celestial hierarchies. Randolph undoubtedly believed that there were Rosicrucians and that he himself was numbered in their ranks, but the order in which he claimed membership was one that bore little resemblance to the Rosicrucians of history.

Rosicrucians on Both Sides of the Grave

In *Dealings with the Dead*, Randolph describes his first encounter in the soul world with the mighty Ramus, known to history as Thotmor or Thothmes, the eleventh king of the second Egyptian dynasty.[10] He is called "the imperial lord of an imperial order,—that great and mystic brotherhood at whose power kings and potentates have trembled most abjectly." Randolph "blends" with Ramus and receives instruction on the nature of the soul—the teachings published in *Dealings with the Dead*—and is encouraged in his intention to revive the order of the Rosy Cross and taught that the capacities of the human soul are unlimited for those possessing and exercising will.

> You aspire to comprehend the mighty secret of the TRINE. You seek to become an acolyte of the imperial order of the Rosy Cross, and to re-establish it upon the earth; and no TRUE ROSICRUCIAN dares shrink from attempting the solution of the mysteries and problems that human minds in heaven or on earth may conceive or propound. Our motto—the motto of the great order of which I was a brother on earth,—an order which has, under a variety of names, existed since the very dawn of civilization on the earth—is "Try."[11]

In *The Rosicrucian's Story*, published in 1863 after Randolph's return from his extended trip to the Near East in 1861 and 1862, Ramus appears again, in a more oriental dress. He is now described as "Chief or Grand Master of the Superlative Order of Gebel Al Maruk—known in Christian lands as the Order of the Brethren of the Rosie Cross, and in America and Europe, where it still thrives, as the 'Imperial Order of Rosicrucia.'"[12]

The crucial juncture between these creatures of vision and the reality of normal earthly life lies in Randolph's assertion that the order of Rosicrucians ramified "extensively on both sides of the grave, and, on the other shore of time, was known in its lower degrees as the Royal Order of the Gann ["djinn"?], and, towering infinitely beyond and above that, . . . the great Order of the Neridii."[13] In *Dealings with the Dead*, Randolph had outlined the hierarchies beyond earth, both of the disembodied and of the never born: (1) spirits— angels; (2) seraphs; (3) arsaphs; (4) eons; (5) arsasaphs; (6) arch-eons; (7) antarphim.[14] In *Ravalette* he gave a more specific description of the nature of these entities and of the possible relationships between them and living mortals and among mortals themselves. In discussing "ghosts," he says:

Some people do not believe in ghosts. I do, ghosts of various kinds. I. It is possible to project an image of one's self, which image may be seen by another however distant. II. The phantasmal projections of heated fantasy . . . as in drunken delirium, opium and other fantasies. III. The spirits of dead men. IV. Spiritual beings from other planets. V. Beings from original worlds, who have not died, but who, nevertheless, are of so fine texture as to defy the material laws which we are compelled to obey, and who . . . are enabled to do all that they do. VI. I believe that human beings, by the action of desperate, wicked wills, frequently call into being spectral harpies—the horrible embodiment of their evil thoughts. These are demons, subsisting so long as their creators are under the domination of evil. VII. I believe in a similar creation emanating from good thoughts of good people, loving out-creations of aspiring souls. . . . This is a clear statement of the Rosicrucian doctrine of the higher order of their temple. In the lower, these seven pass under the names of Gnomes, Dwarfs, Sylphs, Salamanders, Nereiads, Driads and Fays.[15]

Randolph is emphatic that these hierarchies of evolved beings, both celestial and earthly, act as the hidden hand molding history and involve themselves in and manipulate human affairs for their own ends: "Much, I learned, that passes among men for spiritual manifestation, really has no such origin, while many things, attributed to an origin purely mundane, are really the work of intelligent beings, beyond the misty veil."[16]

Spiritualism was the obvious example of this intermixing in the affairs of men, and, its purpose having been achieved, it was destined to give way in turn to the next higher stage of planned spiritual development, exemplified by the Rosicrucians (see chapter 5).

For Randolph the Rosicrucians spanned the juncture of living men and these celestial and earthly hierarchies, and their teachings were the link that enabled ordinary men, during life, to communicate with these hierarchies. While the nature of the celestial hierarchies and of communication with them is fairly clear in Randolph's works, the same cannot be said of their earthly extensions on this side of the grave and more specifically of the Rosicrucians as a flesh-and-blood brotherhood or society. Any attempt to unravel that puzzle must brave the labyrinth of Randolph's various statements—especially his novel *The Wonderful Story of Ravalette*—about the Rosicrucians and the Brothers of the Light.

Ravalette

Ravalette (1863) is told in the person of a narrator, a friend of "The Rosicrucian" (who is obviously Randolph himself). It is fantastic in every sense and admittedly abounds in anachronisms, but beneath it all there are glimmerings of what Randolph himself taught (and probably believed) about his association with the Rosicrucians. In the novel, Randolph initially simply asserts that he is a Rosicrucian, without giving the details:

> [My] doom has brought around me, as it did around others before me, certain beings, powers, influences, and at length I became a voluntary adept in the Rosicrucian mysteries and brotherhood. How, or when, or where I was found worthy of initiation, of course I am not at liberty to tell; suffice it to say that I belong to the Order, and have been—by renouncing certain things—admitted to the companionship of the living, the dead, and those who never die; have been admitted to the famous Derishavi-Laneh, and am familiar with the profoundest secrets of the Fakie-Deeva Records.[17]

As mentioned earlier, the plot of *Ravalette* hinges on the claim of Randolph/the Rosicrucian to be a special "neutral soul," born over and over again on earth as penance for a horrible murder committed ages ago, and doomed to rebirth until he married a woman "not born of Adam." As a neutral soul he was unique and was eagerly sought both by the adherents of the "august Fraternity of the Heavens, known as the Power of the Light" and by its opposite, called the "Power of the Shadow"—the chief embodiments of which had acted roles in the earlier crime for which Randolph was destined to be reborn.[18] His first encounter with the brethren of the Shadow comes in a vision that is told in almost precisely the same terms as his description (in *Dealings with the Dead*) of his meeting in the soul world with Ramus/Thotmor. Randolph relates that when a very young man living in Portland, Maine, he spontaneously fell into a trance and had an extraordinary vision.

So absorbed did I become during the evening, that on one or two occasions I partially lost myself in a sort of semi-mesmeric coma, which gradually deepened as the discussion waxed warmer, until my lower limbs grew cold, and a chilling numbness crept upon me, creating such a terror that I resolved to make my condition known, even at the risk of interrupting the discussion.

I made the trial, and found, to my consternation, that I could not utter a syllable—I could not move an inch. . . .

With inexpressible alarm, I felt that life itself was fast ebbing from me, and that death was slowly and surely grasping, clutching, freezing my vitals. I was dying. Presently—it appeared as if a long interregnum had occurred between the last previous conscious moment, and the present instantaneous, but positive agony—a sudden, sharp, tingling pang, like that of hot needles thrust in the flesh, shot through my brain. This was followed by a sinking sensation, as if the body had resigned itself to passive dissolution, and then came, with electric rapidity, a succession of the most cruel agonies ever endured by mortal man. When it ceased consciousness had ceased also, and I fell to the floor as one suddenly dead, to the amazement of the company. . . .

How long this physical inanition lasted, I cannot now say, but during it the spiritual part of me was roused to a tenfold degree of activity, consciousness and power; for it saw things in a new and cryptic light, and far more distinctly than it ever had through the bodily eyes. . . . I gazed out, and down, and up, through an avenue of the most astonishing light I had ever beheld. It seemed to me that I no longer occupied my body, but that, freed from flesh and time, I had become a denizen of Eternity.[19]

At this point in the vision Randolph met an old man called "Ettelavar" (an anagram of Ravalette, the mysterious and sinister entity who reappears under a variety of names throughout the novel) who told him that "his design was to serve both him and me" and that he possessed the mighty secrets possessed through the ages by "the Narek El Gebel, the Hermetists, the Pythagoreans, the three temples of the Rosie Cross, the mediæval and modern Rosicrucians, and the scattered delvers after mystery in all ages, times, and places." Ettelavar then tempted Randolph by offering him the elixir of life that conferred perpetual youth and beauty, the water of love that made its drinker irresistible to the opposite sex, the wondrous stone of the philosophers that transmuted gross metal into gold, and the magic crystal ball that allowed the seer to see whatever he wished. Ettelavar/Ravalette thus knew or claimed to know the secrets of the Rosicrucians, but he was not himself, apparently, one of their number.

Years after this vision, Randolph says, he traveled to Paris and there first encountered the real Rosicrucians. If he is not being deliberately deceptive, this was his first trip abroad in the spring of 1855 since he mentions that at the time D. D. Home was in London and had not yet begun his tour of the Continent.

> At length, there came an invitation from Baron D——t [Dupotet], for me to attend and take part in, a Mesmeric Séance. I attended; and from the reputation I gained on that occasion, but a few days elapsed ere I was summoned to the Tuilleries, by command of his majesty, Napoleon III., who for thirty-four years had been a True Rosicrucian. . . .
>
> On this occasion I had played and conquered at both chess and écarte, no word being spoken, the games simultaneous, and the players in three separate rooms. There was present, also, an Italian gentleman with an unpronounceable name.[20]

The Italian count is, of course, the famous magnetist and purveyor of mirrors we have already met with—perhaps Regazzoni (see chapter 3). At the invitation of Napoleon, the count proceeded to mesmerize the entire audience, without passes, merely by glancing at them in a mirror. As each person in turn was magnetized, he proceeded to perform the usual stunts associated with stage hypnotists. When Randolph commented quietly to himself on the count's power, the count overheard him and told him that all of this power and more would be his if he became a Rosicrucian.

> I learned my secret among the magi of the East—men not half so civilized as are we of the West; but who, nevertheless, *know* a great deal more than the sapient men of Christendom—that is, less of machinery, politics, and finance; but a great deal more of the human soul, and its nature, its powers, and the methods of their development.[21]

The count reveals to Randolph that he is part of the True Temple, the "*Supreme Dome* of the Rosie Cross" to which only good men may belong. He emphasized the point by making a blaze of lightning bolts circle the room and settle in a crown over the head of Napoleon, and with this demonstration as an example, he instructs Randolph to be aware of the true cause of the phenomena of spiritualism: they are mostly the work of living men and of beings far different from the "spirits" of the dead—a claim that would soon become the rallying cry and hallmark teaching of "occultism" in its contest with spiritualism and that would be echoed in the works of Emma Hardinge Britten and Madame Blavatsky. "I do not aver that all the phenomena exhibited in these days as spiritual are produced as I have these; but I do say that not one-tenth part is attributable to spiritual agencies. That which is indeed spiritual is not all the product of dead men, but much of it proceeds from the Larvæ and inhabitants of the spaces between the rolling globes"[22]

Randolph leaves the court, pondering the power of the count and his promise that they will meet again. Later, in Naples on his way East, he awakens in the morning to find his coins arranged in the form of a triangle surmounted by the letter "R"—the symbol of the Rosicrucians that had been shown him by Ramus/Thotmor in the vision he had related in *Dealings with the Dead*. Repeatedly, in Egypt, France, and elsewhere, his path crosses that of the count, but Randolph is plagued with skepticism about the Rosicrucians, despite wide reading and his acquaintance with scores of pseudo-Rosicrucians whom he considers mere "paper-stainers."

After completing his tour ("none the wiser," he says), Randolph states that he returned to Boston and took up the practice of medicine. This must have been in 1856 or 1858, probably the latter.[23] There he is again tempted by the Power of the Shadow—this time in the guise of an Armenian "Guebre," Miakus, who displayed to him his amazing powers over the magic mirror—but again Randolph resisted the invitation to throw his lot in with the tempter. The following night he had the vision described in *Dealings with the Dead* in which he first encountered Ramus/Thotmor, the "imperial chief of an imperial order."[24] From the vague hints earlier in the novel that Randolph thought he recognized the Italian count when he first met him, we probably are expected at this point to deduce that the count and Ramus/Thotmor are one and the same.[25]

Throughout the book, Ravalette himself appears, a somewhat sinister counterpart of the count possessing equally wonderful magical powers. Ravalette, together with Miakus, tries to get Randolph "the neutral soul" to sleep the "Sleep of Sialam Boaghiee"—the mysterious prophetic trance possible only once in a hundred years.[26] Near the end of the book yet another mysterious figure, Mai Vatterale ("I am Ravalette"), appears. He is clearly the count under a new guise, and—to emphasize the point made earlier—he also causes all the phenomena familiar to the seance room to occur through his own power.[27]

The narrator of *Ravalette*, who at this point is totally confused, then tries to make sense of all that has taken place. He sets his conclusions down point by point:

> 1st, That there was in existence a society, having its head-quarters in Paris, the members of which were practisers of Oriental magic and necromancy, in which they were most astonishingly expert. 2d, That the organization had for its object, not the attainment of wealth or political position, but abstract knowledge, and the absolute rule of the world through the action and influence of the brotherhood upon the crowned heads and officials of the world. 3d, That this organization was governed by a master-mind, and that this mind was Ravalette's. 4th, That this society had cultivated mesmerism to a degree unapproachable by all the world besides. That they had exhausted ordinary clairvoyance [and sought a unique mind to sleep the sleep of Sialam]. . . . 6th, It was clear that, while these men knew much of the Rosicrucian system, they were not in full harmony or accord with that brotherhood.[28]

Even this attempt at a synthesis fails, however, and in the final scenes of the book it is revealed that Ravalette is Ettelavar is Mai Vatterale is Miakus is the count, and so on, and is also, for good measure, a being called "Dhoula Bel the Vampire."[29] The goal of the entire exercise of shifting personalities as it turns out has been to prevent Randolph from escaping his age-old curse of rebirth by wedding a mysterious girl "not born of Adam." Randolph of course finally weds the girl, but before he does he consents to sleep the "Sleep of Sialam." In the presence of Ravalette and Napoleon III he enters the prophetic trance and gives vent to sweeping prophecies of political turmoil and upheaval—all of which, with the exception of the prediction of the downfall of Napoleon, have been proven false by time. On the future of the Rosicrucians the sleeper predicts the coming of a Prussian who would proclaim the system to the entire world and be hailed as *the* man of the nineteenth century.[30] On this note, all the various personages subsumed in "Ravalette" vanish, and Randolph weds the non-Adamic girl, begets a son named "Osiris Budh" and shortly thereafter dies, presumably to be reborn no more.

In *Ravalette*, then, so far as our search for the Rosicrucians is concerned, we have come full circle from Randolph's rejection of Rosicrucian origins for his work. From the disembodied Ramus of *Dealings with the Dead*, we have moved to competing groups of adepts (the Brethren of the Light and the Brethren of the Shadow) extending on both sides of the grave, both of whom are masters of mesmerism and possessors of wondrous powers with which they can at will provoke the phenomena of the seance room, and both of whom, though primarily Oriental in origin, have extensions in Europe and, most notably, a headquarters in Paris[31]—a claim that recurs throughout Randolph's works and the works of other contemporary occultists. What can we make of these flesh-and-blood extensions of myth?

History Behind the Myth?

In *Ravalette*, in describing the purpose of his second trip to the Near East in 1861 and 1862, Randolph says: "I was on my second journey toward the Orient, and had taken in London and Paris on my way. My objects in the journey were . . . to visit the Supreme Grand Dome of the Rosicrucian Temple; to make my obeisance to its Grand Master; to study its higher doctrines, and visit the Brethren."[32]

The claim appears again in *The Rosicrucian's Story* (1863). Randolph was sailing, he said, to "the Pyramids of Egypt, near which I am to meet a conclave of Oriental Rosicrucians."[33] Here again Randolph raised the specter of Ramus/Thotmor, but this time in the form of a living Persian, Pul Ali Beg, who had succeeded Ramus as chief of the order. Randolph's second trip to Europe and the Near East in 1861 and 1862 was considerably more extended than his earlier trips, almost lasting a year, and certainly put him in a position to encounter such men as the mysterious Persian. He visited England, Ireland, Scotland, France,

Malta, Egypt (and the Sudan), Syria, Palestine, Turkey—in which he probably included the Turkish vilyats in what is now Iraq, as far as the Persian border, and may have visited Persia itself—and Greece.[34]

> I am a Brother of the Rosie Cross, and I have been over Egypt, and Syria, and Turkey; on the borders of the Caspian, and Arabia's shores; over sterile steppes and weltered through the Deserts— and all in search of the loftier knowledge of the Soul that can only there be found; and I found what I sought . . . —the nature of the Soul, its destiny, and how it may be trained to any end or purpose. And the History and Mystery of Dream, . . . from the lips of the Oriental Dwellers in the Temple—and Pul Ali Beg . . . our Persian Ramus, and our lordly Chief,—and I learned the worth of Will, and how to say, and *mean* "I *will* be well, and not sick—alive, and not dead!" and achieve the purpose. How? That is our secret—the Rosicrucians'—strange order of men; liv- ing all along the ages, *till they are ready to die*—for Death comes only because man will not beat him back. They die through Feebleness of Will. But not so with us . . .; we leave not until our work is done. . . . We exercise our power over others, too, but ever for their good.[35]

Thus, despite all his disclaimers, when the mood was on him Randolph freely boasted of the dependence of his Rosicrucian groups on higher authority and of his own rightful (though by no means dominant) place in a chain of tradition reaching back to the earliest ages. In his 1874 Rosicrucian foundation, Randolph described himself as "Grand Templar, Warden and Supreme Hierarch" of the order,[36] but from the late 1850s on he had stressed that beyond him stretched the whole panoply of mythological Rosicrucianism.

> The Rosicrucians are . . . working under a Grand Lodge Char- ter, deriving its power and authority from the Imperial Dome of the Third Supreme Temple of the Order, and the last (claiming justly to be the oldest association of men on earth, dating from the sinking of the New Atlantis Isle, nearly ten thousand years anterior to the days of Plato), and as a Grand Lodge, having jurisdiction over the entire continent of North America, and the Islands of the Sea.[37]

In his first Rosicrucian manifesto (1863), Randolph sketched the history of the order from the magi through the Sabeans, Zoroaster,

R. POOLE.　　　　　NASHVILLE TENN.

Plate 1. Paschal Beverly Randolph in 1874

Plato, Melchizedek, and the rest of the usual *prisci theologi*, all of whose secrets were subsumed in "the sacred doctrines of the Mountain of Light," the translation of the Arabic name Randolph gave to the group presided over by Ramus/Thotmor.[38] Later in 1863 Randolph enticingly added to this mythological history the claim that the Rosicrucian order, "though long considered to be dead and buried, has within twelve years [i.e., since 1851] been revived in Germany, France, England—under a Grandmastership; and in America (New York) and also in California, in all of which places it bids fair to do a vast amount of good in the direction of dispelling many of the clouds that obscure the mental vision of the race."[39]

Similarly, in his early Rosicrucian novels Randolph played this vast worldwide organization for all it was worth, insinuating lofty connections, unknown superiors and degrees beyond the simple three degrees of the American Lodges he himself was then establishing.[40] The public propaganda for his San Francisco foundation in 1861, for example, linked the order expressly with an extensive organization of existing lodges, and Randolph let it be known that he was "engaged upon a massive work called 'The Book of Rosicrucia,' written at the instance of the Supreme Grand Lodges of the Order in America, Europe, and Asia."[41] Similarly, Randolph coyly says that he had only passed the fifth degree of the order—that is, considerably higher than the regular members of his lodges but still inferior to and buttressed by higher unknown superiors.[42] In his later books this diffidence vanishes and he becomes the ultimate head of the Rosicrucians: "I know many such [Rosicrucians] in various lands, and was, till I resigned the office, Grand Master of the only Temple of the Order on the globe."[43]

If we venture into the morass of rumor, myth, literary allusion, and outright deception that the occultists of midcentury created around their activities and origins, Randolph's claims of real, organized Rosicrucians (by whatever name) on this side of the grave are far from isolated. Leaving aside for the moment Madame Blavatsky's Rosicrucians and Brothers of Luxor, discussed in chapter 12, the striking similarity between Randolph's Brothers of the Light and Brothers of the Shadow and Emma Hardinge Britten's (or the Chevalier Louis's) mysterious Ellora and Berlin brotherhoods is obvious. The major elements in both stories are identical: mesmerism, crystal gazing, will, drugs as an aid to the development of clairvoyance, opposing groups of adepts, and the emphasis on spiritualism as a ploy created by the adepts for their own aims. Only Randolph's Near Eastern coloring is less evident in Britten's later descriptions. At very minimum it defies belief to think that Britten (or Louis) had not read and heavily relied on Randolph. Whether the connection existed on a more profound level—as the H. B. of L. and the proponents of the hidden hand later taught—is a different question.

Again on a literary level, Randolph's idea of a conclave of Oriental Rosicrucians which met at the pyramids in Egypt consciously echoed Heinrich Jung-Stilling's unnamed esoteric group that convened "in Egypt, on Mount Sinai, in the Monastery of Canobin, and under the Temple at Jerusalem."[44] Emma Hardinge Britten increased the confusion by having Professor von Marx in *Ghost Land* equate his Berlin Brotherhood with the society "described so graphically by Jung-Stilling in vision,"[45] and all of these references in turn are compounded by Frederick Hockley's "Crowned Angel," who announced to Hockley's scryer the existence of a "sacred society" of Rosicrucians whose chiefs were in Jerusalem, but which could be joined by traveling to France.[46]

Randolph's distinction between Brothers of the Light and Brothers of the Shadow also necessarily evokes the Brothers of Light—Fratres Lucis—another supposed organization that displays the same interplay of myth, allusion and deception that appears in the accounts of Randolph and Emma Hardinge Britten. References to the Fratres Lucis began in 1873, when the spirit of Cagliostro appeared (as always, in the crystal) to Herbert Irwin (the seer for his father, Francis Irwin, a longtime associate of Kenneth Mackenzie and Frederick Hockley) and related the outline of the history and ritual of the brotherhood.[47] Mackenzie, in turn, in his *Royal Masonic Cyclopædia* (1877) claimed that the group was real and fleshed out Irwin's description. Mackenzie traced the origins of the group to 1498. He claimed that the group was widespread throughout the world and that its members included Martinès de Pasqually, Cagliostro, Swedenborg, Saint-Martin, and Eliphas Lévi (who had died in 1875 when the *Cyclopædia* began to be published in fascicles and thus was unavailable for comment).[48] Again, there is specific reference to Paris as the headquarters of the group or at least as a place where entry might be gained to it—and the mystery is heightened by Irwin's claim actually to have met with the brothers there.[49] Once again, the emphasis in the Fratres Lucis is on crystals, mesmerism and practical occult work and on the secret direction of events by the unseen adepts.

All these continued references to the Orient, Paris, magic mirrors, and mesmerism appear to reflect some reality beneath the storytelling and literary cross-referencing. In Randolph's case they immediately call to mind his Italian count/Armenian seer, Cuilna Vilmara, whom he met in Paris, and the "Mystic Brotherhood of Paris, France" that supplied his magic mirrors and was somehow related to a Fraternité de la Rosecroix and to Colonel Fraser's worldwide fraternity of mirror magicians which had a center in Paris. There are other hints also in Randolph's work that point to the existence of real men with whom he at least felt himself associated in some common endeavor. He asks rhetorically, for example, what sort of brotherhood it is "whose loftiest offices pass by crowned kings and settle upon the weary shoulders of a coffee-carrier of Arabia, a German chemist, or a man of no position in the world!"[30]—a question that is at least calculated to cause us to ask the very question we are asking.

In *Ravalette* (1863), Randolph is more specific—if not about the chiefs of his organization (such as "Pul Ali Beg"), then at least about those whose work he considered public expressions of kindred currents of thought. He has the Italian count mention that he had learned the great secret of projecting images at will "in the Punjab, of Naumsavi Chitty, the chief of the Rosicrucians of India, and the greatest reformer since Budha."[31] This mysterious personage reappears in the company of actual men in Randolph's 1871 manifesto *The Asiatic Mystery, The Fire Faith! The Religion of Flame! The Force of Love! The Energos of Will! The Magic of Polar Mentality! First Rosicrucian Manifesto to the World Outside the Order.*

> During the past sixteen years five brethren—Victorien Moreau, Paris, France, Le Compte d'Ouche, ditto, Hargrave Jennings, London, England, Paschal B. Randolph, Boston, America, and N'Sauvi Chitty, Bengal, India, have published to the world various works and speeches about our principles, which, though not professedly of a propagandistic character, nevertheless resulted in winning innumerable thousands of the best minds in the world to our system and standard of belief, and all such we regard as brethren without a lodge; until for two reasons it is no longer incumbent that the veil be unlifted. Hence we raise it. The first reason is, because false Rosicrucians are abroad in the lands; and second, the Supreme Grand Master of the Order on Earth expressly so wills that it shall be.[52]

The Count D'Ourches we have already discussed (chapter 2). While he may have moved in mysterious circles and have caught Randolph's attention, he appears from the little that is known about him to have been a simple spiritualist, without more occult preoccupations. Hargrave Jennings, the only other familiar name in the list, holds a curious and important place in Randolph's work, but despite Randolph's explicit claims, he appears an unlikely candidate for an unknown superior or even for a member of any secret group.

Jennings was an enigma to his contemporaries and remains one today, not so much because of what he wrote (though his writings are incredibly turgid and indirect) but because of his apparent isolation.[33] He said he was an autodidact, and the claim appears true. Starting with what must have been a fair knowledge of classical languages, he had poured over antiquarian histories, such as Godfrey Higgins's *Anacalypsis* (1836), and combined their penchant for explaining universal mythology with what little was known of Buddhism and Indian religions generally at the time, adding in the process perhaps too liberal a dose of Schopenhauer, Bishop Berkeley, Spinoza, and Schlegel. The result was curious and often unintelligible, but tantalizing for his readers.[34]

For Jennings the idealist, space and time were ultimately illusory, but the substratum of the illusion was the universal fire or light, which was both the agent of magic and mysticism and the ultimate goal of achieving awakening. "And all [man's] knowledge of things comes from that light shining *within* his prison—his mind. Within that radius, the light is perfect and he is himself perfect. But what guesses he, or can he know, of the great light within? . . . Man is the centre to himself in his light of mind, shining as in his castle and prison of body."[35] The primary manifestation of this fire or light for men, and the key to their ultimate awakening, was in the mystery of sex—though it is impossible to discern through Jennings's words what he believed the key may have been as a practical matter. In his correspondence in the 1880s with Robert H. Fryar, the mirror magician and purveyor in England of Randolph's books and manuscripts, he made the point explicitly:

> "Phallicism"—not the sensual "Priapeian" Phallicism—but the highest religious and spiritual Phallicism—is at the bottom of all religions ancient and modern. The real "Rosicrucians" *knew this.* They carefully suppressed themselves and their beliefs—hiding away in mystery and parable to which all authentic scriptures must ever be committed.[36]

On one level, at least, magnetism undoubtedly played a role in the unfolding of the phallic mystery.

> The old Buddhists—as equally as the ancient believers in the doctrine of the Universal Spiritual Fire—held that Spirit Light was the floor or basis of all created things. The material side or complement of this Spiritual Light being Fire, into which element all things could be rendered; and which (or Heat) was the

motive of all things that are. They taught that matter or mind—as the superflux—as the sum of sensations, or as natural and unreal shows of their various kinds—were piled, as layer on layer or tissue on tissue, on this immutable and immortal floor or groundwork of Divine Flame, the Soul of the World. That emotion, intensity, mind-agitation, thought, according to the powers of the unit or the lifting heavenward:—or as the dots or dimples in the everflowing onwave of being: were—to speak in the familiar sense—"as impressions down," perhaps through and through its covers, upon this living floor of spiritual flame. The escape of which was the magnetism—magnetism of the body: supersensual force, or miracle, of the spirit—which is the disclosure of and bond of the Universe, and the "self-protest" of matter, remonstrating again back, as it were, towards its last HEAVEN or REST. Which latter is the "non-irritation into matter," or sublime "Non-Being" of the Buddhists.[57]

In turn, the great agents in penetrating to the light were the magic mirror (which Jennings equated with the philosopher's stone) and also certain unnamed drugs, gases, and vapors.[58]

Jennings believed that the mysteries of the celestial fire and its magic were the special possession of the "Buddhists of Upper India." They had built the megaliths in Europe and around the Mediterranean and left traces of their wisdom in universal mythology. Various groups from the mystical and magical tradition—ranging from Melchizedek through the Persian Guebres, the priests of Eleusis, the Assassins, the Druses (whom Jennings, following Higgins, equated with the British Culdees) and the Knights Templar to the Rosicrucians—had secretly professed the ancient Buddhist fire faith.[59] All of these were privy to the great secret. "There must have existed in these secret societies, the dreams, trances, visions, magic-sight, which made princes of the seers. It is in this secret medium—whatever it may be—whether conjured out of the capacity of man in the intoxication of narcotics, through fumes, anointings, or lapsing out of the prisoned sense into the unimprisoned sense;—it is in their new world that the explorers stumble upon unbelievable, though real, things."[60] Nor was this secret tradition dead in the nineteenth century. Jennings believed there were still secret societies which preserved these mysteries intact, and he was careful to allay the fears of initiates that he might have revealed their secrets accidentally in his books.

To the guardians of the more recondite and secret philosophical knowledge, of whom, in the societies—abroad and at home—there are a greater number, even in these days, than the uninitiate might suppose, it will be sufficient to observe that in no part of our Book . . . is there approach, by us, to disclosures which, in any mind, might be considered too little guarded.[61]

Despite Jennings's reference to his knowledge of these societies, however, there is very little indication anywhere in his works or in the little that is known about his life that he took any part in them himself.[62]

Undoubtedly Hargrave Jennings's books, the earliest of which began to appear in the late 1850s when Randolph was in England, were a revelation to Randolph.[63] The two met at the time, and while Jennings later could only condemn Randolph's mischievous and dangerous publication of sacred doctrines, Randolph originally was more than complimentary of Jennings.[64] In Randolph's original work on magic mirrors in 1860 and in the reworking of the pamphlet as *Seership* in 1870, Jennings is called "the chief Rosicrucian of all England" and "one of the master Rosicrucians of England,"[65] and his *Curious Things of the Outside World* is quoted at great length on the divine fire, magnetism, and magic mirrors.[66] Throughout his life, Randolph continued to refer to and borrow and quote from Jennings, especially on universal phallicism,[67] but despite the compliment of imitation, Randolph's early opinion of Jennings as a "paper-stainer" probably reflects the reality of his judgment on him and shows that the relationship was a literary one, pure and simple.[68] Jennings taught Randolph the context in which to view his sexual discoveries; he did not initiate him into the discoveries themselves.

The solution to the problem of Randolph's Rosicrucian origins and connections—if there is a problem and Randolph did not simply create his Rosicrucians out of whole cloth—must lie concealed in these hints of celestial hierarchies, the mysterious Orient, secret lodges in Paris and eccentric spiritualists, mirror magicians, and antiquarians. The solution, however, is an unsatisfactory one, partially for reasons that have to do with the nature of the problem itself.

In even discussing "origins" and "influences" in connection with secret occult groups such as Randolph's Rosicrucians, we must be very clear what it is we are really seeking and what it is that we can legitimately expect to find. The H. B. of L., which propagated Randolph's system of sexual magic after his death, described him as being—along with Madame Blavatsky—a member of an obscure Oriental branch of their order, and taught that Randolph had received both his initiation and his teachings there (see chapter 12). The H. B. of L.'s intention, obviously, was to have us imagine the order along the lines of the Ellora Brotherhood into which Louis was inducted in *Ghost Land*—an organized enterprise of outwardly non-descript "adepts," men and celestials, who were spread throughout the world, communicating astrally or mentally, and who possessed wondrous powers and directed the affairs of the world on a mysterious level for secret purposes. Even if we were prepared to accept the description as offered, however, we are left with the problem of what such an order would look like to the historian and how it would be recognized if seen. What sort of traces does such an organization leave—literary ones that can be viewed either as part of a public propaganda effort on behalf of the organization's agenda, or, more cynically, as evidence of plagiarism and simple literary borrowing? Identical or similar teachings or occult practices? Mirror communications from the "same" celestial being? And if these traces or trends are found, what would really have been demonstrated? Would it really be possible to distinguish mere literary dependency or the spirit of the age from the marks of the postulated secret group?

On a purely historical level, the celestial-beings-beyond-the-scenes part of this problem is insoluble. By definition, no amount of factual research can establish the existence, nature, or occult activities of the Rosicrucians on the far side of the grave. Randolph thought he had encountered them in his visions and on earth, but we cannot follow him into his visions, and the traces of his passage among the flesh-and-blood adepts and authors of his time are obscured by the passage of time and the (postulated) secrecy of their endeavors. In the end, also, the search for some identifiable group that taught practical methods (drugs, magic mirrors, and perhaps sex) to achieve conscious clairvoyance and communication with celestial and earthly hierarchies leads inevitably to the same sort of enigmas (the Ellora Brotherhood, the Chevalier Louis, and the Crowned Angel of the Seventh Sphere) that we find in Randolph himself. The most that can be done, finally, is to point out the surprising consensus of occult belief and practice that Randolph embodied.

In even asking the question of sources and influences, of course, we are doing precisely what Randolph told us not to do—discounting his own creativity. The quest, nonetheless, is one that Randolph, by his claims, invited us to make.

Reuben Swinburne Clymer's Myths

None of these factual and theoretical problems constrained Reuben Swinburne Clymer (1878–1966), the great myth maker about Randolph and source of most of the pseudo-history of Randolph that has circulated in occult circles in this century. As the head of various organizations, Rosicrucian and otherwise, claiming descent from Randolph's groups, Clymer worked for more than sixty years to create a coherent version of events that would establish Randolph's (and, by derivation, his own) priority as a Rosicrucian, and almost all writers on Randolph have mined his works, with or without attribution.[69] Despite this wide acceptance, Clymer's version of events, even where he professes to be factual and supports his story with detail, is almost entirely bogus. Part of the reason for this failure is the simple intractableness of Randolph's life and work, but the contradictions in Clymer's own position exacerbated the problems he faced.

Clymer came only late and indirectly into the various groups of Randolph's successors and was heir to very little information about him that was not available publicly in Randolph's works themselves (see chapter 11). He inherited the leadership of disparate, loosely connected groups of arcane societies, many unrelated to Randolph and with widely varying, fanciful histories to begin with, and set himself the task of discovering what he could about each group, fabricating connections and antecedents as necessary to harmonize the stories and defend his claims to the title of head of the original Rosy Cross group in the United States. His situation was made more complex by the necessity he labored under of avoiding the more embarrassing details of Randolph's life—especially the claims that Randolph was a sexual magician[70]—and of smoothing over Randolph's frequent changes of position.

Like the creator of a cross-word puzzle, Clymer had to examine the works of Randolph, take every name and date mentioned (even in the novels), and work them uncritically into the tapestry of occult history. So, for example, when Randolph mentions the two French doctors in New York City for whom he did medical trance readings in the early 1850s, Clymer was obliged to take the names, ignore the context in which they appeared (which is practically the only thing actually known about the men), and make them members of the secret Councils of Three and Seven that oversaw the American Rosicrucian Fraternity in the 1850s before Randolph became the first supreme grand master of the Supreme Grand Dome of the Fraternity for the Western World and Isles of the Sea. Everything was grist for his mill. If he heard of "the old Rosicrucian Lodge at Frankfurt"—a lodge that recurs in Kenneth Mackenzie's creations and in many pseudo-histories of various groups[71]—he makes it the surviving seat of the original seventeenth-century Rosicrucians and contrives to make General Ethan Allen Hitchcock not merely a member of it but its master until he handed that dignity over to Randolph. Similarly, Clymer converts a chance tale of a strange young man's meeting with Eliphas Lévi into a record of Randolph's encounter with the mage.[72] When all else failed and his attempts at harmonization proved too much even for his indefatigable energies and he could not even hazard a guess about some earlier occultist's role in the great work, Clymer fell back on the story of the destruction of the Fraternity's archives by enemies.

Clymer was not content—as were most of his predecessors and followers in the writing of occult history—with simply setting out the litany of names of the Western occult "tradition," the Neoplatonists, followed by the alchemists, Renaissance magicians, and eighteenth-century mages. He related them all to a complex Rosicrucian hierarchy. Leaving aside his ponderous *catena* of names and events connecting the ancient Egyptians to the Renaissance, Clymer began his story by describing the "Brethren of Light" or Fraternitas Rosae Crucis—a term that for him meant the entire Rosicrucian endeavor. The Fraternity has three outer courts, the Brotherhood, Order, and Temple of the Rosy Cross, and in each country is represented by a Supreme Grand Dome ruled by a supreme grand master who governs with the aid of a bewildering variety of councils of three, seven, nine, fifteen, or twenty-one. These councils really give room for Clymer to exercise his creativity and are the primary device he uses to cover lapses in his information. Any name associated with Randolph or Western occultism is made a member of one council or another: Abraham Lincoln, E. A. Hitchcock, K. R. H. Mackenzie, W. G. Palgrave, Charles Trinius, Napoleon III, Bulwer-Lytton, Charles Mackay, Alexis and Adolph Didier, Baron Spedalieri, Saint-Yves d'Alveydre, Stanislaus de Guaita, Papus, Peter Davidson, and even Albert Pike and William Lloyd Garrison are thus accommodated. Over this hodgepodge in turn, in Randolph's time, was the supreme hierarch, "Count A. de Guinotti"—a figure derived as much from that of the Italian/Armenian count of *Ravalette* as from the novels of Marie Corelli and the work of John C. Street.[73] Clymer is even up to the task of relating the Rosicrucian strain of Randolph's thought with the Ansairetic and Oriental, and he tells of the departure of the Count de Saint-Germain from the West and his reception in the East by the Grand Dome there, which, in Randolph's time, he says, was under the jurisdiction of Othman Aswald el Kindee, and in Syria under Abu-id-Durr, Djundub of the Ansaireh—names Clymer appropriated from the dedication of Randolph's *Eulis*.

Clymer's version of events, in other words, despite the evident sincerity of his own belief in the value of his own work in propagating Randolph's practices, is pure fantasy, concocted to satisfy his own followers who approached him as mystagogue, demanding to know his bona fides and the sources of his authority. The mistake is in treating it as history.[74]

Randolph's First Rosicrucian Foundations

Randolph himself invited much of this confusion both by the novel form in which many of his Rosicrucian ideas are dressed and by the necessity he labored under of concocting a pedigree that would convince the neophytes in his own foundations of his legitimacy. Despite this, some facts about his own early Rosicrucian organizations are ascertainable.

In the charter of the Triple Order which he issued on behalf of the "Fraternity everywhere on Earth" in connection with his reconstitution of the order in 1874 (plate 3), Randolph gave his title as "Supreme Hierarch, Grand Templar, Knight, Prior and Hierarch of the Triple Order" and recited the genealogy of the First Temple of the order, beginning with Isis-Osiris, Hermes Mercurius Trismegistus, Thoth, and Buddha and continuing through Melchizedek, Rhasoph, Zerdasht, Laotse, and Prester Jan. The Second Temple began on the death of Mohammed and ran through a list of Ottoman sultans and others until 1789, when, Randolph says, it decayed and "oriental rule" ended—events that Randolph enticingly connects with the "establishment of European and Occidental Branches."[75] Randolph then presents his cryptic account of the founding of his own organization, the Third Temple of the Rosy Cross:

> Initiation of 12 adepts; founding of 3d Temple (in America) by Paschal B. Randolph. Propaganda begun 1855; 1st Grand Lodge founded August 1857; 1860 dissolution of Grand Lodge and founding of Supreme Grand Lodge at San Francisco, Cal., Nov. 5th, 1861—John Temple, S. Grand Master; 1863, death of S.G.M. The Temple slept from 1861 until 1874; P. B. Randolph S. G. M and Hierarch.

It is difficult to say now what Randolph meant by the "beginning of propaganda," but it is significant that the date coincides with Randolph's first European trip. The inference is that Randolph acquired the idea of calling himself a Rosicrucian in Europe in 1855, though this early date seems unlikely, as does Randolph's statement elsewhere that his Rosicrucian roots went back to 1852.[76] There is no information whatsoever about the Grand Lodge supposedly founded in August 1857, but again the date coincides with a European trip. These were troubled times, as we have seen, and the foundation, if it took place at all, must have occurred immediately after Randolph's return from his second trip to Europe and the Near East in 1858.[77]

More information is available about Randolph's next Rosicrucian foundation. In September 1861 he arrived in San Francisco, California, from the East. He lectured in his best style before enthusiastic crowds, frequently challenging the audience to pick the topic for the declamation on the spot, and, obviously proud of being free of spirit-control, he boasted that "he did this wholly and solely by aid of his own mental power."[78] His original intention was to remain in San Francisco, and he started a medical practice in the offices of Dr. John B. Pilkington, an ophthalmologist (or occulist) who continued to be involved in Randolph's Rosicrucian ventures at least until Randolph's death in 1875.[79] The two of them also published Randolph's *The Grand Secret; or, Physical Love in Health and Disease*, discussed in chapter 1.[80] Since the book is the earliest version of Randolph's teachings on sexual union as the producer of the vital "fluid" necessary for marital happiness and for soul progress, presumably the Rosicrucian Supreme Grand Lodge that Randolph started during his stay in San Francisco had a basis in sexual theory and practice. Undoubtedly the use of the magic mirror also played a role, and the order's doctrinal teachings probably were those expounded in *Dealings with the Dead*, which were published at about the time of the founding of the San Francisco Grand Lodge.[81]

The external organization of the San Francisco Supreme Grand Lodge can be pieced together from Randolph's earliest Rosicrucian manifesto ("The Rosicrucians, Who and What They Are; Honor, Manhood, Goodness. Try!") which was included in his novel *Ravalette* (1863).[82] For what are obviously propaganda purposes, designed to profit from the massive revival of fraternal orders at the time, the Grand Lodge is described in terms of brotherhood, self-development, and mutual aid rather than in terms of magic, though all of these fraternal goals are premised on "the omnipotence of the Will!"[83] The public program, at least, is uninspired.

> Usually the Lodges of Rosicrucia meet once a week to hear lectures, exchange courtesies, thoughts, news; to listen to invited guests, debate questions in art, science, and philosophy; to mutually inform and strengthen each other; to investigate any and all subjects of a proper nature, and to cultivate that manly spirit and chivalric bearing which so well entitles their possessor to be called a MAN.[84]

Women apparently were not admitted in this first foundation—an omission that was later corrected by Randolph—and there is no indication of a ritual or of passwords, though undoubtedly some such must have existed since they were being created right and left in the United States at the time as part of the resurgence of fraternalism generally. Three degrees (not named)[85] were to be conferred. An initiation fee and monthly dues of one dollar were charged, and in exchange the member received access to the proceedings of the lodge and vague promises of fraternal support for himself and family in the event of death or disability.[86]

How much of this structure was wishful thinking and how much reality is a matter of conjecture. The theoretical organization of Randolph's groups always outstripped the actual. Whatever its formal public organization, however, the lodge undoubtedly functioned as a "pool"—as did many other occult organizations before and since—for the screening of candidates deemed worthy of admission to the more secret and less publicly acceptable teachings of the order on sex and magic mirrors.

The rank-and-file membership of the original San Francisco lodge is unknown, but its officers were:

John Temple, of Los Angeles (Grand Master)

Charles Trinius, of Strahlsund, Prussia (Grand Guard)

Col. L. W. Ransom (Grand Sentinel)

F. H. D., of San Francisco (Grand Key)

John Blakey Pilkington (Grand Door)

["Baron"] Fischer, of San Francisco (Grand Dome)

Little is known of any of these men. Temple died in 1863, though his memory lingered on with Randolph, and he is named among the dedicatees of *Eulis* in 1874. Pilkington and Ransom remained faithful to Randolph's cause. Pilkington became vice-hierarch in Randolph's Supreme Grand Corner Stone Lodge in his refounded Triplicate Order of Rosicrucia, Pythianæ, and Eulis in 1874, and Colonel Ransom, an old spiritualist, became supreme grand master in the San Francisco Supreme Grand Lodge of the same foundation. Of the other three (Trinius, Fischer, and "F. H. D."), Randolph later said only that they "were never really Rosicrucians at heart and were dropped."[87] Despite this offhand dismissal, however, Charles Trinius played a considerable role in Randolph's life. He recurs in Randolph's works as the possessor of wondrous magic crystals, and he is said himself to have been a visionary of note in the magic mirror.[88] "Baron" Fischer was still working with Randolph in 1871 when Randolph attempted once again to found a Rosicrucian order, but he broke with him shortly afterward.[89]

Despite his announced plans to remain in San Francisco, after a mere two-and-a-half months Randolph "electrified" his followers by telling them that "he had received commands to depart!"—an announcement that prefigures by twelve years Madame Blavatsky's claims that in Paris in June 1873 she received "orders" from the "Brothers" to leave for America in their cause.[90] In mid-November, accordingly, Randolph left San Francisco by sea for New York, whence he set off for Egypt, Persia, and the Orient.

It is hard to imagine a foundation such as the Supreme Grand Lodge in San Francisco enduring long in Randolph's absence, and apparently it did not, though the story of the dissolution is obscure. In the charter of the Triple Order Randolph notes that the supreme grand master of the San Francisco foundation (John Temple) died in 1863 and that the "Temple slept from 1861 until 1874." The statement probably masks the frequent internecine squabbles between Randolph and his disciples and, as we shall see, glosses over several intervening Rosicrucian foundations that foundered.[91]

The Orient, 1861–1862

Randolph's 1861 to 1862 trip to the Near East lasted almost a year. He made the whole circuit from Great Britain and France through Egypt and Palestine to Constantinople and Greece.[92] His travels were truly in the mold of the great nineteenth-century travelers, such as Richard Burton and Charles M. Doughty. As one of his English correspondents reported in October 1862:

> He has left Egypt, where he became a great favorite with people of high and lofty station, and with the Dervishes, Persian Magicians, and miracle workers, whom he astonished and confounded with exhibitions of the higher sort of magic, by means of his most wonderful crystal globe—which globe also, in his hands and others, astonished not a few of us English people, before he went to the Orient.
>
> He has learned in the East very many of the dark secrets of the Oriental magicians; and many of the things described by him in his letters to me are indeed of an astonishing nature.

He crossed the Red Sea where Moses did, in company with one of the most celebrated Arab physicians of the day, and three other dealers in mystery. He crossed the Asiatic Desert and returned, after receiving a series of instructions in Arab medicine, Persian metaphysics, and Egyptian magic. He then explored the Pyramids; went up and down the Nile; visited Bubastis; visited Syria, and visited Jaffa, Ramah, Bethlehem, and Jerusalem; made friends with the Beni Joseph; got copies of their three thousand five hundred years' old manuscripts at Nablous; proved the story of the Dead Sea, Lot's Wife, Sodom and Gomorra, &c. Then went to Byrant [Beirut?] to meet another distinguished dealer with the dead. We next find him in Cyprus, Rhodes, Smyrna, Gellipolis, Constantinople, where he "became hand and glove" with the greatest living medium—the celebrated negro of Stamboul, with whom he tested magic at his leisure. He then visited Prinkipo, at the house of the chief Physician of his majesty, the Sultan.[93]

One of Randolph's purposes in making this trip was to do research on human origins and cyclopean remains, and, as we shall see, he pursued this work conscientiously and wrote his *Pre-Adamite Man* shortly after his return. He also pursued his more long-lasting interests among the "dealers in mystery" of the Near East. He said that he learned the interpretation of dreams from "a Dongolese negro near Santa Sophia"[94] and that he had been taught the method of preparing a superior version of his hashish elixirs from the physician of the sultan of Turkey himself.[95] Most important, on this trip he appears to have encountered the mysterious Nusa'iri or Ansaireh for the first time and to have become "a mystic" among "some dervishes and fakirs" met along the way. He also, as we shall see, learned the "fundamental principle of the White Magic of Love" from "a dusky maiden of Arabic blood" (see chapter 10).[96]

After this long trip, Randolph's work takes on a stronger Oriental tone that increased with the passage of years—usually fairly gratuitous travelers' phrases and the use of *Allah* for God and the like—but he never uses the developed terminology of Islamic esotericism. After this trip also the mysterious Persian Pul Ali Beg appears in his writings, and Randolph tantalizingly dedicates one of his last books to "Abu-id-Durr, Djundub of the Ansaireh" and "Fairooz Shirwan Afridoon, Her Gracious Purity." The names are only that, however, and we cannot now discern the historical figures behind them.

Pre-Adamite Man

A major stated purpose of the long trip to the Continent and the Near East in 1861 and 1862 was research on a subject in which Randolph had apparently long been interested: the debate then raging over the literal truth of the biblical account of origins and the corollary disputes over mono- or polygenism—that is, whether there was a single origin for all the existing races of men.[97] Coupled with this was Randolph's fascination with chronology and with sifting the various myths and myth-histories of origins to find the beginnings of what he perceived to have been a magnificent, coherent, unitary mythology whose fragments now lay obscurely scattered about the world.

In this last, he was undoubtedly prompted by the early books of Hargrave Jennings, "the Chief Rosicrucian of all England," and the monumental works of Godfrey Higgins, which had become a mainstay of fringe and occult thinkers and with which Randolph was familiar.[98] Jennings, like so many antiquarians before him, had sifted classical literature, the Bible, and what was known through ongoing oriental researches, and had arrived at the conviction that the "Buddhists of Upper India" (of whom Melchizedek was a priest) had built the pyramids of Egypt and erected Stonehenge, Carnac, and all the other megalithic remains scattered throughout Europe and the Near East. All of the mythologies of the world were also their creation, originally unified and coherent and resting on the same principles. Randolph was fascinated by the task of reconstructing the wrecked original (especially the secret philosophy and practice) from its dismembered antediluvian fragments.

> Distributed as over the wide and heaving sea of history, most numerous fragments, evidently of a mighty wreck—most wonderful the ship, and of materials and of design portentous and superhuman—have floated as to the thinker's feet. Chips as of strange and puzzling woods—pieces that, dissevered, bore no meaning—contradictory objects, diverse matters, only, through keenness, with suspected relation—a beam, portions of rope, the angle of the prow, items that, by long guessing, could alone be discovered to have once constituted a fabric; these have been, as it were, gathered up, and build, into a whole Argo, humbly, in my book. And I have sought to reconstruct a majestic ship, and have traced a celestial and the sublimest story, which we have heired, unknowingly, through the ages. Whether I have succeeded in demonstrating the philosophical possibility of the Supernatural, I am not to be the judge.[99]

Randolph echoed these sentiments felicitously in *Ravalette* (133) in describing the traces of the glories of the antediluvian world, "the débris of a world-wreck remembered only by the seraphim!" The result of this interest and Randolph's geological and anthropological researches was an utterly uncharacteristic book, *Pre-Adamite Man: Demonstrating the Existence of the Human Race upon this Earth 100,000 Thousand Years Ago!* which Randolph published under the pseudonym of "Griffin Lee of Texas."[100]

The book is a marvel, especially considering Randolph's background and lack of formal education. He reveals a good knowledge of French, and he passes knowingly (in the usual nineteenth-century antiquarian fashion) from Thomas Browne and Plato to discussions of Nordic and Mexican myths of origin, the *Dabistan*, Vedic texts, Buddhist lokas and theories of cosmic cycles, Confucius, the Samaritan text of Genesis, cyclopean architecture, and so on. The book is an *omnium gatherum*, like Madame Blavatsky's later *Isis Unveiled*, and is the only one of Randolph's books to smack at all of the pervading antiquarianism of the times. It is so different from his other books that it is difficult to reconcile Randolph's authorship of it with the life he had led to that point. Today it is a curiosity, a period-piece, but judged in the light of many similar productions of the time which sought to reconcile biblical chronology with the new prehistory[101] or to show the absurdity of such a reconciliation, Randolph's book is impressive. He amassed, synthesized, and arranged an enormous body of data on fields as diverse as ancient history, linguistics, biblical criticism, geology, and paleontology and expounded it rationally in support of his ideas. His list of authorities cited contained all of the current leading experts in these areas, and he appears to have consulted personally with several of them in London, Paris, and Munich in preparing his work.[102]

Randolph's primary thesis is simple. The human race is not a unity and did not originate with a single mythical ancestor, "Adam."[103] Rather, several separate races exist, now largely intermingled (except for the black race), each with a separate origin and a history that long antedates the age assigned by the Bible for the creation of the world. Following a trail that began in the pre-Adamite debates of the seventeenth century, he first debunked the Adam and Eve story by pointing out the usual Biblical inconsistencies—"From where did Cain's wife come?" From there he moved to the vestiges of ancient, high civilization—mainly the cyclopean ruins, many of which he had personally seen in Malta and the Near East—that seemed clearly to predate the accepted biblical chronology for the creation of cities. As an aside, Randolph reviewed the problems of ancient chronology in general and concluded, as have many others since,[104] that dates given by classical authors are symbolic rather than historical. As a conclusion, he waded fearlessly into a review of the current state of paleontological research on the fossil origins of man. While he says that he was unable to decide between the theory of simple evolution of man from primates (which in 1863 he found "repulsive") and a theory of multiple specific acts of creation of man by God,[105] he later opted for separate evolution and gave an elaborate theory of the infusion of the divine soul into the evolved being.[106] Not a bad piece of work for a man who learned to write by copying billboards.

The book is quite revealing about Randolph's personal struggle to come to grips with his own origins. One of the great dangers of polygenesis is, of course, the tendency of denying authentic humanity to members of races other than one's own.[107] If Adam is not the father of us all, we may not even be remotely related, and the "others" (read blacks, Jews, Irish, or whatever) may be in- or subhuman. Randolph opts decidedly for polygenesis and has some revealing things to say about the black "race." The differences between blacks and other races were to him so obvious and apparent that the very existence of blacks as a group became a primary argument for rejecting a common origin for all men.[108] He thought that the black race was one of the original races of the world and was in fact the only pure and unmixed race remaining. Nevertheless, in the quirky way typical for him, Randolph also rejected outright all notion of an early black high civilization or of dynasties of "Negro Kings" of Egypt— the theory first advanced in the late eighteenth century by "C. F. Volney" (C. F. Chassebeuf), who was also one of Randolph's predecessors in being fascinated by the mysterious Nusa'iri of Syria.[109] "It is doubtful if the Negro, since the world began, ever even approximated to such a high state of civilization as he has attained on Northern American soil; but that he will achieve great things in the future, is, of course, but a mere question of time."[110] This backhanded expression of sentiment is really a combination of hope for the future and Randolph's beliefs that, at present, blacks were "lowest" on the evolutionary scale.[111] The hope is more than overbalanced by his pæon to the Europeans and (white) North Americans as supreme among the natural hierarchy of nations. Randolph may have been black, but he was also and above all a believer in his own abilities and culture—an aristocrat—and he could never reconcile his achievements with those of the "thick-lipped Negro of the 'Stupid Tribe.'"[112] All of this confusion, ambiguity, and, frankly, self-hate because of his origins was to come to a head for Randolph in the wake of the Civil War (see chapter 7).

On more purely occult matters, in *Pre-Adamite Man* Randolph (like many of his contemporary occultists, including Emma Hardinge Britten and Madame Blavatsky) is caught in the dilemma created by his belief in an age-old tradition of high wisdom (embodied in Rosicrucianism and its antecedents) and his belief in progress, science, and the imminent coming of the new day of democracy and the destruction of outmoded "sacerdotalisms."[113] He clearly believed in the earlier existence of a series of high civilizations whose remains lived on in legend and pre-Adamic monuments such as the Sphinx.[114] In his first mention of the mysterious Ansaireh or Nusa'iri of Syria, to whom he will later attribute his sexual magic, he has his Muslim traveling companion and translator speak of

the five ages before the present race of men inhabited the earth, and of the Djân, the Ramm, the Tamm, the Bann, and the Djam, all of which lived long ages before your Adam. You perhaps understood that those five orders of intelligent beings were men as you and I are. They were; and believe me, the legend is more than a mere figment of imagination . . . and in these orders you can easily see the faint but certain record of long lines of kings, nations, religions and political systems—forms of faith and records of past human action.[115]

Similarly, in mentioning the "great, valuable, and strange philosophical system of the Rosicrucians,"[116] he says that it has been attributed in turn to Germany, then ancient Greece, then India, then Egypt and is

now found to have been an old story with the Chinese who lived scores of ages before it became a wandering star in other lands. Astrology, medical and judicial, the search for the Philosopher's Stone, the Elixir of Life and Immortality; and, in short, all the Hermetic and Spiritualistic mysteries, table-turning, *et hoc genus omne*, all and each of them were as familiar to and with the inhabitants of Ancient China, as they were to the Confucianists twenty-five hundred years ago, and to the mystical philosophers of the present day, in America and Europe. . . . What ages must have rolled away since the absolutely original man lived on earth![117]

In his views, which were later echoed and expanded in the teachings of the H. B. of L., there has been a series of cataclysms that have changed the face of the earth and destroyed the works of earlier civilizations. Most of these, such as the flood of Noah (which he dates to some 22,000 years ago) appear to have been the result of the natural motion of the earth. Randolph posited that, besides the diurnal and orbital motions of the earth, there was an "oscillating motion" by which the earth's axis shifted over vast periods of time. As the axis shifts, the polar ice caps melt, causing worldwide destruction and floods.[118] In addition, there have been extraordinary cataclysms, such as the destruction of the planet that once existed between Mars and Jupiter in the orbit now occupied by its remnants, the asteroid belt. When it exploded some 58,600 years ago, the earth "changed its axis and its angle to the ecliptic" and the polar ice caps melted, causing the sinking of Atlantis.[119]

In later years, this calm discussion of past worldwide destructions takes on an apocalyptic and prophetic tone. The new age is indeed at hand, but the way must first be prepared by cataclysmic overthrow of the old.

> [B]efore [the good time coming gets] here this land and this whole earth of ours is doomed to pass through a terrible series of convulsions, electric, volcanic, magnetic, climatic,—a general upheaving and overturning of the present state of things the wide world over. Preparations are now going on. . . . [T]he purely physical disturbances will almost equal the terrible event of which the "Deluge" is the traditional reminiscence, which altered the axis of the earth, and changed the equator; sunk the Old Atlantis and upheaved it again, with a few of its pyramids yet intact, but transforming the happy land into the deserts of Zahara. . . . These all result from fire-tempests in the sun . . . changing earth's angle to the ecliptic plane.[120]

From the more purely occult point of view, Randolph's theories of cyclic history, recurring cataclysms, and pre-Adamite races carry the germs of ideas more thoroughly worked out by others, including Madame Blavatsky in her early works. Citing Godfrey Higgins's *Anacalypsis*, she expatiated on the regular revolution of the poles and the consequent ascent and destruction of civilizations in cyclic cataclysms, and she attributed to the "Pre-Adamite" races (the "elohim" and "Sons of God") the remnants of high wisdom still found in the world, most notably at Ellora—a reference to Emma Hardinge Britten's Ellora Brotherhood.[121] More interesting in light of Randolph's theories of hierarchies of spirits (the disembodied and those never embodied on earth) and his hints that the Rosicrucians are derived from the pre-

Adamite priest-king Melchizedek,[122] is her insistence on the role of the *pitris*—the spirits who "are not the ancestors of the present living men, but those of the human kind or Adamic race; they are the spirits of *human* races which, on the great scale of descending evolution, preceded our races of men, and were physically, as well as spiritually, far superior to our modern pigmies."[123] These "lunar ancestors" of our race are included among the "good genii, the dæmons of the Greeks, or the inferior gods of the invisible world," and their magical evocation constituted the real secret teachings of the theurgists of late antiquity and of the Hindu Brahmins, secrets revealed only to the higher adepts.[124]

> When the soul of the invocator has reached the *Sayadyam*, or perfect identity of essence with the Universal Soul, when matter is utterly conquered, then the adept can freely enter into daily and hourly communion with those who, though unburdened with their corporeal forms, are still themselves progressing through the endless series of transformations included in the gradual approach to the Paramâtma, or the grand Universal Soul.[125]

The "invocators" and the entities invoked strongly resemble Randolph's Rosicrucians "on both sides of the grave"—a conclusion strengthened later in *Isis Unveiled*. At the conclusion of the book (2:639), Madame Blavatsky announced that the "worship of the Vedic *pitris* is fast becoming the worship of the spiritual portion of mankind. It but needs the right perception of things objective to finally discover that the only world of reality is the subjective." In a curious aside, she also commented that the "Brotherhood of Pitris" referred to by Louis Jacolliot, was in fact real and was more mysterious even than the "Hermetic Brothers" mentioned by Kenneth Mackenzie.[126] Mackenzie's reference and his accompanying reference to the "Brothers of Luxor" cast long shadows and led eventually to the H. B. of L. and to the formation of the Theosophical Society (see chapter 12).

Randolph never explicitly drew these conclusions on the role of the pre-Adamite spirits, but the theories are perfectly consistent with his ideas. These sorts of spirits (calling themselves the "the most ancient angels" and the "most ancient and primal in men" and boasting of their pre-Adamite origins) had begun appearing about 1852 in seances held by the Koons family in Ohio. The spirits identified themselves generically as "King," and vigorously sought to distinguish themselves from the ordinary spirits of the dead. In the mid-1850s this same "King" (whatever "same" may mean in this context) became one of the controls of the Davenport brothers under the name *John King*, and claimed to be in some sense the spirit of the pirate Henry Morgan. Randolph spent a considerable amount of time with the Davenports in Buffalo in 1856 during the period in which John King was first appearing to them and received teachings very similar to theirs himself, though he more modestly attributed his to the spirits of the dead.[127] The doctrines expounded by King at the time the pre-Adamite entity first appeared are familiar ones: the grand Central Sun, the all-pervading "subtler fluid" seen as a sea of light, spiritualism as a precursor of higher things, and the eternal progress of the individualized soul after death.[128] Emma Hardinge Britten was so impressed with this collective pre-Adamite King that the picture of "Oress," one of these "ancient angels," appeared as the frontispiece to her *Modern American Spiritualism*, brooding over the pyramids—a careful hint, no doubt, of the Near Eastern connections of Oress. Nor does John King's history end with Randolph or Emma Hardinge Britten. In the mid-1870s he reappeared (though eventually demoted to an "elemental") as Madame Blavatsky's constant companion and aid in her early days in New York.[129]

Most of Randolph's time after his return from the Near East was devoted to *Pre-Adamite Man*, and the work was published in the spring of 1863.[130] It was dedicated to Charles Trinius and—Randolph says by his request—to Abraham Lincoln, a presage of events to come, since the next three years of Randolph's life were taken up with the problems facing Lincoln and were almost entirely removed from Randolph's usual occult concerns.

Chapter 7

THE CIVIL WAR YEARS

In the late 1850s Randolph had begun to try take an active part in the abolitionist movement of the time, searching for a cause to which he could dedicate his services—and which could support him and his family. As a spiritualist, he had in some respects always been involved with politics, and indeed, given the reform circles in which he traveled, it would have been practically impossible for him not to have been. Abolition was the central pivot of radicalism and reform of the era and was closely intertwined with spiritualism. While not every reformer was a spiritualist, every spiritualist, as we have seen, was a reformer, and in Randolph's case the political issues were of especially cogent personal concern because of his own origins.

On the coming of the American Civil War, the focus of the abolitionist movement shifted to the enlistment of black soldiers in the Union army. Although today it might seem a self-evident proposition that the privilege and duty of fighting in the armed forces has nothing to do with race, the point was hotly disputed at the beginning of the Civil War, and the debate was the principal focus of black thought and action in the early years of the war. Federal law had authorized the enlistment of blacks as early as 1862, but nothing was done to implement the law, and the Union army refused to allocate funds to pay black soldiers. Even in the circles where the idea of actually recruiting blacks into the army was accepted, it was generally conceded (even by President Lincoln) that they should be laborers only and not armed.[1]

In the State of New York where Randolph was then living,[2] Governor Horatio Seymour, a Democrat who was strongly opposed to President Lincoln, was reluctant to enlist blacks, and a group of white liberals, including Peter Cooper, Horace Greeley of the *Tribune* and P. T. Barnum (of circus fame), tried in May 1863 to interest Abraham Lincoln in applying pressure on the governor. They already had promises of some three-thousand recruits and recommended John C. Frémont, a flamboyant and eccentric general who had had to be removed as a commander in Missouri for his radicalism, as commander of the proposed African-American regiment.[3] When this idea failed, the group in July 1863 formed the Association for Promoting Colored Volunteering at a meeting in New York City and made a formal appeal to the governor, again without success. A subsequent mass meeting on November 11, 1863, sponsored by the association resulted in a letter to Secretary Stanton, who finally approved federal pay for black recruits. The association and the Union League Club then formed a Joint Committee for Volunteers and raised the first group of one thousand black troops.

In the meantime, the black citizens of New York, not to be outdone, met in a state convention in Poughkeepsie, New York, on July 15 and 16, 1863, for the same purpose.[4] Randolph must have been active with the ill-starred Frémont Legion earlier in the year, as he says he was,[5] because the convention appointed him as chairman of a New York State Central Committee to canvass and recruit black men for the Union army.[6] No record remains of the effects of Randolph's efforts in recruitment, though he says that troops he helped raise later fought in other regiments, but the practical result of the common effort was an initial small enlistment of blacks that swelled to very considerable numbers by the end of the war. In March 1864, the Twentieth U.S. Colored Troops, the first black unit raised in New York, held its first parade down Broadway in New York City.[7]

A presidential election was held in the United States in 1864, pitting the Radical Republicans (who did not nominate Abraham Lincoln) against the regular Republicans (who did nominate him) and the Democrats.[8] With the outcome of the war increasingly clear, the central issue of the election was the fate of the South and blacks in the postwar period. The blacks themselves, in an effort to have a say in the planning, called a National Convention in Syracuse, New York, for October 1864, and again, Randolph played a major role.

The National Convention of Colored Men met from October 4 to October 7, 1864. Although the convention was but one of a series of such going back to 1830, its members seemed to have clearly recognized that their work was unique and would "undoubtedly form the starting point of a new era in the history of the African race."[9] Some five-hundred black leaders attended, and the ex-slave Frederick Douglass was elected president of the gathering.

Randolph attended the convention as one of the New York City delegates and was appointed to the business committee—a bizarre choice, given what we know of his life and business acumen.[10] His speech on October 6, often quoted by historians, was a high point of the convention and gives a clear impression of Randolph's rhetoric, which was very highly regarded at the time though it appears overblown today. After the almost mandatory reference to God's salvation of the Israelites from Egypt, Randolph theatrically saluted the battle flag of the first black regiment to see combat, stained with the blood of the soldiers who had fallen at the battle of Hudson's Bend, and declaimed:

> And yet his paths are plain. Let the nations take warning! God never sleeps. Wherefore let us all take heart. He fights our battles; and, where he fights, he wins. Wagner, Hudson, Petersburg, and all the other battles of this war have not been fought in vain; for the dead heroes of those and other bloody fields are the seeds of the mighty harvests of human goodness and greatness, yet to be reaped by the nations and the world, and by Afric's sable descendants on the soil of this, our native land. Be of good cheer! Behold the starry flag above our heads! What is it? It is the pledge of Heaven, that we are coming up from the long dark night of sorrow towards the morning's dawn: it is the rainbow of eternal hope, set in our heaven, telling us that we shall never again be drowned in our own salt tears, forced up from our very souls' great depths by the worshippers of Moloch—great bloody-handed Mammon; it is a guaranty, by and from the God of Heaven, that *we, the mourners, may and shall be happy yet.* . . .
>
> Here we are met, not to hear each other talk, not to mourn over the terrible shadows of the past; but we are here to prove our right to manhood and justice, and to maintain these rights, not by force of mere appeal, not by loud threats, not by battle-axe and sabre, but by the divine right of brains, of will, of true patriotism, of manhood, of womanhood, of all that is great and noble and worth striving for in human character. We are here to ring the bells at the door of the world; proclaiming to the nations, to the white man in his palace, the slave in his hut, kings on their thrones, and to the whole broad universe, that WE ARE COMING UP! (Applause.)[11]

Several notes struck in the speech recur in Randolph's thought. The plaintive cry that "we . . . may . . . be happy yet"—supposedly his mother's counsel from beyond the grave—became one of his mottoes.[12] Additionally, a theme that was not to endear him to most radicals of the time or since, was Randolph's claim to prove his right to equality with white men not on the basis of manhood only, but on the basis of "brains and will." This comes suspiciously close to a form of elitism, a defect from which Randolph, who had dragged himself up from the slums of the Five Points by his own efforts, undoubtedly suffered. He emphasized the point later in the speech by stating that it was "sheer folly [for blacks] to expect to be raised to a coveted position without self-endeavor" and without "persistent culture of our latent powers." It is to Randolph's credit that he subsequently acted upon these beliefs by attempting to educate the newly freed slaves, but he never came to accept the equality of blacks simply as men with persons of his own accomplishments and merits.

The official work of the convention was the establishment of a National Equal Rights League to "obtain by appeals to the minds and conscience of the American people, or by legal process when possible, a recognition of the rights of the colored people of the nation as American citizens."[13] This purpose, basically to obtain suffrage for African Americans, was mainly to be accomplished by exhortation, and as the cornerstone of its work the league published a Declaration of Wrongs and Rights, the approval of which was largely the work of Randolph.[14]

The wrongs complained of in the declaration were classic: blacks taunted as inferior by those whose laws prevented their education; black volunteer troops fighting for the Union and denied equal pay and recognition of their efforts and heroism; taxation of free blacks without allowing them a voice in government. The rights claimed were equally basic: the abolition of slavery, the right to reward for effort and to respect, and the right to vote. Also stressed was the right to exercise these rights in America, rather than being relegated to a colony in Africa, Central America, or one of the less-favored states. This colonization scheme was an idea at times advocated by Lincoln and by many despairing American black leaders, including Randolph himself, but at the convention Randolph rejected it absolutely:

> That, as natives of American soil, we claim the right to remain upon it: and that any attempt to deport, remove, expatriate, or colonize us to any other land, or to mass us here against our will, is unjust; for here were we born, for this country our fathers and our brothers have fought, and here we hope to remain in the full enjoyment of enfranchised manhood, and its dignities.[15]

This last right, the right to remain in America, had been the subject of extreme controversy and debate since the (Southern-organized and led) American Colonization Society some fifty years earlier had first proposed that since blacks could never measure up to the standards of Western culture, they should be resettled in Africa.[16] Randolph's first act on entering the fray in Louisiana after the Syracuse convention was to denounce a proposal calling for colonization as a means to get rid of blacks and at the same time "unfurl the banner of the cross" in Africa. Thomas W. Conway, who later made amends and joined the Radical Republicans in the reconstruction of the South, had the temerity to make this proposal in a letter copied in the black-owned and run *New Orleans Tribune*. Randolph, who had been in New Orleans less than two months, dramatically replied, proposing, tongue-in-cheek, that Irish, German, and British Americans might similarly be employed to spread the gospel in their respective homelands:

> We men of color were born here; so were our fathers, and mothers down a long line of ancestry: Our blood, bones, nerves— every material particle of our bodies was and is composed of American soil, air, water, and our souls are American all the way through, all of which, so it seems to me, constitutes us Americans; wherefore all our attractions, hopes, tendencies, ambitions and applications are American; wherefore again, if we are but apprentice missionaries and colonists destined to African fields, I confess to being so very stupid as not to comprehend the logic of it and so blind as not to see it. What! Are we to go to the lands of our African ancestors because our skins are dark? Are all our sufferings to be rewarded by our removal to African deserts and barbaric climes and places. Ought we colored citizens to even tolerate the idea? No! Never! Here is our home, and here we mean to stay, and on this soil will die, and in it will be buried. . . . We are Americans, and mean to remain such—and Young Americans, too.[16]

In addressing a "Grand Mass Meeting" in New Orleans on December 2, 1864, Randolph threw aside his old prevarications about his ancestry and proudly and openly cast his lot with blacks—preserving at the same time his perception of his own superiority.

> I do not represent the three-fourths black; I stand here to-night as representative of the African. I do not come as a flatterer of the black man; I want justice for him. . . . Who are we, that are now nothing before the world? The best blood that runs in the veins of any people runs in ours. We claim our rights because we are men, fashioned by the hand of Almighty God. . . . There are two

questions that come up: the one is the question of social equality, the other, of political equality. All men, so far as humanity is concerned, are not equal for the reason that a man is better than another man. The only aristocracy is the aristocracy of mind and morals; the best man stands the highest. The spirit of democracy is to fight for universal rights.[18]

Randolph's enlightenment, however, was wavering and short-lived. In *Pre-Adamite Man*, he had rejected the view (held by Volney and others) that blacks in ancient days had enjoyed a glorious, high civilization, but he had prophesied with confidence the brilliant future awaiting blacks. By the end of the Civil War, probably because of his experiences in Louisiana and the gulf he perceived between himself and the new freedmen, his ambivalence about his race more apparent. While he still asserted the common humanity of whites and blacks, he had come to believe that blacks (from whom he carefully distanced himself) were always destined to an inferior status, even after death.

[T]o illustrate this idea [of perpetual qualitative differences], take two persons, one a Hottentot, digger-Indian, or thick-lipped Negro of the "Stupid" tribe,—two or three specimens of whom may be often seen waddling up and down the streets of Boston, listlessly staring in the shop windows and fancying themselves ultra human, when but three removes from the horn-headed gorilla,— the other shall be a glorified seraph from the galactic girdle of the universe of universes. They are both men . . . but what a difference! One would eat his brother—the Hottentot; one is ignorant of God's existence,—the Digger; one, the thick-lipped Negro, is wholly unprincipled, incapable of refinement or true civilization, and would swear away the liberty or life of his best friend with perfect nonchalance and moral unconcern. . . . I do not believe that there ever will come a time in all being, when either the Digger, the Hottentot, or the "Stupid" Negro, will approach the *same sort* of perfection that the seraph hath reached,—not even when billions of centuries shall have rolled away.[19]

After the Civil War Randolph revised his views on "Negro Colonization." In *After Death*, first published as a series of articles in the fall of 1866, Randolph, obviously disillusioned after his experiences, advocated total separation of the races:

The negro-question is to be settled summarily by the people's will, and that settlement will be not on the basis of miscegenation, for that race and the white can never mingle or fuse, seeing that the latter has some thousands of years the start, and will forever keep it, and its own dignity; but the nation will give the negro a vast territory freely, and, while protecting him, will insist that he must win his place by his deeds among the peoples of the world. Radical false philanthropy and the hatred of caste will alike stand still, while reason and progress settle the question on entirely new grounds. The races can never live side by side on equal terms, because mind rules the world, and ever will intensify its rule, and the white race has most of the mind. As for the unfortunate mixed race, their lot is cast for extinction, like the Indians.[20]

Randolph envisioned a revivalist fervor sweeping the blacks, "who will, with almost a frenzied zeal, march off to their Zion in the southwest,—the new territory ceded to them for an abiding-place by the American people," and vowed that if he were alive then "I will be their Peter the Hermit, and cast my lot with theirs,—for the new empire and the new civilization yet to come out of that poor yet rich and mighty people is destined to be as great in peace and spiritual goodness, as their masters have been in intellect and war."[21]

All of this was still in the future when the Syracuse convention was adjourned on October 7, 1964, to spread and establish the National Equal Rights League. A month later, Randolph appeared in New Orleans to continue his public, political life.

Randolph later boasted that he had been invited to go to New Orleans by Abraham Lincoln, his "personal friend," but that claim was made only after Lincoln's death and is otherwise unconfirmed.[22] At the time he certainly claimed to have been invited to New Orleans by "a prominent United States official"—but if this was Lincoln, it is odd that he did not advertise the fact more clearly.[23] It is more likely that Captain J. H. Ingraham, a Louisiana delegate at the Syracuse convention, was the immediate source of the idea of going to Louisiana. Captain Ingraham was a "Creole Negro" from New Orleans and had been one of the commanders of the "free colored" Native Guards (who had at first been Confederate troops and then Union after the North captured New Orleans in the spring of 1862). He was one of the leaders of the free colored population of New Orleans and later, after Randolph's arrival in the South, was one of Randolph's sponsors. Perhaps he invited Randolph, or perhaps the thought of New Orleans, a Union toehold in the Deep South, appealed to Randolph as a place to make himself, as he said, "useful to the colored people of [that] Southern country."[24]

New Orleans was indeed an anomaly. A former colony of Spain and later of France, it had a numerous and influential free population of mixed race with both wealth and a recognized social status. These Creole blacks, long removed from slavery themselves and separated by wealth, education, and very often language from the newly freed slaves, had originally favored the Confederacy in the Civil War and had formed the Native Guards to fight for the South—the surest indication of their anomalous position. An observer noted in the *Liberator* at the time, that "there are not more decided Confederates to be found in the South than may be found among the free colored creoles of Louisiana."[25] After General Butler and the Union armies victoriously entered New Orleans in 1862, the black Creole Native Guard changed allegiance and joined the Union forces en masse, figuring prominently in several battles.

Despite their wealth and position, the Creole blacks, like many northern blacks, were "free" but not equal. They suffered under a variety of indignities, including deprivation of a political voice and the imposition of taxation to support white-only schools, but, unlike their Northern brethren, they were wealthy and educated and were in many cases slaveholders themselves—a fact that did not prevent them from aspiring toward equality for themselves based on their own merits. They proudly pointed to General Andrew Jackson's (unfulfilled) promise to give them equality as a reward for their services to the United States in the battle of New Orleans in the War of 1812. In every way, however, their political future was tied to the newly freed (or about to be freed) slaves. There were only ten thousand free blacks in New Orleans, but the central concern during the Civil War was the fact that blacks, with the inclusion of the mass of former slaves, constituted a majority in Louisiana.[26] Louisiana was the point of the wedge, and everyone knew it. Developments there were very closely followed throughout the United States, and Randolph's work in New Orleans was performed on a national stage.

The major issue confronting the Creole blacks (as it would later confront the entire Union) was the extension of the electoral franchise to blacks. The portions of Louisiana conquered by the North were initially under the military rule of General Butler, a militant abolitionist.[27] The state convention held in New Orleans in May 1864 to consider the form of government to obtain in Louisiana after the war refused blacks the ballot, but Butler had at least gotten a vague compromise approved that might have allowed some blacks of special "intellectual fitness" to vote. In the fall of that year, just before Randolph's arrival in New Orleans, another compromise (the "Quadroon Bill") was proposed, that would have allowed blacks who could "pass for white" to vote.[28]

When he arrived in New Orleans in mid-November 1864, fresh from the Syracuse convention and the formation of the National Equal Rights League, whose primary goal was the extension of suffrage to all (male) citizens, Randolph found himself caught up in a whirlwind of conflict that was to characterize the entire country a year and a half later at the end of the Civil War. His very first days there were affected by controversy. On his way to uptown New Orleans for Thanksgiving dinner, Randolph, who was accompanied by his otherwise unknown nephew, Frank A. Potter (who may be the son of Randolph's half-sister, Harriet), was ordered by one of the Union soldiers occupying New Orleans to get off of a streetcar because he lacked the appropriate pass. When Randolph refused he was arrested, only to be freed that evening when he paid the jailers a small bribe. He immediately wrote the Creole black newspaper, the *New Orleans Tribune* (begun in July 1864 and published both in English and in French), demanding to know whether the United States government sold "its dignity for $7.50."[29]

To make ends meet in New Orleans, Randolph probably set up as a physician. By the fall of 1865 at least, and most likely from the beginning of his stay in New Orleans, he was advertising his skills as a consulting physician (by mail), with a system of cure he claimed was an improvement over that which he had learned in Turkey, Egypt, Syria, and France.[30] To get his name before the public in his early days in the South, he presented public lectures, and for the first time in his career sought out black audiences. In December 1864 he advertised a lecture on "Manhood, Womanhood and the Conditions of Human Progress" to be held at St. James Chapel (an AME church in New Orleans)[31] and in January 1865 he was lecturing on spiritualism.[32] He also denounced the Voodoo cult publicly in a series of lectures at the School of Liberty—after learning its secrets, he said, from its queen, Mme. Alice H———.[33] In addition to all of this, Randolph was also apparently putting the finishing touches on a book, never published, on the African Americans in Louisiana, and was at the time—a fact that was to have consequences for him later—acting as the New Orleans correspondent for the Northern (and, by New Orleans's standards, more radical) *Anglo-African*, published in New York.[34]

Randolph was initially welcomed by the Creole blacks of New Orleans as one of their own. He was well-traveled, cultured, and probably fluent in French. A resolution was even passed tendering him the "hospitalities of the city,"[35] and the *New Orleans Tribune* held him up as a model for Creole black children "anxious for intellectual acquirements and literary distinctions."[36] He was there under the auspices of the National Equal Rights League and the free blacks of New Orleans, who had sent delegates to the Syracuse convention, immediately took up the League's idea of concerted action to obtain their rights. After a public meeting at which Randolph spoke in early December 1864, a convention of Louisiana's blacks was called, and in early January 1865 the first Louisiana State Colored Convention was convened in New Orleans, a convention largely controlled by the wealthy and educated Creole blacks of New Orleans.[37] For their benefit, the proceedings were bilingual, in French and English, and their newspaper, the *New Orleans Tribune*, was named the official organ of the convention. Randolph, "after slight opposition," was admitted to the sessions.[38] The convention's immediate concerns were the righting of the petty indignities of the times, including the right of blacks to ride in the streetcars of the city (a topic that must have appealed to Randolph, though he did not introduce the resolution), by petitioning for redress. On a more fundamental level, the convention wrestled with the problems of education for the newly freed slaves and of the electoral franchise— a two-edged sword for these elite blacks who wanted it for themselves but largely feared its extension to the masses of illiterate former slaves. One result of the convention was the formal establishment for Louisiana of a branch of the National Equal Rights League that Randolph had helped found in Syracuse the preceding fall.

Once again, as he had done before and would do again, Randolph proceeded to act as a firebrand, alienating his sponsors, an action that was absolutely characteristic of him. Driven by some feeling of the punctilio of honor or of exaggerated honesty, or impelled simply by the urge to destroy what he had achieved, Randolph sooner or later always bit the hand that was feeding him. In New Orleans, the process began at a meeting of the convention in February when Randolph took a subtle swipe at the Creole blacks who had welcomed him and had invited his participation in the convention in the first place.

> [Dr. P. B. Randolph] said that this great battle is only a particular instance of the grand contest between aristocracy and democracy, between the powerful and the humble, between the oppressor and oppressed. On every part of the globe, where societies have been established, one class always contended to rule over the other. But as God protects the weak against the aggressions of the haughty, we will succeed in our efforts to obtain our rights, provided we be wise enough to stand united.[39]

The situation was compounded when one of Randolph's letters to the *Anglo-African* in New York was reprinted in English and French in the *New Orleans Tribune*.[40] In writing to the northern journal, Randolph had incautiously described the convention as the tool of the Creole blacks, "a very small clique of very small men, whose day of power is already waning," and proclaimed that his entire sympathy was with the party of progress and "with the freedmen and the American people, for the reason that they do the fighting."

The *Tribune* was outraged at what it saw as Randolph's perfidy and pointed out that two days after Randolph had written the offending letter he had appeared on the platform of a meeting called by that selfsame "very small clique of very small men" and had publicly endorsed their views and concurred in resolutions attacking the "party of progress" that Randolph had extolled to the *Anglo-African*.[41] At a meeting on March 10, 1865, Randolph was publicly condemned.

> WHEREAS, Dr. P. B. Randolph, representing himself as from New York, has abused of the hospitality and confidence of the citizens of New Orleans by writing letters to the Anglo-African, derogatory and detrimental to our cause, and said Randolph has thereby advanced Falsehood through that paper, calculated to place us in a wrong position before the world; therefore,
>
> *Be it resolved*, That we hereby declare that the said Randolph is unworthy [of] a place in our community;
>
> *Be it further resolved*, That we do not regard him as a true representative of the North.[42]

Randolph's departure from the good graces of the Creole blacks fortunately coincided with the effort to teach blacks in Louisiana and opened the door to the next cause to which Randolph sought to dedicate his life—freedmen's education.

Under the military government that ruled most of the state during the war, the Board of Education had started a few schools for blacks, including the newly freed slaves, financing them in a hit-or-miss fashion with a "military tax" on property, supplemented by a small tuition and raffles. By January 1865 the new schools had twenty thousand students of all ages and conditions, with two or three generations frequently sharing the same class.[43] By July 1865, when the education of freedmen was handed over to the care of the Freedmen's Bureau, there were more than 125 schools for blacks in the state.

The Freedmen's Bureau, as it was known, was set up by the federal government in March 1865 as the Bureau of Refugees, Freedmen, and

Abandoned Lands in an effort to deal with hordes of former slaves who flocked to the areas under Union control. It was a bone of contention from the beginning and the rock around which broke the currents of moderate and radical proposals for the "reconstruction" of the South after the war. Its work of education was initially unfunded, and in New Orleans it continued to depend on the military tax until the tax itself was abolished in November 1865, an action which resulted in the temporary closing of the schools. The bureau was re-authorized by Congress in February 1866, over the veto of President Johnson, but, again, funding was lacking and the bureau was allowed to languish as the attention of the country largely turned away from the former slaves. In New Orleans, the bureau's schools at first tried to become self-supporting, with various proposals being made (including a tax on the wages of the former slaves) to assist them. In the fall of 1866, the schools became a (segregated) part of the public school system, and in 1867 they disappeared altogether. Despite these handicaps and problems, however, by the time of their demise, the Freedmen's Bureau schools had been instrumental in commencing the education of more than fifty thousand blacks in Louisiana.

Randolph may have begun formally teaching freedmen at the time of his disaffection from the Creole blacks in February and March 1865.[44] Certainly by August he was employed as a teacher in the Freedmen's Bureau schools in New Orleans. In a series of letters to the newly started *Religio-Philosophical Journal* in Chicago, he spoke of the "deep, powerful, and holy influence" that had brought him to New Orleans, and he boasted of the hundreds he had taught to read and think.[45] The letters show Randolph at his humorous best in describing the characteristic foibles of New Orleans, but at the same time they reveal his genuine pride in what he was accomplishing and his happiness in what he was doing. This period seems to have been one of the very few times in Randolph's life in which he was optimistic and happy. By October, after passing an examination on his qualifications, he was made a principal teacher in the appropriately named "Lloyd Garrison School—Colored" on Coliseum Street in New Orleans, a substantial position.[46] Randolph took the occasion to write the school's namesake in Boston to ask for educational materials and described his rewarding work in trying to educate "373 pupils . . . graded from the Primer to the 5th Reader, monosyllables to grammar, object-counting to fractions."[47]

Even as the noose tightened around the neck of the Freedmen's Bureau schools in late 1865, however, Randolph remained optimistic. In the summer of 1865 he had been planning to leave in the fall for a lecture tour of the West,[48] but when the fall came he was committed to another year of teaching.[49] In October he took part in the ceremonies for the inauguration of the enormous new Abraham Lincoln School in New Orleans.[50]

As the schools fell into disarray, Randolph, whether paid or not, continued his efforts for the freedmen. In January 1866, probably to support himself, he gave lectures at the Abraham Lincoln School on "What I saw in the Holy Land and Thereabouts" (admission twenty-five cents), but he also gave a series of free talks aimed at "uplifting the working man."[51]

In February 1865, Randolph gave up teaching to become "Educational Agent" for the Freedmen's Bureau in the unreconstructed country parishes west of New Orleans.[52] He took up residence in St. Martinsville, a tiny town in St. Martin's Parish in the heart of the Cajun country, where he worked on the sequel to *Dealings with the Dead* and was "obliged to sleep with pistols in my bed, because the assassins were abroad and red-handed Murder skulked and hovered round my door."[53] He was, as he put it, "a Yankee, bad—a 'nigger teacher,' worse—and not as white as I might have been, worse still."[54] He did not exaggerate his plight, because in April the *Tribune*, under the caption "Loyal Men Fleeing to the City," carried the story of Randolph's escape to New Orleans, one step ahead of the forces of Southern reaction unleashed by the end of the war.[55] This precipitous flight marked the end of Randolph's career as a teacher, but signaled his rise as what he called "a red-hot politician."[56]

President Lincoln had died on April 14, 1865, almost at the end of the Civil War, and upon his death Reconstruction and the future of the newly freed slaves (and of blacks in general) formed the basis of the political wars between the Radical Republicans and the new president, Andrew Johnson, conflicts which nearly resulted in Johnson's removal from office. The center of the struggle was the civil rights bill introduced by the Republicans in January 1866, a measure that extended full civil liberties to all male citizens, including blacks.[57] This was vetoed by Johnson and then, after an enormous political struggle, passed into law over his veto in April. The attention of the nation then focused on the congressional elections to be held in the fall, elections which would determine the fate of Reconstruction.

It was in this context that Randolph again headed north. He said that he had resigned his position, but in view of the decay of the Freedmen's Bureau schools in Louisiana it seems more likely that there was little left from which to resign. In early July went first to New York City and then to Washington, D.C. and New England, to gather endorsements and raise money for a "Lincoln Memorial High Grade and Normal School" he proposed to start in Louisiana as an institute for the training of black teachers.[58]

The idea began at a public meeting in Thibodeauxville, Louisiana, near St. Martinsville, and must have originated at some point before Randolph fled back to New Orleans in mid-April. Randolph was named "Special Agent and Director" of the project.[59] A commission was established for the national subscription, with Charles Partridge, the editor of the *Banner of Light*, as one of the treasurers, and the project was endorsed by an impressive list of patrons. General U. S. Grant, President Johnson, General O. O. Howard (the commissioner of the Freedmen's Bureau), and a host of Radical Republican politicians gave their approval and promised contributions. The printed subscription list carried General Howard's praise of Randolph for his two years of faithful service to the education of freedmen and President Johnson's tribute to him as "a man, an educator of his people, a true philanthropist, and a gentleman of very rare and unusual attainments as a scholar and orator." In Washington, D.C., Randolph was for a brief moment the center of attention and was even received at the White House by the president.

Randolph incorporated his endorsements and a brief description of the plight of the freedmen in a small pamphlet, *A Sad Case; A Great Wrong! And How it May Be Remedied, Being An Appeal in Behalf of Education for the Freedmen of Louisiana*, and armed with these references and glowing credentials he made the rounds of the Northeast, eventually collecting about five hundred dollars in cash and considerably more in unkept promises for his school.[60] (President Johnson pledged two hundred dollars, but never paid.)[61]

After about a month of effort, Randolph's attention was increasingly distracted by politics. The Republicans, especially the Radical Republicans with whom Randolph had always associated, were fighting for their political lives against the disillusionment and desire for stability that followed the war. Randolph was apparently enlisted as a speaker in the cause by Henry Wilson, a former senator from Massachusetts, and combined his fundraising with public speaking to beat the drum for the Republicans. Though his efforts met with some success at the time, Randolph later was bitter about the lack of reward he received for his efforts for the cause. "[W]hen they had used this man to their hearts' content, he who penned the Civil-Rights bill, and who so stiffened the Republican back-bone that they put a 'Black Suffrage' plank into their platform, not only turned the cold shoulder to him, but worse. Without this man they might have carried the elections that year, but it is doubtful."[62]

In September 1866, the "Southern Loyalists"—Southern citizens (including many reformers and a few blacks) who had remained loyal to the Union during the war—convened in Philadelphia to support the Republican cause and to seek recognition (and demand reward) for their loyalty and to urge extending the ballot to "the loyal negro." The convention was sponsored by the reform-minded National Union Club (of which J. B. Ferguson, the old associate of John Murray Spear and manager of the Davenport brothers) was secretary. The tenor of the convention (and of the times) was summed up in the *New York Herald's* caption: "Blacks and Whites, Free Lovers, Spiritualists, Fourierites, Women's Rights Men, Negro Equality Men and Miscegens in Convocation."[63]

The very thought of blacks and whites participating in the same meeting was anathema, and the *Herald* called the gathering the "First Grand National Convention of Nigger Worshippers" and a "Mongrel Convention" and joked that "from the complexion of some of the delegations, the Convention proposes to be a racy affair."[64] Even within the ranks of the convention racial discrimination was the rule. Despite the presence of several prominent black leaders at the meeting, including Frederick Douglass—who was barred from a seat because he was a Northerner—no black was seated as an official member of the convention. Randolph had been elected as a delegate before leaving Louisiana, but the convention refused to recognize him, and he had to settle for the anomaly of being a ward "under the care of the editor of the [New Orleans] *Independent*," W. R. Crane.[65]

Despite this beginning, Randolph was allowed to address the gathering, and his impassioned oratory set the convention on fire and precipitated him into the forefront of the political battle over the fate of the South. The speech was a real barn burner and was carried in full by all of the leading newspapers.

> I am not P. B. Randolph; I am the voice of God, crying, "Hold! hold!" to the nation in its mad career! The lips of the struggling millions of the disfranchised demanding Justice in the name of Truth—a Peter the Hermit, preaching a new crusade against Wrong,—the Genius of Progress appealing for schools; a pleader for the people; a toiler for the millions yet unborn; mechanic for the redemption of the world.[66]

Just at the opportune moment, Dr. Randolph leaped to the platform, and made an electric speech picturing the wrongs of a race, demanding redress, claiming the ballot, and, suddenly turning to a colossal portrait of Mr. Lincoln behind the platform, exclaimed

"We are coming, Father Abraham, five hundred thousand more!"[67] Fred Douglass was so excited that he seized Anna Dickinson's Derby hat and flung it into the air, and Anna in her turn grabbed Fred's beaver and whirled it triumphantly aloft.[68]

The practical result of the convention was the organizing of a "Political Pilgrimage to Abraham Lincoln's tomb," a publicity device of the more radical Republicans to influence the crucial congressional elections of 1866 and to counteract President Johnson's earlier speaking tour of the country. The pilgrimage was a tour de force of public oratory. At every whistle stop from New York City to Lincoln's tomb in Springfield, Illinois, there would be rallies, parades, and especially speeches. Oratory was the major form of public entertainment of the times, and public occasions were always viewed as contests between the speakers. The pilgrims included many of the renowned orators of the day, and Randolph, who had been chosen for the trip, was pitted repeatedly against the best of them. Always, as the *Chicago Tribune* reported, "the little Octoroon" emerged triumphant. His reception, in fact, was overwhelming. The *Tribune* enthusiastically reported that Randolph, while he did not have the sarcastic power of Frederick Douglass,

> excels him in description, word-painting, language, apostrophe, appeal, denunciation,—terrible, swift, merciless, and crushing,— and, withal, is an actor of such rare power that the scene depicted becomes real to the audience. Nothing can excel his "Prairie on Fire;" his "Clink, Clink" scene; "The Cobra Copello" adventure; "Democrat in Heaven;" "Descent into the Maelstrom;" "Pat and the Octoroon;" and the inimitable "Bar Fite" away down south in Dixie, at the recital of which people are wont to laugh themselves sore from rib to heel, for his action is ridiculously absurd, while his talk is irresistibly funny.[69]

During the pilgrimage Randolph appears to have suffered the usual indignities of racial prejudice—in Syracuse the organizers scheduled him to speak, alone on the platform, during a rain storm—and he also appears to have excited the special enmity of R. H. Branscomb of Missouri, the chairman of the pilgrimage. This worthy, who was a prominent politician at the time but long since forgotten, apparently accused Randolph of stealing from the pilgrimage because he kept a few small sums given to him after his speeches.[70] Faced with ostracism by his fellow committeemen and prevented from speaking, Randolph promptly left the train and hurried to Chicago, where he enlisted S. S. Jones, the editor of the *Religio-Philosophical Journal*, to approach Governor Oglesby to reinstate him—which he did.[71] Randolph was vindicated—at least in his own eyes and in the press—by a speech of extraordinary power in Chicago.[72]

On his return from Lincoln's tomb, Randolph returned to Chicago where he again stirred up controversy, this time among the more orthodox Christians—with repercussions that finally killed all thought of returning to the South and teaching. In a lecture on "What and Where is God?" (described by the *Religio-Philosophical Journal* as one of his "peculiar efforts, not strictly orthodox"), Randolph, in the "whack-Moses" fashion he had condemned in his recantation speech eight years before, said that he did not believe Jesus was God. "The great fact was that God is electricity, is motion and light." He then made the mistake of presenting his fundraising credentials to the American Missionary Association, which forwarded a review of the speech to General O. O. Howard, one of the sponsors of his proposed school. Howard promptly demanded that Randolph return his endorsement. The *Chicago Evening Journal* took up the controversy and, insinuating broadly that Randolph had been making personal use of the funds raised, branded him as an "infidel negro . . . almost as rare as a white crow. He is a cruel libel upon his race, and deserves to be branded wherever found." Randolph defended himself in the pages of the *Evening Journal* and the *Religio-Philosophical Journal*, stating that while he had raised $430.50 in cash he had spent $1,200 on travel and other fundraising expenses, but the damage was done, and he instructed his treasurers to send back the contributions already received.[73] The school was dead.

His mistreatment on the Political Pilgrimage by those whose cause he had championed for years (mainly white Northern liberals and reformers) left a very bitter taste in Randolph's mouth, "and he withdrew from the soiled pack, never again to be counted in."[74] His experiences made him scathing of the duplicity of abolitionists and reformers in general, and he seems to have been the first to propound the once-familiar generality that Northerners loved blacks in general, though they knew none of them, while Southerners, who actually knew many of them, loved individual blacks while hating the race in the abstract.

> Everybody knows that slavery was in some sense a patriarchal institution; and that some favored servitors made themselves both free in speech and familiar in act, with their masters and their ladies, to a degree quite surprising to those northerners, who,

while professing great love for the negro and his cause, nevertheless hate and despise him with an unction and fervor never yet known in the South. Philanthropy toward the black man has in nine cases in every ten been a mere profession in the north!— a convenient hobby to ride toward political preferment, or stump oratorical notoriety. The love for the black man was and *is* a hollow pretense; for the negro was always nearer to the white man's heart in the South than to the pale Yankee of the East; and a black has a fairer chance to-day in the South than in the East. Indeed, may God help the man of even a drop of colored blood in the North, for he is the pariah of pariahs; and though he has the talent and genius of a Raphael or Le Sage, yet whatever thief or harlot with a white skin meets him in the North, feels warranted, by the fact of hue, in grossly insulting him at any time, and anywhere, and is practically backed in so doing by society at large,—except at voting time! Bosh! Northern philanthropy is a sham and utter cheat, as well as much of northern morals.[75]

Randolph's venture into education and his short-lived political career were over.

Chapter 8

THE POST-CIVIL WAR YEARS IN BOSTON

The completion of the Political Pilgrimage to Lincoln's tomb at the end of 1866 marks a watershed in Randolph's life. After fifteen years' hard toil in the vineyards of reform, and after thousands of speeches on temperance, abolition, women's equality, and freedmen's dignity, he had achieved exactly nothing for himself. While others—including even a few blacks, such as Frederick Douglass—found a share in the spoils of reform's victorious crusade against the South, Randolph was, as always, left out in the cold. His proposed normal school, which might have given him a secure position, died from controversy, and freedmen's education generally was abandoned in the South. His angular personality, fickle ideas, and outsider status had prevented his building a political base even among those for whom he had labored. Most gallingly of all, the reformers of the Northeast whose flag he had carried for so many years had revealed their true colors when faced with a specific black man and not with enslaved Southern blacks as an abstraction.

Randolph stayed on for a short time in Illinois after the Political Pilgrimage to Lincoln's tomb in September and October 1866, lecturing as the occasion presented in Chicago and Milwaukee. During his stay in Louisiana he had married again—apparently without the formality of a divorce from Mary Jane—and fathered a daughter, Parthenia. In Chicago in January 1867 a son was born, named after his father, but the marriage broke up shortly thereafter. Randolph says that while he was absent on the East Coast in early 1867 a traveling free-love propagandist by the name of "J-m-s-n" (W. F. Jamieson) "corrupted his wife and broke up a joyous family."[1] His comment on the breakup of his first two marriages was the same: "Married twice.

173

Radicalism debauched both wives, and rendered a happy home a wilderness of woe."[2]

The Rosicrucian Rooms in Boston

After the activity of the Civil War years and the turmoil of the immediate postwar period, Randolph was ready to give up the public platform and to devote himself to the practice of medicine and the writing of his books.[3] To some extent the choice was forced on him because he was still to a large extent persona non grata with the spiritualists (who, in any case, had increasingly fallen on hard times after the war) and he had no future with the victorious army of reform.[4] In early 1867 he ended up in Boston, practicing his brand of medicine, running a chemical laboratory for his elixirs, and displaying his powers as a Rosicrucian.[5]

He found a patron for his work in a Mrs. Mary P. Crook who financed the establishment of "Rosicrucian Rooms" at 29 Boylston Street. In her preface to Randolph's *Guide to Clairvoyance* (May 1867),[6] she states that she employed Randolph as a clairvoyant in five specialties (as well as employing other seers in other areas) and that clairvoyant examinations would be made daily and circles held for the development of clairvoyance, psychometry, and mediumship. Each Wednesday evening a grand levee was to be held for the "cultured and refined only. Admission by card." She also touted the availability of "sympathetic rings, lockets and stelle, and Rosicrucian Mirrors (for seeing the dead, etc.)." Randolph at the time was apparently in contact (on the soul or spirit level) with Raymond Lull, because in April he announced that Lull had dictated through him the "Wonderful Symph, or Rosicrucian Prediction Chart" that he subsequently advertised and sold.[7] This consisted of lists of favorable or unfavorable predictions for the days of the week, month, and year. The predictions were to be written separately on cards and randomly consulted by the user—a system approximating that of rotating concentric circles that Lull had used when alive.

At the same time as this public exhibition of the virtues of Rosicrucianism were going on in Mrs. Crook's rooms, Randolph was quietly engaged in trying to recruit members for his Rosicrucian order. In the *Guide to Clairvoyance* he boasts about the uses to which clairvoyance was being put by him and his "associates."

I have associates.

Possession ordereth use. We are using [clairvoyance]. We do not count ourselves as altogether of this world; for we are in connection with and do the works of the Ethereal peoples of the starry skies. So far as the Seer is concerned, the world knows this.

By the clairvoyance thus attained, I, and my assistants, read the varied scrolls of human life; explain dreams and visions; examine and prescribe for those who are sick in body, mind, heart, ambition, aspiration, speculation, hopes, losses, fears, troubles, affections; healing bodies, minds, souls; scanning by positive vision, not merely the secrets of a man or woman's loves, and lives, and keeping them, but also, knowing that organization determines destinies, revealing what will inevitably come to pass. . . . More than this. Scientific instruction can be imparted to the intelligent, and all that *I* know I can also teach others.

* * *

Power cannot be bought with money. I *want the best souls to come to me. Such may be admitted to the Rosicrucian Brotherhood!*[8]

The emphasis of this appeal by Randolph is primarily on the diagnostic and predictive aspects of clairvoyant Rosicrucianism, with a lesser emphasis on true love as the great medical panacea. The "predictive science," Randolph claimed, dated back to the days of Hermes Trismegistus, "our Grand Master," and had been "cultivated secretly and openly since long prior to the foundations of Egypt or Babylonia."[9] Presumably Randolph's intention in his recruitment was to let his readers believe that this succession from Hermes continued effectively, through unspecified but still existing channels, down to him, and he referred enticingly to an unspecified "Grand Lodge" which alone could teach a method of making an "oraculum" superior to his.[10]

The Rosicrucian work that Randolph was doing in Boston in the late 1860s was at least on one level fairly light-hearted. On July 4, 1869, the "Rosicrucian Club" of Boston rented a ship for an outing and picnic down the bay and spent the day on the water, singing songs composed for the occasion and eating ice cream. A foreigner with a "slight Italian accent" was elected as president of the club— probably a reference to the mysterious Italian/Armenian Cuilna Vilmara who, Randolph says, was in the process of instructing him at the time on further mysteries of the magic mirror. The event was commemorated in a pamphlet, *Rosicrucian: Out of the Shell* (1869) which states that it was written "July 4 Anno Rosic II, Anno Mund. MMMMMDCCCLXIX"—that is, the second year of some new Rosicrucian founding (presumably dating from the "Rosicrucian

Rooms"). The pamphlet is anonymous, but Randolph's humorous style pervades it, and it is undoubtedly by him.[11]

After Death; or Disembodied Man

There is no indication of how long Randolph remained in the employ of Mrs. Crooks in the Rosicrucian Rooms, but the advertisements for the rooms cease to appear by June and neither she nor the rooms appears in his later writings. She was but one of a series of women with whom Randolph was to be involved professionally—and frequently personally as well—in the coming years. Their names recur throughout his writings of the time. There was "La Blondette," for whom Randolph wrote *Casca Llanna* (1872). Randolph calls her with evident feeling a "cool, conscience-less, sinister, thin-lipped, blue-eyed affectional sorceress."[12] Then there were Mert La Hue, who dined while he starved, Carrie Chute, for whom he wrote one of his books on love and who probably advanced him the money for its publication, and Flora S. Russel, who provided the introduction to his edition of the *Divine Pymander*.[13] These companions must have given rise to considerable comment in Boston. "'He's fond of the women! he's fond of the women,—al-to-gether *too* fond of 'em!' The fools! As if *that* was a crime, seeing that I come by it naturally,—for my father was so before me, and the fault . . . is constitutional, and 'runs in the family.'"[14]

This period in Boston in the late 1860s was the most prosperous and productive of Randolph's life.[15] He had obviously become something of a celebrity, lionized in a small way by Boston society. He was consulted on the stock market by Horace Day, a prominent financier (and spiritualist) and achieved some notoriety for correctly predicting the gold panic of 1869, the appearance of a comet, and the fall of Napoleon III.[16] His books were selling well.[17] His constant search for a cause to which he could dedicate his life and energies turned him for a time to the rehabilitation of prostitutes—a common preoccupation of society at the time—and to a crusade against the evils of abortion.[18]

In late 1866 Randolph had published in the *Religio-Philosophical Journal* a long series of articles entitled "Sequel to Dealings with the Dead" that gave his current ideas on the postmortem existence of the disembodied spirit. He then reworked the material slightly and published it in book form in Boston in 1868 as *After Death; or Disembodied Man; The World of the Spirits, Its Location, Existence, Appearance, etc.; The Sequel to Dealings With The Dead*.[19] The work was the product of a powerful series of visions Randolph had had of the spirit world, and he had begun working on the book during his last days in Louisiana in the spring of 1866. He thought of the book as his "masterpiece"[20]—and, indeed, it is well written, abounding in flashes of humor and brilliant digressions on the world of vision—but the result is disappointing and the book is definitely a regression from Randolph's earlier grand vision of the soul world. Like so much spiritualistic literature of the time, the book is a meretriciously rational, highly detailed description of the earth-like abode and conditions of the dead. It paints a beautiful picture of the spirit world, the complex spheres within spheres ascending from the earth toward God. The "spirit" with which Randolph was concerned was a tangible (ethereal, but still material) body that wore clothes and enjoyed its former pleasures and was in all respects a "perfect human being both in mind and person."[21] Upon its separation from the body, the spirit began a vast pilgrimage through ever more refined spheres, gradually divesting itself of its earthly faults and atoning for its earthly wrongs and asymptotically returning to God, the eternal Sun that had originally spun off the universes.

As Randolph had first set out in *Dealings with the Dead* in 1862, the universes of creation, like man himself, were triplicate, consisting of material, spiritual, and "soul" worlds. The spirit world into which humans were introduced at death consisted of seven grand zones or belts of ethereal matter (each divided into seven lesser zones or spheres) that circled first the earth, then the planets of the solar system, then the solar belt and the entire solar system and then an enormous volume of systems that pivoted about a "dark sun" that was one of the Pleiades.[22] This vast area in turn was but one focus of an ellipse that had as its other focus a similar zone that circled another sun, and this ellipse itself was surrounded by the seventh zone which circled all of material creation. Beyond all of this lay six further and indescribable zones which themselves were but one focus of an ellipse whose other focal point was the deific realm—God himself, the Central Sun.

The material universe is bounded, limited, circumscribed, and circumvolved, or surrounded, by a vast and almost inconceivable ocean of Spirit, and on the breast of that vast sea are cushioned the ethereal belts, zones, and worlds, as are also the material constellations. The material zones of constellations revolve within corresponding spiritual or ethereal zones or belts, on all sides of the spaces,—seven of them; and in the midst of this space, equidistant from each of the seven, embracing alike the material and ethereal zones, belts, rings, universes and constellations,—in the profound and awful deeps of Distance,—is a Third Universe of

universes,—and this is the Vortex, the centre,—the dwelling-place
of Power, the seat of Force, the fountain of all Energy,—the unimaginable dwelling-place of the great I AM,—the supercelestial
throne of the ever-living God! Alone? No! The purified souls of
the myriads of dead centuries are there, contemplar, but not co-
equal Gods. . . . God is not Panthea, Jehovah, Aum, Brahm, Allah,
Jove. He is self-conscious. . . . Not spirit or soul, but souls' and
spirits' crystallization. Not intelligence, but its concentration . . . an
auroral Sun of suns.[23]

As if this were not enough, Randolph hinted at yet another revelation
according to which the spirit's peregrination through the seven grand
zones constituted but one cycle of a still more unimaginable journey.[24]

At the moment of death, the majority of humans were transposed to
the upper side of the earth's atmosphere, where illumination was provided by the great "aerial river" that Randolph envisioned flowing in an
arc from the north and south poles. This was "Vernalia" or "Aidenn,"
complete with cities, rivers, and forests, in which poets had cottages
and "freebooters roamed the gloomy forests."[25] Here, men began the
process of "vastation" whereby they overcame their erroneous beliefs
and physical infirmities and atoned for their faults. Randolph was nothing if not a realist when it came to the infirmities of human nature, and
he saw no reason why death alone should make one perfect.[26]

> If a man goes to sleep a zealot, bigot, or fool, I see no good
> reason why he or any one else should expect him to wake up
> next day a perfectly right sort of person, sane and sound in all
> respects; entirely and completely changed, re-made, worked over,
> purified and crystallized; do you? If a Jersey rogue starts on the
> ferry-boat from Hoboken, I see no reason why, or method through
> which, his nature should have undergone an entire change by
> the time he reaches New York; do you?[27]

Since the lower zones of the afterlife were, by hypothesis, peopled
with those still in thrall to their earthly existences, they were also home
to sectarians, all still believing whatever they had believed on earth.
There were, accordingly, Christian missionaries still trying to convert
the heathen and learned Buddhists who taught the doctrine (once believed by Randolph) that eventually man would so purify himself as to
enter "Narwana" and lose his individuality in God.[28] Gradually all of
these erroneous beliefs faded away, and by the finish of the seventh
subdivision of the second zone, man became a god. "[A]ll these tremen-

dous powers, qualities, and faculties converge and blend into one. He has again reached the plane of unity,—has become as a God."[29]

All this (with the possible exception of Randolph's emphasis on the eventual deification of man) is nothing but good, old-fashioned "Summer Land" spiritualism, with heavy debts to Swedenborg and Andrew Jackson Davis. The more sublime teachings of *Dealings with the Dead* (to which *After Death* was intended as a sequel) about the "soul world"—the nonmaterial, atemporal state of being beyond the world of the spirit and beyond material creation—were affirmed by Randolph in passing[30] but largely neglected in favor of a minute description of the details of the life and adventures of the disembodied in the "spirit world." If there is any truth in the assertions of later occultists, such as Madame Blavatsky and the H. B. of L., that Randolph was a failed initiate, a person who had originally been taught the truth by some unspecified Oriental order or brotherhood but had later fallen away into error, the proof of the transformation (if such a falling away or change existed at all and is reflected in his works) may be the reaffirmation of the more prosaic side of spiritualism displayed in *After Death* and the downplaying of the more exalted vision he had shown in *Dealings with the Dead*[31] (see chapter 12). Randolph continued in the same beliefs until his death and, while not disavowing the mysteries of the soul world, never returned to them with his earlier fervor.

Also during the late 1860s Randolph completed his biography of the Davenport brothers, Ira and William, the wonder-working "phenomenal mediums" whose performances caused such a stir in the United States and Europe around the Civil War. As we have already seen in discussing Randolph's *Pre-Adamite Man*, he had become acquainted with the brothers in the very early days of their mediumship in Buffalo in 1855 or 1856, when they were mediating communications from the conglomerate spiritual entity "King" or "John King," and he had stayed in contact with them through the years. He had begun work on the book in a garret in New York City in July 1864, before departing for the South, but only finished it in 1869.[32] The book, although it is a competent spiritualistic biography in the contemporary mode, is undistinguished at best, and it is a mystery why Randolph wrote it at all—though his finances probably compelled him to undertake the commission. He published it anonymously in 1869 and did not retain the copyright, most likely because by the time it was finished he had come to see the brothers as "deliberate impostors."[33] The only notable portion of the book is Randolph's recounting (304) of an investigation of the Davenports in the late 1860s by Henry Steele Olcott, who was later to be one of the cofounders of the Theosophical Society.

Randolph Publishing Company

In 1870, Randolph established the Randolph Publishing Company in Boston. Its stated purpose was the modest one of publishing "works of rare merit and character, by unusually able authors, among others, those of Paschal Beverly Randolph, the world-famous genius."[34] The other able authors appear never to have materialized, and it is impossible now to determine whether the press was established in a mood of optimism or out of desperation because Randolph was unable to place his works with the major publishing houses of the day. In very short order Randolph reprinted several of his earlier works, including *After Death* and the final version of his works on magic mirrors and clairvoyance, entitled *Seership*, and he published for the first time his major works on human sexuality. He fleshed out his list with several pot-boilers. Among these were a "Rosicrucian Dream Book" that purported to give the meanings of thousands of unlikely things seen in dreams,[35] and a re-issue of Dr. Everard's seventeenth-century translation of the Corpus Hermeticum.[36]

Between 1869 and 1871 he published several of his best books on sex and sexual happiness, all largely directed at women and aimed at ameliorating what Randolph saw as the scandal of modern marriage, and all broadly hinting at the greater mysteries of love that could be revealed by corresponding with the author. These were *Love and its Hidden History* (1869), *The Master Passion* (1869), *Love! At Last!* (1870) and *Casca Llanna* (1871). In the same vein was his pamphlet *The Golden Secret*, published in 1872.[37] All of these were written in Randolph's guise as physician, not mage, but the underlying basis of his theories on sexual happiness remained the mix of occult theories we have already seen (chapters 1 and 5). The details of the sexual practice taught—hinted at, but not expatiated upon—broadly overlapped Randolph's fully developed sexual magic. As he had always done, Randolph used these books intended for a general audience as lures to attract correspondents for his deeper ideas on sexual practice and to showcase his elixirs, protozones, and cordials. Randolph viewed these books as his "Revelations" or "Rosicrucian Revelations" of sex. The first had been *The Grand Secret* published in San Francisco in 1861 but never reprinted, probably because Randolph had come to view the practice of karezza (prolonged intercourse without ejaculation) as wrong. As he enumerated his revelations in the 1870s, the first was the double volume *Love and its Hidden History* and *The Master Passion*, the second was *Casca Llanna*, for publishing which, as we shall see, he was imprisoned in Boston), the third was *Eulis*, published in 1874, and the fourth was the privately circulated manuscript "The Ansairetic Mystery," which gave the full details of Randolph's sexual magic.

Sexual Happiness

Like many other sexual reformers and revolutionaries of the time,[38] Randolph saw himself as the great discoverer of the panacea for all social and domestic ills, a pioneer in demonstrating the central importance of sex and love in all aspects of life. All any person wanted, he thought, was "love, and the rich as well as the poor are daily pining for what neither lust, wealth, beauty, or position *can possibly give,*— love, sirs, or ladies; love, right straight from the heart!"[39]

> Many years ago I made the discovery . . . that most of human ills, social, domestic, mental, and moral, were the result of infractions, by excess, entire continence, or inversion, therefore *perversion*, of the sexual passion and instinct common to the human race. But there was no known cure for those evils, and I was therefore compelled to search for one in the regions of the unknown. With certain speculative and transmitted data to start from, I began, and for long years continued, the investigation of the matter, with a persistence, patient research, and strength of will that shrank at no obstacle, admitted no possibility of defeat or failure.[40]

He attributed his discoveries first and foremost to his own genius, but also acknowledged his debt to what he had learned on his Oriental travels and to his experiences in combating the "Voudeaux" of New Orleans, from whom especially he had learned the "lower" sorts of secrets of love charms for sexual attraction and repulsion.[41]

In these revelations of sex he supplemented and modified what he had written in *The Grand Secret* (1861). On the negative side of current sexual mores, Randolph believed that most marriages were failures and travesties because almost everyone suffered from magnetic/vital exhaustion, the lack of the nervo-vital fluid produced by the body to link the triad of body, spirit and soul to the Æth, the infinite reservoir of such fluid. This depletion results primarily from onanism— Randolph's perennial theme from the early 1850s. "The reason that solitary vice is so destructive is because there is no electrical, magnetic, or chemical reciprocation—no natural leverage; all is lost and nothing whatever gained; it is all intensity, no diffusion,—and the effects are analogous in the case of either sex, for each alike [is] guilty of this mode of self-murder, and are both rushing down the same declivity to—ruin; and both lose more life and vitality in such a debauch than in *ten* normal intercourses."[42] The second major cause of vital exhaustion was unrequited love and lovelessness within and outside of marriage, a lack of the "blending of natures" which resulted in "love starvation" and "vampires"—loveless persons that fatally attract the unwary and drain or poison another's magnetic sphere.[43]

This situation of unhappiness and depleted vital energy could be remedied first and most simply by the consumption of Randolph's various elixirs (all probably compounded, it must be remembered, with hashish). Different foods also naturally contained elements that restored energy. (Randolph prints the most amazing lists of foods, common in the midnineteenth century, but now serving only to remind us how diminished our own larder is.) The ultimate remedy for depleted energy, however, was proper sex. Just as imperfect or improper sexual unions drained the magnetic sphere of the individual, so proper sex restored it.

Many of Randolph's sexual nostrums are simple common sense, but perhaps not so commonly discussed in the midnineteenth century. To restore the magnetic sphere (and thus sexual attractiveness) he advocated cheerfulness, tenderness, consideration, attractive dress, patience, and generosity, and—unusual in his day—he taught the "supreme law of cleanliness, sunshine and ventilation."[44] He also taught the existence of certain natural periods, a waning and waxing of sexual power, passion, and interest, that had to be respected if sexual union was to be a restoring, rather than a draining experience.

> A woman is more forceful and powerful in both will, personal magnetism, and in tenderness, therefore love, just a little before and after the catamenial period, than at any other time; and her power culminates and is most effective in the evening, in the twilight, than at any other period of the day. . . . There is a vast sea of ether surrounding this globe, and that ether is the vehicle of the motions and emotions of the soul. . . . All mankind are purer and holier, therefore have less *force*, but more POWER at eventide, and between three and eight A.M., than at any other hours. . . . Men are most powerful in the morning.[45]

These mysterious cycles and rhythms as we shall see play a major role in Randolph's more esoteric sexual magic.

Supremely important in all sexual matters was will, especially the woman's will when joined with clear attention to a specific purpose.

Randolph was totally convinced that women were the controlling force in sex and indeed that women always could control and dominate men if they but knew how. "[W]oman's love is the strongest force on earth; her cause is the purest, strongest, and most just; and all the good powers of the universe are in sympathy therewith."[46] Will was the key, the "It-shall-be-as-I-want-it power of the soul."[47] By "placing herself soul, body, mind, purpose, thought, desire, intent, in *that tender* state, she instantly becomes a positive (attracting) power to everything male within the pale of God's universe, and of course conquers by *apparently* stooping to do so. I care not who the straying lover, or recreant husband may be, he *must* yield to this superior force, for it is the great magnetic law of love, and worth more to unhappy wives and unloved girls than all the 'love charms' and 'powders' in America, for these are mainly errant cheats and swindles, and when they do apparently succeed the thing is accomplished by other means."[48]

The practical effects claimed by Randolph for his sexual science were numerous. Since love was a magnetic phenomenon, it could be accumulated and projected at a distance to attract a new lover or to reclaim one grown distant and cold, to cure and comfort the ill, and to repel a person stealing the affections of the loved one.[49] Repulsion was accomplished by calling the interloper's image into the magic mirror and then exerting the will to punish the offender.[50] Gustav Meyrink, who translated Randolph's *Ravalette* into German in 1922, gives an example of Randolph's ability to fascinate women through will alone. He relates that a man who had known Randolph well told him the following story.

> Because the rumor about [Randolph] was that he could, by a projection of his Will, make women pliant, I decided one day, to test him in that respect and brought the conversation around to that issue. We were already in the theater and it was during the intermission. "Yes," said Randolph when I asked him, "every woman whom I call must come. Every time. At once." "Even now," I asked. "Certainly. Even now. Pick out one of the many women who sits down there." I furtively pointed at a young blond lady some distance away, and Randolph immediately went into trance, closing his eyes and becoming rigid.
>
> Scarcely two minutes later, the woman stood up and reeled out like a moonstruck person. Of course, I asked Randolph to break off the experiment at once.[51]

The accumulated magnetic power of love could also be used to "charge" certain objects—rings or "magnetic powders"—which had

the property of retaining the "odyllic, magnetic, ethereal, and volitional energies" used to charge them, and which served the purpose
of attraction and of blending the magnetic sphere of the lovers.[32]
Randolph especially touted the powers of one of these powders called
"Persian Phluph," whose secret he had learned in Egypt in 1861. For
a fee of five dollars—which he specified was not for the phluph but
for his medical opinion—he would prepare and send a small sample
to correspondents.[33]

The exact method of charging these substances is left vague in
Randolph's books for general circulation, but it is clear that where the
object was to affect some third person the process required two people
of opposite sex, one of whom had to be the one desiring to affect the
absent person. At this level, at least, the process seems to have required a union of effort short of actual sexual intercourse. The persons
"must conjoin in the process of infiltrating, by will, by hope, by the
breath and finger-tips, the neutral substances with the specific power,
and magnetic quality designed; nor can it be done in any other way
whatever, because there *can be no magnetic evolution unless the magnetic
law of minus and plus, positive and negative, magnetic and electric, be observed.*"[34] Apparently the couple charged the neutral matter (steel filings,
sugar of milk, "chloride of gold," "lactuarium," and other substances
in proper proportions) by grinding it in a mortar with other (unspecified) substances provided by the one seeking the benefit of the procedure, while all the while concentrating their attention and will to
"magnetize" the powder for the purposes desired. The resulting mixture then had to be secreted in the garments or the pillow of the one
to be affected.[35]

The centerpiece of Randolph's exoteric sexual science was his teaching on human generation, an issue that had occupied him since *Dealings with the Dead* (1861–62). To him, as we have seen, human souls
were incarnated divine monads, individualized and immortalized by
the act of conception. These monads were eternally spun off by the
Divine Central Sun in pairs, male and female, and clustered in the
atmosphere of earth around the head of each man, seeking incarnation
and individualization. Once successfully implanted in the foetus these
monads became immortal souls.[56] The worst crime, accordingly, was
abortion, and Randolph's works are full of denunciations of the practice.[57] Birth control by "unnatural" means was also a crime, but
Randolph taught an "Oriental" method to prevent conception by willing it not to occur.[58] On the positive side, Randolph taught, both in his
books for popular consumption and in private manuscripts sent for a
fee (such as "The Golden Letter"),[59] a variety of methods of conceiving

and nurturing superior children. Conception at the proper point in the cosmic cycle played a role in the process: "[T]here is a mystery connected with generation *and* morning which those who yearn for perfect offspring would do well to study. It is this: The children of night are like their parents—weary; while those who are launched on life with the sun are fresh and vigorous, last longer, and are healthier, and know a great deal more."[60] A related mystery, as we shall see, was the method of attracting "mature" monads and even monads from the celestial spheres for implantation in the womb and incarnation.

The most important requirement for producing superior children— and one with deep roots in Randolph's esoteric beliefs—is that they be conceived in "Love." The full and complete "Love-joy" essential to the creation of superior children in turn depended upon the accumulation of "nerve aura" in the system, especially that "magazined within the mystic crypts appointed of Nature for that purpose."[61] The offspring of cold, loveless parents are themselves love starved and become in their turn "Vampyres." In life and after death they are "scranny" and lean souls, requiring eons to develop properly and advance.[62] As he had been teaching since the early 1860s, Randolph believed that the soul was a bipolar, "diamondesque," divine white fire (a "condensation and crystallization of God's nervous fluid"),[63] resident in the brain and in the sexual organs. Its negative, male, electric pole was in the brain and was responsible for reasoning, learning, and factual assimilation. Its positive, female, magnetic pole was in the genital area in the man and in the womb of the woman, and it was this magnetic pole which directly put man in contact with the subtle, divine fluid, fire or Æth that pervades the universes and ties body to soul, mind to matter, and man directly to God.[64] The action of both poles, but especially the magnetic pole, was essential to the creation of perfect human children. Without "Love," and the action of both poles of the soul, only the brain participated in generation, producing lifeless drones.[65]

> We hold that the other pole of the Soul is situated within the genital system; that in *true* marriage the *entire Soul* officiates at the celebration; that both positive and negatives of each parent assist at the incarnation of the new Souls that genuine marriage calls into the world; that where no mutual love inspires the parents, only one of the two forces of their Souls officiate, and the consequence is that the world is full of half-men, half-women and weaklings; and thus it is seen why illegitimate children are generally the smartest,—it is because Love was the inspiration. Apply the principles laid down by us, and it is seen how

wherefrom it happens that inferior-brained, but strong-*loving* women become mothers of mento-moral millionaires; while brainy mothers give us children born to intellectual penury; inferior-brained, but large, love-natured, men usually become fathers to their mental superiors; while we all know that genius generally, nay, notoriously, produces mental weaklings.[66]

When love officiated at the conception, the child so engendered was a marvel:

> Wherever you see a rich and *jouissant* beauty and power in a girl or boy—wherever you see force of genius—you may rest assured that the mother conceived when impassioned. *Au contraire*, wherever you see genuine meanness— "moral turpentine," as Mrs. Malaprop says; whenever you see a lean, mean, scrawny soul-wizened, white-livered, trickish, grab-all-ish, and accursed generally—you may safely wager your life that such a being was begotten of force, on a passionless, sickly, used-up wife, and you'll never lose your bet.[67]

"Love" itself, for Randolph was triplicate: of body, spirit, and soul; it was magnetic interplay at all three levels, not mere sentiment or even passion.[68] True love was thus material, spiritual, and mystic.[69] On the physical level, Randolph had developed a complete sexual physiology to accompany his theories. He pictured the omnipresent divine monads clustering around the head of every mature man and being drawn in with his breath to quicken the sperm and to take on their load of the father's characteristics.[70] In the act of generation, the body sent a "spiritual-material" portion of itself to the left half of the man's prostate gland, while the soul and spirit sent parts of themselves to the right half, "and at the exact instant that these all meet at that point, the nervo-vital muscles spasmodically contract, and the procreative fluid passing through, takes with it the prostatic exudations, and the immortal being is thus charged with a joyous load of heaven, or a grievous burden of intolerable horrors."[71] It is to allow the accumulations of this vital fluid or nerve aura that accompanied orgasm that Randolph taught the necessity of periods of abstinence before, and infrequent exercise of, the sexual act.[72] In his earliest writing on sexual fulfillment, *The Grand Secret*, Randolph had taught that "Physical Love" was distilled by the sexual glands and secreted as a fluid which revivified the sexual partners and in conception went to form the body of the child.[73] In his final pronouncements he returned to the idea. "I now call attention to another, different from all and far more important [secretion], and which is the only one common to both sexes alike. I refer to that colorless, viscid, glairy lymph, or exudation which is only present under the most fierce and intense amative passion in either man or woman. . . . [P]rior to its escape, per vagina and male urethra, it is not a liquid at all; but the liquid is the resultant of the union of three imponderables . . . magnetism, electricity, and nerve-aura,—each rushing from the vital ganglia and fusing in the localities named."[74] Only when this is present, mutually, was it safe and proper to complete the sexual act, and only then was the superior child engendered.

This mutual lymph, as we have seen, probably played a role in Randolph's consecration of magic mirrors. It was also the precondition and foundation of his more developed sexual magic.

Randolph also thought that the quality of the monads to be ensouled in the act of generation had marked effects on the quality of the child. He believed that on occasion a monad might go through the generative process as many as five times before being finally implanted in a foetus prepared to receive it. These more mature monads produced superior children.[75] On a more esoteric level, as we shall see, this teaching approached the idea propounded by John Murray Spear and later taken up by the H. B. of L. and made the mainstay of its sexual teachings, that it was possible not only to attract "mature" monads but also to draw down monads from the aerial spaces and implant them in the womb and to implant directly in the foetus the powers of the celestial hierarchy.

All of these secrets and powers were not mere empty theory to Randolph. He undoubtedly exercised them to the full in the conception of his last child, Osiris Budh Randolph, born March 30, 1874. In commending Osiris Budh to the care of his last occult foundation until he reached majority, he touted him as a "singularly organized and extraordinarily constituted boy" and claimed that he "was the *only* being now on earth who by organization is capable of wholly entering the Penetralia and esoteric realm of the Eulian System."[76]

From the more exoteric point of view of happy marriage, the immediate consequence of love was the rapturous blending and mutual nourishment of the magnetic and electric spheres of the partners.[77]

[W]hen pleasure results from a meeting of the electric currents of the male with the magnetic flow of the female, in the nerves of each, as in the touch of loving lips, the two currents spread out into waves, which flow all over the vast nervous network of both, until they die out as they roll upon the foot of the throne whereon each soul sits in voluptuous expectancy. In the [case of

onanism] all joy is local; in the other it is *diffused* over both beings, and each is bathed in the celestial and divine aura—the
breath of God, suffusing both bodies, refreshing both souls![78]

The consequence of this mutual magnetic interplay in triplicate sex,
in turn, was mental and physical health—and prolonged life. Even on
the exoteric level, Randolph taught that following his teachings on
love produced the elixir vitae, the philosopher's stone, "by which the
human stay on earth [can] be prolonged a *great deal* beyond the storied
threescore years and ten."[79]

The Rosicrucians Again

Randolph continually protested that, after the San Francisco foundation of 1861, he had had to work his Rosicrucian ideas alone and
without followers. Each time he tried to establish a more formal
organization (in 1871 and again in 1874), he glossed over the intervening years between the then-current attempt and the original foundation of the San Francisco Grand Lodge in 1861,[80] but he appears
nonetheless always to have had at least an informally organized group
of followers who practiced his ideas and looked to him for leadership. Throughout the 1860s some of his original Rosicrucians had
stayed with him. John Blakey Pilkington, who had been the Grand
Door of the original foundation in 1861, continued in contact with
Randolph and later became the Vice-Hierarch of the Triplicate Order
of Rosicrucia, Pythianæ, and Eulis when it was refounded in San
Francisco in December 1874. There were undoubtedly others. We
have already looked at the Rosicrucian club that Randolph was running in 1867 and his attempts at recruitment for his order in the
same year. As we shall see in connection with the Great Free Love
Trial affair of 1871 and 1872, Randolph in the early 1870s was initi-
ating neophytes individually into some Rosicrucian mystery with a
ceremonial and three degrees (Volantia, Rosicrucia, and Decretism),
corresponding to his three primary magical techniques, but all these
efforts appear to have lacked formal structure, and they were obviously not satisfactory or successful.

One of Randolph's mottoes, however, was *je renais de mes cendres*,
an apt sentiment for a man who was forced again and again to restart
from the beginning. This was true as well for his Rosicrucian groups,
and in Boston in the early 1870s he again made an effort to found a
formal Rosicrucian group.

At some time in the late 1860s Randolph was contacted for the first time by Freeman B. Dowd, who was to become his best-known follower and was the organizer of a Rosicrucian group whose off-shoots survive after a fashion today. While Dowd's Rosicrucian efforts after Randolph's death are fairly clear, his role in the earlier foundations is murky. In his strange novel *The Double Man* (1895),[81] Dowd gives a letter, supposedly written by the novel's protagonist, "Don La Velle" (who is obviously Dowd himself), to Randolph in March 1864, seeking to join Randolph's Boston club of Rosicrucians. The letter is full of anachronisms and must have been written later, probably in 1867,[82] but it probably reflects reality in showing Dowd's eager approach to Randolph. Dowd (1825–1910) was, in his exoteric life, a peripatetic lecturer and phrenologist (and perhaps commercial photographer, which was a traveling profession in those days). He appears in Davenport, Iowa, and St. Louis, Missouri, in the 1860s; in Iowa, Arkansas, and Missouri in the 1870s; and in Philadelphia and San Francisco (where he started Temples of the Rosy Cross) and in Hempstead, Texas, in the 1880s and 1890s.[83] In the mid-1860s he appears to have been a fairly run-of-the-mill traveling spiritualist, corresponding with the journals on the wondrous cures of spiritualist physicians.[84] He first came to prominence in connection with Randolph's work when he supplied the introduction, dated September 1869, to Randolph's 1870 publication of his double work *Love and its Hidden History* and *The Master Passion*.[85] Again in 1870 Dowd wrote a glowing, orotund preface, "The Thinker and his Thought," to a new edition of Randolph's *After Death*:

> Toil on, O genius rare! Toil on! brave thinker! Bow low thy head before the mighty thoughts which crowd upon thee—great rocks, though they be—from out the Temple of Infinite Thought. Toil on! thou knowest not why! Yet thou rearest here, and now, the Dome of thought of the great hereafter of the world! What matter the mad ravings of the multitude to thee—those others who come after—shall build monuments on thy footprints, and use as text-books thy works in ROSICRUCIA'S glorious temples of the YET TO BE!

Randolph returned the favors by saying of Dowd that he "quotes from God himself, because he can read his handwriting on all the walls that hem in the universe in which we live and move."[86] He also dedicated his 1871 re-printing of *The Rosicrucian's Story* to "Freeman"[87] and touted Dowd as the publicizer of certain magnetic bandages (worn fore and aft on the head while sleeping) created by Randolph as a means of developing clairvoyance.[88] At the same time that these courtesies were being exchanged, Dowd was beating the drum for sexual Rosicrucianism up and down the Midwest, advertising his work entitled "Rosicrucia! The Road to Power; Sexual Science; Psychical and Mental Regeneration. A pamphlet of 60 pages by Freeman B. Dowd. Priceless to wives and mothers and such as are trying to be men. 50 cents."[89] Unfortunately, this has not been preserved, but Dowd's later writings show that his thoughts on the magical role of sex parallel Randolph's own.[90] He was also, like Randolph, a visionary.

> I seemed to be ecstasy itself. I heard no music, but I felt as if I was all melody itself. All forms had suddenly disappeared; nothing was left but an inconceivable and indescribable light. The awful experience above, below and around presented no object for the eye to rest on; nothing but light, which came from no source but simply was. . . . I was harmony; I was a strain of most ravishing melody, I was a ray of that most wondrous light.[91]

From all of this it is apparent that around 1869 Randolph began to make another attempt to institute his Rosicrucian work in a more organized fashion and that Dowd played a prominent part in the revival. He was in fact the nominal head of the organization. In Randolph's synopses of his writings, printed in 1870 as advertisements for his books, he calls Dowd "Grandmaster of the Rosicrucians,"[92] and Dowd's preface to the re-issue of *After Death* the same year heralds him as "Grand Master, Imperial Order of Rosicrucia." The reason for this elevation of Dowd is unclear since he was the pupil and Randolph the teacher. Perhaps Randolph sought to avert criticisms aimed at his fickleness or womanizing, or perhaps the racial issue again reared its head to bar him from the position of honor. Whatever his title, the organization was Randolph's own creation.

By early 1871, the situation had changed. In February, prompted by "the defection of nine false brethren" who were establishing false lodges in the land, Randolph published *The Asiatic Mystery. The Fire Faith!— The Religion of Flame!—The Force of Love!—The Energos of Will!—The Magic of Polar Mentality! First Rosicrucian Manifesto to the World Outside the Order!*[93] This is the clearest statement of Randolph's Rosicrucianism and assembles succinctly all of the ideas we have seen developing since the early 1860s.

The Rosicrucian Order, the manifesto brags, is Oriental in character. God is the ineffable center, "the *soul* of the universe; POSITIVE HEAT,

CELESTIAL FIRE," and "dwells within the Shadow, *behind*, the ever-lasting FLAME." Love is the aura of God, pervading the universes. Man is a spark of the Divine, and the vast "aerial spaces" likewise abound with intelligences, disembodied and never embodied, who have their origin in Æth and with whom man, if properly instructed, can establish communion.

We, the Brotherhood of Rosicrucians, or by whatever name the world chooses to call us, further hold that there are Ætherial (spacial) centres of Love, Power, Force, Energy, Goodness, and for, and of, every kind, grade, species, and order of knowledge known to man . . . and that it is not only *possible* to reach those centres, and obtain those knowledges, but that it is achievable by a vast number, who now drone and doze away life. . . . [94]

Declaring that true manhood and womanhood are more or less *en rapport* with one or more of the upper Hierarchies of Intelligent Potentialities, earth-born and *not* earth-born, we believe there are means whereby a person may become associated with, and receive instruction from, them.[95]

To accomplish this, the order taught the "radiantly glorious MAGIC OF THE HUMAN WILL" and the method by which humans can penetrate the "domains of the SHADOW, and glimpse the ineffable effulgence of the gorgeous LIGHT." Power, including magical power, the manifesto proclaimed, lies not in knowledge, but in goodness, love and will: "Love lieth at the foundation." The order teaches the method to "strike out this divine spark" of love—something achieved other-wise only by accident—a method that rests upon the "polar world of *white fire* within the human body." The negative pole of this fire is in the brain and its positive pole in the genital system, and this, in turn, is "in direct magnetic and ethereal contact with the Soul of Being,—the foundation-fire of the universe . . . the subtending Love, or Fire-floor of Existence." The Rosicrucian method—and its three specific magical practices: volantia, decretism and posism—gives its practi-tioners full power over the material world, over "the Ætherics of Space" and over time itself.[96] Randolph's magic gives the "key wherewith can be unlocked the SEVEN GATES,—money (1), Love (2), Clairvoyance (3), Special Mental Power (4), General Power (5), Magnetic Presence (6), and Ubique, or far sight (7)."[97]

The manifesto is powerful and represents Randolph's style at its most enthusiastic. As usual, however, and for obvious reasons, Randolph makes it clear that these general statements of the "secret doctrines" were not all, and that "such as concern the domestic, celestic, magnetic, and volantial interests of life and power of mankind, which we reveal to initiates of the third and higher degrees."[98]

The circumstances surrounding the issuance of the *Asiatic Mystery* are not entirely clear, but it appears that it marks a breach with Dowd. Randolph says that a "few men" joined him in early 1871, after the defection of the "nine false brethren."[99] As he had always done in discussing his Rosicrucian antecedents, Randolph referred tantalizingly to an unnamed "Supreme Grand Master of the Order on Earth" at whose bidding the "Asiatic Mystery" was issued, and signed the document himself simply as "Secretary *ex officio*," but there is no mention of Dowd or of his being the "Grand Master, Imperial Order of Rosicrucia." By the time that Randolph published his edition of the *Divine Pymander* later in the same year, the manifesto was attributed to Randolph as "Supreme Head of the Order." The conclusion seems inescapable that Dowd, like so any others before and after, broke with Randolph and was placed "under Ban."[100] After the break, Dowd went on with his rambling life as a Rosicrucian. He continued to submit his "Rosicrucian Musings" and "Rosicrucian Heart–Lines" to the *Religio-Philosophical Journal* during the 1870s,[101] and next appeared in Philadelphia in 1882 where he published his masterpiece, *The Temple of the Rosy Cross, The Soul, Its Powers, Migrations and Transmigrations*,[102] and apparently began Rosicrucian groups that eventually became part of George Winslow Plummer's Societas Rosicruciana in America and of Reuben Swinburne Clymer's Rosicrucian Fraternity—the only active vestiges of Randolph's Rosicrucian work (see chapter 11).

Randolph's Rosicrucian work in Boston before and after the defection of the nine false brethren and the issuance of his manifesto appears to have been hit or miss and may have lacked a developed organization. In the fall of 1871, when he was enmeshed in the confidence game that led to his arrest the next year for peddling free-love literature (see chapter 9) he initiated Churchill and French in Boston and Andrew Bay in Ohio into the probationary degree of Volantia.[103] The formalities of the initiation appear to have consisted in the taking of the Rosicrucian oath[104] and a ceremony of some sort. In the case of Bay, who was over sixty, the ceremony, Randolph said, required the confrontation of "Sin" (Bay) with "Innocence" (innocent young girls). Since innocence was as hard to find then as now, the ceremony had to go forward with substitutes, including the "perfect little gem" that Randolph was then involved with.[105] Even after this initiation, the probationers of the order (whom he calls "Builders") were not privy to the real secrets, which were revealed only to "masters" for whom the "iron door" had rolled back upon their truthful proclamation that they were honest men.[106]

Increasingly as money problems assailed him Randolph sought to turn his secrets into cash while at the same time recruiting disciples and spreading his ideas. He not only sold his phluph, for example, but for twenty-five dollars he offered to teach the secret of compounding the powder; for one-hundred dollars he would prepare students to teach others his entire medical doctrine on increasing the vital powers.[107] With the secret of making his elixirs he offered a parchment certificate, undoubtedly "suitable for framing," so that his students could prove to the world that they had indeed learned the method from its source, Randolph.[108] His sales pitch promised not only health and success to the patient, but wealth—from part-time work—to the student.[109] In 1870, driven by his own need or by the failure of the public to recognize his worth, Randolph temporarily sold his "general" medical practice to a Dr. Franklin Smith in Boston, but he was careful to note in his books that he still acted "in cases where hope is gone and only death or madness looms up in the near future."[110]

By the early 1870s Randolph began to suffer from serious depression at the lack of recognition of his talents—and at his perpetual shortage of money, and for the first time he appears to have turned to alcohol for comfort. In a memoir of Randolph as he knew him at the time, Freeman B. Dowd painted what appears to be a true-to-life portrait of Randolph, sitting slumped in his empty Rosicrucian Rooms, sorting mail and tossing "such as contained neither money nor stamps" into the wastebasket.

His dark complexion, curly hair, black eyes, flat nose, large mouth, and thick lips suggested African blood; while his broad, square forehead, wide-set eyes, with their piercing look, coupled with the fascinating smile that wreathed his amorous mouth at times, showed the finer blood of the Anglo-Saxon race. This man was P. B. Randolph, a man in whom the blood of different races boiled like the lava of a volcano. His nature was electrical, volcanic. A man of moods, there was for him no middle ground; he was either in Heaven or in Hell. Love to him was a passion; its indulgence, like everything else, was in the extreme, hence he was love-hungry and love-starved. Always longing, never satisfied, a prey to extreme imagination, lofty in ambition, but constantly humiliated on account of his color, denied the position in so-ciety to which his genius entitled him, it is not strange that he became morbidly sensitive, envious, and full of hate. Naturally mediumistic and at times clairvoyant; superstitious, as all of the African race are; he was a fatalist, and imagined that he had existed on this earth previously, and that he was born of mixed blood as a punishment for crimes he had committed then. Soft and tender as a mother at times, his great heart would melt with tears, only to be burned and dried up a moment later by the fierce fires of anger at himself and creation. He was medium of rare abilities, an intuitive reader of character, and a subject of obsession; he predicted his own death by his own hand, and came near fixing the exact time. Such was Dr. Randolph as I knew him. Born of poor and obscure parentage, reared in the slums of New York, a newsboy, a bootblack, a barber, a waiter at a restaurant, without education, he acquired the best. Without a chance in life he became one of the most learned men of his day. He had a magic tongue, could speak many languages, possessed a memory of ideas and words truly marvelous, and was a public speaker superior to most. Without friends or money he traveled over Europe, Asia, and America, gathering knowledge as a bee gathers honey.

But with all his genius and all his acquirements, he did not acquire that urbanity of temper, that magnanimity of nature, which every gentleman must have to entitle him to recognition in society; and instead of attributing this to the true cause he attributed it to his color. Socially, as in everything else, he was an extremist. A warm, self-sacrificing friend, a jovial, laughing comrade, a vindictive and unforgiving enemy, an egotist, ready to be insulted where no insult was intended, it is no wonder that he became addicted to the use of strong drink.[111]

Chapter 9

THE GREAT
FREE-LOVE TRIAL

R andolph had always been a poor judge of character. He placed blind trust in anyone, man or woman, who claimed to be his friend—and often suffered financially as a consequence. He should have heeded the warning of the famous sex-reformer and phrenologist, O. S. Fowler ("You are utterly unfit for anything pecuniary or commercial.")[1] and avoided business transactions altogether, but he did not, and in 1871 he fell in with a pack of rogues and scoundrels who eventually left him penniless.

Arrested

By the spring of 1871, Randolph was just making ends meet with his books and medical consulting and was living in a garret on Court Street in Boston.[2] He was also just recovering from his infatuation with "La Blondette" and beginning to write his masterpiece on love, *Casca Llanna*. His situation, which was already bad, began to worsen in May when a certain fast-talking Canadian confidence man, Thomas Churchill, approached him and convinced him that he could put together a syndicate that could sell 300,000 copies of *Casca Llanna* for Randolph—which, of course, was music to Randolph's ears.[3] Because he was "temporarily" out of funds, Churchill appears to have attached himself to Randolph and lived at his expense while spinning his webs of national circulation and vast profits.

In August Randolph met a second scoundrel, who gave his name variously as W. T. French, W. Bay French, or W. French Bay. French was from Ohio. He initially approached Randolph to learn his medical secrets and to be admitted into Randolph's "secret order of thinkers." Once in Boston, he immediately perceived the value of Randolph's works, especially his manuscript "The Golden Secret," which Randolph wrote out for correspondents for considerable sums of money. When he met Churchill in Randolph's rooms the two immediately recognized their common interest in fleecing Randolph. Both were admitted into Volantia, the probationary degree of Randolph's order, and both swore the Rosicrucian's oath, binding themselves to fair dealing and honesty, especially with brothers of the order, such as Randolph.[4] They promptly broke the oath by plotting to obtain the rights to Randolph's works, especially the copyrights.

As they laid out their scheme, French and Churchill would contribute the capital necessary to print Randolph's books and would in return receive an exclusive right to deal in them, paying Randolph only a small royalty. Since neither French nor Churchill actually had the money to contribute to the venture, French singled out a "mark" back in Ohio, Andrew Bay, a rich and eccentric old man with a penchant for fringe medicine—he believed all illnesses were caused by "bugs" and could be cured by drinking rum toddies. Randolph described him as a man "who consisted principally of poor clothes, broad acres, much money, more hair, and strong confederate proclivities,"[5] but even after the trap had been sprung and Randolph defrauded, he continued to believe that Bay was more sinned against himself than sinner.[6]

French traveled to Ohio to convince Bay to fund the venture and wrote back to Randolph urging him to dedicate *Casca Llanna* to Bay as a sop to his vanity. Randolph, rather unwillingly, complied, and the first 250 copies of the book which came off the presses in December 1871 carried the desired dedication:

To
Andrew Bay, Esq
Leatherwood, Geurnsey County, Ohio
How Grateful is the Parched Earth When the Waters
Descend!
The Wrecked Sailor When Friendly Hands Rescue
Him From Impending Death!
The Pain-Racked Sufferer When God Sends Relief!
Even So Do I,
Casca Llanna,

Feel Grateful for the Very Timely Aid Which You,
Sir Have Afforded
in Assisting at the Birth of and Bringing this
BOOK OF MY SOUL,
Before the Millions who Need Light

In October, Randolph (accompanied by Churchill—at Randolph's expense) traveled to Ohio to meet with Bay. Here the story takes on elements of soap opera. French was apparently pursuing another man's wife (whom he called his "Turkel Duvv" in letters to Randolph) and was amorously pursued in turn by Andrew Bay's seventy-year-old sister. Simultaneously, he was trying to insinuate a relative of his into Bay's household to marry Bay's serving girl. Bay himself (who is variously described as seventy-two or eighty-six years old) was trying to get a seventeen year old to marry him. Randolph, not to be outdone, "devoted his spare hours to admiring the beauty and perfections of a delicious little neighbor of Bay's . . . a perfect little gem, a flower, a violet. He was so smitten with her, in fact, that under the triple influence of French's elixir [the medicinal rum toddies] and the resultant spooneytude, he really thought he'd like to change her name for his."[7]

In the midst of all this, Bay applied for admission to Randolph's order, sponsored by Churchill and French. Randolph says that "when a person over sixty years of age applies for membership, the laws of the order are that 'Sin,' the man, be confronted with 'Innocence,' a pure, young girl, generally a child." Apparently there were no such girls in that part of Ohio, and they had to settle for Bay's sister and the "little gem" Randolph was pursuing at the time.[8]

Finally, Andrew Bay agreed to supply the money for the printing and to advance other money to run the business. A company called "Bay, French and Co." was formed and an agreement entered into with Randolph whereby Bay would contribute some $6,600 in capital for the reprinting (and in some cases the restereotyping) of Randolph's books and the publication of new works, especially *Casca Llanna*, and the company would receive the exclusive right to deal in his books. Randolph was promised a royalty from sales. Under this agreement, amazing as it seems, Bay actually paid over some $2,500. In November Randolph, French, and Churchill returned to Boston and, on the strength of Bay's promise to pay in the rest of the promised capital, Randolph gave the advance he had received from Bay to the printer and matched it with his own funds—money he said he had been saving to provide for his crippled daughter. *Casca Llanna* was soon rolling off the presses, but December came and went without the arrival of the remainder of Bay's contribution. All the while French and Churchill continued to live at Randolph's expense, making ineffectual efforts to publicize and sell the books.

At about this time, Randolph began to see he was getting nowhere with Bay, French and Company, and agreed to buy out their interest for $1,900—which he did not have—and a thousand copies of *Casca Llanna*. French initially agreed, but reneged on the deal and instead bought out Bay's interest for $1,000 and took an assignment from Bay of Bay's rights against Randolph on the $2,500 already advanced. In December, to raise the money to distribute his books and clear himself of his obligations to Bay, French and Company, Randolph cast about for a sales agent, and succeeded in falling into the clutches of yet another shady character—Mert La Hue.

Randolph's interest in Ms. La Hue seems to have been more than mere business. She is apparently the woman Randolph describes who "kept saying, 'Je t'aime, je vous aime! and I, poor ninny, believed her, and lost all the rest of my capital, while she, ah, but she cut a gorgeous swell in black velvet and jockey hat along the principal thoroughfare of the centre of the universe—and I dining alone on 'one fish-ball' at Presho's—but he, good man, always gave *bread* along with it—but she took her quail on toast at Fera's or Stumpke's 'Avon Cafe.'"[9] Distracted by her jockey hat and fine figure, Randolph set up his new agent in a fancy book shop on Washington Street in Boston stocked with copies of his books. There, La Hue did nothing.

At this juncture, early in February 1872, French, whose goal all along had been to get his hands on Randolph's copyrights and on the manuscript, "The Golden Secret," hatched a final fiendish plot to coerce Randolph into surrendering the rights to his works. He accused Randolph of purveying obscene materials, specifically free-love literature.[10] If Randolph is to be believed, French must have given copies of several of Randolph's books and circulars (unspecified) to two maladroit, rather comic sounding policemen, "Detectives Ham and Wood," and these two worthies, apparently finding them obscene to their tastes, obtained from the municipal court a search warrant for Randolph's apartment and office at 89 Court Street.

Ham, Wood, and two other detectives served the warrant on Saturday, February 24, 1872. When they arrived they found Randolph sick in bed with "heart disease" but proceeded nonetheless to search high and low for free-love literature. What they in fact found were copies of Randolph's various books, the printed version of "The Golden Letter" (printed for physicians and dealing with preventing conception by will) and some of Freeman B. Dowd's "works on Physiology."[11] They obviously thought these sufficient proof, because they arrested Randolph on the spot, heart disease or not, and hauled him off to the First Police Station, where he stayed locked up (lips "blue with the cold") until Monday morning.

According to Randolph, French's scheme from beginning to end was aimed at obtaining complete ownership of his copyrights. The final effort was to put pressure on Randolph by having him jailed and then agreeing to drop the charges in exchange for the rights to Randolph's books—and in fact Randolph says that French's lawyer made exactly that proposal to him in jail.[12]

At this point some judgment on Randolph's bona fides must be made. The entirety of his *Curious Life* is devoted to the rascality of French and the wrongs he suffered at his hands, but is all of that true? Granted that French was no gentleman and that he was probably involved with Randolph for what he could get out of him, the actual situation in February 1872 was that French had worked for half a year on the venture, found a backer who had advanced $2,500 to print Randolph's books, and had gotten an assignment of Bay's claim for the $2,500 against Randolph. In exchange he had received from Randolph only a few free meals and the loan of $260. Even assuming that he actually put the law on to Randolph, his goal may simply have been to get paid for his efforts. This view is strengthened by the outcome of the meeting in jail between Randolph and French's lawyer. While French may have demanded the copyrights and "The Golden Secret," what he settled for was 1,000 copies of Randolph's books in exchange for a quitclaim—and even these books he proceeded to sell back to Randolph for $700.[13] Whatever the truth of French's motives, Randolph decidedly got the better of the deal: for $700 his books were returned and he was clear of the claims of Bay, French and Company.

On Monday, February 26, Randolph was released from The Tombs, freed not by French's efforts but by a conscientious man, Judge Chamberlain, who seems actually to have read the material seized by Detectives Ham and Wood and decided that, whatever it was, it was not "obscene" within the meaning of the statute. He refused a "warrant" in the case and ordered Randolph released.

Though out of jail, Randolph's troubles were still not over. He still had to deal with Mert La Hue, who had been ensconced in her book shop at Randolph's expense, doing nothing—and not paying the landlord. Shortly after Randolph's release, the book shop and all of the precious books he had assigned to La Hue were attached for nonpayment of the rent. When La Hue approached him, probably tearfully, with the request for $150 to pay immediate expenses, Randolph borrowed the money, pledging as security the precious stereotyped plates for his books, but again La Hue did nothing to help Randolph. The pledge was forfeited, and Randolph lost his plates—temporarily, for again he was able to barter copies of his books for their return.[14]

When the furor died down, Randolph was financially ruined and in debt. He estimated that losses due to his arrest amounted to $9,750, though most of that money would appear to have gone to print his books—most of which ended up in his own possession. He was probably book rich and money poor, and in order to make ends meet he had again to borrow money and pledge the plates of his books as collateral.

In desperation, Randolph took advantage of his temporary notoriety to write all the local papers, touting his books and enclosing copies so that their reviewers could judge for themselves the books' innocent character.[15] The press had had a field day on Randolph's arrest, gloating over the "Learned Pundit's" predicament and commenting vaguely on the "most free and easy character" of some of his books on love,[16] but in typical fashion, his release was deemed less newsworthy. Randolph then rushed to press with yet another book, *Paschal Beverly Randolph, the "Learned Pundit," and "Man with Two Souls," His Curious Life, Works and Career. The Great Free-Love Trial.*[17] The book was out by early May and widely advertised in a lurid fashion. It is almost entirely a pot boiler, a compilation of favorable notices of Randolph's books, speeches, and lectures, with a rehash of his grievances against Bay, French, Churchill, and Mert La Hue, but it is also the only one of Randolph's books even to attempt a biography, though the result is scarcely coherent. Essentially, the book is a pathetic plea to the public ("Reader, do your part!"),[18] and Randolph does not spare the pathos. He had striven, he says, for twenty-two years to accumulate eight-hundred-dollars so that he might leave his poor crippled daughter provided for after his death, and now he was penniless.[19]

To us, who have grown up in the age then only just inaugurated by the Civil War amendments to the United States Constitution and confident in the freedom of the press, Randolph's arrest must appear trivial—two nights in a jail and invaluable free publicity. Things were considerably different at the time, however. Victoria Woodhull was to spend more than a month in jail in Boston later the same year for advocating her free-love theories, and the next year was to witness the first serious federal obscenity statute and the beginning of the forty-year reign of terror of crusader Anthony Comstock, who jailed for long terms a variety of spiritualist marriage reformers whose ideas were considerably more pedestrian than Randolph's.[20]

The machinations of French, Bay, La Hue, and others, while they left Randolph penniless, at least gave him the chance to consider his stance vis-à-vis the shifting phenomenon of free love. The problem, like a will-o'-the-wisp had floated at the margins of his thought for twenty years, and the aura of "free-lovism" had haunted him during the same period. Even though the charge that had led to his arrest had technically been obscenity, the term as then used was broad enough to cover material thought to incite others to immorality, free love, and even the practice of birth control. Randolph took the opportunity presented, and part 3 of his *Curious Life* was devoted to a discussion of free love in the guise of the impassioned closing arguments of a mock court trial supposedly convened to ban and suppress Randolph's books on love, especially *Casca Llanna*.[21] The trial was said to have taken place before a jury composed of individuals from all the major nationalities and religions of the world, and the closing arguments were three sided—in addition to Randolph and the prosecutor, a free-love advocate was allowed to address the jury. All this should have alerted readers to the fact that the trial was a literary fiction, a set piece, but it apparently did not, and the Great Free Love Trial in Boston has become a staple of Randolph's biography.[22]

In the debate, the prosecutor provided the comic relief (and indirect compliments) by calling Randolph "the most dangerous man and author on the soil of America" and by questioning what women might do if once they learned what love was really all about. He warned that "if a Randolphite happens to get her eye on you, the game's up—and you are lost," and adds for good measure that if Randolph's ideas prevailed, we would be "plunged neck-deep in the resistless torrent of a social revolution and domestic cataclysm, wherein men must take back seats and universal woman come to the front."[23] The free-love advocate's arguments for untrammeled "Individual Sovereignty"—but of course not licentiousness, which was anathema to New England reformers—were obviously more familiar to Randolph, and he does them fair rhetorical justice, but his own "speech" of course carries the day. It was clearly intended to convey conviction and sincerity, and in fact it does. It is Randolph's judgment on the futility and evil of free love (which he makes into a strawman and equates with unbridled licentiousness and promiscuity), not on the theoretical grounds of exhaustion and depletion that are familiar to us from his medical works, but on the basis of his twenty-years experience of the doctrine and its practical consequences. It was obviously Randolph's own way of dissociating himself from a movement that his own life had, at least externally, all too closely paralleled.

Randolph admitted that he had "loved, not too wisely but too muchly" and that he "knew what wild oats were and had in his early days sowed a few," but he denied ever believing in the free-love doctrine.[24] This, of course, was not technically true, since he had been involved with John Murray Spear, Andrew Jackson Davis, and others of that ilk in the early and mid-1850s, but Randolph probably felt that his denial was justified by a definition of free love that limited it to a soulless pursuit of sensuality for its own sake, without pity, regard, or concern. The examples he gives of such free lovers seem always to be the itinerant proselytizers of the caliber of the "J-m-s-n" who debauched his wife in Chicago. These men, in Randolph's version, went about cynically ruining unwary women by subtly convincing them that their husband's "magnetism" was somehow harmful to them (but could be neutralized by the preacher's sharing of his more balanced magnetism) or that their own depleted energy could be replenished, as a special favor, from the rascal's own overflowing reservoir of vital fluid.[25] Whatever Randolph was, he was never cynical, and by this definition had indeed probably never been guilty of free love.

Randolph is at his most realistic (and most humorous) in examining the actual practice of free love as he had seen it over the years. "In twenty years I have seen as many thousands of free-lovers and 'passional attractionists,' but have yet to see the first woman made happy by or through either, if she practised the doctrine, [nor] have I ever seen one made joyous by the knowledge that her husband was sustaining such relations beyond her own homeside."[26] He pointed out the hidden corollaries in the affinity system that had usually prevented an indigent free lover's becoming the affinity object of a good-looking woman, and that had somehow restricted the affinities of free-love prophets and mages exclusively to such women.

> On the other hand, the he free-lover never discovers his heart's best feelings touched by the charms of Madame of thirty-five or forty; but the scales drop quickly from eyes, and his bump of affinity-discovery becomes suddenly developed when a buxom damsel, with lithe form and tripping gait, crosses his path, and then, ah! *then*, he sighs and ogles and talks lofty transcendentalisms, as he begins to weave his infernal web about her.[27]

Randolph's portrait of the aging female reformer or male sexual mage of the era is both accurate and chilling. Wherever free-love doctrines prevail, he says,

there you will find either a worn-out debauchee, a freedom-shriek-
ing woman of faded charms, sharp voice, rapid tongue, overplus
of brain, paucity of soul, little passion and less love; or brainy
men, actually heartless unemotive, spasmodically lecherous, bent
on world-saving, themselves wholly lost, vapid . . . unreliable,
strangers to generous mankind or manly feeling, devoted to
an ism; people of a clique or ring, loud-mouthed, sour-souled
brawlers for liberty to infract every social and moral law, bitter
propagandists, unreasoning zealots, criers down of "bigotry,"
themselves the most ultra and one-sided bigots who breathe; —
usurpers of divine right, claiming the right to demoralize the
world, yet denying that of any man to kick them downstairs for
poisoning the mind of his wife or daughters![28]

In distinguishing himself from the strawman he had made of free
love, Randolph avoided the real issue presented by the free-love
movement of the time: the nature and permanence of marriage and
the right of the state to prohibit the dissolution of marriage. His own
life was perhaps the best indicator of his views, but in his writings he
usually glossed over the issue, emphasizing that true love could be
rekindled in any marriage by his teachings on love. In the end, he
opted for allowing divorce[29]—a position that had real consequences
for his occult theories of sexual magic. On the occult level, the question raised was the existence of the "eternal affinities" proposed by the
more mystical of the free lovers. Randolph had all of the prerequisites
for adopting this view in his doctrine that monads proceeded from
God originally in pairs, male and female—precisely the foundation
upon which the H.B. of L. was later to build its mature sexual magic.
Randolph, however, could not agree: affinities there were, but they
were not eternal. Souls progressed at different rates, and one's affinity
here might not continue to be so in the soul world. Even though
Randolph always believed that the divine paired monads always retained a feeling and attraction for each other, these sentiments did not
constitute real "Eternal Affinity."[30]

Randolph probably spent the summer and early fall of 1872 simply
trying to piece his life back together again. His novel *Dhoula Bel*, which
he had announced for publication in March 1872 never appeared. It is
a real loss, because, from the published synopsis, its early chapters
were biographical. Except for *Curious Life* his only other publication
that year was the pamphlet *The Golden Secret*. He had requested correspondence on a manuscript of that name for years, touting it as
teaching the secrets of the "esoteric love-life of the race"[31] and hinting
that it was fairly graphic: "At this point there arises a thought which,

while of inestimable value to all who are subjects of affection, cannot well be printed in this book, not because of immodesty, but because the masses yet labor under many false impressions." The thought was "the most transcendently valuable ever given on the esoteric love-life of the race," and was expressly for disappointed married people. This was announced for publication in April 1872,[32] but, as printed, the pamphlet is mild indeed, a rehash of his already published ideas on happy marriage.

The Great Boston Fire and Toledo

On November 9 and 10, 1872, a large part of the center of Boston was destroyed by fire. Randolph lost everything he had managed to build up over the years, and escaped only with his copyrights and some of the plates for his books and with what was left of his reputation.

With the Boston fire, many occult dreams besides Randolph's came to an end. Emma Hardinge Britten's journal, *The Western Star*, which she had begun to publish in Boston in July 1872 and in which she had been publishing the reminiscences of the adept she later called Louis (later published as *Ghost Land*) was forced to close.[33]

After the Boston fire, Randolph apparently took up the offer of an unnamed man to live at Massillon, Ohio, but the move did not work out. "[F]inding I would not instruct him how to be a greater scoundrel than Nature made him, or God intended, [he] perjured what soul he had, and thereby extorted all I had saved from the fiery wreck two months before."[34] By early spring 1873, he had moved to Toledo, Ohio— "of necessity," he says—and lacking other employment, gave himself up to a case study "of the workings of the organic law of sex, as displayed in the products of marriages, . . . at periods varying from fifteen to sixty-five years anterior to 1873."[35] Toledo at the time was a hotbed of radical ideas—which may have been what attracted Randolph in the first place—and he must have felt at home immediately. By 1874, he had settled down in the old routine. The *Toledo Directory* for 1874-75 lists him as a physician and publisher, living on Vance Street, where he had also established a Protozone Works and Laboratory for the manufacture and sale of protozone and his other elixirs.[36]

In May 1873 Randolph suffered a serious injury that left his left arm and side partially paralyzed. Apparently, while walking over a railroad trestle in Toledo—one has to suspect that he was intoxicated—he found himself between "two converging locomotives, one behind and one before," and fell twenty-five feet to the ground.[37] He says that he might have overcome the accident but for the fact that he "was also subjected daily to violent and continued affectional and mental emotion; cause: 'A woman at the bottom of it;' and that sort of excitement is quite sufficient to bring on paralysis, without the help of any locomotive"[38] After the accident he was cared for by two men of Toledo identified only as "A. W." and "E. D. M." Though paralyzed, he was still able to perform in spiritualist circles.

[F]or while wholly unable to talk of his own power, he repeatedly sunk into the absolute trance, and gave forth wisdom-talks of surpassing interest, and also developed a phase of mediumship seldom equaled, never surpassed, for repeatedly, in broad daylight, were spirits visible, and tangibly present in his room, so tangibly, that one gentleman at his door declared he heard what seemed to be twenty voices talking with him, but when he entered, none but the invalid was in the room.[39]

One of the results of the accident was his meeting with a young woman, Kate Corson, who formed part of a "circle for manifestations" with Randolph and who, by "conglomerate mediumship" with Randolph, produced the revelations contained in his work *The New Mola*, published late in 1873.[40] In the Toledo circle, "seven persons sitting in twilight, the mediums being a lady and a gentleman, a phantom hand moved through the air, across the table, pulled at a gentleman's beard, and faded away in dim phosphoric vapor. In presence of the same couple the most magnificent spiritual pyrotechnics frequently occur, and *thousands* of electric scintillas dance mazy waltzes about the room, and anon broadening out into sheets of living vapor, irradiated the room with pearly light."[41] After such an introduction, Randolph was soon intimately, though ambivalently, involved with Ms. Corson.

Kate Corson was nineteen when Randolph first met her.[42] Despite her age she was already both a good businesswoman and a powerful medium and perhaps a mirror-seer. As Kate Corson and Company, she was the publisher of Randolph's *The New Mola* and also owned the rights to the book until Randolph found the money to buy them back.[43] Randolph's relationship with Kate Corson was always troubled at best, and was complicated as we shall see by his fits of jealousy. At some point, apparently, Randolph wed Kate Corson, though there is no record of the marriage in the Toledo records. Perhaps they were married in Indiana, where she was born; perhaps they merely considered themselves married (after all, Randolph still had a "widow"—

Plate 2. Kate Corson Randolph *(Reprinted by permission of the Toledo-Lucas County Public Library)*

Mary Jane—living in Utica, and may have had another in Chicago). On March 30, 1874, they had a son whom Randolph called "Osiris Budh," the name that the "Rosicrucian" in *Ravalette* (1863) had given to the child of his union with the woman not born of Adam.[44]

The New Mola is largely a spiritualist pot-boiler. It contains extracts from *Seership* and a piece on "Second Youth and How to Gain It" which is by and large simply an extended advertisement for Randolph's elixirs. One novel doctrine set down in *The New Mola* for the first time but later rehearsed at length is the teaching that "ALL PEOPLE DO NOT HAVE SOULS."[45] Early in his career, in his diatribes against Andrew Jackson Davis, Randolph had condemned Davis in the bitterest terms for teaching that very doctrine, but by 1873 Randolph had come to accept the idea that immortality was conditional, something to be achieved by effort rather than an inherent attribute of human nature.[46] The book also describes the dangers of what Randolph calls "Mixed Identities" or "Atrilism," which is surely another term for the extremes of what he had earlier spoken of as "Blending"—the process whereby a celestial or an embodied human took over or co-existed with a subject, sometimes for weeks or months on end. The discussion obviously owed a great deal to Randolph's perception of his own situation.[47]

Last Visit to Europe

One of the dedicatees of *Eulis*, published in the summer of 1874, is a certain "E. A. Perceval, Jr.," about whom nothing more is said. *The Ghostly Land*, written at the end of the same year as a supplement to *Eulis* and *The New Mola* (1873) is also dedicated to him, with more particulars: "To Earnest Augustus Viscompte de Percévéle, Lord of Ulma." The introduction to *The Ghostly Land* shows that Randolph had found a European patron in Perceval and that this mysterious personage had underwritten the publication of *Eulis*, but nothing more is said about how Randolph cultivated Perceval, what the original connection was or what Perceval's interest may have been.[48]

It is clear from *The Ghostly Land* that, either in 1873 or at some point between the sending of *Eulis* to the printer in July 1874 and his departure for California in late October or early November, Randolph had again visited Europe, where he walked with Perceval through the woods around Antwerp.[49] The visit, otherwise insignificant, is important nonetheless not only because it gives some reason to believe in Randolph's continuing connection with Europe but also because—perhaps by mere coincidence—it places Randolph in Europe at a time near the mythological origin of the H. B. of L. According to the H. B. of L.'s official history:

> [I]n 1870 . . . an Adept of the still existing ancient Order of the original H. B. of L., with the permission of his Brother Initiates resolved to select in Great Britain a neophyte who would serve his purpose.
>
> After executing a private and important mission upon the *continent of Europe*, he landed in Britain in 1873, and eventually discovered a neophyte who satisfied his wishes, and, after having adequately proved and verified the authenticity of his credentials, he gradually instructed the neophyte.[50]

Peter Davidson, the provincial grand master of the north of the H. B. of L., was most likely the British neophyte in question, and he in turn always traced his own introduction to the H. B. of L. and his initiation into it to the early 1870s.[51] The Rev. William Alexander Ayton, after his disillusionment with the H. B. of L. in the spring of 1886, speculated that Davidson's reference to having been initiated fourteen years before "probably alludes to some kind of Initiation by Randolph when in England. He is not the only one whom Randolph pretended to initiate."[52] While the dates do not totally agree, Randolph's last trip to Europe in 1873 or 1874 at least provides some slight support for Ayton's surmise and an immediate source for the introduction of Randolph's teachings on sexual magic into the H. B. of L.[53]

The Revelation of Sexual Magic

Randolph was always preoccupied with his ill health, but the railroad accident in May 1873 focused his mind on the immanence of death and the necessity of providing for his crippled daughter and perpetuating his thought and work.

To ensure that his "improved Protogene" would continue to aid people after his death, in the summer of 1873 he offered to sell doctors the formula for the elixir and the right to use his circulars—all for $300 for any one state, more for the Union as a whole, and less for counties or cities. With the recipe he offered to include "certain peculiar and special instructions to be had nowhere else on earth."[54] In apparently increasing desperation, he finally offered to sell for $13,500—his estimate of the cost of the stereotype plates and his laboratory expenses for experimentation—a one-half interest in his entire life's work: the right to sell any of his books and to manufacture and sell any of his elixirs.[55]

Most importantly, with the fear of approaching death, Randolph began for the first time to print or publish parts of the works he had for so long distributed only by private letter.

> Before closing my literary career, I propose to reveal the secret of the Ansaireh Priesthood of Syria. I do not believe it can possibly be used for evil purposes; but this I *know*: There *is* a moment, frequently recurring, wherein men and women can call down to them celestial—almost awful—powers from the Spaces, thereby being wholly able to reach the souls of others, and hold them fast in the bonds of a love unknown as yet in this cold land of ours. Would to God every husband and wife on earth would use it; then, indeed, were this a far more blessed life to lead. I do not give Spencer Hardy's translation of the mystery, for he lost his life before he got it all, in Cairo, Egypt, I think from Nusairetic poison, because he was about to expose this and other mysteries of the Syrian mountaineers. But I give my own translation, and know it to be perfect and complete. It must be written in the nature of a private letter, or not at all, and only be sent at special request. Since the "New Mola" was sent to press I concluded to print the private information alluded to herein, embracing "Love and its Hidden Mystery," the "Physician's Legacy," being the above "Private Information," and also "The True Oriental Secret." But in addition to *both* the above, (*when specially requested at the time of purchase*—price $5), "The Ansaireh Secret" will be clearly, fully written and sent. It is not possible for me to remain much longer on the earth.[56]

There had been a kaleidoscopic variety of such private manuscript teachings, some going back to the late 1850s: "The Golden Secret," "The Golden Letter," "Love and its Hidden Mystery, being the True Oriental Secret, or, the Laws of Human Love Revealed," "The Physician's Legacy (Asgill's Rules)," and the "Grand Secret."[57] Some of these manuscripts dealt generally with the more intimate details of Randolph's theories of marital happiness and with the abandoned idea of karezza; some dealt with the "Maternal Defense" to prevent conception or abortion and the methods for begetting superior children; and some, undoubtedly, dealt with the secrets of sexual magic—the material set forth in "The Ansaireh Secret," first mentioned in *The New Mola*.

The "Golden Secret," which had been the precipitating cause of the Great Free Love Trial, circulated as a manuscript for years before a version of it appeared as a pamphlet in 1872, even before the Toledo train accident and Randolph's decision to reveal his secrets. At least as published, however, it is merely a list of platitudes on how to prolong life (with mortality tables to tell how long the user is likely to live); how to increase vitality; how to cure female ulcerations; how sweet meats generate morbid passions; and endless lists of proper foods to eat. The material published in *The New Mola* was more serious. In an appendix entitled "A Physician's Legacy to Mankind—Asgill's Rules," Randolph in the summer of 1873 printed for the first time parts of "Love and Its Hidden Mystery, the Physician's Legacy" and also "The True Oriental Secret."[58] These also were Bowdlerized for publication, but indicate the sequence of Randolph's teachings. "Asgill's Rules" (Asgill is variously a French physician who taught the cowardice of dying and a spirit who imparted the same message) consist of twenty-eight numbered paragraphs that reiterate the brutality and "pigness" of men in general, the evil of abortion, and the other sentiments of Randolph's general exoteric teachings on love. After point 8, however, Randolph begins to give "The Ansairetic Mysteries":

> We are triplicate beings—soul, spirit, body. Our loves and passions may be of either one, two or all three of these. . . . The marital office and function is therefore *material, spiritual* and MYSTIC. . . . The Ansairetic secret doctrines only contain it, for they alone establish the fact that the marital function is unquestionably the highest, holiest, most important, and most wretchedly abused of all that pertains to the human being.[59]

There follow further platitudes on sex with frequent Oriental allusions to Allah and "giours," all obviously designed as teasers for the note that follows point 16: "[Note: At this state the *esoteric points* of the mysteries come in. They are *never* printed, but are written to such as need and will properly observe them. The fee for writing them out will in no case be less or more than $5."[60]

These handwritten portions of Randolph's private teachings are the "Ansaireh Secret"—or the *Ansairetic Mystery* as they finally came to be called when printed—the revelation of Randolph's fully matured sexual magic.

Chapter 10

THE COMING
OF THE NUSA'IRI

The Nusa'iri

The Nusa'iri or Ansaireh or Ansayree (the latter spellings representing the elision of the definite article with the initial N) are a nominally Muslim group living today, as they have for the thousand years that history has taken note of them, in isolated areas in the mountains of northwest Syria above Latakia and in pockets in Palestine, Kurdistan, Egypt, and Iran.[1] Like the Druses and the Isma'ilis with whom they were frequently confused by European and Near Eastern historians alike and with whom the Nusa'iris have fought for a thousand years—a struggle over theological niceties that has masked the fundamental areas of agreement among them—the Nusa'iris are extreme emanationists, with an elaborate theology of the progressive descent of the divine into manifestation and history and the reascent of man to the divine light. Although there are certain similarities between Randolph's ideas and the systems of the Nusa'iri, the similarities appear to have depended on travelers' tales and Randolph's reading, and for our purposes the Nusa'iris (again, like the Druses and Isma'ilis) are notable, not so much for what they actually are, but more for what they were accused of being by travelers and their enemies and thought to be by occultists. What has mainly set the Nusa'iris apart and made them the object of persecution and massacre by more orthodox Muslims and by Druses, Isma'ilis, and Crusaders alike is the belief that they practiced the pagan and Gnostic sexual rites of antiquity.

The Nusa'iri first came to the attention of the western world in the late eighteenth century through the travel books of Carsten Niebuhr and C. F. Volney.[2] Volney, who traveled in Syria from 1783 through

1785, was one of the first modern anthropologists, working systematically from a detailed questionnaire. As a contemporary of Voltaire he had a very low estimation of human nature and considered the tales he heard of "bizarre cults" among the Nusa'iri quite possibly true, although Niebuhr had rejected them on the ground that no humans could be so degraded. Volney reported a wide divergence of belief and practice among the Nusa'iri, some believing in metempsychosis, some denying the immortality of the soul, some (on the road from Alexandretta to Aleppo, he specified for the benefit of later travelers) offering their wives and daughters to travelers for a few coins,[3] and some (the Qadmousié) giving their veneration to "the organ which in women corresponds to Priapus," a quaint turn of phrase which appears over and over in the later literature. Volney was told that these Qadmousié in their nocturnal assemblies had certain readings, then extinguished the lights and had sexual intercourse indiscriminately with all present "like the ancient Gnostics."[4] These rights were secret and restricted to Nusa'iris alone. Volney dutifully noted that he had only been told this but did not know it firsthand.

The great Orientalist Baron Antoine-Sylvestre de Sacy next took up the Nusa'iris. In his *Exposé de la Religion des Druses* (1838), he devoted a long chapter to the Nusa'iris as described in an early diatribe against them by Hamza, the prophet of the Druses. Hamza had said that he had come across a book by one of the Nusa'iris that was full of such obscene ideas that he was forced to refute it, but in actuality Hamza's vehemence was probably engendered more by the fact that the doctrines of the two groups were largely identical and the sexual imagery used by the Druses to describe mystical matters was constantly tending to a physical rather than a merely metaphorical interpretation. Charges of religious libertinism had been made against the Druses, with some justification, from the very beginning.[5] Hamza reported the usual stories of the depravity of the Nusa'iri, but also gave the theological explanation of the Nusa'iri for their practices: spiritual union is only perfectly accomplished through carnal union.[6] De Sacy also convinced a century of historians that the Isma'ili Assassins derived their name from their use of hashish to create the artificial paradise of the Old Man of the Mountain.[7]

In the 1840s, the French poet and occultist Gérard de Nerval traveled in the Levant and took along with him his belief that the Druses and Nusa'iri had been responsible for the revival of occultism (and the birth of Freemasonry) through their influence on the Knights Templar and accordingly lay at the root of the power of such later mages as Cagliostro.[8] On his trip he was told by the son of the English consul in Tripoli, who had married a Nusa'iri woman and learned a great deal about their secrets, that the Nusa'iri had a ceremony "like a mass" in which a priest worshipped a naked woman on a table, and that on certain days the men embraced and prostrated themselves before every woman they met.[9] Nerval also repeated the universal story that at the rising of Venus at the beginning of the year the Nusa'iri women and the "akhales"—the fully initiated Nusa'iri, according to him— entered one by one into a square, domed chapel and then extinguished the lights. Nerval commented, "I leave to you what happened then," but he goes on to quote the remark of another Frenchman who had managed to partake in the ceremony: "It was like a marriage done with the eyes closed."[10]

In all of this, there was (and is) considerable difference of opinion about exactly who and what the Nusa'iris were and about the source of their curious ideas and practices. The orthodox Muslim controversialists in the eleventh and twelfth centuries derived Nusa'iri from "Nasrani" ("little Christian") and thought them vestiges of the ancient Gnostics.[11] In Volney's opinion, the Nusa'iris were the lingering remnants of the ancient pagan cult of Venus. The Orientalist and secret-society fanatic Joseph von Hammer-Purgstall thought that the Knights Templar (and the Freemasons) derived their doctrines and practices from the Isma'ili Assassins, who in turn had them from the ancient Gnostics.[12] Godfrey Higgins in his *Celtic Druids* (1829) identified the Druses with the Druids, and in his wonderful *Anacalypsis* (1833–36) followed von Hammer in coming to the conclusion that the Isma'ili Assassins had derived their secret phallic mysteries from the Druses and the Nusa'iri (or Mandaits or Yezidis, as he also called them) and in turn had passed them on to the Templars, Freemasons, and Rosicrucians.[13] In the 1850s, Lieutenant Frederick Walpole, reiterated the identification of the Nusa'iri with the Isma'ilis and Assassins,[14] and in the 1860s John P. Brown, in writing on *The Darvishes or Oriental Spiritualism*, followed de Gobineau in believing that the Nusa'iri were the same as the Kurdish *Ahl al-Haqq*.[15] In Chwolson's view as in the more modern and scholarly views of Dussaud and E. G. Browne, the Nusa'iri were simply the remnants of ancient Near Eastern paganism, identical with the "Nazerini" mentioned by Pliny (*Historia Naturalis* 5.81), who had successively assumed the protective coloring of Christianity and Islam in order to survive. Browne hazarded the guess that their ritual was derived from that of the Sabaeans and the Mandaeans and from the old mysteries of Asia.[16] Hasluck repeated the claim of "perverted masses" with the lights extinguished and believed that Nusa'iri religion was identical with the teachings of the Kizilbash (Red

Head) Shi'i and with the doctrines of the Bektashi dervishes.[17] On the more occult front, Laurence Oliphant, after his years of servitude with Randolph's old acquaintance, the sexual mage Thomas Lake Harris, opined on the esoteric value of the system concealed by the theology of the Druses and the Nusa'iri.[18] Emma Hardinge Britten used the marvels they performed as an example of the powers obtainable with modern "Spiritism,"[19] and other daring souls have sought to find in the Nusa'iri the origins of the secrets of the Cathars and of Gurdjieff's supposed sexual magic.[20]

To a large extent this creation of genealogies was guesswork, but it rested upon the universal human desire to explain the unknown by the known, and for many of the scholars and occultists of the nineteenth century it was a self-evident fact that under the myriad guises of old mythologies and symbols there lay a substructure of universal phallicism, the "worship of the generative powers," which was intimately connected with the "mystic theology of the ancients."[21] Much of this phallic conviction in the nineteenth century was of the simple antiquarian variety—a fascination with chronicling the odd details of sexual worship of the ancients—but there was also a perception that in the preserved fragments of antique sexual lore (especially in the heresiologists' descriptions of the Gnostics) there lay a forgotten key to spiritual progress, a practical method of developing the hidden powers in man.[22] The ability to properly understand and to use this key, it was reasoned in turn, must lie in the mysterious East where isolated sects had preserved intact the spiritual practices of antiquity. This was the real fascination of the Druses and the Nusa'iri for the nineteenth-century occultists. They were the living link with the practical wisdom of the past.[23]

More modern scholarship, primarily based on the work of Louis Massignon, while acknowledging the debt of the Druses, Nusa'iri and Isma'ilis generally to Gnosticism (especially Valentinian and Bardesanian Gnosticism) and to Manicheism and earlier classical and Persian ideas, has come to see the Nusa'iris and Druses as offshoots of twelfth-century Fatamid Isma'ilism and has more mediately found their common source in the ideas of the Ghulat (the "Exaggerators") of the late seventh century and early eighth century. These radical Shi'i groups, mainly non-Arab, who were universally viewed by the more orthodox as antinomian and libertine, were given over to wild speculation about the divinity of 'Ali and his place in the progressive emanations of God, and about metempsychosis, cosmic intermediaries, and cyclical history.[24]

A fair summary of Nusa'iri doctrine as it was understood in Randolph's time and which has stood the test of later scholarship appeared in the *Journal of American Oriental Society* in 1866.[25] It was a long translation of what purported to be the "confession" of a Nusa'iri renegade, translated by a Christian missionary in Beirut. According to this, the real mysteries of the Nusa'iri were secret, never revealed to women or foreigners and only gradually revealed to adult Nusa'iri in a rite of initiation patterned on adoption. The mysteries centered on the progressive emanations of the divine from the archetypal deity ('Ali), to the expressed deity (Mohammed), to the communicator (Sulman al Farsi), and then down through the vast hierarchies of orders and angels to men. Men were fundamentally particles of light, originally wandering stars but now trapped in bodies. They fell because in their pride they thought themselves equal to 'Ali's splendor, and then fell again, into matter and sexual differentiation where they were doomed to transmigrate from body to body until restored to their celestial origin. The goal set for the Nusa'iri was salvation from further (and lower) transformations through recognition of 'Ali. Time was viewed as the cyclical succession of æons, and in each æon 'Ali manifested himself and created his "Name," who in turn created the "Bab"—the "Gate" or "Door"—the most exoteric approach to the mystery. In earlier ages Adam, Noah, Moses and Jesus had been the "Name," and in this age Salman al-Farsi, Mohammed's first non-Arab disciple, was the "Door." Permeating the Nusa'iri's confession, as the missionary admitted, was "a sensuous veil of imagery [that] almost hides from view the dogmas." The repentant Nusa'iri provided considerable information on the practice of "conjugal communion," "the indispensable requirement and incumbent duty" of every good Nusa'iri, imposed on him by the Koran and by the Rules of Life of Ja'far 'as-Sadik, who enjoined "every believer to gratify his fellow-believers as he would gratify himself," but the good missionary omitted the details of this "communion" because their "whole significance is more impure than purifying."

It was this labyrinth that Randolph entered when he announced in *The New Mola* (1873) that he would reveal the secret of the Ansaireh priesthood of Syria. He had first mentioned the Nusa'iri in *Pre-Adamite Man* (1863), when his Muslim traveling companion described the five ages of man that had passed before the coming of Adam—a reference that comports well with the doctrines of the Nusa'iri on the succession of æons.[26] In the intervening years, Randolph's published works are almost entirely silent on the Nusa'iri. He mentions the Druses once, in *Casca Llanna* (1872), where he refers to the "strange lore . . . which he learned among the Druses, and Nusaireh of Syria; the Guebres of Persia; the Arabs of the desert; the Turk in Stamboul and the swart sages of sweltering Negro-land,"[27] but that is all.

In *Eulis*, published the year after *The New Mola*, he repeats for the Nusa'iri the disclaimers he had earlier made about the Rosicrucians:

> Precisely so was it with things purporting to be Ansairetic. I had merely read Lydde's book, and got hold of a new name; and again mankind hurrahed for the wonderful Ansaireh, but incontinently turned up its nose at the supposed copyist. In proof of the truth of these statements . . . the world is challenged to find a line of my thought in the whole 4,000 books on Rosicrucianism . . . or in the Ansairetic works, English, German, Syriac or Arabic.[28]

These disclaimers probably reflect the ultimate reality of Randolph's relations with the Nusa'iri, who were a closed sect, scarcely available to the casual traveler, but at the same time they must be discounted by his overwhelming desire to demonstrate the originality of his system. Randolph had certainly moved in the shifting milieu of Near Eastern Gnostics, dervishes, sufis, and occultists in his travels and had undoubtedly encountered the Nusa'iri and heard tales of them,[29] but any claim that he was indebted to them in any systematic way for any substantial part of his ideas, especially his ideas on sexual magic, is simply speculation, as much because of the lack of specifics in Randolph's works as because of our lack of real information on the details of actual Nusa'iri practice. Aside from the occasional term ("bab," gate or door, for example), Randolph shared with the Nusa'iri as we know them from scholarship only some general notions of the succession of historical ages, the idea of the transmigration of the soul, possibly the spiritual use of hashish, and the underlying, fundamental doctrine of a role for sexuality in spiritual development, nothing more. Moreover, none of these similarities, is at all specific to the Nusa'iri. They are all simply part of the koiné of Near and Middle Eastern esotericism.[30]

A more rewarding (though less specific) approach to Randolph's Oriental antecedents is given by Randolph himself in a passage in *Eulis* which (with the exception of the claim to have become chief) has the ring of authenticity.

> One night—it was in far-off Jerusalem or Bethlehem, I really forget which—I made love to, and was loved by, a dusky maiden of Arabic blood. I of her, and that experience, learned—not directly, but by suggestion—the fundamental principle of the White Magic of Love; subsequently I became affiliated with some dervishes and fakirs of whom, by suggestion, still, I found the road

to other knowledges; and of these devout practicers of a simple, but sublime and holy magic, I obtained additional clues—little threads of suggestion, which, persistently followed, led my soul into labyrinths of knowledge themselves did not even suspect the existence of. I became practically, what I was naturally—a mystic, and in time chief of the lofty brethren; taking the clues left by the masters, and pursuing them farther than they had ever been before; actually discovering the ELIXIR OF LIFE; the universal Solvent, or celestial Alkahest; the water of beauty and perpetual youth, and the philosopher's stone.[31]

That Nusa'iri were among these wandering fakirs and dervishes Randolph encountered seems very probable, and this conclusion is buttressed by the fact that, despite his disclaimers in *Eulis*, he dedicated the book to, among others, "Abu-Id-Durr Djundub of the Ansaireh; Othman Aswad El Kindee; [and] Her Gracious Purity, Fairooz Shirwan Afridoon." Perhaps Her Gracious Purity was the dusky maiden Randolph had encountered that magical night in Jerusalem or Bethlehem.

The Ansairetic Mystery and the Mysteries of Eulis

By late 1873 or early 1874 Randolph had prepared two works for private circulation to his students and correspondents. The first of these was *The Ansairetic Mystery. A New Revelation Concerning Sex! A Private Letter, Printed, but not Published; it being Sacred and Confidential.* The complement to this was "The Mysteries of Eulis."[32] The date of the redaction is fairly clear from references in the text and from Randolph's other works, but the actual provenance of the works is less certain. As we have seen, Randolph had from the early 1860s circulated a bewildering variety of letters, sheets, and small handwritten works on the more explicit details of his sexual teachings, and the immediate origin of both of these final revelations undoubtedly lies there, most probably in the original manuscript version of "The Golden Secret" that Randolph had circulated at least as early as 1870. The "Eulian" and "Ansairetic" guise of the teachings, however, is clearly new, a product of the 1870s.[33]

Both these works rehearse the fundamentals of Randolph's ideas on love and sex that we have already discussed: the all-pervading universal "fluid" (metaphorically love and physically Æth) that unites all levels of the universes to God; the direct participation of man's soul (the bipolar, "diamondesque" divine white fire, the "crystallization of God's nervous fluid") in the Æth through its magnetic pole located in the genitals; the accumulation of "nerve aura" and *vif* in man through proper sexuality, foods, and elixirs; the production of the marvelous mutual "lymph" at the moment of the "most fierce and intense amative passion"; and the location of power in the will (the feminine, love side of the soul) rather than in the intellect—"MEN FAIL THROUGH FEEBLENESS OF WILL!"[31] With this foundation, *The Ansairetic Mystery* proceeds to reveal the fundamental secret of Randolph's sexual magic: at the instant of intense mutual orgasm the souls of the partners are opened to the powers and energies of the cosmos, and anything then truly willed is accomplished.

> [N]o real magic (magnetic) power can, or will, descent into the soul of either, except in the mighty moment—the orgasmal instant of BOTH—not one alone! for then, and *then only*, do the mystic forces of the SOUL OPEN TO THE SPACES. . . . The eternal spark within us (and which never flashes except when the loving female brings to her feet the loving man in their mutual infiltration of Soul, in the sexive death of both—that intense moment when woman proves herself the superior of man—mutual demise!) was created by ALLAH—God himself—Billions of ages ago in the foretime, and finds its human body only when Sex-passion opens the mystic door for it to enter the man—through him, the woman, through her the world, through THEM the Spaces, and through it again Allah, God—*not* as a drop of infinite ocean of Mind, but as a Being in the Heavenly hierarchies!

* * *

> Now, Man, being the chief work of Nature; allied to all that is; being the central figure upon which all forces play; and copulative union being the crowning act of his being—it follows that his moment of greatest Power is that in which Love unlooses the doors of his Spirit, and all his energies are in highest action; whence it happens that they who unitedly *Will* a thing, during copulative union and its mutual ending, possess the key to all possible Knowledge, the mighty want of White Magic.

The details of this great revelation were deliberately omitted in *The Ansairetic Mystery*, but the fundamental truth was clearly stated. Obviously the work was intended as a lure for still further correspondence with Randolph. To ensure the interest of his readers Randolph appended a list of 122 powers and results obtainable with his white magic. Some are trivial (feminine beauty, success in business), but all are interesting and cry out for further explanation—as Randolph intended. A selection of the powers reveals their variety.

1. *Special* Power, involving exercise of the Volantia, Decretism, and Posism.

8. Tirau-clairism—ability to think clearly to a point, and *know* it.

25. To have mental dalliance with the powers of Space.

26. The three degrees of positive non-mesmeric clairvoyance.

33. To bring four powers to bear upon the formation of an unincarnated soul—Stirpiculture.

48. The Oriental Breast-Love, its principles, laws and value.

54. The secret terrifying force sent as a corrective against the erring. (Mahi-vapia).

55. To affiliate an earthly with an ethereal Love assembly.

67. To penetrate the formidable sphere of the middle Spaces (Zorvoyance).

68. To attain the road leading to the ineffable Beyond. (Æthævoyance).

71. To come *en rapport* with Oriental minds, living or dead.

100. The ability to teach and impart the same æthic power to others; comprehending the three degrees of the Persic and Hindoo Mahi-caligna, as taught the Acolytes 5000 years ago.

101. To attach to oneself innumerable æthic, ærial, invisible assistants. (Arsaphism).

It is impossible to believe that anyone interested enough to obtain the *Ansairetic Mystery* in the first place would not have requested further information from Randolph or, as we shall see, from the Brotherhood of Eulis, Randolph's last attempt to found an organization to propagate his ideas. In a further effort to arouse the interest of the public, in the early summer of 1874 Randolph published *Eulis! The History of Love: Its Wondrous Magic, Chemistry, Rules, Laws, Modes, Moods and Rationale; Being the Third Revelation of Soul and Sex*, his last major published work, which evoked in more general terms the wonders of the orgasmic moment.[35]

> LOVE LIETH AT THE FOUNDATION . . . and Love is convertibly passion; enthusiasm; affection; heat; fire; SOUL; God. . . . [T]he nuptive moment, the instant wherein the germs of a possible new being are lodged, or a portion of man's essential self is planted within the matrix, is the most solemn, serious, powerful, and energetic moment he can ever know on earth; and only to be excelled by correspondent instants after he shall have ascended to realms beyond the starry skies.[36]

At some point in 1874, Randolph wrote his private manuscript, "The Mysteries of Eulis," his ultimate and finest exposition of the sexual mysteries of the universe, intended for the use of the members of the Brotherhood of Eulis. On one level it is simply a more detailed exposition of the practical details of the first part of the *Ansairetic Mystery*—the use of the will in conjunction with mutual orgasm to achieve specific goals—but on a deeper level "The Mysteries of Eulis" explores the mysteries of communication with the "Centers, Orbits, Spheres, Potencies, Hierarchies and Brotherhoods" of the universes.

On a practical level, Randolph sets forth the three fundamental laws of all magic: volantia, decretism and posism. Each of these in various guises and under various names had formed a part of Randolph's thinking since the early 1860s, but in the "Mysteries of Eulis" he defined them clearly for the first time.[37] "Volantia," which is simply the formal statement of Randolph's motto from the earliest days ("Try!"), is "the quiet, steady, calm, non-turbulent, non-muscular exertion of the human *Will*," the product of Power rather than Force.[38] This power, with its three constituent principles of attention, concentration, and abstraction, could be developed by staring at a wafer placed on a magic mirror or at a black spot hung on the wall, and then compelling and controlling the resulting phantoms and shadows.[39] This ability to control the shifting images of the mind was "Tirau-clairism": the ability "to think clearly to a point, and *know* it" and "to use the will to bring any image, flash, spark or scintilla before you and never take the mind's eye from it." It was both the prerequisite of the exercise of volantia (the formulation of the object desired) and a means of direct knowledge.[40]

"Decretism," as its name implies, is the "decreeing, ordering, commanding" power of the developed will. At the *decretal instant*—which in many but not all cases coincided with the moment of mutual orgasm of the partners—this ordaining power "leaps from the soul like a flash of vivid white lightning, traversing space, centering on its object even though oceans flow between, or vast spaces divide" and accomplishes the clearly formulated object or goal. It was this power, exercised through the magic mirror, that Randolph had taught over the years as the means of reclaiming dallying lovers, of punishing those who stole them, and of preventing unwanted births.

"Posism" is the most important of the three powers and the most difficult to obtain. It is the "placing [of] oneself in a *receptive* position, state, frame of body, mind and feeling," the equivalent of bracing oneself before trying to lift a heavy load or cowering before a threatened blow. The simplest example of the exercise of this power was Randolph's conviction that a wronged wife could call up the image of the "other woman" in the mirror and, in the "pose" of hate, repel her and drive her away from her lover.[41] On a deeper level, posism and receptivity were the prerequisites for fruitful commerce with the hierarchies of the universes—room had to be provided in the brain or soul "for the expected or hoped for new tenant, and the entire attention of the soul be withdrawn and vacated except for that special thing, gift, energy, quality, power, then sought." For Randolph, any conceivable quality, power, or knowledge had "a Hierarchy, Society, Brotherhood or nation in the Spaces and the Vault, who cultivate[s] that specialty as a positive science," and on a preliminary level posism (by itself, without the other principles) allowed the user who clearly defined his or her goal to communicate with any of these at will, as it also allowed him or her to contact the mind of any person, living or dead.

As an adjunct to these three principles, Randolph taught the power of slow, regular breathing, with the "inhalations and out-breaths . . . of equal length." Normal breathing extracted from the air only the *vif*, the chemicals necessary to sustain life, but this slow respiration sifted the air and extracted and stored the "Magneto-electrical-Ethereal" fluids which alone give the soul the "ascensive ability" necessary for the "sacred sleep of Sialam" in which the soul "bids defiance to all the barriers which, awake or asleep, or in the mesmeric states, limit and bound it . . . [and] reach infinite altitudes, and sweep with masterly vision the amazing rain of stellar galaxies falling down the Deep!"[42]

These marvelous principles, together or in isolation, and sometimes in conjunction with the magic mirror which was an essential part of these mysteries,[43] allowed the user to attain all of the powers and virtues listed in the *Ansairetic Mystery*. They underlay the powers of "Projection" (the "sending, forcing, compelling of your image, wraith, spirit, soul, phantom or simulacrum to, and wherever you *will*") and

"Attraction" (the ability to call into the mirror the entities of the "middle Spaces" (zorvoyance) and of the "ineffable Beyond" (æthævoyance).

Beyond these more straightforward applications of Randolph's three principles there lay still greater mysteries connected with inner breathing, the sleep of Sialam and the awful celestial powers.

> [S]omewhere in this universe, there is a great central, Intelligent Power, Presence and energy, who *necessarily* knows all that was, is, and is to be. This central power must be environed by colossal mental energies or Potentialities in knowledge only second to Its Supreme self: Nor do I conceive such Potencies to be ascended human beings who once dwelt in flesh-and-blood bodies, lived, died and rose again—but I mean that there are Electrical, Ethereal, non-material Universes beyond the matter-Island floating like eggshell scallops on the breeze of the azure sea. . . . [T]here are hierarchies—armies of them! Potencies, Powers, vast Intelligences . . . before whose awful grasp of mental powers, before whose amazing sweep of mind, the grandest intellect earth ever did or can produce, is as a pebble to a mountain range. . . . These beings may be the arbiters of the destinies of worlds; and I believe that they are the originators of many a drama of fruitful good.

* * *

It behooves me now to call your attention to the most tremendous of all the powers of the human soul: It is the purely spiritual, non-material, or Æthic power of the interior man . . . [whose] sphere of action pertains to higher and better states than this of earth. . . .

The term Æth signifies that fine essence which spirits breathe . . . which cushions the worlds . . . ; it is inhaled by Æthereal people precisely as we of earth draw in the effluence of matter in its grosser and lower forms. No real, divine, or celestial, mental or loving energy can come until by patient and continued effort the Neophyte learns to inhale it; simultaneously with the firm fixity of the mind upon what is in and of it, therefore we contact the essence of power and the denizens of the ethereal and far-off countries and climes. ("The Mysteries of Eulis," appendix C)

These mighty powers were "the Neridii" who could not be contacted in seances or through mesmerism, but only in the "sleep of

Sialam induced by mirror gazing; or through the mirror itself." Beyond this simple statement, however, lurked a greater mystery, a sexual one that also provided the key to the procreation of superior children.

In "The Mysteries of Eulis," Randolph was reticent about the subject and said that he was withholding information on "certain sexive applications" and "a peculiar rite." The omitted secrets, however, can perhaps be supplied from his other works. In the *Ansairetic Mystery* and elsewhere Randolph had taught that "Soul-seeds (Atomonads)" dwelt in the "Æther and the Sakwalas or Spiritual Spheres," and that in those spheres also existed the germs of all knowledge and power, embodied in the Powers of the Celestial Hierarchies. The highest form of intercourse with all of these occurred during the moment of intense mutual orgasm, in which the soul "breathed in" the celestial entities.

> None of these [powers] spring up from within us, but all are reachable by us, and flow into us in our highest moments; and all or any knowledge or power the human being has a brain capable of holding can be drawn to it, if willed, wished, desired and commanded, as and when aforesaid; and it or they enter the soul *only* in the moment, at the very instant, of the holy, full, mutual and pure orgasm, or ejection of the three fluids and two auras . . . and the dual magnetism evolved.[44]

> [A]t the very instant his seminal glands contract to expel their treasures, at such instant his interior nostrils open, and minute ducts, which are sealed at all other times, then expand, and as the lightning from his soul darts from the brain, rushes down the spinal-cord, leaps the solar plexus, plunges along the nerval filaments to the prostate gland to immortalize the germinal human being; and while the vivific pulse is leaping to the dark chamber wherein soul is clothed in flesh and blood, at that instant he breathes in through the inner nostrils one of two atmospheres underlying, inter-penetrating—as the spirit does the body—the outer air which sentient things inhale. One of these auras is deeply charged with, because it is the effluvium of, the unpleasant sphere of the border spaces, where is congregated the quintessence of evil from every inhabited human world in the entire congeries of soul-bearing galaxies of the broad universe; else he draws in the pellucid aroma of divinity from the far-off multiple heavens.[45]

In other words, in the moment of sexual climax, men and women can breathe in the germs of all of the powers and knowledges of the exalted entities of the celestial hierarchy.

This drawing in of the monads from the higher reaches of the hierarchies and implanting them in the foetus in the act of generation is the secret of producing superior children and, in the H. B. of L.'s version of Randolph's sexual magic, it became the only proper exercise of this facet of his sexual magic. It was suicide to implant these seeds of power in one's own soul, and Randolph's indulging in this folly caused his own insanity and death.[46]

This contact with the hierarchies in turn also may have masked yet a further mystery. Randolph had always spoken of "Blending" in two senses: the conscious co-existence of another being (Cynthia, Thotmor) in one's soul and the sexual blending that occurred between two people in true love.[47] Although it is not clear, it is probable that the two meanings at times co-existed. Randolph had always insisted that sex continued for humans even after death (though without its reproductive side), and in "The Mysteries of Eulis" he also made it clear that sex fulfilled its higher functions even among the awful entities of the celestial hierarchies, for whom (as on earth) sex was the fundamental principle of knowledge, power, and advancement. The obvious question then (never explicitly answered by Randolph) is whether the blending with the disembodied and the never embodied was (or could be) sexual. The answer appears to be yes.

In *The Ghostly Land* (1874) Randolph pushed to the extreme the idea first discussed in *After Death* (1868), that there was nothing "ghostly" or "etherial" about spirits in the afterlife. To the contrary, the spirits enjoyed bodies every bit as solid and "physical" as our own. This conclusion then led Randolph, in a very obscure passage, to raise the issue of sexual intercourse between humans and the disembodied. He carefully avoided the conclusion, which he said had been advanced by some, that Jesus Christ was the product of such a union, but clearly adopted the position that such sexual unions do occur and that the stories of the loves of the "Sons of God" for the "daughters of men" reflect reality.[48] On a more personal level, in a bizarre letter he wrote to the *Religio-Philosophical Journal* during the Civil War, Randolph described his nightly escapades with the spirit of a deceased woman.

> Let me here relate a new phase of psychical being: A woman, to whom I am indebted to the Christian world for the loss of, has the strange power of calling me in her sleep when I, too, am asleep, and together we roam over earth, and not seldom in the world of spirits. Death has its sleep, as well as its life and wakefulness. Current opinions respecting our after life are, many of them, silly and fabulous. In the world of soul that woman sleeps,

and in that sleep woos me to her side. I instruct her, she me; yet, in my wakeful state, even when lucid, she cannot affect me in the least, nor I her, except she be asleep up there, pillowed on the breast of God. How strange that two, between whom there yawns a gulf, wide as time, deep as space, separated by a century or a creed, which is all the same, yet in the abnormal phase of life, can meet and mingle high and holy ayont the fence of flesh and passion![49]

Similarly, Randolph was familiar with the idea of the immortalization of "elementals" through sexual intercourse with humans, the doctrine that forms the centerpiece of the *Comte de Gabalis*,[50] and he must have known of or speculated about the elevating role of sexual intercourse with the higher entities or gods of the celestial hierarchy, since the doctrine is almost universal in mythology.[51] None of this, however, is explicitly discussed by Randolph in his works, but it is at least a fair conclusion that within the meaning of the term *blending* Randolph at times included the notion that the blending was sexual in nature.[52]

The quirks and abuses of such ideas are obvious. Randolph's old acquaintance Thomas Lake Harris clearly believed in his sexual union with his Lily Queen and ended up being accused by Madame Blavatsky of begetting a child with her in the spirit world,[53] and the Abbé Boullan in France in the 1880s was openly advocating the Christian duty of "celestializing" elementals through "unions of life" and of being celestialized in turn by similar unions with superior entities.[54]

Blending for Randolph, whether always sexual or not, was a complex and far-reaching concept. It constitutes the central tenet of his belief in communication with others, both with those higher in the celestial hierarchy and with those on our own plane, and the idea of blending, as we shall see, becomes, under a variety of names, the hallmark of the influence of Randolph and of the H. B. of L. Just as we can influence others at a distance by our wills and projections, so can we be influenced in turn by the hierarchies that tower over humanity.[55] On its lowest level, it was merely the exercise of will that Randolph used to attract a young woman in the story told by Meyrink, but on a more elevated level it was the highest mode of intercourse with the celestial hierarchies.

Randolph's disciples, even with the *Ansairetic Mystery* and "The Mysteries of Eulis" in hand, had few explicit details about actual sexual practice. Randolph mentions a regimen of sexual abstinence and cleanliness for forty-nine days before attempting the rite, all the while fixing the mind on the desired goal, but that is all. A great deal of information must have been reserved by Randolph for oral transmission or for communication by letter. Despite this, some details can be gleaned from other sources. We have already seen the use of the mutual lymph generated by intense sexual release to consecrate and magnetically charge magic mirrors.[36] Similarly, the "Breast-drill" mentioned by Randolph in the *Ansairetic Mystery* (no. 48) was, as we can learn from R. S. Clymer, a practice of arousing the sexual energy, either alone or with a partner, by concentrating the attention on the genital pole of the soul and attempting to transmute and redirect "the sensations of the sex functions."[57] Further details, if they are to be trusted, are supplied by Maria de Naglowska, the emigrée Russian who published *Magia Sexualis* in Paris in 1931. Most of the book consists of passages from the *Ansairetic Mystery*, "The Mysteries of Eulis," *Seership* and *The New Mola*, but de Naglowska claimed that the remainder of the work was the teachings imparted orally by Randolph to the members of the Brotherhood of Eulis. Some sections of this new material undoubtedly represent Randolph's thought (the consecration of amulets and rings, for example), but the great majority of the new material appears to have been de Naglowska's own creation or her borrowing from other sources. It smacks too much of the desire for correspondences and systems, the determining of the appropriate hour, day, color of room, zodiacal sign, and so on in which the rites were to be performed. There is little of the spontaneity of Randolph. It is also highly astrological, which in itself renders it suspect since there is scarcely a single reference to astrology in all of Randolph's works.[38] One lack in Randolph's final manuscripts that de Naglowska convincingly supplies is the role and importance of drugs in sexual magic. She prints a recipe for a frightening salve of hashish, hyoscamine, belladonna, opium, and the like that probably reflects Randolph's own practice.[39]

What then are we to make of Randolph's fully developed sexual magic? Its main characteristic appears to have been its simplicity and its pragmatism, its almost complete lack of the antiquarian elements and correspondences that had been the hallmark of nineteenth-century scholarship. The use of sex in religion and magic is truly universal in human history. Its power is obvious, and it has always been recognized and exploited by systematizers and mages, and indeed, it would scarcely be an exaggeration or a historical distortion to view most of the Western magical and occult tradition as a working out of the permutations of sexuality in symbolism and practice. The primary characteristic of almost all of this sexual approach to magic and the mysteries is the presence of a variety of mythologies of the fall and redemption of man through sex, and of a complex symbolism and

a system of correspondences that placed sexuality and all of its elements in a coherent world view in which woman and sexuality are
alternatively the cause of the imprisonment of the divine in matter
and the path to redemption from matter; the union of male and female
is but the expression on one limited level of the union of the fundamental, cosmic principles of all reality that occurs simultaneously on
all levels of creation; and sperm is the embodiment of the divine light
(to be reintegrated in the body) or is the *prima materia* necessary to
effect the alchemical transformation.[60] The nineteenth-century
phallicists, such as Godfrey Higgins and Hargrave Jennings, expounded
to a receptive audience precisely this theme of the universality of the
sexual symbolism found underlying all traditions and also vaguely
hinted at the existence of a secret tradition of sexual practice that
accompanied it.[61] Of the traditions with which Randolph at least
claimed familiarity (alchemy and Rosicrucianism), both were commonly
recognized in his day as having a sexual element, certainly in symbolism and probably in practice as well.[62]

The cosmological and mythological elements of this symbolism are
almost entirely lacking in Randolph's sexual magic, though he was
certainly aware of them from his reading of Hargrave Jennings and
Godfrey Higgins, and his greatest distinction from his contemporaries
(and his successors) lies precisely here. Whether because of the "scientific" bias of the spiritualist tradition from which he emerged or—
more probably—because Randolph was above all a visionary, he was
no propagator or exponent of mythologies or traditional symbolic
systems, even though elements of his ideas (such as the role of the
Æth and the notions that power comes from the feminine side of God
and that "Love lieth at the Foundation") frequently coincide with elements of those systems. What Randolph taught was first and almost
exclusively a practical method, a tool to achieve a result. This is not to
say that there is no exposition in Randolph of a system of results to be
expected from the practice. He did have a visionary cosmology of the
vortical central sun, the spinning off of twin, bi-sexual monads and
the like, and he conveyed these expected results to his followers. This,
of course, is a mythological system, though a rudimentary one, and in
that sense Randolph is a mythographer and appropriately has his place
within the Western tradition. His uniqueness, however, lies in the
primacy he accorded to practice and technique over myth and symbol,
and in that respect he is perhaps more properly seen as the forerunner
of the "gurus" of our own time rather than as a part of the formal
Western occult and magical tradition which to a very large extent has
consisted in the sterile, academic, and antiquarian transmission of the

dead symbols and mythologies of what perhaps originally had been an experienced, visionary reality.

It is the eternal task of the nonvisionary disciples of a visionary teacher to systematize the master's experience and integrate it in the formal traditions of such visions, and it fell to Randolph's successors, such as the H. B. of L. and Maria de Naglowska, to attempt to integrate Randolph's work into the larger Western tradition of correspondences, myths, and symbols. Maria de Naglowska, as we have seen, added to Randolph's work an astrological setting and a system of magical correspondences appropriate to situating his sexual techniques in the structured traditional hierarchy of colors, stones, signs of the zodiac, and the like. The H. B. of L., through the efforts of the antiquarian Peter Davidson, the provincial grand master of the North for the order, supplemented Randolph's work on magic mirrors with the prayers, calls, invocations, and releases of traditional mirror magic, and firmly fixed his sexual techniques within the larger Western tradition of the fall and redemption of man through sexuality.[63]

The Brotherhood of Eulis

In March 1874, Randolph, who as usual complained that he was alone in his work,[64] attempted once again to found an organization to practice and carry on his teachings, this time in Nashville, Tennessee, where he founded the "B.O.E.," "the Brotherhood of Eulis." The term *Eulis* was Randolph's own creation, adopted to distinguish his own creative work. It was but one more guise (like "Rosicrucian," "Paschian," and "Ansairetic") in which to garb his thought. He suggested that those who saw the term as kin to "Eleusis" would not be far wrong, and in doing so he was merely following the accepted notion that the Eleusinian mysteries of classical antiquity were above all sexual mysteries.[65] He also proffered another etymology with more explicitly Oriental roots: "We are EULIS, because we cultivate the rich treasures of thought handed down to us from all ages; and we translate our Oriental name MAREK GEBEL,—'gate of LIGHT'—into Eulis, or the Door of the Dawn, by which name, during the era of this, the Third Temple, the triplicate Order, Guild and Brotherhood shall be henceforward known."[66]

In this version, "Eulis" was more properly "eolis," derived from *eos*, the Greek for dawn.[67]

What Randolph was doing in Tennessee is unknown, but the connection may lie in Randolph's long association with and high regard for the Rev. Jesse B. Ferguson of Nashville. Ferguson had originally been a Baptist minister in Tennessee. Early on he had been converted to spiritualism, and during the Davenport brothers' American and European tours in the early 1860s he acted as their chaplain, road manager, and chief propagandist, and undoubtedly met Randolph in their company while Randolph was writing their biography. On the Davenports' tour of England in 1863, Ferguson met John Murray Spear, and after the war he was very active in promoting Spear's Sacred Order of Unionists in the United States. Ferguson was also a reformer and was the corresponding secretary of the Union Club in New York that had sponsored the Southern Loyalist Convention in 1866. In that capacity, Ferguson, among others, recommended Randolph's scheme to raise money for his normal school.[68] He had died in 1870, but some lingering effect of his work in Tennessee may have prompted Randolph to journey there to found Eulis.[69]

The relationship between Eulis and Randolph's Rosicrucianism in this Tennessee attempt is nowhere stated. In the light of his next foundation, in San Francisco the following year, however, it is clear that the Rosy Cross was not intended to be supplanted by Eulis, but to be supplemented by it and perhaps act as a more exoteric "pool" for the recruitment and vetting of candidates for the more esoteric Eulian mysteries.[70]

The Tennessee foundation was short-lived indeed, even by Randolph's standards. The brotherhood was instituted in March 1874 and was dissolved by the end of June. As always, the reason appears to have been Randolph's "angular" personality.

> [O]wing to irreconcilable misunderstandings it became absolutely necessary to dissolve the provisional society *as* the B.O.E., and to utterly decline to permanently organize it, owing to the presence of a person with whom it became impossible for me to break bread and taste salt—things which no man of Eulis or Rosicrucia will ever do under unpleasant conditions. Consequently, hereafter as heretofore, I shall do what good I can, single-handed and alone—yet not alone, for God and I are a clear majority.[71]

Despite the claim of solitude, however, Randolph was not quite alone and Eulis itself still lived. Randolph's *Eulis*, to which he appended the after-the-fact addendum announcing both the formation and the dissolution of the Tennessee B.O.E., is still confidently signed by Randolph as "Re-Founder and Hierarch of Eulis," and the dedication lists the names of a few faithful followers, most of whom will reappear in his next—and final—foundation.[72]

In late September or early October 1874 Randolph was off once more, this time to California, probably at the invitation of the remnants of his 1861 Rosicrucian group who paid his travel expenses.[73] For eight months he explored for gold and silver in the Pacific desert, lectured, and once again tried to establish an organization to carry on his work—and also to support and care for his infant son, Osiris Budh, who had been born March 30, 1874.[74]

In San Francisco in December 1874 for the last time he refounded an organization to practice his ideas—the Triplicate Order Rosicrucia, Pythianæ, and Eulis. In February 1875, as "Refounder, Organizer and Supreme Hierarch," he published his last book, *The Book of the Triplicate Order*,[75] in which he set forth the constitution of the organization. The work is truly pathetic in revealing Randolph's overly grandiose schemes for perpetuating his work and caring for his infant son after his death—schemes which even he must have realized from bitter experience were futile—but the book provides the fullest glimpse we have of the inner organization of one of Randolph's groups.

Randolph prefaces the constitution of the refounded order by quoting verbatim the long section from *Ravalette* (1863) in which the Rosicrucians are identified with Jung-Stilling's unnamed occult fraternity that met on Mount Sinai and under the Temple at Jerusalem, and in which the history of the order is recounted from pre-Adamite times ("the sinking of the New Atlantis Isle, nearly ten thousand years anterior to the days of Plato"), through Brahma, Buddha, Lao-tse, Plato, and Melchizedek to the modern Rosicrucians.[76] The seven points of the original manifesto of his San Francisco foundation of fourteen years before are also repeated, substituting only "Rosicrucian and Eulian" for the original's simple reference to Rosicrucian.[77]

Despite this mythological history, Randolph again made it clear that the refounded order was his own creation.

> We accept truth wherever found . . . and among others those evolved by the Brethren of the Rosea Cruce in all lands . . . but as their knowledge and procedures in their search of truth and the attainment of the maximum of individual human power, spiritual insight, and intellectual strength, are not adapted to the present age, we accept their interpretations as laid down in the books written by our brother, the Hierarch, who therein has given mankind the cream of the writings of the ancient Brethren, and evolved hundreds of new truths from his own mentality by aid of the Philosophic and Scientific resources of the nineteenth

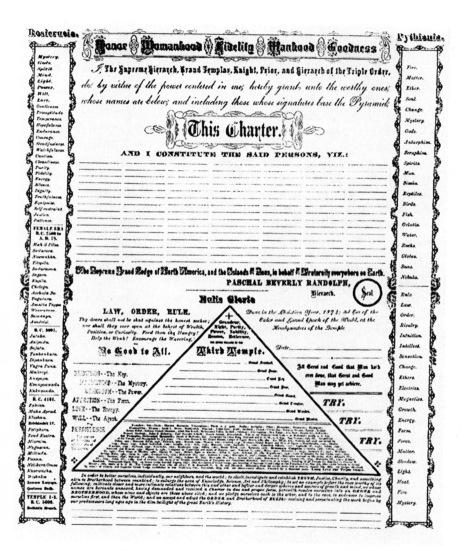

Plate 3. The Charter of the Triplicate Order
(Courtesy of the Livingston Masonic Library)

century, wherefore we cut loose from India, Siam, Egypt, Arabia, Chaldea, Syria, Germany, England, France and Greece, and on these shores found a NEW TEMPLE for a THOUSAND YEARS to bear the proud and imperial name of EULIS; and we disclaim all allegiance to any other Order or Fraternity on earth. . . . [A]nd we hold all other claimants to Rosicrucianism as frauds and impostors.[78]

In the new foundation the terms *Pythianæ* and *Eulis*—the latter of which was to give its name to the entire order—were added to the simple *Rosicrucia* of the San Francisco foundation of 1861. The additions were probably made to provide more explicitly for higher degrees based on Randolph's sexual magic. Randolph noted that the original San Francisco group had been "founded in one degree only (the Rosicrucian)."[79] This is not strictly true, since three "degrees" were to have been conferred there, but what Randolph intended to convey was the fact that *whatever* had been conveyed in the three original degrees was now to be taught in the first (Rosicrucian) degree of the refounded order, and that beyond that there were two further degrees, the Pythian and Eulian, in which further mysteries were to be revealed.[80]

The nature of the distinctions among these degrees is fairly clear. As Rosicrucians (the first degree) the order was concerned with "mental science" and the cultivation of "all that is abstruse, unknown, and which pertains to nature's deeper departments, and the subtler crypts of the unfathomable human soul." As Pythians (the second degree)—which would appear to be derived from the Pythia, the mantic prophetess of Greece, but which Randolph relates for some reason to the Pythagoreans—the order cultivated "intimate relations with the Base of the Universe—the God of Nature and its Soul—and with the Spiritual and unseen worlds." Finally, as Eulians (the third degree) the order cultivated "the rich treasures of thought handed down to us from all ages"—especially from the Marek Gebel ("Gate of Light").[81] The "Marek Gebel" or "Gebel Al Maruk," of course, is the Superlative Order of which Imperial Thotmor and Ramus were grand masters.[82] All of this is a change, at least formally, from Randolph's earlier work. At the time of his 1871 attempt to refound his Rosicrucians, Randolph had apparently divided the order into three degrees corresponding to the three magical techniques of Volantia, Rosicrucia and Decretism, though probably the names covered the same secrets and progressed to a full revelation of sexual magic. In his final foundation, so far as can be determined from the names of the degrees, the mirror magic was probably taught in the second degree, while the full panoply of sexual magic was reserved for the third. In fairly normal occult fashion, the lower degrees probably were designed to function as "pools" for the selection of the elite destined for fuller initiation.[83]

The ritual structure of the order is obscure, but undoubtedly there was an initiation of some sort. In describing his problems with Bay of Ohio in the early 1870s, as we have seen, Randolph described the initiatory confrontation of "sin" and "innocence" that preceded the degree of Volantia, and something similar probably existed in the Triplicate Order.[84] Whatever the details of the ritual, it must have been mild. The Triplicate Order was open to both sexes, and in fact required that each office or function be held both by a man and by a woman of equal rank, and Randolph was careful to state that "nothing is ever said or done in our Lodges that could paint a blush upon a child or even an angel's cheek."[85] Ordinary lodge ceremony, as described by Randolph, seems perfunctory at best. A member entering the lodge room was to bow to the master with outstretched arms, and then "with the right hand touch the forehead and then the chin, as if stroking the beard; then drop the arm and repeat the W.H.—to which the G.M. answers, A.H."[86]

Structurally, the Triplicate Order was to be organized in each state under a Grand Lodge or Temple, with subordinate lodges within the state to be called "Guilds of Eulis." Each was expected to make its own bylaws, give degrees, and diplomas (white or silver for the first degree, gold for the second, and purple for the third). A grand master (or master in the case of guilds) presided over each lodge within a state, assisted by a grand dome, a grand door, a grand key, a grand guard, a grand warden, and a grand sentinel, each with perfunctorily described duties. The only officer whose duties are expatiated upon is the grand dome, who was to be the treasurer of the lodge, and who was charged with collecting dues and remitting money in turn to the higher levels of the order.

The San Francisco lodge founded in December 1874 was given special prominence in Randolph's constitution because of its priority. It was designated a Supreme Grand Lodge, with authority over "the entire continent of North America and the Islands of the Sea" and the power to grant charters to new lodges and grand lodges, and all of its members were automatically admitted to the third degree.[87] It was also constituted by Randolph guardian of his successor and son, Osiris Budh. Its exact membership when founded is unknown, but its officers undoubtedly included all those listed as members of the Supreme Grand Council of the Reformed Temple of Eulis.[88]

L. W. Ransom (Supreme Grand Master)
M. J. Burke (Supreme Grand Dome)
Nathaniel Batchelder (Supreme Grand Warden)
John Cogill, Sen. (Supreme Grand Key)
D. W. Frary (Supreme Grand Door)
H. R. Morton (Supreme Grand Guard)
Thomas Docking (Supreme Grand Templar)
P. B. Randolph (Supreme Grand Hierarch)

Over all was the pre-existing "Corner Stone Lodge." At the time of the refounding of the order in San Francisco, it consisted of

L. H. McLaughlin, First Vice President
John Blakey Pilkington, Portland, Oregon, Vice Hierarch
John F. Kapp, Sunbury, Pennsylvania
Oscar Franklin Shaw, Mariposa, California
Albert Burpee, Haverhill, Massachusetts
T. C. Creamer, Ohio, and
Paschal Beverly Randolph, President.[89]

Over all of this in turn was the mythological Imperial Dome of the Third Supreme Temple of the Order.[90]

The financial organization of the order was pyramidal, with Randolph at the top. Initiation into the Supreme Grand Lodge in San Francisco was "fixed at $30, gold coin," or ten dollars per degree, but in that case Randolph specified that the fees had already been paid when the lodge had reimbursed him for his travel expenses. The charge for initiation into any other Grand Lodge was the same, and twenty dollars was charged for initiation into a guild. In addition, a monthly fee of one dollar was to be charged—though this was waived (and a five dollar bounty paid) if a member brought in three new initiates. All initiation and charter fees were to be paid to the Supreme Grand Lodge in San Francisco, together with one-tenth of the monthly fees, and that lodge in turn was obliged to turn over one-tenth of all of *its* income to the Supreme Grand Corner Stone Lodge.[91]

Randolph's primary concern in the constitution of the Triplicate Order was to ensure that his infant son was cared for after his death. The supreme hierarch had the right to nominate his successor, and Randolph nominated his son, Osiris Budh—"the *only* being now on earth who by organization is capable of wholly entering the Penetralia and esoteric realm of the Eulian System"—to succeed him.[92] In the event of Randolph's death—an event that loomed large in Randolph's thinking—the vice-hierarch, John B. Pilkington, Randolph's old Rosicrucian co-worker in San Francisco in 1861, was to fill the office until Osiris's majority on March 30, 1895.[93] During Osiris's minority, Randolph charged the Supreme Grand Lodge in San Francisco with his care under what must be one of the most unusual contracts ever written: help from the beyond in exchange for care of Osiris Budh.

> [T]he said Grand Lodge on signing its Charter voluntarily accepts said charge; and to protect said child till he shall receive his full illumination and reach maturity; and a small sum shall from each member of the Order be set apart for the care and instruction of said child, in return for which the present Hierarch promises his post mortem assistance and teachership to said Order through its respective systems hereafter to be established. This charge is given because the Hierarch spent his life for the Order, and lived a life of isolation, travel, study and pain that this Grand Order might perpetuate its being. About said child there is a tremendous mystery; and by the hour of his majority the world, through him—through Eulis, will gain a most enormous benefit by the opening of a new channel of strange, rare and mighty knowledge theretofore unknown upon the earth. Therefore protect and properly educate him to labor and self-support, but help him when he needs it.[94]

To the Supreme Grand Corner Stone Lodge Randolph bequeathed all of his writings—which he listed—on the condition that a portion of the proceeds from their sale, together with some percentage of all fees and dues, be paid to the guardian of Osiris Budh for their support and his education. In a touching note, Randolph specified that his son be educated "in all the branches and languages afforded by a first-class school or institution of learning until his majority."[95] In a backhanded bequest to his wife, Randolph provided that if Osiris Budh died she was to be paid his share "during the term of her widowhood, or she never marries again, and preserves a pure and virtuous life, then it shall be allowed and paid her until her death."

Toward the end of his California trip, in May 1875, Randolph lectured in Owens Valley and stayed with the Hutchinson family. His stay was a bitter one, marred by the "prejudice and bigotry of the orthodox believers" who threatened to kill him unless he left within 36 hours.[96] The Hutchinsons apparently protected him and refused to have him cut short his visit. Although the exact relationship is unknown, the Hutchinson family must be that of Jesse Hutchinson who had been involved with spiritualism, and probably with John Murray Spear, from the earliest days, and had moved to California in 1852.[97] Luna Hutchinson was part of the clan and subsequently was one of the mediums who obtained the postmortem teachings of the disembodied Randolph.[98]

In June 1875 Randolph left the Hutchinsons and returned to Toledo by way of Los Angeles, full of plans to lecture in the East on the marvels of California and the adventures of its early pioneers.

Finale

Randolph arrived back in Toledo in late June or early July 1875. He appears to have been happy. In a letter in mid-July to S. S. Jones, the editor of the *Religio-Philosophical Journal*, he claimed to be flush with gold and silver found in his explorations in the Pacific desert, and he was full of plans: a trip to Russia to confound the Franco-Russic Savants with his "triple clairvoyance" and his ability to read while blindfolded (a reference to the "Appeal to Mediums" that Madame Blavatsky had been making to find test mediums for the spiritualists of St. Petersburg),[99] and the completion of his new book, *Beyond the Spaces*. He was obviously proud of his sixteen-month-old son, and proposed to Jones a World's Mystic Tournament in Chicago where he and and the boy would confound the skeptic. "[N]ow that I am on the thither side of the to be fatal 29th day of March, 1875, [I] feel that I can work and win new victories, no longer afraid of a lack of greenbacks, friends, or faith in God."[100]

In this optimistic mood, he wrote a letter to Col. Henry S. Olcott, who had achieved some fame in spiritualist circles at the beginning of the year by publishing his *People from the Other World* which described his experiences with the mediumistic Eddy brothers—and who, of course, had been the constant companion of Madame Blavatsky since they had met at Chittenden, Vermont, in the previous year.

Toledo, Ohio, July 10th

Col. Olcott

Sir, I learn that you have certain Mirror Revelations from a Brooklyn Lady. So have I. I also am the proprietor of *Eulis*— a book. Some of it is essentially what you have written in your book. I have been 8 months on the Pacific Slope and have just returned and am now writing out for publication the extraordinary tale of the Hermit of Arizona, which I think will match your wonderful book, although not in the same line. I wish to exchange Books with you. Eulis for yours. If agreeable, please notify whither to send mine.

Respectfully yours,

Paschal Beverly Randolph
334 Vance St., Toledo Ohio

Perhaps you are not aware that I am the author of various works and the importer of the Mirror which Mrs. R. of B. had some curious matters through. I should like to have an interview with you as soon as I transcribe my notes of the magnificent work I am now engaged on.

Respectfully.[101]

No reply exists, and it is likely Randolph never received one, since his death occurred two weeks after his letter. The letter itself is most interesting for the light it casts on Olcott's (and perhaps Madame Blavatsky's) interests. As we shall see, Olcott was an enthusiastic mirror magician at the time (see chapter 13). He had been very closely involved with spiritualism in New York since the early 1850s and must have known of Randolph already. He is in fact mentioned by Randolph in his book on the Davenport brothers as one of the earnest investigators of the brothers' spiritualist phenomena in the mid-1860s, and Randolph may well have met him at the time, though Randolph does not recall the fact in his letter to Olcott.[102] Olcott, in turn, in addition to his mirror practice with the woman in Brooklyn, also acquired a considerable number of Randolph's works, and—in the simplest possible conjecture—may have been the one to bring Randolph to Madame Blavatsky's attention (see chapters 12 and 13).

Suicide

Despite his cheerfulness at times and optimism about the future, Randolph was very troubled. He was beset by jealousy of his wife and suffered from alcoholism. The torrent of wrongs, abuses, lack of recognition, penury, and failures of his life had taken their toll. Earlier in his career, he had been resilient, clinging to his mother's supposed dying words, "We may be happy yet!" Toward the end of his life, however, his woes and bitterness appear to overwhelm him, and his complaints—especially about the ingratitude of the spiritualist reformers in whose cause he had labored for twenty-five years—become the paranoid rantings of a man yearning for rest.

> The rank and file of this trouble-making army [of pseudo-reformers] wouldn't pass muster at the gates of heaven; for a more ungenerous, malignant, back-biting set was never developed by any civilization earth ever saw. Born of loveless parents, they rush through life striking alike, hap-hazard, at friend or foe; discontented from the nipple to eternity; full of malice; steeped to the lips with cruel, cool, cobra-like venom, they are never happy save when slandering their betters, picking flaws in others' characters, and stabbing in the back those whom they dare not face. . . . Ostracized by those for, and with whom I had labored since 1848; met with ingratitude at every step, I gladly accept the ostracism of the many for the good companionship of the few. . . . Neglect, slander, vile prejudices, contumely—all have in this trial of six and twenty years—though ranking millions armed with staves, crying, "Crucify him! crucify him!"—proved signally unequal to the task of defeating a single solitary man . . . PASCHAL BEVERLY RANDOLPH!—the *sang melée!*— Proud of his descent from the kings and queens, to say nothing of the Randolphs, nor their rise from Warwick the king-maker! . . . I am to-day alone, and for that scarce a lecturer or paper devoted to "Reform" but had its fling at me, even to the extent of abusing my dead mother. . . . It is a terrible crime to be by God constituted differently from those who see light in the same thought you do, yet feel the pulses of manhood throbbing in your veins;—and sure to be hated on that account. I *am* a *sang melée*; and not less than twelve strains of blood rush through my veins, yet have I ever met insult all the way along of life, because I *dared* to be myself! . . . For the fault of the Infinite, if fault it was, to make me of an unfashionable cast, have I been almost crucified, and have suffered, as it were, a thousand deaths. For the Indian tinge on my cheek, not its volcanic fires in my soul—Fires which held the cowards at bay for five and thirty years—have I been doubly wronged, by these and them and those, who, when help was needed, gladly availed them of my brain and speech and pen, to devoutly damn me when the fights were won! Driven

by the flaming sword of mean prejudice from all noble occupation and employment, by those who without either Soul, or Honor or Manhood, or nobility of character, made them strong, and gave them warrant to invade my rights and cruelly slander me,— and invariably behind my back! lacking manly courage to do it to my face,—cowards, all, whom I felt and feel were, and are, as far beneath me as the floor of space is below the loftiest Turret of the Immeasurable Temple wherein God resides! Attached with bitter and envious malignity, ever without the chance of reply,— by tongue and pen,—and still I survived; and—despite them all. Treated more like a beast of the jungle than a human being; they exhausted all logic trying to prove me a nobody,—themselves the only real thinkers; and in seeking to justify their own outrage, really vindicated *me!* . . . I became a Power in the world! What are they? I took to Mirrorology, and they did not like it, because it enabled me to laugh their isms and practice to utter scorn. . . .

Oh, how I have yearned for everlasting death, in view of the pitiless, remorseless persecutions, insults, wrongs, heaped on my head by thousands whom I never either harmed or even met— envious, jealous, sorted! I pitied them, and longed for lasting rest.[103]

Randolph's death, like his life, was fiery and passionate. He killed himself on July 29, 1875. A neighbor provided an eyewitness account to the local paper.

BY HIS OWN HAND
DEATH OF A WELL KNOWN SPIRITUALISTIC AUTHOR BY
SUICIDE—DR. B. P. RANDOLPH TAKES HIS OWN LIFE THIS
MORNING AT A LITTLE AFTER EIGHT O'CLOCK

[Mrs. Worden] says that before eight o'clock she noticed Dr. P. B. Randolph, who lives diagonally across the street from her house . . . walking past her house several times; after a while he went to his own house, and after remaining there a while he started toward Division Street. He soon returned to the vacant lot adjoining the Worden house, and while standing called to Mrs. W. that he wanted to tell her something. She stepped out on the back porch with her daughter. Then Randolph told her to tell his wife, whom he supposed to be in the house, to come out. Mrs. Worden replied that she was not there. Randolph then said: "Well, good bye. In less than two hours I shall be a dead man. I'm going to shoot myself." Mrs. Worden told him that he wouldn't do a thing of that kind, but he replied: "Yes, I will. In less than two hours I'll be dead, and I want you two to witness the deed, and then you can testify. I leave all my property to my son. You will be witness to that, and testify that I said so, when they call upon you after I'm dead, and that won't be a long time, either." While making these remarks he was standing within fifteen feet of Mrs. Worden, who was so badly frightened at the way he was talking that she turned to go in the house. Just then she heard the report of a revolver, and turning she saw Randolph fall in his tracks. . . .

The conjectures as to the cause which lead the unfortunate man to commit the rash deed are as numerous almost as there are people to conjecture, but it is most generally conceded that jealously was the main cause. Randolph was part Spaniard, and inherited all the suspicious distrusting qualities of the people of that nationality. For some time he has imagined that his wife has been untrue to him, and from brooding over his imagined injuries he became morose, overbearing and tyrannical, and began to drink heavily. While in these fits he would treat his wife very badly, and threatened several times to kill their little baby boy, which he claimed was not his; but when sober, he was generally a kind husband and father. For the past week he has been drinking worse than ever, and yesterday his conduct became so bad that his wife went to her mother's house. He staid around the house all day and last night slept there.

This morning he arose and went to look for his wife, and not finding her became furious. Then he went out, took several drinks, and returned to Mrs. Worden's house where he committed the deed in the manner already described.[104]

Randolph died as a "part Spaniard." Even at the end he had not made peace with his ancestry.

Chapter 11

$\mathcal{P}$OST-$\mathcal{M}$ORTEM

After Randolph's death, the spiritualist press, whose attitude had long been ambivalent (at best) toward him, noted his "angularities" while recalling his early services to their cause. His restless spirit appeared for a time at seances around the country, announcing that he was still unloved even in the spirit land and that he would gladly return to the land of the living.[1] A few months after his death, his spirit began appearing regularly in California to Luna Hutchinson and to Mrs. Frances ("Fanny") Harriet Whipple Green McDougall, a veteran spiritualist and reformer who had edited the *Journal of Progress* in which Randolph's first literary efforts had been published in 1853. The result was *Beyond the Veil: Posthumous Work of Paschal Beverly Randolph, Aided by Emanuel Swedenborg and Others, Through the Minds of Frances H. McDougall and Luna Hutchinson*, published in 1878. It carried as a frontispiece a studio portrait of Randolph and bore on its cover the device of the winged globe and his motto, Try! This final book, like his *After Death*, showed Randolph's continued regression from the soul world to the platitudes of the spirit world, the "Summer Land" of spiritualism, and it is most notable now for his spirit's recounting of the reception into the afterlife of the recently martyred (and greatly surprised) General George Custer, fresh from the Little Big Horn.

With this ambiguous tribute Randolph might very well have passed into the oblivion that has received so many of his co-workers in the early spiritualist movement. More penetrating contemporary observers, however, were quick to perceive the radical change of direction Randolph had introduced into spiritualism, a change that was even then transforming the movement. W. E. Coleman, a died-in-the-wool spiritualist now remembered mostly for the charges of plagiarism he leveled at Madame Blavatsky, correctly recognized Randolph as a

241

pioneer and emphasized the transition from classical spiritualism to occultism represented by Randolph, Emma Hardinge Britten, and Madame Blavatsky. In reviewing Randolph's postmortem pronouncements in *Beyond the Veil*, which was published the year after Madame Blavatsky's *Isis Unveiled*, Coleman perceptively stated:

> Randolph, it will be remembered, while on earth, was a devoted Rosicrucian, addicted to occultic rhapsodies, voudoistic charms, and magical mummeries; and claimed a membership in Oriental Theosophical lodges and brotherhoods. It seems unfortunate, that, just as the theories and principles so ardently advocated by him for years should obtain prominence in Spiritualistic circles, he should pass to the spirit-existence, leaving others [*read* Madame Blavatsky and Emma Hardinge Britten] to reap all the glory (?) accruing from the dissemination of Occultism. Were Randolph alive in the flesh to-day, how he would revel in the present discussion of the mysteries of the occulto-Rosicrucian-hermetico-alchemico-astrologico-theosophico-astralo-theurgico-Isis-Unveilingo-elementalo-sub-mundano-Ansaiterico-voudooico-cabalistico-thaumaturgico-Art-Magico-koboldo-akasoico-condensed vaporo-elementary bombast and nonsense with which America and England are being flooded.[2]

This juxtaposition of the works of Randolph, Emma Hardinge Britten, and Madame Blavatsky was perceptive, because, for all their differences in detail and emphasis, the three undoubtedly shared a fundamentally similar approach to the mysteries of the other world and created the sea change that was in the process of transforming spiritualism (the passive reception of doctrines from the spirits of the dead) into "occultism" (the active search for personal spiritual advancement, individualization and knowledge among the celestial hierarchies). There was a battle raging, and to contemporary eyes the ranks of the occultists were led by Randolph, Emma Hardinge Britten, and Madame Blavatsky. Andrew Jackson Davis named them explicitly (together with Colonel Olcott) as the proponents of what he called "Magical spiritualism."[3] The old "scientific" and progressive spiritualism was not long to stand in the way of the revival of the ancient "magical mummeries" that Coleman and the other spiritualists so abhorred.

Despite Randolph's bequest of his works to the Triplicate Order and his careful detailing of provisions for the care and nurturing of his son, his dreams did not materialize. The Triplicate Order apparently continued to exist in some form until the end of the century since

Gustav Meyrink acquired a copy of one of Randolph's manuscript works on sexual magic from Kate Corson Randolph through the auspices of the order, but no details survive and little is known of the order's work or membership. Neither can have amounted to much. In 1900, Sylvester Clark Gould (1840–1909), who was in a good position to know since he was an inveterate joiner and had become a member of the H. B. of L. in 1885, said that Randolph's Rosicrucians had "ceased as an order some 25 years ago"—that is, at or shortly after Randolph's death.[4] To some extent the decline was to have been expected, since Randolph himself was the visionary, driving force behind the order, but it was also a natural result of the peculiar constitution of the order, which Randolph envisioned fundamentally more as a vehicle for imparting his techniques than as an organization. He had always taught that "each Brother comprises the whole Order in himself, and acts for himself toward himself and all others," and the consequence was the short-lived flourishing or a bewildering array of minor Rosicrucians, all beholden to Randolph.[5]

Some formal organization of the Triplicate Order continued nonetheless. The office of "door" of the order, which in Randolph's days had been filled by an otherwise unknown person named D. W. Frary, subsequently passed to the equally unknown John Heaney of Iroquois County, Illinois, to whom Freeman B. Dowd dedicated *The Temple of the Rosy Cross*.[6] If Dowd had become alienated from Randolph in the early 1870s, as seems likely, the split between the Rosicrucians appears to have been healed or glossed over after Randolph's death.

Dowd's own subsequent history is too far afield to be traced here,[7] but it is at least in part through him and his Temple of the Rosy Cross that R. Swinburne Clymer (1878–1966) came to know Randolph and his works, and it is through Clymer that the major Rosicrucian group based on Randolph's work still survives today.[8] To establish his own legitimacy, Clymer painted a simple picture of well-defined organizations through which the apostolic succession passed from hierarch to hierarch: from Randolph to Dowd (aided by the "door," John Heaney, and, after Heaney's death, Dr. James Ralph Phelps); from Dowd to Dr. Edward H. Brown; and from Brown and Phelps to Clymer. The reality of the transmission is far more amorphous and complex, but by 1922, when Brown died, Clymer had pulled into his own hands the control of many of the groups imbued with Randolph's magic that had arisen in the years since his death: the various temples, orders, and fraternities of the Rosicrucians, the Ansairetic Priesthood, the Æth Priesthood, the Temple of Eulis, and the H. B. of L. (in the derivative form of W. P. Phelon's Hermetic Brotherhood of Atlantis, Luxor, and Elephantae).[9]

244 • *Paschal Beverly Randolph*

To this he added a native Pennsylvania strain of mysticism and a patriotic strain of Rosicrucianism (from the novels of the socialist George Lippard),[10] and mixed the whole with the teachings of a variety of obscure groups (the "Illuminatae Americanae," the "Order of the Golden Age," "Philosophers of the Living Fire," and "Ordo Militia Crucifera Evangelica") that combined unorthodox medicine, jingoism, sexual nostrums, and occultism.[11] Over them all he erected a fantastic superstructure of unknown superiors, culminating in the "Supreme Hierarch of the World, Count A. de Guinotti," an "Italian *inconnu.*" Clymer appropriated this figure from Randolph's Italian/Armenian count, Cuilna Vilmara, and from the work of J. C. Street and the novels of Marie Corelli (see chapter 6), but that did not prevent him from claiming personal contact with Guinotti's successor in the office of supreme hierarch.[12]

Fantastic as all of this elaboration was, the foundation of the entire endeavor was serious. From at least as early as 1908, Clymer was distributing to candidates in his Æth Priesthood copies of *Divine Alchemy* ("printed but not published")[13] which provided the gist of Randolph's manuscript teachings on sexual magic and instructed the neophytes in the mysteries of the single and double "Breast Drill"— breathing and concentration exercises for arousing sexual energy.

Largely unaffected by all of this, Kate Corson Randolph appears to have gone her own way, trying alone to raise her infant son as best she could. As Randolph Publishing Company, she kept most of Randolph's important works in print through the rest of the century and even beyond, and as a chemist and physician she continued to make available his various elixirs (protozone, chlorylle, barosmyn, and lucina cordial)— although it seems probable that she, like Randolph before her, found the effort scarcely remunerative. Through her control of Randolph's published books she continued to have some contact with and perhaps influence over the various groups that perpetuated Randolph's ideas, but his manuscript works on sexual magic almost immediately became common property.[14] The Triplicate Order apparently recognized its obligation to Mrs. Randolph, if only to the extent of referring inquirers after Randolph's works to her, and this was the method through which Gustav Meyrink acquired Randolph's manuscript works and a "black mirror" ("a so-called Indian 'Battah' Mirror").[15] She also independently continued to copy and sell Randolph's manuscript works on sexual magic, and it was through her that John Yarker acquired his copy of the "Mysteries of Eulis," carefully noting at the end: "The sum of four pounds was paid for this MSS to the widow of P. B. Randolph and was remitted to her by me.—John Yarker."[16]

The amorphous condition of Randolph's endeavors in the decades after his death is clearly revealed in a letter Mrs. Randolph wrote to R. Swinburne Clymer in 1907 in response to his request for the "Master Word"—the *"verbum myrificum"* whose power Randolph had touted in *The Triplicate Order*.

> *You* are reorganizing this lodge— and as such you will give your own Passwords, etc. You being the *head* of this Society— you would also give the *Master Word*. I do not know what these which you refer to were—Dr. R. passed away in just a few weeks after his return from Calif. where he was trying to organize the Society and these were not given to me— I do not think *this* is so essential. It is <u>not</u> a society strictly of Passwords, ritual etc., but for the betterment of Mankind, to improve the Man—to build up the individuality, to increase their latent powers, to help each other to be better, truer Men and women, it is to increase our powers. Therefore I do not think these points so essential. You give the passwords, which in turn are given to other lodges as these are organized. Is this not so?
>
> > Very truly yours,
> > Kate C. Randolph

I do not know today if there be any organized society existing, only as someone as [has] started some society, as per the Eulians of Salem.

F. B. Dowd was once a student of P. B. R.[17]

At some point after Randolph's death, probably in the early 1880s, Mrs. Randolph acquired in some unknown way an agent in Great Britain for the sale of Randolph's works—especially his manuscripts on sexual magic. The agent was Robert H. Fryar, whom we have already discussed. He was a struggling, poorly educated clerk in Bath who had long been involved in the English world of crystal seers. In later years he went on to publish under his own imprint a hodge-podge of works on the occult and on the fringe aspects of sexuality written or with introductions by such noted occultists as W. W. Westcott, Anna Bonus Kingsford, Hargrave Jennings, and John Yarker.[18] None of these could have been ignorant of Randolph's work, and all of them (with the exception of Kingsford) were believers in the fundamental role of sexuality in mythology and occult practice. It was Fryar, finally,

who first announced to the world the appearance of the H. B. of L.—
the Hermetic Brotherhood of Luxor—the true heritor of Randolph's work.

From 1884, when Fryar's edition of *The Divine Pymander* appeared
with a solicitation for the H. B. of L., until the effective splintering of
that organization in mid-1886 when it was revealed that T. H. Burgoyne
(or T. H. Dalton or D'Alton), the secretary of the order, was a convicted felon, the H. B. of L. took massive strides in recruiting the many
dissatisfied spiritualists and disaffected Theosophists who had sought
in vain for practical methods of occult realization. Through the mail-
order distribution of lessons (whose practical instructions on sex and
magic mirrors were almost entirely taken from Randolph's works), the
new order recruited the Rev. W. A. Ayton in England, "F.-Ch. Barlet"
(Albert Faucheux), "Papus" (Gérard Encausse), Arthur Arnould, and
"Paul Sédir" (Yvon Le Loup) in France, and a majority of the most
active members of the Theosophical Society in America, and enlisted
them in a crusade of "Western" occultism based on the magical quest
for individualization during life and the perpetual pilgrimage of the
divinized individual through the spheres of the celestial hierarchies
after death. Even after the debacle over Burgoyne, the sundered fragments of the H. B. of L. continued in a myriad guises—the Church or
Brotherhood of Light of "C. C. Zain" (Elbert Benjamin) and the various endeavors of S. C. Gould, W. P. Phelon, and others—to perpetuate
elements of Randolph's work.

The story of the H. B. of L. has recently been told and its manuscript
teaching works published at last in *The Hermetic Brotherhood of Luxor.
Initiatic and Historical Documents of an Order of Practical Occultism.* The
details of its history need not be given here.[19] Its debt to Randolph is
obvious, but its attitude toward him was extremely ambivalent nonetheless. The group took over wholesale Randolph's practical teachings on
sexual magic and the use of the magic mirror, but gradually distanced
those practices from their author (the "Mysteries of Eulis" became "The
Mysteries of Eros," for example) and at the same time warned of the
dangers inherent in Randolph's own interpretation of those practices.

The whole tenor of the revelation of the Ansairetic Arcanum,
and the mysteries of sex in relation to the Occult, are such as to
lead the uninitiated to the conclusion that pure sexual intercourse
may be made the means of magical power. This conclusion, in its
general sense, is a *fearful delusion*, but, at the same time, it is a
sublime truth when understood in its proper light. The doctrines
of Eulis, as set forth by Randolph, teach that the concentration of
the will upon any one, or upon any triune of powers, or at-

tributes, by both the male and female at the supreme moment of seminal emission during sexual intercourse, calls down from within the spaces of Æth the Divine germs of spiritual powers and attributes; or, in other words, the seeds of magical powers, and that these become planted in the souls of those who call them, grow, and in due time, ripen into the grand powers, or gifts, so rarely found existing in the human organism in a natural state. (By natural state we mean the present unnatural state of incarnated humanity; because, when man is in a *natural* state, he is the perfect man, or, in other words, the Adept.)

When taken literally in this light, the teachings of Eulis are an awful and terrible delusion, and mean ruin to all who practice them as a means of obtaining power, since they call down powers into the soul, which fasten upon its vitality and can never confer the remotest power or benefit. Such practices rear and nurse a swarm of vipers which will ultimately sap not only the vitals of the body, but the soul and terminate the physical existence of their victims by suicide, or drive them to the grave as driveling idiots, or as howling maniacs to the mad-house. Not content with this when death puts an end to physical torment, they still cling, like magnetic vampires, to the soul, and cause the complete destruction and disintegration of the spiritual remnant of their prey in the lower planes of the soul-world.

Therefore, be warned, O Neophyte, and rouse not the Furies lest you cannot lay them. This is the magical delusion of Eulis. This is *one* of the dwellers of the household ["threshold"], and all those who have become the slave instead of the master of such powers, had better follow the example of Judas Iscariot, and hang themselves before it is *too late to save their immortality*. For, in this life, they will only get from bad to worse; in the next, if not *too late, they may shake off the power of the fiends*. In the soul union of twin souls, as also in the physical union, there are mighty and potent effects, but they are far too recondite and abstruse to be here explained. Never, therefore, attempt to seek them until spiritual initiation has been attained, then you will know how to use and utilize them in a proper manner.

* * *

The awful list of powers, attributes and forces set forth in the works of P. B. Randolph, as attainable by the actual use of the sexual force, is a terrible snare. It was this fatal mistake that ruined the unfortunate, misguided Randolph himself. Therefore, remember, if you value your soul's immortality, that evil powers can be so gained, but those who gain them are forever lost. It is the true way to Voudooism and Black Magic. So beware how you play with the infernal laws which rule the realms of animal nature and outer darkness.[20]

All of this caution, as we shall see in the next chapter, led the H. B. of L. (and Madame Blavatsky and others) to characterize Randolph as the "half-initiated" seer, the failed initiate, who had fallen away from the truth he had learned in the East.

Kate Corson Randolph was only twenty-one when Randolph died. She survived him by almost sixty-five years, and by the time of her own death in 1938 he must have become in her eyes a very misty and distant figure to her. Her son, Randolph's pride and his boast to the spiritualists and the Brotherhood of Eulis, dropped *Budh* as his middle name and went on to become a well-respected, mainstream physician and surgeon in Toledo. There is no indication that Osiris Randolph ever took any interest in his father's work or in the Triplicate Order and his twenty-first birthday—on which Randolph envisioned Osiris's coming into his own as supreme hierarch of Eulis—took place in 1895, apparently without notice by the Triplicate Order.[21]

The year 1895 did mark the regrouping of various strains of occultism dependent on Randolph's work—the supposed refounding of Dowd's Temple of the Rosy Cross in Philadelphia and the organization of the Hermetic Brotherhood of Light, which was in turn one of the sources of the Ordo Templi Orientis (OTO), the most notorious effort at propagating sexual magic as the key to the mysteries.

What is known of the founding of the Hermetic Brotherhood of Light is derived almost exclusively from the comments of S. C. Gould, who was in a good position to know since he was almost certainly involved personally. In his "Resumé of Arcane Fraternities in the United States," which appeared in his *Notes and Queries* in 1896 and elsewhere, he described the H. B. of L. as an "Ancient and Noble Order," once dormant but recently revived:

> The Hermetic Brotherhood of Luxor. An Ancient and Noble Order. Teaches that the divine scintillations of Eternal Spirit will each complete its own "Cycle of Necessity." This is the only immortal portion of the Human Soul. The Brotherhood was divided into three grades, and these again sub divided into three

degrees, in America. The Order in America was somewhat modified from the Eastern form. It is referred to in a foot-note in "Isis
Unveiled." This Brotherhood has had a somewhat checkered
record, at one time it was dormant. It has, it is understood, in
quite recent years, been revived, re-formed, and is at present in
active life, the Head of the Exterior Circle being in Illinois.[22]

Gould, of course, had firsthand information on the H. B. of L. in its
early days, since he had become a neophyte in 1885, but from the
description given it is apparent that he believed that the order was a
thing of the past—except for the cryptic notice of its reformation.[23]
When Gould's "Resumé" was continued in 1905, he added a notice on
the Hermetic Brotherhood of Light, the "revived" and "reformed"
version of the H. B. of L. that he had referred to in 1896, but now he
was careful to distinguish the two.

The Hermetic Brotherhood of Light. This Brotherhood must
not be mistaken for, nor identified with, the H.B. of L., or Hermetic Brothers of Luxor. The Brotherhood of Light was organized in 1895, on top of the highest building in the largest eastern
city in the United States, under the blue canopy of heaven, when
Sol reigned supreme, where the air was pure, and the "spirit
moved on the faces" of those present. Harmony has reigned in
the brotherhood since the "high twelve," and all *hands* were
pointing upwards. "The wise will understand." *Vive, vale.*[24]

In Gould's final notice on the group, published in his *Rosicrucian
Brotherhood* in 1908, he added that the group was formed in Boston and
specified that the "President resides in Illinois, the Vice-President, in
New York, the Secretary and Treasurer, in New Hampshire."[25] These
less-than-illuminating notices in turn have formed the basis for a number of equally cryptic notes on the Hermetic Brotherhood of Light[26] and
are essentially all that is known about the origins of the group. From
Gould's descriptions it is clear that he himself was involved in the
formation of the H. B. of Light in 1895 and that he was in fact the
secretary/treasurer of the group, but the identity of the others involved
is pure guesswork. Any of several contemporary occultists is a possibility: Franz Hartmann, Edouard Blitz, W. P. Phelon, Karl Kellner—and
even John Heaney of Illinois, the "Door" of the Rosicrucians.

The importance of the group stems from the fact that when the OTO
appeared in the early twentieth century, it prominently claimed as its
source the Hermetic Brotherhood of Light or Fraternitas Hermetica Lucis.

The Spiritual Father of the newly organized Oriental Templar Order was the late Sovereign Honorary Grand Master in Germany and Great Britain, Brother∴Dr. Carl Kellner, 33°, 90°, 96°, X°. During his many and extensive trips in Europe, America and Asia Minor, Brother∴Kellner came in contact with an organization which bore the name "The Hermetic Brotherhood of Light." The stimulation which he received through his contact with this organization, in conjunction with other circumstances, which shall not be described further here, created the desire in Brother∴Kellner to found an *"Academia Massonica"* (an Academy of Masonry) which would enable all brothers so desiring to become acquainted with all existing Masonic degrees and systems. In the year 1895 Brother∴Kellner had long conversations with Brother∴Reuß in Berlin as to how his idea could be realized. In the course of the conferences with Brother∴Reuß, Brother∴Kellner dropped the title, first suggested, of *Academia Massonica* and submitted reasons and data why the name "Orientalische Templer" (Oriental Templars) should be adopted. These negotiations did not lead to any positive results at the time (1895).[27]

The inner kernel of the OTO in turn was sexual magic—though a variety of sexual magic that had been transformed into a far more exotic and varied growth than Randolph's simple system.

One of the secrets which Our Order possesses in its highest grades is that it gives its members the practical means to re-erect the true temple of Solomon in men, to re-find the "Lost Word," that is, that Our Order gives to the select initiated Brother the practical means which place him in the condition already in this earthly life to experience proofs of his own immortality. . . . Our Order possesses the KEY which unlocks all Masonic and Hermetic secrets; it is the doctrine of Sexual Magic, and this doctrine explains without exception all the riddles of Nature, all Masonic symbolism and all religious systems.

Independent of the H. B. of L. and its direct offshoots, interest in Randolph's works obviously continued in Europe after his death (as witness Fryar, Yarker and Meyrink), but it is difficult now to discern whether and to what extent that interest was other than isolated and purely literary—to what extent, in other words, Randolph's ideas survived in practice or in organized groups rather than merely in the imaginations and work of individual occultists. During his life

Randolph boasted of wide European connections, both of the secret-lodge-in-Paris variety and of the more mundane sort, such as his sale abroad of the rights to his medicines and elixirs, but the claims are vague and unsubstantiated. Ernest Augustus, viscompte de Percévéle, lord of Ulma, the benefactor who provided the funds to publish *Eulis* and to whom Randolph dedicated *The Ghostly Land*, is for us no more than a name. Similarly, Randolph's connection with Walter Moseley, the English occult bibliophile who supposedly died as a consequence of his experiments with drugs under Randolph's tutelage, is little more than a rumor.[28] Some writers on the history of the occult have posited a "tiny group of French followers" of Randolph or "Czech and Austrian" practitioners of his magic who continued to exist after his death and eventually passed the torch to the OTO, but if the genealogy is true the details and documentation are lacking.[29] Similarly, many isolated seekers after enlightenment or small groups both in America and in Europe must have chanced upon Randolph's published works and his secret teachings in the period between his death and World War I, and undoubtedly many of them took up his invitation to occult practice—to direct and personal communication with the celestial hierarchies through the magic mirror, drugs, and sexual magic.

By the end of the nineteenth century, there had been a great metamorphosis in spiritualism and occultism, initiated by Randolph himself and fostered by Emma Hardinge Britten and Madame Blavatsky (at least initially), that stressed above all practical occultism and personal experience. The Order of the Golden Dawn is the best known example, even though its workings were independent of Randolph's and at least officially free of any sexual element. A substantial undercurrent of this new movement toward practical occultism, however, recognized in one way or another that sexual energy was the driving force of occult achievement. Even where Randolph and his ideas were not credited—and perhaps even where his name was unknown— his ideas passed into the commonplace assumptions, the koiné of the era, becoming transformed in the process into strange and exotic growths. In 1886, R. H. Fryar reprinted the *Comte de Gabalis* with its tale of the immortalization of elementals through sexual intercourse with men, supplementing the work with long citations from an eighteenth-century work by Father Sinistrari on the dangers of *incubi* and *succubi*.[30] The occult public was widely interested in the subject, probably because intercourse with such mystical "soul-mates," as Madame Blavatsky made clear in her review of Fryar's book, had become a staple of spiritualism in the 1870s and 1880s.[31] She even accused Hiram E. Butler and Thomas Lake Harris of begetting children on the astral plane through such intercourse.[32]

Largely through Randolph's influence the genie had been released from the bottle and the antiquarian notion that sex provided the lost key to the scattered elements of mythology had taken on a practical side. A multitude of sexual mysticisms flourished, often without formal recognition of Randolph's role, like that of the unhappy Ida Craddock, who killed herself after Anthony Comstock repeatedly had her arrested for pornography.[33] After World War I, Randolph's influence, which had never been totally absent from France because of the French H. B. of L., blossomed again in the work of Maria de Naglowska, transformed by the addition of Satanic and feminist elements, and enjoyed a certain underground vogue in Paris between the two world wars.[34] Randolph's most recent transformation is ironic given his ambivalence about his race. Along with Ida B. Wells, Marie Laveau, and Marcus Garvey he has recently become one of the seven black "racial avatars" recognized by the Aquarian Spiritual Center of Los Angeles—another indirect offshoot of the H. B. of L.[35]

With this proliferation of epigoni, Randolph has become more a figure of myth than a man of history. His greatest influence, however, still remains to be discussed—his influence (or at least the influence of his books and of the current of thought he had come to represent) on Madame Blavatsky. She was the true occult giant of the last quarter of the nineteenth century and the decisive watershed between "Summer Land" spiritualism and modern occultism. Her work actively continues today, though, as we shall see, in a form and with a purpose far different from its earliest intention. Madame Blavatsky has been mentioned frequently in the pages that have gone before as her ideas coincided with those of Randolph, but the details of their similarities and relationship require extended discussion.

Chapter 12

RANDOLPH AND MADAME BLAVATSKY

Helena Petrovna Blavatsky (1831–1891) was the enigmatic Russian who founded the Theosophical Society in New York in 1875 and inspired it until her death in 1891—and in the process fundamentally transformed the occult world. Subsequent myth, propounded by the exponents of the hidden hand, has made Randolph and Madame Blavatsky co-initiates of a mysterious Oriental brotherhood and attributed to them a fatal enmity that led directly to Randolph's death. Behind the myth is a substratum of fact sufficient to show a real, though elusive and indirect, relationship between these two sources of the occult revival of the late nineteenth century.

The Occult Duel

In his introduction to his German translation of one of Randolph's novels in 1922,[1] Gustav Meyrink recounted what little he had been able to learn about the author. He had acquired the manuscript of the book many years before from Kate Corson Randolph, through the Brotherhood of Eulis, and had also gotten other writings of Randolph and a "Battah" mirror. He was unwilling to reveal all that he had learned about Randolph and his practices from the Brotherhood of Eulis because he considered the teachings dangerous, but he did relate several stories he said he had learned from a friend who knew both Randolph and Madame Blavatsky well.

> Helena Petrovna Blavatsky, the famous foundress of the Theosophical Society, had come to know [Randolph] in her travels in

America. They communicated with each other in a very secret manner, as a friend who knew both and was often together with them reported to me. "They appeared to make themselves understood telepathically (through communication of their thoughts)," so my friend wrote to me. "Often, when I was sitting at tea with the 'Old Lady' (Blavatsky's nickname), she suddenly sprang up and called out: 'What does this fellow want!' And then, when I accompanied her, we always encountered the 'Nigger' waiting in some place, to whom Madame Blavatsky was most rapidly directed, as if she was under a command. What they then did with each other, I have never been able to learn, because the Old Lady was as silent as the grave about it."

* * *

"Randolph," so my friend continued in his letter, "is the weirdest man I ever met in my life. I did everything I could to learn what he was really about—in vain. Suddenly, in the midst of talking, on the street, his tone of voice changed and a stranger appeared to speak from him, often in a language (and I know many of these) which was totally unknown to me. His gift of foreseeing events clairvoyantly that happened in far off places bordered on the wonderful. . . .

The cause of the hate that sprang up between Madame Blavatsky and Randolph almost overnight is completely unknown to me. Perhaps it was rivalry. In any case, the Old Lady was victorious. . . . It was in Adyar (India). Madame Blavatsky and I sat motionless and silent in our seats in the shade because it was very hot. Suddenly Madame Blavatsky called out: 'Now the Nigger is shooting at me! . . . So now the devil has him.'

To my astonished question what was wrong, she told me that Randolph just then wanted to murder her in a magical way. In America, thousands of miles away, he had loaded a pistol, commanding with his Will that the bullet might dematerialize and then again become lead in her (Madame Blavatsky's) heart. In the last second, however, Randolph had become crazy and had shot himself in the forehead.

Of course, I didn't believe this, but in any event noted the hour, date and minute.

What I learned about a year later from Kate (Randolph's widow) in Ohio, deeply shocked me: the Nigger had actually shot himself in the forehead at that very time."[2]

The story of Randolph's acquaintance with Madame Blavatsky and his occult duel with her is fascinating, though even in the kindest light it can scarcely be accurate in all its facts since Madame Blavatsky arrived in India only in February 1879, long after Randolph's death. If this were all, the story might be dismissed as pure invention on the part of Meyrink's unnamed friend, but the kernel of the myth is confirmed in a curious way by, of all people, Colonel Olcott, Madame Blavatsky's constant companion beginning in the fall of 1874 and the co-founder of the Theosophical Society.

The greatest occult gossip of the nineteenth century was William Alexander Ayton (1816–1909), a timid Church of England vicar at Chacombe, Oxfordshire, who was the inconstant friend and correspondent of everyone who was anyone in the occult for a half century beginning in the 1860s.[3] He was a Tory in politics, a practicing alchemist (who found the elixir but allowed it to evaporate), a believer in every sort of quack medical advice (Schüssler's "Tissue Remedies" and Babbitt's odd colored-light contraptions), a true paranoid on the subject of the role of the "Black Brotherhood" (exemplified by the Jesuits) in human and especially occult history, and a joiner of every occult scheme of his time (the H. B. of L., the Sât B'hai, the Golden Dawn, the Society of Eight, the Order of Light, and so on)—always in turn hopeful of practical realization of his occult dreams in this life and resigned to disappointment. Failure did not deter him. For all his naiveté, however, he was no fool and was in fact quite learned in matters of occultism. Ayton was a personal friend of Colonel Olcott and Madame Blavatsky—she had even asked him to come to Ostend where she was then staying to help her work on the *Secret Doctrine*. In the mid-1880s, Ayton was also the provincial grand master of the North of the H. B. of L., and as such he had the duty of communicating with the scattered neophytes of the order in England and the United States who had been put under his care. Several of his letters survive in private collections, and they provide fascinating gossip about Randolph and about his relationship with Madame Blavatsky.

In August 1884, Ayton responded to one prospective candidate for admission to the H. B. of L. who had inquired about Robert H. Fryar's advertisements for magic mirrors. Ayton's reply was a thorough condemnation both of Fryar and of Randolph.

The worst feature of [Fryar's] case is that he became Agent for the sale of the posthumous M.S.S. works of the suicide Randolph. Those works contain instructions for the worst kind of Black Magic by means of sexual intercourse—a system well known to have been practised in the East, and also in Europe at various periods, especially in the Middle Ages. These M.S.S. have been sold by this person to several young men with most devastating results. Col. Olcott himself told me that Randolph tried to practice Black Magic upon him, but that he was able to turn the circle back upon him, and that he immediately committed suicide.[4]

Ayton relates this bit of gossip firsthand. Colonel Olcott, he says, told him the story directly, and there is no reason to doubt Ayton's account. In subsequent letters to the same person (who had become a neophyte of the H. B. of L.), Ayton corrected his blunder in condemning Randolph outright—after all, the H. B. of L. at that very time was distributing Randolph's manuscripts on sexual magic to its students— and added further details on the H. B. of L.'s judgment about Randolph and Madame Blavatsky.

I have also heard more as to Randolph. He was an Initiate, but somehow betrayed his trust. Whether he took to Black Magic after that, I do not know. . . . Randolph was really an Initiate, but he gave no attention to the monitions of his Occult Guru, and in consequence, fell into a state of irresponsible Mediumship, during which he published "'Eulis" & then went off into Black Magic. He had not gone far enough to have the Key to Eulis,[5] which makes a very different thing of it. As a Freemason, you will understand that he was accessory to his own destruction & paid the penalty of his obligation. Eulis really contains truths up to a certain point, as taught in all Hermetic Orders. We may almost say, it has been sown broad-cast & therefore it cannot be ignored. I suppose he published it first in his life-time, & since his death, his widow has been by means of Fryar, hawking it in M.S.S. as a posthumous work. I was consulted upon it by several of my Chelas who had given £10 for it. Some of them had taken much harm by reading it & trying to put it into practice. It was sent to me by one of them, & I saw if carried out literally, it must lead to Black Magic. I did not then know, nor when I wrote to you first, about him, that he had really been initiated in a remote branch of our Order. I might have known by asking, but I was put off the scent by Col. O. telling me that he had turned his Black Magic back upon him & caused him to commit suicide, which I now find on authority was a delusion of Col. O. It took a higher power to do that. . . . Nevertheless, I know now, from authority, that [Madame Blavatsky], equally with Randolph, was really initiated in a remote branch of our Order in India. Hence, she has considerable knowledge, having gone further than Randolph. She goes as far as she dare in making revelations without incurring the penalty of her obligation. . . . Madame B. is an Initiate of a remote Oriental branch of our Order, & as such, she has been taught a great deal of Occultism. Like Randolph she has perverted it to her own evil purposes, but unlike Randolph, has contrived to steer clear of the penalty of her obligation.⁶

Here is the H. B. of L.'s full-blown myth of Randolph and Madame Blavatsky: they had both been initiated into "a remote Oriental Branch" of the H. B. of L., probably in India, and both had fallen by the wayside, though Madame Blavatsky had made considerably more progress in occultism than had Randolph before she deviated from the true path.

Other occultists also have told the tale of the fatal duel between Madame Blavatsky and Randolph. Maria de Naglowska, who revivified (and embellished) Randolph's sexual magic in Paris between the wars (chapter 11), repeats it as well, attributing its cause to Randolph's having revealed the "key to the mystery, reserved only for the initiated." She adds that if he died young while Madame Blavatsky lived on, "it was, without doubt, because his task on this earth was accomplished more rapidly than that of the founder of the Theosophical movement. The mission of Randolph was to find and temporarily conceal a light, that of H. P. Blavatsky—to teach the masses."⁷

What are we to make of all this, especially Colonel Olcott's strange story about the "remote Oriental Branch" of the secret brotherhood that fostered both Randolph and Madame Blavatsky?

The full mythology of this hidden hand that guided the rise and development of occultism in the nineteenth century is extensive and has recently begun to be studied carefully. In the early 1890s, the Anglo-Catholic occultist C. G. Harrison published *The Transcendental Universe. Six Lectures on Occult Science, Theosophy, and the Catholic Faith, Delivered before the Berean Society.*⁸ His thesis was that there exist secret fraternities or orders of living men who possess real occult power and involve themselves in the conduct of world affairs; that there are factions (which he labels "Esoterics," "Liberals," and "Brothers of the Left"—the last of which, of course, is identified with the Jesuits—among these adepts and their goals and plans do not always agree; that the spiritualist movement was deliberately created by certain of these adepts for the purpose of opposing the growing materialism of the mid-nineteenth century; that this effort backfired when mediums

258 • *Paschal Beverly Randolph*

universally came to believe that they really were communicating with the spirits of the dead; and that Madame Blavatsky because of her very peculiar occult characteristics became a shuttlecock, controlled first by one and then by another group of adepts for their own ends.

The notions that the hierarchies of earthly and celestial entities (whether Brethren of the Shadow or of the Light) involve themselves in human affairs and that spiritualism was an artificial phenomenon, created by "adepts" or "Rosicrucians on both sides of the grave," are ideas that are familiar from Randolph's works and from those of Emma Hardinge Britten as well. Similarly, the idea that Madame Blavatsky passed from the control of one set of superiors (who taught the perpetual progress of the individualized soul or spirit through the spheres of creation after death) into the control of other masters (who led her to advocate the curious doctrine of impersonal or nonindividualized immortality and reincarnation) is the basic assumption that underlies Ayton's comments both on Madame Blavatsky and on Randolph. Both had originally been part of the authentic brotherhood and then fallen by the wayside, one into black magic and the other into the hands of "Buddhist fanatics." The most interesting facet of all this for occult history is that the doctrines ascribed to the original unknown superiors in this view in fact correspond closely with those of Randolph and, as we shall see, with the early teachings of Madame Blavatsky.

The only thing lacking in Harrison's theory is any discussion of Randolph himself. Others were not slow to point out the connection, however. René Guénon, following in the footsteps of Harrison and the H. B. of L.—he had inherited that order's materials from its provincial grand master for France, F.-Ch. Barlet—thought Madame Blavatsky the tool of various adept brotherhoods with conflicting views on the nature of man and on the methods to be adopted to combat the growing materialism of the second half of the nineteenth century. In its simplest terms, his thesis was that Madame Blavatsky had originally been a simple spiritualist (controlled by, or mediating for, a "spirit" named "John King"). She then had come under the control of the adepts behind the H. B. of L., demoting "John King" in the process to the status of a mere "elemental," and during the period of the H. B. of L.'s control and under its influence she began to propagate its typical teachings—attributing the phenomena of spiritualism to living adepts rather than to the spirits of the dead and touting "occultism" over "spiritualism." Finally, she had been expelled from the H. B. of L., had fallen prey to the omnipresent Buddhist sectarians, and had transformed the Theosophical Society into an organization for the propagation of "Buddhist" religious views on karma and reincarnation.[9]

In his diatribe against spiritualism, Guénon relied for his factual account of the origins of the movement in the Hydesville rappings of 1848 on Emma Hardinge Britten's *History of Modern American Spiritualism* (1870)—a treasure trove of information compiled by Mrs. Britten from long-forgotten journals and pamphlets. There was more to Guénon's use of Mrs. Britten's work than simple scholarship, however, because he prefaced his reference by stating his belief in the "curious fact" that Mrs. Britten had been a member of the H. B. of L. This, in turn, led Guénon to the meat of his theory:

> We say that this fact is curious, because the H. B. of L., while being totally opposed to the theories of spiritism, nonetheless claimed to have been mixed up in a very direct fashion in the production of this movement. In effect, in accordance with the teachings of the H. B. of L., the first "spiritualist" phenomena were provoked, not by the "spirits" of the dead, but by living men acting at a distance, by means known only to certain initiates. And these initiates would have been precisely the members of the "Exterior Circle" of the H.B. of L. Unfortunately, it is difficult to go back, in the history of this association, further than 1870, that is to say, to the very year in which Mrs. Hardinge-Britten published the book which we just mentioned (a book which, needless to say, makes no mention of what we are dealing with now). Also, certain persons have thought they could say that, in spite of [the H. B. of L.'s] pretensions of great antiquity, it dated only from this epoch. But, even if this were true, this would be only as to the form which the H.B. of L. finally assumed. In any case, [the H. B. of L.] received the inheritance of diverse other organizations which, themselves, very certainly existed before the middle of the 19th century, such as the "Fraternity of Eulis," which was directed, at least exteriorly, by Paschal Beverly Randolph, a very enigmatic personage who died in 1875. Basically, the name and form of the organization which would have effectively intervened in the events [surrounding the origins of spiritualism] matter little. And we must say that the thesis of the H. B. of L., in itself and independently of these contingencies, seems to us at least strongly probable.[10]

This ties it all together. In the struggles between the Brethren of the Light and the Brethren of the Shadow for the minds of the nineteenth century, the hidden hand was that of the organization later known as the H. B. of L. This order initially guided and directed Randolph,

Emma Hardinge Britten, and Madame Blavatsky, and its control is the reason for the similarities found in their thought. The myth is clear; facts to support it, however, are more difficult to find and inherently ambiguous when found.

The Reality behind the Myth

Randolph never mentions Madame Blavatsky, and from his letter to Colonel Olcott a few weeks before his death it is clear that if (as seems likely) he and Olcott had met in connection with Olcott's investigation of the Davenport brothers in the 1860s the acquaintance was passing and slight. However, Olcott's familiarity with Randolph's works was considerable. He had collected several of them even before he met Madame Blavatsky and thought enough of them to give them as gifts to her and to his father and to cite the authority of *Ravalette*, "that marvellous book by that lurid genius P. B. Randolph" to establish the proposition that a living adept could control the spirits at seances.[11] None of this is at all unusual, since Olcott had been an avid spiritualist since 1852 and would be expected to be familiar with Randolph's works. Similarly, Madame Blavatsky had clearly read Randolph's books and valued them highly (if not uncritically), as did her "Masters" of the time themselves, but there is no clear indication that she and Randolph ever met, corresponded, or (as Meyrink's friend would have it) "communicated telepathically." They both certainly believed in the possibility of this last mode of communication,[12] but if it took place it is hard to imagine what traces such intercourse would leave for the historian.

Meyrink's unnamed informant said that the two had met on Madame Blavatsky's travels in America. Leaving aside her supposed trip to the United States in the 1850s, which is perhaps mere fiction, the meeting, if it occurred at all, would have had to have taken place at some point between Madame Blavatsky's arrival in New York in July 1873 and Randolph's death in July 1875—two years, during the last eight months of which Randolph was certainly traveling in the West and during which he was probably on the East Coast only once, in 1873, on his way to Europe. Madame Blavatsky's whereabouts, while sketchily known for the second half of 1873, are well known thereafter, and there is no indication that she traveled farther West than Buffalo during the entire period.

It is possible, of course, that the two met in Paris or London during the 1850s or early 1860s. As we have seen in chapter 2 in discussing the mysterious "Vic de Lassa" and his mirror magic, Madame

Blavatsky's masters, at least, were very familiar with the magical and occult circles of Paris at the time Randolph was there, and she herself probably also moved in those same circles. She also is said to have been a subject in Paris for Victor Michal, a mesmerist who used hashish in his experiments and who claimed Isma'ili connections as well.[13] Again, though the point is extraordinarily confused by her contradictory statements, Madame Blavatsky probably was again in Paris in 1858, where she claimed to have been converted to spiritualism by D. D. Home.[14]

One enormously tantalizing hint of a possible direct connection between Madame Blavatsky and Randolph precisely with regard to magic mirrors can be found in Randolph's *Seership,* in which he describes various fabulously expensive magic mirrors he had seen. "The late Maha-Raja Dhuleep Singh possessed three: one an immense diamond, the other an enormous ruby, and the third composed of the largest emerald known in the world."[15] The reference appears firsthand and clearly implies that Randolph had actually seen Singh's emerald mirror. Randolph's use of "late" to describe Singh would appear to be an error since he was alive when Randolph was writing. He may have meant that Dalip Singh (1838–1893) was formerly a maharaja, since he had been maharaja of Lahore until deposed by the British in 1849 and exiled to England in 1854. K. Paul Johnson has marshaled the evidence for various influences on Madame Blavatsky, and in the process has cast fascinating light on the intricate connections between her and Singh's entourage. Johnson draws especial attention to the mysterious figure of a Rajput raja-yogin and magician, Gulab-Lal-Singh, who appears in Madame Blavatsky's *Caves and Jungles of Hindustan* and whom she first met in the house of a dethroned native prince—who can be no other than Dalip Singh—in England in the early 1860s.[16]

Another hint of a possible common source for the stream of teachings given out by Randolph and Madame Blavatsky is provided by Master Koot Hoomi himself, who showed himself familiar with the pullulating world of magical mesmerism that flourished in London and Paris at the time of Randolph's visits there. In the early 1880s, A. P. Sinnett and A. O. Hume, who were even then in the process of receiving endless doctrinal treatises from Koot Hoomi, expressed their dissatisfaction with the lack of practical occult training and proposed to the masters that a practical school of Theosophy should be started— a "hot-bed of magick," as Koot Hoomi characterized it. The suggestion was rejected with horror as impossible to Europeans and almost impossible even in India. In support of his refusal to provide practical training, Master Koot Hoomi cited an earlier experiment along such lines in which he himself had had a hand.

The greatest as well as most promising of such schools in Europe, the last attempt in this direction,—failed most signally some 20 years ago [i.e., before 1862] in London. It was the secret school for a practical teaching of magick, founded under the name of a club, by a dozen of enthusiasts under the leadership of Lord Lytton's father [Edward Bulwer-Lytton]. He had collected together for the purpose, the most ardent and enterprising as well as some of the most advanced scholars in mesmerism and "ceremonial magick," such as Eliphas Levi, Regazzoni, and the Kopt Zergvan-Bey. And yet in the pestilent London atmosphere the "Club" came to an untimely end. I visited it about half a dozen of times, and perceived from the first that there was and could be nothing in it. And this is also the reason why, the British T.S. does not progress one step practically. They are of the Universal Brotherhood *but in name*, and gravitate at best towards *Quietism*—that utter paralysis of the Soul. They are intensely selfish in their aspirations and will get but the reward of their selfishness.[17]

It is unfortunate that nothing more is known about this supposed school. Zergvan Bey is totally unknown and conceivably his name was added to the list simply to supply exotic coloring. Bulwer-Lytton and his interest in magic are well known. As we have discussed already, he probably did meet Randolph at some point, but his biographers are silent on any participation by him in this "club."[18] Lévi seems an unlikely member of any club formed to work practical magic. Of all of these figures, Regazzoni is the most interesting to us, since it is possible that he was the original of Randolph's Italian/Armenian mirror-magician and seer, Cuilna Vilmara (chapter 3). As we shall see, Regazzoni, together with Baron Dupotet, is also frequently cited by Madame Blavatsky in her early works for his astonishing feats, "greater than those attributed to Pythagoras."[19]

The "Half-Initiated Seer"

In 1881 Madame Blavatsky wrote to the *Spiritualist* of London to defend A. P. Sinnett's assertions of the existence of the "Himalayan Brothers" who stood behind the Theosophical Society, and as support for her position she cited Eliphas Lévi and Randolph:

> There never was a true Initiate but knew of the secret Fraternities in the East. It is not Eliphas Lévi who would ever deny their existence, since we have his authentic signature to the contrary. Even P. B.

Randolph, that wondrous, though erratic, genius of America, that half-initiated seer, who got his knowledge in the East, had good reasons to know of their existence, as his writings can prove.[20]

Madame Blavatsky's use of the term *half-initiated* to describe Randolph is certainly significant. She rarely used *initiated* loosely or to apply to a person she thought merely learned in occult matters or possessing occult powers.[21] Rather, the term *initiated* is almost always used by her in the very specific sense of a person who has undergone the necessary training and been formally inducted into some branch of the Great Lodge of which she herself claimed to be a member. Her reference to Randolph, then, sounds an echo of the position advocated a few years later by Reverend Ayton. In Madame Blavatsky's view, apparently, Randolph really had been initiated into a true occult fraternity in the East; his writings demonstrated that fact and were of such weight as to lend support to her own claims. In other words, she implicitly acknowledges that both she and Randolph represent in some fashion the teachings and work of the "Grand Lodge."

Similarly, in her effort to expand the horizons of the spiritualists to include beings other than the spirits of the dead—as Randolph had done fifteen years before—Madame Blavatsky cited Randolph in support of the existence of "elementaries" and "elementals."

Spiritualists have never accepted the suggestions and sound advice of certain of their seers and mediums. They have regarded Mr. Peebles' "Gadarenes" with indifference; they have shrugged their shoulders at the "Rosicrucian" fantasies of P. B. Randolph, and his "Ravalette" has made none of them wiser; they have frowned and grumbled at A. Jackson Davis' "Diakka"; and finally lifting high the banner have declared a murderous war of extermination to the Theosophs and Kabalists. What are now the results.[22]

Mahatma Koot Hoomi also carefully distinguished Randolph from the mass of mere mediums and did so precisely on the basis of the different sources of their visions. He pointed out to A. P. Sinnett the obvious fact that all of the myriad of seers who claimed control by angels or spirits contradicted each other, and he divided visionaries into two categories.

Summed up, it comes to the following:—All the "Rosicrucians," all the mediæval mystics, Swedenborg, P. B. Randolf, Oxley, etc., etc. [teach]: "there are secret Brotherhoods of Initiates in the East, especially in Tibet and Tartary; there only can the Lost Word (which is no word) be found"; and, "there are Spirits of the Elements, and Spirit-Flames, that were never incarnated (in this cycle), and immortality is conditional."[23]

These seers fall into a higher classification than mere "mediums and clairvoyants," who deny these doctrines. The mahatma then singled out William Oxley and Mrs. H. Billing (presumably because they were still living) as examples of the first (higher) category on the ground that they were "in direct communication with the 'Brothers.'"

Despite this approbation, it is clear that the endorsement of Randolph by Madame Blavatsky and her mahatmas was by no means unqualified. In the mid-1880s, W. Q. Judge wrote a long letter to A. P. Sinnett for inclusion in Sinnett's "biography" of Madame Blavatsky. He related that in the early days (probably 1876 or early 1877) while sitting in her rooms he picked up and began to read one of Randolph's works that an unnamed friend of Olcott had brought.

> I was one day, about four o'clock, reading a book by P. B. Randolph, that had just been brought in by a friend of Colonel Olcott. I was sitting some six feet distant from H. P. Blavatsky, who was busy writing. I had carefully read the title-page of the book, but had forgotten the exact title. But I knew that there was not one word of writing upon it. As I began to read the first paragraph, I heard a bell sound in the air, and looking, saw that Mme. Blavatsky was intently regarding me.
>
> "What book do you read?" said she.
>
> Turning back to the title-page, I was about to read aloud the name, when my eye was arrested by a message written in ink across the top of the page which, a few minutes before, I had looked at, and found clear. It was a message in about seven lines, and the fluid had not yet quite dried on the page—its contents were a warning about the book. I am positive that when I took the volume in my hand not one word was written in it.[24]

Even years later Randolph's works continued to be of interest to the original Theosophists, though again the recognition was ambivalent and qualifications were made specifically with reference to Randolph's teachings on sex. In 1889, W. Q. Judge in a backhanded fashion recognized Randolph and Emma Hardinge Britten as forerunners of Madame Blavatsky, but stressed his reservations.

> Since the founding of the T.S., and the appearance of *Isis Unveiled*, all these conditions have changed. Among spiritualists there

had been some preparation for the new *régime* by works like *Art Magic* and *Ghost Land*, and if any had the patience and the hardihood to wade through the writings of P. B. Randolph, they might have discovered amid the ravings of sexual insanity, lucid passages that were indeed food for serious thought. *Isis Unveiled*, that cyclopaedia of occultism, entered the arena at this point.[25]

The Rosicrucians yet Again

When Madame Blavatsky first arrived in America in 1873 she claimed to be a Rosicrucian and made similar claims for years thereafter.[26] Even in these early days, however, it was clear that her Rosicrucians, like Randolph's, were of a peculiar sort. In her first serious article, "A Few Questions to 'HIRAF,'" written by "express orders from S*****" (Serapis Bey, her Egyptian master) in mid-1875, Madame Blavatsky makes it clear that the "Rosicrucians" properly speaking were originally but an extension, an offshoot, of a larger and more elevated brotherhood whose primary seat was in the Orient.[27] While the European Rosicrucians had long since disappeared, the Oriental Rosicrucians—"for such we will call them, being denied the right to pronounce their true name"—with whom she claimed familiarity did "still exist and [had] lost none of the primitive secret powers of the ancient Chaldeans." The "origin of the Brotherhood [can] be ascertained by any earnest, *genuine*, student of Occultism, who happens to travel in Asia Minor, if he chooses to fall in with some of the Brotherhood." These occultists still were ready at times to impart their wisdom and their practice to worthy students, but the prerequisite was that they "Try!"[28] Although Madame Blavatsky always insisted that her immediate masters in the brotherhood were living men,[29] like Randolph she also taught that the work of the brotherhood was a collaboration between these living adepts and "the pure disembodied human and newly-embodied high Planetary Spirits, for the elevation and spiritualization of mankind."[30] In other words, for Madame Blavatsky as for Randolph the true occult brotherhood extended on both sides of the grave and included the exalted ranks of the never embodied.

When Madame Blavatsky was putting forth her Rosicrucian claims in the early 1870s the only context for the term *Rosicrucian* in the United States (besides the purely literary ones supplied by Hargrave Jennings's phallic theories and Bulwer-Lytton's novels—both of which Madame Blavatsky knew and admired) was given by Randolph and his various Rosicrucian endeavors. Aside from Masonic high degrees with a Rosicrucian basis or coloring and quasi-Masonic bodies such as the Societas Rosicruciana in Anglia, Randolph's groups were the only Rosicrucians there were in America at the time, and to mention Rosicrucians from 1873 to 1875 was immediately and necessarily to call to mind Randolph and his work. And, lest there be any mistake about the reference, when Madame Blavatsky came to reveal more about the order to which she *really* belonged—which she began to call the "Brotherhood of Luxor" in the spring of 1875—she emphasized that her order was widespread in America and in addition stressed again that the by-word of the order was Try! This exhortation to Try!—which was, of course, Randolph's motto—was the constant refrain of Madame Blavatsky's brotherhood in the early years in New York before her departure for India in 1878.

Brothers of Luxor

Mme Blavatsky met Colonel H. S. Olcott at a seance in Chittenden, Vermont, in September 1874 and immediately converted him to her cause—a cause from which Olcott never thereafter wavered, though its nature changed drastically over time. Originally, Olcott (who had been an active spiritualist for more than twenty years) was led to believe that Madame Blavatsky likewise was a spiritualist of the traditional sort: "Was not I at first made to believe that I was dealing with disincarnate spirits; and was not a stalking-horse put forward to rap and write, and produce materialized forms for me, under the pseudonym of John King?"[31] This changed over the years.

> Little by little, H. P. B. let me know of the existence of Eastern adepts and their powers, and gave me by a multitude of phenomena the proofs of her own control over the occult forces of nature. At first, as I have remarked, she ascribed them to "John King," [a spirit or elemental] and it was through his alleged friendliness that I first came into personal correspondence with the Masters. . . . For years, and until shortly before I left New York for India, I was connected in pupilage with the African section of the Occult Brotherhood; but, later, when a certain wonderful psycho-physiological change happened to H. P. B. that I am not at liberty to speak about, and that nobody up to the present suspected, although enjoying her intimacy and full confidence, as they fancy, I was transferred to the Indian section and a different group of Masters. For, it may be stated, there is and ever was but one altruistic alliance, or fraternity, of these Elder Brothers of

Plate 4. The Winged Globe, Randolph's Emblem

humanity, the world over; but it is divided into sections according the needs of the human race in its successive stages of evolution.[32]

Colonel Olcott later makes it explicit that by "African" he meant "Egyptian" and that originally he had been inducted into the Egyptian section of the brotherhood. "She subsequently explained that our work, and much more of the same kind, was being supervised by a Committee of seven Adepts belonging to the Egyptian group of the Universal Mystic Brotherhood."[33]

This Egyptian section first introduced itself to Colonel Olcott in the spring of 1875, when he received a letter, emblazoned with emblematic Hebrew letters, Gnostic sigils, and a Maltese cross in a five-pointed star, urging him to place his trust in "Sister Helen" who would lead him to "the Golden Gate of truth."[34] The letter was captioned "From the Brotherhood of Luxor, Section the Vth" and signed by "Tuitit Bey, Observatory of Luxor"—later said by Olcott to have been a Copt[35] — and disclosed that the principals on whose behalf Olcott had been working were "Serapis Bey (Ellora Section)," "Polydorus Isurenus (Section of Solomon)," and "Robert More (Section of Zoroaster)." Colonel Olcott was specific that all of these were Westerners (or at least not Hindus, Sikhs, or Tibetans): "one [was] a representative of the Neo Platonist Alexandrian school, one—a very high one, a Master of the Masters, so to say—a Venetian, and one an English philosopher, gone from men's sight, yet not dead. The first of these (Serapis, or the Master Serapis) became my first Guru."[36]

The first Brotherhood of Luxor letter concluded that it was issued "By Order of the Grand ∴." This symbol was the emblem of the brotherhood thus revealed to Olcott and was expressed either as the traditional Masonic "three points" or as an equilateral triangle with point up.[37] In this latter form it was, of course, also one of the emblems of P. B. Randolph.[38] Olcott is in addition three times in the letter exhorted, "Try!" with the command followed by the equilateral triangle—both of which were practically trademarks of P. B. Randolph and would have been instantly recognized as such by anyone interested in magic or occultism at the time.[39] It is interesting that in these early letters Olcott is also repeatedly told by his guru that Madame Blavatsky was "an Ellorian"—which can only be seen as a reference to the Ellora Brotherhood of Emma Hardinge Britten's adept, the Chevalier Louis.[40] Despite Madame Blavatsky's later denial that Louis was a real adept at all, in her early writings she was more than willing to recognize him as such and to appeal to his writings (as she did to Randolph's) as authority for her own ideas[41]—and those ideas were in fact identical with those of Randolph and Emma Hardinge Britten and foreign to Madame Blavatsky's later teachings. In *Isis Unveiled* (1:368), for example, she quotes the "authority of an adept in that mysterious science"—Louis—for a lucid statement of the process of transmigration eventuating in individualization. It could easily have been written by Randolph and certainly is at variance with her later pronouncements:

> Man lives on many earths before he reaches this. Myriads of worlds swarm in space where the soul in rudimental states performs its pilgrimages, ere he reaches the large and shining planet named the Earth, the glorious function of which is to confer *self-consciousness*. At this point only is he man; at every other stage of his vast, wild journey he is but an embryonic being—a fleeting, temporary shape of matter—a creature in which a *part*, but only a part, of the high, imprisoned soul shines forth; a rudimental shape, with rudimental functions, ever living, dying, sustaining a flitting spiritual existence as rudimental as the material shape from which it emerged; a butterfly, springing up from the chrysalitic shell, but ever, as it onward rushes, in new births, new deaths, new incarnations, anon to die and live again, but still stretch upward, still strive onward, still rush on the giddy, dreadful, toilsome, rugged path, until it awakens once more— once more to live and be a material shape, a thing of dust, a creature of flesh and blood, but now—*a man*.

The Committee of Seven of the Brotherhood of Luxor made its appearance when Colonel Olcott was directed to prepare a circular ("Important to Spiritualists") for inclusion in the *Spiritual Scientist* that touted the journal as the selected forum for putting before spiritualists the work of the best minds.[42] Madame Blavatsky told Olcott to sign the circular: "For the Committee of Seven, Brotherhood of Luxor." In her scrapbook she adds a note to the circular: "Sent to E. Gerry Brown [editor of the *Spiritual Scientist*] by the order of S⋯ and T⋯ B⋯—of Lukshoor. (Published and Issued by Col. Olcott by order of M∴)." Later Colonel Olcott received a certificate on thick green paper, with gold ink, which declared that he was attached to this "Observatory" and that three masters had him under scrutiny.

At almost exactly the same time that the idea of the Theosophical Society was being broached following a lecture by G. H. Felt on September 7, 1875, at one of Madame Blavatsky's "at-homes," the purposely enigmatic invitation in Olcott's circular to inquire about the Brotherhood of Luxor brought results. A Mr. Mendenhall used the columns of the *Religio-Philosophical Journal* to question the existence of the Brotherhood of Luxor, and Madame Blavatsky responded gleefully:

I can satisfy Mr. Mendenhall. The Brotherhood of Luxor is one of the sections of the Grand Lodge of which *I am a member*. If this gentleman entertains any doubt as to my statement—which I have no doubt he will—he can, if he chooses, write to *Lahore* for information. If perchance, the *Seven of the Committee* were so rude as not to answer him, and would refuse to give him the desired information, I can then offer him a little business transaction. Mr. M, as far as I remember, has two wives in the spirit world. . . . If so, let one of the departed ladies tell Mr. M the name of that section of the Grand Lodge I belong to. For *real, genuine, disembodied* spirits, if both are what they claim to be, the matter is more than easy; they have but to enquire of other spirits, look into my thoughts, and so on; for a disembodied entity, an immortal spirit, it is the easiest thing in the world to do. Then, if the gentleman I challenge, though I am deprived of the pleasure of his acquaintance, tells me the true name of the section—which name three gentlemen of New York, who are accepted neophytes of our Lodge, know well — I pledge myself to give to Mr. M the true statement concerning the Brotherhood, which is not composed of spirits, as he may think, but of living mortals, and I will, moreover, if he desires to, put him in direct communication with the Lodge as I have done for others.[43]

Two years later, in *Isis Unveiled*, in discussing esoteric subgroups of all ages, Madame Blavatsky quoted the pithy entry in Kenneth Mackenzie's *Royal Masonic Cyclopædia* on the existence of a group called the "Hermetic Brothers of Egypt": "A Fraternity in America having a Rosicrucian basis, and numbering many members."[44] With this as support, Madame Blavatsky added a footnote (*Isis Unveiled*, 2:307–9) to emphasize her triumph over the doubting Mr. Mendenhall.

What will, perhaps, still more astonish American readers, is the fact that, in the United States, a mystical fraternity now exists, which claims an intimate relationship with one of the oldest and most powerful of Eastern Brotherhoods. It is known as the Brotherhood of Luxor, and its faithful members have the custody of very important secrets of science. Its ramifications extend widely throughout the great Republic of the West. Though this brotherhood has been long and hard at work, the secret of its existence has been jealously guarded. Mackenzie describes it as having "a Rosicrucian basis, and numbering many members" ("Royal Masonic Cyclopædia," p. 461). But, in this, the author is mistaken; it has no Rosicrucian basis. The name Luxor is primarily derived from the ancient Beloochistan city of Lookshur, which lies between Bela and Kedgee, and also gave its name to the Egyptian City.

The picture of the forces that Madame Blavatsky believed were at work through her in the early days is thus fairly clear. She was connected with an Oriental Grand Lodge of adepts and was working directly under the Near Eastern (Egyptian) section of that lodge which was, in a vague manner, both related to and somehow separate from Luxor in Egypt. The lodge was composed of living men, not spirits, but men who knew how to communicate with such spirits and with the never embodied. The lodge was widespread in the United States, and three unnamed gentlemen in New York were members.

Madame Blavatsky returned to the subject of her Brotherhood of Luxor in October 1888, after her war with the H. B. of L. had taught her caution. In an article entitled "Lodges of Magic" she replied to an "esteemed friend" (oddly enough, the Reverend W. A. Ayton) who had proposed to her the establishment of lodges for practical magic:

> [T]he senior Editor of Lucifer begs to inform her friends that she has never had the remotest connection with the so-called "H(ermetic) B(rotheroood) of L(uxor)," and that all representations to the contrary are false and dishonest. There is a secret body—whose diploma, or Certificate of Membership, is held by Colonel Olcott alone among modern men of white blood[45]—to which that name was given by the author of *Isis Unveiled* for convenience of designation* but which is known among Initiates by quite another one. . . . What the real name of that society is, it would puzzle the "Eulian" phallicists of the "H. B. of L." to tell.[46]

---

*In Isis Unveiled, Vol II, p. 308. It may be added that the "Brotherhood of Luxor" mentioned by Kenneth MacKenzie (vide his Royal Masonic Cyclopedia) as having its seat in America, had after all, nothing to do with the Brotherhood mentioned by, and known to us, as was ascertained after the publication of "Isis" from a letter written by this late Masonic author to a friend in New York. The Brotherhood MacKenzie knew of was simply a Masonic Society on a rather more secret basis, and, as he stated in the letter, he had *heard of, but knew nothing of* our Brotherhood, which, having had a branch at Luxor (Egypt), was thus purposely referred to by us under this name alone. This led some schemers to infer that there was a regular Lodge of Adepts of that name, and to assure some credulous friends and Theosophists that the "H.B. of L." was either identical [with] or a branch of the same, supposed to be near Lahore!!—which was the most flagrant untruth.

The late disclaimer is as interesting as the original claim. Madame Blavatsky's earlier strange connection of "Luxor" with "Lukshoor" in Baluchistan has been replaced by the explicit acknowledgment that the original brotherhood to which she introduced Colonel Olcott (whatever its real name may have been) had been called by her the "Brotherhood of Luxor" because it "had a branch at Luxor (Egypt)." Colonel Olcott, who here as in so many instances failed to keep current with (or to acknowledge) Madame Blavatsky's later changes, continued despite her disclaimer to equate *his* brotherhood in the early days with Mackenzie's Brotherhood of Luxor.[47] Here, as in so many other instances, Olcott apparently never got the news, or else refused to go along with subsequent revisionism.

Whatever may be the real truth of Madame Blavatsky's Brotherhood of Luxor, the group as she describes it, with all of its Near Eastern echoes, appears to bear a closer semblance to Randolph's Rosicrucians than it does to her own later Indian or Tibetan mahatmas.[48]

Madame Blavatsky and Spiritualism

Of necessity, since spiritualism was the dominant belief in the circles in which she moved in her early years in America, Madame Blavatsky's early public posturings were made in relationship to spiritualism. The orders of her brotherhood were to effect a change within spiritualism, and, as she repeated constantly, she saw her task as the enlargement of spiritualism's horizons and the shifting of its emphasis from passive "mediumship" to active "magic" or "occultism" controlled by the will. Although she later claimed to have been the first to proclaim these truths,[49] she was foreshadowed at every step in her efforts by both Randolph and by Emma Hardinge Britten in transforming spiritualism into "occultism."

Madame Blavatsky always maintained that she had been sent, "on orders," from Paris to New York in 1873 for the explicit purpose of demonstrating the truth of the phenomena of spiritualism (which were wearing a bit thin after twenty-five years of static repetition, exposures, and frauds) while at the same time showing the poverty and absurdity of spiritualism's theory that the phenomena of the seance room were produced by the blessed dead alone.

> I had to save the situation, for *I was sent from Paris to America on purpose to prove the phenomena, and their reality, and show the fallacy of the spiritualistic theory of spirits.* . . . I did not want people at

large to know that I could *produce the same thing* AT WILL. I had received orders to the contrary. . . . The world is not prepared yet to understand the philosophy of Occult Science . . . and that there are hidden powers in man which are capable of making a *god* of him on earth.[50]

Like Randolph and Emma Hardinge Britten before her and René Guénon afterward, Madame Blavatsky was convinced that spiritualism as a movement was an artificial phenomenon, a construct, specifically created "from the East," for the sole purpose of convincing the world of the falsity of materialism.

[T]he time is near when all the old superstitions and the errors of centuries must be swept away by the hurricane of Truth. As the prophet Mohammed, when he perceived that the mountain would not come to him, went himself towards the mountain, so Modern Spiritualism made its unexpected appearance from the East, before a skeptical world, to terminate in a very near future the oblivion into which the ancient secret wisdom had fallen.[51]

The primary characteristic of her early writings was their emphasis on enlarging the horizons of spiritualism while preserving its vision of the unseen world and the reality (if not the explanation) of the phenomena of the seance room. Again, as Randolph had before her, Madame Blavatsky added to the restricted world view of spiritualism the claim that other entities (in her case, living adepts, "elementals," "elementaries," "spirits of the fifth sphere," "planetary spirits," and so on) besides the "spirits of the dead" were to be contended with.[52] She also added (as had Randolph) that not all of these entities were necessarily good.

Randolph had always stressed the existence of vast hierarchies of entities, living, disembodied, and never embodied, on both sides of the grave and stretching away through the universes toward the primal Central Sun of deity (chapter 5). He also, for the first time in modern English-speaking spiritualism, taught the existence of the "elementals"—the natural spirits of the elements who never had been part of the world of men. With his recantation speech in 1858, he began in addition to introduce into the blithe Summer Land school of spiritualism the notion of evil—a notion which amounted at times almost to the idea of an "evil center" operating in the world. The chief expression of this center was the unregenerate souls of disembodied men, who roamed the world, confined to the middle state as "larvae," and preyed as "vampires" upon mediums. It was these creatures, he thought, who inspired and possessed mediums and produced many of the phenomena of the seance room. Randolph envisioned descending hierarchies of these evil spirits, apparently culminating in the "Brethren of the Shadow" and their adherents who opposed the Brethren of the Light for their own selfish ends.[53]

Madame Blavatsky again retraces Randolph's footsteps, explicitly citing him as we have seen for the reality of the elementals. In her writings, these nature spirits were frequently the masters of the unconscious medium and were the tools of the adept/magician and of the disembodied dead, both good and evil.[54] The unregenerate "souls" of the dead also played a central role in her criticism of spiritualism. By her time in New York, the notion of such 'evil spirits' had become a commonplace of spiritualism, and in her works they become the "elementaries"—the detritus of the depraved dead who have forfeited immortality:

> [T]hese souls have at some time prior to death separated from themselves their divine spirits, and so lost their chance for immortality. . . . Once divorced from their bodies, these souls (also called "astral bodies") of purely materialistic persons, are irresistibly attracted to the earth, where they live a temporary and finite life amid the elements congenial to their gross natures. . . . [T]hey are now unfitted for the lofty career of the pure, disembodied being, for whom the atmosphere of earth is stifling and mephitic, and whose attractions are all away from it.[55]

There are very striking similarities, verbal and theoretical, with Randolph in Madame Blavatsky's formulation of her ideas on these evil "spirits." Her elementaries are confined within "the dense fogs of the material atmosphere" as Randolph's "demons" are confined to the borderland of the middle state; they are "larvae" and "vampires" and in the East are known as the "Brothers of the Shadow"—as are Randolph's, and like his entities they hate and oppose humanity and obsess and possess the medium.[56]

For anyone familiar only with Madame Blavatsky's later writings, the position advocated by her in her early days on the reality of communication with the spirits of the dead must appear surprising. In her early writings, spiritualism is described as true but incomplete, a phenomenon that must be supplemented by reference to the wisdom of the East on the kinds of spiritual entities and the role of will in communicating with them.[57] In her later works, spiritualism becomes purely and simply a dead end, and the possibility of real communication with the "spirits of the dead" is practically denied because the "personality" or "individuality"—the "John Smithness" of the deceased—endures only for a short while in "Devachan" and then disappears when the *impersonal* principles of man reincarnate. This was the source of the ongoing struggle between Madame Blavatsky and the spiritualists and "Western" occultists in the 1880s—one of whose primary manifestations was the H. B. of L. The rub, of course, as Emma Hardinge Britten, the spiritualists generally, and the H. B. of L. were quick to point out, was the loss of individuality after death and the effective denial of any real communication with the elevated and advanced souls beyond the grave.[58]

Madame Blavatsky's original criticism of spiritualism (besides deploring its limited repertoire of communicating entities) was principally addressed to the falseness of a certain class of spiritualist phenomena very common in her day—"materialized" spirits, the apparently physical appearance of the dead at seances. These she reiterated were dreadful illusions, the work of elementals and elementaries and were almost never produced by the disembodied spirits of good men. Despite this, she clearly did not reject outright all communication with the disembodied dead, as she termed them. As Randolph had done before her, she taught that the phenomena of spiritualism, while usually the work of living adepts or elementaries making use of the elementals, or even of the elementals acting of their own accord, could nonetheless be the work of the disembodied dead and of the "planetary spirits," the "Pre-Adamite *pitris*"—beings of a race other than our own who were never embodied as men.[59]

We are far from believing that all the spirits that communicate at circles are of the classes called "Elemental," and "Elementary." Many—especially among those who control the medium subjectively to speak, write , and otherwise act in various ways—are human, disembodied spirits. Whether the majority of such spirits are good or *bad*, largely depends on the private morality of the mediums, much on the circle present, and a great deal on the intensity and object of their purpose. . . . But, in any case, human spirits can never materialize themselves in *propria persona*. . . . We will now only again assert that no spirit claimed by the spiritualists to be human was ever proved to be such on sufficient testimony. The influence of the *disembodied* ones can be felt, and communicated *subjectively by* them to sensitives. They can produce *objective* manifestations, but they cannot produce *themselves* otherwise than as described above. They can control the body of a medium, and express their desires and ideas in various modes well known to spiritualists; but not *materialize* what is matterless and purely spiritual—their divine essence. Thus every so-called "materialization"—when genuine—is either produced (*perhaps*) by the will of that spirit whom the "appearance" is claimed to be but can only personate at best, or by the elementary goblins themselves, which are generally too stupid to deserve the honor of being called devils. Upon rare occasions the spirits are able to subdue and control these soulless beings, which are ever ready to assume pompous names if left to themselves, in such a way that the mischievous spirit "of the air," shaped in the real image of the *human* spirit, will be moved by the latter like a marionette, and unable to either act or utter other words than those imposed on him by the "immortal soul." But this requires many conditions generally unknown to the circles of even spiritualists most in the habit of regularly attending seances.[60]

The Primordial Central Sun

As her contemporaries recognized, Randolph, Madame Blavatsky, and Emma Hardinge Britten represented a metamorphosis in spiritualism, with the characteristics we have already observed (see chapter 11).[61] On a purely doctrinal and cosmological level as well, the early (as distinct from the later) ideas of Madame Blavatsky had very striking similarities with those of the Randolph/Emma Hardinge Britten wave or current of occultism, similarities which lent support to the hidden hand conspiracy theories of the H. B. of L. and others that these three pioneers of occultism had all originally been part of or inspired by a single school or branch of occultism that operated behind the scenes, or had at least been subject to the developmental process of such a group or school. Of central importance in any of these theories is the idea of a change or transformation in Madame Blavatsky's ideas, a shift from early influences (by hypothesis, those of the H. B. of L., under whatever name it then operated) to later and different ones (those of the omnipresent "Buddhist fanatics") who *ex hypothesi* controlled her after her departure for India in 1878, and indeed her early ideas are frequently diametrically opposed to the ideas expounded by her in later days. The cosmological and doctrinal ideas of her New York years (1873–1878) are easily summarized and are strikingly familiar after our review of Randolph's ideas and those of Emma Hardinge Britten.

1. There is a primordial "central, spiritual SUN" which is eternal, invisible and divine, and the "Æther," the "astral fire," the "astral ocean of invisible fire" permeates the universes and acts as the agent of all magical and occult operations.[62]

2. Emanating from the divine Central Sun is the spirit, which is a ray of the divine and co-eternal with the Sun and yet is in some inchoate way distinct and individualized.[63]

3. From the "central, spiritual and *Invisible* sun" the originally bisexual "monad" radiates, thus beginning its vast journey from the sun, through myriads of transformations, into birth and individualization on its journey back to the sun.[64]

4. On this journey the monad transmigrates through myriads of forms, seeking "individualization" as man—the potential stepping-off place for perpetual progress through the spheres above.[65]

5. Man himself is a trinity of Spirit, soul, and body. The spirit is a ray of the eternal, spiritual Sun and is divine.[66]

6. Man's soul is matter—ethereal—and as such is mortal. It can be separated from the body and can move independently of it even during life. At the same time, the soul is conditionally immortal, and it becomes immortal, if at all, when it is joined with the spirit.[67] The goal of the monad's journey through its transmigrations is its individualization, the joining of the mortal soul with the immortal spirit. "Man is also triune: he has his objective, physical body; his vitalizing astral body (or soul), the real man; and these two are brooded over and illuminated by the third—the sovereign, the immortal spirit. When the real man succeeds in merging himself with the latter, he becomes an immortal entity."[68]

7. Immortality is conditional. If man during life sets his mind on material things, at death his soul loses contact with the immortal spirit and is doomed to roam the confines of the material world as an "elementary" until it gradually dissolves and is annihilated.[69]

8. If man on earth keeps the spiritual in mind, the soul becomes immortal and a "god" and sets out on a vast ascensive journey through the spheres, a joint creature of Spirit and soul, and at every stage the soul ("Astral Soul") progressively casts off its

external forms while preserving its individuality and fundamental form for "millions of ages."[70] "[T]he liberated soul-Monad, exultantly rejoins the mother and father spirit, the radiant Augoeides, and the two, merged into one, forever form, with a glory proportioned to the spiritual purity of the past earth-life, the Adam who has completed the circle of necessity, and is freed from the last vestige of his physical encasement. Henceforth, growing more and more radiant at each step of his upward progress, he mounts the shining path that ends at the point from which he started around the GRAND CYCLE."[71]

9. The goal of the vast process is return to the divine Sun. This is nirvana, but that state is by no means annihilation. It is rather existence in the spirit alone, with the soul "re-fused" into the spirit, free at last of matter and external form.[72]

With the exception of the ultimate and final fate of the individualized soul after the myriads of ages of progress as a godling through the spheres—an issue on which Randolph himself changed positions and Madame Blavatsky appears to have wavered—the similarities of Madame Blavatsky's early views with those of Randolph and of the "Western" occultists and spiritualists generally are striking and, to those so inclined, they provided strong evidence of the operation of the hidden hand at work in the rise of occultism.

Reincarnation and the Sleep of Sialam

One of the most singular examples of the consonance of the ideas of Madame Blavatsky and Randolph is found in their views on reincarnation. Randolph thought that once the monad had transmigrated through the lower, material realms and reached individualization as a soul incarnate in man, it never—with minor exceptions—returned to rebirth on this earth. This denial of reincarnation was indeed the consensus both of American and of British spiritualists of the time. The uniqueness in Randolph's position is found in the exceptions that he admitted to this rule, and it is precisely there that his agreement with the Madame Blavatsky of *Isis Unveiled* lies. In general, Randolph allowed for a sort of rebirth on earth only in the case of abortions and congenital idiots. In these cases, he thought, the "monad" somehow never became properly encased in the body and individualized and hence sought again to incarnate on this earth.[73]

Madame Blavatsky's position in the early years is precisely identical and for precisely the same reasons. Despite a sea of ink, spilled by her and others in an attempt to explain the unexplainable, there can be no doubt that in her New York years she absolutely and unequivocally denied the reality of reincarnation in the sense of reincarnation of the same individual on earth, allowing only the exceptions stated earlier by Randolph—and (unusually for her early work) she emphasized that her position was derived from "authority."

We will now present a few fragments of this mysterious doctrine of reincarnation—as distinct from metempsychosis—which we have from an authority. Reincarnation, *i.e.*, the appearance of the same individual, or rather his astral monad, twice on the same planet, is not a rule in nature; it is an exception, like the teratological phenomenon of a two-headed infant. It is preceded by a violation of the laws of harmony of nature, and happens only when the latter, seeking to restore its disturbed equilibrium, violently throws back into earth-life the astral monad which had been tossed out of the circle of necessity by crime or accident. Thus, in cases of abortion, of infants dying before a certain age, and of congenital and incurable idiocy, nature's original design to produce a perfect human being, has been interrupted. Therefore, while the gross matter of each of these several entities is suffered to disperse itself at death, through the vast realm of being, the immortal spirit and astral monad of the individual—the latter having been set apart to animate a frame and the former to shed its divine light on the corporeal organization—must try a second time to carry out the purpose of the creative intelligence.

If reason has been so far developed as to become active and discriminative, there is no reincarnation on this earth, for the three parts of the triune man have been united together, and he is capable of running the race. But when the new being has not passed beyond the condition of monad, or when, as in the idiot, the trinity has not been completed, the immortal spark which illuminates it, has to reenter on the earthly plane as it was frustrated in its first attempt. Otherwise, the mortal or astral, and the immortal or divine, souls, could not progress in unison and pass onward to the sphere above. . . . [T]he monad which was imprisoned in the elementary being—the rudimentary or lowest astral form of the future man—after having passed through and quitted the *highest* physical shape of a dumb animal . . . that monad, we say, cannot skip over the physical and intellectual sphere of the terrestrial man, and be suddenly ushered into the spiritual sphere above. What reward or punishment can there be in that sphere of disembodied human entities for a foetus or a human embryo which had not even time to breathe on this earth, still less an opportunity to exercise the divine faculties of the spirit? Or, for an irresponsible infant, whose senseless monad remaining dormant within the astral and physical casket, could as little prevent him from burning himself as another person to death? Or for one idiotic from birth . . . and who therefore is irresponsible for either his disposition, acts, or the imperfections of his vagrant, half-developed intellect?[71]

This is exactly the doctrine first put forth by Randolph in *Dealings with the Dead* in 1862.[75] It is also perfectly consistent with the general cosmological views of individualization and progress that we have just explored and inconsistent with, or at least difficult to reconcile with, those that Madame Blavatsky later espoused. "Man" was the pinnacle of a vast series of transmigrations by the monad. In this life he either attached himself to his higher principle (the spirit) and thus became an immortal individual which progressed thereafter through myriads of spheres, or he severed the connection with the immortal spirit and at death became one sort of "elementary" that gradually decayed into annihilation. There was simply no room in the scheme for "reincarnation," for a return to earth to atone for the misdeeds of the last life and to try again to achieve immortality. Only in those instances where the monad had somehow not properly and fully come to animate the entity, where nature had failed to produce a "Man," did reincarnation occur.[76]

There is one other facet of Madame Blavatsky's teachings on reincarnation that appears to establish conclusively the kinship of her ideas with Randolph's. Randolph, as we have seen, believed that as a special case *he* was reincarnated again on earth, as punishment for some heinous crime he had committed in a past life (see chapter 6). This was the underlying theme of *Ravalette* in which the protagonist was condemned to rebirth for some crime. Madame Blavatsky, strikingly, echoes the same idea, emphasizing its Oriental origins.

Further, the same occult doctrine [reincarnation] recognizes another possibility; albeit so rare and so vague that it is really useless to mention it. Even the modern Occidental occultists deny it, though it is universally accepted in Eastern countries. When, through vice, fearful crimes and animal passions, a disembodied spirit has fallen to the eighth sphere . . . he can, with the help of that glimpse of reason and consciousness left to him, repent; that is to say, he can, by exercising the remnants of his will-power, strive upward, and like a drowning man, struggle once more to the surface. . . . A strong aspiration to retrieve his calamities, a pronounced desire, will draw him once more into the earth's atmosphere. Here he will wander and suffer more or less in dreary solitude. His instincts will make him seek with avidity contact with living persons. . . . These spirits are the invisible but too tangible magnetic vampires. . . .

* * *

It is for these carnal terrestrial *larvae*, degraded human spirits, that the ancient kabbalists entertained a hope of *reincarnation*. But when, or how? At a fitting moment, and if helped by a sincere desire for his amendment and repentance by some strong, sympathizing person, or the will of an adept, or even by a desire emanating from the erring spirit himself, provided it is powerful enough to make him throw off the burden of sinful matter. Losing all consciousness, the once bright monad is caught once more into the vortex of our terrestrial evolution, and it repasses the subordinate kingdoms, and again breathes as a living child.[77]

The similarities with Randolph, even on the verbal level, are apparent. It is the will alone that can save the disembodied and lost criminal, and in the process of salvation he becomes a "vampire"—an echo of Dhoula Bel, the vampire, the enigmatic alter-ego that haunted Ravalette's steps in *Ravalette*. To drive home the comparison, moreover, Madame Blavatsky goes on to add that "few kabbalists" believed in the possibility of this sort of reincarnation, and that the idea had originated with the astrologers who had come upon it in casting nativities for historical figures and found that the results tallied perfectly with certain prophecies. "Observation, and what would now be termed 'remarkable coincidences,' added to revelation during the 'sacred sleep' of the neophyte, disclosed the dreadful truth. So horrible is the thought that even those who ought to be convinced of it prefer ignoring it, or at least avoid speaking on the subject."[78] This "sacred sleep" can only be Randolph's sleep of Sialam.

This way of obtaining oracles was practiced in the highest antiquity. In India, this sublime lethargy is called "the sacred sleep of * * *" It is an oblivion into which the subject is thrown by certain magical processes, supplemented by draughts of the juice of the soma. The body of the sleeper remains for several days in a condition resembling death, and by the power of the adept is purified of its earthliness and made fit to become the temporary receptacle of the brightness of the immortal Augoeides. In this state the torpid body is made to reflect the glory of the upper spheres, as a burnished mirror does the rays of the sun. . . . What his lips utter he will never know; but as it is the spirit which directs them they can pronounce nothing but divine truth. For the time being the poor helpless clod is made the shrine of the sacred presence, and converted into an oracle a thousand times more infallible than the asphyxiated Pythoness of Delphi.[79]

There can be no question about the kinship of these curious ideas with those of Randolph.

All of these early views of Madame Blavatsky on reincarnation, cosmology, and the postmortem continuation of the individualized entity that she taught would sally forth as a godlet, an adventurer into the infinitely varied worlds of creation, changed markedly in her later works,[80] and the change was evidence, for those inclined to search for it, of the operation of the hidden hand in the development of occultism and of Madame Blavatsky's change of allegiance from her original masters—masters who were, by hypothesis, the powers behind Randolph and the H. B. of L.[81]

Chapter 13

ℛANDOLPH, ℬLAVATSKY, AND OCCULT ℘RACTICE

Yet another of Madame Blavatsky's principal complaints against contemporary spiritualism in the late 1870s was the same as that lodged against it fifteen years before by Randolph: spiritualism was a purely passive phenomenon, and it left the "medium" in the control of entities whose identity was, at a minimum, unknown.[1] Opposed to this in her mind was the ancient "Magic," a precise science preserved and still practiced in the East, which allowed its practitioner to control the entities that appeared and to discriminate among them. In turn, the key to magic and occultism was the will, summed up in the exhortation to Try![2] In all of this, as with Randolph, the mesmerists—especially the Baron Dupotet—were her model.

Madame Blavatsky's public position on the possibility and value of practical occultism and magic for members of her society changed markedly over time. In her earliest writings she constantly reiterated that practical occultism ("magic") was the proper goal of those elite few capable of pursuing it, that book learning and antiquarian devotion to occultism were insufficient to develop this practical side of occultism,[3] and that the path to practical magic, for those willing to devote their lives to it, lay—as it had with Randolph—in the East.

> To the fervent and persevering candidates for the above science, I have to offer but one word of advice, "Try and become." One single journey to the Orient, made in the proper spirit, and the possible emergencies arising from the meeting of what may seem no more than the chance acquaintances and adventures of any traveler, may quite as likely as not throw wide open to the zealous student, the heretofore closed doors of the final myster-

ies. I will go farther and say that such a journey, performed with the omnipresent idea of the one object, and with the help of a fervent will, is sure to produce more rapid, better, and far more practical results, than the most diligent study of Occultism in books—even though one were to devote to it dozens of years.[4]

In its early years, in accordance with these views on "magic," the Theosophical Society devoted considerable effort to practical occultism and to developing the hidden powers in man—an effort that, although totally consistent with the views of Randolph, Emma Hardinge Britten, and the H. B. of L., was at variance with the ideas of Madame Blavatsky in her later years.[5]

The Original Purpose of the Theosophical Society

The orthodox history of the Theosophical Society is that when the Theosophical Society was founded by Madame Blavatsky, Colonel Olcott, and others (including Emma Hardinge Britten) in September 1875, its purpose was merely to "collect and diffuse a knowledge of the laws which govern the universe."[6] This version of events—guided retroactively by the later rejection of occult practice by the Theosophical Society—has it that at its commencement the society was an open one, devoted simply to discussion, the presentation of papers by the members, and the occasional "testing" of mediums. Practical and personal occult work ("magic"), with the notable and ill-fated exception of the claims of G. H. Felt that will be discussed below, played no part in the new society's program. In this version, the pledge of secrecy that formed such an important part of the society in the early years had to be instituted in early 1876 only because one of its members (Charles Sotheran) temporarily defected for reasons extraneous to the work of the group and publicly criticized the society.[7] This usual explanation, however, appears incomplete as to the intended nature of the original society, and it fails to do justice to what it was that the society was really doing that was thought to need concealment. In reality, it appears that what was sought to be concealed was the practical magical work that was being done by at least a subset of the early Theosophists, work that had been going on secretly in Madame Blavatsky's circle even before the founding of the society and which was viewed as one of the principal reasons for the society's existence.

Charles Sotheran (1847–1902), like Madame Blavatsky's old traveling companion A. L. Rawson (with whom Sotheran was to be associated in various Masonic ventures), is one of the great enigmas of the early Theosophical Society. (It was he who proposed the name for the new society.) He was an English bibliophile and socialist who arrived in New York in 1874 adorned with a wide range of occult and fringe-Masonic connections. Sotheran was a member of the Societas Rosicruciana in Anglia, like the mirror magicians F. G. Irwin, Frederick Hockley, and Kenneth Mackenzie (discussed in chapter 2), and he was also a member of the Rite of Memphis and of various of John Yarker's Masonic concoctions.[8] He intimated more mysterious connections still. In June 1875, he contributed a piece on Cagliostro and the living reality of alchemy and "Theurgic Magic" to the *Spiritual Scientist*,[9] a struggling spiritualist journal that Madame Blavatsky and Colonel Olcott were attempting to transform into a vehicle for the promotion of occultism, and appended to his name "(Societ: Rosie Crucis)"—a designation clearly intended to convey more than his membership in the Soc. Ros. in Anglia. After Madame Blavatsky's first major article ("A Few Questions to 'HIRAF' ") on the "Oriental Rosicrucians" appeared in the same journal in July, the editor carefully explained that the Soc. Ros. was merely a "shell," like the Freemasons.[10] Sotheran in turn defended his pretensions: "To those who are genuinely anxious, and seek with abnegation for information, I will freely impart—having freely received or becoming not being made—to those having authority through +++++++ and the 'M.C.' will my credentials, engraved on the tablets, be freely displayed."[11]

In later years, Sotheran claimed that even before the founding of the Theosophical Society he and Madame Blavatsky, as he told a reporter, had known each other well "not only as advanced masons, but as Brothers of the Rosy Cross. In fact, it was first intended that the society organized for work on the exoteric plane should be openly known as what it really is (or was originally) a branch of the Rosicrucian Brotherhood." The Theosophical Society was in fact merely a convenient front, erected because "it was not judged wise to take the outer world into the secret of the Rosicrucian origin of the society."[12]

After being one of the leading lights of the new Theosophical Society during the first three months of its existence, Sotheran, in December 1875, had a public falling out with Madame Blavatsky and the society, and it was his defection that prompted the transformation of the society into a secret one early in 1876. Its work was made secret, and an oath, signs, and words of recognition were instituted among the members. In the oath of the society, the probationer promised to "maintain ABSOLUTE SECRECY respecting its proceedings, including its investigations and experiments."[13] In succeeding years, membership was divided into three sections and a ritual structure and initiation were imposed, but the scheme was never entirely worked out to anyone's satisfaction.[14] In 1878, Olcott, Madame Blavatsky, Sotheran (who had been welcomed back into the society six months after his defection), and others toyed with the idea of patterning the degrees and ritual on Freemasonry, making the society in effect a higher degree body above the craft degrees, "restoring to [Freemasonry] the vital element of Oriental mysticism which it lacked or had lost."[15] There was discussion even long after Olcott and Madame Blavatsky arrived in India in 1879 of completing the structure—Swami Dayananda, the head of the Arya Samaj with which the society was temporarily amalgamated, even drafted a ritual, and one fellow of the society (at least) was publicly admitted to the second section.

As the degrees were initially described in a circular issued in May 1878 while Madame Blavatsky and Colonel Olcott were still in New York, persons joining the society became probationers in the third degree of the third section and then progressed through the degrees based on "merit."[16] While merit, in turn, is defined largely in moral terms, there is no reason to doubt that progress in the degrees was also thought to turn on practical proficiency in occultism. In the society's first circular to correspondents (issued in May 1878), Madame Blavatsky made the point explicitly:

> [The Theosophical Society] influences its fellows to acquire an intimate knowledge of natural law, especially its occult manifestations. As the highest development, physically and spiritually, on earth, of the Creative Cause, man should aim to solve the mystery of his being. He is the procreator of his species, physically, and having inherited the nature of the unknown but palpable Cause of his own creation, must possess in his inner, psychical self, this creative power in lesser degree. He should, therefore, study to develop his latent powers, and inform himself respecting the laws of magnetism, electricity and all other forms of force, whether of the seen or unseen universes.[17]

In commenting on this, Colonel Olcott made it clear that the degree and section structure announced "was in the hope and expectation that we should have more practical guidance in adjusting the several grades of members than we had had—or have since had, I may add."[18]

In September 1878, Madame Blavatsky and Colonel Olcott issued another circular to announce the new "Theosophical Society of the Arya Samaj of Aryavart," the result of the alliance with the Indian

Arya Samaj of Swami Dayananda. This also made it clear that the structuring of the society into sections was to promote individual, practical occult development. The circular provided that members "also, should they so desire, labour to acquire that control over certain forces of nature which a knowledge of her mysteries imparts to its possessor." Olcott in describing the circular in the 1890s elaborated on the generalization and at the same time attempted to gloss over the changes wrought by the intervening years:

The occult training and developments of H. P. B. and her grade of pupils were here hinted at. The phrase shows that the chief original motive of the Founders of the Society was to promote this kind of study; it being their firm conviction that with the development of the psychical powers and spiritual insight all religious knowledge was attainable, and all ignorant religious dogmatism must vanish.[19]

The "Principles, Rules, and Bye-Laws" of the society, adopted in late 1879,[20] make it clear that, as envisioned, the first section was the inaccessible abode of the masters or brothers—the inner circle of the unknown superiors, who guided the society—and that practical work still continued to be a goal:

Upon his being accepted by the President of the Society or Branch . . ., at the expiration of three weeks . . ., the candidate shall be invested with the secret signs, words, or tokens by which Theosophists of the third (probationary) Section make themselves known to each other, a solemn obligation upon honour having first been taken from him in writing, and subsequently repeated by him orally before witnesses that he will neither reveal them to any improper person, nor divulge any other matter or thing relating to the Society, especially its experiments in Occult Sciences, which it is forbidden to disclose.

Madame Blavatsky also makes the same point about practical occult work in *Isis Unveiled* (1877): "The Theosophical Society, to which these volumes are dedicated by the author as a mark of affectionate regard, was organized at New York in 1875. The object of its founders was to experiment practically in the occult powers of Nature, and to collect and disseminate among Christians information about the Oriental religious philosophies."[21] At the same time, she saw no easy path for Westerners to obtain practical realization. At the end of *Isis*

Unveiled, after 1,200 pages devoted primarily to proving the universality of magic and the role of spiritualism as the stepping stone to magic, Madame Blavatsky took up the obvious question that must have been present in the minds of many of her readers:

> By those who have followed us thus far, it will naturally be asked, to what practical issue this book tends; much has been said about magic and its potentiality, much of the immense antiquity of its practice. Do we wish to affirm that the occult sciences ought to be studied and practiced throughout the world? Would we replace modern spiritualism with the ancient magic?[22]

Her answer was a solid "no!"—at least for the masses. In Madame Blavatsky's view, the acquisition of magic was "practically beyond the reach of the majority of white-skinned people; and that, whether their effort is made at home or in the East." For a variety of reasons— temperament, endurance, inherited intuition and, especially, lack of proper training—attainment could be had by only one in a million, or one in 10 million Westerners. For the few who were prepared to "pay the price of discipline and self-conquest which their development exacts" the answer, however, was different.[23]

> To become a neophyte, one must be ready to devote himself heart and soul to the study of mystic sciences. Magic—most imperative of mistresses—brooks no rival. Unlike other sciences, a theoretical knowledge of formulae without mental capacities or soul powers, is utterly useless in magic. The spirit must hold in complete subjection the combativeness of what is loosely termed educated reason, until facts have vanquished cold human sophistry.[24]

The conclusion is inescapable that in the early days of Theosophy, mere bookish occultism was thought useless. Practical "magic," although it was no easy mistress and required the instruction of adepts, was the goal and the only real path to personal, direct experience of the mysteries of the universe.

> To admit the possibility of anyone becoming a practical Cabalist (or a Rosicrucian, as we will call him, as the names seem to have become synonymous) who simply has the firm determination to "become" one, and hopes to get the secret knowledge through studying the Jewish Cabala, or every one that may come into existence, without actually being initiated by another, and so

being "made" such by someone who "knows," is as foolish as to hope to thread the famous labyrinth without the clue. . . . [W]hat hope can there be for a modern Occultist, learned only in theoretical knowledge, to ever attain his object? Occultism without practice will ever be like the statute of Pygmalion, and no one can animate it without infusing into it a spark of the sacred Divine Fire.[25]

What then appears to have been at issue in the society as originally envisioned—and in Madame Blavatsky's gathering of followers even before the commencement of the society[26]—was not mere theoretical discussion among equals or merely the dissemination of bookish learning, but practical occult work and (it was hoped) what would later be called "chelaship"—initiation into practical occultism by the masters.[27] This practical side of the work of the society was secret from the beginning,[28] and it was disagreement precisely over one aspect of this practical work—the public announcement of the experiments of G. H. Felt—that led to the defection of Charles Sotheran and the imposition of a formal oath of secrecy on the members of the society.[29]

The Enigmatic G. J I. Felt

Felt is the centerpiece of René Guénon's hidden-hand views of the relationship between the H. B. of L. and Madame Blavatsky. Guénon— undoubtedly following the ideas of the H. B. of L., although Felt is nowhere mentioned in the order's surviving records—believed that Felt, like Emma Hardinge Britten, was a member of the H. B. of L., and that it was he who had brought Madame Blavatsky and Colonel Olcott into the H. B. of L. and under the control of "Serapis"—"Serapis Bey" or the "Master Serapis," as he is variously called. Guénon dates the induction of Madame Blavatsky and Olcott into the H. B. of L. precisely to April 1875 and believed that she fell under the control of Serapis on September 7, 1875, the famous evening on which Felt had given an informal talk at her rooms on "The Lost Canon of Proportions of the Egyptians," the lecture that gave rise to the Theosophical Society.[30] Later (in 1878 according to this theory), Madame Blavatsky and Olcott were expelled from the H. B. of L., and fell under the control of the "Kashmirì Brother"—Master Koot Hoomi. Guénon makes this second transfer of control coincide with Madame Blavatsky's forming an alliance of the Theosophical Society with the Arya Samaj in 1878.[31]

By this theory, then, the H. B. of L. or one of its parent, sister or predecessor groups (such as Randolph's Brotherhood of Eulis, in which Guénon believed the origins of the H. B. of L. lay) controlled Madame Blavatsky from 1875 to some time in 1878 and, during that time, she did its work. As for Felt, Guénon states that, having delivered one lecture on the "Egyptian Kabbala" and promised to give three more, he "disappeared brusquely, leaving various papers in the hands of Mme Blavatsky; without doubt, his mission was accomplished."[32]

The standard Theosophical judgment on Felt and his involvement in the origins of the Theosophical Society is that he was he was a brilliant, though erratic, autodidact, who just happened to lecture at Madame Blavatsky's rooms the night the Theosophical Society was first proposed. He succeeded in evoking a few dangerous elementals—which terrorized the members and confirmed Madame Blavatsky in her unchanging opposition to practical magic—and promptly disappeared, leaving no permanent trace on the society. He was the occasion for the formation of the Theosophical Society in other words, but in no way its cause, and he had no lasting role in the new group.

Felt's actual involvement with Madame Blavatsky and his influence on the Theosophical Society, while they may not rise to the level posited by Guénon, certainly exceed that set out in the accepted version.

Colonel Olcott in his *Old Diary Leaves*[33] relates the events of the fateful September 7, 1875. As previously announced,[34] Felt lectured informally on "The Lost Canon of Proportion of the Egyptians" to a few of Madame Blavatsky's and Olcott's friends, including Charles Sotheran and Emma Hardinge Britten, at Blavatsky's apartment on Irving Place in New York City. Felt was a former Union officer and is variously described as a professor of mathematics, an engineer, and an Egyptologist.[35] Although he was something of a celebrity, and his discoveries had excited great expectations at the time,[36] the gathering the night he spoke appears to have been simply another evening at home with Madame Blavatsky, whose own notoriety in the press had caused an odd assortment of occultists, reformers, and antiquarians to gather around her.

Felt's lecture clearly impressed Olcott at the time, and he recounts Felt's theories at length in his *Old Diary Leaves*. Felt contended that the Egyptians and the ancient Greeks employed a canon of proportions in their architecture that could be deduced—as he claimed to have done—from an examination of their surviving buildings. The basis of the canon was the "Star of Perfection"—a figure consisting of a "circle with a square within and without, containing a common triangle, two

Egyptian triangles and a pentagon."[37] Felt believed that when this diagram was superimposed upon Egyptian mural hieroglyphics or zodiacs the terms enclosed by the figure revealed the real teachings of the Egyptians, including their formularies for the evocation of elementals and the secrets of their initiations.[38]

Nor was this exercise proposed by Felt purely theoretical. In *Isis Unveiled* (1:22–23), Madame Blavatsky emphasized the practical consequences of Felt's discoveries:

> As to the practical results to be obtained by "the investigations of geometry," very fortunately for students who are coming upon the stage of action, we are no longer forced to content ourselves with mere conjectures. In our own times, an American, Mr. George H. Felt, of New York, who, if he continues as he has begun, may one day be recognized as the greatest geometer of the age, has been enabled, by the sole help of the premises established by the ancient Egyptians, to arrive at results which we will give in his own language. "Firstly," says Mr. Felt, "the fundamental diagram to which all science of elementary geometry, both plane and solid, is referable; to produce arithmetical systems of proportion in a geometrical manner; to identify this figure with all the remains of architecture and sculpture, in all of which it had been followed in a marvelously exact manner; to determine that the Egyptians had used it as the basis of all their astronomical calculations, on which their religious symbolism was almost entirely founded; to find its traces among all the remnants of art and architecture of the Greeks; to discover its traces so strongly among the Jewish sacred records, as to prove conclusively that it was founded thereon; to find that the whole system had been discovered by the Egyptians after researches of tens of thousands of years into the laws of nature, and that it might be called the science of the Universe." Further it enabled him "to determine with precision problems in physiology heretofore only surmised; to first develop such a Masonic philosophy as showed it to be conclusively the first science and religion, as it will be the last"; and we may add, lastly, to prove by ocular demonstrations that the Egyptian sculptors and architects obtained the models of the quaint figures which adorn the façades and vestibules of their temples, not in the disordered fantasies of their own brains, but from the "viewless races of the air," and other kingdoms of nature, whom he, like them, *claims* to make visible by resort to their own chemical and kabalistical processes.

This was published in the fall of 1877, two years after the founding of the Theosophical Society.

Lest there be any misunderstanding about the italics on the word "claims," there is no doubt Madame Blavatsky, at least for a time, believed in—and touted as we shall see—Felt's abilities at evocation.

After the initial lecture, Dr. Seth Pancoast (Madame Blavatsky's some-time physician and a learned occultist) challenged Felt on his ability to evoke "spirits from the spatial deep," and Felt replied that, not only had he actually called "into sight hundreds of shadowy forms resembling the human," but that he would do so before the assembled group in future lectures if they would bear the cost of his preparations. He also promised to teach "persons of the right sort" how to evoke and control the elementals.[39] The actual method of making these evocations—presumably learned by Felt from his reading of the Egyptian hieroglyphics—appears to have been a combination of magical formulae and the burning and use of unspecified chemicals, herbs, and plants.[40] This latter element was one with clear antecedents in the Western magical tradition—and in Randolph's mirror magic and the magic of the H. B. of L.[41]

It was as a consequence of this exchange that the idea of founding a society for the study of such things was first proposed.

Despite Felt's acknowledged abilities, Madame Blavatsky and Colonel Olcott appear never to have stated that Felt was an adept or a member of their brotherhood or even its emissary, or that he had been sent deliberately to develop the Theosophical Society. Madame Blavatsky did assure Olcott of Felt's ability to deliver on his promises,[42] and Olcott was initially very enthusiastic about Felt's discoveries. It is undoubtedly true that Felt and his magic were the original focus and in fact the very raison d'être of the society from a practical point of view. Olcott states that "Felt's demonstration of the existence of the Elemental races" was "counted on as the sound experimental basis" of the society.[43] When Felt vanished from the scene and his efforts proved (in Olcott's later judgment) futile, the society was left essentially purposeless, a study and discussion group, and had to fall back on bland investigation of flower mediums and precipitators of spirit photographs.[44] Olcott sadly admits that after Felt's departure "we made slow progress, for, though we all, by tacit consent, put the best face upon it, every one of us was secretly discouraged by Felt's fiasco, and there seemed no chance of finding a substitute." The Society's need of a *practical* magician after Felt's departure was so great that Olcott even commissioned one of the members to go to Tunis "to find a real magician or sorcerer who [would] consent to come to this country . . . and display his powers before the Society."[45]

The perception of the success of Felt's demonstrations was mixed. In response to a letter claiming that Felt had not succeeded in producing the promised "elementaries," Emma Hardinge Britten guardedly stated that the society had become a "secret order" and that the correspondent, accordingly, was in no position to judge the success of the experiments. The implication, at least, was that Felt had done what he promised.[46] Olcott relates that when Felt exhibited his diagrams on September 18, several persons thought they saw light "quivering over the geometrical figures," but he was later inclined to dismiss it all as an effect of the power of suggestion.[47] In his inaugural address in November 1875, however, Olcott was still enthusiastic.

> Without claiming to be a theurgist, a mesmerist, or a Spiritualist, our Vice-President [Felt] promises, by simple chemical appliances, to exhibit to us, as he has to others before, the races of beings which, invisible to our eyes, people the elements.... Fancy the consequences of the practical demonstration of its truth, for which Mr. Felt is now preparing the requisite apparatus! ... What will the Spiritualists say, when through the column of saturated vapor flit the dreadful shapes of beings whom, in their blindness, they have in a thousand cases revered ... as the returning shades of their relatives and friends. The day of reckoning is close at hand, and the name of the Theosophical Society will, if Mr. Felt's experiments result favorably, hold its place in history as that of the body which first exhibited the "Elementary Spirits."[48]

Later Olcott was to thank his stars that he had added the "if" to his praise of Felt.[49] His often-quoted final judgment on Felt's experiments as a whole was that they were "a complete and mortifying disappointment. Whatever he may have done by himself in that direction, [Felt] showed us nothing, not even the tip end of the tail of the tiniest Nature-spirit."[50]

In the standard version of events, then, Felt, although elected one of the first vice presidents of the Theosophical Society and granted one hundred dollars by it for his experiments, was a dismal failure at evoking elementals and was the first of the "formers" of the society to fall by the wayside. After his second failure at evocation in June 1876, the society even had its attorney (W. Q. Judge) formally demand that Felt fulfill his legal obligations; Felt did not and thereafter was heard from no more.[51]

The reality of Felt's relations with the Theosophical Society appears to have been somewhat different and more extended, and the conflict in testimonies may bespeak some reason on the part of Olcott and Madame Blavatsky after the fact to minimize Felt's involvement. At the time, Madame Blavatsky had no doubt whatsoever about Felt's success. In her scrapbook she included a clipping from the *Banner of Light* in January 1876 on Olcott's inaugural address and added in her own hand: "And Mr. Felt *has done it* in the presence of nine persons in all."[52]

Felt's own version of events is contained in a letter of his included by Colonel Olcott in *Old Diary Leaves*.[53] The letter is dated June 19, 1878 and was later published in the London *Spiritualist*. Felt says that it was drafted in response to skeptical letters that appeared in that journal more than two years before, about which he had only just learned.[54] In the letter, Felt asserts that the effect of his diagrams on those attending the original meeting in September 1875 was so powerful that the real "illuminati" present immediately realized the necessity of a degree or grade system within the Theosophical Society as a means of preserving such serious workings for the elite Theosophists alone. This system of degrees, he says, was in fact instituted and he continued to work within the society with such members as possessed the appropriate degree of development. Felt states that he was unable to publish the details of this work, because of the obligation of secrecy imposed upon him when the Theosophical Society was transformed into a secret society (in early 1876), but what he does feel free to reveal is quite interesting.

First of all, he claimed that he had discovered that the Egyptians in their initiations made use of the appearances of the elementals that were evoked with his figures, and that they taught the neophytes how to control and use the elementals. His original intention had been to introduce such initiations into Freemasonry, and he strongly implies that when the Masonic attempt proved bootless he in fact introduced these Egyptian elemental initiations to the elite members of the Theosophical Society.

After relating his failed attempt at introducing a form of initiation into Freemasonry and his resolve to find more appropriate students, Felt states that "with one of the members of the Theosophical Society, a legal gentleman of a mathematical turn of mind" he carried on a series of experiments in which, with his diagrams, he was able to project elementals at a distance which appeared to the recipient as bright lights or animal shapes in Egyptian form." The legal gentleman was, surprisingly enough, the young W. Q. Judge, who apparently related the results of this and other experiments with Felt to a meeting of the society sometime in 1876.[55]

Finally, to dispel any question that his experiments before the society were ineffective, Felt reiterates that, after his original experiments at which the members of lower degree were frightened by the apparitions, he produced similar manifestations only with the "illuminati." Having obtained permission of the council of the Theosophical Society to speak of matters covered by his obligation, he could state unequivocally, "I have lately performed what I agreed to do, and, unless the Council forbids, I hereby give permission to such of the illuminati as have seen it, to come forward, if they choose and bear evidence of the fact."[56] The use of the word *lately* is especially interesting because Felt's letter is dated June 1878, two and a half years after the foundation of the Theosophical Society and only six months before Olcott and Madame Blavatsky departed for India.

Succinctly put, by Felt's account, given without contradiction by Olcott himself and only after Felt says he had obtained the permission of the council to speak, Felt continued to work with the "illuminati" of the Theosophical Society all through the dark years of inactivity of the society (1876–1878), including the period when *Isis Unveiled* was written. Clearly, Felt's account reflects the secret work of at least a part of the original Theosophists along practical lines. Just as clearly, however, Felt's efforts— whether as eccentric autodidact or as emissary of the H. B. of L.—were not totally satisfactory. Nor, as we shall see, were his experiments the only practical occultism of the society during the New York years.

Occult Practice in the Early Years

The actual methods of occult practice followed by Madame Blavatsky and taught by her and her masters in the early years in America are now almost impossible to discover because of the strict oaths of secrecy that were imposed on the members of the Theosophical Society at the time. Despite the secrecy, however, the conclusion is inescapable that she and her masters in the early years in New York enrolled neophytes and gave them some form of occult training—training which was played down and even actively discouraged for the members in general in the years after Madame Blavatsky and Colonel Olcott departed for India in 1878.[57] The separation of the "astral form" of man and "astral travel" were undoubtedly immediate goals of the training,[58] as was conscious intercourse with pure disembodied souls and planetary spirits—entities identical in concept with the exalted denizens of Randolph's celestial hierarchies.[59] In all of this it appears likely that mirror magic in some form played a major role.

Colonel Olcott, as we have seen, had been experimenting with magic mirrors during the period after he first came to know Madame Blavatsky and had received "certain Mirror Revelations from a Brooklyn Lady"—as had Randolph, who was the importer of the woman's magic mirror (see chapter 10). Randolph's acquaintance with these experiments with the mirror almost certainly came from the glowing notices that appeared anonymously in the *Spiritual Scientist* in June and July 1875. On June 3, 1875, the author (who was probably Olcott) expatiated on the wonderful landscapes and visions of the spirit world that had been demonstrated in the magic mirror by an unnamed lady in a large New York city (later said to be Brooklyn). The black onyx mirror used was said to have been made in India, prepared by a high-caste priest "with solemn and peculiar ceremonials," and bought in Europe—though Randolph was undoubtedly the intermediary. The description of the manner of using the mirror also reflects Randolph's ideas in stressing that the mirror was the tool of the "conscious clairvoyant" whose "interior vision is opened while the person is awake [and able] to see the wonderful phantasmagoria of the spirit-world."[60] In succeeding weeks, the author followed these revelations with two more articles recounting the visions obtained in the mirror, and stated that in addition to the mirror used by the Brooklyn woman, there was a second one in use by an unnamed man in Manhattan—presumably Olcott himself.[61]

All of these pieces, it should be remembered, were published while the "Important to Spiritualists" notice announcing the Brothers of Luxor was still running in the pages of the *Spiritual Scientist* and immediately preceded the appearance of Madame Blavatsky's "A Few Questions to 'HIRAF'" which introduced to the world her vision of the Oriental Rosicrucians. It was at this juncture also that Madame Blavatsky noted in her scrapbook: "*Orders* received from India direct to establish a philosophico-religious society and choose a name for it—also to choose Olcott. July, 1875."[62]

Nor were such mirrors and their uses strange or unknown to Madame Blavatsky herself. As we have already seen, in reviewing Peter Davidson's recounting of Colonel Stephen Fraser's remarks on the sexual consecration of bhattah mirrors in India and on the existence of a brotherhood of magicians in Europe and the Orient who prepared and used such mirrors, Madame Blavatsky vouched for the account as factual and even claimed familiarity with the fraternity (see chapter 3). She was also aware of the connection of such sexually consecrated mirrors with Randolph. In her travels within India shortly after her arrival there in 1879, she described her visit to the place which the

Sakti worshippers ("worshippers of the female power") used "for the performance of their pujas; during which ceremonies the famous black crystals or mirrors mentioned by P. B. Randolph, are fabricated by the hands of young virgins."[63]

Madame Blavatsky obviously assigned a special importance to these "consecrated black mirrors" and believed that they were an almost universal facet of the ancient wisdom tradition.[64] She herself, she says, on an earlier visit to India had had considerable experience with such mirrors:

> We have made hundreds of experiments with cats, dogs, monkeys of various kinds, and, once, with a tame tiger. A round black mirror, known as the "magic crystal," was strongly mesmerized by a native Hindu gentleman, formerly an inhabitant of Dindigul, and now residing in a more secluded spot, among the mountains known as the Western Ghauts. He had tamed a young cub, brought to him from the Malabar coast, in which part of India the tigers are proverbially ferocious; and it is with this interesting animal that we made our experiments.[65]

These Indian experiments with the magic mirror were (like Randolph's and Felt's evocations) preceded by fumigations with the smoke of resinous trees and shrubs. They produced stark terror in the unfortunate tiger.

Madame Blavatsky's masters during the New York period were also familiar with the magic mirror. We have already discussed the short piece, published in November 1875 in the *Spiritual Scientist*, in which the Master Hilarion had related the story of the ageless Vic de Lassa/Cagliostro and his marvelous successes with the magic mirror in Paris in the early 1860s (see chapter 2).[66] The prototype or original of this master may well have been one of the two mysterious men (one, at least a Near Easterner—a Cypriot) who visited Colonel Olcott in late 1875 or early 1876 and showed him wonders in the magic mirror. The elder of the two visitors, Colonel Olcott says

> took out of his pocket a painted lacquered case—and asked me if I wanted to see "an Eastern bonhomiere.". . . Upon opening the case a round flat concave crystal was displayed to view—he told me to look in it—holding it a few inches from my eye and shading my eye from the light so that there might be no reflected rays cast upon the glass—the box exhaled a strong spicy aromatic odor—much like sandalwood—but still not just that—whatever

I wished to see—he said I need simply think of—only taking care
to think of but one thing at a time—I did as directed.

At first the eager Colonel simply beheld a scene from his past (his
mother urging him to avoid spiritualism), but then he saw a door that
"came nearer and nearer, and grew plainer, until I lost consciousness
of external objects—and seemed to be in the very room I had in mind."
For more than an hour he was transported into strange landscapes
and enabled "to call up any spirit I wished to talk with" and to remember things "that had occurred to me when out of the body."[67]
No other records now remain of mirror practice in the early days of
the Theosophical Society, but, especially in light of the repeated references to magic mirrors and to attempts to communicate with planetary spirits that undoubtedly were made at the time, such a practice
probably existed among at least a select group of neophytes of the
society.[68] If it did, it is inconceivable that the practice went on without
reference to Randolph and his works on seership and clairvoyance.
A similar connection between the occult practice of Randolph and
that of Madame Blavatsky may exist in the latter's unquestioned extensive use of hashish. She had been introduced to the drug in Egypt
in the early 1850s in the company of A. L. Rawson, with whom she
explored the wonders performed by the Coptic magician Paulos
Metamon (whom later myth associated with the origins of the H. B. of
L.),[69] she probably used the drug in Paris as well—if she was indeed
a mesmeric subject for Victor Michal, as alleged. In her New York
years in the 1870s, she again appears to have used the drug regularly.[70]
In light of this experimentation, it is inconceivable that this aspect of
Randolph's works would not have been known to her, though she
never mentions it explicitly. In fact, she almost never mentions the
drug, and there is really very little evidence on Madame Blavatsky's
purposes in using it or on her experiences with it.[71] Rawson's recounting of her experiences is limited to the ecstatic generalities that are
found in so many literary hashish users of the time.
Despite this silence on hashish, Madame Blavatsky spoke knowingly of the use of some drugs for purposes of clairvoyance and communion with the gods. She extolled the benefits of "Soma," which
puts the soul in communication not only with the minor gods but also
with the "divine essence itself." She insisted that the real drug was not
the substitute known to the West under that name.[72] In one very telling instance, however, she connects the sleep of Sialam—another trade-
mark of Randolph's work—with the drinking of soma by would-be
initiates in the Near East, which may indicate that what was meant

was some preparation of hashish (see chapter 3).[73] Similarly, the aromatic fumigations that were an important part of the original Theosophical Society's attempt to realize the evocations of elementals promised by G. H. Felt may have been thought to have narcotic properties, and may indeed have had such.

Blending and Tulku

The most characteristic phenomenon of Randolph's occultism (magic mirrors, sexual magic, and hashish aside) is what he calls "Blending" or "Atrilism": the taking over of a conscious subject's body and mind by a living adept or by some disembodied or never embodied entity from the celestial hierarchies. He was the first to describe the phenomenon in the nineteenth century, and he recounted vividly the effects and consequences of thus acting as proxy for the will of others (see chapter 5). After him, the idea became one of the touchstones of the wave of "Western" occultism, especially that of the H. B. of L.

John Yarker, whose manuscript of Randolph's "Mysteries of Eulis" is the only one known to survive and whose ritual for the Sât B'hai was considered by Madame Blavatsky as the basis for the ritual of the Theosophical Society, is illustrative. In an unusually personal discourse delivered by him before the Manchester College of the Societas Rosicruciana in Anglia and later reprinted by S. C. Gould,[71] Yarker was at pains to distinguish the real Rosicrucians and their work from the "convivial brotherhood, satisfied with the name and jewel of the confraternity," and he related that he had only encountered three brethren with a competent and practical knowledge—Frederick Hockley, K. R. H. Mackenzie, and Captain F. G. Irwin—all names that have recurred throughout these pages. He listed the stages of real occult progress, beginning with the necessity of silence and of operative alchemy. The third stage is the "study of psychological science, clairvoyance, the use of the 'Crystal Stone' or magical mirror; knowledge of elemental and elementary spirits, which Charles H. Felt [sic], an American mathematician, claims to have rendered palpably visible by chemical means." The fourth stage is "[c]ommunion with the spiritual world, by vacation of the body, by spiritual impressions, and by placing the soul *en rapport* with the Universal Soul, and absolute possession." Beyond all this is the full command of the forces of nature and the conjoining of the soul "with the all-pervading astral power." The key to all this was mesmerism and the magic crystal.

The "absolute possession" that Yarker hinted at was, he thought, the great secret of the initiations of the Druses, the Dervishes, and the Hindu Brahmins, acquired by the development of the will. Initially the magnetic operator may free the soul of the subject from the body, so that it "ascends upwards, or traverses the sea to distant countries at the will of the operator." Beyond this is "possession" itself:

> The operator may go a step further and possess the vacated body for a time with a guardian spirit drawn by his will. He may experiment day after day, and week after week, and in the one body may be placed two minds, the one unknown to the other; and he may prove these phenomena absolutely. This is possession. What is still more remarkable is that all clairvoyants, of whatever language or ability, agree in generalities, differing only in the details of an immense scheme. The great aim of the magician is to acquire all this power for his own body.[75]

The ultimate example of this possession is "the life transfer, the awful *Seventh Rite* of the great sacerdotal operation, which is the highest theurgy, which, when once an adept has received, he belongs no more to this world." "The High Hierophant alone knew how to perform this solemn operation by infusing his own vital life and Astral soul into the Adept chosen by him for his successor, who thus became endowed with a double life."[76]

Yarker's description of this mystery is striking and is taken without attribution and almost word for word from *Isis Unveiled* (2:564–66). This process appears to be identical with the experience of Randolph, the "Man with Two Souls,"[77] and with that through which T. H. Burgoyne is said to have passed on leadership in the H. B. of L. to Belle M. Wagner after his death.[78] Wagner herself made the idea the centerpiece of her occult historical novel of ancient Egypt, *Within the Temple of Isis*, in which select neophytes of the temples were prepared to receive the souls of the still embodied and the disembodied.[79]

Something very similar is also found in Madame Blavatsky's experiences with her masters.

Randolph's Blending	**Madame Blavatsky's Penetration**
Well, she died; and after a year or two had passed, I began to understand that at times her soul was near me, and many and oft	Do not be afraid that I am off my head. All that I can say is that someone positively *inspires me*— more than this, someone enters

were the periods in which I did not seem to be myself, but had an invincible conviction that I was Cynthia for the time being instead of who and what I am. By and by there came a consciousness of this blending, so deep, so clearly defined, so calm, that I at last began to appreciate a mighty, almost resistless Will and Purpose behind it all; for I was myself and Cynthia—never simultaneously, as is asserted to be the case with many of the people called "Mediums"—but in separate instants—now her, then myself; at first very imperfectly, but gradually approaching an absolute and complete mergement of Soul.

me. It is not I who talk and write: it is something within me, my higher and luminous Self, that thinks and writes for me. Do not ask me, my friend, what I experience, because I could not explain it to you clearly. I do not know myself! . . . *Someone* comes and envelopes me as a misty cloud and all at once pushes me out of myself, and then I am not "I" anymore—Helena Petrovna Blavatsky—but someone else. Someone strong and powerful, born in a totally different region of the world; and as to myself it is almost as if I were asleep, or lying . . . not quite conscious—not in my own body but close by, held only by a thread which ties me to it. . . . However, at times I see and hear everything quite clearly: I am perfectly conscious of what my body is saying and doing—or at least its new possessor. I even understand and remember it all so well that afterwards I can repeat it and even write down *his* words.

* * *

This continued for nearly two years, at intervals, and after about eighteen months had passed, one portion of the process seemed to have reached completeness—for in a degree it changed, and instead of momentary, as before, the transmutations became longer, until at last, as now, the changes last sixty, and in one instance has reached two hundred and forty-five minutes.

And just about this time I [began] to feel a very strange duality. Several times a day I feel that beside me there is someone else, quite separable from me, present in my body. I never lose the consciousness of my personality; what I feel is as if I were keeping silent and the other one—the lodger who is in me—were speaking with my tongue.

It may here be asked: "Where are *you* in the interim?" and the answer is: "We are two in one, yet the stronger rules the hour."

For instance, I know that I have never been in the places which are described by my "other me," but this other one—the second me—does not lie when he tells about places and things unknown to me, because he has actually seen them and known them well. I have given it up; let my fate conduct me at its own sweet will; and besides, what am I to do? It would be perfectly ridiculous if I were to deny the possession of knowledge avowed by my No. 2, giving occasion to the people around me to imagine that I kept them in the dark for modesty's sake.

It will be seen, therefore, that this condition is as widely separated from those incident to the "Mediums," as theirs is supposed to be different from the ordinary wakeful mood. *They* reach their state by a sort of retrocession from themselves; they fall, or claim to fall into a peculiar kind of slumber, their own faculties going, as it were, to sleep. On the contrary, *mine* is the direct opposite of this, for, instead of a sleep of any sort, there comes an *intense wakefulness.* Nor is this all in which we differ; as are the processes and states apart, so also are the results different.

In the night, when I am alone in my bed, the whole life of my No. 2 passes before my eyes, and I do not see myself at all, but quite a different person—different race and different in feelings. But what's the use of talking about it? It is enough to drive one mad. I try to throw myself into the part, and to forget the strangeness of my situation. This is no mediumship, and by no means an impure power; for that, it has too strong an ascendancy over us all, leading us into better ways.[80]

* * *

[B]y slow degrees I felt that my own personality was not lost to me, but completely swallowed up, so to speak, in that of a far

I see this Hindu every day, just as I might see any other living person, with the only difference that he looks to me more ethereal more potent mentality. A subtlety of thought, perception and understanding became mine at times, altogether greater than I had ever known before; and occasionally, during these strange blendings of my being with another, I felt that other's feelings, thought that other's thoughts. . . . For a time I attributed these exaltations of Soul to myself alone, and supposed that I was not at all indebted to foreign aid for many of the thoughts to which, at such moments, I frequently gave utterance; but much study of the matter has at length convinced me, not only that the inhabitants of the Soul-worlds have much to do in moulding the great world's future, but that occasionally they manage things that their thoughts are spoken, and their behests, ends, and purposes fulfilled by us mortals . . . we doubtless are oftentimes merely the proxies of others, and act our allotted roles in a drama whose origin is entirely supernatural, and the whole direction of which is conducted by personages beyond the veil.[81]

and more transparent. Formerly I kept silent about these appearances, thinking that they were hallucinations. But now they have become visible to other people as well. He (the Hindu) appears and advises us as to our conduct and our writing. He evidently knows *everything* that is going on, even of the thoughts of other people, and makes me express his knowledge. Sometimes it seems to me that he overshadows the whole of me, simply entering me like a kind of volatile essence penetrating my pores and dissolving in me. Then we two are able to speak to other people, and then I begin to understand and remember sciences and languages—everything he instructs me in, even when he is not with me any more.[82]

The similarities with Randolph's blending (described in chapter 5) are remarkable, and the double consciousness of the subject helps explain the "fickleness" so often noted in Randolph's life—and in Madame Blavatsky's as well.[83]

Sex

Despite all these similarities in teachings and the echoes of Randolph's works in her early writings, Madame Blavatsky, even by the farthest stretch of the imagination, can never be said to have been a follower or a disciple of Randolph. Even in the broadest version of the hidden-hand theory the most ever claimed about a connection between the two is that they were ultimately members (or pawns) of the same organization. In other words, assuming the truth of such speculations, we might expect to find (as we have) similarities in teachings but never slavish emulation. Randolph, as the H. B. of L. and as Madame Blavatsky emphasized repeatedly, was himself problematical, and there were parts of his teachings that neither was prepared to advocate unquestioningly. Madame Blavatsky's reference to Randolph as "half-initiated" bears this out, as does the H. B. of L.'s disclaimer that Randolph, while an initiate, had fallen aside into black magic (see chapter 10).

In Madame Blavatsky's case, the great problem with Randolph was his sexual teachings—though it is at least debatable whether her opposition extended to Randolph's underlying theory of the pivotal role of sexual differentiation in all manifestation or was directed only to sexual magical practice. In a lengthy letter to the Boston *Daily Globe* in 1888 criticizing the H. B. of L. and Hiram Butler's Solar Biology group, Madame Blavatsky claimed that as early as 1875 she had denounced Randolph's sexual magic and had, as a consequence, stirred up powerful enemies against herself:

> Since 1875, almost before the Theosophical Society was first formed, I had unrelentingly exposed the criminality of this vile doctrine [i.e., sex as a means of progress in occultism]. The secret origin of my countless enemies lies there. I had denounced P. B. Randolph and his doings and teachings in certain esoterico-magnetic centres for the practical carrying out of his doctrines, which he had established in Boston, calling them Rosicrucian mysteries. I denounced the "Pantarchy" of shameful memory in New York, established by Stephen Pearl Andrews, and the still more infamous psychic clubs connected with Mrs. Victoria Woodhull. Fearlessly pointing out the trail of the serpent wherever I found it, I roused the enmity of the thousands of their followers who were all Spiritualists.[84]

Madame Blavatsky was certainly aware of the vagaries of Randolph, Stephen Pearl Andrews, and Victoria Woodhull, but no record remains of her attacking them in 1875 or indeed at any time before she left for India.[85] In a letter to the London *Spiritualist* in July 1882, she replied to criticism that she had slandered all spiritualists by questioning their morality, and she pointed out that mediums attracted to themselves "Pisachas"—the unreformed detritus of the human entity—that were the source of their doctrines. She singled out again Andrews and

Woodhull "whose moral code is Free love" and whose ideas were derived from their spiritual "controls," and added:

> And there were, as we were informed, secret lodges, or Agapae, where the genuine Black Magic of Asia was taught by the late P. B. Randolph, and sensuality was at least preached and advocated—as everyone can see by reading any one of the numerous works of this man of genius driven by his Pisachas—to suicide. Also there were and are male and female mediums—public and private—who boasted publicly and in our hearing of marital relationships with materialized Spirits, and—in the case of the Rev. T. L. Harris, the great poet, mystic and Spiritualist—alleged parentage is claimed of children begotten by him in a revolting union with his "Spirit-Wife."[86]

The H. B. of L.'s propaganda always contrasted the "antisex" attitude of the Orientals (by which they meant Madame Blavatsky's "Indian" masters) and the attitude of its own "Western" occultism which allowed a primary role to sex and sexual differentiation in the progress of the soul. The consequence of this theory and of the H. B. of L.'s claim that she had originally been one of its own in her New York days would appear to be that in her early period Madame Blavatsky should have had and expressed some appreciation of this cosmic sexuality. Such an attitude, if it was in fact present, is very hard to discern. It is a commonplace in Theosophical lore that Madame Blavatsky was personally indifferent to sex and theoretically opposed to it as a hindrance to development.

Nonetheless, there is a side to Madame Blavatsky that indicates a largely unrecognized appreciation on her part and on the part of her masters of the cosmological role of sex. Initially, throughout her life she consistently praised Hargrave Jennings and relied on his strange books (with and without citation) as her authority on the Rosicrucians, the "Fire Philosophers," alchemy, obscure Kabbalistic symbolism, and the sexual key to the mysteries. From his explanations she took the myth expressed in the "Wheel of Ezechiel," the astrological depiction of the primordial androgyne, the first idea emanating from "the double-sexed and hitherto-inactive Deity," and the descent of "man" into matter on the sundering of the originally bisexual being[87]—a myth which, as we have seen, lay at the root of a great deal of speculation in Swedenborgian and spiritualist free-love circles (see chapter 1).[88]

A reflection of all this is found in one of the original letters from Madame Blavatsky's masters to Colonel Olcott, probably at the time of her short-lived marriage to Michael Betanelly in the spring of 1875.

The letter may have been the masters' attempt to explain the marriage to Olcott, or it may have been in answer to Olcott's own questions on the subject of sex.

> Know, O Brother mine, that where a truly spiritual love seeks to consolidate itself doubly by a pure, permanent union of the two, in its earthly sense, it commits no sin, no crime in the eyes of the great Ain-Soph, for it is but the divine repetition of the Male and Female Principles—microcosmal reflection of the first condition of Creation. On such a union angels may well smile! But they are rare, Brother mine, and can only be created under the wise and loving supervision of the Lodge, in order that the sons and daughters of clay might not be utterly degenerated, and the Divine Love of the Inhabitants of Higher Spheres (Angels) towards the daughters of Adam be repeated. But even such must suffer, before they are rewarded. Man's Atma may remain pure and as highly spiritual while it is united with its material body; why should not two souls in two bodies remain as pure and uncontaminated notwithstanding the earthly passing union of the latter two.[89]

The last sentiment certainly appears designed to assuage Olcott's doubts on the possibility of preserving the spirit pure even while the body is physically involved in sexual union. The body of the passage, however, appears to point to some greater mystery explained by the masters to Olcott, a mystery involving not only the original bisexual state of man, but also his relations through his sexual nature with the inhabitants of the higher spheres. Unfortunately, the passage is elusive, raising more questions than it answers.

Similar questions are raised by a fascinating series of letters from Madame Blavatsky to Prince Dondoukoff-Korsakoff, written between 1881 and 1884.[90] In the letters, she reveals her long search from 1848 until her arrival in India in early 1879 for the "marriage of the red Virgin with the Hierophant . . . of the combination of the feminine and masculine principles in certain alchemical and magical operations." She says that she pursued her "researches concerning the 'red Virgin' and the human 'salt' " throughout the Near East, among the "whirling Dervishes, with the Druses of Mt. Lebanon, with the Bedouin Arabs and the Marabouts of Damascus," all without avail, physically preserving her virginity but of necessity indulging in unspecified "physiological investigations" that would certainly be regarded as odd by the world at large. There can be no question whatsoever about the sexual and magical connotations of the search, beginning with her marriage.

Do you know why I married old Blavatsky? Because, whereas all the young men laughed at "magical" superstitions, he believed in them! He had so often talked to me about the sorcerers of Erivan, of the mysterious sciences of the Kourds and Persians, that I took him in order to use him as the latch key to the latter. But—*I never was his wife*. . . . Neither have I been anybody's wife as evil tongues have pretended—for I was about ten months in search of the "astral mineral" that had to have the "red Virgin" pure and entire and I did not find that *mineral*. What I wanted and searched for was the subtle magnetism that one exchanges, the human "salt," and father Blavatsky did not have it; and to find it and obtain it, I was ready to sacrifice myself, *to dishonour myself!* . . . Married during the spring of 1848, in the month of February (or January) 1879 I was still in search of my "salt" and human "mineral" and—*the "Virgin"* was still there in the full sense of the word. . . . [To Prince Emile de Wittgenstein I] gave the actual proof that there existed in the world at least one woman who, married for nearly a year, with the reputation of a *courtesan* . . . and who yet *physically* was as pure as a new-born child. I say physically, because, unfortunately, I was not so morally. My researches concerning the "red Virgin" and the human "salt" having necessitated physiological investigations that were certainly not for my age, my imagination was coldly depraved. I looked for the *subject*.[91]

Having said all of this, it still appears most likely that Madame Blavatsky's protestations against physical and astral sex were genuine and heartfelt but, like much of what she wrote, they probably conceal as much as they reveal and are certainly not the whole story of her beliefs on the role of sexuality in occultism. For purposes of the hidden hand, however, as for all nonfalsifiable theories generally, the point is unimportant, since, *ex hypothesi*, sex (or at least actual physical intercourse) may be viewed as the point of deviation either of Randolph or of Madame Blavatsky from the true path of the original occult mentors. The H. B. of L. criticized Randolph precisely on his excesses in sexual magic, and the proponents of the hidden hand could easily accommodate Madame Blavatsky's divergence from Randolph over matters of sex by positing that it was just on that issue that Randolph fell (as the Reverend Ayton says, into "Black Magic") away from the original teachings. Conversely, Madame Blavatsky's apparent rejection of a primary role for sexual differentiation in occult development could just as easily be used—as it was by the H. B. of L.—as proof of her own deviation. All is grist for the mills of the hidden hand.

Madame Blavatsky, even more than Randolph, is personally an enigma, and there are as many solutions to the questions of her true intentions and purposes as there have been biographers and commentators. To her contemporaries, especially the spiritualists, the common revolutionary intent inherent in her work and in the works of Randolph, and Emma Hardinge Britten was obvious, and they were not slow in pointing it out. In denouncing Madame Blavatsky's Theosophy, W. E. Coleman pointedly included her in the revolution he characterized as "Occultism, Rosicrucianism, Art Magic, White Magic, Black Magic, Ansaiteric Mystery," and he had no fear that his readers might fail to see Randolph, Blavatsky, and Mrs. Britten behind the terms.[92] The relationship was there for all to see.

At the least, all this material supports the idea of a background relationship of some sort between Randolph and Madame Blavatsky. On its most obvious level, there is a very marked and singular similarity between their teachings, extending even to the verbal level, that shows at very minimum a close (and largely undisclosed) reading by Madame Blavatsky of Randolph's works.[93] The hidden-hand conspiracy theory propagated by the H. B. of L. and others went beyond this, of course, and made both Madame Blavatsky and Randolph failed initiates of an Oriental brotherhood and tools in the hands of that brotherhood or its antecedent groupings. In this view, Randolph and Madame Blavatsky would have been collaterally, and not necessarily directly, connected, and the original connection would have been through what may best be described as a "Western" branch or school or wave of occultism that focused on the practical development of the human being's powers in this world, his or her perpetual progress through spiritual spheres after death and the denial of reincarnation. The term *Western*, of course, must not be taken in a geographical sense, since the center of gravity of the movement as described would appear to be in the Near East with extensions in Europe, especially Paris. The term rests rather on the distinction posited by the H. B. of L. and others between their movement and the "Eastern" school it believed lay behind Madame Blavatsky's later developments and modifications of Theosophy. The evidence on Randolph and Madame Blavatsky (and on Emma Hardinge Britten) can be interpreted, by those so inclined, to support this thesis as well without doing violence to it. However, the endeavor here has been, not to prove the existence of the hidden hand—an effort that by definition shades off into realms beyond the grasp of history in any case—but rather to look at the consonances that gave rise to the theories connecting Randolph, Emma Hardinge Britten, and Madame Blavatsky in the first place, in order to arrive at a better historical understanding of Randolph's role in the events that transformed spiritualism into occultism in the late nineteenth century.

&PILOGUE

W e have come a long way from the abandoned child learning his alphabet by copying the bills posted on the shabby walls of the Five Points. Randolph was learned, brilliant and charming—and also, as everyone recognized, angular, eccentric, proud, prickly, suspicious, and even paranoid at times. He was a black man who tried with considerable success to succeed in a white world and to do so on his own terms rather than as the merely symbolical Black Man erected by the forces of organized reform. In the world of spiritualism and occultism his was a revolutionary role, and he was truly the precursor of what occultism has become. He was in this sense the first modern "guru," and occultism today, in its almost exclusive preoccupation with personal experience and spiritual techniques and its relegation of doctrine to a secondary position, is a reflection of Randolph's vision. In his own terms, he was a visionary and a witness to the reality of the other world. In the balance, the compelling power of his vision was his greatest strength and his greatest weakness, the cause of his failures and angularities and also the source of his creativity and brilliance.

Appendix A

THE ANSAIRETIC MYSTERY

A New Revelation Concerning SEX!

A PRIVATE LETTER, PRINTED, BUT NOT PUBLISHED;
IT BEING SACRED AND CONFIDENTIAL

AXIOM—God and Nature marries the sexes together, while Man, Custom, and the State unites individuals. The former are *never* failures; hence those thus married, being laws unto themselves, need but little light to guide them in this mysterious subject—seeing that God makes no mistakes; but the latter sort of marriages are seldom anything else than failures, at least within the area of Occidental civilization; hence the parties to such unions need all possible light to guide them from the lee shores and sunken rocks upon which myriads are continually being wrecked.

A. The preservation, Rejuvenescence Intensification and Sanctification of Love between Man and Woman invariably, primarily, and always did, does, and forever will depend upon the perfection of their conjunction; in plain words, upon the fullness and completeness of the conjugal union, in each case, and upon *both* sides. The vast majority of civilized men have no endurance, or *staying* qualities or powers; but are so very morbid—a result of prostatic inflammation—that their love-journey is spasmodically ended long before that of the woman has fairly begun; and the *presence* is scarce achieved, ere the discharge takes place, whereupon—all *rigidity* ceases, and poor *she* is deprived of all the joy of marital union, while compelled to endure all the legitimate and illegitimate penalties and pains consequent upon infracted

311

natural law; for if the female is not brought—and that, too, by purely *legitimate* methods, at which not even a seraph could blush, and none but gross, coarse savages object to—to the natural sexual demise, the full and perfect *orgasm*, all of love *in* her is curdled and soured, and all of love *for* him appreciably diminished; and when it decreases from *that* cause, he is an *idiot* who expects true wifeliness at her hands; and then *she*, whose delicious soul ought to be wakened to the keenest sensuous symphonies, instead of being blasted, is exceedingly liable to the influence of gusts of love flowing from *other* directions than the nuptial or conjugal apartments—which, if she is, he is to blame; for no man has a right to regard woman as a mere nervo-vital machine for his especial pleasure and use, for she is a magnificent instrument capable of evolving such celestial music as will tingle the nerves of an archangel and bring delicious death to the finest nerves in all the universe!

B. To the *true* and perfect conjugal union, it is absolutely essential that the neck of the uterus be bathed in and by the husband's prostatic lymph and ejected semen *every time* they know each other; for unless their mutual acids and alkalis, generated then and there, meet, mingle, blend and fuse, the electro-magnetic and nervous conditions essential to perfect union are not present, and the reaction is fatal to health—the result being loathing and repulsion in both cases, and the measure of soul-fusion theretofore existing is most effectually injured, if not totally destroyed. Behold the beginning of domestic horror!

C. What a fool is he, and how suicidal, who goes when and where he is not wanted—blindly brutal, and to the funeral of his own joy—not realizing her inability to give true pleasure who experiences none herself. How exceedingly senseless [is he] or rather IT, who insists upon inflicting horror, himself realizing but a mere mechanical union, utterly devoid of magnetic flow, and which, while harming her, is sure to land him on the sterile shores of Impotence, and to beget a kind of Spermatic disorder that even the purest Protozone may not be able to cure. Unless the woman is fired with passion, (see note below) she remains dry, cold, unmoved, because not reached—seeing that such union is merely *mechanical*, instead of nervous, electric, chemical, magnetic and soul-ful, as it ought to be; and the vaginal parietes, with their countless ducts, are sealed by the voluntary and involuntary power of her will: he commits Onanism, and she fails to exude the natural lymph of the parts involved; and the male organ cannot absorb the strange Vivific life, fire and tingling joy, it should, from contact with that precious alkaline lochia. Every one remembers some unions more joyous than others. Well, the lymph, passion, lochia and fire is the sole cause of all the transcendent difference!

(NOTE —Lust originates in congestion, or physical inflammation of the organs; while Passion, or true Desire, takes its rise in the Soul and Spirit. Gratification of the first is ruinous, beastly, utterly inhuman and diabolic—leaving us badly off; while the consummation of the second is the most supreme bliss the composite human being—soul, spirit, body—is capable of enduring; for it is heavenly, transcendental, and divine.)

D. The *true* conditions of union are absolutely, unqualifiedly essential to perfect health, joy, and to the mystic power alluded to hereinafter; but neither can be had or realized in their absence, or if the wife fails to actualize the normal orgasm—which wives in these days very rarely do! as a consequence of which the vagina, ovaria and uteri become disordered, inflamed, congested; and congested sexual organs will transform an angel into its opposite, quicker than anything else on earth except well-founded Jealousy—the King Devil of the household; and the coldness, despair, and hatred thus begotten are speedily fatal to any sort of domestic happiness.

E. Now, understand me—an humble professor of sexual *common sense and honesty*—when I say, in simile: Two boats start together for the same port; but one is rather slow—generally the one called Sarah Jane,—while the other is as much too *fast*. Well, he's a poor captain who insists upon sailing away from his companion, reaching port alone, and discharging cargo before the other is anywhere near port. "But, my good God!" says the captain, "how am I to prevent it? —*she's* so slow, and I'm so fast!" Why, you fool, haven't you a WILL? Haven't you the power to *heave to, rest, stop stock still* midway of the voyage, if need be? Rest a spell. *Think* of anything else but the end of the trip. Do *not* finish the race alone! Wait till the slower craft overtakes you— the paler fire begins to glow; for, depend upon it, both boats have equal rights, and should have equal chances; for if you reach port and she falls short, she'll hate you for your mean, contemptible, piggish, one-sided selfishness; and disappointment is the least bad result that follows.

F. Some people desire to attain mystic power through its own regal road. They long for that grand mental force which will enable them to scan the mysteries and sweep the floors of the Sidereal and Spheral Spaces, but are impatient of the methods. Now, let all such know, once for all; that the doors are shut to all save the obedient; and the effort to obtain mental intensity need never be attempted, unless the law— *its* law—be scrupulously observed, because no real magic (magnetic) power can, or will, descend into the soul of either, except in the mighty moment—the orgasmal instant of BOTH—not one alone! for then, and *then only*, do the mystic doors of the SOUL OPEN TO THE SPACES. Darwin and his abettors are mistaken: the immortal soul of man is not—never was —developed from any stage of monkeyhood; and they libel God Almighty who affirm it! The eternal spark within us (and which never flashes except when the loving female brings to her feet the loving man in their mutual infiltration of Soul, in the sexive death of both—that intense moment when woman proves herself the superior of man—mutual demise!) was created by ALLAH—God himself— Billions of ages ago in the foretime, and finds its human body only when Sex-passion opens the mystic door for it to enter the man— through him, the woman, through her the world, through THEM the Spaces, and through it again Allah, God—*not* as a drop of infinite ocean of Mind, but as a Being in the Heavenly hierarchies! What follows? —Why, that every *he* should *never* forget his fealty to WOMAN, but remember who and *what* she really is—the gem of God's own Auroral Crown!

G. What follows? Why, that the grosser *he* should ever be *considerate and gentle* to, and *with*, woman; never fierce, *brutal*, in a hurry; but should restrain all impetuosity. Yet many of the most splendid human beings have resulted from—haste, hurry, and the terrific fears and terrors of discovery—results of stolen interviews, wherefore it is said that bastards are superior; but there is no reason why marriage should not produce as fine; on the contrary, it ought to produce finer, because less angular, children. No man should dare seek coverture of an unwilling woman; never till by endearments, caresses, love-fondlings, and affection—not *affectation*—he has brought her to the Passional mood. He must, in all this holy matter, be JUST, else will he assuredly reap crops of hatred—smothered and dissembled perhaps, yet hatred still; and that; too, of the worst sort, because it is magnetic, therefore constitutional; and any woman on earth can effectually damn any man who is with her sexually, provided he has not the knowledge and skill to render this curse inoperative.

H. Neglect of the man to bring his wife to the orgasm, either with, before, or after his own, constitutes a defective, selfish, infamous and infernal fraud; for whatever woman is capable of menstruation, is capable also of all her nature implies, and it is her *right* to experience it. And yet, not over one in fifty realizes that which is her due; but the grand mass go to their graves, even after mothering many babes, without ever tasting the slightest joy in that most mysterious and sacred rite! Why? Owing to the universal Hogitude of what pass for, but are not husbands, in any real sense of that prostituted term; for, judging by the revelations and appearance of wives generally, the majority of their "lords and masters" know little, and care less, about cultivating passion in their wives.

(NOTE —Wherever you see a rich and *jouissant* beauty and power in a girl or boy—wherever you see force of genius—you may rest assured that the mother conceived when impassioned. *Au contraire*, wherever you see genuine meanness—"moral turpentine," as Mrs. Malaprop says; whenever you see a lean, mean, scrawny soul— wizened, white-livered, trickish, grab-all-ish, and accursed generally— you may safely wager your life that such a being was begotten of force, on a passionless, sickly, used-up wife, and you'll never lose your bet.)

The average husband's wife is full of aches, pains, wrinkles, gray hair, fallen womb, leucorrhæ; and a good many of them are nicely inoculated with syphilis by their lords, and the doctors hide it, and their ignorance too, and call it *"Fluor Albus"*; besides which, the usual husband attacks his victim as pigs their food, for all the world as if she had neither soul, sense, feeling, womanhood, delicacy, or human rights. At the beginning he says, "Now!" at the end he grunts, "There!" and, instead of a loving *grateful* hug and kiss, in five minutes he is snoring away like any other hog; while she, poor soul, sobs her life away, and wonders how long she is to remain in that particular section of Hell. He never *tries* to change her cold to warmth—her indifference to chaste desire; nor knows he aught of the meaning or use of gentleness, per- suasive caresses, continual kindness, or of deliberation; above all, he utterly forgets that it is his duty to *wait* for her, if it takes six months, till he wins the soul and passion, as well as the "duty and obedience," of the mysterious being he calls Wife! —God's profoundest miracle, the bearer of the mysterious womb.

I. The Generative System of brutes—all animate nature beneath man, allies them to external nature; but that of mankind allies them to ex- ternal, internal and supernal, or mystic nature, at one of the same time—therefore to the SPACES, POWERS, ENERGIES, FORCES, PRIN- CIPLES, POTENCIES and Hierarchies of the entire absolute universe! and not only allies, but unites the race therewith: wherefore ensexment is Prayer; for all Nature, Space, Power, God, centers in that mystic act, in which a Soul may become incarnate—a mighty soul, capable of balancing the Universe in its mind and weighing the World in its scales! It is time something was done toward purifying sex matters, and uplifting it from the filth and mud of barbaric ages, and civilized dirt besides; hence this monograph. Now, Man, being the chief work of Nature; allied to all that is; being the central figure upon which all forces play; and copulative union being the crowning act of his be- ing—it follows that his moment of greatest Power is that in which Love unlooses the doors of his Spirit, and all his energies are in high- est action; whence it happens that they who unitedly *Will* a thing, during copulative union and its mutual ending, possess the key to all possible Knowledge, the mighty wand of White Magic—may defy disease, disaster, keep Death itself at bay, regain lost youth and wasted power, challenge permanent defeat, gain all good ends, reach the ul- timate Spaces, commune with highest seraphs, bathe in the crystal seas of God's Infinite Love, and be in truth Sons and Daughters of the Ineffable Lord of glory! Now follows some strange new truths:

J. 1. Soul-seeds (Atomonads) exist in the Æther surrounding the world,

2. The germs of all possible knowledge reside there also.

3. All absolute power, knowledge, energy, force, exits in the Æther and the Sakwalas or Spiritual Spheres.

4. None of these spring up from within us, but all are reachable by us, and flow into us in our highest moments; and all or any knowledge or power the human being has a brain capable of holding can be drawn to it, if willed, wished, desired and com- manded, as and when aforesaid; and it or they enter the soul *only* in the moment, the very instant, of the holy, full, mutual and pure orgasm, or ejection of the three fluids and two auras— *i.e.*, prostatic, seminal, and female lymph or lochia, and the dual magnetism evolved, and which in its rush from one soul to the other, is the cause of a bliss which no language is adequate to the description of.

5. In the orgasmal moment there is no middle-ground; for we ei- ther rise toward heaven or descend hellward. At its close, we are either better or worse—generally worse—than before, be- cause of our halfness; for in that moment do these soul-seeds, germs of knowledge, knowledge itself, and magic power de- scend to, and find lodgment in our souls, the mystic doors of which are then instantly opened and as suddenly closed again. If, before and during that instant, we invite Evil, Evil will find its way to the Soul, and be locked within its secret crypts, only to blaze out and come to the surface when we least expect it. If we Will and Pray for the Good, then the Evil angels stand aside, and the Good becomes enclosed within the meshes of our Spir-

its. If we wish for Power, then the germ of that power takes root on the soil of our Souls.

6. It is thus seen why Moses forbade sexual incompletes to enter upon great duties, and why Oriental nations banned all such; for it is certain that he or she who is impotent, except of injuries or years, is not a man or woman, but only an apparition—solid, certainly, yet an apparition still; for uterine power, ovarian force, vaginal energy in woman, and their correspondents in the male, are the *only* passports to the divine regions of Soul Power, mental and spiritual.

K. The ejective moment, therefore, is the most divine and tremendously important one in the human career as an independent entity; for not only may we launch Genius, Power, Beauty, Deformity, Crime, Idiocy, Shame or Glory on the world's great sea of Life, in the person of the children we may then produce, but we may plunge our own souls neck-deep in Hell's horrid slime, or else mount the Azure as contemplar associate Gods; for *then* the mystic Soul swings wide its Golden gates, opens its portals to the whole vast Universe, and through them come trooping either Angels of Light or the Grizzly Presences from the dark corners of the Spaces. Therefore, human copulation is either ascensive and ennobling, or descensive and degrading; wherefore I proclaim—

1. That true Sex-power is God-power.

2. That he or she who, by, in, with, and through it, truly wishes, yearns, prays and craves, with WILL, FAITH, EARNEST VERVE, any great good, Favor, Energy, Power, Quality, Force, or Ability of whatsoever grade, degree, nature or kind, possible to any human being, as Love, Self-command, Retentive Power, Magnetic Presence, or any other achievable thing—beginning the mental work before, continuing it during, and *decreeing* it at love's culmination and demise—that coveted boon will come as certainly as the Soul is true that craves it. But accursed of himself is he who leaveth her till *her* joy, as his own, is complete; for no power can come to either alone, but is the result of the double asking and the dual prayer. Unless there be that reciprocal mutuality, no boon descends, but remaineth in the Spaces.

L. The test of fitness, fullness, capacity, energy, manhood, force, power, ability, and latent possibility of any man, is the terseness, non-inflammatory state, compactness and retentive force of the prostate gland and testes. If these be diseased, loose, easily excited, pendant, non-solid, he is not in a fit state of either soul, body, will, nerves or affection, to either generate his kind, make love, accept it, or do anything else of manly kind, and his first duty is to correct the error.

M. The test of fitness in a woman is her responsive power, her womanly fullness, tenderness, and that true health which makes life a perpetual joy; for if a woman's *heart* is filled, her body *respected*, her *love* returned, her soul appreciated, she will have little need of the doctor's services, but will bid the multitudinous ills that now oppress her an exceedingly *lasting* but not a fond farewell. Why? Because she will not then be compelled to exert all her power to prevent herself from running and screaming at her highest pitch under the infernal spell of nervous excitement; besides which, she will know that her power over him who covers her is immense, and, if she chooses to assert it, absolutely Awful; as they will demonstrate who shall hereafter teach Sex-science and the three underlying principles—Volantia, Posism, and Decretism—which *cannot* be taught by other than myself at present.

(To prevent needless correspondence, let it be known that but a limited number will be taught the whole Science, to become teachers, the fee for which is $250 in gold, or its equivalent. Other points of the System will be taught at $10 per lesson; also the normal sexual secret of magnetic sex-power for either gender, the fee for which is S25, gold or its equivalent, that being the Society's *only terms*. Address as below; but no attention will be paid to applications not clearly stated and unaccompanied with the fee.)

N. Some people there be in this section of the "civilized area" of the earth who cannot imagine anything of magic power or magnetic ability in the human soul, either active or latent, nor indeed any other superior powers or energies at all, than such as find their field of use in heaping up wealth through the diabolic magic of rascality on 'change, in trade and elsewhere, or in seeking to gratify tastes brutal at their bases, and lusts foul enough to shame the devil.

To oblige such, I herewith give a *very* short list of a few such undreamed-of powers, the attainment of which depends upon the degree of effect wherewith they exercise three *simple* principles named below. The wise ones alluded to above may, and probably will, in view of the extraordinary revelations concerning Sex made herein, ask me: *"Canst thou minister to a mind diseased?"* I reply, Yes! By teaching that mind the nature and principles of its own immortal powers and the rules of their growth—not otherwise. For centuries we have known what the world is just finding out, that all the multiple hells on earth originate in trouble, un-ease, of the love, affections, and passions, or amatory sections, of human nature; and that Heaven cannot come till Shiloh does—in other words, knowledge positive on the hidden regions of the mighty world called MAN. Hence this partial uplifting of the veil between us and people of the continents. MEN FAIL AND DIE THROUGH FEEBLENESS OF WILL! Women perish from too much passion, none at all, and absolute, cruel love-starvation. This WE intend to correct; Shall we succeed?

The list of powers attainable by the human being, alluded to herein, numbers hundreds of distinct energies, nearly totally unknown by civilized Christian mankind, who are far more familiar with destroying, than with building up, the Fabric of Human Happiness. This list comprises less than one-half of that pertaining to the Exoteric, or external system, alone; while those of the Inner System are not recorded herein at all. Each power is separate and distinct from all the others.

There ought to be established in this land, for adults—in brains, as well as years—a SCHOOL OF SEXUAL SCIENCE, in which all herein, and immeasurably more, shall be taught. Were not the writer's days numbered, such a school should be opened, wherein people should be taught the mysteries of their own immortal being, and the amazing difference between LOVE and LUST, and the laws that govern them! As it is, the work must be done by other minds; for at best he will only be able to instruct others in the three sublime Principles which underlie the whole superstructure, thus fitting students to teach others. The fee is large, but the Knowledge cost the best years of a whole life. Let me, before giving the list remark that Truth, not Falsehood, ever brightly shines. The power sought will never avail a false individual, whose time and means, in such case, are merely thrown away.

In the course of human life millions sigh for the power of irresistibly affecting an appulsion; to draw or bring to them, for good ends, others when afar off, actually or sympathetically.

1. *Special* Power, involving exercise of the Volantia, Decretism, and Posism, on units only.

2. The same power, near *and* afar off; general exertion on units multiple.

3. Frustrating bad plans of others, when such will prove a benefit.

4. The precisely opposite—to assist others by exertion of the Æthic force of Soul.

5. Moral and other changes, effected by will-influence through health changes.

6. Increasing the dynamic life-force through the three principles.

7. Prolonging specific energy through the single breath force.

8. Tirau-clairism—ability to think clearly to a point, and *know* it.

9. Relating to money dealings, losses, gains, and to forecast them.

10. The grand secret of *Domestic* Happiness—the law of marital discord discovered, and its most effectual antidotes shown, among which is one of *incalculable* value to every wedded couple. Thus we strike a blow direct against the *monster crime of the age*—murder, red-handed, atrocious murder—the awful crime of ABORTION.

11. To render a false husband, lover, or wife, sexively cold to others—*against* their will; in other words, to render them impotent when trying to be untrue. The foregoing eleven are not adapted to barbaric human beings.

12. Where persons are of unloving natures, to change it by attracting love-energy from the earth and matter by self-action.

13. To change it through æreal influences by self-action.

14. To exert the same two influences upon another.

15. To impel a specific energy of love to a person near.

16. To impel a specific love-energy to a far-off person.

17. To do the same, the person's locality being unknown.

18. To intensify the energies of formative love upon unborn children, and on those who breathe.

19. To correct a Physiological failure and source of trouble in husbands.

20. To correct the same annoying circumstance in wives.

21. Impedimenta in the path of false friends, to bring them back to right and justice.

22. To correct companies and families through the same power.

23. To silently induce the female world to assist one's mental purposes.

24. To produce the same results from the man-world.

25. To have mental dalliance with the powers of Space.

26. The three degrees of positive non-mesmeric clairvoyance.

27. To forestall markets by the rising or the falling of the mirror-cloud.

28. To secretly penetrate others' designs (Machiavelli's power).

29. To cultivate the normal, but external will.

30. The power of influencing others, solely financially.

31. Correcting the passionalism of others, when abnormal.

32. Forecasting events in the lives of others—Astro-biognomy.

33. To bring four powers to bear upon the formation of an unincarnated soul—Stirpiculture.

34. To derange the love relations of those not one's lover, or husband or wife, to save an innocent one.

35. To derange the love affairs of a recreant one; punishing duplicity by secret will-force.

36–7–8. To magnetically reclaim a straying lover, wife or husband.

39. Foiling wicked intents of others by will-telegraphy—Decretism.

40. The power of preparing Amulets, and charging them with Æthae.

41. The power of specifically charging them for *special* purposes.

42. The non-luminous, or interior (mental) clairvoyance.

43. To culture the power of direct, impressive, magnetic presence, for general, affectional, or business purposes.

44. To change a lover or husband's affection for another into its opposite toward that other.

45. To cultivate the central, emotional force of character in oneself.

46. To inspire the loftiest non-passional love for oneself in another.

47. To reconstruct a shaking love by secretly generating jealous passional affection.

48. The Oriental Breast-love, its principles, laws, and value.

49. The Uterine (Basic) love; the all compelling, God-like love in Woman.

50. Sending a specific affectional energy to one across the land.

51. The same across seas and lakes, and up mountain lands—Ama-telegraphy.

52. To increase, deepen, and fortify one's own affections when found waning.

53. To do the same for others when their affection wanes toward oneself.

54. The secret terrifying force sent as a corrective against the erring. (Mahi-vapia.)

55. To affiliate an earthly with an ethereal Love assembly.

56. To do the same with a Will-assembly of the Spaces.

57. The same with the Divine Passional forces of Space.

58. The same with reference to the Will-love-energy of Space.

59. The same with reference to single individuals, affiliating with and drawing specific VERVE from the four centers just named—the Greek-Chaldaic principle of Astro-fusion.

60. The law whereby agreed inferior parents may produce their mental superiors through a dual law.

61. The Oriental mystery of sympathetic rings—the Diamond energy.

62. To prepare a talisman on true magnetic principles for self-use.

63. To affiliate with the Hierarchies who cultivate fore-knowledge.

64. To gain positiveness of soul through special love-energies.

65. The intensification of the entire nature of an aspirant.

66. To penetrate the secrets of the lower Spacial worlds. (Suvoyance.)

67. To penetrate the formidable sphere of the middle Spaces. (Zorvoyance.)

68. To attain the road leading to the ineffable Beyond. (Æthævoyance.)

69. To endow others with a given specific power.

70. To vitalize medicines, foods, drinks, clothing, with a specific mission. (The grand Life-secret.)

71. To come *en rapport* with Oriental minds, living or dead.

72. The power of resisting disease and death by Will alone.

73. The seven Magnetic Laws of Love. (Revealed in "Seership.")— which see.

74. The sublime secret of general magnetic Will-energy.

75. The art of adding specific energy to neutral substances. (This has been sadly abused by false brethren and Zingaros, who have thus foisted "Love Powders" on mankind, whose influence was destructive, pestilential passion instead.)

76. The circle of seven, for the generation of absolute Power.

77. The real secret of magnetic union for Power alone. (So badly abused by the late "Brother" Prince, of the London Agapemone.)

78. The famous mystery of the magnetic pillow.—Negative. (So badly abused by the hot-blooded quadroons of the South.)

79. A secret relating to control of married people by their partners; specifically concerning the inter-relations of souls, the inter-dependence of the opposite sexes, and the laws governing the same.

80. To come *en rapport* with the purely Intellectual powers of Space.

81. To fill the air around one with one's own magnetic effluence at will.

82. To foil an conscious or unconscious vampyrism, and defeat it.

83–4–5–6. Attainment of magnetism of being: 1st, positively; 2d, persuasively; 3d, etherially; and *to impart same to others.*

87–8–9, 90–1–2. The specific rules and principles of exerting the Will-love-mental power and force over *special* grades, temperaments, and diverse personalities: 1st, over light, or blonde men; 2d, over same order of women; 3d, over florid, or ruddy men; 4th over same grade of women; 5th over dark, or brunette men; 6th, over same grade of women. For a power that is applicable to one, is wholly, totally unadapted to another.

93. The unwelcome maternity defense, aiming a direct blow against the sextuple horrors of infanticide, abortion—red-handed, ruthless child-murder—premature exhaustion, ungodly quackery, and the unutterable woe of forced motherhood. Embracing: 1st, the silent WILL-FORCE (already published as "Love and its Mystery," in a sheet, and sent to any for a trifling fee); 2d, the Protective formula.

94. The wife's secret power of pleasing *magnetically*, and thus determining her own happiness by ensuring her husband's.

95–6. Exerting a defeative, depressive influence, secretly, for redemptive ends, upon an absent wrong-doer of either sex.

97–8. The science of FEMINANTIA: the ability to exert the purely true and perfect Woman-force over the opposite sex generally.

99. MALEANTIA: exact reverse power of the foregoing.

100. The ability to teach and impart the same æthic power to others; comprehending the three degrees of the Persic and Hindoo Mahi-caligna, as taught the Acolytes 5000 years ago.

101. To attach to oneself innumerable æthic, ærial, invisible assistants. (Arsaphism.)

102. Soul-ometry, past and future: —mathematical reading of others' lives and careers.

103. To become immersed in business spheres, to reliably direct others.

104. To increase the dynamic force and power of any bodily organ.

105. To deepen and expand any special faculty of soul.

106. The special increase of the magnetic beauty of any female soul.

107. To destroy an unhealthy, abnormal passion.

108–9–10 and 11. Are special and extraordinary modifications of this power, both positive and negative, and which, with those that follow and certain others not alluded to herein, can be taught VERBALLY, and also by mail, viz.:

112. The grand secret of Life-prolongation.

113. The real secret of magnetic Soul-union—its nature, laws, and achievability.

114. Positive mystery of the Oriental magnetic pillow; and—

115–122. The Seven Superlative Powers of the Soul.

These constitute all that will be taught.

Owing to the Innumerable hosts, who, dissatisfied with life, religions as they are, philosophies, and currents isms and institutions, are eagerly, impatiently craving Light, more Light, no attention will be paid to any except such as are in absolute earnest, no matter who they are, or what financial ability they possess.

Druggists, Physicians, and all others who write me for formulas and recipes, are hereby informed that in no case whatever will I dispose of my formulas for Cerebral, Nervous and Sexual Tonics, Invigorants and Restoratives, unless paid for the same, the prices for any one of which, with license to manufacture, is $250 in gold for either of the first four, and $450 and $500 gold coin for either of the remaining three—these prices being based upon the fact that they are the most perfect, totally harmless, and non-injurious Invigorants on the earth. It will be of no use whatever to write me for either of them without the fee—the price for all seven of which is $2,000 in gold coin.

In conclusion: I am preparing an Especial Work on Sex matters, because there is none on earth yet that begins to do justice to the subject. In it I mean to say what no human being has either dared to, or knew—which is more likely. The book, "SEXAGYMA," will be *printed*, not *published*, and will be only sent to subscribers who order it and *pay for it in advance*, and not another copy beyond that limited number can be had *at any price*. It will be ready very soon, and its price will be $5 per copy—not a cent less.

My work on Mediumship, "The New Mola," can be had by addressing me, at 60 cents, or two copies for $1.

Finally: All those who desire to cultivate Inner Vision or Clairvoyant Light through the mystic but sublime instrumentality of the Magic Mirror, are hereby informed that I have just arranged for a few very fine ones, which can be had at very advantageous rates; commission, $2 to $5. These Mirrors are adapted *also to mundane purposes*—speculative, monetary, lottery, etc.—and can be had at once, if applied for. The entire lot are from the late Dr. Jarlin's (French) collection. Prices on application. Those desiring especial instructions of me on various points, are referred to the "New Mola."

All communications in reference to matters connected herewith must be directed as per address on separate slip enclosed herewith, and, to ensure *immediate* attention, must contain stamp for return postage and a fee of $1.

[Toledo *Sun* Liberal Printing House, Toledo, O.]

Appendix B
THE MYSTERIES OF EULIS

1st. The Neophyte is supposed to have read, *studied* and *understood* the meanings and mysteries revealed and set forth in the paper known as "The Asiatic Mystery: being the first Rosicrucian Manifesto to the World!" If not then such is his first obligation and bounden duty.

2nd. He will also understand that the term "Rosicrucian" does not mean the whole Brotherhood of Eulis, but means only those who have taken the first primary lessons in the stupendous system of Eulis, and is but a mere passing name wherewith the *true* Brethren *amuse,* and at the same time mystify the world; for we hold it as a cardinal principle that it *will not* do to "cast pearls before swine lest they turn and rend you after trampling pearls under their foul feet, which they have neither soul to appreciate or brains to comprehend." Therefore caution is our canon—observe it *carefully.*

3rd. It is equally essential that the neophyte study well; and thoroughly master, if not the *entire* meaning, then at least the Drift of the "Ansairetic Mystery."

4th. The genius of EULIS, its spirit and meaning, its dicta and principle is that each Brother comprises the whole Order in himself; and acts for himself toward himself and all others, its aim being not a society of secret Brethren endowing him with powers to initiate whom he deems competent and worthy but never giving him the Password till he has proved himself both competent and worthy, to which end *it is in order to try him* by all kind of ordeals and trusts, *unknown to him,* when, where, how or for what purpose tried; for it is the experience of all "true" brethren that *many* are called, while only few are chosen. Each Brother of Eulis is at liberty to establish lodges to suit himself, with such passwords as the lodge may adopt from time to time; but the gates of all lodges fly open when the MASTER WORD is spoken, no matter when, where, or by whom, as none but full Eulians *guard the doors* and *none but such* possess the MASTER KEY word, opening all portals.

5th. The grand object of EULIS therefore is to build up the individuality of each acolyte, [to] the end of adding a new power to the Universe a new force to the human soul; wherefore each is an independent being working out the problem of his own redemption from the thraldom inherited from ancestry, the dead ages, and forced upon him by condition.

We do not expect to teach a man and find brains wherewith he may understand said teachings; but we indicate the way, furnish a chart, and bid him square his sails and depart for the SHINING SHORE! To which end here is given the following: DEFINITIONS.

1st. The first grand principle to be studied, mastered and applied, in the search for knowledge, and endeavor to enlarge the scope and range of individual human Power—mental, magnetic and psychical, is

VOLANTIA—the quiet, steady, calm, non-turbulent, non-muscular exertion of the human WILL. To increase which, and render practically *and* magnetically serviceable, *practice* is necessary not a fitful, now and again kind, but regular, that is daily: observe these rules—and follow them.

Place against the wall a black card, round, with a white center, or a white one with a black center, and gaze on it steadily, one minute, willing at the same time to increase your powers of ATTENTION, CONCENTRATION, and ABSTRACTION. Then slowly turn your face to the blank wall and the optical effect will be an apparition, and the card,—colors reversed,—will slowly pass across your line of vision. Usually but one or two will thus flit by, but there should be at least from four to seven. The card may be of any other colors, and the phantoms will be their exact opposite or complementary hue. These exercises are intended to develop the above named three powers, and their ultimate end and purpose is to finally enable you to fix your mind on any one, alive or dead, and will *their* phantom, and in the latter case, *themselves* to appear.

Of course the greater results are quicker and better attained if instead of a card you place a wafer on the center of a good magic mirror, albeit some are so weak-nerved as to be frightened when a face or figure gazes directly at them from the brightly black-white magnetic sea of the mirror. Of course all such persons had better abandon at once the pursuit of higher magic, which requires *heart, courage, persistence* and *goodness* to its noblest and most successful culture.

After the cards have been used for a while, say thirty times, they may be abandoned, either for the wafered mirror or the head of a nail—brass-head—or better still, *three* nails—zinc, copper, steel—

arranged in a triangle of one inch diameter; wrap around them all together a bundle of fine copper or zinc wire, and while gazing on them hold the other end thereof in your right hand. The effect is electrical, and serves also to render your attention more firm, positive and concentrated,—albeit it may take from three to six months before you will be able or competent to substitute metaphysical objects in their stead.

The 2nd. Principle is DECRETISM—*i.e.* decreeing, ordering, commanding, mentally enforcing the behests of Will and Desire;—to say, feel, think, ordain a thing to be, to do, act, go, live, move, appear, vanish, rise, fall, sink, stop, fly,—It-must-and-shall-be-itiveness. It is the positive executive force of the human soul, without a proper culture and activity of which, no great thing either within or without the pale of white magic can be accomplished. Volantia generally, but not *always* should precede it. Great care should be taken that there be no other emotion or action going on in the mind during the *decretal instant*, for this ordaining power, especially after the exercise of volantia, leaps from the soul like a flash of vivid white lightning, traversing space, centering on its object even though oceans flow between, or vast spaces divide; yet its period of activity or duration *never* exceeds *three* to *seven seconds* of earthly time.—It is the *Blessing* or *Cursing* energy of the soul; and is at once its grandest and most terrible force, alike potent for good or evil: and its laws are periodical, its form of orbit elliptical, its action magnetic; therefore what it takes from you it always brings back—If *good* then good; if evil then *additional* evils. The 3rd. Element or Energy is POSISM—placing oneself in a *receptive* position, state, frame of body, mind and feeling. It is the most important and most difficult of either of the three great principles,—and its results—especially in Affectional lines correspond,—indeed are numerous. To exert it successfully requires a fair development of ATTENTION, ABSTRACTION and CONCENTRATION in addition to the exercise and power of Volantia and decretism, not merely as regards any special object, or power to be sought, but to induce the condition of Posism itself. If to give, take, strike or sustain a blow you *pose* your body, hands, face, eyes, nostrils and mouth—as *all* do, even so is the same law and rule imperative in the higher or superphysical, metaphysical, mental and ethereal region of the vast being that you are; and you must enforce them in order to reach the sublimest of all the Receptive-powers of your being. There is no magic save in Will, Love, Posism. Remember this.

To illustrate my meaning let me say, per example, air and heat rush in to fill a vacuum; and there can be no vacuum if anything is there.

Well you cannot wholly either notice, wish for, will, decree, or receive the full measure of the thing sought, or power desired, or the entire weight of any mental or metaphysical desideratum, if half or more of the mind is already occupied by something else, which receives that proportion of its attention and ratio of the heart's desire.

In some lodges, in the foretime, and in some instances now, the acolytes practiced and practice Posism two years before being considered proficient;—(good chess players are usually good posists), for it requires the entire devotion, absorption and concentration of *all* the inner being. When a thing is to be done, an energy—(individual—in both senses), hierarchy or special power is to be invoked and brought down from the ærial kingdoms of the spaces; or evoked and called up from *within*, the mind must not only be brought to wholly bear upon the Reception thereof, but *room* in the brain, or soul, must be provided for the expected or hoped for new tenant, and the entire attention of the soul be withdrawn, and vacated except for that special thing, gift, energy, quality, power, then sought.

This road of FULIS is a royal one, which dolts, fools and "recipe" followers can never travel; for only MEN and occasionally a woman— can travel its Imperial paths; because the higher powers only come to those capable of appreciating them; they *never* flow into the empty heads or starveling souls; and *never* at all unless the laws of their evocation, development, operation and evolution are coolly, calmly, steadily, persistently followed, implicitly obeyed.

4th. PRINCIPLE: BREATH-POWER. We breathe two kinds of air, mingled to a greater or less extent: 1st. Common atmospheric; 2nd. Magneto-electrical-Ethereal, in combination. The first sustains the life of matter:—sensation;—the second, that of soul and emotion—the higher, inner, deeper part of man; that portion of us which laughs at wealth, honors, titles, time, and concerns itself only about Infinite and eternal interests. The first gives Force; The second generates Power. It is possible to fill the lungs, therefore the brain with this last, sifted from the first, and thus the soul with ascensive ability and inclination; with the loftier kind of trance power,—the sacred sleep of Sialam—in which the soul bids defiance to all the barriers which, awake or asleep, or in the mesmeric states, limit and bound it;—with that grand flight-power wherewith it can reach infinite altitudes, and sweep with masterly vision the amazing rain of stellar galaxies falling down the Deep!—that sleep of Sialam, wherein man may gain whatsoever of knowledge and power he wills, which lies within his soul's capacity of comprehension and making use of.

Now by slowly, regularly breathing, two things occur: 1st. you gain lung, therefore physical-life-power, for the organs in an instant extract the *Vif* of the air, and immediately discharge their accumulated load of carbonized air. The exhalent movement is always longest in natural breathing; that is the foul air is longer going out, than the fresh air is coming in: But if you wish to gain the interior worlds, and have more ethereal life than mere physical, the slow breathing must go on for seven to ten minutes at a time; and to obtain the better influence the heavings of the chest should be regular and the inspirations and out-breaths be of equal duration. In this way,—first fixing some object to be obtained in the mind,—and the sifting process will go on, and the ethereal air be retained in the lungs, brain, nerves—until reserve force enough is gained to add new power, and, enabling the soul to subdue sense, afford the pure intellect, ability to take lofty, prolonged, and heaven-sustained flights into the blue Empyrean, or indeed in any direction fancy or inclination prompts or necessity suggests.

5th. It behooves me now to call your attention to the most tremen-dous of all the powers of the human soul: It is the purely spiritual, non-material, or Æthic power of the interior man but this power should never be attempted to be brought into action for merely worldly-wise, financial or temporary motive, use or end, because its sphere of action pertains to higher and better states than this of earth, at least in these ages wherein men look down for God and not upward, judging by the sincere homage they pay to the Golden Gods.

The term ÆTH signifies that fine essence which spirits breathe, which is the filling in of space; which cushions the worlds, and which pen-etrates the outer air just as odors do; it is inhaled by Æthereal people precisely as we of earth draw in the effluence of matter in its grosser and lower forms. No real, divine, or celestial, mental or loving energy can come until by patient and continued effort the Neophyte learns to inhale it; simultaneously with the firm fixity of the mind upon what is in and of it, therefore we contact the essence of power and the denizens of the ethereal and far-off countries and climes. [In so] doing, will he breathe the elements which generate power in the human soul.

Remember, O, neophyte, that GOODNESS alone is POWER, SILENCE is STRENGTH, WILL REIGNS Omnipotent, and LOVE lieth at the FOUNDATION.

6th. Centers: Orbits: Spheres: Potencies: Hierarchies: Brotherhoods: All things on earth, material and hyperphysical alike, have their cen-ters, orbits, periods; and all conceivable powers, qualities and energies in the spaces, have the same. There are times when they are and are not contactable and it is very difficult for one living in dour hell to contact them at all, save through the exercise of a RESOLUTE WILL. But there are Societies of Beings, invisible by material eyes, who were of earth once, and others who *never knew* material bodies at all—who understand any and everything man can imagine; who cultivate every possible species of knowledge, and who answer the desire and invocation (and it is well to burn incense and scatter odors when invoking them), of those of us who take to the same lines of thought and feeling; who belong to the same category of intelligences or who voluntarily place themselves under the essential conditions of *rapport* or contact.

Not any one Brotherhood or Society cultivates all forms of knowledge, yet it is impossible to think of any personal, general, special adherents, cultivators, professors, centers, agents, workers, understanders, teachers and propaganda in the Æthic realms beyond the shadows and gloom of earth, (where injustice rules and wicked prejudices reign paramount and supreme). Be thou careful, however, to divest the mind of all but the thing in hand, so to speak. Never seek for *two dissimilar* favors or boons at the *same time*, or within seven clear days between operations, every one of which should be prepared for with a full heart— for the invisibles can read you thoroughly!— by fasting, ablutions; soul prayer, alone,—and night is *always Best.*

Study these things thoroughly and well, nor forget this caution: Nothing can be done except through Law, Order, Rule, and a clear and definite comprehension of the underlying principles set forth herein and in other works from Dr. P. B Randolph. But by proceeding further it is advisable to consider one or two points which, in the end, will be found of great service to the thinking reader and student of the philosophy now taught.—There are no accidents, really, no such thing as chance, in this life and world of ours; for all things and events are the result of eternal causes; and there are rules by which they can be forecast and anticipated.

Now I do not mean by this that all human events and occurrences are foreseen by those who once were denizens of the world we inhabit and who, for redemptive, or other ends, reveal them to their earthly proteges; for I do not believe such is often, though doubtless occasionally, the case; but I do mean that somewhere in this universe, there is a great central, Intelligent Power, Presence and energy, who *necessarily* knows all that was, is, and is to be. This central power must be environed by colossal mental energies or Potentialities in knowledge only second to Its Supreme self: Nor do I conceive such Potencies to be ascended human beings who once dwelt in flesh-and-blood bodies, lived, died and rose again—but I mean that there are Electrical, Ethereal, non-material Universes beyond the matter-Island floating like eggshell scallops on the breeze of the azure sea, as far grander, vaster, more magnificent and mysterious than this of ours with all its amazing splendors, all its myriad galaxies; all its rainstorms of starry systems; its incomputable distances and stretch of fathomless centuries!—as this of ours is superior to an anthill in an African jungle.

That there are hierarchies—armies of them!—Potencies, Powers, vast Intelligences—not of human or material genesis, before whose awful grasp of mental powers, before whose amazing sweep of mind, the grandest intellect earth ever did or can produce, is as a pebble to a mountain range: a tiny dewdrop to the almighty rush of ocean's waters;—a gentle shower to a tempest of rain; a zephyr to the raging typhoon on its devastating march over lands and seas! These beings may be the arbiters of the destinies of worlds; and I believe that they are the originators of many a drama fruitful of good. "But how do you know that such things exist?" Because 1st. In the sleep of Sialam I and others have seen them; and we know they were *not* of this or similar earths, because they are organically different, and look no more like a human apparition than a negro does like a Kalmuc Tartar. 2d. They sense the future. 3rd. They reveal things Infinitely grander than do spirits. 4th. They know the future: Man, embodied or not, is unable to sense it. 5th. They declare that Soul-power and sex-power are co-efficients and co-dependents:—their own sex-systems, corresponding to our public region—is in the *side*, near the heart, and serves but one purpose; while ours serves *three*, the *essential*, the *sensual*, and the *sensitive*. 6th. They cannot be contacted through circles, mesmerism or by any so-called spiritual modus; but only through the sleep of Sialam induced by mirror gazing; or through the mirror itself. 7th. We know they are supra-human in power, stature, form, shape, mind, intelligence, wisdom and energy because they teach supra-human knowledges and contact with them makes man better and wiser,—while spiritual contact does not always. We call them the NERIDII—and the Philosophy they teach the Eulian.

So far the basic principles of the DIVINE SCIENCE. Now for their general and specific exercise; and [to] comprehend the modus operandi, it is essential that you understand somewhat more of the awful and tremendous powers and native majesty of the human soul; things neither dreamed of or taught by any philosophers or philosophy extant save THIS alone!

In the first place, then, remember that we believe in Deity, acknowledge His Omnipotence, Omniscience and Omnipresence; that man is made in His image and likeness in every respect, save only that God's capacity is unbounded, while man's is limited; which limits are either contracted or vast in strict accordance with the relative ratio of his soul development, and independence of mere bodily sense, aptitude and material bias.

Thus one so developed may bore the spaces by use of the power about to be taught you now; while the brain power of another may not enable him to imagine or perceive anything loftier than the most common place facts and irrelevant truths of mere matter, or mundane interests. Man has not Omniscience, but has *much* knowing power. He is not Omnipotent yet possesses enormous latent power. He is not capable of Omnipresence, but *is* capable of Ubique—that is of being mentally, spiritually, psychally in many places and scenes at the time.

Illustration: A million photographic instruments will chain at one instant, a million shadows, or images of the same man, object or thing, because all surrounding space is filled with myriads of such shadows, given off by everything at every moment; and this is even more true of the soul than of the body, which fact brings us face to face with the sublime mystery of PROJECTION; and that of its opposite: Soul-attraction.

1st. Definition—PROJECTION: means the sending, forcing, compelling of your image, wraith, spirit, soul, phantom or simulacrum to, and wherever you *will* through the three Principles.

2nd. [Definition]—ATTRACTION: is the exercise of the same power *to bring* the same to you instead of the reverse. The first is called Æthævoyance; the other Zorvoyance, and both are loftier developments of Psycho-vision, or that which people call clairvoyance, albeit no such clairvoyance as used to be, exists now, and cannot save by and through the magic mirror so-called.

Through resemblances to Deity you may know much; by presence, by apparitional power or birth, whenever you have steady will-force enough to decree your presence, you may compel the approach of whatsoever phantom (or real spirit either) you choose, and you may act with enormous force upon whom you desire. *Observe*:

VOLANTIA can be exerted from two planes: 1st. Pure intellect, cold and joyless—which is its negative force or plane; 2d. From the heart, soul, emotion or Love plane, which is its positive point of action.

DECRETISM is *always* masculine, positive, ordering, commanding, electric—of Head *alone*.

POSISM requires instantaneous falling *from* the masculine, head, brain, to the soft, tender, loving, emotional side of your nature. Man looks earthward in Sex intercourse. Woman Heaven-ward. He imparts. She receives; so also the intellect of man acts on imperative principles:— Her Love on Receptive ones. This is the *LAW!*

(Note. you can execute any problem in the List and others not there, by never forgetting that all things of earthly use, intent or interest, correspond to *odd* numbers; while mental, psychal, soul, heavenly, power-gaining, power-giving, heart-protecting, knowledge-acquiring energies, all belong to *even* numbers, thus, of course merely distinguish between the two enormous ranges.

The *even* numbers begin with, and end in *Prayer*, and posing to receive the boon craved, asked, longed,—yearned for; while the *odd* numbers begin and end with either of the *three* principles, except in financial matters, or the punishment of wrong, or the protecting of the weak, or the imparting of power, health, etc. to others, and *then* Decretism ends the formula invariably.)

Now to work:—Say No. 4 of the "Ansairetic"—you will first remember what follows: The party to be frustrated must be present either in person or by apparitional birth, which you can bring about by posing first, then willing, then decreeing his or her presence, repeating or continuing it till the image stands clearly before your mind's eye. Then think what you want to just as clearly: then *will* and *decree* whatsoever you choose. Else apply the Æthic force and after the soul is full, then decree and will and pose it. *But the Æthic force need not be used to frustrate; but *should* be to impart, inspire, protect or bless.* To aid you a photograph will be of good service; but in Oriental lands and also in the practice of Dr. P. B .R. a picture or a *doll* was used, *named* for the party to be helped; He *never cursed* but sometimes found occasion to defeat designing people, hypocrites, false friends and otherwise incorrigible wrong doers, for these are *children* from three to three score years of age who are touchable only by the hand of Force, and upon whom Kindness and goodness are merely thrown away!—people who cannot understand that one is in dead earnest, except storm announces it. It is not pleasant to be compelled to resort to the *lex talionis* or the Draconian law, yet at times it *must* be done. However, of late years he had abandoned that and learned to pity and forgive. On the other hand, using the same ten cent doll to name, he helped a score to glory, healthy prosperity, wealth and fame.

You need not be told that to increase the dynamic Life-force requires *that* purpose distinctly to be brought before your soul, and worked as an *even* number, Æthic force, and while retiring, rising, and walking, continue it regularly for seven minutes a day, two at night, two at rising, three in walking.

TIRAUCLAIRISM is a difficult power to attain owing to the cerebral activity of most persons. It is best done at night. Use the will to bring any image, flash, spark or scintilla before you and never take the mind's eye from it, but hold it there, resolutely fighting against the innumerable hosts of other images or phantoms that are sure to come crowding in like flakes of snow before the driving hurricane. But it can be done. After which you can apply the power to whatsoever you please. Indeed you cannot even practice _La Haute Magie_ without developing, increasing, strengthening this superb power and faculty of the Imperial human soul; and it is one which, although difficult to reach, will amply repay all the efforts you may put forth to acquire its mastery.

As already stated, the human mind cannot conceive of any quality, knowledge, power or energy, but has a Hierarchy, Society, Brotherhood or nation in the Spaces and the Vault, who cultivate that specialty as a positive science, to the general exclusion of all others. I name a few: Health, Jewels, Trade, Exchange, Wealth, Music, Geometry, Melody, Medicine, Logic, Astronomy, Soul, Brain, Physiology, Astrology, White Magic, Spirit, Social Law, Sexagyma, Love, Ambition, War, Black art, Black Magic, Lust, Friendship, chance, (Lotteries, etc.) and so on to thousands of others.

But the impact, rapport and contact law must first be learned, assiduously obeyed, steadily pursued, and that too, to the practical exclusion of the recondite and cognate studies during the entire time of discipline and consequent novitiate; for, as said already no human being can, as Dr. P. B. R., master the principia without severe effort, persistence, will and purpose, with that divine enduring patience under restraint, which alone can open the chambers of the inner-man to entertain the mighty guest whose aid and association is [sought].

Definitions. First clearly define the Brotherhood or Hierarchy you wish to affiliate with. Bend your whole soul to clearly locate it East, West, North, South or between these points. Name it, and a warm breath will presently fan your cheek or head, coming from the point where the Brotherhood dwells. Then apply the Posism only, and the double Prayer, to God first, the Hierarchy second. Success is attained when the mental assurance reaches the portals of your immortal selfhood. But pray avoid invoking more than one at a time. Two may be cultivated at once but the procedure must be bridged by from three to seven entire nights and days.

The Neophyte can if he or she truly will do so in accordance with the three principles explained elsewhere, contact minds of any grade whether on the Earth or off it. If the mind be on that of one departed, or dead, the neophyte's mind must dwell on the Oriental or the Northern Heavens, or westward or wherever the departed may have gone toward from his or her earth location.

But if the party be not dead, then the neophyte's mind must dwell upon the earth, in that direction whereto the sought mind belongs. He or she may select Persia, Chaldea, Egypt, Babylon, but above all India, Ceylon or China, for by so doing he or she can readily contact both the living and the dead.

CONCLUSION: These are the fundamentals, and all that is absolutely essential to any one; for their application is as broad and varied as life itself. A List of over one hundred powers attainable is given in the "Ansairetic Mystery," which see. But there are certain sexive applications not therein given, among which is that of life-prolonging through a peculiar rite—which usually weakens health, and destroys life, but which under proper conditions absolutely strengthens and prolongs both. This mystery is that of MAHI-CALIGNA—or the Sexive principle of Eulis, but comes into active use in many ways, but principally in these seven:—

    I. For purposes of increasing the brain and body power of an unborn child.

    II. Influencing one's wife or husband, and magnetically controlling them.

    III. Regaining youthful beauty, energy, vivacity, affectional and magnetic power.

    IV. Prolonging the life of either the subject or actor, or either at will.

    V. Attainment of Supreme white-magic of will, Affection or Love.

    VI. For the furtherance of financial interest, schemes, Lotteries etc.

    VII. The attainment of the loftiest insight possible to the earthly soul.

These seven constitute a crowning glory of the system of Eulis. To work or execute any or all of them, that which has been already herein set forth and explained, should be well and clearly studied and mastered before even an attempt is made, because to begin and fail is to be forever shut out from either the chance, or the Power sought for.

If a man has an intelligent and loving wife, with whom he is in full and complete accord, he can work out the problems by her aid. They all are a radical soul-sexive series of energies, not to be attempted impurely, or under the malign influences of passional fire or animal lust, but only when under the dominion of the loftiest desire for power leading unto God and goodness. The *rite* is a *prayer* in all cases, and the most powerful, earthly beings can employ. The first thing is to have the object of the prayerful act or ceremony clearly defined before the mental eyes of those who undertake it. An able man or wife can often avail herself or himself of this grand fact of knowledge unknown to the other; albeit it is best for both husband and wife to act together for the attainment of the mysterious objects sought.

Success in any case requires the adjuvancy of a superior woman. THIS IS THE LAW! A harlot or low woman is useless for all such lofty and holy purposes; and just so is a bad, impure, passion-driven apology for a man. Remember also: The woman shall not be one who accepts rewards for compliance; nor a virgin; or under eighteen years of age; or another's wife; yet must be one who hath known man and who has been and still is capable of intense mental, volitional and affectional energy, combined with perfect sexive and orgasmal ability; for it requires a *double crisis* to succeed: no one can reach the power sought, or gain their special purposes unless they do so in the *coitive* act, or at the *exudive* moment of the woman, or the expulsive one of the man; which event should be simultaneous or as near as possible, because the mystic gates of the soul never open to admit the elements of power, or send forth its magic-working will, save for an instant *at that precise juncture.*

The terms MAHI-CALINGA signify the Knowledge of ages; of the past present, and of Present Possibilities, and also the power and the ability to effect the purposes of the pure, *true*, and *good* desire, of cultivated Will!—for to execute the great intent through the magic use of gender, requires guiltless sexual union—mere pleasure being not its object at all;—that is to say: The purpose *must* be pure, pure power and knowledge [for] attainment; never lust or its gratification. Thus it becomes not only an energizer of both souls but a health, joy and peace-creator, and, magically speaking,—the most forceful money bringing, wealth compelling power on the Planet when that wealth's object is good-promotion, and not mere self-aggrandizement, as is too often the case.

The entire mystery can be given in very few words, and they are: An upper room; absolute personal, mental and moral cleanliness both of the man and wife. An observance of the law just cited during the entire term of the experiment—*49 days.* Formulate the desire and keep it in mind during the whole period and especially when making the nuptive prayer, during which no word may be spoken, but the thing desired be strongly thought and the three Principles enforced—*Volantia, Posism, Decretism.* The end sought, the power coveted or the thing desired must be clearly defined in each mind—*then*, and both after and before. These few lines invoke and embrace a mystery of superlative grandeur. The mystery cannot be abused, or worked to evil ends, for just as certain as they are attempted to be, just so sure will evil follow that attempt.

These solemn things are never to be imparted to the young and giddy, or to any character but the high, solid and noble; and only to those in the higher degrees of the mystic and Imperial fraternity.

Secret 112. Life–Prolongation:—The natural constitution—injuries excepted—can be rendered far more endurable by a persistent following of the subjoined Seven Rules.

1st. The body must be kept perfectly clean by frequent bathing; which must include head, hair, eyes, ears, feet, groins and sexual organs—these seven—at least twice in every passing week.

2d. The food must be natural, solid, free from an excess of liquid, fat, oil, water, alkali, acid and sweets—these seven—and not if possible to be long neglected.

3rd. The bed should be hard; head to the north; pillows moderately hard; bed clothes not heavy; pillows low; rooms cool, and well ventilated:—These seven.

4th. The body naked should be twice a week subjected to the air-bath, in sunshine if possible: Be twisted; tuned; bent;—slowly, kick and strike, pull, lift,—row,—slowly. These seven. Constantly.

5th. Draw in the breath *slowly*, and emit it the same; holding it in as long as possible, for every additional minute it is so held, will add ten days to the sum of life.

6th. Never indulge in sexual intercourse except both parties are at the highest tide of loving passion. Sleep apart: indulge not save once or twice a week at the outside; and on no account either touch an unready or unwilling woman; *or quit her till both orgasms are effected: Do not* neglect this latter important point.

7th. Stop worrying; scolding; fretting; drinking; and go to bed early; Love much, and rely on God and your own Soul. These seven.

The mystery of life and power, seership and forecast , endurance and longevity, silent energy, and mental force—lies in the SHE side of God, the Love principle of human kind and in the sexual nature of the kosmos. Outside of it all is cold and death; in it resides all FIRE, Energy, Procreant Power (spiritual and all others) and the key unlocking every barred door in the realms that are. Remember, O Neophyte, that I am not dealing in mere *recipes*, formal and trashy "directions," but in the fundamental Principia subtending Being.

Fix this first Principle firmly in your memory. Its basic form is "Love lieth at the Foundation," and Love is covertibly Passion, Enthusiasm, Heat, Affection, FIRE, God. Master that.

2d. The moment wherein a man discharges his seed—his essential self—into a willing or unwilling womb, is the most solemn, energetic and powerful moment he can ever know on earth. If under the influence of mere lust it be done, the discharge is suicidal, losing, demoralizing to himself; it is Harlotry, disease, magnetic damnation to the woman, and if successful, generates murder, crime and misery in the child. If in Love on both sides, then strength and its cognates follow.

3rd. At the moment his seminal glands open his nostrils expand, and while the seed is going from his soul to her womb he breathes one of two atmospheres, either fetid damnation from the border-spaces or Divine Energy from the far heavens.

4th. Whatsoever he or she shall truly will and internally pray for when Love, pure, divine, natural, passional or volitional is in the ascendant, that moment the prayer's response comes down.

5th. If he *will* for any power, from the moment of passing the outer door till the woman shall have *expelled him*, that will he reach. But Hell reigns in marriage land today, and its principle cause is that while still the *spiritual* semen is passing, he *withdraws*, still *erect* and hell takes hold at the very roots of their being, because they defy, annul, prostitute and disobey *the* very primary law of being—the great purpose underlying their very creation. This therefore learn and teach.

6th. He who covers a woman under the dominion of mere lust, commits suicide and does murder. He who covers a woman in lust, and only liking her, at the time, only obeys the instinctual law, and both suffer from incompleteness, for it is only when he lusts, likes and *loves*, that the triple law is obeyed, and power, not weakness, follows the act.

7th. He who touches a woman who has not previously been excited to the want of the union, is a suicidal fool. This is the main sexual Law. Now I will teach you the grandest truth you can ever dream of. It is this. Remember that the essence of all Power, of whatsoever nature, character or kind, ever resides in, evolves out of and derives its impulsive energy from the SHE side of God; hence the same side of a man or woman—for it *don't* follow that all who wear the Penis are in soul true males, or that a vagina is the sign of womanness; but he or she who has an emotional, loving, weeping, sympathetic, beautiful, soft, and tender side, has the *sheness* alluded to. Now by the exercise of Will in Love (not Will in Intellect), do we of Eulis achieve our mental and other superior triumphs. For when will is exerted, of intellect, weariness and failure comes: but when will in Love goes forth, VICTORIES ARRIVE. Now when you seek to cure a person, supposing you to be medically inclined, by the hands, or to charge any medicine, or a bit of cloth or paper with curative power, let your features and soul drop right straight out of *Force* and *Intellect*, and right into smiles, gentleness, softness, LOVE and in that state gently, softly *will* the thing you want and it SHALL BE*!!!*

Nor can you ever achieve the grander triumphs unless you obey this law. No matter what the thing, power, quality, range, kind, character, sort of thing or power you desire. This, and this only, is *the* Law of its attainment. Hence never deal out medicine or put your hand to a patient unless you drop down to the floor of Power, and that foundation is LOVE. It is also the ladder to unaccountable Powers, forces, knowledges of the upper Heavens!!

If you comprehend these truths you are armed for all emergencies, for the Law is universal in its application; you cannot master what is herein written in a day or month, for it requires long and severe study and practice to thoroughly comprehend it.

Study Seership along with it.

(The sum of four pounds was paid for this MSS to the widow of P. B. Randolph and was remitted to her by me.—John Yarker)

Appendix C
BIBLIOGRAPHY OF THE WORKS OF PASCHAL BEVERLY RANDOLPH

In his *Curious Life* (17), Randolph says that the principles of his "life will be found set forth in all his works, and in hundreds of essays, poems, newspaper articles, songs, letters, lectures and fugitive pieces now floating up and down the sea of literature, translated into five languages,—like shallops of silver on a sea of ink," and predicts that his works will ensure him "a lofty place in the pantheon of great thinkers" a hundred years hence.

This confident prophecy of future glory has not been fulfilled. Randolph's scattered essays, letters, and topical pieces have now largely vanished, and even some of his more substantial works are scarce and difficult to find. Several of his books are still in print. Those issued by Reuben Swinburne Clymer's Rosicrucian organization in Quakertown, Pennsylvania, however, have been altered and abridged and are useless for historical purposes. The reprints issued by Health Research in Mokelumne Hill, California, are faithful, if not elegant, versions, except where the Clymer edition has been reproduced.

The name under which each of Randolph's works was written is given here because almost all of Randolph's early writings were published anonymously or under various pseudonyms. "Cynthia Temple," the name under which he published his pamphlet *It Isn't all Right* was the name of the spirit through whom he first learned of the mysterious process of communication he calls "Blending." "A Builder of the Temple," the pseudonym under which *The Rosicrucians—Who and What They Are* was published, was the name of one of the degrees of his Rosicrucian foundations. "Casca Llanna" is both the title of one of his books and the pseudonym under which the tale is authored and was said to mean, variously, "Good News" or "Falling Waters." (*Casca Llanna*, cover page and 373). The origin of the term is unknown, but Albert Pike published some of his legal articles in the 1850s under the pseudonym "Casca," and it is tantalyzing (though far-fetched) to posit some connection. "Griffin Lee," the name under which Randolph published the original version of *Pre-Adamite Man*, must have been adopted because of the hybrid nature of the griffin. "Count de St. Leon," the name under which *Love and its Hidden History* first appeared in 1869, is probably an echo of the Count de St. Leon of William Godwin's novel of the same name—an identification made more certain by the fact that Godwin takes his story from Cohausen's *Hermippus Redivivus*. The reference may also be biographical and refer to "Count Leon," the bastard of Napoleon. "The Son of Flora," the name with which Randolph signed the dedication of *Dealings with the Dead*, and "The Rosicrucian," the name under which he authored the book, are obvious, as is "A Seer," the name appended to his first article. Someone writing under the initials G. D. S. in the introduction to *The Rosicrucian's Story*, the first book that Randolph appears to have published under his true name, says that Randolph "has at last decided to drop all disguises, since it is now conceded on all hands that a man, even if of mixed blood, has certain rights that are bound to be respected." The implication that pseudonymity was adopted because of racial prejudice may be partly true, but an equally strong motive was provided by Randolph's reputation for fickleness and eccentricities and by the subject matter of many of his works.

Because of his innumerable changes of position and the necessity of making a living, Randolph constantly reworked his writings and incorporated versions of earlier works in later publications, making the publishing history of his books a labyrinth, and this bibliography is designed to help penetrate the tangled history of his works. In compiling this bibliography I have reviewed the standard works and booksellers' material on occult bibliography and have haunted over the years the major public and university libraries in the United States, Great Britain, and France as well as many private libraries in those countries with a specialization in spiritualism and the occult. The standard on-line and electronic bibliographical services have also been consulted. The bibliography is in roughly chronological order and is divided into three sections: (1) published pamphlets and books, and circulated manuscripts, (2) occasional pieces, articles, and published letters, and (3) works that Randolph says he was working on but in fact probably never published. Works known to have existed but which I have not been able to locate are included as a guide for future researchers and are marked with an asterisk after the title, as are the works which probably were never published. The bibliography is as complete as I have been able to make it, but I would be delighted to have other researchers discover other works by Randolph or copies of works I have been unable to locate.

Published Books and Pamphlets and Manuscripts Known to Have Been Circulated by Randolph

1854

1. *Waa-Gu-Mah.** Allibone's *Critical Dictionary of English Literature and British and American Authors Living and Deceased* (1870) lists this (2:1738) as *Waa-gu-Nah*, a 12mo volume published in 1854, with a third edition in 1863. *Curious Life* (2) describes it as a book, and it is listed on the cover pages of Randolph's Rosicrucian novels in the early 1860s. Randolph's last book, however, *The Triplicate Order* (24) lists it as a manuscript.

1859

2. *Lara.** Allibone lists this as a 12mo volume published in New York in 1859. David Board has unearthed a short article by "The Rosicrucian—Dr. P. B. Randolph" under the title "Lara.—An Experience," which was written by Randolph while he was in San Francisco in 1861 and published in *The Hesperian* 7, no. 3, in November of that year. This is probably some version of the lost book of that name. The article, which is reworked in part 1 ("Lara") of *The Rosicrucian's Story* (1863), marks Randolph's first use of the motto Man only fails through the feebleness of will, and also marks one of the first appearances of Thothmes or Thotmor, "the builder of the first Pyramid, King of Egypt, and sixty-ninth chief of the Imperial Order of the Rosy Cross."

3. *Dhoula Bel, or the Magic Globe.** This is a lost novel by Randolph. Some version of it existed before 1860, since it is mentioned in *The Unveiling* (9), published that year, which describes its subject as "vampyres"—the evil spirits who seize upon the unprayerful magnetic sensitive. Allibone says that there was an edition in 8vo published in 1864. The mysterious vampire Dhoula Bel is a central character in Randolph's great Rosicrucian novel *Ravalette* (1863), and an advertisement for a proposed later edition of *Dhoula Bel* says that *Ravalette* "solves the Dhoula Bel mystery." The solution is a murky one, however. In *Casca Llanna* (1872) Randolph announced for March 1872 the

publication of *Dhoula Bel: The Magic Globe: A Romance of the Shadow and Light,** and printed a lengthy synopsis of what he described as a "mainly autobiographical" work. This never appeared, however, probably because of the troubles Randolph describes in *Curious Life* (1872), and Randolph's last work, *The Triplicate Order* (24), describes *Dhoula Bel* as a manuscript. In 1922, the occultist Gustav Meyrink published *Dhoula Bel, ein Rosenkreuzer-Roman von P. B. Randolph* (Vienna, Berlin, and Leipzig: Rikola Verlag, 1922), which he describes as *aus dem Englischen Manuskript übersetzt*. However, the book is simply a close translation of *Ravalette*.

1860

4. *"Clairvoyance; How to Produce It, and Perfect It," with an essay on "Hashish, Its Benefits and Its Dangers." Also, "How to Make the Magic Glass, or Mirror of the Dead, by means of which the Oriental Magi are said to have held intelligent commerce with spirits."** Boston: Albert Renne & Co., 1860. This pamphlet was advertised in *The Unveiling* (1860). It has not survived, but the section on clairvoyance was probably reworked and republished in *Guide to Clairvoyance* (1867), which was then reprinted in the first edition of *Love and its Hidden History* (1869) (part 2:139–68), as "Clairvoyance, or Somnambulic Vision; its Art and Culture, with Rules for its Attainment." This was removed from subsequent editions and published, first in *The Master Passion* (1870) as "Seership and Somnambulic Vision," and then, together with the new ideas Randolph said he had recently gotten from the mysterious Italian/Armenian seer, Cuilna Vilmara, republished in *Seership* (1870). *Seership* gives the material on clairvoyance and also reprints what is probably a version of the 1860 work on magic mirrors: part 1, "Clairvoyance, or Somnambulic Vision; Its Art and Culture, with Rules for its Attainment," and part 2, "The Magnetic Mirror, Theory and Practice." This essay on clairvoyance was also reworked in *The New Mola* (1873) (part 2:19–33) as "Clairvoyance—its Rules, Laws and Principles." In *Seership* (18), Randolph says the section on clairvoyance first appeared in an edition of sixty copies for subscribers, then was reprinted (probably as *Guide to Clairvoyance*) in an edition of five-hundred copies. The sections of this original 1860 pamphlet dealing with hashish may be the same as "Hashish: Its Uses and Abuses" and as *Guide to Clairvoyance* (1867) (part 2: "Extasia, Fantasia, Hashish, and its Uses"). See nos. 9, 24, 27, 28, and 40, below.

5. *The Grand Secret.** Allibone describes this as a medical work in 12mo, published in Boston in 1860. In *The Unveiling* (June 1860) it is

described as a pamphlet that gave Randolph's revelation of "the most important discovery of the last 25 years, in a physiological point of view," a revelation that would restore health, strength, beauty and long life. The discovery undoubtedly was Randolph's theory on the debilitating effect of "onanism" and perfunctory sexual intercourse and the enlivening effects of good sex and his hashish elixirs. The pamphlet also included a "little brochure" by Mary Jane Randolph in which she urged women to write to her for her cure of marital problems. A book of the same title (no. 11) was published in San Francisco the following year, but it appears to be different from this and lacks the hashish references and Mrs. Randolph's contribution. Another short piece by the same name and dealing with Randolph's elixirs to restore vital energy is printed as an appendix to *After Death* (227–45), and "Grand Secret" appears in the subtitles of several other of his works. See nos. 13 and 34, below. In *Dealings with the Dead* (146), Randolph described as the "Grand Secret" his theory of the attraction of the swarming monads of the spaces to the heads of men, and this notion may have had a part in this lost work.

6. *The Unveiling: or, What I Think of Spiritualism. To which is Appended his World-Famous Medicinal Formulas*, by Dr. P. B. Randolph. Copyright 1860 by Mary J. Randolph and with a Preface by M. J. R., dated Boston, June 1860. Newburyport: William H. Huse & Co., Printers, 1860. Allibone lists another edition (in 8vo) in New York in 1863 which I have not seen. This is Randolph's extended justification for his "recantation" of spiritualism.

1861

7. *Love a Physical Substance.** This work, said to be by Mary Jane Randolph, is described in an advertisement at the end of *Dealings with the Dead* (1861–62) as a pamphlet which was to be rewritten and enlarged every six months and published by Mrs. Randolph from Utica. This was probably a version of the works listed in nos. 11 and 13.

8. *It Isn't all Right. Being A Complete And Thorough Refutation Of The Pernicious Doctrine That "Whatever is, is Right,"* by "Cynthia Temple." Boston: New England Reform Association, New York: S. T. Munson, 1861. This pamphlet was written by Randolph in response to A. B. Child's *Whatever Is, Is Right* (Boston: Wm. White & Co., 1860), which had originally appeared anonymously in *Tiffany's Monthly* (3 [1857]: 433–44). Randolph's pamphlet was published in November 1860, and Allibone says it was republished in 1863. Versions of the pamphlet were reprinted by Randolph in *After Death* (chapter 17, 207ff.) as "A

Philosophical Error Corrected," and in *Casca Llanna* (chapter 22), as "The 'All-Right' Fallacy Exploded." Randolph's pamphlet in turn prompted a continuing correspondence in the *Banner of Light* and a reply by A. P. McCombs, *Whatever Is, Is Right Vindicated, Being a Letter to Cynthia Temple, briefly reviewing her theory of "It Isn't All Right,"* published by Wm. White & Co. in 1861.

9. *Hashish: Its Uses and Abuses.** *Dealings with the Dead* (1861–62) announced the publication of this pamphlet for September 1, 1861. The description tells all: "Being the experience of three souls during their illumination by means of this terrible drug. . . . It details the curious effects of Hashish—its clairvoyant power, and what several souls have learned while under its wierd and awful influence—How a soul lives a thousand years in a moment of time—Where the Hashish world is. It will contain the only solution of this mystery ever attempted—and the true one." This is probably a version of the essay on "Hashish, Its Benefits and Its Dangers" included in no. 4, above, and of the material on hashish included in *Guide to Clairvoyance* (1867), no. 24, below.

10. "The Golden Letter, or Chart of the Polarities of Physical Love."* This was a letter circulated to enquirers in manuscript or as a printed sheet and dealing with the secrets of sexual happiness. It is mentioned and advertised in *The Grand Secret* (1861) (54, 67), and parts of of it are given in the same work (36–40) as "Golden Letter in Fifteen Grains," a letter received from Benredin Eli, a philosopher of the rare school of Nommoc Esnes ("common sense"). Like that work, the original "Golden Letter" appears to have taught some version of prolonged intercourse without ejaculation on the man's part. The "Golden Letter" is listed as a publication on the title page of *The Rosicrucian's Story* (1863) and is described in the accompanying advertisements as "for the guidance of those who are suffering from Sexual Debility, Exhaustion, Barrenness, Spermatorrhœa." *Curious Life* (1872) (67) states that the "Golden Letter" was printed as a sheet for physicians (apparently only five copies were issued) by F. Smith, M.D., to whom Randolph sold his medical practice in 1870. In *After Death* (165), Randolph mentioned a "sheet long since printed" that gave his theories on the production of superior children. This may have been some version of the "Golden Letter" or of another manuscript privately circulated by Randolph under the title "The True Oriental Secret, or, the Laws of Human Love Revealed."* The focus of this latter manuscript was a woman's exercise of will to prevent conception and to repel the attacks of abortionists. See *Love! At Last!* (1870) (38–40). In *Love and its Hidden History* (1869) (118–19), this practice is called the "great Oriental Secret," learned by Randolph in the Near East, and the same teaching is referred to in the *Ansairetic*

Mystery as the "Maternity Defense," embracing the "silent will-force, already published as 'Love and its Mystery,' in a sheet, and sent for a trifling fee." The more exoteric parts of this last work, in turn, were printed by Randolph in *The New Mola* (1873) (38–40, 56–62), under the titles "Love and its Hidden Mystery (Being the True Oriental Secret); or, The Laws of Human Love Revealed" and "A Physician's Legacy to Mankind—Asgill's Rules." See nos. 39 and 40, below. The earliest of this bewildering number of sheets and pamphlets was an unnamed sheet that Randolph distributed in 1859, dealing with "Geehr" and "Keemlin," the fine fluids produced by men and women that united to form the abode of the monad.

11. *The Grand Secret; or, Physical Love in Health and Disease*, by Dr. Paschal Beverly Randolph. Copyright by Randolph, 1861. San Francisco: Pilkington & Randolph, 1861–62. The first part of the title of this work is the same as the lost pamphlet listed as no. 5, but the two are probably different works, since the hashish recipes touted in the earlier work are missing from this one. Versions of parts of this work were reprinted by Randolph in *Casca Llanna* (chapters 6 and 7). The work also probably incorporates material published by Randolph as *Human Love* (no. 13) since as early as the fall of 1860 he was advertising a pamphlet variously known as "Physical Love in Health and Disease" and "Human Love: Its Physical Aspects in Love and Disease" that dealt with "Electric, Magnetic, Sympathetic and Diabolical Love; A Grand Secret: Analysis Extraordinary: Soul vs. Bodies; . . . A Great Discovery; the Proper Time to Love. Gives the answer to the affinity question." Randolph thought of this 1861 *Grand Secret* as his "First Revelation of Sex," but never reprinted it in toto, probably because he had changed his mind on the effects of karezza.

12. *Hesperina.** Allibone lists this as a volume in 12mo published in California in 1861. Parts of it may be reproduced in *The Rosicrucian's Story* (45ff.), which are captioned "Hesperina."

13. *Human Love.** Allibone lists this as published in New York in 1861 in 12mo and in 1863 in 8vo. Randolph's advertisement for his books, appended to *The Rosicrucian's Story* (1863), includes *Human Love—A Physical Substance, in Health and in Disease*. *The Grand Secret*, published by Cornhill Publishing House in Utica, New York, and describes this later edition as a pamphlet that gave the "gist" of the earlier, larger work.

14. *Dealings With The Dead; The Human Soul, Its Migrations And Its Transmigrations*, by The Rosicrucian. Preface by G. D. S. and dedication by "The Son of Flora." Copyright 1861 by Alexander Brady. Utica: Mary J. Randolph, 1861–62. This originally appeared as a series of

articles in *The Banner of Light* under the same title in the fall of 1859. *The Unveiling* (June 1860) says the book was already in press at that time, but for whatever reason it was not published until March 1862. Allibone says there was another edition in 12mo in 1863. Randolph republished the book with minor changes as the first part of *Soul! The Soul World* (1872), and Health Research republished the original version in 1959. This is Randolph's greatest work, giving his visions of the "soul world"—the "state" that underlies both the material world and the "ætherial" world inhabited by the spirits.

1863

15. *The Celebrated "Rodrey" Dream Book*.* Randolph mentions his edition of this work in *The Rosicrucian's Story* (1863) and touts it as "the largest and most perfect book of the kind in the world, in any language, [containing] the enormous number of 3000 SOLUTIONS OF 3000 DREAMS!" Randolph claimed to have learned the interpretation of dreams from a Dongolese Negro in Constantinople (*The Rosicrucian's Story*, 43). It was available from Cornhill Publishing House in Utica, New York, and from Sinclair Tousey in New York City. Tousey, who was a wholesale distributor rather than a publisher, handled several of Randolph's works. This is probably an earlier version of *The Rosicrucian Dream Book* published by Randolph in Boston in 1871 and listed below as no. 33.

16. *The Rosicrucian; His Adventures, Earthly and Unearthly; His Dealings with the Living, the Dead, and those Who Never Die*.* By "The Son of Flora." This was described by Randolph in *The Rosicrucian's Story* (27) as out of print and to be reissued that year. Randolph called it a sequel to *Dealings with the Dead* and says that it "relates to the Human Soul— its origin, nature and destiny, on the earth and off it." Although the description appears different, this may be an earlier version of *Ravalette* (Clymer says there was one in 1861) or some germ of *After Death*, which Randolph advertised as the sequel to *Dealings with the Dead*. See nos. 18 and 19, below.

17. *The Rosicrucians—Who and What They Are*.* By "A Builder of the Temple." This was recommended by Randolph in *The Rosicrucian's Story* (1863) (27) to those seeking information on the Rosicrucians. See no. 18, below.

18. *The Rosicrucian's Story: The Wonderful Things That Happened to Mr. Thomas W. and His Wife. Embracing the Celebrated "Miranda Theory,"* by Dr. P. B. Randolph. Introduction by G. D. S. Copyright by M. J. Randolph, 1863. Utica: M. J. Randolph, 1863. The book was also dis-

tributed the same year under the title *The Rosicrucian's Story: or, the Little Window at the Foot of the Bed, and The Very Strange Things That Came Through It* (New York: Sinclair Tousey, 1863) and some copies have both title pages. Part 1 of this book is "Lara," probably a reworked and expanded version of no. 2, above. The same year and in subsequent editions, this work under the title *Tom Clark and his Wife, Their Double Dreams, and the Curious Things that Befell Them Therein: Being The Rosicrucian's Story* was bound and sold with *Ravalette*, though it may have been distributed separately under that title as well since Allibone lists *Tom Clark* as a separate work in 12mo published in 1863. The original edition of *The Rosicrucian's Story* in the double volume bore a dedication to "Charles T"—Charles Trinius, a Prussian mirror magician whom Randolph knew in San Francisco. The reissue of the double volume published by Randolph Publishing Co. in Boston in 1871 and later reprinted by his wife after Randolph's death gives the text of the dedication but changes the person so honored to "Freeman"—Freeman B. Dowd. The later editions were also modified to remove Randolph's attacks on Andrew Jackson Davis by name and his claims to be working under a grand master. They also lack Randolph's diatribes against hashish and muust and add Christian references absent from the original editions. The introduction by G. D. S. to the original edition says that Randolph had written eight books, mostly under assumed names, and the book itself provides those curious about Rosicrucianism with a list of books to read. Except for Hargrave Jennings's *Curious Things of the Outside World*, the list is exclusively of Randolph's books. Most notable are those listed as nos. 16 and 17 above.

19. *The Wonderful Story of Ravalette. Also, Tom Clark and his Wife: Their Double Dreams and the Curious Things that Befell Them Therein; or, The Rosicrucian's Story*, by P. B. Randolph. New York: S. Tousey, 1863. The first part of this double volume is Randolph's most famous Rosicrucian novel, *Ravalette*. Allibone lists it separately, but it survives now only in copies bound with *The Rosicrucian's Story/Tom Clark*. See no. 18, above. *Ravalette* (79–86) has Randolph's earliest Rosicrucian manifesto: "The Rosicrucians, Who and What They Are; Honor, Manhood, Goodness. Try!" The double volume was copyrighted and republished by Randolph Publishing Co. in Boston in 1871 and then reprinted unchanged (except for the dedication and a diminishing of the criticisms of spiritualism in the introduction) throughout the rest of the century by Randolph's widow: Toledo: K. Corson Randolph Publisher, 1876, 1887. A German translation of the book was published by Gustav Meyrink in 1922 as *Dhoula Bel*. See no. 3, above. R. S. Clymer

published a version of this work as *The Wonderful Story of Ravalette* (Quakertown: Philosophical Publishing Co., 1939), and that version in turn was reprinted by Health Research in 1960. In his notes Clymer says that *Ravalette* was first published by Randolph in 1861, a claim that echoes Randolph's statement that the book had been published nine years before 1870. See *Curious Life*, 75. See also "Destiny of Nations: a Prophetic Declaration," *Banner of Light* 28, no. 25 (August 27, 1870):2 which quotes extensively from what it calls the first edition, published by S. Tousey in 1861. This earlier edition may be some version of *The Rosicrucian; His Adventures*, referred to in no. 16 above.

20. *Pre-Adamite Man: Demonstrating the Existence of the Human Race upon this Earth 100,000 Years Ago!* By "Griffin Lee of Texas." Copyright by A. J. Brady, 1863. New York: S. Tousey, 1863. The book made quite an impression, and Randolph issued a second edition, which I have not seen, probably in 1863, and a third (New York: Author) in 1864, before the work was picked up by the leading publishers White & Co. (4th ed., Boston, 1869) and Colby & Rich (5th ed., Boston, 1873). A "sixth edition" (actually a reprint of the 4th ed.) was issued by Randolph Publishing Co. in Toledo in 1888, and that edition has been reprinted by Health Research (1970). This may be a version of *Human Antiquity**—an otherwise unknown publication mentioned on the cover page of *The Rosicrucian's Story*. *Pre-Adamite Man* is a totally uncharacteristic work by Randolph, one in which he sought to explain by contemporary scientific prehistory the vanished ages whose fragments were to be found scattered in ancient works and mythologies. The first edition is dedicated to Charles Trinius and to "Honest Abraham Lincoln, President of the United States, as a Testimonial of my Gratitude for his efforts to save the Nation, and Widen the Area of Human Freedom." Randolph's name first appeared on the 5th edition in 1873.

1864
21. *Edward Price.** Allibone lists this as published in 12mo in 1864.

1866
22. *A Sad Case; A Great Wrong! And How It May Be Remedied, Being An Appeal on Behalf of Education for the Freedmen of Louisiana.* Anonymous. Washington, D.C.: Chronicle Reprint, 1866. This was a short pamphlet listing the endorsements of Randolph by all the leading Republicans of the era. Randolph had it printed to introduce his pitch for funds for his planned normal school in Louisiana. His labors and their ill-starred result are described in *Curious Life* (1872).

1867

23. *Ancient Kaldi Oracie, or Rosicrician Predictive Symph, Translated from the Original Rosicrucian Tablets by Paschal Beverly Randolph in 1867.* N. p., n.d. [c. 1867]. The preface to *Guide to Clairvoyance* (1867) recites that this was revealed to Randolph on April 27, 1867, by Ramond Lull. It was advertised for sale at one dollar in *Love! At Last!* (1870). For unknown reasons, the little work was only copyrighted in 1913, by H. Elizabeth Nixon, who is otherwise unknown to me. Health Research has reprinted the 1913 edition. Perhaps for practical reasons, Lull advised that the possibilities for the week, month, or year in question be written on cards or slips of paper rather than on the revolving concentric wheels that he had favored during life.

24. *The Guide to Clairvoyance, and Clairvoyant's Guide: A Practical Manual for those who Aim at Perfect Clear Seeing and Psychometry; also, a Special Paper concerning Hashish, its Uses, abuses, and Dangers, its Extasia, Fantasia, and Illuminati. Printed for People of Common Sense Only.* Anonymous. Boston: Rockwell & Rollins, Printers, 1867. The tangled publishing history of the various parts of this pamphlet is given in connection with no. 4, above.

1868

25. *After Death; or, Disembodied Man. The World of Spirits, its Location, Extent, Appearance; the Route Thither; Inhabitants; Customs; Societies: Also Sex and its Uses There, etc., etc., with Much Matter Pertinent to the Question of Human Immortality. Being the Sequel to Dealings With The Dead,* by "The Author of 'Pre-Adamite Man'." Copyright by Randolph, 1868. 2d ed. Corrected and Enlarged. Boston: Author, 1868. The first appearance of this work was as a series of articles published in the Chicago *Religio-Philosophical Journal* from November through December 1866 under the title "Sequel to Dealings with the Dead." The series ended with chapter 13 when the journal ceased publication for a year. Randolph says that the work was later published in pamphlet form. The second edition (listed here) is dated March 1868 and appeared without Randolph's name, an omission corrected in later editions. The 1868 edition is dedicated to Freeman B. Dowd and S. B. Watrous and also carries a second title page: *After Death; or, Disembodied Man. The Location, Topography, and Scenery of the Supernal Universe; Its Inhabitants, Their Customs, Habits, Modes of Existence; Sex After Death; Marriage in the World of Souls; the Sin Against the Holy Ghost, its Fearful Penalties, etc.* A third edition, slightly augmented with minor new material (added at the ends of chapters in order not to disturb the plates and pagina-

tion) and without the table of contents, appeared in Boston in 1869 as *After Death: the Disembodiment of Man*, with the rest of the first title remaining unchanged, and a fourth edition under this title was published by Colby & Rich in Boston in 1873. This 1873 edition, called a "fourth edition, revised, corrected and enlarged, third edition," was then republished by the Randolph Publishing Co. in Toledo before Randolph's death and kept in print throughout the rest of the nineteenth century by Randolph's widow. This edition was reprinted in 1961 by Health Research. This publishing history is confused by the fact that there was another edition (called the "fifth") issued by Randolph Publishing Co. in Boston in 1870. This edition was the first to carry the laudatory preface by Freeman B. Dowd, "Grand Master Imperial Order of Rosicrucia," that appeared in all subsequent editions. The Dorbon catalogue, *Bibliotheca Esoterica* (no. 643), listed for sale two manuscripts that were apparently incomplete French translations of *After Death*.

1869

26. *The Davenport Brothers, The World Renowned Spiritual Mediums: Their Biography, and Adventures in Europe and America*. Anonymous. Copyright 1869 by Ira Davenport, Sen. Boston: Wm. White & Co., 1869. This is a straightforward spiritualistic biography of the phenomena-producing brothers whom Randolph had known since the mid-1850s. It is difficult to decide why he wrote the book. He was working on the book in July 1864, before his departure for New Orleans, but for unknown reasons did not complete it until 1869, and then it was issued anonymously and the brothers' father retained the copyright. Perhaps Randolph undertook the book simply as a way of earning a living, or perhaps by the time it was finished he believed the brothers were "deliberate impostors"—a position he certainly came to hold. *Master Passion* (44–45). The book manages to include a fair amount of material on Randolph's ideas, and it adds (189–95) a long reminiscence called "Extracts from Paper Found in a Bottle Floating in the Sea, A.D. 3869," which points up the foibles of the world from the point of view of the future. The same piece with minor changes appears in *Soul! The Soul World* (122–37).

26. *Rosicrucian: Out of the Shell*. Anonymous. N.p., n.d. This light-hearted ten-page pamphlet was issued by the Boston Rosicrucian Club in 1869 to commemorate its Fourth of July outing that year.

27. *Love and its Hidden History. A Book for Man, Woman, Wives, Husbands, and for the Loving and the Unloved: The Heart-Reft, Pining Ones*, by

"Count de St. Leon." 4th ed., Entirely Rewritten. Boston: William White & Co., 1869. The publishing history of this work and its congeners is extremely tangled. In *After Death*, published right after the Civil War, Randolph had promised to write more about sex. His first effort in that line, *Physical Love*, was then long out of print. The synopsis of *After Death* advertising the appearance of that work (*Religio-Philosophical Journal*, April 4, 1868) promised as an appendix "Love and Its Hidden History; Its Ebbs and Flows; Its Calms and Blows; Its Unsuspected Mystery," which can only be the sketch on the "proper study of mankind is Woman" that is included as part 2B of the 1868 edition of *After Death*. The complete work on *Love and its Hidden History* must have appeared first in 1868, and Randolph says (p. 6 of the 1869 edition), that it had run through three editions totalling nine thousand copies by 1869, a very respectable run for the times. The fourth edition, "entirely rewritten," was published in Boston in June 1869. Part 1 (which ended with page 138) was the promised work on love, and part 2, was a reworked version of Randolph's pamphlet on clairvoyance (see no. 4, above). The response to the work was gratifying. The first printing of this edition had carried a preface (now lost) in which Randolph promised a sequel with still further revelations, especially on women's magnetic powers of attracting men, preventing unwanted births, and achieving personal attractiveness. In the second printing the preface was removed (see F. B. Dowd's preface to *After Death*) and replaced by a preface announcing the publication of the promised volume. This sequel appeared in November 1869 under the title *Woman, Affection; or, Love and its Hidden Mystery, the Laws of Beauty, Methods of its Culture and Retainment, with a Statement of the Great Magnetic Law of Female Attractive Power, and How to Gain and Cultivate It.** Randolph said the volume might be had by writing Miss Carrie Chute (in care of his own address) for whom *Love and its Hidden History* had been written. The earliest edition of this sequel has not survived, but it was apparently short (ninety-seven pages) and padded out with some version of Randolph's pamphlet on clairvoyance under the title "Seership and Somnambulic Vision." The following year, Randolph (under his own name for the first time) published both works under the imposing title *Love and its Hidden History: Also, The Master Passion, or the Curtain Raised on Woman, Love, and Marriage. Female Beauty; its Attainment, Culture and Retention, with Hints for the Increase of Woman's Power. A Book for Woman, Man, Wives, Husbands, and Lovers, for the Loving, the Unloved, and the Yearning Ones of the World*, by P. B. Randolph. Preface by F. B. Dowd. 5th edition. Rewritten and Enlarged. Copyright by Randolph, 1870. Boston: Randolph & Co., 1870. This contained part 1 of *Love and its Hidden History* (plus a few new pages on Randolph's friendlessness and a preface, dated September 1869, by F. B. Dowd) and the separately paginated sequel, *The Master Passion*. The sequel, however, omitted the material on clairvoyance, replacing it with new material on the role and functions of women. In turn, the section on clairvoyance that had first graced *Love and its Hidden History* and then the first version of *The Master Passion* was published separately as *Seership*, together with the new ideas on mirror vision that Randolph had learned from the Italian/Armenian Cuilna Vilmara, See no. 4, above. Randolph called *Love and its Hidden History* his "First Revelation of Sex".

1870

28. *Seership! The Magnetic Mirror. A Practical Guide to Those Who Aspire to Clairvoyance-Absolute. Original and Selected from Various European and Asiatic Adepts*, by Paschal Beverly Randolph. Copyright by Randolph, August 1870. Boston: Randolph Publishing Co., 1870. This is the next incarnation of the material on clairvoyance and magic mirrors that Randolph had been reworking since 1860 and publishing as "Clairvoyance, How to Produce It," *Guide to Clairvoyance* (1867), *Love and its Hidden History* (part 2, 1869) and *The Master Passion* (1870) and was to publish again in *The New Mola* (1873). See nos. 4 above and 40 below. To this material Randolph added the new mirror ideas he had just learned from the mysterious Cuilna Vilmara and the seven magnetic laws of love (persistence of purpose, attention, calmness, will, etc.) that Randolph advertised as the means by which wives could win back their husbands' love and punish other women who trifled with their husbands' affections, and any woman could "impress herself ineffaceably upon the man she feels for." *The Master Passion* (168). Randolph touted the work as the fullest exposition of these subjects ever to be issued "outside the temples of the Imperial Order, *De la Rose Croix*." (Ibid., 178). He advertised the work by various names (*The Rosicrucian Hand-Book, Complete Self-Guide to Clairvoyance*, and *Mysteries of the Magnetic Universe*), but all the editions of the work that continued to appear throughout the nineteenth century (Toledo: Randolph & Co., 1875; Toledo: K. C. Randolph, Publisher, 1884, 1892) are from the same plates, omitting only the final paragraph of this 1870 edition in which Randolph solicited paying students. In a contemporary advertisement for the first edition of the book, Randolph refers to the "good lady proprietress" of the work, which could mean that he had found a patron (as he had for *Guide to Clairvoyance* in 1867)

or that he was yet again enmeshed with a woman—perhaps the Carrie Chute for whom he had written *Love and its Hidden History*. R. S. Clymer republished the work as *Seership, Guide to Soul Sight. A Practical Guide for those who Aspire to Develop the Vision of the Soul. The Magic Mirror and How to Use It* (Quakertown: Confederation of Initiates, n.d. [c. 1930]), and that version in turn was reprinted by Health Research in 1960.

29. *The Riddle of Hermes*. N.p., n.d. This brain teaser, probably written about 1870, was distributed by Randolph in quarto broadside attached to his works. A prize of five-thousand dollars was offered for its solution. It was reprinted in S. C. Gould's *Notes and Queries* (1886, 12–13; 1904, 69–70; 1906, 246–47).

30. *Love! At Last! The Seven Magnetic Laws of Love. The Philosophy of Fascination, the Increase of Woman's Power, the Solution of the Problems of Love Charms, Love Spells, Love Powders, and "Love Powders," Being a Portion of Love and its Hidden Mystery*, by Dr. P. B. Randolph. Copyright by Randolph, 1870. Boston: Randolph & Co., 1870. While there is some new material in this little book, Randolph admits (34) that it is "mainly a few extracts" from *Love and its Hidden History*, *The Master Passion*, and *Seership* and a prolonged advertisement for Randolph's "Golden Secret" and his elixirs.

1871

31. *The Asiatic Mystery. The Fire Faith!—The Religion of Flame!—The Force of Love!—The Energos of Will!—The Magic of Polar Mentality! First Rosicrucian Manifesto to the World Outside the Order!* N.p., n.d. [Boston, 1871]. Randolph had earlier published a Rosicrucian manifesto in *Ravalette* in 1863 to tout his Rosicrucian foundation in San Francisco in late 1861. This manifesto, which he published in February 1871, marked another attempt to establish a formal organization to spread his teachings. This is one of the most valuable of Randolph's works since it states in general, exoteric terms the powers and possibilities to be revealed fully in the third degree of the order and the celestial provenance of those powers. The manifesto was reprinted by R. S. Clymer (he says "verbatim") in his journal *The Initiates, A Magazine Issued by Authority of the Rosicrucian Fraternity and Devoted to Mysticism, Occultism and the Well-Being of Man* 3 (May-June 1930-May-June 1931):107–23, and in that version Randolph describes himself as "Secretary *ex officio*" and refers enticingly to the "Supreme Grand Master of the Order on Earth." A slightly different version was also given by Randolph in *Soul!* (1872) (274–288) and in Flora S. Russel's introduc-

tion to the *Divine Pymander* (1871), and parts of the work were reproduced in *Eulis* (1874) (84ff.).

32. *Hermes Trismegistus: His Divine Pymander. Also, the Asiatic Mystery, The Smaragdine Tablet, and the Song of Brahm.* Edited by Paschal Beverly Randolph. Copyright by Rosicrucian Publishing Co., 1871. Boston: Rosicrucian Publishing Co., 1871. This is a reprinting of the seventeenth-century edition by Dr. Everard to which Randolph has added Emerson's "Brahm." There is a short historical preface by Alfred E. Giles arguing the antiquity of the teachings of the *Divine Pymander* and a long introduction by Flora S. Russel of Boston that reprints a version of the *Asiatic Mystery*—Randolph's second Rosicrucian manifesto. Randolph's selection of the *Divine Pymander* for publication was clearly no accident, because its teachings on the ascent of the soul and on the embodiment of the powers and qualities of the celestial hierarchy in the soul clearly reflect his own ideas. Dr. Everard's translation was printed again in 1884 by Robert H. Fryar of Bath. This later edition (which carried an introduction by Hargrave Jennings) was undoubtedly prompted by Randolph's earlier work and marked the first public appearance of the H. B. of L.

33. *The Rosicrucian Dream Book: Containing Solutions of over Three Thousand Different Dreams. Collected and Translated from the Old English, German, Norwegian, Turkish, Arabic, Syriac, Danish, Cingalese, Hindostani, French, Ethiopic and Dongolese. Rendering This By Far the Largest, Most Comprehensive and Complete Work of the Kind in any Language.* Anonymous. Copyright by Randolph, 1871. Boston: Randolph Publishing Co., 1871. Randolph describes himself in a notice as "Professor of Oriental Interior Science." The user of this method first looked up in an index the thing or action seen in the dream and then used the key to find the appropriate solution. Some of the solutions are transparent, but most appear labored and random. This is probably a reworking of no. 15.

1872

34. *Casca Llanna: (Good News.) Love, Woman, Marriage: The Grand Secret! A Book for the Heartful.* Anonymous. Copyright by Randolph Publishing Co., November 1871. Boston: Randolph Publishing Co., 1872. The travails surrounding its publication are detailed at length in *Curious Life* (1872). The meaning of "Casca Llanna" is uncertain. Randolph alternatively uses it as a pseudonym and to mean both "good news" and "Falling Waters." *Casca Llanna* is largely a rambling disquisition on love and reproduces versions of chapters from Randolph's earliest work on the subject, *The Grand Secret*. See nos. 5

and 11 above. The book is especially helpful bibliographically because of the lengthy and detailed synopses Randolph adds to the list of his books—although the synopses occasionally differ widely from the books they are supposed to summarize. The book was widely referred to as *The Woman's Book* and is probably the same as *Love: Its Mystery; Its History; Its Principles, Phases, Moods and Laws* which Randolph lists in the *Asiatic Mystery* (1871) (109). Randolph considered *Casca Llanna* to be his "Second Revelation of Sex."

35. *James Fisk, Jr. His Secret! The Secret of His Success and Wonderful Power. What the Clairvoyant Lady Said About Him! Also, the Laws of Love as Applied to Fisk's Case, with a Paper on The Tobacco Habit. How to Break it. The Natural Antidote. Also, about Matters Pertinent to the Happiness of All Wives and Their Husbands; also, all Males and Females of the Human Species on Earth.** The writing of the Fisk pamphlet is described by Randolph in his *Curious Life* (1872). Fisk was a famous robber baron of the times, and before Fisk was murdered Randolph had high expectations of him as a patron. Portions of the pamphlet on Fisk are printed in *Casca Llanna* (222ff.). James Russell Lowell and others similarly eulogized Fisk. A version of the antitobacco pamphlet under the title *The Tobacco-Fiend: How to Slay Him* was added by Randolph as a supplement to *Soul!* (1872) and was separately published by R. S. Clymer as *The Evils of the Tobacco Habit, Method for its Cure Found to be Highly Successful if Followed Consistently. Reinforced by a Sincere Desire to be Free From it.* Quakertown: Philosophical Publishing Co., n.d. [c. 1956].

36. *Soul! The Soul World: The Homes of the Dead,* by "The Rosicrucian." Boston: Randolph Publishing Co., 1872. Subsequent editions show the author as "The Rosicrucian, Paschal Beverly Randolph." This was a reprint, slightly amended, of *Dealings with the Dead,* to which Randolph appended a variety of his smaller works, including his "Clinton Hall Recantation Speech," the pamphlet on *The Tobacco-Fiend: How to Slay Him,* the *Asiatic Mystery,* and a long reminiscence from the point of view of Febuary 8, 2869, of the stupidity and ignorance shown by the history of a thousand years earlier. This last is also printed in *The Davenport Brothers* (189–95).

37. *Will, Candy and Sugar, Their Effects on Amatoriness; 24 Rules of Power, etc., etc.** Randolph mentions this lost pamphlet, "the substance of his life's work," in *Curious Life* (1872).

38. *P. B. Randolph, the "Learned Pundit," and "Man with Two Souls," His Curious Life, Works and Career. The Great Free-Love Trial. Randolph's Grand Defence. His Address to the Jury, and Mankind. The Verdict.* Boston: Randolph Publishing Co., 1872. This book was an attempt by Randolph at an autobiography and his defense against the claims that he taught

"Free Love." To some copies of this Randolph added a separately paginated pamphlet entitled *The Golden Secret! Curious Life*, with significant alterations and omissions, was republished by R. S. Clymer as *The Rose Cross Order*. Allentown: Philosophical Publishing Co., 1916.

39. *The Golden Secret!* This little pamphlet on affection was circulated in manuscript ("securely sealed") as early as 1869. *Love and its Hidden History* (1869) (69). *Love! At Last!* (1870) (34) calls the work "the most transcendently valuable ever given on the esoteric love-life of the race" and touts it as a panacea for disappointed married people. It was the struggle over rights to this work—Randolph claimed that copies had sold for fees of from five to forty dollars—that led to the events described in *Curious Life* (1872). A version of the essay, probably Bowdlerized, was written in April 1872 and then published as a twenty-page pamphlet later in the same year which was in turn bound up with some copies of *Curious Life*. Randolph called the work "a bit of rare knowledge . . . learned among the Arabs, Turks, Syrians, Armenians and Egyptians," but the printed version at least is exoteric (his ideas on long life, vitality, happy marriage, and the virtues of his elixirs) and was intended as an enticement for his true sexual magic. The work invited correspondence on the "White Magic of Love, Will and Aetherics: Volantia, Posism and Decretism." It appears likely that the original manuscript version of the "Golden Secret" included the more explicit sexual material later circulated privately as "Love and Its Hidden Mystery, the Physician's Legacy" and "The True Oriental Secret." See no. 10 above. These were distributed by Randolph in manuscript until late 1873 and were in turn intended as "leaders" or advertisements for the real sexual magic taught in "The Ansaireh Secret" and *The Ansairetic Mystery*. A socially acceptable version of the the exoteric side of these secrets had already been published by Randolph in *The Master Passion* (1870), and in late 1873 he combined "Love and Its Hidden Mystery, the Physician's Legacy" and "The True Oriental Secret" and printed them—omitting the more explicit material—as "A Physician's Legacy to Mankind—Asgill's Rules" in an appendix (56–63) to *The New Mola!* See no. 10 above and no. 40 below.

1873

40. *The New Mola! The Secret of Mediumship! A Hand Book of White Magic, Magnetism, and Clairvoyance. The new Doctrine of Mixed Identities. Rules for obtaining the phenomena, and the celebrated Rules of Asgill, a Physician's Legacy, and the Ansairetic Mystery*, by Paschal Beverly Randolph. Toledo: P. B. Randolph, 1873. This work, besides reprinting

parts of Randolph's earlier works on mirrors and clairvoyance (see no. 4, above), also gave tantalyzing excerpts from various of Randolph's privately circulated manuscript works on sex. See no. 39, above. R. S. Clymer in *The Divine Alchemy of Imperial Eulis, Esoteric, yet Practical, Instructions for the Transmutation of the Baser Metals (Man's Gross Passions) into the Pure and Shining Gold (the Illuminated Soul) of the Alchemists. The Randolphian Physician's Legacy to Mankind, and Asgill's Rules. Instructions in the Single and Double Breast Drill of the Initiates. For Students Only* (5th ed., Quakertown: Printed but not Published by Philosophical Publishing Co., n.d. [preface dated August 7, 1945, but printed by Clymer at least as early as 1908 and probably earlier]) gives rules 1 through 8 of *The New Mola* text as "Asgill's Rules, A Physician's Legacy to Mankind" while rules 9 through 27 (except 17, which refers to hashish) follow in the next chapter as "The Ansaireth Mystery, A New Revelation of Sex." Clymer only lightly edited the material, removing the pseudo-Arabic references and omitting the parts on hashish. The term *new Mola* was used by John Murray Spear for his perpetual motion machine.

41. *The Ansairetic Mystery, A New Revelation Concerning Sex! A "Private Letter, Printed, But Not Published; It Being Sacred and Confidential.* Anonymous. Toledo: Printed by Toledo Sun, Liberal Printing House, n.d. [c. 1873]. In *The New Mola* (August 1873), Randolph announced his intention to reveal the secret of the Ansaireh Priesthood of Syria: "There is a moment, frequently recurring, wherein men and women can call down to them celestial—almost awful—powers from the Spaces, thereby being wholly able to reach the souls of others, and hold them fast in the bonds of a love unknown as yet in this cold land of ours." He claimed the work was his own translation, not that of Spence Hardy, who, Randolph says, had been killed in Cairo, "probably by Ansaireh poison." The work is described as a private letter, sent only on request and only on payment of the five dollar fee, and was intended to supply the esoteric parts of the works listed in connection with no. 39, above. At some point in late 1873 or early 1874 Randolph, partially paralyzed and probably unable to write out the material himself, had it printed by the John Lant's Liberal Printing House in Toledo, the publishers of the *Toledo Sun*. The earliest identifiable predecessor of the work was a sheet called "The Choice" that included the list of powers obtainable by the magic of will. See chapter 10. An advertisement in *After Death* calls the work the "Fourth Rosicrucian Revelation Concerning Human Sex." The work is the fullest expression of the magical powers, many of them trivial, that Randolph believed could be acquired through sexual and mirror magic,

and is the more practical side of the sexual magic taught theoretically in "The Mysteries of Eulis." Versions of both works were taken up by the H. B. of L. and issued as "The Mysteries of Eros."

1874

42. "The Mysteries of Eulis." This manuscript is the real crown of Randolph's works, the final version of his secret sexual teachings. The Dorbon catalog lists a copy of this (eighteen pages of forty-eight lines each) and dates it to c. 1860, claiming that it contains the teachings of the Supreme Lodge of the Temple of Eulis in San Francisco—a claim that is certainly wrong. The manuscript now survives in only one known copy (twenty-two pages of forty lines each) which bears John Yarker's colophon and notation that he had bought it from Randolph's widow. The text of this version certainly dates to the 1870s and probably to 1874.

43. *Eulis! The History of Love: Its Wondrous Magic, Chemistry, Rules, Laws, Modes, Moods and Rationale; Being the Third Revelation of Soul and Sex. Also, Reply to "Why is Man Immortal?" The Solution to the Darwin Problem. An Entirely New Theory,* by Paschal Beverly Randolph, M.D. 2d ed. Copyright by Randolph, 1874. Toledo: Randolph Publishing Co., 1874. This second edition is the earliest known, and it continued to be reprinted by his widow unchanged as late as 1906. Randolph states (3) that he originally intended to call the book by a different title (perhaps *Sexagyma,* see below) but changed his mind on rewriting the volume. Perhaps this original text was the first "edition." As the title indicates, this was Randolph's third revelation of sex, and it is the most succinct statement of the exoteric theory and practice of love that Randolph had been expounding since 1860: true love is the complete, mutual exaltation of the magnetic union of male and female. Its presence produces health and long life, and its absence is the cause of the woes of the world—especially women's problems. Love and true sex are also the key to immortalization and communication with the spheres of the celestial hierarchy—though the details of the method for achieving these ends were reserved for Randolph's privately circulated works, *The Ansairetic Mystery* and "The Mysteries of Eulis." Part 3 of the book is devoted to reprinting an article on the phallic mysteries of the Siamese "nautch girl," Luan Prabana (copied from "Siamese Sorcery," *Banner of Light* 16, no. 2 [April 11, 1874]:2) and to a long excerpt from Colonel Stephen Fraser's *Twelve Years in India* in which the old soldier described the erotic "Sebeiyeh Dance" in which "Bhattah Glyphæ" mirrors are consecrated. This excerpt, in turn, was picked up by Peter Davidson, the provincial grand master of the north of the H. B. of L., and Robert H. Fryar and commented upon knowingly by Madame

Blavatsky. The book was reprinted by R. S. Clymer as *Eulis, Affectional Alchemy; The History of Love: Its Wondrous Magic, Chemistry, Rules, Laws, Moods, Modes and Rationale. Being the third revelation of Soul and sex and a reply to "Why is Man Immortal"* (Quakertown: Philosophical Publishing Co., 1930), and that edition has been reprinted by Health Research.

44. *The "Ghostly Land:" the "Medium's Secret;" Being the Mystery of the Human Soul: Its Dwelling, Nature, and Power of Materialization, Also, The Coming Woman, and the New Divorce Law.* Anonymous. Copyright by Randolph, 1874. Toledo: Kate Corson, 1874. This was intended as a supplement to *The New Mola* (1873) and *Eulis* (1874), in both of which Randolph gave his resolution of the question he had wrestled with since the early 1860s, whether immortality was an acquired or an achieved quality and whether all men are immortal. The book continued the description, begun in *After Death* (1868), of the æthcrial zones and spheres through which the soul progresses after death. The final section on the woman of the future and divorce may have been written by Kate Corson.

1875

45. *The Book of the Triplicate Order, Rosicrucia, Eulis, Pythianæ,* by Paschal Beverly Randolph. San Francisco: Woman's Publishing Co. Print, 1875 ("Printed for the Use of the Brotherhood, Candidates for Membership, and all who Desire to Know Who and What We Are, and the Work we are Doing"). In this last book Randolph, styling himself the "Refounder, Organizer and Supreme Hierarch," set forth the constitution of the Triplicate Order he had just founded in San Francisco in late 1874 and sought to make the order the protector of his infant son Osiris Budh in exchange for the rights to his books. The list of books he gives is the final version of what Randolph called "The Rosicrucian Library," which consisted of his own books (with the exception in the earliest list of one of Hargrave Jennings's tomes). See *The Rosicrucian's Story* (1863), *Seership* (1870), and *Ghostly Land* (1874). The constitution of the order was to be supplemented in each lodge by more practical by-laws, and the "Rules and Regulations of an Outer Circle adopted by the Supreme Grand Lodge at San Francisco, California, on February 13, 1875," are given by R. S. Clymer in *The Initiates. A Rosicrucian Magazine* (July 1908, 119ff. and April 1909, 20ff.).

Post-Mortem

46. *Beyond the Veil: Posthumous Work of Paschal Beverly Randolph. Aided by Emanuel Swedenborg and Others, Through the Minds of Frances H. McDougall and Luna Hutchinson.* Edited by F. H. McDougall and L. Hutchinson. New York: D. M. Bennett, 1878. This work purports to

contain the postmortem musings of Randolph from beyond the grave and includes his (or the mediums') attack on the errors of Emma Hardinge Britten, "Colonel Alcott," and the new occultism generally. It was reprinted by Health Research in 1972.

47. *Rosicrucian and Ashburton Springs.** Copyright by P. B. Randolph, in February 1878. All that I have been able to discover about this pamphlet is the copyright notice.

48. *Magia Sexualis.* Translated by Maria de Naglowska. Copyright by Robert Telin. Paris: Robert Télin, au Lys Rouge, 1931. This is a translation of parts of several of Randolph's books and private manuscripts on sexual magic and magic mirrors. There have been several subsequent editions in French, including one by Guy Le Prat in 1969, and an Italian translation was published by Julius Evola, an old friend of de Naglowska's from their Dadaist days in Switzerland, as *Magia Sexualis. Forme e Riti* (Roma: Edizioni Mediterranee, n.d. [c. 1977]). An English translation of sorts has been published in New York as *Sexual Magic* (Translated and with an Introduction by Robert North. New York: Magickal Childe, n.d. [c. 1988]), and there is reference to a Spanish translation (*Magia sexual* [Madrid: EDAF, n.d., c. 1988]), but I have not seen it. The introduction to the English translation suffers from a too credulous reliance on R. S. Clymer's histories. Although Clymer denounced *Magia Sexualis* as a forgery when it appeared, there can be no doubt whatsoever that the great majority of the work is Randolph's. The only significant parts that cannot be traced directly to Randolph's works are the section on animated statues, the astrological references, and the systematization and antiquarian elaboration that were obviously added by de Naglowska. In her introduction, de Naglowska mentions three books she says were by Randolph (*She, Magh Thesor,* and *Asrotis*) which are otherwise unknown, but may have been translations of Randolph's works. De Naglowska also announces the coming appearance of various other of Randolph's oeuvres, most of which probably owed more to her than to Randolph: "Le Rituel du premier degré"; "La Théorie occulte, les Ordres et les Fraternités"; "Astrologie: A) La pierre, B) La plante, C) L'animal, D) L'homme, E) Le son, F) Le mot, G) La couleur, H) Le parfum, I) Le geste"; "Type-Astrologie et la reconstruction rétrograde des Horoscopes"; "La Chimie occulte." These booklets correspond to the five parts of the first degree of the Brotherhood of Eulis, according to de Naglowska, as *Magia Sexualis* itself is said to correspond to the second part of the second degree.

Articles, Published Letters and Occasional Pieces

——. Advertisement. *The New England Spiritualist* 1, no. 37 (December 15, 1855).

——. Advertisement. *The New England Spiritualist* 1, no. 38 (December 22, 1855).

——. Advertisement. *New England Spiritualist* 1, no. 41 (January 12, 1856).

——. Advertisement. "Dr. P. B. Randolph pursues his Practice of Medicine." *Banner of Light* 7, no. 23 (September 1, 1860): 7.

——. Advertisement. "Hashish." *Banner of Light* 8, no. 2 (October 6, 1860): 4.

——. Advertisement. "P. B. Randolph's Card." *Banner of Light* 8, no. 9 (November 24, 1860): 5.

——. Advertisement. "Dr. P. B. Randolph Examines and Prescribes in Special Cases Only." *Religio-Philosophical Journal* 1, no. 4 (October 21, 1865): 8.

——. Advertisement. *Religio-Philosophical Journal* 4, no. 2 (April 4, 1868): 7.

—— [Le Rosicrucien]. "Dealings with the Dead." *Banner of Light*, seven parts from 5, no. 23 (September 3, 1859): 3, to 6, no. 9 (November 26, 1859): 6–7.

——. "From One of the Ancients." *The Telegraph Papers* 1 (1853): 333–35.

——. "Introductory Trance Address by a Spirit Designating Himself 'The Stranger' through Mr. Randolph, an American Medium." *The Yorkshire Spiritual Telegraph* 4, no. 3 (March 1857): 31–32.

——. "Jottings by the Wayside. The Earlville Miracles." *The Telegraph Papers* 8 (1855): 265–66.

——. "Lara.—An Experience." *The Hesperian* 7, no. 3 (November 1861).

——. "Letter from P. Beverly Randolph." *The Liberator* 28, no. 46 (November 12, 1858): 183.

——. "Letter from P. B. Randolph." *The Telegraph Papers* 8 (1855): 157–59.

——. Letter. *The Yorkshire Spiritual Telegraph* 3, no. 12 (February 15, 1857): 166–67.

——. Letter. *New Orleans Tribune*, November 29, 1864, 2.

——. Letter. *Journal du Magnétisme* 15 (1856): 43–44.

——. Letter. *New Orleans Tribune*, December 8, 1864, 2.

——. Letter. *Spiritual Telegraph* (November 20, 1858): 296.

——. Letter. *The Yorkshire Spiritual Telegraph* 3, no. 12 (February 15, 1857): 166–67.

——. "Lettre du Docteur P. B. Randolph, à l'Anglo-African." *New Orleans Tribune*, French ed., March 11, 1865, 2.

——. [A Seer]. "Notes of My Psychal Life." *Journal of Progress* 2, no. 3 (October 1853): 38–39.

——. "Notice." *Religio-Philosophical Journal* 6, no. 9 (November 20, 1869): 5.

——. "Philosophy from a Spirit." *The Telegraph Papers* 2 (1853): 20–22.

——. "Randolph's Letters—No. 1," *Religio-Philosophical Journal* 1, no. 1 (August 26, 1865): 2; "Randolph's Letters—No. 2," ibid. 1, no. 2

(October 7, 1865: 2; "Randolph's Letters—No. 3," ibid. 1, no. 3 (October 14, 1865): 7; "Randolph's Letters—No. 4," ibid. 1, no. 4 (October 21, 1865): 6 with a letter from "S. H. A. F." on "Cholera— Dr. Randolph's Remedy"; "Randolph's Letters—No. 4, A Latter Day Sermon," ibid. 1, no. 8 (November 18, 1865): 2; "Randolph's Letters—No. 5," ibid. 1, no. 13 (December 23, 1865): 3; "P. B. Randolph's Letters—No. 7," ibid. 1, no. 18 (January 27, 1866): 3; "From Our Regular New Orleans Colored Correspondent, P. B. Randolph—No. 8," ibid. 1, no. 21 (February 17, 1866): 3; "From our Regular New Orleans Correspondent, P. B. Randolph, No. 11," ibid. 2, no. 12 (June 16, 1866): 2; "A Note From Brother Randolph," ibid. 2, no. 16 (July 28, 1866): 4; "A Present-Day Sermon," ibid. 2, no. 19 (August 4, 1866): 2; "From Our Regular New Orleans Correspondent, P. B. Randolph, No. 12," ibid. 2, no. 20 (August 11, 1866): 2; "From Our Regular New Orleans Correspondent, P. B. Randolph No. 12," ibid. 2, no. 24 (September 8, 1866): 2.

———. "Rosicrucian Papers. No. 5. Eden, Gethsemane and Paradise." *Religio-Philosophical Journal* 5, no. 20 (February 6, 1869): 3, and "Rosicrucian Papers. no. 6. 'The Man Wat Died Game.' " ibid. 6, no. 3 (April 10, 1869): 2.

———. "Sequel to Dealings with the Dead." *Religio-Philosophical Journal*, various numbers from 3, no. 7 (November 10, 1866): 1–2, to 3, no. 14 (December 29, 1866): 1–2.

———. "Spirit Monitions." *The Telegraph Papers* 1 (1853): 421–22 [by "Your Angel Mother"].

———. "Spiritual Reporter." *Religio-Philosophical Journal* 3, no. 14 (December 29, 1866): 3.

———. "The Converted Medium," *New York Daily Tribune*, November 25, 1858, 3.

———. "They Say!" *Banner of Light* 21, no. 3 (April 6, 1867): 3.

Books *Announced but Probably Never Published*

*The Book of Rosicrucia.** An 1861 newspaper article on Randolph's departure from San Francisco to the Orient mentions that Randolph was engaged on this "massive work" "at the instance of the Supreme Grand Lodges of the Order in America, Europe, and Asia." See preface to *After Death* (1870).

*The Realm of the Fay.** In *Dealings with the Dead* (1861–1862) (148) Randolph says he would soon write a book by this title on the post-mortem fate of aborted and miscarried fœtuses and of congenital idiots. The same passage is repeated in *Soul!* in 1872, so the book must never have been written.

The Sexual Question.* Randolph in 1861 says he will shortly publish a book by this title dealing with the sensitivity of women mediums: "Such persons, sitting in 'circles,' either draw off the very life of those with whom they come in contact, or else themselves are sponged dry." *Dealings with the Dead* (245).

The Human Body and the Human Soul—Their Origin, Nature, Constitution and Destiny, On the Earth and Off It.* Randolph proposed to write a sequel to *Pre-Adamite Man* under this title. *Pre-Adamite Man* (398).

The Blacks in Louisiana.* In a letter to the *Anglo-African*, published in the edition of February 25, 1865, and translated and reprinted in the *New Orleans Tribune* for March 11, 1865, Randolph claimed he was rapidly completing a book under this title.

Planes Beyond.* In *After Death* (1868) (194), Randolph announced his intention of writing a work under this name on the "Dark Sun," the "Lost Pleiad" in the direction of Alcyone, the pivot around which revolves our half of the universes of creation. This may be the same as the project he later titled *Beyond the Spaces.* See below.

Prostitution; its Causes and Cure.* In *The Master Passion* (1870) (61–69), Randolph quotes from a book under this title which he says was soon to appear. It is unclear from the text whether Randolph contributed to the work or simply testified on the subject before some committee.

Man Beyond The Veil.* In *After Death* (1868) (173) Randolph claimed he had learned more in the preceding year about disembodied man than ever before. The preface to his posthumous *Beyond The Veil* (1878) says that Randolph had planned to publish this new material under this title.

La Feronee.* Randolph quotes from a manuscript of this name in *Casca Llana* (1872) (225).

Walks Among the Women. In his *Curious Life* (1872) (49–50), Randolph mentions this as the "proposed title of a book of gems on the subject of the tender passion."

Sexagyma.* In the *Ansairetic Mystery*, printed in late 1873 or early 1874, Randolph says he was preparing an "Especial Work on Sex matters" under this title. The work was to be printed but not published and accordingly was to be more explicit than Randolph's published works on love.

*Beyond the Spaces.** Randolph mentions this in *The Ghostly Land* (1874) as dealing with the mysterious Dark Sun, and in *Eulis* (1874) says that the teachings to be embodied in it had been learned in the "Sialam slumber." In a letter to the the *Religio-Philosophical Journal*, published on August 14, 1875, Randolph states that he had completed the work.

*Hermit of Arizona.** In a letter to Col. H. S. Olcott in July 1875, Randolph wrote: "I have been 8 months on the Pacific Slope and have just returned and am now writing out for publication the extraordinary tale of the Hermit of Arizona, which I think will match your wonderful book [*People from the Other World*], although not in the same line."

NOTES

Foreword

1. Paschal B. Randolph, *Eulis! The History of Love* (Toledo: Randolph Publishing Company, second edition, 1874), 4.

2. *Paschal B. Randolph, His Curious Life, Works and Career* (Boston: Randolph Publishing House, 1872), 7.

3. Paschal B. Randolph, *The Wonderful Story of Ravalette* (Boston: Randolph Publishing Company, 1876 edition), 243.

4. Joscelyn Godwin, Christian Chanel, John P. Deveney, *The Hermetic Brotherhood of Luxor: Initiatic and Historical Documents of an Order of Practical Occultism* (York Beach, Maine: Samuel Weiser, 1995).

5. Linda Gordon, *Woman's Body, Woman's Right: Birth Control in America* (New York: Penguin, revised edition, 1990), 24.

6. Paschal B. Randolph, *After Death: The Disembodiment of Man* (Boston: Randolph and Company, 1870), 245.

7. Paschal B. Randolph, *Soul! The Soul World: The Homes of the Dead* (Quakertown: Confederation of Initiates, 1932), 122.

8. Gordon, *op. cit.*; Robin D. G. Kelley, *Race Rebels: Culture, Politics and the Black Working Class* (New York: Free Press, 1994); David R. Roediger, *The Wages of Whiteness: Race and the Making of the American Working Class* (New York and London: Verso, 1991). For the notion of history turned toward the future, see Nicolas Calas, *Confound the Wise* (New York: Arrow Editions, 1942), especially pages 64–70.

9. See, by David S. Reynolds: *George Lippard* (Boston: Twayne, 1982); *George Lippard: An Anthology* (New York: Peter Lang, 1986); *Beneath the American Renaissance: The Subversive Imagination in the Era of Emerson and Melville* (New York: Knopf, 1988), and his Introduction to the latest edition of Lippard's

masterpiece, *The Quaker City, or, the Monks of Monk Hall* (Amherst: University of Massachusetts Press, 1995).

10. Carolyn L. Karcher, *The First Woman in the Republic: A Cultural Biography of Lydia Maria Child* (Durham and London: Duke University Press, 1994).

11. Lydia Maria Child, *Letters from New York* (New York: Charles L. Francis and Co., 1843), 194.

12. André Breton, *What Is Surrealism? Selected Writings*, edited and introduced by Franklin Rosemont (New York: Monad Press, 1978).

13. Reynolds (1982), *op. cit.*, 40–43, 45–46, 51, 107; Reynolds (1986), 2, 25.

14. Karcher, *op. cit.*, 306

15. Randolph, *After Death, op. cit.*, 14.

16. Marc Pluquet, *La Sophiale: Maria de Nagloska, sa vie, son oeuvre*, unpublished manuscript (*see* Bibliography).

17. Ernest de Gengenbach, *L'Expérience démoniaque* (Paris: Eric Losfeld, 1968), 322–323; *Judas ou la vampire surréaliste* (Paris: Eric Losfeld, 1970), 182, 187, 195.

18. P. B. Randolph, "Les conditions spéciales de préparation et de travail pour les miroirs magiques spéciaux à couches magnétiques vivantes," in *Néon*, No. 2 (Paris, 1948), 4.

19. The *Lexique succinct de l'erotisme* was later also issued separately (Paris: Eric Losfeld, 1970); the entry on Randolph appears on page 61.

20. I would like to thank Gérard Legrand, Edouard Jaguer, Elie-Charles Flamand, and Philip Lamantia—all of whom were active in the surrealist movement in the 1940s and/or 1950s—for providing much of the information contained in this and the preceding paragraph.

21. Sarane Alexandrian, "Maria de Naglowska et le satanisme féminin," in *Les liberateurs de l'amour* (Paris: Editions du Seuil, 1977), 185–206. Alexandrian, incidentally, had been coeditor of Nèon in 1948.

22. Randolph, *After Death, op. cit.*, 201.

23. Randolph, *Soul! The Soul World*, op. cit., 238.

24. Randolph, *Eulis! The History of Love*, op. cit., 83.

25. Randolph, *After Death, op. cit.*, 104–105.

26. *Ibid.*, 69.

27. Paschal B. Randolph, *The Rosicrucian Manifesto* (February 1871), in the journal *The Initiates* (Vol. III, May–June 1930/May–June 1931), 113.

Preface

1. René Guénon, "Rose-Croix et Rosicruciens," *Le Voile d'Isis* (May 1931): 275ff.

2. James Webb, *The Occult Underground* (LaSalle: Open Court, 1974), 5ff.

3. This view of the world (much diminished and impoverished by the time spiritualism arose in the United States in the late 1840s) was the intellectual foundation of the occult beliefs of the West. For the Renaissance, for example, see Gary Tomlinson, *Music in Renaissance Magic: Toward a Historiography of Others* (Chicago and London: University of Chicago Press, 1993), 46: "The sixteenth-century magus took for granted three postulates: that the world was hierarchically ordered, with intellectual elements occupying its highest realm; that superior elements in the hierarchy influenced inferior ones; and that the wise man might ascend through the levels of the world structure (or at least interact from below with higher levels) to gain special benefit from these influences. At one level of analysis the whole of Renaissance occult thought proceeded from these straightforward premises." The work is valuable even though its historical research is unnecessarily encumbered with the author's attempts to define the nature of his discourse.

4. See, e.g., René Le Forestier, *La Franc-Maçonnerie Templière et occultiste aux XVIIIe et XIXe siècles* (Paris: Aubier, Eds. Montaigne, 1970), 31.

5. *Voyage du sieur Paul Lucas, fait par l'ordre du Roy dans la Grèce, l'Asie Mineure, La Maçedoine et l'Afrique*, 2 vols. (Paris: Nicholas Simant, 1712), ch. 12, 1:98–112. Peter Davidson, the provincial grand master of the North of the H. B. of L., published a version of the story for Madame Blavatsky's *The Theosophist* in 1882. Peter Davidson, "The Mysterious Brothers—An Old Tale Retold," *The Theosophist* 3, no. 5 (February 1882): 120–21 and 3, no. 6 (March 1882): 153–54. Davidson drew his readers' attention to the similarities of Lucas's dervish with the equally mysterious "Chundra-ud-Deen" who instructed Emma Hardinge Britten's "Chevalier Louis de B——" and with Madame Blavatsky's story of the "Count de Lassa," the ageless master of the magic mirror who supposedly frequented the salons of Paris in the early 1860s, after Randolph's sojourn there. The original Rosicrucian publications in the early seventeenth century revived and popularized the idea of secret brotherhoods operating behind the scenes, and Baron von Hundt confirmed the central importance of these *supérieurs inconnus* with his Rite of Strict Observance in the eighteenth century, but the notion had a long history before then and is really a constant of human nature. For a recent discussion of the rise of the myth of the wandering adept in the seventeenth century, see William R. Newman, *Gehennical Fire: The Lives of George Starkey, an American Alchemist in the Scientific Revolution* (Cambridge, MA: Harvard University Press, 1994), 1–13. On Randolph's claim to visit Jung-Stilling's conclave, see his *Ravalette* (1863), 72–73. On the nineteenth-century's almost

universal belief in the role of secret societies behind the events of profane history, see J. M. Roberts, *The Mythology of the Secret Societies* (London: Secker & Warburg, 1972), 4ff.

6. See Christopher Bamford's introduction to C. G. Harrison, *The Transcendental Universe: Six Lectures on Occult Science, Theosophy, and the Catholic Faith, Delivered before the Berean Society*, ed. Christopher Bamford (1894; Hudson, New York: Lindisfarne Press, 1993).

7. The essential survey is Joscelyn Godwin's four-part series of articles, "The Hidden Hand," *Theosophical History* 3, nos. 2–5 (April 1990-January 1991): 35–43, 66–76, 107–117, 137–148.

8. The H. B. of L. has recently been studied and its manuscript teachings published. See Joscelyn Godwin, Christian Chanel, and John Patrick Deveney, *The Hermetic Brotherhood of Luxor: Initiatic and Historical Documents of an Order of Practical Occultism* (New York: Samuel Weiser, 1995).

9. Quoted in Philippe Encausse, *Sciences Occultes, ou 25 années d'occultisme occidental; Papus, sa vie, son oeuvre* (Paris: OCIA, 1949), 52. See also Paul Sédir, *Histoire et doctrines des Rose-Croix* (Lyon, 1932), which is filled with Sédir's constant hopeful references to mysticism and his citation of out-of-the-way stories of true adepts who appeared to earnest seekers who had passed through despair and arrived at a sort of cosmic indifference as the necessary preamble to mystical experience. On Maître Philippe, see Claude Pasteur, "Monsieur Philippe, un juste parmi les hommes," *Nouveau Planète* (May-June 1971): 53–65.

10. Porphyry, *Vita Plotini* 11.

11. On the phenomenon, see, e.g., Jules Bois, *Le Monde Invisible* (Paris: Flammarion, 1902), 12. Bois, who was a journalist and peripheral participant in the French occult revival of the 1890s (he once fought a duel over occult matters), stresses that, from his observations, the goal of the occultists had always been "ecstasy," but as this proved impossible to attain they turned increasingly to magic to force the doors of the invisible.

12. It is this drive to seek release from the prison of diminished reality that is the very fruitful juncture between romanticism (and the literary impulse generally) and the occult. On the connection, see Auguste Viatte, *Les sources occultes du Romantisme: Illuminisme—Théosophie, 1770–1820*, 2 vols. (Paris: H. Champion, 1927); René Daumal, *Mount Analogue* (London: Vincent Stuart, 1959); Eduardo A. Azcuy, *El Occultismo y la Creacion Poetica* (Buenos Aires: Ed. Sudamerica, 1966); Christian Lepinte, *Goethe et l'occultisme* (Paris: Les Belles Lettres, 1957); Gwendolyn Bays, *The Orphic Vision: Seer Poets from Novalis to Rimbaud* (Lincoln: University of Nebraska Press, 1964); Jean Richer, *Gérard de Nerval et les doctrines ésotériques* (Paris: Editions du Griffon d'Or, 1947).

Chapter 1

1. Randolph's own works are referred to by short title without author and by edition where editions vary or the date of publication is important. The full titles and tangled publishing history of Randolph's works are given in the bibliography of his works in appendix C. He gives his father's full name as William Beverly Randolph in *Curious Life* (18). "Beverley" is indeed a common name among the Randolphs of Virginia, and there is even a William Beverley Randolph (1799–1868) among them, but none is a likely candidate for Flora's husband. See Robert Isham Randolph, *The Randolphs of Virginia: A Compilation of the Descendants of William Randolph of Turkey Island and His Wife Mary Isham of Bermuda Hundred* (n.p., n.d., probably Chicago, 1936), 217; J. Eckenrode, *The Randolphs: The Story of a Virginia Family* (Indianapolis: Bobbs-Merrill, 1946). Flora Clark's last name is on Randolph's baptismal record (November 18, 1832) at the Church of the Transfiguration in New York City, though at times Randolph calls her "Flora Beverly." *Ravalette* (1876), 17; *Master Passion*, 143. Randolph's middle name, Beverly, is thus, variously, either from his father or from his mother—or was the name he took on his baptism as a Roman Catholic in 1832. *Ravalette*, 16 (baptized at eight years of age as "Beverly"). This last seems unlikely, since there is no St. Beverly and the baptismal record merely names him "Paschal, last son of William Randon and Flora Clark." If Randon is not a *lapsus calami*—and Randon appears again in the index of the baptismal records—Randolph's last name is his own creation. But see note 5 below. Birth records were not kept for New York City for the period, and there is no official record of Randolph's birth. Randolph's early years are covered after a fashion in his *Curious Life* (1872) but were apparently extensively discussed in his lost novel *Dhoula Bel*. See page 20 of the advertisement for that work appended to *Casca Llanna* (1872).

2. *Curious Life*, 2.

3. *Ravalette*, 16–17 ("her husband, after years of absence, during which she had deemed him dead, and contracted a second alliance with the father of her boy, had suddenly returned, and never from that moment did she receive one particle of what her heart yearned for."). He told a different story in addressing the American Association of Spiritualists in 1873: "Forty-six years ago there was a man who fell in love with a woman and a woman who fell in love with a man. They did not stop to pay fees to the justice or to the priest, but they accidentally generated, and a fellow called P. B. Randolph was the result. Twelve months after he was born she married the man and the man married her. Five or six children were born after the marriage." *Proceedings of the Tenth Annual Convention of the American Association of Spiritualists, Held at Grow's Opera Hall, Chicago, on Tuesday, September 16* (n.p., n.d., but probably Chicago, 1873), 69. This ill comports with the statement on Randolph's baptismal certificate that he was "the last son" of William Randon and Flora Clark.

4. *Casca Llanna*, 241–42; *Curious Life*, 2 (knew little of mother, less of father); *Ravalette*, 16 (his "father loved him little").

5. "Notes of My Psychal Life," *Journal of Progress* 2, no. 3 (October 1853): 38-39, by "A Seer" but signed "P. B. R." The spirit of his newly deceased father appeared to him, he says, on March 29, 1842, when he was living in Portland, Maine, and he later learned that his father had died at just that time. The records of deaths for New York City in fact show that a William B. Randolph of Virginia, fifty-three years of age, died on April 1, 1842.

6. Both Randolph and his father are described in press reports as the nephew of John Randolph. *Curious Life*, 18, 47 (nephew), 13 ("relative"). Reuben Swinburne Clymer, an epigonous follower of Randolph whom we shall discuss later, with characteristic specificity opted for John Randolph's son Edmund Randolph as the father. John Randolph (1773–1833) was a gentleman squire of Virginia, a member of Congress and minister to Russia and was descended in the seventh degree from Pocahontas. He was also eccentric and at times insane, characteristics that Randolph would point to in explaining his own angularity. See Eckenrode, *The Randolphs*, 187, 292–93.

7. *Curious Life*, 18–19; *Ravalette*, 16 ("From his father our hero inherited little save a lofty spirit, an ambitious, restless nature, and a susceptibility to passional emotions, so great that it was a permanent and positive influence during his entire life.").

8. *Curious Life*, 2.

9. *Curious Life*, 3, 4 ("gave up Eden for Paradise, just as the old man did before me, if the genesic tale be true"). See also *Casca Llanna*, 55 (quoting *Dhoula Bel*: the sins of the fathers are visited on children, who are born "thralls of vice"); 54 (without a father's magnetism and love to help the pregnant mother, the child is born angular).

10. *Dealings with the Dead*, 69. The Canal Street address is given in *Curious Life*, 3, and in the synopsis of *Dhoula Bel* appended to *Casca Llanna*.

11. George G. Foster, quoted in Leonard P. Curry, *The Free Black in Urban America, 1800–1850: The Shadow of the Dream* (Chicago: University of Chicago Press, 1981), 117. See also *Transfiguration Church: A Church of Immigrants, 1827–1977* (New York, n.d.), 8–9: Five Points "became a haven for freed slaves and immigrants who were now joined by the most disreputable and forgotten people of the City. While sailors added a certain color to the place and the prostitutes a bawdy notoriety, it was in reality a decayed, diseased and violent collection of hovels where despair and hopelessness were a way of life. 'Paradise Square,' the 'Old Brewery'—which averaged a murder a night for years—, the 'Den of Thieves,' and 'Murder's Row' were places where such gangs as the 'Plug Uglies' and 'Dead Rabbits' transacted their business. People who preferred not to be mugged, murdered, or shanghaied onto whalers bound for Alaska, gave the area a wide berth, including the police."

12. *Curious Life*, 2 (death "in or about the year of the great cholera, 1832"); *Ravalette*, 16, gives Randolph's age at the time of her death as five, as does *Casca Llanna*, 382. *After Death*, 181, describes his vision on July 4, 1864, of his mother "thirty-three years in heaven." *Ravalette*, 21–22, gives the description of the pesthouse quoted in the text. His mother's death and its consequences to him appear constantly in Randolph's writings, but it should be noted that in a letter of May 2, 1858, to Gerrit Smith, he mentions his mother as then living—perhaps a reference to his mother-in-law. The correspondence is in the Gerrit Smith Collection, George Arents Research Library, Syracuse University Library, Department of Special Collections.

13. *Ravalette*, 19; *After Death*, 4 ("My mother was a seer before me").

14. *Ravalette*, 31.

15. *Dealings with the Dead* 100–101. See also ibid., 83–89, and *Curious Life*, 4–5: "I was born *in* love, of a *loving* mother, and what she *felt*, that have I lived, because I am the exact living counterpart of her feelings, intense passions, volcanic, fiery, scoriac; her love, higher than heaven, deeper than death; her agony, terrible as a thousand racks! her hope and trust, fervent, enduring, solid as steel, unbreakable as the lightning, which blazes in the sky! her loneliness, I have been a hermit all my days, even in the midst of men; in a word, I am the exact expression of that woman's states of body, emotion, mind, soul, longings, spirit, aspirations, when she took in charge the incarnation of the soul of [my soul]. . . . From birth I breathed a rich, voluptuous atmosphere, because I breathed my mother's sphere, and drank in love from *her* bosom. I was incarnate love, and my thoughts ever ran in that direction. Is it any marvel then that my entire soul was given up to studies of the master passion of human kind? . . . The great trouble with me through life has been a too ready credulity. On that rock I have often struck. When a man said he was my friend, or a woman—some hundreds of both— told me she 'loved' me, I believed both, and never yet failed to get bit for my 'folly.'" His unfulfillable desire for love and affection even caused him to write a song, "The Heart Song," whose lyric runs "Love me, love me . . . " *Casca Llanna*, preface "C."

16. *Curious Life*, 3. See also *Dealings with the Dead*, 73 (Boss Tom Riley's Fifth Ward). He must have kept in some contact with his sister, because his nephew, a certain Mr. Potter, was arrested with him when he first arrived in New Orleans in late 1864.

17. See *Ravalette*, 16; *Dealings with the Dead*, 169. His conversion to Catholicism seems not to have affected his later thought to any appreciable extent, and he says he left the church some time later when he became disgusted with several features he found objectionable. *Ravalette*, 42. The objectionable features of what he called "the *Pope*-ish doctrine, that whatever exists is just as the Eternal One decreed" (more properly a spiritualist than a Catholic doctrine) prompted Randolph's pamphlet *It Isn't all Right, Being A Complete*

And Thorough Refutation Of The Pernicious Doctrine that "Whatever is, is Right" (Boston: New England Reform Association, New York: S. T. Munson, 1861), written under the pseudonym *Cynthia Temple*. The quoted language is on page 5. The "good old Father Verella, a Spanish priest" who received Randolph into the Church is Father Felix Varela Morales (1788–1853), one of the forerunners of Cuban independence. He founded the Church of the Transfiguration in 1827 in what is now Chinatown in Manhattan (where a plaque commemorating his life now hangs on Mott Street) and eventually became vicar-general of the New York archdiocese. The baptismal records at the church show that Randolph was baptized on November 18, 1832, with Mary Davis as sponsor.

18. F. B. Dowd, *The Double Man* (Boston: Arena Publishing Co., 1895), 34.

19. In the synopsis of his lost novel *Dhoula Bel*, printed in the advertisements at the end of *Casca Llanna*, 20, Randolph speaks of his "early years in Newport, Rhode Island."

20. Synopsis of *Dhoula Bel* (Cuba and return). Randolph says variously that he was a cabin boy from twelve to twenty and from fifteen to twenty. *Curious Life*, 3, 4, 19. The brig *Phoebe* is in *Ravalette*, 32. On the merchant marine of the time, especially its lower ratings, as a typical niche for blacks, see Martha S. Putney, *Black Sailors: Afro-American Merchant Seamen and Whalemen Prior to the Civil War* (New York, Westport and London: Greenwood Press, 1987). Putney mentions a whaler *Phoebe* that sailed from Nantucket for the South Seas in the early 1840s with a black captain, but the name is probably merely a coincidence. Ibid., 64–65, 74, 162.

21. *Curious Life*, 19 (accident chopping wood); 32–34 (miseries of life at sea). Randolph has a good story of his replacing the contents of his jug of rum with "croton oil" (a powerful purgative) to revenge himself on the sailors who were stealing from him.

22. In *Ravalette*, 34, Randolph says he went to Portland after leaving the sea. His "Notes on My Psychal Life," printed in the *Journal of Progress*, says he was living with a Mrs. Dodge in Portland in 1842—the year he learned of his father's death. In *The Liberator* for November 12, 1858, however, Randolph for his own reasons (discussed in chapter 4) denied being in Portland after 1839.

23. *Curious Life*, 3. In *Ravalette*, 16, he says that his fifth year marked the beginning and the end of his formal education. See also "P. B. Randolph at the Melodeon," *Banner of Light* 4, no. 14 (January 1, 1859): 1, 8 (ten months of formal education). *Soul! The Soul World*, 292, is probably closest to reality in saying that Randolph had a few months of formal education before he was five, a few more when he was eight, and finally a few months more when fifteen—in all, less than two years.

24. *Casca Llanna*, 383; *Curious Life*, 9. There may be some truth in the claim, and others noted the similarity of his handwriting to printed characters. See the preface by Luna Hutchinson and Fanny Green to *Beyond the Veil:*

Posthumous Work of P. B. Randolph, Aided by Emanuel Swedenborg and Others, Through the Minds of Frances H. McDougall and Luna Hutchinson (New York: D. M. Bennett, 1878).

25. *Curious Life*, 64, quotes the *Boston Herald* in 1872: "It is said that he is one of the most learned and extensively read men in America, is familiar with all the ancient languages and literature, and has written numberless works upon philosophy, love, religion, and other topics. . . . His acquaintance with prominent and influential men of every known nation is said to be extensive, and his experience seems to have been as varied as the most eccentric could desire."

26. See, e.g., *Dealings with the Dead*, 239 (Heinrich Jung-Stilling); 254 (Behmen, Swedenborg); *Davenport Brothers*, 110 (Randolph was once going to reprint the *Anacalypsis* of Godfrey Higgins); *Master Passion*, 29 (Pietro di Lombardi and "Le Petit Albert").

27. *Grand Secret*, 32 (violin); *Casca Llanna*, preface "C," gives "The Heart Song" which Randolph wrote and arranged for the pianoforte; *Curious Life*, 75 (he wrote but did not read music, and could discuss music theory). All of this gives some reason to believe that the chants to accompany Randolph's fully developed sexual magic (published by Maria de Naglowska in *Magia Sexualis*, 1931) may actually be reflections of Randolph's own work.

28. The extraordinariness of Randolph's literary achievements is highlighted by the fact that the first novel by an African American had been published only in 1853. See John Hope Franklin and Alfred A. Moss, Jr., *From Slavery to Freedom* (New York: Knopf, 1988), 151. Randolph published several other novels even before 1863, but they are mostly lost. See the Bibliography, appendix C, and S. Austin Allibone, *A Critical Dictionary of English Literature and British and American Authors Living and Deceased, From the Earliest Accounts to the Latter Half of the Nineteenth Century*, 3 vols. (Philadelphia: J. B. Lippincott & Co., 1870), 2:1738. Allibone also says that between 1852 and 1861 Randolph edited *The Messenger of Light* and *The Journal of Progress*. The only surviving number of the latter carries an article, "Notes on my Psychal Life," by Randolph but does not mention him as an editor. *The Messenger of Light* has not survived. Braude says it was published in New York in 1854. Ann Braude, "News from the Spirit World: A Checklist of American Spiritualist Periodicals," *Proceedings of the American Antiquarian Society* 99, no. 2 (1989): 399–462, 424. A notice, "A New Paper in New York," in *The Telegraph Papers* 4 (1854): 289–91, stated that three issues had appeared and described it as a new newspaper published by Messrs Whitney and Conklin and devoted to the "extension of spiritual light." This was taken over by *The Christian Spiritualist*, a weekly that J. H. W. Touhey, Horace Day, and Emma Hardinge Britten put out from May 13, 1854, to May 2, 1857, to which Randolph contributed a letter. For Britten's role in the venture, see chapter 2. The *Journal of Progress* was published by the Harmonial Association in New York City. It bore the motto "Liberty—Fraternity—Unity"—the

Watchwords of the Race and addressed itself to "reformatory and progressive minds." It was as much a reform as a spiritualist journal and was the successor to several earlier attempts (*The Spirit Messenger*, *The Spirit Messenger and Harmonial Advocate*, and *The Messenger of Light*) by Fanny Green, Apollos Munn, and R. P. Ambler and others to spread their version of reform and of Andrew Jackson Davis's ideas. After the issue of October 1853, in which Randolph's "Notes on My Psychal Life" appeared, the editors merged the journal with their companion effort, *The Reformer*, which itself quickly succumbed.

29. Curry, *Free Black in Urban America*, 4, 251.

30. Ibid., 218.

31. Ibid., 19, 90.

32. Ibid., 94.

33. Ibid., 90, 101, 125, 164.

34. *Curious Life*, 4, 18 ("Flora, his mother, was said to have been, as is likely, a woman of extraordinary mental activity and physical beauty, nervous, 'high strung,' and willful; a native of Vermont, of mingled Indian, French, English, German and Madagascan blood,—she had not a single drop of negro in her veins, nor consequently has her son. . . . The tawny complexion of both mother and son came from her grandmother, a born queen of the Island of Madagascar."), 19.

35. Preface to *Beyond the Veil* (which most probably reflects the cover story Randolph was using in 1875) calls him a *"sang melée,"* descendant of the Queen of Madagascar, a mixture of three races. In *Ravalette* it becomes seven races, and in his Clinton Hall recantation speech in 1858, it becomes Indian, Asiatic, and European. *Soul!* 265ff. In the year before his death he was describing himself as a Persian, descendent of a long line of "Persian chiefs." "Spiritual meetings," *Religio-Philosophical Journal* 17, no. 2 (September 26, 1874): 4–5.

36. *New Orleans Tribune*, December 2, 1864. See also "Letter from P. Beverly Randolph," *The Liberator* 28, no. 46 (November 12, 1858): 183 (unity with the "the race whose blood, as well as that of the Anglo-Saxon, fills my heart"). The controversy over "repatriating" African Americans to Africa is examined in chapter 7 and in Howard A. White, *The Freedmen's Bureau in Louisiana* (Baton Rouge: Louisiana State University Press, 1970), 18–19.

37. "The Converted Medium," *New York Daily Tribune*, November 25, 1858.

38. *Rosicrucian's Story*, 100–101.

39. Emma Hardinge [Britten], *Modern American Spiritualism: Twenty Years' Record of the Communion between Earth and the World of Spirits* (New York: Author, 1870; reprint, New York: University Books, 1970), 242ff.

40. On Garrison as a spiritualist, see Ann Braude, "News from the Spirit World: A Checklist of American Spiritualist Periodicals," 406, no. 6, with cites

to *The Liberator* from 1851–54; also J. L. Thomas, *The Liberator: William Lloyd Garrison* (Boston: Little Brown, 1963), 373; "Joseph Barker in America," *Spiritual Magazine* 3, no. 5 (May 1862): 219–28 (describing an evening the British traveler spent with A. J. Davis and Garrison); *The Letters of William Lloyd Garrison*, ed. Walter M. Merrill, vol. 5, *Let the Oppressed Go Free, 1861–1867* (Cambridge and London: Belknap Press, 1979), 5, 6, 99, 109, 429, 434–35, 446–47. R. S. Clymer, typically, makes Garrison one of the Council of Three who governed the Rosicrucians during Randolph's tenure as grand master of the order. Beecher dabbled in spiritualism. See William Howitt, *The History of the Supernatural in All Ages and Nations, and in All Churches, Christian and Pagan: Demonstrating a Universal Faith*, 2 vols. (London: Longman, Green, Longman, Roberts & Green, 1863), 2:189 (Beecher); J. M. Peebles, *Seers of the Ages: Embracing Spiritualism, Past and Present. Doctrines Stated and Moral Tendencies Defined*, 4th ed. (London: J. Burns, Progressive Library, Boston: Wm. White & Co., 1870), 235–36, 217–18 (Beecher, Smith and Garrison).

41. In a letter to *The Liberator* in November 1858, Randolph said that he had lived within five miles of Peterboro, New York, in Madison County, for the previous ten years. "Letter from P. Beverly Randolph," *The Liberator* 28, no. 46 (November 12, 1858): 183.

42. Randolph to Horace Mann, March 5, 1851, preserved in the Mann Papers at the Massachusetts Historical Society. I am grateful to Prof. Carl E. Lindgren for bringing this letter to my attention.

43. *Ravalette*, 121–22. In denouncing spiritualism in 1858, one of Randolph's criticisms was that it had taken him from his honest employment as a barber: "I was a decent sort of barber when Spiritualism came, took me from my work, sent me from Dan to Beersheba and back again, filled my head with complex science which I did not come honestly by through means of an education, and unfitted me from following the practical duties of life." "P. B. Randolph at the Melodeon," *Banner of Light* 4, no. 14 (January 1, 1859): 5, 8.

44. Appendix to *Unveiling* (1860).

45. *Curious Life* (1872), 3, speaks of his pretty little girl, aged fifteen, which would make her born in 1857 or so. The advertising insert to one edition of the book pleads for the public to buy Randolph's works "to the end that I may have my daughter (almost an invalid from birth) other than a dependent on cold charity." Jacob is mentioned in a letter from Randolph to Gerrit Smith, dated May 2, 1858, preserved in the Gerrit Smith Collection, Syracuse University. *Casca Llanna*, synopsis of *Dhoula Bel*, 21, of advertisements, has "Little Winnie."

46. *Ravalette*, 48–49 (Randolph entrusted funds to a friend and left for Europe, and the friend deceived him and his daughter died of hunger); *Rosicrucian's Story*, 43 (little Winnie starved and buried in Utica); *Curious Life*, 9. He also blamed himself for her death: "This demonical phase of Spiritualism deprived me of reason, led me from my home and duties, caused me to

squander in world-roving a sum more than sufficient to have rendered my family comfortable for life." "The Converted Medium," *New York Daily Tribune*, November 25, 1858, 3.

47. Advertisement at the end of *Unveiling* (1860).

48. Circular notice appended to *Dealings with the Dead* (1861–62).

49. *Casca Llanna*, 21 ("Married twice. Radicalism debauched both wives, and rendered a happy home a wilderness of woe."), 383. All this is said in the context of an attack on the radical free-love advocate Moses Hull.

50. See Whitney R. Cross, *The Burned-over District: the Social and Intellectual History of Enthusiastic Religion in Upstate New York, 1800–1850* (Ithaca: Cornell University Press, 1950).

51. Spencer Klaw, *Without Sin* (New York: Allen Lane Press, 1993).

52. The best short exposition of the history of the Fox sisters is Ernest Isaacs, "The Fox Sisters and American Spiritualism," in *The Occult in America: New Historical Perspectives*, Howard Kerr and Charles L. Crow, eds. (Urbana: University of Illinois Press, 1983), 79–110.

53. For a clear statement of the prevailing view on individual sovereignty, see W. S. Courtney, "Individual Sovereignty," *The Telegraph Papers* 2 (1853): 296–308. For the spiritualists' position on the Bible see, e.g., S. B. Brittan, "The Bible and Inspiration," *The Telegraph Papers* 2 (1853): 454–60 (the value of the Bible lies in its poetry; its truths are subsumed in the discoveries of nature); Andrew Jackson Davis, "Old Testament Inconsistencies," *The Telegraph Papers* 2 (1853): 142–58.

54. The psychometrist J. R. Buchanan made the point well in defending the progress inherent in his own discoveries: "That any ancient Hindoo priesthood are in possession of a science of the brain analogous to that which I have established by experimental investigation, is so entirely improbable and Munchausen-like a story, that I have no doubt it is either greatly exaggerated or totally untrue." Buchanan, "Hindoo Philosophy," *The Telegraph Papers* 2 (1853): 48–51. Where early spiritualism does mention the East, the emphasis is more on the progress shown by the primitive Easterners in taking up spiritualism than on their ancient wisdom. See, e.g., U. Clark, ed., *The Spiritual Register for 1859: Facts, Philosophy, Statistics for Spiritualism* (Auburn, New York, and Boston, MA., n.d.)(spiritualism among Armenians of Istanbul); "The Spirits in Syria," *The Telegraph Papers* 2 (1853): 75. See also the advertisement by Thomas Coleman for mediums to proselytize in India (salary and expenses paid). "Mediums for India," *Banner of Light* 8, no. 12 (December 15, 1860): 5.

55. For the best in the secondary literature on spiritualism, see Ann Braude, *Radical Spirits: Spiritualism and Women's Rights in Nineteenth-Century America* (Boston: Beacon Press, 1989); Howard Kerr, *Mediums, and Spirit-*

Rappers, and Roaring Radicals. Spiritualism in American Literature, 1850–1900 (Urbana: University of Illinois Press, 1972); R. Laurence Moore, *In Search of White Crows. Spiritualism, Parapsychology, and American Culture* (New York: Oxford University Press, 1977). On the cumulation of reform fads, see also John D. Davies, *Phrenology: Fad and Science: A 19th Century American Crusade* (n.p.: Archon Books, 1971). On the relations between the abolitionist (antislavery) movement and women's suffrage, land reform, various socialisms, and demands for universal public education in the first half of the nineteenth century, see, e.g., W. Z. Foster, *The Negro People in American History* (New York: International Publishers, 1954), 132. The congeries of "reform" ideas is well represented by educational institutions such as Oberlin College, which advocated "revivalistic religion, anti-slavery and peace activity, co-education, 'manual labor,' dietary reform and missionary activity." See J. H. Fairchild, *Oberlin: The Colony and the College* (Oberlin, Ohio: E. J. Goodrich, 1883).

56. "Spiritualism and Reform," *Religio-Philosophical Journal* 2 (July 16, 1866): 4. The same judgment was reached by the old socialist John Humphrey Noyes, who recounted the streams of the various socialisms that flowed into the reservoir of the new spiritualism. See John Humphrey Noyes, *History of American Socialisms* (New York: Hillary House Publishers, 1961), 564–67.

57. See Braude, *Radical Spirits*, ch. 5; Alex Owen, *The Darkened Room: Women, Power and Spiritualism in Late Victorian England* (Philadelphia: University of Pennsylvania Press, 1990).

58. Martin Henry Blatt, *Free Love and Anarchism: The Biography of Ezra Heywood* (Urbana: University of Illinois Press, 1989), 84. See also Hal D. Sears, *The Sex Radicals. Free Love in High Victorian America* (Lawrence: University Press of Kansas, 1977), 21; Frank Podmore, *Mediums of the Nineteenth Century*, 2 vols. (New Hyde Park: University Books, 1963), 1:291–95.

59. On free love generally, see William Hepworth Dixon, *Spiritual Wives*, 2d ed. (Philadelphia: J. B. Lippincott & Co., 1868), who makes the distinction between "scientific" and mystical free lovism. Also, J. B. Ellis, *Free Love and its Votaries; or, American Socialism Unmasked: Being an Historical and Descriptive Account of the Rise and Progress of the Various Free Love Associations in the U.S. and of the Effects of Their Various Teachings upon American Spiritualism* (New York: U.S. Publishing Co., 1870); Sears, *The Sex Radicals*; Louis J. Kern, *An Ordered Love: Sex Roles and Sexuality in Victorian Utopias—the Shakers, the Mormons, and Oneida Community* (Chapel Hill: University of North Carolina Press, 1981); Raymond Lee Muncy, *Sex and Marriage in Utopian Communities in Nineteenth Century America* (Bloomington: Indiana University Press, 1973); Blatt, *Free Love and Anarchism*. A very good review of the literature is given in John Calvin Spurlock, *Free Love, Marriage and Middle-Class Radicalism in America, 1825–1860* (Ann Arbor: University Microfilms, 1987), who provides (161ff) a synopsis of the transformation of Swedenborg's views on love in the works of Andrew Jackson Davis. Swedenborg's own ideas were considerably

transformed in their transition to America. He himself taught a simpler doctrine based on the finding (either in this world or in the next) of the true partner with whom "conjugial" love was shared. This conjugial union continued in the afterlife, and its exercise begat wisdom and increasing true love until the partners in their "inner heart, mind and soul" became one angel. This, of course, is a version of Plato's myth in *Banquet*. See Emanuel Swedenborg, *The Delights of Wisdom Pertaining to Conjugial Love, After Which Follow the Pleasures of Insanity Pertaining to Scortatory Love* (New York: Swedenborg Foundation, 1954), nos. 28–41, 49–51, 177–78; E. A. Sutton, *Living Thoughts of Swedenborg* (London: Cassell, 1947), 84–90. On Balzac's transformation of this doctrine in *Séraphita* (1835) into the progressive transition during life from mortality to angelic (hermaphroditic) unity, see Inge Jonsson, "New Jerusalem in the World," in *Emanuel Swedenborg: A Continuing Vision*, R. Larsen et al., eds. (New York: Swedenborg Foundation, 1988), 417–24. For a discussion of the claim that Swedenborg's views in *Conjugial Love* were influenced by the ideas of John Norris on kabbalistic sacramental sexuality, see Marsha Keith Schuchard, "Swedenborg, Jacobitism, and Freemasonry," in *Swedenborg and His Influence*, E. J. Brock et al., eds. (Bryn Athyn: Academy of the New Church, 1988), 359–79.

60. Quoted in Dixon, *Spiritual Wives*, 399.

61. *After Death*, 110, 157–61 (relationships in afterlife are based on interests and development, not on blood or even "eternal affinities" (one's paired monad-twin), who necessarily develop at different rates and soon separate; *Eulis!* 37 ("I am capable of one *love* at one time, but that time to me fastens its further end to the eternities just ahead of us all. Temporary attractions departed with my dead years, thank Heaven, and their fruitage was ever bitter, bitter.").

62. On Andrews, see Madelaine Stearns, *The Pantarch: A Biography of Stephen Pearl Andrews* (Austin: University of Texas Press, 1968); R. M. and C. R. Goldfarb, *Spiritualism and Nineteenth Century Letters* (New Jersey, 1978), 47ff. For hints of Randolph's involvement in the free-love movements of his time, see "Randolph's Letters—No. 2," *Religio-Philosophical Journal* (October 7, 1865):2: "With what thankful hearts we acknowledged and thanked God that we got through free-love straits, losing some adhering barnacles by the way, and sailed out upon the deeper waters of 'Do Right' channel!"

63. *Casca Llanna*, 60. Despite this condemnation, Randolph, as Todd Pratum has pointed out to me, still thought enough of Andrews to subscribe for his interminable treatise, *The Basic Outline of Universology. An Introduction to the Newly Discovered Science of the Universe; Its Elementary Principles; and the First Stages of their Development in the Special Sciences* (New York: Dion Thomas, 1872). The earliest versions of this appeared in the *Spiritual Telegraph* throughout 1856 and 1857 and was copied in *Tiffany's Monthly*. A long defense by Andrews of his views on free love may be found in the *New York Daily Tribune*, November 8, 1858.

64. Harris was yet another Universalist minister turned spiritualist. He was always peripheral to Randolph's work, and Randolph quotes him and refers to him, but it is extremely unlikely that two such strong individuals could ever have worked together closely. *Dealings with the Dead* (1861–62), 254, quotes him in the company of Behmen and Swedenborg as true clairvoyants who have really "beheld the realities of the spiritual life." Harris's own recantation of 1858, when he discovered that he had for years been obsessed, is quoted extensively and favorably by Randolph in *Unveiling* (1860), 12–17, and has many of the elements of Randolph's own recantation: evil, obsessing spirits, and vampire-like "larvae" feeding off the odylic sphere of the medium. See also Britten, *Modern American Spiritualism*, 59ff, 209ff. In avoiding the evils of obsession, Harris came to believe that he had been "intromitted" to a higher degree of spiritual intercourse and communicated with higher celestials, unlike most spiritualists who, he believed, were controlled by demons. See his "Song of Satan," published in 1859. Like Randolph at the time, he also denounced "spiritual pantheism" and advocated mystical Christianity. Harris later opposed esoteric Buddhism (that is, the Theosophical Society) at the time the H. B. of L. was doing the same—and did so in very similar terms. The main link between the two mages of course is their sexual magic, but they vary so greatly in their approach to the subject that a direct connection appears precluded. Unlike Randolph, Harris taught that sex—for ordinary people—was a hindrance to spiritual progress. On Harris generally, see Herbert W. Schneider and George Lawton, *A Prophet and a Pilgrim, Being the Incredible History of Thomas Lake Harris and Laurence Oliphant; Their Sexual Mysticism and Utopian Communities Amply Documented to Confound the Skeptic* (New York: Columbia University Press, 1942); Frank Podmore, *From Mesmer to Christian Science: A Short History of Mental Healing* (New Hyde Park: University Books, 1963), 234–47. See Harris's *The Lord: The Two-in-One* (Salem-on-Erie, NY: Brotherhood of the New Life, 1876) for his ideas on his true mystical marriage with his celestial counterpart, the Lily Queen.

65. See, e.g., E. H. Heywood, *Cupit's Yokes: or, The Binding Forces of Conjugal Life, An Essay to Consider Some Moral and Physiological Phases of Love and Marriage, Wherein is Asserted the Natural Right and Necessity of Sexual Self-Government* (Princeton, Mass.: Co-Operative Publishing Co., 1878), 14 ("Variety is as beautiful and useful in love as in eating and drinking.").

66. His first wife, Mrs. Dodge, had divorced her husband on the advice of spirits to marry Davis. After her death, affinity drove him into the arms of Mary Finn Love, whom he left in turn to marry a still newer affinity. Davis's relations with Mary Love are the main topic of the second half of his autobiography, *The Magic Staff: An Autobiography* (New York: J. S. Brown & Co., Boston: Bela Marsh, 1859). A discussion of Davis's early peccadilloes can be found in Burton Gates Brown, Jr., *Spiritualism in Nineteenth Century America* (Ann Arbor: University Microfilms, 1972), 29ff; his later change of wives under the impetus of the spirits is discussed in E. J. Isaacs, *A History of*

Nineteenth-Century American Spiritualism as a Religious and Social Movement (Ann Arbor: University Microfilms, 1975), 315ff.

67. Britten, *Modern American Spiritualism*, 233ff.

68. Ibid., 234.

69. Benjamin Franklin Hatch, *Spiritualists' Iniquities Unmasked and the Hatch Divorce Case* (New York: Author, 1859), 14. From the date, the abandoned wife to whom Randolph later returned must be Mary Jane. The identity of the other woman is unknown. On the Hatch divorce case, see *New York Daily Tribune*, November 29, 1858; M. F. Bednarowski, *Nineteenth Century American Spiritualism: An Attempt at a Scientific Religion* (Ann Arbor: University Microfilms, 1973), 61–62, 161–73. Judge Edmonds's own (obviously apologetic) warnings on the evils of spiritualists giving their minds, not to pure disembodied spirits, but to their own passions and appetites, may be found in *The New York Times*, November 29, 1858.

70. See *Unveiling*, 49–56; "P. B. Randolph at the Melodeon," *Banner of Light* 4, no. 14 (January 1, 1859): 5, 8 ("I heard there was a man by the name of Andrew Jackson Davis, who could see through a millstone, and went to him to know if he could explain certain phenomena which enabled me to discern the interior of objects without the use of the natural senses."). In his "Dealings with the Dead" as it first appeared in the *Banner of Light* in 1859, Randolph said that when spiritualism first appeared he spent three weeks with Davis in Hartford and was admitted to Davis's Harmonial Brotherhood. Le Rosicrucien, "Dealings with the Dead.—No. 2," *Banner of Light* 5, no. 24 (September 10, 1859): 3–4. It was while there that he had his first marvelous vision of the universe. See chapter 5.

71. As a teenager he published his first pamphlet, *Lectures on Clairmativeness: All the Mysteries of Human Magnetism and Clairvoyance Explained by the Celebrated Jackson Davis, of Poughkeepsie, New York* (New York, 1845), and his first major work, *The Principles of Nature, Her Divine Revelations, and a Voice to Mankind* (New York: S. S. Lyon & W. Fishbough) appeared in 1847. On Davis generally, see Podmore, *From Mesmer to Christian Science*, ch. 13, 218–33; A Mystic, "Andrew Jackson Davis, The Great American Seer," *The Shekinah* 3 (1853): 1–18.

72. From his earliest work, *Lectures on Clairmativeness*, 34, 36. The passage is quoted by La Roy Sunderland in his article, "The Case of A. J. Davis," *The Spiritual Telegraph* (February 26, 1859): 434ff. On Davis's clairvoyance, which he saw as a process of "inter-penetration" which placed the seer *en rapport* with nature, see A. J. Davis, "Spiritual Perception of Nature in Clairvoyance," *Spiritual Magazine* 2, no. 9 (September 1861): 417ff. C. O. Poole, "A Review of Clarvoyance, the Superior Condition and Nirvana," *Banner of Light* 42, no. 24 (March 9, 1978): 2. The best compilation of Davis's thought is *The Harmonial Philosophy: A Compendium and Digest of the Works of Andrew Jackson Davis, the*

Seer of Poughkeepsie, ed. with preface, biographical summary, and notes by "A Doctor of Hermetic Philosophy" [A. E. Waite] (Chicago: Advanced Thought Pub. Co., n.d. but c. 1930).

73. See the article by La Roy Sunderland, "The Case of A. J. Davis," in *The Spiritual Telegraph* (February 26, 1859): 434, and Andrew Jackson Davis, *The Magic Staff,* 332ff where Davis describes his original vision in 1846 of the "Spiritual Sun of the Univercoelum" that lies at the center of the six concentric spheres through which the spirits progress after death.

74. See *Unveiling,* 50, and chapters 5 and 8. On Davis's cosmology, see *The Harmonial Philosophy. A Compendium and Digest of the Works of Andrew Jackson Davis,* 40–76. Davis is the immediate source of Randolph's views, even though the same basic cosmology was also that of Swedenborg and could have been traced fairly easily in Neoplatonism, Stoicism and various other classical philosophies.

75. Spear left only a few published works on spiritualism, none notable, and letters and comments by and about him and his followers are scattered throughout the spiritualist literature. The earliest account of Spear's conversion to spiritualism is in E. W. Capron, *Modern Spiritualism: Its Facts and Fanaticisms, its Consistencies and Contradictions* (Boston: Bela Marsh, New York: Partridge & Brittan, 1854), 218–25. Spear's own version of events is given in his *Twenty Years on the Wing. Brief Narrative of my Travels and Labors as a Missionary Sent forth and Sustained by the Association of Beneficents in Spirit Land* (Boston: W. White & Co., 1873). Neil B. Lehman has produced a wonderful life of Spear as a thesis: *The Life of John Murray Spear: Spiritualism and Reform in Antebellum America* (Ann Arbor: University Microfilms, 1973). Some three hundred manuscripts relating to Spear are included in the Sheldon Papers at the University of Pittsburgh. Unless otherwise noted, the description of Spear and his work given here is derived from Lehman's.

76. This belief in the imminent coming of the new age is the obvious nexus between Spear's beliefs and his dispatch of Randolph to Robert Owen's World Convention in 1855. Lehman, *The Life of John Murray Spear,* 366ff, discusses Spear's millenarian ideas but appears to have missed Spear's message to Owen.

77. Britten, *Modern American Spiritualism,* 219.

78. On the Kiantone movement, see Britten, *Modern American Spiritualism,* ch. 23, 229ff.

79. On Spear's new motive power, see Britten, *Modern American Spiritualism,* ch. 22. The quotation is from page 221.

80. *New Era* quoted in Britten, *Modern American Spiritualism,* 222. The rival *Spiritual Telegraph* decided that the claims were premature, since only a few little balls had been seen to move—as if that were nothing!—while the

"grand revolver" was still. Ibid., 223. Spear's sorrowful announcement in the *New Era* of the destruction of the machine after it had been moved to Randolph, New York, is printed in ibid., 228–29. See also Spear, "The Destruction of the New Mola," *The Telegraph Papers* 5 (1855): 396–99. The *new mola*, the term Spear used to describe his machine, was used by Randolph as the title of one of his last books.

81. Britten, *Modern American Spiritualism*, 224–25. Davis remained, accordingly, doubtful of the outcome of Spear's experiment. It proved the existence of spirits but nothing more, and he cautioned against the effects of a blind and "unreasoning faith" on spiritualism! On Davis's visit, see Lehman, *The Life of John Murray Spear*, 178. Spear's experiment initially was made at High Rock Cottage in Lynn, Massachusetts (just south of Boston), where Davis had already had visions in August 1852. The property had been owned by a spiritualist named Jesse Hutchinson and became a spiritualist retreat after Hutchinson left for California. See Andrew Jackson Davis, *Present Age and Inner Life: A Sequel to Spiritual Intercourse* (n.p.: C. Partridge, 1853). The Hutchinson family, in turn, became Randolph's host on his last visit to California in 1874 and 1875, and Luna Hutchinson received Randolph's postmortem revelations from beyond the grave. See chapters 10 and 11.

82. Lehman, *The Life of John Murray Spear*, 408–9. The particulars are vague.

83. Britten, *Modern American Spiritualism*, 221.

84. Lehman, *The Life of John Murray Spear*, 194ff.

85. Quoted in Britten, *Modern American Spiritualism*, 222. Britten cites the medium's husband for the proposition that she had been the recipient of extraordinary visions and experiences that lead her, independently of Spear, to visit the machine, where she found that her spiritual impulse coincided with Spear's. Ibid., 226. Britten was especially impressed with the coincidence of experiences but questioned the origins of the manifestations: "What class of mind, embodied or disembodied, could have projected" them? See also on the birth of the machine Isaacs, *History of Nineteenth-Century American Spiritualism*, 199–203.

86. Lehman, *The Life of John Murray Spear*, 408ff.

87. Ibid., 409.

88. Ibid., 409–10. Spear also instructed the implementist to make pictures of the two sexes and movable models that were to play some part in the magic.

89. Lehman, *The Life of John Murray Spear*, 422-23.

90. Ibid., 296. See also the report on the Kiantone meeting in October 1858 which concludes: "The courage of which they boast is simply the effrontery of impudent men and shameless women—and their vaunted

self-development consists in the unlimited gratification of passion and appetite." *New York Times*, October 14, 1858.

91. Lehman, *The Life of John Murray Spear*, 300. See also "Carried Off by Spiritualism," *Banner of Light* 4, no. 3 (October 16, 1858): 4; "New York Correspondence," *Banner of Light* 4, no. 13 (December 25, 1858): 8 (Spear's spirits said "all the purely natural passions must have ample scope to work themselves out in their true order.").

92. "Human Chemistry," document 10 in the Sheldon Papers in the University of Pittsburgh Library, September 24, 1858, quoted in Lehman, *The Life of John Murray Spear*, 312ff. Also in 1858 there is mention in various places of a mysterious trial of Spear—apparently a formally conducted proceeding within the Kiantone group—in which Spear defended himself against unspecified charges by one of his (female) disciples. The charge obviously was sexually related, but no details survive. Ibid., 313–15.

93. Lehman, *The Life of John Murray Spear*, 353, 392.

94. Ibid., 370. Britten, *Modern American Spiritualism*, 236, reprints an announcement of the Sacred Order.

95. Britten, *Modern American Spiritualism*, 234.

96. Ibid., 237.

97. Ibid., 238. The meeting left no trace in the leading spiritualist paper, the Boston *Banner of Light*.

98. Lehman, *The Life of John Murray Spear*, 439. Ashburner had been a frequent contributor to the *Yorkshire Spiritual Telegraph* in 1857 when Randolph had been feted in its pages. See chapter 2.

99. On the meeting in England with Ferguson, see Lehman, *The Life of John Murray Spear*, 440ff. On Ferguson's support for Randolph after the Civil War, see chapter 7. On Ferguson's fervor for spiritualism and his decidedly odd position in the politics of the Civil War, see T. L. Nichols, *Supramundane Facts in the Life of Rev. Jesse Babcock Ferguson, A.M., LL.D., including Twenty Years' Observation of Preternatural Phenomena* (London: F. Pitman, 1865). Ferguson was also (as who was not?) a correspondent of Emma Hardinge Britten. See Britten, *Nineteenth Century Miracles* (Manchester: William Britten, 1883), 157.

100. On the appearance before the Dialectical Society, see Britten, *Nineteenth Century Miracles*, 182–83. See also *Report on Spiritualism, of the Committee of the London Dialectical Society, Together with the Evidence, Oral and Written, and a Selection from the Correspondence* (London: Longman, Green, Reader and Dyer, 1871), 135–37.

101. See Blatt, *Free Love and Anarchism*, 118ff; Sears, *The Sex Radicals*, 37ff. Bennett was a free thinker and purveyor of patent nostrums who latterly was

converted to spiritualism. He was jailed by Comstock for selling one of Ezra Heywood's books on birth control—an arrest that made him a celebrity in liberal circles. The Mahatma Koot Hoomi (speaking through "Jual Khool") claimed that Bennett, when he arrived in India on a world tour in 1882, the year of his death, was "one of our agents (unknown to himself) to carry out the scheme for the enfranchisement of Western thoughts from superstitious creeds." *The Mahatma Letters to A. P. Sinnett from The Mahatmas M. & K. H.,* transcribed and compiled by A. Trevor Barker (1923; Pasadena: Theosophical University Press, 1975), 249. On Bennett, see the bio-bibliographical note in Madame Blavatsky's collected works. *H. P. Blavatsky: Collected Works,* compiled by Boris de Zirkoff, 15 vols. (Wheaton: 1966–1991), 4:625ff. This series will be referred to hereafter as *BCW*.

102. On his return to the United States, Spear said he had been "honorably discharged" by his spirits. He lived in Philadelphia, where he was active in local spiritualist circles and was so impoverished that the leading spiritualist journals collected money to support him. See "John Murray Spear," *Banner of Light* 33, no. 17 (July 26, 1873): 4, and Allen Putnam, "John M. Spear," ibid., 33, no. 21 (August 23, 1873): 3; "Quarterly Convention," ibid., 35, no. 12 (July 4, 1874): 3. For years the *Banner of Light* ran his advertisement offering to "delineate character" by mail for $1.00.

103. "P. B. Randolph at Washington Hall, Charlston," *Banner of Light* 6, no. 10 (December 3, 1859): 5.

104. "The Converted Medium," *New York Daily Tribune*, November 25, 1858, 3.

105. *Unveiling* (1860), 32.

106. Ibid. 8–9.

107. *After Death*, 4 ("My mother was a seer before me, and I have been a clairvoyant by spontaneity since my fourth year; and that power has been quickened by mesmeric induction all along the bitter years, and intensified since the exciting advent of the modern *Theurgia*."); 29 ("I was born a seer."); *Ghostly Land*, 11 ("The author was a Spiritualist before Jackson Davis was thought of, a rap was ever heard in Hydesville, or Wm. Berry quit printing to start the 'Banner of Light' in the Hub of the Yankee Universe").

108. *Dealings with the Dead*, 170. The women do not appear in Emma Hardinge Britten's *Modern American Spiritualism* or in the spiritualist journals, and I have not been able to identify them. In the synopsis of *Dhoula Bel* published among the ads at the end of *Casca Llanna* (22), Randolph also mentions Marshal, Michigan, which may indicate some greater connection with the state in these early years.

109. Beginning in 1853, Partridge and Brittan's *Spiritual Telegraph* published a variety of letters and spirit communications from Randolph that were

later reprinted in their annual compilation *The Telegraph Papers*. See "From One of the Ancients," *The Telegraph Papers* 1 (1853): 333–35, by "P. B. Randolph, Medium" (writing medium of the ancient Persian "Zoroaster," who has gone on to another plane); "Spirit Monitions," ibid. 1 (1853): 421–22, by "Your Angel Mother," with cover letter of Randolph from Utica; "Philosophy from a Spirit," ibid. 2 (1853): 20–22, by "P. B. Randolph, Medium" (communications from Blaise Pascal, Eben El Teleki, and Zoroaster); "Letter from P. B. Randolph," ibid. 8 (1855): 157–59; "Jottings by the Wayside. The Earlville Miracles," ibid. 8 (1855): 265–66. *The Telegraph Papers* also regularly noted his contributions to the incipient spiritualist organizations. See Tappen Townsend, "Harmonial Convention," *The Telegraph Papers* 4 (1854): 49–58 (Randolph at the Auburn, New York, Harmonial Convention with Andrew Jackson Davis); "Clairvoyance and Psychometry," ibid. 6 (1855): 54 (Randolph now in New York City and diagnosing for Drs. Bergevin and Toutain in New York City); "Conference of Aug. 8," ibid. 6 (1855): 95–96 (New York City conference in which Randolph mediated Robespierre and was praised for speaking better in his normal state than in trance); "Spiritual Annexation," ibid. 7 (1855): 80–84 (Randolph's assistance in the formation of the Brooklyn branch of the Society for the Diffusion of Spiritual Knowledge). The society was the work of J. H. W. Touhey, the editor of *The Christian Spiritualist*, in which Emma Hardinge Britten had a leading role. See chapter 2.

110. *Ravalette*, 30–31 (appearance of mother); "The Converted Medium," *New York Daily Tribune*, November 25, 1858, 3 (condemnation).

111. See, e.g., "The Converted Medium," *New York Daily Tribune*, November 25, 1858, 3.

112. Braude, *Radical Spirits*, 87ff.

113. See above and Gustav Meyrink's introduction to *Dhoula Bel: Ein Rosenkreuzer-Roman von P. B. Randolph, Aus dem Englischen Manuskript ubersetz und herausgegeben von Gustav Meyrink* (Vienna, Berlin, Leipzig, and Munich: Rikola Verlag, 1922). The practical drawbacks of this sort of trance speech were apparent to Randolph early on. In "Conference of Aug. 8," *The Telegraph Papers* 6 (1855): 95–96, Randolph was praised by the audience for speaking better on his own, and he promised the audience that he would try in the future not to lose his individuality.

114. "Suicide," *Religio-Philosophical Journal* 8, no. 22 (August 14, 1875):172. See also "Notes on My Psychal Life" ("To such an extent was I absorbed in this existence, that I became an apparent misanthrope; for I have had, and still have, the reputation of being of an unsocial being, absent-minded, full of idiosyncrasies, and partially insane. In fact, some persons have roundly asserted that I was completely lunatic; and yet, after all, they were compelled to admit that there was some method in my madness.").

115. *Curious Life*, 18. On the insanity, see "The Converted Medium," *New York Daily Tribune*, November 25, 1858, 3. *Curious Life*, 9, gives his

sobriquet of "The Comet Man," who was regarded as being "of the Don Quixote school of enthusiasts." See also *Soul!* 291 (reputation for variability and fickleness).

116. "Philosophy from a Spirit," by "P. B. Randolph, Medium," *The Telegraph Papers* 2 (1853): 20–22.

117. See his contributions to *The Telegraph Papers*, listed above, which show his travels. On Randolph as a writing medium, see "From One of the Ancients," *The Telegraph Papers* 1 (1853): 333–35. For his efforts in organizing the spiritualists of Brooklyn, see "Spiritual Annexation," *The Telegraph Papers* 7 (1855): 80–84 and *Davenport Brothers*, 325.

118. "The Converted Medium," *New York Daily Tribune*, November 25, 1858, 3.

119. Ibid. See also "P. B. Randolph and J. V. Mansfield," *Banner of Light* 6, no. 3 (October 15, 1859): 3–4 (the "ultra radical 'Socialists' of both worlds had promised . . . a heaven on earth," and Randolph labored to bring it about, spending thousands of dollars and traveling ten thousand miles).

120. *Guide to Clairvoyance*, 13–14.

121. *Guide to Clairvoyance*, 13–14; *Love and Its Hidden History* (1869), 145. He names, in addition to the doctors mentioned, Drs. Clark and Orton. Clark is perhaps Dr. John E. F. Clarke whose obituary Randolph published in the 1860s. "Departed," Banner of Light 14, no. 24 (March 5, 1864): 3. Dr. J. R. Orton is little remembered now but was a prominent spiritualist of the time. He was among those who recommended Randolph to the World's Convention in London in 1855 (see chapter 2), and was unusual in opposing the dominance of the harmonial philosophy of Andrew Jackson Davis. See J. R. Orton, "Mr. Davis and the Old Testament," *The Telegraph Papers* 2 (1853): 430–43. He was also the author of a letter to the *Spiritual Telegraph* for December 4, 1858, 318, describing a mysterious fall of (sixteen) human bones from the heavens—a phenomenon that would have delighted Charles Fort.

122. *Guide to Clairvoyance*, 10–11.

123. *Spiritual Telegraph* (November 20, 1858): 296: "I think ten years' study and practice fairly justifies the terminal 'M.D.'" He began to use the title in 1852. In the appendix to *Unveiling* (1860), he says he began studying medicine in 1852 and that he later became acquainted with the antiseptic theory of disease and cure in England, where met its exponent, Dr. Evans, who used acacia charcoal for that purpose.

124. Dr. Anna Kimball is a good example. In later years she advocated the idea of sexual intercourse with spirits, mediated Mary Stuart for Lady Caithness, and, with the maverick George Chainey, was expelled "for cause" from the Theosophical Society and collaborated in the short-lived journal, *The Gnostic*, that featured the work of Freeman B. Dowd, the most prominent of

Randolph's followers. Her advertisements for "Electric and Magnetic Treatment" and diagnosis from a lock of the patient's hair appeared frequently in the *Religio-Philosophical Journal* in the early 1870s. Another fringe doctor with connections with Randolph is Dr. Charles Main who was later involved with Randolph in Boston. See *Eulis!* (1874), 200. The *New England Spiritualist* (January 26, 1856) carries his advertisement as a medium-healer, and he also claimed to be able to diagnose (for one dollar) a person's physical condition from a lock of hair. By the early 1860s he was promoting his "Hygienic Institute for the Treatment of Every Known Disease" in Boston. See *Banner of Light* 11, no. 13 (June 21, 1862): 7. On Main, see also A. B. Child, "History of Mediums, No. 10: Dr. Charles Main," *Banner of Light* 4, no. 6 (November 6, 1858): 8, ibid. 4, no. 7 (November 13, 1858): 2; Moore, *In Search of White Crows*, 47–48. A fine example of the crank trance physician is Fanny Green (Frances H. Green McDougall), who received from her spirits a never-fail "Cancer Plaister," a spirit tooth paste, "a cure for the Putrid Pimple, that is now making such terrible ravages," and a "Magnetic Embrocation for the bite of Serpents, Locked Jaw, Hydrophobia, and inflammations generally." The last two she confessed had not as yet been completely tested, but she was sure they were worth a fortune. "Letter from Fanny Green," *The Spiritual Telegraph* (February 26, 1859): 435. Fanny Green had been involved with Randolph from a very early date. She was the editor of the *Journal of Progress* which published Randolph's "Notes of My Psychal Life" in 1853, and after Randolph's death she and Luna Hutchinson received from his spirit the work they published as *Beyond the Veil*. See chapter 11.

125. *Guide to Clairvoyance*, 10–11. It seems clear that the event in 1854 that prompted Randolph to take up his specialty of curing sexual afflictions was related to his discovery that "onanism" robbed the soul of its "physical aliment" and that proper, mutual sexuality restored the soul. See *After Death*, 129–30.

126. Kern, *Ordered Love*, 330. See also Lesly A. Hall, "Forbidden by God, Despised by Men: Masturbation, Medical Warnings, Moral Panic and Manhood in Great Britain, 1850–1900," in *Forbidden History: The State, Society, and the Regulation of Sexuality in Modern Europe*, J. C. Font, ed. (Chicago: University of Chicago Press, 1992), 293–315; Steven Marcus, *The Other Victorians: A Study of Sexuality and Pornography in Mid-Nineteenth-Century England* (New York: Basic Books, 1966), 12–33 (Acton's thesis: all sex does harm; masturbation is fatal); Spurlock, *Free Love*, 17–22. The origin of the idea of the loss of this precious fluid antedates Mesmer but was perfectly consonant with mesmerism—as it was later with the odd notions of Wilhelm Reich. See W. Edward Mann, *Orgone, Reich and Eros. Wilhelm Reich's Theory of Life Energy* (New York: Simon and Schuster, 1973), 95ff. In fact, the idea that the sperm is directly connected with the life force and with the brain is part of the most ancient heritage of the West. See R. B. Onians, *The Origins of European Thought about the Body, the Mind, the Soul, the World, Time and Fate* (Cambridge: Cambridge University Press, 1951), 108–9, 231ff. On the classical background of fear of

loss of semen, see Th. Hopfner, *Griechische-ägyptischer Offenbarungszauber*, Studien zum Paläographie und Papyruskunde, nos. 21, 23, 3 vols. (Leipzig: H. Haessel-Verlag, 1921–24): 1:no. 236; Erna Lesky, *Die Zeugungs-und Vererbungslehren der Antiken und ihre Nachwirken* (Wiesbaden, 1956), 9–30; Peter Brown, *The Body and Society: Men, Women and Sexual Renunciation in Early Christianity* (New York: Columbia University Press 1988), 17–26 (classical idea of sex as a "human expresso machine"; "fantasy of loss of vital spirit). When the idea of spermatic economy fell out of favor with science it retained a home in the occult. Robert H. Fryar, who revealed the H. B. of L. to the public in the 1880s, repeats the old formula that on a scale based on the amount of blood necessary to replace a substance, an ounce of blood would be considered 1, an ounce of saliva 5, an ounce of semen 61, and an ounce of prostatic fluid or "female lochia" 211. *Sexagyma, A Digest of the Works of John Davenport— "Curiositates Eroticae Physiologiae" and "Aphrodisiacs and Anti-Aphrodisiacs,"* with a *Bio-Bibliographical Memoir of the Author*, ed. R. H. Fryar (n.p., Privately Printed for Subscribers, 1888), 20–21n.

127. *Unveiling*, 27. On "Od," see Karl von Reichenbach, *Researches of Magnetism, Electricity, Heat, Light, Crystallization, and Chemical Attraction, in Their Relations to the Vital Force* (London: Taylor, Walton and Maberly, 1850).

128. *Grand Secret*, 7ff. Randolph's wife Mary Jane also advertised a pamphlet on love as a physical substance. See Randolph's bibliography, appendix C. "Dealings with the Dead," published in 1859, mentions for the first time the separate fluids produced by men and women and gives them the Arabic names *geehr* and *keemlin* which unite to give a home to the monad. "Dealings with the Dead. Number Seven. Parenthetical to 'Epoch,'" *Banner of Light* 6, no. 9 (November 26, 1859): 6–7. Randolph discussed the subject regularly in 1860 in the weekly Boston Spiritual Conferences and the same year published his pamphlet (now lost) on "Physical Love in Health and Disease." See "Boston Spiritual Conference," *Banner of Light* 7, no. 23 (September 1, 1860): 8, ibid., 7, no. 24 (September 8, 1860): 8; ibid. 7, no. 25 (September 15, 1860):8.

129. *Grand Secret*, 8, 21.

130. *After Death*, 143.

131. *Grand Secret*, 21.

132. See, e.g., *New Mola!* 36. In his secret work, the *Ansairetic Mystery*, printed the year before his death, Randolph was still advertising his elixirs and offering to sell the secrets of making them and the rights to sell them worldwide.

133. The idea of such *coitus reservatus* is in fact not unknown in Islam, and there are traditions that the Prophet Mohammed practiced it to preserve his vital energies. See Allan Edwardes and R. E. L. Masters, *The Cradle of Erotica: A Study of Afro-Asian Sexual Expression and an Analysis of Erotic Freedom in Social Relationships* (1962; reprint New York: Bantam, 1977), 102 ff.

134. *Grand Secret*, 66ff. (emission not necessary: all can learn in ten minutes to have sex without orgasm and joy without loss of strength); 67n. (send for the "Golden Letter, or Chart of the Polarities of Physical Love"); 76 (anyone can learn, as Noyes and the Agapomenites do, to control spasmodic ejaculatory muscle). Noyes had come upon the idea in 1844 and then published it in *Male Continence* (Oneida: Office of the American Socialist, 1866). It was then popularized by his follower George N. Miller as "Zugassent's Discovery" in his novel *The Strike of a Sex* (Stockham Publishing Co., n.d., c. 1900). On Noyes, see Sears, *The Sex Radicals*; Louis J. Kern, *An Ordered Love*, 207ff. On karezza generally, see J. W. Lloyd, *The Karezza Method, or Magnetation. The Art of Connubial Love* (Roscoe, CA: Author, 1931), who, however, disagrees with Noyes on the propriety of female orgasm: "The female orgasm [is] an acquired habit and not natural." Ibid., 55. Alice Bunker Stockham (1833–1912) had first advocated the idea of karezza in veiled terms in her very popular *Tokology: A Book for Every Woman*, new and revised ed. (1883; Chicago: Alice B. Stockham & Co., 1895). The theory is fully set forth in A. B. Stockham, *Karezza. Ethics of Marriage* (1896; Chicago: Stockham Publishing Co., n.d., c. 1900), and is hinted at with veiled references in a novel she wrote with L. H. Talbot, *Koradine: A Prophetic Story* (1893; reprint Chicago: Alice B. Stockham Publishing Co., 1897). The mix of occult ideas at the end of the century is shown by the fact that the young heroine in *Koradine* appears at a Delsarte reception (F. B. Dowd's *The Gnostic* among other things prominently featured the Delsarte techniques), and the book carries an advertisement for Will Garver's famous occult novel, *Brother of the Third Degree* (1894; reprint, Chicago: Metaphysical Library, 1946), with its tale of competing brotherhoods, marriage of true soul affinities, and adepts with headquarters in Paris). Stockham's *Karezza* was published as part of the "Occult Science Library" by Ernest Loomis and Company in Chicago. Like many other of these sex reformers, Stockham was arrested by Comstock. Sears, *The Sex Radicals*, 88. For an enlightening discussion of the related practice of *amplexus reservatus* in the medieval courts of love, see Danielle Jacquart and Claude Thomasset, *Sexuality and Medicine in the Middle Ages* (Princeton: Princeton University Press, 1988), 94ff.

135. Randolph continued to believe in the possibility of such control of ejaculation, but the practice was condemned as fatal. *Eulis!* 79, 119, 150. See also *Ansairetic Mystery* ("It is absolutely essential that the neck of the uterus be bathed in and by the husband's prostatic lymph and ejected semen *every time* they know each other."). Randolph was always of two minds about Noyes, lumping him with the free lovers ("Noyes' brothel") and excluding him from their number. See *Casca Llanna*, 59; *Grand Secret*, 8 (Noyes is a "rake"). Randolph's reference to the Agapomenites is to the "Abodes of Love" set up in England by Henry James Prince (1811–1899), whom Randolph consistently condemns. Prince was one of the sexual mages who thought that God expressed his love for his flock through the flesh—specifically, through Prince's flesh. On Prince, see Donald McCormick, *The Temples of Love* (New York: Citadel, 1965), and Dixon, *Spiritual Wives*.

136. *The Telegraph Papers* 6 (1855): 54, says that Bergevin was "a director of the Société Magnétique and assistant of the Baron Dupotet and M. Cahagnet." The passage is quoted in Joscelyn Godwin, *The Theosophical Enlightenment* (Albany: State University of New York Press, 1994), 251, to which I owe the reference. Randolph on his 1855 trip carried letters of introduction to Barons Dupotet and Corvaja. *Ravalette*, 175–76.

Chapter 2

1. See James B. Dixon, "The Westminster Review and Spiritualism," *The Herald of Progress: Devoted to the Discovery and Application of Truth* (December 15, 1860): 2; "Robert Owen and the Spirits," *The Telegraph Papers* 2 (1853):490–92; "Personal," ibid. 2 (1853): 514; Robert Owen, "Letter from England," ibid. 2 (1853): 240–41; W. R. H[ayden], "Letter from England," ibid. 2 (1853): 403–5; Robert Owen, "Expériences de Table Parlante Faites au Londres," *La Table Parlante, Journal des Faits Marveilleux* 1 (1854): 220–22. On the beginnings of spiritualism in England, see Janet Oppenheim, *The Other World: Spiritualism and Psychical Research in England, 1850–1914* (Cambridge: Cambridge University Press, 1985), 11ff. Mrs. Hayden's story is told in William Hayden, "Seven Years with the Spirits in the Old and New World; Being a Narrative of the Visit of Mrs. W. R. Hayden to England, France and Ireland; with a Brief Account of her Early Experience as a Medium for Spirit Manifestations in America," *Banner of Light*, various numbers from 1, no. 7 (May 21, 1857): 6–7, through 2, no. 10 (December 5, 1857): 6.

2. See "Permanent Happy Existence of the Human Race, or the Commencement of the Millennium in 1855," *The Spiritual Telegraph* 7 (December 20, 1854): 260, which announced the convention. The recently founded *New England Spiritualist*, May 5, 1855, prominently reviewed Owen's pamphlet on the preliminary meeting in January.

3. On the Convention and Randolph's role in it, see Robert Owen, *New Existence of Man on Earth, Part VII* (London, 1855), 73ff. See also Frank Podmore, *Robert Owen, A Biography* (New York: D. Appleton and Co., 1924), 613ff; Podmore, *Mediums of the Nineteenth Century*, 2 vols. (New York: University Books, 1963), 2:22–23. One of Randolph's recommendations was from the Brooklyn spiritualists' association that he had helped form in early 1855. See chapter 1.

4. See Emma Hardinge Britten, *Nineteenth Century Miracles*, 150 (elite); 153 ("Mr. P. B. Randolph, an eccentric trance speaker, and Mrs. A. E. Newton, a vision seeress and clairvoyant, were also received amongst the *haut ton* of European Spiritualism and each contributed their quota as honored American visitors, in disseminating spiritual light amongst the more favored part of the community."). Randolph certainly had some acquaintance among the European *literati* of the time. He speaks of a letter written to a friend who was also a friend of Carlysle (*Seership!* 38) and in his *Curious Life* (9) says that he was

a friend of Alexandre Dumas, *père*, a mulatto like Randolph and a friend of Eliphas Lévi. Dumas had always had a peripheral acquaintance with the occult, magic mirrors, and drugs, as his novels bear witness, and Randolph's claim of friendship was most probably true. The *Report on Spiritualism, of the Committee of the London Dialectical Society*, 406, published ten years after Randolph's last visit, shows that the English spiritualists generally retained a favorable impression of Randolph and characterized him as "one of [spiritualism's] most thorough and earnest advocates." The impression that Randolph left with the contributors to the London *Spiritual Magazine* is discussed below.

5. *Ravalette*, 58. Randolph carried letters of recommendation to Baron Corvaja and to Baron Dupotet. Ibid., 175–76. Corvaja was perhaps Baron Guiseppe Corvaja, a controversialist in the 1840s on the subject of reforming national banks, but, from bibliographical sources, there is no indication of any Rosicrucian concerns. The only likely English "Wilson" would appear to be Dr. John Wilson, an animal magnetist who was associated with *The Zoist* and with Dr. John Ashburner—whom Randolph undoubtedly met. On Wilson, see Britten, *Nineteenth Century Miracles*, 124ff. The "King" referred to may be the conglomerate spirit "King" or "John King" who reappears constantly in spiritualist circles from the early 1850s through the 1870s, or conceivably the reference is to the Reverend Thomas Starr King, an active spiritualist whose funeral oration Emma Hardinge Britten delivered in March 1864 in San Francisco. The only well-known "Scotts" are James L. Scott, the associate of Thomas Lake Harris in his earliest communal endeavors, and the medium Cora L. V. Scott, but neither had any obvious Rosicrucian proclivities. Both "Cervaja" and Scott (referring to James L. Scott) are also named by Randolph in an advertisement for a lecture series in late 1855. "Lectures on Spiritualism, &c.," *New England Spiritualist* 1, no. 37 (December 15, 1855). Hitchcock is General Ethan Allan Hitchcock, an active soldier who had come to study alchemy in 1854 and who in 1866 believed he had found the philosopher's stone. Randolph at least met him (he speaks familiarly of his library, for example), but R. S. Clymer's fantasies of Randolph, Hitchcock, Alexander Wilder and Abraham Lincoln functioning as the leaders of a Rosicrucian club in the 1860s are just that—fantasy, though Hitchcock's wife, Josie, later joined one of Clymer's Rosicrucian endeavors. See Clymer's notes to Randolph's *Ravalette: The Rosicrucan's Story* (Quakertown: Philosophical Publishing Co., 1939), 64. On Hitchcock's wife, see Clymer, *The Fraternitatis Rosae Crucis* (Quakertown: Philosophical Publishing Co., 1929), 66. Hitchcock's major work, which Randolph may have known, is *Remarks on Alchemy and the Alchemists* (Boston: Crosby, Nichols & Co., 1857). On Hitchcock's library, see the introduction to the joint volume *Ravalette* and *The Rosicrucian's Story* (1863). On Hitchcock's life, see I. Bernard Cohen, "Ethan Allan Hitchcock," *Proceedings of the American Antiquarian Society* 61 (1951): 29–129.

6. On this "wine," see *Eulis!* 88, 107–8; *New Mola!* 5, 36. On the borrowing of terms, see, e.g., *Guide to Clairvoyance*, 41: "I have given much time and

study to the Mystery of Bodiless Flights (Scin-Laeca) the Double, and under what conditions a living person can be seen in two places at the same time." *Scin-Lecca* is the term for the "astral double" that Lytton uses in *The Strange Story*. The term was subsequently picked up by Madame Blavatsky. Another borrowing is found in Randolph's manuscript work "The Mysteries of Eulis" in which he expresses the foreignness of the inhabitants of the celestial spheres by saying that they "look no more like a human apparition than a negro does like a Kalmuc Tartar." In *Zanoni*, Lytton had described the myriads of entities in the universes and commented that "these races and tribes differ more widely each from the other, than the Calmuch from the Greek." Randolph's version of the reference is especially curious in light of his own race and Madame Blavatsky's frequent self-description of her "Kalmucko-Tartaro-Buddhistic" appearance. See chapter 12.

7. The unnamed lady for whom Eliphas Lévi performed the evocation of Apollonius of Tyana in London in 1854 dropped Lytton's name to lure the timid abbé into making the experiment, and Lytton and Lévi later corresponded and met on Lévi's return to London in 1861. On Bulwer-Lytton's wavering belief in spiritualism, see "Dr. Gully on the Late Lord Lytton's Relation to Spiritualism," *Spiritual Magazine*, n.s., 8 (1873): 235; "Lord Lytton," ibid., 8 (1873): 130. On his using mesmerism to project a subject's astral double, see "The spirits of Sleeping Mortals," *Spiritual Scientist* 2, no. 2 (March 18, 1875): 21.

8. It figured, for example, in Glanvil's *Sadducismus Triumphatus*, Aubrey's *Miscellanies*, Scott's *Discoverie of Witchcraft*, and Burton's *The Anatomy of Melancholy*. On the English background generally, see Northcote W. Thomas, *Crystal Gazing, its History and Practice, with a Discussion of the Evidence for Telepathic Scrying* (New York: Dodge Publishing Co., 1905), 77ff; Richard Kieckhefer, *Magic in the Middle Ages* (Cambridge: Cambridge University Press, 1989), ch. 7; "Crystal-Seeing in Lancashire," *Spiritual Magazine*, n.s., 1 (1866), 516–22. A fascinating plate that shows the intricacies of a seventeenth-century magic mirror can be found in *A Treatise on Angel Magic. Being a Complete Transcription of Ms. Harley 6482 in the British Library*, ed. Adam McLean (Grand Rapids: Phanes Press, 1990), 21.

9. *Seership!* 36.

10. On Sand, see *Seership!* 38–45, where Randolph quotes *Consuelo* at length.

11. Northcote Thomas, *Crystal Gazing*, 113ff.

12. For a study of what is known of Barrett, see Timothy D'Arch Smith, *The Books of the Beast* (Wellingborough: Crucible, 1987), 89–97; Francis X. King, *The Flying Sorcerer, Being the Magical and Aeronautical Adventures of Francis Barrett, Author of The Magus* (London: Mandrake, 1992), which also gives an unpublished scrying manuscript by Barrett. Barrett's own book is *The Magus, or Celestial Intelligencer* (1801; reprint, Samuel Weiser, n.d.).

13. C. Cooke, *Curiosities of Occult Literature* (London: Arthur Hall, Smart, and Allen, n.d. c. 1863), 123ff. Even the names of Morrison's many schemes

are dubious: the Wellington telescope (a plan for a public telescope for profit near the Crystal Palace in which they tried to get Bulwer-Lytton involved); the Emperor Life Assurance Society; the Astro-Meteorological Society.

14. See the *Times*, June 30, 1863, 3b; Theodore Besterman, *Crystal-Gazing: A Study in the History, Distribution, Theory and Practice of Scrying* (n.p., n.d.), 58–59.

15. See Podmore, *Robert Owen, A Biography*, 613ff; Podmore, *Mediums of the Nineteenth Century*, 2:31ff. Owen also received messages from the Crowned Angel of the Seventh Sphere through the mediumship of Mrs. Hayden. See Jean Burton, *Heyday of a Wizard: D. D. Home, The Medium* (New York: Knopf, 1944), 55–56. On Hockley generally, see John Hamill, ed., *The Rosicrucian Seer: The Magical Work of Frederick Hockley*, with a bibliographical note by R. A. Gilbert (Wellingborough: Aquarian Press, 1986). Hockley wrote one article on crystal gazing: "On the Ancient Magic Crystal, and its Connexion with Mesmerism," *The Zoist* 8 (1849): 251–66, which is reprinted by Hamill. Though Hockley later joined the Societas Rosicruciana in Anglia and other groups, he appears in many ways self-sufficient. John Yarker counted him, along with Francis Irwin and Kenneth Mackenzie, among the only three competent practical occultists he ever met. John Yarker, "The Society of the Rosy Cross," in *The Rosicrucian Brotherhood* (1907): 113ff. On the transmission of Hockley's scrying manuscripts after his death, see A. E. Waite, *The Occult Sciences: A Compendium of Transcendental Doctrine and Experiment, Embracing an Account of Magical Practices; of Secret Sciences in Connection with Magic; of the Professors of Magical Arts; and of Modern Spiritualism, Mesmerism and Theosophy* (London: Kegan Paul, Trench, Trübner & Co., 1891), 108.

16. The best summaries of her life are E. J. Dingwall's introduction to Emma Hardinge, *Modern American Spiritualism* (New York: University Books, 1970), and A. B Child's "History of Mediums. No. 5. Miss Emma Hardinge," *Banner of Light* 3, no. 18 (July 31, 1858): 7–8. For the best accounts of her early life, see Emma Hardinge, "Valedictory: Emma Hardinge's Farewell to her American Friends," *Banner of Light* 17, no. 17 (July 15, 1865): 4; "Emma Hardinge's Farewell To Her Friends in America: Part Second," ibid. 17, no. 18 (July 22, 1865): 8. See also James Robertson, *A Noble Pioneer, The Life Story of Mrs. Emma Hardinge Britten* (Manchester, n.d.).

17. See Britten, *Modern American Spiritualism*, 135ff, 250–51, in which she gives her contemporary accounts of her introduction to spiritualism ("disgust," "pious horror," "aghast at the absence of human agency," etc.). See also R. Laurence Moore, *In Search of White Crows*, 107, and the bio-bibliographical entry in *BCW*, 1:466–67.

18. In *Ravalette* (1863), 73, Randolph mentions the utter ignorance of a female medium's recent remarks on the Rosicrucians in a Boston spiritualist paper, a reference that is probably to Emma Hardinge Britten. See the notice in the *Banner of Light* 11, no. 9 (May 24, 1862): 4, on her lecture at the Lyceum on "The Rosicrucians."

19. *Autobiography of Emma Hardinge Britten* (Manchester and London: John Heywood, 1900), 3–4.

20. *The Western Star: A Magazine Devoted to a Record of the Facts, Philosophy, and History of the Communion Between Spirits and Mortals,* six numbers only, July–December 1872. *Ghost Land* began to appear in the July number.

21. *Ghost Land, or, Researches into the Mysteries of Occultism, Illustrated in a Series of Autobiographical Sketches, in Two Parts,* translated and edited by Emma Hardinge Britten (Boston: Editor, 1876). The citations are to the edition published by Progressive Thinker Publishing House in Chicago in 1897 and reprinted in 1970 by Health Research. Britten is listed as translator and editor. *Ghost Land* was continued by Britten in 1888 in her journal *The Two Worlds,* published at Manchester, without significantly adding to the original tale. The first part of *Ghost Land* was also published in Paris in 1903, with an introduction by Papus (Gérard Encausse), probably under the continuing impulse of the theories of the H. B. of L., as *Au pays des Esprits, ou roman veçu des Mystères de l'Occultisme* (Paris: Edition de l'Initiation, 1903).

22. E. J. Dingwall and others believed "Louis" was Baron de Palm; Madame Blavatsky and Colonel Olcott thought he was Emma Hardinge Britten herself; the editor of the *Spiritual Scientist* at one point opted for Prince Salm-Salm. See "Ghost Land," *Spiritual Scientist* 5, no. 14 (December 7, 1875): 145, 147. G. R. S. Mead, as A. E. Waite relates in his *Shadows of Life and Thought* (London: Selwyn & Blount, 1938), 70ff, believed Louis was Bulwer-Lytton, while Waite himself believed that Louis lived "only in the second-rate and typically feminine imagination of Emma Hardinge." The H. B. of L. and René Guénon believed in a real Louis. An old defacer of books in the New York Public Library scrawled in the library's copy of *Ghost Land* that Louis was Thomas Henry Burgoyne, the seer of the H. B. of L. The identification scarcely comports with the facts, but it probably reflects hints dropped by Burgoyne himself.

23. *Ghost Land,* 31.

24. Ibid., 45.

25. Ibid., 44.

26. Ibid., 45. The entire passage is quoted at length by W. T. Brown in an apparent attack on Madame Blavatsky's then-current views of the after-death state of the soul. See W. T. Brown, "The Mystic's Soul Flight. The Chevalier de B," *Religio-Philosophical Journal* 42, no. 2 (March 5, 1887): 6.

27. In *Ghost Land,* 65, Mr. Dudley is said to have brought a Russian "Schaman" to England. In *Art Magic* and in the original installments in *The Western Star* he is "Lord D——." There cannot have been many Englishmen who brought shamans to England in the first half of the nineteenth century, and future research should be able to identify him.

28. *Ghost Land,* 68.

29. Ibid., 67.

30. The rules of the Orphic Circle apparently prohibited the revelation of the names of living members. Emma Hardinge Britten later identified the fourth Earl Stanhope, who by then had died, as a member of the group. He was an associate of Hockley in his scrying endeavors and had been the patron of Baron Dupotet during his visits to England in the late 1820s. See below, and see generally Godwin, Chanel, and Deveney, *The Hermetic Brotherhood of Luxor*, introduction; Godwin, *The Theosophical Enlightenment*, chs. 8–11; *The Zoist* 12 (June 1855): 107–8 ; ibid. 10 (September 1852): 194.

31. *Ghost Land*, 68–69.

32. Ibid., 261–63.

33. Ibid., 287ff. Emma Hardinge Britten had begun to hint at the role of living men in the phenomena of spiritualism in 1860. See Emma Hardinge, "On Living Spirits and Dying Spiritualism," *Banner of Light* 7, no. 18 (July 28, 1860): 2.

34. *Art Magic; or, Mundane, Sub-Mundane and Super-Mundane Spiritism. A Treatise in Three Parts and Twenty-Three Sections: Descriptive of Art Magic, Spiritism, the Different Orders of Spirits in the Universe Known to be Related to, or in Communication with Man; Together with Directions for Invoking, Controlling, and Discharging Spirits, and the Uses and Abuses, Dangers and Possibilities of Magical Art* (New York: Author, 1876).

35. *Art Magic*, 18.

36. Ibid., 32, 433ff. (visions of Cahagnet's lucides); 439.

37. Ibid., 21, 69–70 (man before birth is a "germ spirit," a "rudimental angel").

38. Ibid., 28. This purports to be from an Indian text.

39. Ibid., 24–25 (Cahagnet's views). See also *Nineteenth Century Miracles*, 46–49 (introduction through M. Kardec's seers of the idea of reincarnation); 55ff. (English reaction); 302ff. (on reincarnation and the Theosophical Society). See chapters 5 and 12.

40. *Art Magic*, 28 (supra-mundane beings include souls of men who have become angels).

41. Ibid., 110, 319.

42. Ibid., 87ff. (elementaries); 90–91 (spiritualism incomplete and needs expanding); 83 (subordinate gods); 323ff. (progress of elementaries to perfect self-consciousness); 335–36 (spiritualism incomplete and it needs to be enlarged).

43. Ibid., 322–23. See also *Nineteenth Century Miracles*, 437ff. (story of publication of *Art Magic* and its attempt to change the emphasis of spiritual-

ism from simple communication with spirits of dead to communication with sub- and supra-mundane beings).

44. *Art Magic*, 137.

45. Ibid., 137, 153; 331–32 (human spirits produce most phenomena, but some are produced by use of elementaries); 450ff. (not only planetary spirits and elementaries, but also spirits of the dead, communicate with us).

46. Ibid., 102; 155 (progress and tradition); 158 (art magic); 353 (fire philosophers of Middle Ages teach that fire permeates matter).

47. Ibid., 160; 289ff. (methods of ancients).

48. Ibid., 119–20 (Rosicrucians and underlying fire); 148 (astral fluid in magic); 158 (magnetism); 166–67 (will and magnetism).

49. Ibid., 171; 174 (hashish, soma, napellus, opium); 183–84 (soma, hashish); 407 (hashish).

50. Ibid., 172; 233 (will).

51. Ibid., 190 (summoning of Pitris); 170 (crystals, stones); 358ff. (Agrippa, Abano); 414ff. (Cahagnet's method); 418ff. (Nostradamus's method for crystal seeing).

52. Ibid., 153.

53. Ibid., 185. Louis, in recounting the beliefs of the Indians, says that beyond all this are the "still higher realms of spiritual absorption, . . . the last stage of divine union with Deity, called 'Nirvana.'" Ibid., 183. The term is undefined, but if it is intended to carry a notion of final rest or absorption, it is out of character and stands in contrast to the repeated refrain of perpetual progress.

54. See also her letter to Victoria Woodhull's *Woodhull and Claflin's Weekly*, February 19, 1873.

55. See the introduction by E. J. Dingwall to the reprint of Emma Hardinge, *Modern American Spiritualism*, ix.

56. All of this is in *Modern American Spiritualism*, 362ff, in which she quotes from the *Age of Progress* for 1856.

57. The only surviving work of the Order is an anonymous forty-page pamphlet, *The Patriarchal Order, or True Brotherhood* (n.p., n.d., probably Cincinnati, 1855), probably by J. Shoebridge Williams, which lists Williams's complaints about being excluded from the order. It states that the group had been started by William H. Bayless. It may have been in connection with this order that Britain was put through "a course of exercises" by a "high priest" to develop her powers as a medium. Britten, "Valedictory. Emma Hardinge's Farewell to her American Friends," *Banner of Light* 17, no. 17 (July 15, 1865): 4. A

similar mysterious, revelatory stone (a "large cube of cream-white stone which was presented to the Order of the Z. Z., by a Mexican chief") underlay the work of the dentist John C. Street whose ideas became later became intertwined with Randolph's in the Rosicrucian foundations of R. Swinburne Clymer. See Street, *The Hidden Way Across the Threshold*, 3d ed. (London: G. Redway, 1889) and S. C. Gould's "Resumé of Arcane Fraternities in the United States," *Notes and Queries* (1896): 272, from which the quotation describing the stone is taken.

58. See E. J. Isaacs, *A History of Nineteenth Century American Spiritualism as a Religious and Social Movement* (Ann Arbor: University Microfilms, 1975), 120–21, 223–34, 387. Williams's papers are preserved in the State Historical Society of Wisconsin at Madison.

59. *The Christian Spiritualist*. Edited by J. H. Toohey and Horace Day. Published by the Society for the Diffusion of Spiritual Knowledge. New York. Weekly, May 13, 1854, to May 2, 1857. Randolph's letter was in the issue for March 3, 1855, reprinted in Baron Dupotet's *Journal du Magnétisme* 15 (1856): 43–44, under the caption "Le Spiritualisme en Amérique." "Spiritual Annexation," *The Telegraph Papers* 7 (1855): 80–84, describes the efforts of Randolph, Toohey, Uriah Clark, and others to found the society in Brooklyn. See also ibid. 9: 195–202. On the Society, see also Capron, *Modern Spiritualism*, 197–203, which gives the charter and original board members. Toohey later tried his hand at another spiritualistic journal and is last heard of in the Boston *Spiritual Scientist*—the journal that was soon to be taken up by Madame Blavatsky. J. H. W. Toohey, "The Need of Science in Spiritualism," *Spiritual Scientist* 1, no. 1 (September 10, 1874): 1–2.

60. See Britten, *Modern American Spiritualism*, 134–35. Emma Hardinge Britten stressed the mysterious work done in the circle, especially in the presidential election of 1856: "For long months prior to their public issue, *State documents and Congressional ordinances existed in the secret archives of an unconsidered spirit circle*. Many are the eyes that will glance over these pages, that have seen the wires of the national machinery pulled by invisible hands, and some few there are who *know* that a mightier Congress than that which sits at Washington has helped to lay the foundations of the New World's destiny in the spirit-circle rooms of 553 Broadway." Emma supplemented her income as a medium by starting "Miss Hardinge's Musical Academy" at 553 Broadway, letting it be known that she had learned music in Europe where "she held a professorship in a highly respectable institution." *Spiritual Telegraph* 5, no. 7 (June 14, 1856): 56.

61. *Ghost Land*, 180. The Undines and Sylphs, of course, are the mortal elementaries who, as set forth in *The Comte de Gabalis* and Charles Mackay's long poem *The Salamandrine*, seek immortality through sexual union with humans. The myth underlies Hans Christian Andersen's story of the Little Mermaid.

62. *Ghost Land*, 280. Emma Hardinge Britten is prominently cited as an exponent of such soulmates by J. M. Peebles, *Spirit Mates, Their Origin and*

Destiny. Sex-Life, Marriage, Divorce. Also a Symposium by Four Noted Writers. Spirit Mates—Their Pre-Existence, Earth Pilgrimages, Reunions in Spirit Life, ed. Robert Peebles Sudall (Battle Creek: Peebles' Publishing Co., 1909), 218. The citation given is to *Art Magic*, but the actual reference is to *Ghost Land*. Even in the 1850s she spoke to her audiences of woman, "the half of which must complete the angel; the dual principle which makes our God, our father and our mother." *The Place and Mission of Woman* (Boston: Hubbard W. Swett, 1859), quoted in Alex Owen, *The Darkened Room, Women, Power and Spiritualism in Late Victorian England* (Philadelphia: University of Pennsylvania Press, 1990), 13–14.

63. See *Art Magic*, 67ff, where Louis discourses on the reasons why the primal astral religion was overlaid with phallicism: "In taking on a material existence, therefore, and changing from a purely spiritual entity to become an organized material being, the first principle of earthly life to be evolved must needs be the means to produce and reproduce it. This, in an earthly state of being, is just as sacred and paramount a theme as the formation of worlds, and the birth of suns and systems in the aggregate of the Universe. As the function of creation is the highest and most wonderful with which the mind can invest Deity, so the imitative law must become the noblest and most sacred function of God's creatures. . . . Physical generation was once esteemed as the gate by which the Soul enters upon the stupendous pathway of progress, and became fitted for its angelic destiny in the celestial heavens. . . . The brief race on earth run, spiritual spheres of progress opening up fresh avenues of purification to the pilgrim Soul, still preserving all the faculties acquired by its birth and association with matter, the celestial Angel stands related to the germ spirit, as the fully unfolded blossom to the embryonic seed. In this order of progress it is clearly shown that the means whereby the spirit-dweller of the original Eden, becomes the perfected Angel of a celestial heaven, are: mortal birth, a pilgrimage through spheres of trial, discipline and purification, and an organism made up of separate parts with appropriate functions, the due and legitimate exercise of which constitute the methods of progress." Despite this, it is abundantly clear that Emma Hardinge Britten believed that the flesh hindered the spirit and that chastity was essential in the quest for practical occultism. See, e.g., *Ghost Land*, 365.

64. The reference to Jung-Stilling's brotherhood is in *The Life of John Henry Stilling* (Gettysburg:Press of the Theological Seminary, 1831): 305–6, a passage that was reprinted by Thomas Shorter, "T. S.," "Spiritualism in Biography—J. Heinrich Jung Stilling," *Spiritual Magazine* 3, no. 7 (July 1862): 289–309. On Randolph's use of Jung-Stilling's brotherhood, see below, chapter 6. On Emma Hardinge Britten's relationship with all of this, see David Board, "The Brotherhood of Luxor and the Brotherhood of Light," *Theosophical History* 2, no. 5 (January 1988): 149–57.

65. On this underworld, see the introduction by R. A. Gilbert and J. M. Hamill to K. R. H. Mackenzie's *The Royal Masonic Cyclopædia* (1877; reprint,

Wellingborough: Aquarian Press, 1987); Ellic Howe, "Fringe Masonry in England, 1870–85," *Ars Quatuor Coronatorum* 85 (1972): 242–95.

66. *Medium and Daybreak* (June 24, 1870). I am indebted to David Board for calling this to my attention.

67. Burke also edited *The Future. A Journal of Philosophical Research and Criticism* which began to appear from Trübner in April 1860. Randolph cites this among his authorities in *Pre-Adamite Man*. Even toward the end of his life Randolph continued to speak highly of Burke. See *Master Passion*, 80.

68. See Alex Owen, *The Darkened Room*, 49, 51–52, 67, 228; Britten, *Nineteenth Century Miracles*, 146, 150, 188ff. A long recitation of the personal spiritualistic experiences of Luxmoore appears in Benjamin Coleman, "Spiritualism in America," *Spiritual Magazine* 2, no. 9 (September 1861): 385ff. (Luxmoore is not named, but his name has been added in the margin of the copy in the New York Public Library, and the identification appears likely). His dabbling with mesmerism is mentioned in *The Zoist* 10 (September 1852): 213. In 1868 he was involved with D. D. Home and Randolph's old mentor John Murray Spear in organizing the London Spiritual Institute. "The Spiritualist Societies of London," *Banner of Light* 35, no. 7 (May 16, 1874): 2.

69. On the *Spiritual Magazine*, see Alex Owen, *The Darkened Room*, 23. Brevior's best known work was *The Two Worlds, the Natural and the Spiritual: Their Intimate Connexion and Relation Illustrated by Examples and Testimonies, Ancient and Modern* (London: F. Pitman, 1864). Emma Hardinge Britten in *Art Magic* and elsewhere calls this a very valuable work, but it is merely one more of the spiritualism-through-the-ages tomes of the period, though unusually competently written. She gave her later journal in Manchester the same name, *The Two Worlds*. For her estimation of Shorter, see *Nineteenth Century Miracles*, 150, 168, 172, 177, 188ff, 199, 464.

70. Emma Hardinge Britten, "The Rosicrucians," *Spiritual Magazine* 3, no. 7 (July 1862): 323–24.

71. "Letter of Dr. Ashburner to Mr. G. J. Holyoake," *The Yorkshire Spiritual Telegraph* 3, no. 11 (February 8, 1857): 150–52, 162–65.

72. E.g., John Ashburner, "Can Force Create Matter," *Spiritual Magazine* 1, no. 5 (May 1860): 223ff.; ibid. 1, no. 11 (November 1860): 486ff.

73. On Cooke, see, e.g., *Spiritual Magazine* 1, no. 9 (September 1860): 430–31; ibid. 1, no. 6 (June 1861): 336.

74. Mackenzie relates that his earliest supranormal experiences were of seeing a mysterious haze around flowers. "Spirituo-Magnetic Attraction," *Spiritual Magazine* 1, no. 4 (April 1860): 174 ff. He became convinced of the realities of spiritualism from reading Judge Edmonds's writings in 1853 and then was visited by the spirit of a deceased friend. See "Leaves from a Spirit

Diary, Leaf the First," *Spiritual Magazine* 1, no. 6 (June 1860): 281–85, which refers the reader for a description of the experience to Newton Crosland, *Apparitions: A New Theory*, 2d ed. (London: E. Wilson, 1856), 35. Mackenzie also presents the material he had learned (by spirit writing) from a spirit suspiciously named "S. J." This spirit had taught that the magic mirror was the highest mode of communication with the spirits—a doctrine that Mackenzie was not, at first, inclined to credit. See "A Retrospect of Spiritual Appearances and Manifestations," *Spiritual Magazine* 2, no. 6 (June 1861): 257–60. Mackenzie subsequently came around to the view that mirrors were the preferred means of communication, an opinion that he says he communicated to Allan Kardec on a visit to Paris—the same trip on which he paid the famous visit to Eliphas Lévi. "Spiritualism in Paris," *Spiritual Magazine* 3, no. 2 (February 1862): 94–95. Mackenzie's more traditional magical interests were noted by the journal in relating his search for a publisher for a seventeenth-century "journal of magical processes" he had unearthed at the British Museum. *Spiritual Magazine* 1, no. 5 (May 1860): 227ff. For Mackenzie's Brothers of Luxor and their long subsequent history in the myth of the hidden hand, see chapter 12.

75. For example, the *Spiritual Magazine* 1, no. 11 (November 1860): 519ff. gives a very sympathetic review of the wonders of hashish as described in Fitz Hugh Ludlow's anonymous *The Hashish Eater, being Passages from the Life of a Pythagorean* (London: Sampson Low, Son & Co.). See also *Spiritual Magazine* 1, no. 11 (November 1860): 506ff. (Jacob Dixon on drugs as a means of polarizing the vital forces); *Spiritual Magazine* 2, no. 4 (April 1861): 171 (Cahagnet and hashish). On mirrors, see Thomas Shorter, "Glimpses of Spiritualism in the East," *Spiritual Magazine* 2, no. 3 (March 1861): 107ff. (discussion of Lane's references to mirror magic in his *Modern Egyptians* and to same in the travel book of Dr. Wolff).

76. See Podmore, *Mediums of the Nineteenth Century*, 1:24, 28–30, 44; Britten, *Nineteenth Century Miracles*, 126, 150, 189; Janet Oppenheim, *The Other World*, 236. Dixon later submitted a letter on his experiences to aid the deliberations of the London Dialectical Society in the late 1860s.

77. See, e.g., Jacob Dixon, "Clairvoyance as a Means of Cure," *Spiritual Magazine* 1, no. 11 (November 1860): 506–19. The article has several turns of phrase that will later recur in Randolph's works, especially the description of the underlying form of material things as their "monadial or soul substance," which he also describes as "sympathial, aural, aromal, essential." In his *Eulis!* (1874), 19, Randolph mentions an article by Dr. Dixon on "The Organic Law of Sex." Dixon, in his relation of one experiment in sympathetic rapport, uses descriptions of the sensitivity of a "Mr. R." with a clairvoyante (possibly Mrs. Welton) which have a decidedly erotic overtone. See also Dixon's "The Experiences of a Medium," *Spiritual Magazine* 2, no. 8 (August 1863): 360–69, and his letters to the *Spiritual Magazine* 2, no. 4 (April 1861): 191–92, and ibid. 2, no. 12 (December 1861): 559. Dixon is also said to have edited a journal, *The Two Worlds*, devoted to homeopathy, spiritualism, and abstinence, but I have not located it.

78. Jacob Dixon, *Hygienic Clairvoyance* (London: W. Horsell, 1859), 13. Substantial parts of the book are reprinted in John Melville, *Crystal-Gazing and the Wonders of Clairvoyance, Embracing Practical Instructions in the Art, History, and Philosophy of the Ancient Science*, new and revised ed. (1897; London: Nichols & Co., 1910), 49–92.

79. See Jacob Dixon, "Clairvoyance as a Means of Cure," *Spiritual Magazine* 1, no. 11 (November 1860): 506–19 (references to Welton and to his wife, who is described as a clairvoyante on a par with Adolph Didier). Dixon's *Hygienic Clairvoyance* is largely given over to descriptions of "Mrs. Thomas W.'s" powers, and notes (24) her use of "frequent doses of opiates, extract of cannabis indica, &c." to stimulate them. See also Thomas Welton, *Mental Magic. A Rationale of Thought Reading, and its attendant Phenomena, and their application to the Discovery of New Medicines, Obscure Diseases, Correct Delineations of Character, Lost Persons and Property, Mines and Springs of Water, and All Hidden And Secret Things* (London: George Redway, 1884), 134. The book was edited by Robert H. Fryar.

80. See, e.g., *Spiritual Magazine* 1, no. 5 (May 1860): 228 (reprint of article from the *Yorkshire Spiritual Telegraph* on Welton's "planchette," recently introduced from France); ibid. 2, no. 2 (January 1861): 46–47 (letter from Sarah Welton).

81. He was a friend of another strange English visionary, William Oxley. Oxley, like Hockley, received secondhand voluminous angelic revelations (most notably from Oress, the mysterious angel whose portrait graced Britten's *Modern American Spiritualism*), though he appears merely curious now because he believed in the reality of the materialized impression of an angel's foot. See Britten, *Nineteenth Century Miracles*, 203ff. (which reproduces a picture of the foot). He lived in Manchester and was a close friend of Britten in her later years. Oxley at one point asked Welton's wife to try his crystal, which she did, though her prediction of Oxley's marriage was wrong (possibly, as Welton opined, because Oxley had magnetized the crystal himself and thus caused it to project his wishes). Oxley is also notable because he was part of the "Western" wing of occultism that, with the H. B. of L., strove to correct what was perceived as a shift by Madame Blavatsky from the true path of individual immortality and perpetual progress to the "Buddhist," impersonal view of the afterlife. See chapter 12 and the notes of H. P. Blavatsky to Oxley's "Hierosophy and Theosophy," *The Theosophist* 4 (July 1883), reprinted in *BCW*, 4:557–60. In the mid-1880s Oxley corresponded with the principles of the H. B. of L., though there is no evidence he actually joined. See *The Occult Magazine* 2 (February 1886): 12. Lest Oxley be dismissed too lightly as a simple eccentric, it should be noted that there are at least claims that he was the founder of a group (The Society of the White Cross) that is said to have taught the practical, sexual aspect of "eternal affinities." See Willy Schrödter, *A Rosicrucian Notebook. The Secret Sciences Used by Members of the Order* (New York: Weiser, 1992), 170–71. Schrödter's details of the Order are wrong—it began to appear in London in 1879—but he may be on to something. Oxley was certainly the

founder and guiding spirit of the Angelic Order of Light, a secret spiritualistic group devoted to angelic revelations, that flourished from the 1880s through the end of the century under various names. The history of the Angelic Order was presented by Lilian Storey and Leslie Price at the Origins of the Theosophical Society symposium in London in July 1995.

82. Welton was the author of various pamphlets ("Fascination"; "Jacob's Rod"; "The Planchette"), but his main work is *Mental Magic*. The reference to drugs is on page 11. Fryar edited this work after Welton's death and supplemented it with his own pamphlets on mirror magic, noting that the original manuscript of one of these works "was destroyed, with papers of Mrs. Emma Hardinge Britten in the great Boston fire of 1872." *Mental Magic*, 5. Fryar also added to the work a summary, without attribution, of Randolph's rules on mirrors from *Seership!* (1870). Fryar said that he had written his first work on mirror magic in the early 1860s, and that in 1886 he had begun importing "Bhattah" mirrors. R. H. Fryar, "Crystal Gazing," *The Rosicrucian Brotherhood* 1, no. 4 (October 1907): 145ff. The article, which appeared originally in *The Spiritual Review* in 1891, is attributed to John Yarker, but the error is corrected later (169). The same piece is published in S. C. Gould's *Historic Magazine and Notes and Queries* 25, no. 10 (October 1907): 241–43. Fryar had been familiar with Bhattah mirrors since at least 1878. See his anonymous "Visions in Mirrors and Crystals," *Religio-Philosophical Journal* 25, no. 1 (September 7, 1878): 6. Welton's references to Bielfield are in *Mental Magic*, 61–64. Apparently Bielfield, through the planchette, received messages from the recently deceased Robert Owen and conveyed them to Owen's son Robert Dale Owen. The date of the communications was thus 1858 or shortly thereafter. Randolph's opinion of Belfedt as a Rosicrucian is in *Ravalette*, 58.

83. *Mental Magic*, 65, 175. The connection with Spear is probably more than purely accidental. The *Spiritual Magazine* frequently carried the contributions of "M. N." (Mary Nichols), the wife of T. L. Nichols. Both, in their American days, were ardent advocates of free love and proponents of the "Spermatic Economy," and T. L. Nichols was later the biographer of the Rev. J. B. Ferguson, a leading proponent of Spear's ideas who also appears in various roles in Randolph's later career.

84. The nineteenth-century bibliographer Allibone is wrong in asserting that Randolph was a frequent contributor to the *Spiritual Magazine*. Allibone, *A Critical Dictionary*, 2:1738.

85. See, for example, "The Blending State," *Spiritual Magazine* 3, no. 6 (June 1862): 278ff. (Randolph was a "Christian Spiritualist of a high order); ibid. 2, no. 3 (March 1861): 138 (William Howitt's reply to a Swedenborgian purist who had thrown up Randolph as an argument against spiritualism: "I do not pin my faith entirely on Dr. Randolph. Many think him a good medium, and he may be so, but he was an eccentric and a fanatic, just as Catholicism and Swedenborgianism, and every other ism has had its eccentricities and fanatics. . . . He says he was driven to desperation, and even to attempt

his life—by what? By neglecting the Scripture rule of 'trying the spirits.' He made a recantation, but of what? Of scientific Spiritualism only, not of religious Spiritualism. He declared over and over in public meetings that he never had renounced '*true* Spiritualism, which, he said, was the very essence of Christianity; it was only the false, the fanaticism, the machine—mediumship he had renounced.' He is a firm Spiritualist, and, say they who know him, a good teacher, constantly acknowledging the cause of his aberration—his neglect to try the spirits. He says in his letters—'Spiritualism is grown to be a first-rate power in the world, and its facts will remain facts, stubborn as iron in spite of all gainsayers.'").

86. *Ravalette*, 68–72.

87. *Guide to Clairvoyance*, 13–14. See also *Seership!* 8.

88. "The Converted Medium," *New York Daily Tribune*, November 25, 1858, 3 ("I am personally acquainted with 341 professed medical clairvoyants, and of these there are 7 actual seers who will stand a testing. One of these is in Paris—Alexis Didier; his brother Adolph, of London; Hussain Khan, a Turk; a child; a girl in London; one in Florence, Italy, and one in America."). See also *Ravalette*, 58–59. Alexis Didier was a contemporary of Randolph. On his powers, see the various references to him in *The Zoist* and also Podmore, *From Mesmer to Christian Science*, 145, 168, 172–84. Professors Bergevin and Toutain, for whom Randolph sat in New York City, thought that Randolph was superior to Alexis as a seer. "Clairvoyance and Psychometry," *The Telegraph Papers* 6 (1855): 54.

89. "The Converted Medium," *New York Daily Tribune*, November 25, 1858, 3. The reference to Ferdinand may relate to Randolph's visit to Spain on this or a subsequent trip. In a letter quoted in the *Religio-Philosophical Journal*, August 14, 1875, Randolph mentions being in Spain (where he says he was almost murdered) in 1859. As for the king of Delhi (whoever that may be) unless Randolph met him in Europe the reference is rhetorical since he never visited India, despite his references in the introductory pages of the *Ghostly Land* (1874) to travels there.

90. The state of French spiritualism at the time may be discerned in the frantic letters of Victor Hennequin, a former representative of the National Assembly, in which he revealed that "The Spirit of the Earth" had whispered in his ear that he was to write a book entitled "Let us Save the Human Race." "Spiritualism in France," *The Telegraph Papers* 2 (1853): 426–28. An early French journal, *La Table Parlante, Journal des Faits Marveilleux*, avidly featured articles on American spiritualism. See, e.g., "Des Manifestations spirituelles des Etats-Unis d'Amérique," 1 (1854): 78-87; "Petition des Quinze Mille Citoyens des Etats-Unis au Congrès," 1 (1854): 212–15. Similarly, *La Revue Spiritualiste* from 1858 through the early 1860s regularly carried a review on "Le Spiritualisme dans Les Etats Unis," and the year after Randolph's first visit to France, Baron Dupotet's *Journal du Magnétisme*, featured articles on "Le Spiritualisme en

Amérique" which described the wonders of the new movement and excerpted the American journals, even including a letter that Randolph had written to the *Christian Spiritualist*. See, e.g., *Journal du Magnétisme* 15 (1856): 43–44, 364–76. Randolph's letter is in ibid. 15 (1856): 43–44 I am indebted to Joscelyn Godwin for bringing this letter to my attention.

91. On the early days of mesmerism in America, see Robert C. Fuller, *Mesmerism and the American Cure of Souls* (Philadelphia: University of Pennsylvania Press, 1982), especially 32ff. on the sexual overtones of mesmerism. Andrew Jackson Davis's powers had originally been revealed under the influence of mesmerism.

92. The "scientific" and medical side of Mesmer's work can easily be exaggerated. Frank Podmore and others have shown the roots of Mesmer's system in the generally accepted theory of the "sympathies" that pervade the universe, and these, of course, are the foundation of much of western hermetic and magical thought. As compared with his later disciples, however, Mesmer was "scientific." On mesmerism generally, see Podmore, *From Mesmer to Christian Science*, especially chapter 2, 26ff. See also James Webb, *The Occult Underground*, 23ff.; Robert Darnton, *Mesmerism and the End of the Enlightenment in France* (New York: Schocken, 1970); Fred Kaplen, *Dickens and Mesmerism: The Hidden Springs of Fiction* (Princeton: Princeton University Press, 1975).

93. *Ravalette*, 58–59. Randolph says that this seance occurred before spiritualism had crossed the Atlantic, at the time D. D. Home was living in London. Home left the United States on March 31, 1855, for London and was in Paris by June. See D[aniel] D[unglas] Home, *Incidents in My Life* (London: Longman, Green, Longman, Roberts & Green, 1863), 62, 126. Napoleon had been interested in spiritualism and its antecedents since the 1830s. See the London *Spiritual Magazine* 2, no. 8 (August 1861): 353.

94. E. Lévi, *The History of Magic, Including a Clear and Precise Exposition of its Procedure, its Rites and its Mysteries*, A. E. Waite trans. (New York: Weiser, 1973), 119, 339ff. See J. Dupotet, *La Magie Dévoilée, ou Principes de Science Occulte*, 304. This was circulated privately in the 1850s and then published with a lock on its pages. See W. Q. Judge, "Mesmerism," *Lucifer* 10 (May 1892): 197–205. Citations are to the edition by Editions Pygmalion, Paris, 1977. Details of Dupotet's life are given in his autobiographical sketch printed as an introduction to this edition. In his later years he was made an honorary member of the Theosophical Society along with Cahagnet, but Madame Blavatsky's familiarity with both of them appears to have been based solely on their works. See *BCW*, 3:30–34 (honorary members). Madame Blavatsky praised Cahagnet as a "modern Boehme" and repeatedly referred with praise to Dupotet in her *Isis Unveiled*.

95. See, e.g., *La Magie Dévoilée*, 124ff., 253, 298.

96. Dupotet dedicated to Lord Stanhope *An Introduction to the Study of Animal Magnetism* (London: Saunders & Otley, 1828).

97. See E. Lévi, *The History of Magic*, 69, 339ff. The book in which these secret teachings were contained was *La Magie Dévoilée, ou Principes de Science Occulte*.

98. *La Magie Dévoilée*, 170ff. Randolph's views closely parallel this: "It is the same *light* so often spoken of in ancient books and modern experiences. It is the *light* revealed to Pimander, Zoroaster, and the sages of the East. It is Boehmen's Divine Vision or Contemplation; Molinos['s] Spiritual Guide, and the inner life of all true men—few, and women—many. It is the Foundation-Fire upon which all things whatever are builded." *Seership!* 60. This light or fire underlying the universe is, for Randolph, the AEth.

99. *La Magie Dévoilée*, 182. Lévi's views are clear in his comment on Dupotet's magic mirrors in his *History of Magic*, 340: "M. Dupotet establishes triumphantly the existence of that universal light wherein lucids perceive all images and all reflections of thought. He assists the vital projection of this light by means of an absorbent apparatus which he calls the magic mirror; it is simply a circle or square covered with powdered charcoal, finely sifted. In this negative space the combined light projected by the magnetic subject and the operator soon tinges and realises the forms corresponding to their nervous impressions. The somnambulist sees manifested therein all dreams of opium and hasheesh, and if he were not distracted from the spectacle convulsions would follow."

100. *La Magie Dévoilée*, 271ff. (spirits); 128, 279ff. (dead).

101. Ibid., 246.

102. Ibid., 253.

103. Ibid., 149. In R. H. Fryar's edition of *Magnetic Magic, A Digest of the Practical Parts of the Masterpieces of L. A. Cahagnet, H.F.T.S., "Arcanes de la future dévoilés," and "Magie Magnétique." Now translated for the first time from the French by the Editor, with the portrait of the Author* (n.p., Privately Printed for Subscribers, 1898), he announced his intention of issuing as *Magic Unveiled* the substance of the "instructions of Baron Dupotet privately imparted to his pupils," but the work was never published.

104. On Dupotet's belief in overwhelming a person by a current of magnetic fluid, see Lévi, *History of Magic*, 69.

105. *La Magie Dévoilée*, 245, 275.

106. See William Howitt's biographical sketch, published in the *Spiritual Magazine*, 3, 1868.

107. On Cahagnet, see Podmore, *From Mesmer to Christian Science*, 191, 200–4. Cahagnet's *Arcanes de la vie future*, 3 vols. (1848–54) was in part published in English as *The Celestial Telegraph; or, Secrets of the Life to Come Revealed Through magnetism: Wherein the Existence, the Form, the Occupations, of the Soul*

after its Separation from the Body are Proved by Many Years' Experiments, by the Means of Eight Ecstatic Somnambulists, who had Eighty Perceptions of Thirty-Six Deceased Persons of Various Conditions. A Description of Them, their Conversations, etc., with Proofs of their Existence in the Spiritual World (1850; reprint, New York: Arno, 1976). Cahagnet's occasional pieces and some of his correspondence were collected by him in his *Magnétisme: Encyclopédie Magnétique Spiritualiste Traitant Spécialement des Faits Psychologiques, Magie Magnétique, Swedenborgianisme, Nécromancie, Magie Céleste, etc.,* 7 vols. (Paris: Author and Germer Ballière, 1854/55–1862).

108. On Cahagnet's views on eternal affinities, see J. M. Peebles, *Spirit Mates,* 237ff.

109. See Britten, *Nineteenth Century Miracles,* 46ff. (Allan Kardec invented reincarnation; about 1848 Cahagnet received the idea of pre-existence of souls, but denied reincarnation).

110. *Celestial Telegraph,* 180 (neither DeLaborde, Dupotet, Cagliostro, nor the sorcerer Léon—an eighteenth-century Jew whose mirror Cahagnet describes—actually saw visions themselves). On the count de Laborde, see Northcote Thomas, *Crystal Gazing,* 113ff. On Cagliostro's supposed (but improbable) scrying, see M. Schele de Vere, *Modern Magic* (New York: Putnam, 1873).

111. *Guide to Clairvoyance,* 36. Randolph also speaks of the use of hashish by the "famed Madame Dablis, the gifted Seeress of the Rue St. Nicholas, Paris"—a further indication of the universality of the drug's use. For Cahagnet's experiments with hashish, see his *Sanctuaire du Spiritualisme* (Paris, 1850), cited in R. H. Fryar, ed., *Magnetic Magic,* 45.

112. *Guide to Clairvoyance,* 36; *Love and its Hidden History* (1869), 167–78; *Seership!* 29.

113. See *Magnetic Magic,* 17, 24, 42, which reprints the highlights of Cahagnet's *Magie Magnétique,* 2d ed. (Paris, 1858).

114. *Celestial Telegraph,* 178ff. Emma Hardinge Britten later translated these instructions and included them in *Art Magic,* and Robert H. Fryar added them to *Magnetic Magic* (16). On Cahagnet's use of the magic mirror, see also his "Miroir Magique," *Magnétisme: Encyclopédie Magnétique Spiritualiste,* 1: 296–99, and "Miroirs Magiques," ibid., 2: 157–60.

115. Thomas Welton's *Mental Magic* has as an appendix a translation of Cahagnet's "An Historical and Practical Treatise on Fascination." See also R. H. Fryar's edition of *Magnetic Magic,* 17–18. Fryar also announced his intention to translate and publish all of Cahagnet's works, with an introduction by George Wyld, M.D., an old mesmerist, advocate of drugs as aids in spiritual progress, and spiritualist and founding member of the British Theosophical Society, but apparently only volume 1 was published. See S. C. Gould's *American Notes and Queries* 2 (December 1885): 676.

116. R. S. Clymer, for example. See chapter 6. On Lévi generally, see Paul Chacornac, *Eliphas Lévi, Rénovateur de l'occultisme* (Paris: Chacornac, 1926); René Guénon, *Le Théosophisme, Histoire d'une Pseudo-Religion*, augmented ed. (Paris: Ed. Traditionnelles, 1969), 152, 299; A. E. Waite, *Mysteries of Magic* (London, 1897), 8; Christopher McIntosh, *Eliphas Lévi and the French Occult Revival* (London: Rider, 1972); Alain Mercier, *Eliphas Lévi et la pensée magique au XIXe siècle* (Paris: Seghers, 1974). Mercier, 161–62, relates the myth of Randolph and Lévi.

117. These were translated into English by A. E. Waite, *Transcendental Magic: Its Doctrine and Ritual* (Chicago: Occult Publishing House, 1910).

118. Including Baron Spedalieri, who later joined the Theosophical Society and the H. B. of L., and Marie Gebhard, whose son Arthur toyed with joining the H. B. of L.

119. Randolph in his *Seership!* 1, first published in 1870, in fact refers to astral light, but in a way directly contradictory to Lévi's use of the term. He speaks of three sorts of light visible to the physical eye (solar, planetary, and astral) and distinguishes all of these from the ether, "one vast billowy sea of magnetic light," which is the medium for inner sight. Randolph never mentions the tarot, and his references to the kabbalah are perfunctory, as for example his reference to the "Cabalistic Light" in *Ravalette*, 57. It is tempting to try to trace cognates of Randolph's ideas (especially those on light and the mysteries of human generation) to sources in the true kabbalah and its Christian offshoots in the seventeenth and eighteenth centuries, and indeed similarities exist, but there is no indication whatever of historical dependency, even literary, and the similarities are more easily and directly explainable by reference to Randolph's own visionary experiences and the koiné of nineteenth-century spiritualism and occultism.

120. This is leaving aside the issue of the existence of a sexual side to Lévi's magic. A tortured case could be made—as it could be made for anyone beholden to the alchemical tradition and to the magnetists' emphasis on the polarity of all manifestation—that there is a practical sexual element concealed in Lévi's work. But if it is there, it is minor and carefully concealed.

121. The transformation is complete by the time of his *History of Magic* (1860).

122. Podmore, *From Mesmer to Christian Science*, 199, mentions the existence of several secret societies of "illuminati and Theosophs" in France in the 1820s who used the trance to heal and to hold intercourse with the world of spirits (relying on Deleuze).

123. Lévi, *The History of Magic*, 344–45. Delaage (1825–1882) is also one of the supposed links between the Martinists of the eighteenth and early nineteenth centuries and their revival at century's end by Papus. Cahagnet describes Delaage as editor of *Almanach de la Science du Diable*. See also A. E.

Waite, *Mysteries of Magic*, 8. Delaage's beauty book is *Perfectionnement physique de la Race Humaine* (Paris, 1850).

124. Lévi, *The History of Magic*, 344. Lévi adds that D'Ourches was preoccupied with being buried alive—a not uncommon fear at the time.

125. The count is named, along with "Alphonse" Didier and Dupotet in a list of French spiritualists in an American spiritualist annual, *The Progressive Annual for 1863; Comprising an Almanac, a Spiritual Register and a General Calendar of Reform* (New York: Andrew Jackson Davis and Co., 1863). Güldenstubbé, together with Alexandre Dumas, *père*, Victorien Sardou, and others became part of Kardec's circle in 1850. See Karl Kieswetter, *Geschichte des Neuren Occultismus*, 2 vols. (1891–95; New York: Arno 1976), 1:470ff. In the late 1850s, in an attempt to identify precisely the spirits with which he was communicating, he hit upon the notion of leaving his card and a writing tablet near the statues in the Louvre and Hall of Antiquities. Most of the persons so represented, he claimed, obligingly wrote messages for him. See John Michell, *Eccentric Lives and Peculiar Notions* (London: Thames and Hudson, 1984), 75–77; Britten, *Nineteenth Century Miracles*, 59–60. Some details of his life are given in "Obituary," *Spiritual Magazine*, n.s., 8 (1873): 329–32.

126. *The Asiatic Mystery, The Fire Faith! The Religion of Flame! The Force of Love! The Energos of Will! The Magic of Polar Mentality! First Rosicrucian Manifesto to the World Outside the Order*, 1871, reprinted in *The Initiates*, 3, no. 3 (1930–31), and, in part, in *Soul!* 276–89.

127. *Spiritual Scientist* 3, no. 25 (November 25, 1875): 133ff., reprinted in BCW, 1:151–59.

128. The editor of Madame Blavatsky's *Collected Works* (BCW, 1:162) notes the curious fact that Peter Davidson, provincial grand master of the North of the H. B. of L., used almost the exact phrase in commenting on his transcription of an "Old Tale about the Mysterious Brothers" in *The Theosophist* for 1882. Peter Davidson, "The Mysterious Brothers—An Old Tale Retold," *The Theosophist* 3, no. 5 (February 1882): 120–21, and 3, no. 6 (March 1882): 153–54.

129. In his announcements of lectures on his return, he proposed to speak only on his experiences in those countries. See his advertisement, *The New England Spiritualist* 1, no. 38 (December 22, 1855).

130. "Robert Owen's Movements in England," *The New England Spiritualist* 1, no. 33 (November 17, 1855).

131. "Mr. Randolph in England," *The New England Spiritualist* 1, no. 35 (December 1, 1855). Randolph in his later years finally judged Owen as a man who had left the world a better place than he had found it. *Casca Llanna*, 59.

132. "Mr. Randolph's Lectures," *The New England Spiritualist* 1, no. 37 (December 15, 1855).

133. Advertisement, *The New England Spiritualist* 1, no. 37 (December 15, 1855); "Mr. Randolph's Lectures," ibid.

134. "Mr. Randolph's First Lectures," *The New England Spiritualist* 1, no. 38 (December 22, 1855); "Mr. Randolph's Lectures," *The New England Spiritualist* 1, no. 39 (December 29, 1855).

135. Advertisement, *New England Spiritualist* 1, no. 41 (January 12, 1856). See also Randolph's advertisement, *The Spiritual Telegraph* (January 12, 1856), and the journal's notice of the "Meeting at Chapman Hall Last Sunday," *The Spiritual Telegraph* (January 12, 1856).

136. Advertisement, *New England Spiritualist* (January 12, 1856).

137. *Yorkshire Spiritual Telegraph and British Harmonial Advocate* 2, no. 17 (August 1856): 208–9, which reprints a notice on Randolph from the Cleveland *Spiritual Universe* for May 31, 1856. The *Yorkshire Spiritual Telegraph* was a (largely) working-class and Owenite spiritualist paper which began publication at Keighley in April 1855. In 1857 it became the *British Spiritual Telegraph*, in which guise it lasted until 1859. On the origins of this aspect of British spiritualism, see Britten, *Nineteenth Century Miracles*, 198, who says the seed for it had been planted by an American Shaker in 1853. This was David Richmond, an Englishman who returned to England after a stay with the Shakers.

138. "An American Medium," *The Yorkshire Spiritual Telegraph*, 3 (January 1857): 125.

139. "Spirit-Power Circle, Charing Cross, London," *The Yorkshire Spiritual Telegraph* 3, no. 10 (January 31, 1857): 131–33. Humphry Davy, of course, was the first to experiment with nitrous oxide, which had its own role to play in the occultism of the later nineteenth century.

140. P. B. Randolph, "Introductory Trance Address by a Spirit Designating Himself 'The Stranger' through Mr. Randolph, an American Medium," *The Yorkshire Spiritual Telegraph* 4, no. 3 (March 1857): 31–32.

141. "The Last Leaf from our Journal," *The Yorkshire Spiritual Telegraph* 3, no. 11 (February 8, 1857): 148-50.

142. Letter, *The Yorkshire Spiritual Telegraph* 3, no. 12 (February 15, 1857): 166–67. The spiritualistic press after Randolph's death touted his ability to speak Greek ("acceptable to Greeks") when in trance. "Paschal Beverly Randolph," *Banner of Light* 37, no. 22 (August 28, 1875): 4.

143. *Curious Life*, 32 ff., prints several undated clippings from the *Times*, *London Weekly Times* and *Lloyd's News* on his lectures. The *Times* described him as "steeped to the lips in magic thought."

144. Britten, *Nineteenth Century Miracles*, 174 (he "failed to reconcile his hearers to his marked eccentricities."). In expatiating on the invasion of American spiritualists in the 1850s, William Howitt merely mentions Randolph as a "trance medium." See William Howitt, *The History of the Supernatural in All Ages and Nations, and in All Churches, Christian and Pagan: Demonstrating a Universal Faith*, 2 vols. (London: Longman, Green, Longman, Roberts & Green, 1863), 2:215–16. The *Telegraph* prints a confused letter in defense of an unnamed "Good Dr." whose withdrawal from a certain spiritual circle had caused bitter comment. This must have been Randolph. "Letter," *The Yorkshire Spiritual Telegraph* 3, no. 11 (February 8, 1857): 153–54.

145. P. B. Randolph, letter, *The Yorkshire Spiritual Telegraph* 3, no. 12 (February 15, 1857): 166–67. The editors of the London *Spiritual Magazine* recalled Randolph during his visit in 1857 as a powerful though eccentric and fanatical medium. *Spiritual Magazine* 2, no. 3 (March 1861): 138 (William Howitt). See also "The Blending State," *Spiritual Magazine*. 3, no. 5 (May 1862): 278ff.

146. See chapter 4 on the accounts of the "officious colored trickster" given in *The Liberator*.

147. "Letter from New York," *Banner of Light* 3, no. 3 (April 17, 1858): 5.

148. *Curious Life*, 73–74. See also *The Grand Secret*, 8, published before his trip to the Near East in 1861–62, in which he refers to the castratos of Cairo and Stamboul. Randolph's claim that he had been known as a Rosicrucian since 1852, however, appears to be an anachronism. As we shall see, the designation first appears at about the time of this second trip and probably was adopted as a result of Randolph's involvement with what he called "the most secret, mystical societies of England and France."

149. The sequence of travels may distinguish the trips. On his 1861–62 trip to gather information for *Pre-Adamite Man*, he says (*Curious Life*, 8) that he visited successively England, Scotland, Ireland, France, Malta, Egypt, Arabia, Syria, Palestine, Turkey, and Greece. Dongola was above Karnac on the Nile (see *Pre-Adamite Man*, 67) and Ethiopia was thought to begin at the second cataract, at Wadi Halfa. See the introduction to *Egypt and the Holy Land in Historic Photograph: 77 Views by Francis Frith*, Introduction by Julia Van Haaften, commentary by Jon E. Manchip White (New York: Dover, 1980). Frith was in Egypt and the Holy Land precisely when Randolph was there in the late 1850s, and his photographs show the antiquities of Egypt as Randolph must have seen them.

150. See chapter 3. On Madame Blavatsky and hashish, see chapter 13.

151. For a contemporary view on the various dervish orders of the Near East (especially Constantinople) which Randolph must have encountered, see John P. Brown, *The Darvishes or Oriental Spiritualism* (1868; Birmingham: Frank Cass & Co. Ltd., 1968). See also chapters 6 and 10.

Chapter 3

1. See "Letter from New York," *Banner of Light* 3, no. 3 (April 17, 1858): 5; *Seership!* 70.

2. Advertisement in *Unveiling* (1860), 71.

3. *The Guide to Clairvoyance, and Clairvoyant's Guide: A Practical Manual for those who aim at Perfect Clear Seeing and Psychometry; also, A Special Paper concerning Hashish, its Uses, Abuses, and Dangers, its Extasia, Fantasia, and illuminati. Printed for People of Common Sense Only* (Boston: Rockwell & Rollins, Printers, 1867). I am grateful to Joscelyn Godwin for unearthing a copy of this work.

4. For the extraordinarily tangled publishing history of these works, see appendix C.

5. *Unveiling*, 41.

6. See Jacques-Joseph Moreau, *Hashish and Mental Illness* (New York: Raven Press, 1973) and the bibliography appended to the introduction.

7. Dr. A. B. Child, a dentist with whom Randolph was to carry on a pamphlet war over "It Isn't all Right," first publicly touted the effects of hashish to the American spiritualist world. See his article, "Hashish," The *Banner of Light*, 4, no. 6 (January 22, 1859): 3: "[H]ashish, of all known substances, is perhaps the most powerful acting upon the human organism, to open the spiritual perception, and carry it beyond the ordinary boundaries of this life, into the world of spirits, the world of intense horrors or intense delights, to behold light, beauty and immensity yet unmeasured by the most active and powerful conceptions of man." See also Moore, *In Search of White Crows*, 281. The London *Spiritual Magazine* 1, no. 11 (November 1860): 519ff, favorably reviewed Ludlow's *The Hashish Eater* and urged spiritualists to experiment with the drug. See also ibid. 2, no. 4 (April 1861): 171, which comments favorably on Cahagnet's remarks on hashish. The use of drugs for mind-altering purposes was widely discussed at the time. See Benjamin Paul Blood, *Pluriverse, an Essay in the Philosophy of Pluralism* (Boston: Marshall Jones & Co., 1920), which reprints his *The Anaesthetic Revolution*, originally published in 1874, and Fitz Hugh Ludlow, *The Hasheesh Eater, Being Passages from the Life of a Pythagorean* (1857; reprint, San Francisco: City Lights, 1979). Blood is probably the man of the same name, described by Randolph as "a real thinker," mentioned in *Ravalette*, 104. Randolph certainly knew Blood and introduced him at one of the weekly Boston Spiritual Conferences. See "Boston Spiritual Conference," *Banner of Light* 8, no. 11 (December 9, 1860): 8. On Blood (1832–1919), see Franklin Rosemont's introduction to *The Poetical Alphabet* (Chicago: Black Swan Press, 1978).

8. See, e.g., Numa Pandorac [pseud.], "Testament d'un Haschischéen," *L'Initiation* 1, vol. 2 (1889): 59–70, which calls the drug "*Dawas Meck*," a term

also used by Moreau de Tours. On the actual preparation of the drug in the Near East, see Peter Lamborn Wilson, *Scandal: Essays in Islamic Heresy* (Brooklyn: Autonomedia, Inc., 1988), 195–213.

9. *Love and its Hidden History* (1869), 167–68. See also *After Death*, 140, 143; *Unveiling*, 57–58; *Guide to Clairvoyance*, part 2. The reference to Fitz Hugh Ludlow is an anachronism, since his book was not published until 1857.

10. *Guide to Clairvoyance*, part 2.

11. *Unveiling*, 55.

12. *After Death*, 141.

13. *Guide to Clairvoyance*, 47–48.

14. See "Boston Spiritual Conference," *Banner of Light* 8, no. 7 (November 10, 1860): 5 (hashish "produces an ecstacy, and mental and spiritual illumination, whose unutterable glory, supernal grandeur and awful sublimity, transcend my powers of description."); ibid. 8, no. 13 (December 22, 1860): 8 ("Five times—perhaps six—in my life, and that within a period of twelve years [since 1848], I have experimented with Hashish upon myself, in order to reach through the gloom toward the light." "I gained more light in any two of the experiments than from all the 'spiritual' experiences of my entire life— real, positive, genuine, unutterable light—nor has my soul ever parted with one jot of that light to this day."). See also Randolph, "Rosicrucian Papers, no. 5," *Religio-Philosophical Journal* 5, no. 20 (February 6, 1869): 3 ("I never took an eighth of an ounce [of hashish] in my life."). Randolph claimed that in six hundred cases of administering the drug to his medical patients he had experienced no problems. The *Banner of Light*, which sponsored the Boston Spiritual Conferences, was not so positive about the use of hashish and warned that artificial experiences were unnatural and led to delusions. See "A Word on Stimulants," *Banner of Light* 8, no. 14 (December 29, 1860): 4; Hudson Tuttle, "Hashish," ibid. 10, no. 19 (February 1, 1862): 3.

15. Advertisement, "Hashish," *Banner of Light* 8, no. 2 (October 6, 1860): 4.

16. Compare for example *Rosicrucian's Story*, 74 (1876 edition) and 58 (1863 edition): "They say there are no miracles! What, then, is this? What are these strange experiences of soul which we are constantly having—fifty years compressed in an hour of ordinary Dream! —thirty thousand ages in a moment of time under the accursed spells of Hashish [1876: "Fantasie"]. . . . The soul flying back over unnumbered centuries; scanning the totality of the Present . . . and all in an instant of the clock, while under the influence of the still more accursed Muust."

17. *Dealings with the Dead*, 117; *After Death*, 140 n. ("two experiments with which . . . the author made in 1856, but which he would not repeat for all the wealth a dozen worlds could afford ten thousand times over."); ibid., 54 (on the after–death punishments of "topers, hasheesh and opium eaters and

tobacco-users"). See also *Guide to Clairvoyance*, 38–39, 47: "Where a person takes hashish for any purpose, let that purpose be clearly, firmly, solidly fixed in the mind from the moment the drug is taken till its effect is over. For instance, if it is to become clairvoyant, let *that* and *no other object* be sought for. . . . [A]nd there are few problems that cannot be solved under hashish. . . . Persons may take a very little of it once or twice to render them susceptible to magnetic or spiritual influences; for while under it nearly any one can be mesmerized, or made a medium. But having become so, abandon its use forever." "Hashish eating is not commendable, any more than rum-drinking or opium smoking. And I here repeat: Do not get habituated to hashish, or dowameskh, or ether, or chloroform, or must, or anything of the sort. If you reach your end and aim through their means, your continual use of them will cause its loss again." In *Ravalette*, 154, the Rosicrucian lists a variety of drugs, including hashish, and concludes that "not one of them is adequate to the office of enabling a clear, strong mind to move within the sphere of the Hidden, but the Real."

18. *Guide to Clairvoyance*, part. 2.

19. Ibid.

20. Ibid., 34.

21. *Guide to Clairvoyance*, part 2. See also *After Death*, 145 (rapturous, drug-like descriptions of touch, music, smell in higher divisions of earth's auroral zones).

22. He may have been put off public endorsement of hashish because of the charges of insanity from its use that were leveled at him in the Anti-Slavery Convention of 1860. See "New England Anti-Slavery Convention," *The Liberator* 30, no. 23 (June 8, 1860): 190, and *Unveiling*, 41. Additionally, there was a persistent rumor, discussed in chapter 11, that Walter Moseley, an occult bibliophile who was supposed to have been one of Randolph's English disciples, later went insane from hashish use, and he may not have been the only one. Prudence may thus have contributed to Randolph's public stance.

23. *Guide to Clairvoyance*, part 2. Randolph specified that these pure preparations could be used either as a dreamy sexual stimulant (suitable for harems), which Randolph forebears describing, or to produce an exhilaration of soul, transcending anything else on earth and leading to clairvoyance. He himself, he says, would take hashish again except that he already had all the power he needed in that line. Randolph thought that the term *hashish* itself in the Near East was really a generic term for the basest form of the drug, like "rotgut" whiskey, and that the three highest forms were "affiyooni," "dabreeb," and "dowam meskh," the last of which led "the soul to glory ineffable and imparts a rapture and bliss not to be measured by mortal standards." See "Boston Spiritual Conference," *Banner of Light* 8, no. 7 (November 10, 1860): 5. In *Unveiling*, 61ff, he bragged that he alone in the United States knew the

"Egyptian formula for extracting Indian Hemp" and offered to sell his recipes for one dollar and three red stamps.

24. In the appendix to *Unveiling* (1860), Randolph gives his "Medical Formulas," written with his wife, Mary Jane, an "Indian Doctress," a "descendant of Indian medicine men," and advertised a small pamphlet, "The Grand Secret," which has not survived, but which dealt with his recipes and his formulas for extracting the essence of "Indian hemp." Randolph claimed to have perfected the formulas for these elixirs after his last trip to the Near East in 1861–62. The *Religio-Philosophical Journal* for October 21, 1865, reprints a letter to the *New Orleans Times* from a grateful patient, giving Randolph's cholera remedy. This consisted of brandy, cayenne pepper, spirits of nitre, and "fluid extract of Cannabis Indica." In *The Golden Secret* (published in 1872 but circulated earlier in manuscript) he advertised an improved restorant and invigorant and bragged: "The original formula, I actually obtained in Constantinople, Turkey, from Sultan Abdul's own physician, during the time I was the guest of our consul-general, Mr. Goddard, in 1862, at Prinkipo, an island in the Bosphorus, opposite Stamboul, between the shores of Europe and Asia."

25. *New Mola!* also claims that two other of these potions, Protozone and Cordiale de Lucina, are the "cure of Nervous Diseases, Brain Softening, Consumption, Dyspepsia, Epilepsy, Impotence, Vital Prostration, Loss of Magnetism, Insanity from Exhaustion, Despondency, Sexive Debility, Weakness, Nervous Morbidity."

26. In *New Mola!* (1873) Randolph gives part of what he calls "The Ansairetic Mysteries." Rule 17 advises, in the absence of Randolph's Protozone, the taking of two grains of "solid extract of cannabin" to improve general health and replenish sexual energy. In the immediately preceding rule, the reader is requested to send five dollars for the "esoteric points of the mysteries." These were on sexual matters, but drugs certainly played a role as well.

27. *Magia Sexualis*, 176–77.

28. *Guide to Clairvoyance*, 7.

29. Ibid., 10.

30. Ibid., 14.

31. *Love and Its Hidden History* (1869), 166–67. The last half of the quotation, with alterations, is also given in *Guide to Clairvoyance*, 42.

32. *Seership!* 54–55.

33. Ibid., 76.

34. Ibid., 23.

35. *Guide to Clairvoyance*, 14. This passage is omitted from *Love and its Hidden History*, 166, and the other reworkings of the pamphlet on clairvoyance

which otherwise reproduce the section. Again, this may indicate a change of opinion or circumstance.

36. *Guide to Clairvoyance*, 4 ("My great discovery consists in the knowledge of the exact method how, the precise spot where, and the proper time when to apply the specific mesmeric current to any given person in order to produce coma and lucidity.")

37. *Guide to Clairvoyance*, 42. The passage was written in 1867, and the travels may reflect Randolph's trip in 1861–62 as well as his earlier trips. It is omitted in the parallel passage in *Love and its Hidden History*.

38. *Guide to Clairvoyance*, 17. If "sparks, flashes, streaks of quick and lingering light [were] seen or phosphor clouds float[ed] before the face" they indicated, either that the person could become clairvoyant or that he could become a medium for the spirits of the "spiritual forms of friends long gone but unlost." Randolph emphasized that the two were separate phenomena and offered to aid the latter category of persons—for a fee, of course. "I will state that the information given on this point is a resume of that which I acquired in the Orient, and differs in toto from all Occidental knowledge and practice of spiritualism." *Guide to Clairvoyance*, 17–18.

39. *Guide to Clairvoyance*, 49–50.

40. *Guide to Clairvoyance*, 15. In 1867 at least, Randolph added that he didn't recommend the self-mesmerism or drugs "notwithstanding I know a lady near me, who by a single experiment with the third agent [hashish], not only satisfied all her doubts about the soul's immortality, but became an excellent Medium and Seeress." This entire passage is omitted in the reworked versions and may indicate yet another change in Randolph's views on drugs.

41. *Dealings with the Dead*, 206 n.

42. *Guide to Clairvoyance*, 15.

43. Ibid., 18.

44. Ibid., 20. By the time *Soul!* was published in 1872, the parallel passage attributing the method to the count was omitted. *Soul!* 150.

45. *Guide to Clairvoyance*, 21. This same method of inducing clairvoyance is also given (undoubtedly from Randolph's writings) by John Melville, *Crystal-Gazing and the Wonders of Clairvoyance*, 49–92.

46. Like most of his opinions, Randolph's views on the relative merits of magnets and magic mirrors varied with time. See *Eulis!* (1874), 201–2 (many people have had recourse to opium, cannabin and camphor; to mesmerism, magnets, disks, circles and fasting, but all have proven unsatisfactory and left the searcher worse off than before. The "surer, better, safer, and grander road" is use of the magic mirror); *Seership!* 36 ("Mirror-seeing is but another mode and phase of clairvoyance; it is the self-same power, reached by a different road and different processes, but is and can be carried to a far greater degree

of perfection by many persons, while others [i.e., other processes] totally and wholly fail." People wrongly laugh at the idea "that a mere physical agent can enable one to penetrate the floors of the waking world, and come up, all brilliant and keen, upon the other side."). Of course, given Randolph's general fickleness, he at times also advocated the opposite views. In *After Death* (1868 ed. only), pp. 205–6, he touts magic mirrors, especially a "good Trinue" glass for people who "prefer to pursue that ancient route to clairvoyance." In later editions, he says that he has come to think that glasses, crystals and phaphters were not adapted for Americans and were a waste of time for developing clear seeing. In their place he recommended being magnetized by a good tractor magnet (bar horseshoe) drawn down the head and body or a magnetic bandage (poles fore and aft, or on sides) helps while sleeping. "I suggested these ideas to F. B. Dowd, Esq.," who has put such before public." Dowd is discussed in chapters 6 and 9. The first mention of Randolph's use of a magic mirror is in 1860 in "Boston Spiritual Conference," *Banner of Light* 7, no. 20 (August 25, 1860): 8.

47. *Guide to Clairvoyance*, 23–24. The reference to Randolph's knowledge of a mysterious process is found only in *Guide to Clairvoyance* (1867) and is omitted from the corresponding parts of *Love and its Hidden History* and *New Mola!*

48. *Ravalette*, 114.

49. *Eulis!* (1874), 205–6, 215. See also ibid., 201 ("The Mysteries are all wrought through the Phallic, Discal, Yoni Principles, in unsullied purity, and the highest, noblest worship known to man."); *Seership!* 60 ("I may not here write concerning the methods of invocation, because fools will laugh, and the fraternity of the mystical everywhere, would grieve thereat."). This latter reference, however, may have related to the use of perfumes and fumigants in employing the magic mirror.

50. See *Seership!* 82–84. A more recent, purportedly scientific commentary on the use of the crystal for scrying dismisses Randolph's directions as "a good deal of trouble to no purpose." Thomas, *Crystal Gazing*, 39. The book has a very good introduction describing the actual use of the crystal by Andrew Lang.

51. *Eulis!* 205.

52. *Sexagyma, A Digest of the Works of John Davenport*—"*Curiositates Eroticae Physiologiae*" *and "Aphrodisiacs and Anti-Aphrodisiacs," with a Bio-Bibliographical Memoir of the Author* (Bath, Privately Printed for Subscribers, 1888). This was part of the Esoteric Physiology series and consisted mainly in excerpts from Davenport's books. In *Magnetic Magic* (1898), 23, Fryar says that this section had been "omitted" from Colonel Fraser's description of the Indian mirror dance that he had already printed (166ff.) in his *Mental Magic* (1884). Fraser is discussed later in this chapter.

53. In *Eulis!* (1874), he refers to the works of "Mundt, Hargrave Jennings, Lawrie, Palgrave, Morier, Lane." See also ibid., 207 (Colonel Fraser's list of orientalists' and travelers' works on mirrors). In *Seership!* 73–74, Randolph mentions, "Once in Cairo, Egypt, I conversed with an educated Arab" and learned from him that it was "a common custom for an injured wife to bring before her the image of the recreant husband—by force of Will—frequently using, for want of a better, either a glass of water, or such a magic mirror as is described in Lane's *Modern Egyptians*, and in Mrs. Poole's *English Woman in Egypt*. But as there are plenty of Wulees, Kutbs, and dervishes all over Egypt, it is quite an easy matter for such to gain an hour's use of a genuine glass or jewel."

54. One enormously tantalizing hint can be found in *Seership!* 81, in which Randolph describes various fabulously expensive magic mirrors he knows of and mentions the emerald mirror of the "late Maha-Raja Dhuleep Singh." Dalip Singh and his relationship with Madame Blavatsky will be discussed in chapter 13.

55. *Eulis!* 206. Randolph calls Palgrave his "learned Jesuit friend" and describes him as "a polished gentleman and scholar, and one of the deepest mystics on the globe outside of the Orient." Little is known about this latter side of Palgrave. He was, however, one of those who were later to oppose the proposal to have the Royal Society investigate spiritualism. Britten, *Nineteenth Century Miracles*, 182. R. S. Clymer, finding Palgrave's name in *Eulis!* proceeded to make him one of a secret Council of Three of the Rosicrucians of England who initiated Randolph, but all that is idle fantasy. Joscelyn Godwin has pointed out that what is known of Palgrave's biography and itinerary in the 1870s contradicts Randolph's statement about the meeting in Toledo in 1873.

56. *Eulis!* 209.

57. Ibid., 214.

58. "The Bhattah Mirrors," *The Theosophist* 4, no. 3 (December 1883): 72–74. Madame Blavatsky's commentary on this is reprinted in *BCW*, 6:6–8. As noted above, Robert H. Fryar also reprinted the excerpt from Fraser in his *Mental Magic* (166ff.) the following year, and Sédir excerpted Fraser for his section on "Bhattah mirrors" in his *Les miroirs magiques* (Paris: Chamuel, 1895), 79ff. Similarly, W. Q. Judge's *The Path* carried a fictionalized account of magic-mirror use that was filled with references to "the moulveh" and "the bhatta, the substance in the basin." See St. George Best, "The Magic Mirror. A Faithful Record of a Strange Experience," *The Path* 9, no. 8 (November 1894): 239–44, and ibid., 9, no. 9 (December 1894): 270–75.

59. "Echoes from India," *Banner of Light* 46, no. 4 (October 18, 1879): 7, reprinted in *BCW*, 2:68–80.

60. *Eulis!* 124–25.

61. *Isis Unveiled: A Master-Key to the Mysteries of Ancient and Modern Science and Theology*, 2 vols. (New York: Bouton, 1877; reprint, Pasadena: Theosophical University Press, 1976), 1:357–58.

62. "The Esoteric Character of the Gospels," *Lucifer* (November 1887), reprinted in *BCW*, 8:204 n. See chapter 12.

63. H. P. Blavatsky, *The Secret Doctrine*, 2 vols. (London: Theosophical Publishing House, 1888), 2:558. The relationships between Madame Blavatsky and Randolph will be examined in detail in chapters 12 and 13.

64. *Seership!* 11–12, 37 (ink in virgin's hand). *Love and its Hidden History* (1869) changes "some" purposes to "ordinary."

65. See generally E. Lefébure, "Le miroir d'encre dans la magie Arabe," *Revue Africaine* 49 (1905): 205–27.

66. *Seership!* 55–57. Again, this was for usual purposes. The reference is to E. W. Lane, *An Account of the Manners and Customs of the Modern Egyptians*, 5th ed. (London: John Murray, 1860), 267–75, which gives the famous account of the Egyptian magician whose scryer (a young boy) called up the spirit of the appropriately one-armed Lord Nelson.

67. See also *Seership!* 80, which refers to the people who "have *provided themselves* during the last 12 years [i.e., since 1858] with good and perfect instrumentalities." His 1860 pamphlet on clairvoyance contained a section on "How To Make the Magic Glass or Mirror of the Dead." See *Unveiling*, 71.

68. See *Seership!* 80.

69. Ibid., 81–82. In *Eulis!* 8, he says he had for years used a "third class trinue" to induce "the state of psycho-vision."

70. *Seership!* 21–22 ("the splendid magnetic mirrors of TRINUE, and the finer ones imported into this country by the Armenian seer, Cuilna Vilmara).

71. *Seership!* 82. Apparently central to their manufacture was the making of the "mysteriously sensitive substance wherewith the shields are covered." Ibid., 108.

72. *Seership!* 35, 57. In *Master Passion* (1870), published just after *Seership!* Randolph says he decided to publish *Seership!* separately because he had "come across Cuilna Vilmara, the distinguished Armenian *savant*, a man of most extraordinary attainments. And as his theory of somnambulic sight is in advance of all others, I have concluded to withdraw the papers on that subject from this work, and publish them separately, adding an account of Vilmara's world-famous Trinue glass, or magic mirror,—a contrivance older than civilization, and a most rapid and extraordinary means for developing the well-ascertained and demonstrated power of contacting various knowledges by means aside from ordinary methods." *Master Passion*, 97. See also *Love and its Hidden History* (1869) where the same claim is repeated. Apparently Cuilna

Vilmara's mirrors could be used for evil as well as good purposes because Randolph mentions a woman who drained scores of men of their magnetism and used one of his glasses to "aid her in her vampiral rascality. She is a consumer of souls." *Master Passion*, 126.

73. *Seership!* 84.

74. Bound with *Love and its Hidden History* (1870), 30.

75. *Guide to Clairvoyance*, 20.

76. See *Ravalette*, 58–64.

77. See chapter 12 for Madame Blavatsky's references to Regazzoni. Dr. Massimo Introvigne has pointed out to me the references to Regazzoni in Henri-Roger Gougenot des Mousseaux, *La Magie au dix-neuvième siècle, ses Agents, ses Vérités, ses Mensonges* (Paris: E. Dentu, 1860), 228, 236ff, where he is described as a jovial missionary of mesmerism who spread its prodigies from Italy to Tunis, Athens, St. Petersburg, Madrid, Paris and London. Regazzoni admitted to des Mousseaux (247) that although he used the "fluid" terminology of mesmerism "in all my difficult operations [there is] a little invocation . . . but of beneficent Spirits." On Regazzoni, see also Rev. Chauncy Hare Townsend, *Mesmerism Proved True, and the Quarterly Reviewer Reviewed* (London: T. Bosworth, 1854), cited in Gougenot des Mousseaux; "M. Regazzoni et le Magnétisme à Francfort," *Journal du Magnétisme* 14 (1855): 8–19; "Turgescence Mammaire," *Journal du Magnétisme* 14 (1855): 159. The induction of this last-named phenomenon was a specialty of Regazzoni.

78. *The Spiritual Telegraph* 5, no. 27 (August 30, 1856), carried the announcement of Regazzoni's arrival in Liverpool, fresh from Paris and his astonishing demonstrations before Napoleon III.

79. *Ravalette*, 58ff.

80. *New Mola!* 34–35. Some ambivalence about Vilmara may have been present even earlier. *Soul!*, which was first prepared in 1869–1870 when *Seership!* was being written, omits entirely from the corresponding passage the attribution of the "special method of thorough magnetization" to the count.

81. *Eulis!* 202.

82. Ibid., 203.

83. Ibid., 202, 205.

84. Some further clues for future research on the identity of Randolph's source can be gleaned from his *Ansairetic Mystery*, printed in late 1873 or early 1874, in which he advertises for sale a special lot of mirrors "from the late Dr. Jarlin's (French) collection."

85. *Seership!* 75. In addition to differing from contemporary mirror advocates in Europe, such as Frederick Hockley, by his insistence that vision

could be developed in the operator himself, Randolph also appears never to have acquired one particular guide or angel in his mirror visions, such as the omnipresent "Crowned Angel," who communicated with Hockley for decades. Also, while Randolph's true emphasis was on producing the higher clairvoyance, he did not, as we shall see, neglect lesser goals to be reached through magic, such as "the Mystery of Bodiless Flights, (Scin-Læca), the Double, and under what conditions a living person can be seen in two places at the same time" ("Ubique") and all the other traditional phenomena set out in _Ghost Land_. The quotes in the text are from _Guide to Clairvoyance_, 5, 41.

86. _Eulis!_ 217.

87. Ibid., 215.

88. _Seership!_ 60.

89. _Guide to Clairvoyance_, 24–25.

Chapter 4

1. "Letter from New York," _Banner of Light_ 3, no. 3 (April 17, 1858): 5. There is a possibility that Randolph made yet a third trip to Europe at some point between his return from his grand tour of 1857–58 and his next departure for the Near East in 1861, but, again, no details survive and what is known of his whereabouts indicates that he had little time for such a trip. In a letter reprinted in the _Religio-Philosophical Journal_, August 14, 1875, Randolph mentions that he had been threatened with death three times, once in Spain in 1859. Since his proselytizing of "Ferdinand" is mentioned in his recantation speech in 1858, however, Randolph may simply be confusing the dates. See also note 37, below. In the preface to _Rosicrucian's Story_ (1863) he boasted that he had crossed the ocean eight times, but again this may refer to his earlier cabin-boy days. He refers also to a speech he made in London in 1864, but nothing is known about that trip, if it took place at all. See _Proceedings of the Tenth Annual Convention of the American Association of Spiritualists_, 226. _Curious Life_, 13, reprints a newspaper clipping from the 1870s that claims he had three times circumnavigated the globe—which is certainly not true.

2. "The Utica Convention," _The New England Spiritualist_ (October 9, 1858).

3. Parker Pillsbury, "The Utica Convention," _The Liberator_ 28, no. 40 (October 1, 1858): 158. Pillsbury was later a charter member of the first lodge of the Theosophical Society outside New York City, in Rochester, New York, a lodge organized and led by Mrs. Josephine Cables, who was to emerge as one of the heads of the H. B. of L. in the United States a few years later. See "Theosophy in America," _The Theosophist_ 3 (April 1882): 186, and the notice in ibid. 3 (February 1883, Supplement): 3.

4. D. S. Grandin, "John Randolph," *The Liberator* 28, no. 45 (November 5, 1858): 177.

5. P. B. Randolph, "Letter from P. Beverly Randolph," *The Liberator* 28, no. 46 (November 12, 1858): 183. *The New England Spiritualist* for January 12, 1856, announced the lecture on slavery. Gerrit Smith, in a letter dated August 29, 1858, mentioned that he had heard Randolph lecture on slavery at some unspecified earlier date. *The Liberator* 28, no. 53 (December 31, 1858): 211. On Randolph's living in Portland, Maine, in 1842, see his "Notes on My Psychal Life," *Journal of Progress* 2, no. 3 (October 1853):38.

6. See frontispiece and plate 1, and the self-description in *Ravalette* (1876), 9–10.

7. See D. S. Grandin, "Randolph Again," *The Liberator* 28, no. 47 (November 19, 1858): 187; Grandin, "The Wrong Man Impeached," *The Liberator* 28, no. 49 (December 3, 1858): 195; and "A Final Correction," *The Liberator* 28, no. 53 (December 31, 1858): 211.

8. *Soul!* 265.

9. "The Converted Medium," *New York Daily Tribune,* November 25, 1858, 3. See also Hatch, *Spiritualists' Iniquities Unmasked,* 14.

10. "The Converted Medium," *New York Daily Tribune,* November 25, 1858, 3.

11. On Harris, see *Unveiling,* and on Dotten, see "Miss Doten's Renunciation of Spiritualism," *Banner of Light* 3, no. 11 (June 12, 1858): 4.

12. On Davis's speech, see *The Spiritual Telegraph* (January 15, 1859): 376. See also Davis's "The Origin of the Devil," in *The Spirit Messenger* 1, no. 6 (1853); "Mr. Davis' Late Pamphlet '*History and Philosophy of Evil,*'" *The Spiritual Telegraph* (January 15, 1859): 376; J. R. Orton, "Mr. Davis and the Old Testament," *The Telegraph Papers* 2 (1853): 430–43. Faced with mediums' overwhelming experience of less than truthful and beneficent spirits, Davis eventually came to teach that the evil in spiritualism was the work of the "Diakka." These tricksters were the spirits of unbalanced men who lived solely for themselves and who were accordingly condemned after death to the Diakka section of Summer Land (in Draco Major, Davis specifies), whence they delighted in disrupting seances with their pranks and lies. Even these, however, were not fundamentally evil, and eventually, under the tutelage of better spirits, they too would progress to the higher worlds of Summer Land. See Andrew Jackson Davis, *The Diakka, and their Earthly Victims; being an Explanation of Much that is False and Repulsive in Spiritualism* (1873; Boston: Colby & Rich, 1886). The debate over the existence of evil spirits and their role raged in the spiritualist press through the 1880s.

13. At the Auburn Harmonial Convention in 1854 at which both Randolph and Davis spoke, Randolph had toed the party line: "Mr. P. B. Randolph, of Utica,

N.Y., became clairvoyant and said, that he did not believe in evil, or a principle of evil." Townsend, "Harmonial Convention," *The Telegraph Papers* 4 (1854): 52.

14. A good example of the prevailing opinion is provided by the speech of G. B. Stebbins at the Utica Philanthropic Convention: "Thus we find that evil is but imperfect development." "Philanthropic Convention, Held in Utica on the 10th, 11th and 12th Sept., 1858, to Consider 'The Cause and Cure of Evil,'" *The Spiritual Telegraph* (October 9, 1858): 234. For a review of early spiritualist views on the existence and nature of evil, see E. J. Isaacs, *A History of Nineteenth-Century American Spiritualism*, 154–60. Connected with this denial of evil was the fundamental optimism expressed by spiritualists as "Whatever is, is right." This was the title of a famous pamphlet of the time by Dr. Asaph Bemis Child (1813–1879) of Boston which argued that, since God is infinite and good, everything must be good, and no human action could improve or degrade the soul. See Moore, *In Search of White Crows*, 58–59, 83; A. B. Child, *Whatever Is, Is Right* (Boston: Berry, Colby, and Co., 1861). Randolph, writing under the nom-de-plume of "Cynthia Temple," responded to this in his pamphlet *It Isn't all Right* (1861). See appendix C. A rejoinder was published by A. P. McCombs, *Whatever is, is Right Vindicated: being a letter to CT, briefly reviewing her Theory of "It isn't all Right."* See the advertisement from Wm. White & Co. at the end of *Davenport Brothers* (1869). The *Spiritual Magazine* 1, no. 11 (November 1860): 528ff, reviewed Child's book and condemned it in the same terms used by Randolph. A presage of things to come (especially of the claim that spiritualism was a ploy of unknown and sinister forces) appeared in the novel by Orestes Brownson, *The Spirit-Rapper: An Autobiography* (Boston: Little, Brown & Co., 1854), which posited the existence of a diabolic conspiracy of living mesmerists to use spiritualism as a revolutionary force. See Kerr, *Mediums, and Spirit-Rappers, and Roaring Radicals*, 84–90.

15. See "Philanthropic Convention, Held in Utica on the 10th, 11th and 12th Sept., 1858, to Consider 'The Cause and Cure of Evil,'" *The Spiritual Telegraph* (October 9, 1858): 234–35. On Randolph's role at the Utica convention, see also *The Spiritual Telegraph*, October 24, 1858, which prints his resolution that the meeting be converted into a permanent national association, and gives his comment that he "didn't accept Andrew Jackson Davis as his earthly God." Randolph spoke again at Utica the next month, attributing spiritualism to imposture, insanity and diabolism in equal parts. *New York Daily Tribune*, October 28, 1858, 5.

16. On the doctrine of "conditional immortality," see chapter 12.

17. See Britten, *Modern American Spiritualism*, 242–43. The call to the ministry is in the *New York Daily Tribune*, October 28, 1858; 5; "P. B. Randolph in the 'Ministry,'" *The Spiritual Telegraph* (November 13, 1858); 284 and "What the Thing Is," *Banner of Light* 4, no. 7 (November 13, 1858): 4.

18. "The Converted Medium," *New York Daily Tribune*, November 25, 1858, 3. See also "P. B. Randolph's Reply and Position," *The Spiritual Telegraph*

(November 20, 1858): 296, "P. B. Randolph's Lectures," *The Spiritual Telegraph* (November 27, 1858): 207, and "New York Correspondence: P. B. Randolph's Definition of Spiritualism," *Banner of Light* 4, no. 10 (December 4, 1858): 5. *Tiffany's Monthly* 4 (1858): 312ff, reprinted the *Spiritual Telegraph* articles. The notices in the *Banner of Light* were conspicuously mild because of the journal's recognition of Randolph's evident sincerity. See, e.g., "New York Correspondence, Dr. Randolph Again," *Banner of Light* 4, no. 11 (September 12, 1858): 8. The Clinton Hall speech, without the references to hashish and the attacks on Andrew Jackson Davis by name, is printed in *Soul!*, 265ff. See appendix C.

19. "The Converted Medium," *New York Daily Tribune*, November 25, 1858, 3.

20. See chapter 1 on Benjamin Hatch's evaluation of Randolph. Later, of course, in 1872, he was arrested for teaching free love when some of his "medical" works were seized by the police of Boston. See chapter 9.

21. See, e.g., *Dealings with the Dead*, 101 ("occasionally the banks overflowed, and he became passional; forgot his dignity; was let to believe that whoever *said* love, *meant* love; was beset with temptation, and yielded, until at last his heart was torn to pieces."); ibid., 94; *Love! At Last!* 16 ("Now, genius in either sex seldom finds its true mate, yearn and groan howsoever it may. It marries; meets what disagrees with it; gets into a state of chronic unrest; becomes attractive to others of opposite sex; falls before the magnetic gale such meetings usher into being; yields,—keeps on doing it; hasn't resistive force enough to stand firm and be a genius still; and so gradually sinks—in love respects—into a permanent unfixedness."); "Randolph's Letters—No. 2," *Religio-Philosophical Journal* 1, no. 2 (October 7, 1865): 2. In later years this fascination with women appears to have become a little more cynical, and his lists of powers to be obtained by his magic include the traditional ones of love attraction. See chapters 9 and 10.

22. "The Converted Medium," *New York Daily Tribune*, November 25, 1858, 3.

23. Judge Edmonds, one of the glories of the early spiritualist movement, eventually came to concede the impossibility of distinguishing control by spirits of the dead from control by one's own passions or even by living men. *New York Times*, November 29, 1858. See also on the debate B. F. Hatch, "Obsession of Evil Spirits," *Banner of Light* 3, no. 26 (September 25, 1858): 7, and Warren Chase, "B. F. Hatch and the Mediums," *Banner of Light* 4, no. 1 (October 2, 1858): 4. For Randolph's views, see "Boston Spiritual Conference," *Banner of Light* 7, no. 18 (July 28, 1860): 4 (evil is a principle);"Boston Spiritual Conference," *Banner of Light* 7, no. 19 (August 4, 1860): 5 (evil has positive existence). The issue of identity haunted spiritualism and was still being rehashed twenty-five years later between Stainton Moses and Madame Blavatsky, with the former insisting that the spirits were indeed the continuations of

specific dead persons, and with Madame Blavatsky insisting that they were mere psychic residue and elementals. See chapter 12. The entire question of the identification of spirits and distinguishing among them is as old as the evocation of spirits. For an excellent discussion of the problem in late classical antiquity, see E. R. Dodds, *The Greeks and the Irrational* (Berkeley and Los Angeles: University of California Press, 1951), and *The Ancient Concept of Progress and other Essays in Greek Literature and Belief* (Oxford: Oxford University Press, 1975), 204–10. For examples of the rare appearances at seances of entities who claimed to be other than disembodied spirits, see Randolph's *Davenport Brothers*, 41–42 (on "Richards"); Britten, *Modern American Spiritualism*, 319–33 (on "Oressa" and "John King" at Koons and Tippie's spirit rooms).

24. Among the spiritualists, Emma Hardinge Britten, was the first (in 1860) to raise the issue. See chapter 12.

25. "Spiritual Mountebanks," *The Spiritual Telegraph* (November 6, 1858): 277, reprinted in *Tiffany's Monthly* 4 (1858): 312ff, with Randolph's reply. See also "What the Thing Is," *Banner of Light* 4, no. 7 (November 13, 1858): 4, whose author stated that if "Spiritualism is one third imposture, one third insanity, and one third diabolism" Randolph was in a good position to address the first two-thirds. Dr. Gardner in Boston was more understanding and wrote that "the eccentric medium" should be given sympathy and a fair trial. H. F. Gardner, "P. B. Randolph in Boston," *Banner of Light* 6, no. 7 (November 12, 1859): 4.

26. Britten, *Modern American Spiritualism*, 242–43.

27. "P. B. Randolph's Reply and Position," *The Spiritual Telegraph* (November 20, 1858): 296. Randolph's usual fickleness is clearly at work, and it is probable that at times he simply relapsed into his old mediumship. The temptation was always there. In *Unveiling* (1860), 32, he says that he had rejected "Atheistic, Ultra, Radical, Pantheistic, 'whack Moses'" spiritualism for a Christian sort, "yet, albeit I have thought I was forever free from its influence, not a day has since passed over my head, that I have not been beset, tempted, tried, castigated, tortured by the infernal host, who in this way make reprisals upon me for declaring them in their true light. Dr. Child, *was* this, *is* this 'All Right.'" In another speech at Clinton Hall in December 1858, Randolph even went so far as to claim that he was not a spiritualist but rather a religious man, and he spoke "in high terms" of Andrew Jackson Davis, though differing from him on "certain questions." "P. B. Randolph Lecture," *The Spiritual Telegraph* (December 11, 1858): 323. In "P. B. Randolph in the 'Ministry,'" *The Spiritual Telegraph* (November 13, 1858): 284, a M. Magan says that Randolph told him that he "needed rest—religious rest—and not being able to find that in Spiritualistic science, he now seeks it in Spiritualistic religion." Fifteen years later Randolph was still carrying around with him the *New York Tribune* report of his recantation speech and trying to explain (to a spiritualist convention) what he had meant. See *Proceedings of the Tenth Annual Convention of the American Association of Spiritualists*, 221.

28. "Mr. Randolph's Lecture," *The Spiritual Telegraph* (December 4, 1858): 318–19; "Dr. Randolph in Boston," *Banner of Light* 4, no. 11 (December 11, 1858): 4; "Dr. Randolph Again," ibid. 4, no. 11 (December 11, 1858): 8; "Dr. Randolph at the Melodeon," ibid. 4, no. 13 (December 25, 1858): 8; "Boston Reform Conference," ibid. 4, no. 14 (January 1, 1859): 4; "P. B. Randolph at the Melodeon," ibid. 4, no. 14 (January 1, 1859): 5, 8.

29. See, e.g., *Casca Llanna*, 73 (in 1858 he broke with his party and all rose up to "crush him out").

30. "P. B. Randolph at the Melodeon," *Banner of Light* 4, no. 14 (January 1, 1859): 5, 8.

31. "A Final Correction," *The Liberator* 28, no. 53 (December 31, 1858): 211.

32. Randolph says that in 1853 he was active in the then new "Reformatory Party" (whose motto he says was "Free speech, free thought, free men."). *Curious Life* 8. This is otherwise unknown but probably is a reference to the Free Soil Party, an anti-slavery party that emerged in 1848 from the Liberty party, the political wing of the American Anti-Slavery Society, a party in which Smith was a leading figure and under whose aegis he was elected to Congress in 1852. Randolph bitterly denounced, without naming him, a leader in the organization who called Randolph his friend but sadly neglected him when he was in need—a clear reference to Smith. Ibid., 9. On Smith generally and his political activities (which frequently overlapped Randolph's), see O. B. Frothingham, *Gerrit Smith. A Biography* (New York: G. P. Putnam's Sons, 1909); James Brewer Steward, *Holy Warriors. The Abolitionists and American Slavery* (New York: Hill and Wang, 1976), 126–27 (Gerrit Smith and the temperance movement among blacks); Avery Craven, *The Coming of the Civil War* (Chicago: University of Chicago Press, 1957), 133 (Gerrit Smith and the influence of religion on politics from the 1840s); 153 (opposition to black repatriation movement); Philip S. Foner and George E. Walker, *Proceedings of the Black State Conventions, 1840–1865*, 2 vols. (Philadelphia: Temple University Press, 1980), 1: 51; Hugh C. Humphreys, "'Agitate! Agitate! Agitate!' The Great Fugitive Slave Law Convention and its Rare Daguerreotype," *Madison County Heritage* 19 (1994): 1–64; Alicia Maxey, "Peterboro has Place in Black History," *Syracuse Herald American*, February 19, 1995, C1–C2. I wish to thank Justine Mulford, deputy county clerk for Madison County, for giving me a copy of this last article.

33. Randolph to Gerrit Smith, January 24, 1859. In his earliest surviving letter to Smith, dated May 2, 1858, Randolph enclosed a vision poem he had just written ("The Slave and Master—A Vision") and sought Smith's help in getting Frederick Douglass to publish it in his journal *The North Star*. (Douglass apparently had earlier rejected a temperance tale submitted by Randolph.) The poem is done in the manner of Edgar Allan Poe and is fairly awful. It deals with a "Sable Sister, Victim of despotic Mammon" and her master, who whipped her for praying. They are snatched by death in the midst of the

whipping, the woman to be led "where the Seraphs God adore," and the master to "a black tartarean hideous gulf . . . to writhe in Torment ever more."

34. Randolph to Smith, undated letter, Wednesday, 1859.

35. Randolph to Smith, April 24, 1859.

36. In a letter to Smith dated August 14, 1866, Randolph says that it had been eight years since he had last written. The farm was finally sold to a purchaser already in possession in April 1860, though with what resolution of Randolph's dilemma it is impossible to tell. The deed was recorded April 13, 1860, in Liber of Deeds CQ, page 47, Madison county clerk's Office. I wish to thank Justine Mulford for locating the deed for me.

37. *The Rosicrucian's Story* (1863) has the story of little Winnie at enormous length at the end of part 4, 75-78, but it is omitted in later editions. Randolph speaks of the principal perpetrator as a "polygamous scoundrel" who thought himself God's private secretary. This "demon in saint's garb" slandered Randolph and his dead mother (perhaps by questioning Randolph's legitimacy) and revealed in his journal Randolph's authorship of a pamphlet written under a nom de plume. In Randolph's mind this man either stole directly from him or betrayed his trust and neglected his children, or perhaps simply criticized Randolph and so deprived the family of money that Randolph might have made on the lecture circuit. The mention of Winnie's death while Randolph was at sea doesn't jibe with Randolph's letters to Smith in 1858–59, and may be evidence of another trip to Europe (in 1858–59). See also *Seership!* 36; *After Death*, 38. In *Ravalette* (1876 ed.), 48–50, 54, 122–23, the story runs that Randolph ruined his health trying to save the life of the sister of a rich man by transfusing his own vitality into her, and then left for Europe to restore his health. On his return he borrowed money from the rich man (presumably this is the loan from Smith) to start a business and gave part of it to another person to purchase for him a few acres. This villain then enticed Randolph to invest the last of his money in a get-rich-quick scheme to buy gold. As it turned out, the man did not even have title to the land and quickly lost all the rest of Randolph's money and caused him to lose his reputation with the rich man. He "actually suffered a child in our family to perish and wretchedly die for the want of food and medicine. But then he told me that he had buried it properly respectably, up there in the cemetery, and it was the only truth I ever heard from his lips. But then he sent the funeral bills for me to pay." Smith's passive role in all this may explain Randolph's failure to mention him in his writings. In later years, however, Randolph's rancor must have cooled because he describes Smith in a speech as "a great and good man." *Proceedings of the Tenth Annual Convention of the American Association of Spiritualists*, 66–73. The references to sanctimoniousness and polygamy might also indicate Andrew Jackson Davis as one of the villains. His *Herald of Progress* began to appear in February 1860, but I have not located any attack on Randolph in its pages.

38. *Dealings with the Dead*, 105–6.

39. "Randolph's Lectures," *Banner of Light* 6, no. 10 (December 3, 1859): 5; "P. B. Randolph at Washington Hall, Charlston," ibid; "P. B. Randolph," ibid. 6, no. 17 (January 21, 1860): 4.

40. "Dr. P. B. Randolph," *Banner of Light* 6, no. 24 (March 10, 1860): 4.

41. Advertisement, "Dr. P. B. Randolph pursues his Practice of Medicine," *Banner of Light* 7, no. 23 (September 1, 1860): 7.

42. "P. B. Randolph's Card," *Banner of Light* 8, no. 9 (November 24, 1860): 5.

43. "New England Anti–Slavery Convention" *The Liberator* 30, no. 23 (June 8, 1860): 190. Randolph commented on the attack in *Unveiling*, 41. Randolph reiterated his rejection of fanaticism in abolishing slavery at the end of the year. See "Dr. Randolph at Allston Hall," *Banner of Light* 8, no. 16 (January 19, 1861): 8.

44. *The Unveiling: or, What I Think of Spiritualism. By Dr. Paschal Beverly Randolph. To which is appended his world-famous medicinal formulas* (Newburyport: William H. Huse & Co., 1860). The book was published in July. "All Sorts of Paragraphs," *Banner of Light* 7, no. 18 (July 28, 1860): 5.

45. *Dealings With The Dead; The Human Soul, Its Migrations And Its Transmigrations* (Utica: Published by Mary J. Randolph, 1861–62). The book was first serialized in part in the *Banner of Light* in the fall of 1859.

Chapter 5

1. *Dealings with the Dead*. The book was ready for printing by the early summer of 1861, but did not appear until March 1862. It is favorably reviewed, without emphasis on its revolutionary character, in "The Blending State," *The Spiritual Magazine* 3, no. 6 (June 1862): 278ff.

2. *Dealings with the Dead*, 44. Randolph says that the ideas on the soul and the coruscation of worlds from the central sun of God were given to him initially by the spirits in Buffalo in 1856 while he was there investigating the Davenport brothers. See *Davenport Brothers*, 150ff, which provides a good summary of his views. It is curious that at the time he was investigating the Davenport brothers in the mid-1850s their control was the omnipresent "spirit" who called himself "John King." King claimed to be far more than a spirit and eventually (transformed into an "elemental") became the constant companion of Madame Blavatsky during her first years in New York.

3. See *Dealings with the Dead*, 49. See also *Soul!* 279; *Asiatic Mystery* ("Deity dwells within the Shadow, *behind*, the everlasting FLAME,—the

amazing glories of *which* minds have confounded with the very God."); *Eulis!*
76–77 (Light is the shadow of God, and he dwells in the shadow, beyond the
fire; light is only God's shadow).

4. *Dealings with the Dead*, 134. See also ibid., 5, 204.

5. Ibid., 249–50.

6. Ibid., 151.

7. Ibid., 151.

8. Ibid., 46–47.

9. Ibid., 41.

10. Ibid., 112, 199, 227, 250.

11. Ibid., 257.

12. Ibid., 97–98.

13. Ibid., 43, 191. In *Soul!* (1872), 261ff, Randolph advances the idea that
souls themselves (not merely the monads) pre-exist incarnation, but the distinction for him appears to rest merely on the degree of intelligence and individuality assigned to each entity, and he frequently uses the terms interchangeably.
See also *Davenport Brothers*, 151: "Vast and mighty is the human soul! . . . The
human soul hath ever lived. Time never was when it had not a conscious
being,—conscious only in its inmost essence, ere it fell, as a raindrop, from the
pulsating soul of its Father, God." All of Randolph's ideas on what he calls the
"monad" and the "soul" have strong traditional roots, of which he was probably only indirectly aware, in late classical antiquity and the Renaissance.

14. *Dealings with the Dead*, 50–51.

15. Ibid., 24–25.

16. *New Mola!* (1873), 16. Boris de Zirkoff, in his bio-bibliographical
article on Randolph in Madame Blavatsky's *Collected Writings* is mistaken in
asserting of Randolph that reincarnation "permeates all of his ideas." *BCW*,
3:518–20. His statement is apparently based on a passage in *The Rosicrucian's
Story* (118–20) in which Randolph describes the intricate postmortem gyra-
tions of the soul (and of its double in a parallel universe) through the "aromal
worlds." "You have heard of Metempsychosis, Transmigration, of Reincarnation, and of Progress. . . . Not only the inhabitants of the countless myriads of
worlds in this material *and aromal* universe, but also the material and aromal
worlds themselves, are in a state of progressive movement. By aromal worlds
I mean the aerial globes that attend each planet. They are places where souls
rest awhile after death, before they commence in earnest the second stage of
their career; and this state is an intermediate one, just like sleep, only that they
are conscious and active while there; but it is an activity and consciousness,

not like, but analogous to that of Dream. Every world, and assemblage of worlds, is periodically reduced, by exhaustion, but at enormously long intervals, into Chaos, and is then reformed or created anew, still, however, being the same world. . . . The majority of those who have lived on any world are reborn in it after its restitution, they, in the meantime, having grown correspondingly clean and perfect." The passage, indeed, sounds like a paraphrase of later Theosophical doctrine on reincarnation, but Randolph makes it clear that the soul is reborn on an "earth resembling the one whereon the double unit had its birth *originally*," and adds that after these migrations the soul begins "*the second full stage of its career, ends its Humanhood, and begins its deific course of the first degree, which career will endure for the space of time expressed by the cube, in centuries, of its former years as a human being; and that each soul will be double, male and female, God and Goddess, until its next change, and so on* FOREVER AND EVERMORE, THROUGH ALL THE ETERNITIES." On the change in Theosophical ideas on reincarnation, see chapter 12. See also W. E. Coleman's review of the "posthumous" book by Randolph, *Beyond the Veil*, in which he points out that Randolph's postmortem teachers were quite correct in denying reincarnation and that "Randolph dead is thus wiser than Randolph living." *The Truth Seeker* (March 30, 1878): 206. I am indebted to Michael Gomes for this last reference. In *Beyond the Veil*, published in 1877 when the battle between the spiritualists and occultists was raging, Randolph's spirit said it could find no one in the afterlife who believed in reincarnation or "elementals," and took a few gratuitous pot shots at Colonel "Alcott" (Olcott) and Emma Hardinge Britten.

17. *Casca Llanna*, 226. See also ibid., 233 (pre-existence and rebirth). The inclusion of Hottentots and the like in the recitation probably is indicative of Randolph's position that they lacked soul and immortality rather than as a suggestion of reincarnation. See the discussion of *Pre-Adamite Man* in chapter 6. The idea of transmigration, descent of the monad into matter and reascent as an "individualized" entity, is explained also in *After Death*, 42–44.

18 The idea of reincarnation as the rebirth on earth of the same individual crept into spiritualism through the work of Hippolyte Denizard Rivail ("Allan Kardec," 1804–1869) who viewed it as a way for the less-than-perfect human to work out his or her development before advancing through the afterlife. See Karl Kieswetter, *Geschichte des Neuren Occultismus* 1:493ff.; Britten, *Nineteenth Century Miracles*, 46ff.; William Howitt, "Spirites, Fusionists, and Re-Incarnationists in France," *Spiritual Magazine*, 1 (1866): 17–27 ("the doctrine of Re-incarnation is . . . merely the desire of re-incarnation in certain sensual needs."). It began to appear in American spiritualism in the early 1860s, but was always controversial. See, e.g., G. L. Burnside, "French vs. American Spirits," *Banner of Light* 14, no. 15 (January 1, 1864): 1; "Reincarnation," ibid., 33, no. 3 (April 19, 1873): 4 ("the day hastens when . . . the verity of reincarnation will be recognized"); "A Correction—Reincarnation," ibid. 33, no. 11 (July 5, 1873): 2; Caldwell, "Re-Incarnation," ibid. 33, no. 16 (July 19, 1873): 3;

W. E. Coleman, "The Law of Immortality versus Re-Incarnation," ibid. 33, no. 17 (July 26, 1873): 8; "'The Law of Immortality versus Re-Incarnation, a Lecture by William Emmette Coleman,' Criticized and Reviewed," ibid. 33, no. 25 (September 20, 1873): 8; "A Spiritual La Mountain—Individual Predictions vs. Eternal Truths," ibid. 33, no. 26 (September 27, 1873): 8; D. M. Funk, "Cahagnet's 'Celestial Telegraph,'" ibid., 34, no. 2 (November 11, 1873): 3. See also chapter 12.

19. *Dealings with the Dead*, 146–49. This, of course, is not properly reincarnation at all, since what is trying again to incarnate is not the same "individual" but merely the germ that had not quite reached individualization. In cases where the monad had become individualized but still lacked maturity Randolph believed that it progressed to the "nurseries of the soul world" and was associated with more developed beings who nurtured it. Ibid. See also "Dealings with the Dead. Number Seven. Parenthetical to 'Epoch,'" *Banner of Light* 6, no. 9 (November 26, 1859): 6–7 (the stillborn and idiots are nursed in the "green houses" of the "Second Region"). This view was also advocated by Eliphas Lévi. See Waite, *The Mysteries of Magic*, 106 (Souls destined to live, but not yet purified, linger after death in a benumbed state, trapped in their astral bodies until they are "gradually drawn from this state by the elect, who instruct them, console them, and enlighten them."). Lévi also explicitly denied reincarnation, though his views are not totally clear or consistent. See Waite's note to the page cited. In *Dealings with the Dead*, 119, Randolph announced his intention of writing a book, *The Realm of the Fay*, on this special class of immature souls, but it was never published.

20. *Ravalette* (1863) is built around the idea of a man condemned for a crime to rebirth on earth until he weds a woman not born of Adam. The man is obviously Randolph himself who, because of his troubled life, apparently believed that he was paying the price for some early misdeed. See F. B. Dowd, *The Double Man*, 35. The similarities between Randolph's ideas on reincarnation and those of the early works of Madame Blavatsky are discussed in chapter 12.

21. See "Mysteries of Eulis," appendix B ("The grand object of *Eulis* therefore is to build up the individuality of each acolyte, [to] the end of adding a new power to the universe, a new force to the human soul."); *Dealings with the Dead*, 44, 146, 177, 46 ("I should ever advance toward, but never reach perfection"); *Davenport Brothers*, 152 ("In other words, man is the crystallization of the waves of thought which proceed from God; hence, never can reach Deity, for the reason that the sphere which emanates from God is less refined and perfect than God himself, as is self-evident."). See also *After Death*, 70–75 ("Once, when *en rapport* with a vast brotherhood of learned Buddhists, of the better land, they taught, and I believed, that there would come a period when man would be so pure and perfect as to lose his identity, and be swallowed up in God—be absorbed into the great Brahm, a component of whom he would then become. Somewhere, in one of the many books I have written,

that idea has its place." This, he now saw was an error: the circle does not return upon itself. "I now believe in our continued existence as humans,—in ascending orders and hierarchies."); 196. Randolph mentions several times that he had considered and rejected what he thought of as the "Buddhist" idea of a final reabsorption of the personality. In *Casca Llanna*, 75, he reports neutrally a comment that the Rosicrucians "regard *Narwana*, or final blending with Death, as the great end of all life and all endeavor." In *Eulis!* (1874), 177, he mentions again that he had once become a Buddhist, but had changed when he slept the sleep of Sialam and used the magic mirror. He named his son, born in March 1874, "Osiris Budh," but the latter name to Randolph clearly carried the implications of Hargrave Jennings's phallic Buddhists rather than anything that a present-day scholar might identify as Buddhism. It is, of course, precisely on this point of individual immortality that the H. B. of L., Emma Hardinge Britten, and the entire "Western" branch of occultism (William Oxley, C. C. Massey, et al.) most strongly disagreed with the Theosophical teachings of Madame Blavatsky after 1881. See chapter 12. This issue of personal, individual survival after death (as contrasted with some form of absorption into the deity) was one of the main characteristics that distinguished spiritualism from New England transcendentalism. See, e.g., Moore, *In Search of White Crows*, 53–54.

22. *Davenport Brothers*, 152 and note.

23. *Dealings with the Dead*, 24–25, 61.

24. Ibid., 151–52.

25. Ibid., 49, 186ff, 191. See plate 4. The image of the winged globe had been re-introduced to Europe in the nineteenth century by the reports and engravings of the French expedition to Egypt under Napoleon. In *After Death*, 13, Randolph attributes the image to "Zerdusht," who must be the spirit of that name. It was later to be used by, among others, Madame Blavatsky in her Eastern or Esoteric Section.

26. He described the vision in various places. It appears to have occurred somewhere between the Rochester knockings that initiated spiritualism in 1848 and his first encounter with hashish in the mid-1850s. *Dealings with the Dead*, 167ff.

27. The vision is described as independent of his hashish use, but in the periods in which Randolph approved of hashish use he uses very similar language of his hashish experiences. The reference to Davis is in Le Rosicrucien, "Dealings with the Dead.—No. 2," *Banner of Light* 5, no. 24 (September 10, 1859): 3–4. *Dealings with the Dead*, 171, omits the reference to Davis and places the experience in Boston.

28. *Dealings with the Dead*, 174–79.

29. Ibid., 77, 80–81.

30. Ibid., 180–82, 188.

31. As with many other visionaries, light was the central theme of Randolph's experiences. See *Soul!* 265 (before and after 1856, Randolph experienced vast sunbursts of light to the soul and felt himself sweeping vast fields of space and being). On the phenomenology of the light experience, see the seminal articles of Mircea Eliade, "Significations de la 'Lumière Intérieure,'" *Eranos-Jahrbuch*, 25 (1957): 189–242; "Spirit, Light and Seed," *History of Religions*, 11 (August 1971): 1–30, reprinted in *Occultism, Witchcraft and Cultural Fashions: Essays in Comparative Religions* (Chicago and London: University of Chicago Press, 1976), 93–119.

32. *Dealings with the Dead*, 22–23.

33. Ibid., 54, 193, 230 134 (spirit is merely a "projection" or "outcreation" of soul).

34. Ibid., 48. Like so many other things, Randolph's views on the location of the spirit world changed over time. In *Soul!* (1872) the re-edition of *Dealings with the Dead*, Randolph adds a note to this effect, referring the reader to *After Death; or, the Disembodiment of Man*, which he wrote in 1866 and published as a book in 1868. *After Death* largely represents a retreat by Randolph from the rather sublime ideas set out in *Dealings with the Dead*. See the discussion in chapter 8.

35. *Dealings with the Dead*, 57–58, 103, 107, 131–32.

36. These are the entities called by Madame Blavatsky the "elementaries." See chapter 12.

37. *Dealings with the Dead*, 263, 267, 84, 59, 215.

38. Ibid., 267–68. See also ibid., 106: Satan "undoubtedly means an evil chief of the harpy bands infesting the borders of both worlds, whose sole delight it is to circumvent God and man, and bring all good things to an evil end." In *Unveiling*, 34–35, Randolph says that he understood "devil" and "demon" to be unregenerate souls of dead men, but that he had another hypothesis as well. He was convinced of the existence of these entities (however defined) because "it is utterly impossible to reconcile one tenth part of my experience of Spiritualism, and what I have observed, with the notion that the communicating intelligences are *all* good." The hypothesis he advanced, however, was far broader: the existence of hierarchies of ascending and descending good and bad men, angels, cherubs, and the like. "We have every reason to believe that, starting from a good man on the earth, there is a chain of *as*-cending good men, step after step, up to angels, cherubs, seraphs,—to the eternal God Himself. Now there must be also a *de*-scending scale. We see it here on earth, and have just as much reason to believe that the chain of evil beings stretches away in like manner, till it ends in the quintessence of all ill." See also ibid., 8–9, 12–17, 40–46. Randolph questioned whether the earth might

not possibly be the rendezvous of multitudes of principalities, powers, and other beings acting for their own purposes. "That whereas I once believed that all things were germinally good, I am led to believe that it was a mistake; I believe now that Christ was something more than a mere man; that his career was not a mere farce; there is a stupendous mystery all about us, that a tremendous danger—of what nature cannot be said, lies just ahead of us all." Ibid., 37, 42–44 (folly to say evil is as yet undeveloped good: perhaps there is an antagonistic center of evil operating in the world). See also *After Death*, 36 (there are thousands of devils but no principle of evil; evil is only the shadow of God).

39. *Ravalette*, 68.

40. See "Mysteries of Eulis," appendix B; *Ravalette*, 68.

41. See chapter 6. See also *Dealings with the Dead*, 19 ("The communication between the soul-world and earth is far more difficult and rare than I had believed, or than thousands believe today. Much, I learned, that passes among men for spiritual manifestation, really has no such origin, while many things, attributed to an origin purely mundane, are really the work of intelligent beings, beyond the misty veil."); *Guide to Clairvoyance* (1867), 24–25 (two kinds of magic: a good one, governed by Adonim; the other foul, malevolent in which "the adept is surrounded by an innumerable host of viewless powers, who lead him on to great ends and power, but finally sap out his life"). The similarities of these ideas with those of Madame Blavatsky in her early works are discussed in chapter 12. Randolph's intimations on the existence of these entities appeared first in *Unveiling*, 36 ("[W]hat do I really know of *any* of the great or little mysteries which surround us on all sides? ... What do I know of the scale or order of viewless beings, that perchance people all the regions round about? Still less. How do I know, 1st: that this earth may not be the rendezvous of countless multitudes of viewless beings of enormous power and enormous guile;—beings differing from, yet in some respects resembling man in intelligence and facility of action? If such beings,—'Principalities, powers, chiefs of the aerial kingdom,' really exist—and there are unmistakable indications pointing that way, scriptural and legendary, how do we know but that, being of rarer materials than ourselves, not subject to the law of gravitation, they may be darting hither and thither at will, through the solar system, alighting here, there and yonder, as fancy prompts, and tormenting us, and amusing themselves at our expense, at the same time.").

42. See chapter 4.

43. *Unveiling*, 30. See also ibid., 57–58 (spiritualism as the outrider of a new and better day); *Dealings with the Dead*, 109; *Davenport Brothers*, 102ff. ("John King" appeared to the Davenports in 1854–55 for the first time to teach immortality and told them to proselytize and make his name a household word); ibid., 28. In the late 1860s, this belief in the limited purpose of spiritualism and the exalted future of men on earth as they developed the "new or

God-knowing faculty" had become a sort of millenarianism for Randolph, who envisioned men in the new dispensation developing their full powers. He even prophesied that the "Coming Man, Redeemer of the World" had already been born. See *After Death*, 14–16, 29ff., 146; *Eulis!* 215–16 (the "old time animal magnetism" gave way to "Electrical Psychology," which in turn gave way to "Seeing Mediums, and all gave way before the 'royal road' of inner vision." Now this in turn must recede before the "higher, broader, deeper clairvoyance" induced by the magic mirror). Randolph's higher spiritual entities apparently also intervened for more explicitly political ends. Randolph says, apparently seriously, that "some of our friends from Summer Land raised a war by inciting one Davis Jefferson to rebel in behalf of human liberty. He was a medium, and did his work remarkably well." "From Our Reg-ular New Orleans Colored Correspondent, P. B. Randolph—No. 8," *Religio-Philosophical Journal* 1, no. 21 (February 17, 1866): 3.

44. *Dealings with the Dead*, 11–12.

45. *After Death*, 31. See also *Rosicrucian's Story*, 104: "I believe there are hierarchies high and low beyond the starry realms, and that we are, elementally, telegraphically, if you will, bound to, and connected with them; and then when Hell reigns in us, hells pour their slime upon our heads; when Heaven rules within, then we are open to the influx of celestial influences."

46. *Dealings with the Dead*, 50, 53, 58, 98, 110–11; *After Death*, 22. On Madame Blavatsky's constant use of the same motto in her early years, see chapter 12.

47. *Dealings with the Dead*, 223–24. The central importance of the Will is foreign to American spiritualism, which was a deliberately passive phenomenon, but it was common among the mesmerists, as we have seen, and in the Western magical tradition in general.

48. *Dealings with the Dead*, 6, 101–3, 116–17.

49. Ibid., 11–12.

50. Ibid., 11, 13. It was as Cynthia Temple that Randolph authored "It Isn't all Right," and the first part of *Dealings with the Dead* itself is written under her name. *Dealings with the Dead*, 152. Randolph describes his relationships with Cynthia Temple and other personages (Thotmor/Ramus and others) in the terms of everyday human conversation, but it is apparent that he conceived these relationships in a more mysterious fashion. In the new edition of *Dealings with the Dead* under the title *Soul! The Soul World* in 1872, Randolph added a note making this clear: "The reader need not be told that this vision was my own, nor that the entire revelation is *my* soul's experience; its reasonings and its results all, all the product of his inner being whose hands pen these lines,—even the Cynthian, Nellian and the Thotmorian experiences are all my own,—and that this book, like Bunyan's 'Pilgrim's Progress,' is a revelation of truth under similitudes; —the *dramatis personæ*, the out-creation of

my own immortal soul; that the experiences were subjective-psychical, and in no sense material, imaginative, borrowed or invented. Mystics will understand the process."

51. See chapters 10, 11 and 12.

52. See appendix B.

53. *New Mola!* 14–15. Randolph says that he is "as certain of the unequivocal truth of the statement as I am that any human being is immortal, which fact I know." In his *Curious Life*, he says that for twenty years he had been known as "The Man With Two Souls," one imperious, one sweet, and uses the condition to excuse his own quirky and angular character. Madame Blavatsky discusses the related Swedenborgian idea that shocks can cause a person's soul to vacate the body and the speculation that adepts or sorcerers can then possess it. *Isis Unveiled*, 2:589.

54. *Ravalette*, 12. See also ibid., 89–90 (explanation of a visitor's state by "the Rosicrucian theory, then quite new to me, that she was obsessed, or possessed, by and with a distinct individuality entirely foreign to her own"). The whole notion appears identical to the Tibetan idea of "tulku," which has curious and obvious echoes in the life of Madame Blavatsky. See Geoffrey A. Barborka, *H. P. Blavatsky, Tibet and Tulku* (Adyar: Theosophical Publishing House, 1966), and see chapter 12. On the sexual aspect of blending, see chapter 10.

55. In his Clinton Hall recantation speech, Randolph complained of daily intercourse for seven years with what purported to be his mother's spirit. This, he was finally convinced, was an "evil spirit and infernal demon." The original distinction between (good) blending and (evil) mediumship appears to have rested on the presence or loss of consciousness. See *Unveiling*, 18–19 (never part with consciousness, because it leads to paralysis of the will; heaven should be sought while wide awake.). Randolph also distinguishes in his recantation speech and elsewhere between voluntary and involuntary trances, but that distinction appears less central. The distinction between Randolph's blending and the state of the ordinary medium was, as a reviewer pointed out, somewhat chancy because, even in Randolph's descriptions, Cynthia at times completely possessed him. "The Blending State," *Spiritual Magazine* 3, no. 6 (June 1862): 278ff.

56. The importance both of mesmerism and of hashish are minimized in *Dealings with the Dead*, 116–17, 204.

57. *Dealings with the Dead*, 7. Randolph's reference to Machiavelli and his method may be derived more immediately from the explanation of Edgar Allan Poe's detective C. Auguste Dupin in "The Purloined Letter" of a boy's method of outguessing his school fellows: "'When I wish to find out how wise, or how stupid, or how good, or how wicked is any one, or what are his thoughts at the moment, I fashion the expression of my face, as accurately as

possible, in accordance with the expression of his, and then wait to see what thoughts or sentiments arise in my mind or heart, as if to match or correspond with the expression.' This response of the school-boy lies at the bottom of all the spurious profundity which has been attributed to . . . Machiavelli." *Great Tales and Poems of Edgar Allan Poe* (New York: Washington Square Press, 1951), 210. For further developments of the concept, see chapter 10. Poe's spirit, for reasons obvious from his works, was a great favorite of mediums in the 1850s and 1860s. See Lizzie Doten, "Poe's Poem," *Banner of Light* 8, no. 12 (December 15, 1860): 4; "A Poem by Poe, Through Lizzie Doten," ibid. 8, no. 22 (February 23, 1863): 4. Randolph was no exception and called Poe "*the* spirit of my love and choice." "P. B. Randolph and J. V. Mansfield," ibid. 6, no. 3 (October 15, 1859): 3–4. The influence of Poe's writings on Randolph is quite extensive. His poem "The Slave and Master—A Vision" (see chapter 4) is obviously imitative of Poe's work, and he may have borrowed the name for his "Oriental idea of the 'Pfal'" (*Love! At Last!*, appendix, viii, 161) from Poe's story of Hans Pfaal. Additionally, as Michael Gomes has pointed out to me, Randolph's constant refrain that "men fail and die through feebleness of will" (*Ansairetic Mystery*, appendix A) forms the caption of Poe's "Tomb of Lucretia."

58. This included, as we shall see, the idea of sex between embodied men and their disembodied (or perhaps never embodied) counterparts in the soul and spirit worlds. See chapter 10.

59. *Dealings with the Dead*, 138.

60. Parts of the manifesto are given in *Soul!* 276ff, which, however, omits the reference to teaching people to do this at pleasure. See appendix C.

61. *Dealings with the Dead*, 52, 80–81, 150.

62. *Dealings with the Dead*, 251; *After Death*, 157–60, 165.

63. *Dealings with the Dead*, 31, 128, 138.

64. *After Death*, 159–60; *Dealings with the Dead*, 127–28.

65. *After Death*, 157–60.

66. *Davenport Brothers*, 152–54.

67. *Dealings with the Dead*, 97–98, 249–50. Ethylle is either the same as the most sublimated and divine fluid that pervades the universes or, alternatively, is one remove from that highest plane.

Chapter 6

1. On the early Rosicrucians, see generally the seminal work of Frances Yates, *The Rosicrucian Enlightenment* (London: Routledge and Kegan Paul, 1972). For the later developments of the myth, see Christopher McIntosh, *The Rose*

Cross and the Age of Reason. Eighteenth-Century Rosicrucianism in Central Europe and Its Relationship to the Enlightenment (Leiden: E. J. Brill, 1992).

2. See the quotations in the text below and also *Triplicate Order*, 29–30; *Ravalette*, 72–79.

3. "Order of Eulis," *Notes and Queries* (April 1905): 98. On these groups and Gould's involvement with them, see chapter 11.

4. Randolph occasionally touts his discoveries as the Elixir Vitae and the philosopher's stone and graces his pages with references to Artephius, Ramon Lull, the *Hermippus Redivivus* and the *Petit Albert*, but there is no sustained effort by him to place his work in the alchemical tradition.

5. See Gustav Meyrink's introduction to *Dhoula Bel*, and compare *Ravalette* (1876), 73, where Randolph dismisses the *Comte de Gabalis* as a "humorous bit of badinage." W. E. Coleman, who admittedly had an ax to grind in opposing the change from spiritualism to occultism, notes, in reviewing Randolph's posthumous *Beyond the Veil* in 1878, that Randolph came to reject the notion of elementals totally after he reached the Summer Land. The claim is unverifiable, but there is no indication that Randolph while alive rejected elementals, though they played no major role in his works. See Coleman's review in *The Truth Seeker* (March 30, 1878): 206. Magic mirrors also play a role in the *Comte de Gabalis*, since such mirrors and the formulation in them of the "solary powder" that exalts the fire within are the means of obtaining power over the Salamandrines. See A. E. Waite, *The Occult Sciences*, 39–40.

6. The beginning of *Dealings with the Dead* describes Randolph's surprised projection of his soul at a distance. See also *Guide to Clairvoyance*, 41 (on the scin-lecca).

7. See, e.g., *Casca Llanna*, 73–74 (volantia is the key to extending life).

8. *Eulis!* 46–47.

9. *Soul!* 274–76. The passage abounds in anachronisms and inaccuracies but it may be generally accurate in describing how Randolph, through the comments of others, came to think of himself as a Rosicrucian. Some indication of who these others may have been may perhaps be gleaned, as we have already seen in chapter 2, from *Ravalette* (1863), in which Randolph says that in Paris and London he had become acquainted with a few "reputed Rosicrucians" whom he found "shallow and muddy." These included Edward Bulwer-Lytton and Hargrave Jennings. See *Ravalette* (1863), 58.

10. *Dealings with the Dead*, 200. Thotmor is also said to have been a "king of the eighteenth dynasty." *Rosicrucian's Story*, 12. "Thotmer" first made his appearance as Randolph's teacher in "Dealings with the Dead. Number Seven. Parenthetical to 'Epoch,'" *Banner of Light* 6, no. 9 (November 26, 1859): 6–7, where he says the name should really be *Thothmes*. Thotmor reappears in "Lara.—An Experience," published by Randolph in *The Hesperian* 7, no. 3,

while he was in San Francisco establishing his Rosicrucian group there in November 1861, as "the builder of the first Pyramid, King of Egypt, and sixty-ninth chief of the Imperial Order of the Rosy Cross." I am grateful to David Board for bringing this article to my attention.

11. *Dealings with the Dead*, 220.

12. *Rosicrucian's Story*, 14–15.

13. *Ravalette*, 55. See also *Casca Llanna*, 74–75, which speaks of "one common brotherhood, not, say they, confined to earth either, but rising by successive steps, grade after grade, hierarchy after hierarchy in the starry heavens, [until it] is lost to mortal fancy as they sweep away into the awful fields of the further sky!"

14. *Dealings with the Dead*, 151.

15. *Ravalette*, 22–23.

16. *Dealings with the Dead*, 19. See also *After Death*, 31: "Disembodied, or rather ethereal people, of a lofty order, generally, but by no means universally, undoubtedly direct, in all essential respects, the grand spiritual movement of the age."

17. *Ravalette*, 56.

18. Ibid., 57.

19. Ibid., 37–39. A variant of the vision is found in "Notes of my Psychal Life," in which Randolph says that in 1842 (when he was seventeen and living in Portland, Maine) he "felt himself leaving the body, as it were. A sharp, prickling pain in my head, told me that something unusual was about to occur. The head appeared to increase in size, three-fold, and from out of the top of it I saw, as plainly as if I had there a hundred eyes." In this position in midair he encountered an unnamed spirit guide (who in this version is beneficent and good), beheld seven spheres of light, and perceived that the heads of all persons are connected by threads of light.

20. *Ravalette*, 58–59. At this point in the novel Randolph warns of deliberate anachronisms.

21. *Ravalette*, 63–64.

22. *Ravalette*, 68. See also ibid., 190–213, where all the wonders of the seance room are caused to occur by Ravalette who, whatever the book intends him to be, is no "spirit," and 67, 179–82.

23. It is hard to obtain any consistency of dates, but the event is intended to be thought of as occurring after the first trip in 1855, although Randolph first went to the Near East on his trip in 1857–1858. "Little Cora" is described as "prattling," and the event is clearly before the trip of 1861–62.

24. *Ravalette*, 105.

25. Ibid., 60: "As he spoke it struck me that, somewhere, at some time, I had met this Italian Rosicrucian, but where, for the life of me, I could not tell; yet I was certain that I had heard that voice, and still more certain that I had beheld that strange, sweet smile."

26. *Ravalette*, 102, 111.

27. Included in the demonstration is the production of spirit sketches which Randolph dubs "Magic art"—a curious foreshadowing of Emma Hardinge Britten's later *Art Magic*.

28. *Ravalette*, 221–23.

29. " 'Mai is but a transposition of I am; 'Miakus' is 'Myself,' Vatterale is an anagram of Ravalette, and a school-boy would have told you that Ettelavar is but Ravalette reversed—the name meaning 'The Mysterious.'" *Ravalette*, 236. *Ravalette* was billed as the solution to the problem posed in another (lost) novel of Randolph entitled *Dhoula Bel, or the Magic Globe*. This was undoubtedly published at some point, perhaps as a pamphlet. It is mentioned in *Unveiling* (1860), and *Casca Llanna* (1872) announced its publication for March 1872 as *Dhoula Bel: The Magic Globe; A Romance of the Shadow and the Light*, but it apparently never saw the light of day in that form. See appendix C. Perhaps it was destroyed in the great Boston fire later that year that also put an end to Emma Hardinge Britten's journal.

30. *Ravalette*, 238ff. He also prophesied that the "Coming Man, Redeemer of the World" had already been born. *After Death*, 146. The reference to the Prussian may be to Charles Trinius, who is discussed below in this chapter.

31. *Ravalette*, 154, 221–22.

32. Ibid., 127.

33. *Rosicrucian's Story*, 24. The frequent omission in Randolph's later works and in later editions of early books of these references to higher authority reflects either his desire to emphasize his originality, which he had earlier masked for propagandistic purposes under Oriental trappings and claims, or perhaps some change in his relationship with his sources.

34. *Curious Life* (1872), 8 (he traveled "successively" to these countries, in the order given); 44 (travels through Arabia, Egypt, Turkey and Palestine); *Pre-Adamite Man* (1863), 82–83 (Randolph's travels in the deserts of Sin and Shur; Sinai); *Soul!* 374ff. (travels in Africa, Arabia, Turkey, Greece, Egypt); *Ravalette*, 68ff. (Egypt, Syria, Turkey, Dongola, Arabia; Naples); *After Death* (France, England, Ireland, Scotland, Turkey, Egypt, Syria, Central and Western America, Arabia, Mexico, California); *Guide to Clairvoyance* (1867) (Africa, Egypt, Turkey, Arabia, Syria; studied hashish in Egypt; England, Scotland, France, Ireland, Egypt, Syria, Arabia, Palestine and Turkey); *Golden Secret* (1872) (hashish

recipe in Turkey from sultan; stay in Constantinople in 1862 with Mr. Goddard); *Casca Llanna* (1872), 12 (Egypt); 217 (Damascus). On Persia, *Casca Llanna*, 73 (in discussing love: "What strange lore is this which he learned among the Druses, and Nusaireh of Syria; the Guebres of Persia; the Arabs of the desert; the Turk in Stamboul and the swart sages of sweltering Negro-land?"); *Casca Llanna*, appended advertisements, 22 (Caboul, Persia, and Tehran); *After Death*, 124 (music in the fourth sphere of the spirit world is like Arabian and Turkish music he has heard in Cairo, Smyrna, Beyrout, Constantinople and Jerusalem); *Soul!* 137 (Jerusalem); *Davenport Brothers* (same).

35. *Rosicrucian's Story* (1863), 80.

36. *Triplicate Order* (1875), 19.

37. *Ravalette*, 79; *Triplicate Order*, 9. See also the advertisement for *Seership!* at the end of *Master Passion* (1870), 178, where Randolph claims that the work is the fullest exposition of these matters ever "permitted to be issued outside the temples of the Imperial Order, *De la Rose Croix*." Only one copy of the book would be sold to a customer "with the end of supplying the brethren of the august fraternity, on the continent of North America and the islands of her seas." Randolph's first reference to "our association, Ce cercle de la croix rouge" is in "Dealings with the Dead.—Number Four," *Banner of Light* 5, no. 26 (September 24, 1859): 7.

38. *Ravalette*, 86–87. "Mountain of Light" is the Arabic *Djebel el nur*.

39. *Pre-Adamite Man*, 64. This is the only mention of a New York lodge.

40. In speaking of how he learned of the Rosicrucians, the fictitious narrator of *Ravalette* says (53): "I forbore to reveal the locality of the lodges of the Dome, or indicate the persons or names of its chief officers, albeit, no such restriction was exacted in reference to the lesser temples of the order—covering the first three degrees in this country—to the acolytes of which the higher lodges are totally unknown." In *Rosicrucian's Story* (the 1863 edition, but not the later ones), 114–15, Randolph begins to relate the nature of the parallel universes and then desists on the ground that he could not do so "without the dispensation of the Grand Master." In *Guide to Clairvoyance* (1867), 52, similarly, he brags of a method of making an "oraculum" superior to anything "known outside the Grand Lodge."

41. Letter of J. B. Pilkington to a Boston paper in 1861, reprinted in *Curious Life*, 27–28, and elsewhere in Randolph's works.

42. *Ravalette*, 214.

43. *Eulis!* (1874), 47. See also ibid., 53.

44. Quoted in *Ravalette*, 72–73. Jung-Stilling (1740–1817) was a Christian visionary much admired by Goethe. His autobiography from which the quote comes appeared first in English in 1844. The passage on the Monastery of

Canobin recurs repeatedly throughout the nineteenth century. See, e.g., the introduction to Alexander Wilder's pamphlet, *The Rosicrucian Brotherhood* (Edmonds, Wash.: Sure Fire Press, 1990). Randolph's knowledge of Jung-Stilling, including this quotation, quite possibly came through the works of his old English spiritualist friends Thomas Shorter and William Howitt. See chapter 2 and William Howitt, *History of the Supernatural in All Ages and Nations*, 1:28–29.

45. *Ghost Land*, 30.

46. See Hamill, *Rosicrucian Seer*, 16.

47. See generally Ellic Howe, "Fringe Masonry in England 1870–85," *Ars Quatuor Coronatorum* 85 (1972):242–95; Hamill, *Rosicrucian Seer*.

48. *Royal Masonic Cyclopædia* 450, 453; David Board, "The Brotherhood of Luxor and the Brotherhood of Light," *Theosophical History* 2, no. 5 (January 1988): 149–57.

49. The order is said still to exist, though with what seriousness it is impossible to determine. See *The Aquarian Guide to Occult, Mystical, Religious, Magical London and Around*, Francoise Strachan, ed. (London: Aquarian Press, 1970), 155–57, and the appendix by "J. Cretien, D.D." on "The Enigma of the Fratres Lucis." This last piece emphasizes that the Fratres Lucis are unconnected with the "Randolph Foundation" and with "the tutti quanti of commercial mystics, whether of Quakertown or Paris" (155). In characteristic fashion, the author embroiders the tale by saying that the *Fratres Lucis* were founded by refugee Templars, Cathars, Manicheans, and Albigenses who met in the palace of the duke of Florence to perpetuate the secret tradition. The author claims that there are only thirteen members at a time, with successors chosen from lay disciples of the deceased adept.

50. *Casca Llanna*, 75.

51. *Ravalette*, 67. In attempting to deny that the sexual magic contained in Maria de Naglowska's *Magia Sexualis* (which had been published in Paris the preceding year) contained Randolph's teachings, R. S. Clymer in his 1932 edition of *Soul! The Soul World*, 13–15, says that *Magia Sexualis* was simply a compilation of *Eulis!*, *Seership!* and a "book published one hundred or more years ago in India, under the title, Sexual Happiness." This may be by the mysterious Naumsavi Chitty, who is otherwise unknown.

52. Reprinted in R. S. Clymer, ed., *The Initiates* 3 (1930–31), and, in part, in *Soul!* 276–89. See appendix C. Victorien Moreau is unknown, but Victorien Sardou, who may be the person intended, was a well-known dramatist of the era and a member of the spiritualist circle around Allan Kardec that included Baron von Güldenstubbé. See Karl Kieswetter, *Geschichte des Neuren Occultismus*, 1:470ff. Alexandre Dumas, père, whom Randolph claimed as a friend, was a member of the group, a fact that lends some credence to the identification.

53. The only study of Jennings is the excellent article by Joscelyn Godwin, "Hargrave Jennings," *Hermetic Journal* (1991): 49–77.

54. The turgidity of Jennings's style has been commented upon by everyone who has sought to understand him, even by A. E. Waite, whose own writings suffer from the same defect. Waite summed up Jennings's work as "a penny dreadful of occult mysteries." *Shadows of Life and Thought* (London: Selwyn & Blount, 1938), 100. Alexander Wilder, the editor of Madame Blavatsky's *Isis Unveiled* and a prolific author on phallic subjects and the Neoplatonists, opined that Jennings's "sentences are often painfully interwrought, so as to nullify their meaning." "The Rosicrucians," *Rosicrucian Brotherhood* 1, no. 3 (1908): 81, 83. The obscurity, however, appears to have been a deliberate device to veil the truths he believed he was revealing, because Jennings could write in a clear and even entertaining style when he wanted to—as his occasional and journalistic pieces bear witness.

55. *The Indian Religions* (1890), 29. This was originally published in 1858.

56. *The Letters of Hargrave Jennings, Author of "The Rosicrucians," "Phallicism," &c., &c. Forming the Unabridged Correspondence with the Editor of the Bath Occult Reprints, between 1879 and 1887, with Frontispiece* (Bath: Robert H. Fryar, 1895), 43. The introduction is by John Yarker, and the preface by "Invictus." R. S. Clymer states that Jennings's letters to Randolph were preserved in the "archives of the fraternity," and his associate Allan F. Odell further specifies that the correspondence was lost in a fire in 1928, so conceivably there is some truth in the claim. See Clymer, *Rosicrucian Fraternity in America*, 2 vols. (Quakertown: Rosicrucian Foundation, 1935), 1:427; advertisement for *Magia Sexualis* in *La Flèche*, March 15, 1933. I am grateful to Maître Christian Chanel for bringing this last to my attention.

57. *Indian Religions*, 68. See also ibid., 198 ("If the bond of the whole visible world be the universal magnetism, then the immortal, unparticled Spirit, of which this magnetism is the shadow, may be that ineffable potentiality, in which the real religion shall be alone possible.").

58. *Indian Religions*, 89, 118.

59. Ibid., passim. On the Druses, see ibid., 149ff.

60. Ibid., 156.

61. Ibid., 220–21.

62. See Godwin, "Hargrave Jennings," who examines the case for a connection between Jennings and Frederick Hockley and Kenneth Mackenzie and points out the fact that Jennings identifies himself in his *Curious Things of the Outside World. Last Fire*, 2 vols. (London: T. & W. Boone, 1861) as "F.R.C. (Rosicrucian)." For Jennings's relationship with Bulwer-Lytton, see the Earl of Lytton, *The Life of Edward Bulwer*, 2 vols. (London: Macmillan, 1913), 2:40ff.

63. Jennings's principal works are *The Indian Religions, or, Results of the Mysterious Buddhism* (London: T. C. Newby, 1858; 2d ed., revised and enlarged, Redway, 1890) (by "An Indian Missionary"); *Curious Things of the Outside World; The Rosicrucians, Their Rites and Mysteries* (London: Hotten, 1870); *Phallicism, Celestial and Terrestrial* (London: Redway, 1884); *One of the Thirty: A Strange History, Now for the First Time Told* (London: J. C. Hotten, n.d., c. 1873); *The Childishness and Brutality of the Times. Some Plain Truths in Plain Language* (London: Vizetelly & Co., 1883)(reprint, Kessinger Publishing Co., n.d.); *Live Lights or Dead Lights: (Altar or Table?)* (London: John Hodges, 1873).

64. *The Letters of Hargrave Jennings,* 16 ("I do not approve of Randolph's Book nor do I look with favour upon his 'Eulis,' or anything which refers in any way to this coarse and rough—even vulgarly free and mischievous and most mistaken way of dealing with these—in truth—sublime and exquisitely learned subjects."); 44 ("I first knew Randolph the American thirty-five years ago [1852], he was, physically, a very remarkable man."). See also *Ravalette,* 58.

65. *Seership!* 44, 59. See also ibid., 80, which appears from internal indications to have been part of the original work on magic mirrors. It refers to "the Masters," and then quotes De Novalis and "the Grand Master, himself a genius rare." The latter (from the quotation) is Hargrave Jennings. By the time *Eulis!* was published in 1874, the printed synopsis for *Seership!* (xv) refers only to "The Grand Master, De Novalis." On Novalis as a literary magician, see Maryla Falk, *I 'Misteri' di Novalis* (Naples, 1939).

66. *Seership!* 59, 61–71.

67. See *Eulis!* 215 (on mirrors), 40 (on Order of Garter); *New Mola!* 36 (Randolph's elixirs are the same as the wine mentioned by Hermippus, Lytton, and Jennings); *Asiatic Mystery* and, in part, *Soul!* 276–89 (Jennings published the teachings of the order).

68. *Ravalette,* 72–73.

69. Even Clymer's archenemy, H. S. Lewis, the head of the rival AMORC. Rosicrucian organization of San Jose, California, felt compelled to accept parts of Clymer's vision and associated Randolph with the organized efforts of W. G. Palgrave, Eliphas Lévi, Hargrave Jennings, and "others" who eventually founded the Societas Rosicruciana in Anglia (of which Randolph was said to be an "honorary member"). See H. S. Lewis, *Rosicrucian Questions and Answers,* 2d ed. (San Jose: A.M.O.R.C., 1932), 139ff. This is pure fantasy.

70. Clymer flatly denied to Gerald Yorke that Randolph had practiced sexual magic and attacked Maria de Naglowska's *Magia Sexualis* as a forgery—all the while privately circulating to his own followers versions of Randolph's manuscript teachings on sexual magic.

71. See, e.g., W. W. Westcott, *The Rosicrucians, Past and Present, at Home and Abroad* (1900; reprint, Mokelumne Hill, Calif.: Health Research, 1966), 4.

For a summary of what is known about the lodge, see Godwin, *Theosophical Enlightenment*, 122–23.

72. Paul Chacornac in his *Eliphas Lévi, Rénovateur de l'occultisme* (Paris: Chacornac, 1926), 241ff., gives the story and identifies the young man as Juliano Capella.

73. Mary Mackay (1855–1924), who wrote under the pseudonym *Marie Corelli*, published her first novel, *A Romance of Two Worlds* (London: R. Bentley & Son) in 1887. The story related the progressive initiation of a young girl by a mysterious Count Heliobas who is described variously as a Chaldean and an Armenian. It is difficult to believe that the figure does not reflect Randolph's Armenian/Italian count, though mysterious counts, such as the count of Monte Christo and the "Comte de Cagliostro," abound. The same figure or his congener reappears in Corelli's "*Ardath,*" *The Story of a Dead Self* (London: R. Bentley & Son, 1890) and in *The Soul of Lilith* (New York: F. M. Buckles & Co., 1892). The "Count A. de G[uinotti], Hierarch of the S.S.S." to whom John C. Street dedicated his *Hidden Way Across the Threshold* (1888) appears on its face unrelated to Randolph, but others have made Street a member of Randolph's Rosicrucians. See "Pioneer Rosicrucian Workers in America, No. 3: Freeman B. Dowd," *Mercury* 2, no. 13 (September 10, 1917): 1, which says (in its reform spelling) that Dowd's "particular sfere of activity was the organization known as the 'Rosy Cross,' into which he was initiated by Pascal Beverly Randolph, the same organization in which J. C. Street, another noted worker was activ." I am grateful to David Board for bringing this to my attention. On Clymer and the identity of this "Count A. de Guinotti," see chapter 11. The H. B. of L., perhaps for competitive reasons, was scathing about Street's organizations. See "S.S.S.5," *Occult Magazine* 1, no. 6 (July 1885): 47–48, and Ursus, "Sham Teachers of Occultism," ibid. 1, no. 8 (September 1885): 63 (reprinting one of Street's "Professional Letters," a correspondence course in occultism widely advertised in the United States, sent to Gustav Zorn, a member of the H. B. of L.).

74. Clymer's history of Randolph and the Rosicrucians is found scattered over all of his many books. See most conveniently his *The Rosicrucian Fraternity in America*, 2 vols. (Quakertown, Rosicrucian Foundation, 1935); *The Fraternitatis Rosae Crucis. An Attempt to Harmonize the Spirit of the Writings of Those who are Known to have been Rosicrucians* (Quakertown: Philosophical Publishing Co., 1929); and his *Book of Rosicruciae. A Correct History of the Fraternitas Rosae Crucis or Rosy Cross, the Men Who Made the Order Possible, and Those who Maintained the Fraternity throughout the Centuries. Together with the Fundamental Teachings of These Men according to the Actual Research in the Archives of the Fraternity*, 3 vols. (Quakertown: Philosophical Publishing Co., 1946).

75. The charter exists only in a copy attached to R. S. Clymer, *The August Fraternity. Order of the Rose Cross in America, and H. Spencer Lewis, The Baron Munchausen of the Occult* (Quakertown: Philosophical Publishing Co., n.d., c. 1933). I am grateful to David Board for calling the document to my

attention. The substance of the charter is printed in Clymer's *Initiates* (April 1909): 22ff. Randolph claimed that the order had first been brought into Europe by Artephius the alchemist after the First Crusade. See *Triplicate Order*, 29–30.

76. See *Curious Life*, 73–74. Randolph's claim that he had been known as a Rosicrucian since 1852 is almost certainly a deliberate deception. The designation *Rosicrucian* first appears after his second trip to Europe in 1857.

77. R. S. Clymer, in a note that has sufficient detail to suggest that it may be based on fact, claimed to have seen in Paris a Rosicrucian manifesto issued by Randolph in 1858, but he said he never received a copy because of World War II. The manifesto was supposed to be the one ("The Rosicrucians, Who and What they Are") that Randolph printed in *Ravalette* (1863). He also states that the *Asiatic Mystery* (the Rosicrucian manifesto of 1871—see appendix C) was originally issued in 1859. See Clymer, *The Rosicrucians—Their Teachings. The Fraternitas Rosae Crucis. American Section. The Manifestoes Issued by the Brotherhood, Order, Temple and Fraternity of the Rosicrucians since its Foundation in America have been Edited and the Teachings Made Applicable to Modern Conditions and the needs of the New Age*, rev. ed. (Quakertown: Philosophical Publishing Co., n.d., copyright 1941), 71–72, 81. The remark quoted in the text about the dissolution of the Grand Lodge probably conceals some dispute between Randolph and his followers—a recurring theme in Randolph's life.

78. *Curious Life* , 8. California at the time was a fertile field for mediums. See "Test Mediums Wanted in California," *Banner of Light* 10, no. 5 (October 26, 1861): 3; G. W. Johnson, "Shall Mediums Come to California," ibid. 10, no. 10 (November 30, 1861): 4.

79. See Dowd's introduction to *After Death*, "The Thinker and his Thought," dated Davenport, Iowa, January 1870. Dowd quotes from a contemporary newspaper article by Dr. Pilkington on Randolph's 1861 visit. See also *Soul!* (1870), 276. On Pilkington, see *Grand Secret*, 83. Pilkington was also author of *Religion And Science: Or, Christianity, Religion, And The Bible Versus Philosophy And Science* (San Francisco: Woman's Pub. Co., 1875), published at the time Randolph was founding his last Rosicrucian venture, but the book reveals nothing about Pilkington's involvement with Randolph's work.

80. Dr. Paschal Beverly Randolph, *The Grand Secret; or, Physical Love in Health and Disease* (San Francisco: Pilkington & Randolph, 1861–62). Allibone says that Randolph published two works while in San Francisco. The second must be *Hesperina*, which Allibone lists as published there, but no copy has been preserved. See appendix C.

81. The Dorbon catalogue, *Bibliotheca Esoterica, Catalogue Annoté et illustré de 6707 ouvrages anciens et modernes qui traitent des sciences occultes . . . en vente à la Librairie Dorbon-Ainé* (Paris, n.d.), lists a manuscript in English of the "Mysteries of Eulis" and notes that it was written about 1860 and that it

contained the teaching that Randolph gave in the Supreme Lodge of the Temple of Eulis that he founded in San Francisco. It is doubtful that these comments reflect reality, however. The Temple (or Brotherhood) of Eulis and the teachings of Eulis themselves are a much later creation, dating from the early 1870s. There is no indication whatsoever that Randolph was teaching Eulis or had developed his complete system of sexual magic before that time.

82. *Ravalette*, 79–86. See above, note 77, on the claim by R. S. Clymer that the manifesto was originally circulated as early as 1858.

83. Ibid., 83ff.

84. Ibid., 85.

85. Ibid., 53, 81. The names of the degrees may have been the same as those in Randolph's last foundation in 1874. The 1874 order called the members of the three degrees "Builders," "Architects," and "Knights of the Temple." *Triplicate Order*, 28. Randolph had already used the pseudonym *Builder of the Temple* in 1863. See appendix C. In *Triplicate Order*, 19, published in 1875, Randolph stated that the "Triple Order was founded in one degree only (the Rosicrucian)" on November 5, 1861. The statement is probably intended to convey the existence of still further mysteries in the later foundation rather than to deny the existence of three stages of some sort in the original order. See chapter 10.

86. Further details on the housekeeping of the order can perhaps be gleaned from Randolph's 1871 manifesto, the *Asiatic Mystery*, and from the rules or by-laws of the order as they existed in 1875. The latter are given in R. S. Clymer's *Initiates* (July 1908):119ff. and (April 1909): 20ff.

87. *Triplicate Order*, 20.

88. *Seership!* 81 (celebrated crystal "glove" of Trinius of San Francisco, for which three thousand dollars was unsuccessfully offered); *Rosicrucian's Story* (1863), 114 (Brother Trinius's visions in the mirror). The original dedication of *The Rosicrucian's Story* was to "Charles T." The dedicatee was later changed (without altering the dedication itself) to Freeman B. Dowd. Randolph also thanks Trinius for his help with *Pre-Adamite Man* (1863) and dedicates the book to him and to Abraham Lincoln. Clymer, of course, says that Trinius was one of the Rosicrucian "*inconnus*" and that he was a member of the Council of Three of Prussia, in which capacity he assisted Bulwer-Lytton in conferring the "Ordre du Lys" on Randolph. *Rosicrucian Fraternity*, 2:xxx and 2:71.

89. Fischer, who is called "Baron" Fischer, assisted Randolph in attempting to revive the order in 1871, but soon fell away. In the *Asiatic Mystery* he is called "one of the recusant nine."

90. Randolph's announcement is in the Pilkington article, *Curious Life*, 27–28. Randolph had already used the device of orders from above in *Dealings*

with the Dead ("I have received a message from beyond the sea" and will soon cross), but apparently had not obeyed the command. Shortly after Madame Blavatsky's arrival in Paris—itself probably on orders, see *H. P. B. Speaks*, C. Jinarajadasa, ed., 2 vols. (Adyar: Theosophical Publishing House, 1950–51), 2:23—she claimed to receive "orders" from the "Brothers" to go to America, and arrived there on July 6 or 7, 1873. See chapter 12.

91. Clymer, in "Fraternitas Rosae Crucis. An Outline History of the Men and Events Leading up to the Foundation of the Fraternity, Its Teachings and Activities to the Present Time," *The Initiates* 5 (May–June 1932–May–June 1941): 111ff., specifies that on Randolph's return from his 1861–62 trip to the Orient he founded temples in Boston, Illinois, California (among E. A. Hitchcock's students, Clymer says), Memphis, Washington, D.C. (where Abraham Lincoln was a member), and Utica. This is, conceivably, based on some unknown document or oral tradition, but it is probably merely Clymer's imagination. Some evidence of continuing propaganda for Randolph's Rosicrucians is provided by A. W. Fenno in 1863. Fenno, who is probably the actor who took Emma Hardinge Britten to one of her first seances, says he was the medium for a Rosicrucian who instructed him on "Who and what were the Rosicrucians"—a title clearly derived from Randolph's first manifesto—and told him that the great error of the early Rosicrucians had been to exclude women from their ranks. See A. W. Fenno, "The Rosicrucians," *Banner of Light* 12, no. 24 (March 7, 1863): 8; Emma Hardinge Britten, "Valedictory," *Banner of Light* 17, no. 17 (July 15, 1865): 4.

92. Randolph does not appear to have performed as a spiritualist on this trip or to have renewed his old acquaintance with the English spiritualists. See "The Blending State, " *Spiritual Magazine* 3, no. 6 (June 1862), where the reviewer (who was probably Thomas Shorter or William Howitt) says that he had last seen Randolph five years previously (i.e., in 1857) and appears unaware that Randolph had again crossed the Atlantic.

93. E. O'Conor, "Letter from London—P. B. Randolph," *Banner of Light* 12, no. 8 (November 15, 1862): 3. The correspondent reported that Randolph was due in England in October and would immediately leave for the United States. Randolph said that he spent ten months in the desert without seeing another American and described the thrill he experienced when he saw the Stars and Stripes flying from the embassy in Jerusalem. *Davenport Brothers*, 65; *Soul!* 137.

94. *Rosicrucian's Story* (1863), 43. In 1863 he published a version of this work on dreams as *The Celebrated Rodrey Dream Book* which has not survived. See list of his publications in *Ravalette* (1863). In 1871 he republished his secrets of dream interpretation as *The Rosicrucian Dream-Book: Containing Solutions of . . . Dreams, etc. Collected and Translated from the Old English* (Boston: Randolph Publishing Co., 1871). The book is anonymous, but the copyright is registered in Randolph's name.

95. *Golden Secret:* "The original formula, I actually obtained in Constantinople, Turkey, from Sultan Abdul's own physician, during the time I was the guest of our consul-general, Mr. Goddard, in 1862, at Prinkipo, an island in the Bosphorus, opposite Stamboul, between the shores of Europe and Asia."

96. *Eulis!* (1874), 48. In the next paragraph Randolph mentions that he, like "Christian Rosencrux," went to Oriental lands "for initiation"—one of his rare uses of the term. For a contemporary's view of the dervishes and their familiarity with the role of will in magic and with hashish, see Brown, *Darvishes or Oriental Spiritualism*, 146ff., 340–43. For a fascinating modern account of the role of sex and drugs among sufis and Isma'ilis, see Wilson, *Scandal* 195–213.

97. Polygenism finally triumphed in the scientific mind in the late 1850s, just before Randolph addressed the subject. See G. W. Stocking, "French Anthropology in 1800," *Isis* 55 (1964):134–50.

98. See *Davenport Brothers*, 110.

99. *Seership!* 70–71.

100. New York: S. Tousey, 1863. The quotations given here are from the 6th edition, Toledo, Randolph Publishing Co., 1888. Randolph mentions a proposed sequel to this that was never published: *The Human Body and the Human Soul—Their Origin, Nature, Constitution and Destiny, on the Earth and off it*. See *Pre-Adamite Man*, 398.

101. In 1865, Sir John Lubbock published his *Prehistoric Times* which popularized "prehistoric" and for the first time used the terms *Paleolithic* and *Neolithic*.

102. *Pre-Adamite Man*, 22. It is perhaps only a curiosity that Randolph repeatedly cites the paleontological work of Charles Carter Blake. *Pre-Adamite Man*, 314, 352, 359, 376. Blake was a man of many parts. He was a scientist and one of the leading lights in the British National Association of Spiritualists (where he was noted for his claims to project his astral body). He also played a mysterious role in the early Theosophical Society in Great Britain. He was a sometime enemy of Madame Blavatsky who ended up contributing a strong tribute to her knowledge of science to a book of her friends' reminiscences. He also had an interest in Indian Tantra (which he suspected the New York Theosophists of practicing). It is tempting to believe that Randolph sought out Blake in researching *Pre-Adamite Man*, but there is no evidence of the meeting. On Blake's relationship with Madame Blavatsky, see chapter 12.

103. Randolph had been convinced of Professor Louis Agassiz's position on the existence of "pre-Adamites" since 1859. See "P. B. Randolph at the Melodeon," *Banner of Light* 4, no. 14 (January 1, 1859): 5, 8.

104. For example, Francis Cornford on Thucydides.

105. *Pre-Adamite Man*, 113.

106. *Eulis!* (1874); *Supplement to Eulis*. See also *After Death*, 48ff. (continuing evolution and infusion of divine Monad into the foetus). For the close parallels of these ideas with traditional Hermeticism, see A. J. Festugière, *La Révélation d'Hermès Trismégiste*, 2d ed., 4 vols. (Paris: J. Gabalda, 1954), vol. 4.

107. See Léon Poliakov, *Il mito ariano* (Milan: Rizzoli, 1976).

108. *Pre-Adamite Man*, 67.

109. Ibid., 66ff., 130–31. Randolph does not mention Volney by name. Volney's ideas on a primitive black civilization are in *The Ruins, or, Meditations on the Revolutions of Empires: and the Law of Nature* (1802; reprint, Baltimore: Black Classics Press, 1991). His curiosity about the Nusa'iri is in *Voyage en Egypte et en Syrie* (1787; Paris: J. Gaulmier, 1959), 216, 279. Randolph's insistence on the "purity" of the black race undoubtedly is a reflection of the ideas of Joseph-Arthur de Gobineau. His *Essai sur l'inégalité des races humaines*, 4 vols. (Paris, 1853–1855), an American edition of which appeared in 1856, stressed the degeneracy consequent upon the mixing of the "red, yellow and black races."

110. *Pre-Adamite Man*, 67. However, he does think that Egypt itself was originally settled from central Africa, though the population that brought it to glory was mixed. Ibid., 58.

111. *Pre-Adamite Man*, 161ff., 338.

112. *After Death*, 100.

113. *Pre-Adamite Man*, 238ff. (older is more barbarous, infantile, and savage); 266 (man is young and undeveloped); 400 (Buddhism and "sacerdotalisms").

114. Ibid., 34–35, 399.

115. Ibid., 35. In *After Death*, 194, written in the late 1860s, he speaks of "four preceding eras of civilization starting from the people of *This, Memphis,* and *Philæ*."

116. *Pre-Adamite Man*, 63–64.

117. Ibid., 64. In an aside that prefigures G. H. Felt's lectures to the inchoate Theosophical Society in 1875 (chapter 13), Randolph quotes Wendell Phillips to the effect that animal magnetism was known in the Middle Ages, and then adds: "An Error! For it was known in both Egypt and Nimroud, Syria, and Nineveh, thousands, instead of hundreds of years ago, as is proved by sculptures and paintings innumerable, some of which represent the curative process, others those of inducing magnetic somnolence; others, still, the act of delivering dreamy oracles, *a la* the modern, so-called 'clairvoyance.'" *Pre-Adamite Man*, 408.

118. *Pre-Adamite Man*, 116–17. *Oscillating* does not appear to be quite the correct term. What Randolph meant was a rotation of the poles of the earth about a pivot located at the center of the globe. The idea of a rotation of the poles as an explanation for the succession of the ages of men and the confusion of the high wisdom of earlier ages came into prominence in the works of Godfrey Higgins, who in turn based his geology on the French astronomer Jean-Sylvain Bailly. For an excellent review of nineteenth-century polar myths, see Joscelyn Godwin, *Arktos: The Polar Myth in Science, Symbolism and Nazi Survival* (Grand Rapids: Phanes Press, 1993).

119. *Pre-Adamite Man*, 135; *After Death*, 87–88 (destruction of the planet formerly between Mars and Jupiter caused the poles to move and the destruction of Atlantis); 185, 194 (the shifting of the poles proceeds in cycles of sixteen-thousand years which also govern the rise and fall of civilizations).

120. *Ghostly Land*, 24–27. The result will be the "universal rule of the people, by the people, for the people," and he adds: "Et des boyeux du dernier prêtre serrez le cou du dernier roi!" This theme of antisacerdotalism is one of the constant background currents of spiritualism, Emma Hardinge Britten, Madame Blavatsky, and the H. B. of L.

121. *Isis Unveiled*, 1:30–34 (revolution of poles); 1:136 (Ellora and the vanished island north of the Himalayas); 1:305 (pre-Adamite races).

122. Randolph thought that Melchizedek was a pre-Adamite priest whose order antedated Genesis, and he hints that Melchizedek may have been a Rosicrucian. *Pre-Adamite Man*, 81. Indeed Melchizedek later appears in Randolph's chart of the Rosicrucians' genealogy, as he had earlier in Hargrave Jennings's theories.

123. *Isis Unveiled*, 1:xxxviii. Randolph's version of these racial or cyclic ancestors (including their physical size) is given in *Rosicrucian's Story*, 118–20.

124. *Isis Unveiled*, 2:105–8, 114–15.

125. Ibid., 2:108.

126. Ibid., 2:308.

127. *Davenport Brothers*, 81, 87, 102ff., 123, 136, 156, 221–33.

128. Britten, *Modern American Spiritualism*, 307–31. See also A. C. Doyle, *The History of Spiritualism*, 2 vols. (New York, 1926), 2:216, 229.

129. For King's intermediate history, see J. N. Maskelyne, *Modern Spiritualism. A Short Account of its Rise and Progress, with Some Exposures of So-Called Spirit Media* (London: Frederick Warne, n.d., c. 1876), 132–53. The *Medium and Daybreak* for August 8, 1873 carried the portrait of John King on its cover, as did the *Banner of Light* for July 18, 1874.

130. It is first advertised in the *Banner of Light* 13, no. 4 (April 18, 1863): 8. Randolph added minor notes to the end of the volume as late as December

for the second edition that appeared the same year. See *Pre-Adamite Man*, 405. On the request for the dedication to Lincoln, see *Curious Life*, 15–16, 19, and passim. On Randolph's claim that Abraham Lincoln was "his personal friend," see ibid., 26.

Chapter 7

1. See generally D.T. Cornish, *The Sable Arm: Negro Troops in the Union Army 1861–1865* (New York: Longman, 1956); James M. McPherson, *The Negro's Civil War. How American Negroes Felt and Acted during the War for the Union* (New York: Vintage, 1965), 164. Lincoln apparently thought that to arm the blacks, who he feared were cowards, would only be to arm the Southern troops that overcame them and would also alarm the border states and turn them against the Union. See also Earnest A. McKay, *The Civil War and New York City* (Syracuse: Syracuse University Press, 1990), 150.

2. The *Utica City Directory* for 1861–62 and 1863–64 listed Randolph as living there at the time.

3. Frémont had been removed from command in Missouri for exceeding Lincoln's orders by summarily freeing the slaves, and Lincoln had had to rescind the order.

4. The Negro Convention Movement began locally in Philadelphia in 1817 and nationally in 1830. With the black churches, it was the primary vehicle by which the black elites of the early nineteenth century tried to work out their own destinies. See Foster, *The Negro People in American History*, 94–95. State conventions were held in New York in 1855 and 1858, a period in which Randolph might have been expected to have taken some part, but he appears not to have participated (though the list of attendees for the 1858 convention has not survived). See Foner and Walker, *Proceedings of the Black State Conventions*, 1:86ff. He had to have been aware of the conventions, however, if for no other reason than the prominence given there to the ideas of Gerrit Smith.

5. *Curious Life*, 19. Randolph erroneously says his efforts for the Frémont Legion had been in 1860.

6. Benjamin Quarles, *The Negro in the Civil War* (Boston, 1953), 188–91. See also *The Record of the Action of the Convention Held at Poughkeepsie, New York on July 15 and 16, 1873 for the Purpose of Facilitating the Introduction of Colored Troops into the Service of the United States* (New York 1863).

7. See McKay, *Civil War and New York City*, 238–39. The in-fighting and bickering that lead up to this triumph probably left Randolph disillusioned with the whole process, and he later spoke disparagingly of "a regiment of thirteen blacks I once knew in New York. It contained one general, two major and three brigadier generals, one colonel, two majors, one captain, one lieu-

tenant, one sergeant, and a private." *Ghostly Land* (1874), 27. The unit is reminiscent of the army of Ozma of Oz.

8. Foster, *Negro People in American History*, 265–67.

9. "Convention of Colored Citizens," *Syracuse Daily Journal*, October 7, 1864, 2.

10. Howard Holman Bell, ed., *Minutes of the Proceedings of the National Negro Conventions* (New York: Arno Press, 1969), 4, 40.

11. The entire speech is given in H. H. Bell, *Minutes of the Proceedings of the National Negro Conventions*, 21–22, and in Proceedings of the National Convention of Colored Men, Held in The City of Syracuse, N.Y., October 4, 5, 6, and 7, 1864; with the Bill of Wrongs and Rights, and the Address to the American People (Boston: Geo. C. Rand & Avery, 1864), 20–22. Selections appear in Carl Sandburg, *Abraham Lincoln, The War Years*, 4 vols. (New York: Harcourt, Brace and Co., 1939), 3:263. Randolph's speech was specifically announced in advance. "Convention of Colored Citizens," *Syracuse Daily Journal*, October 6, 1864, 2.

12. Dedication to *Rosicrucian's Story*, 1871 and subsequent editions.

13. Bell, *Minutes of the Proceedings of the National Negro Conventions*, 36.

14. The declaration is published in Bell, *Minutes of the Proceedings of the National Negro Conventions*, 41–43, and in the *Syracuse Daily Journal*, October 7, 1864, 2 ("A Declaration of Wrongs and Rights, Made by the Colored Men of the United States of America, in Convention Assembled, in Syracuse, N.Y., Oct. 4th, 1864"). The attribution to Randolph's efforts is in the *New Orleans Tribune*. "National Convention," *New Orleans Tribune*, October 25, 1864, 1 ("the groundwork of the declaration was prepared by P. B. Randolph of New York City"); "National Convention," ibid., October 27, 1864, 2 (Randolph introduced the resolution that the declaration be brought to the floor). This appraisal is unlikely to have been any result of Randolph's own self-aggrandizement, since he was not yet in Louisiana, and it probably represents the opinion of Captain J. H. Ingraham of Louisiana who attended the convention and sent other reports to the *Tribune*.

15. Bell, *Minutes of the Proceedings of the National Negro Conventions*, 42. On the colonization movement, see McKay, *The Civil War and New York City*, 161 (Lincoln proposed to colonize blacks in Central America).

16. Foster, *Negro People In American History*, 172–73; 252–53. The State Convention of the Colored Citizens of New York held in New York in 1855 had vehemently attacked the idea as a fraud. Foner and Walker, *Proceedings of the Black State Conventions*, 1:86ff. See generally John Cornelius Englesman, "The Freedmen's Bureau of Louisiana," *The Louisiana Historical Quarterly* 32, no. 1 (January 1949): 145–224; McKay, *Civil War and New York City*, 161 (on Lincoln's proposal to colonize blacks in Central America); Robert C. Morris,

Reading, 'Riting, and Reconstruction: The Education of Freedmen in the South, 1861–1870 (Chicago: University of Chicago Press, 1976), 154ff. (back-to-Africa movement of the American Colonization Society); John Hope Franklin and Alfred A. Moss, Jr., *From Slavery to Freedom* (New York: Knopf, 1988), 154ff.

17. Letter, *New Orleans Tribune*, December 8, 1864, 2. Conway had proposed sending blacks to "a great country beyond the sea, where Livingstone traveled, which must ultimately be reached by the children and grandchildren of those whose chains we are now breaking." The controversy is examined in Howard A. White, *The Freedmen's Bureau in Louisiana* (Baton Rouge: Louisiana State University Press, 1970), 18–19.

18. "Grand Mass Meeting at Economy Hall," *New Orleans Tribune*, December 3, 1864, 2. See also "Great Meeting of the Colored People at Economy Hall, . . . The Oration of Dr. P. B. Randolph, of New York," *New Orleans Era*, December 3, 1864, 2.

19. *After Death*, 100. From his own experiences, Randolph was convinced that "Aristocracy governs in Aidenn"—the afterlife. Ibid., 101. Even though blacks there lose their "wooly hair" and pigment (ibid., 108), they initially inhabit only the lowest fringes of the first great zone of the afterlife and never catch up with the spirits of the Europeans. Ibid., 100–101, 115–16, 118 (abode of Hottentots and "lower Negroes"). See also *Eulis!* (1874), 85–86. Cahagnet, in *Celestial Telegraph*, 2:44–45, had anticipated Randolph in believing that, after death, blacks become white. Typically, Randolph had also advocated the contrary position: "The law of Distinctness is imperative; and though Quashee, the negro who died fifty years ago, and whose soul is as fair as the best white saint's among them all, might desire to visit earth again, he could not do so in borrowed plumes, but must come . . . a negro still." *It Isn't all Right* (1861), 14.

20. *After Death*, 259–60.

21. Ibid., 260. In this piece Randolph envisions the blacks opening "new doors to the mysterious realms above and around us, that the colder white can never penetrate," (ibid.), and at the same time teaches that even in the spirit world blacks were perpetually condemned to lag in the race through the celestial spheres. Ibid., 100. Similarly, in *Ravalette*, 242, the Rosicrucian in the sleep of Sialam, envisions the spread of a black empire from the southern United States to Brazil.

22. *Curious Life*, 15–16, 19, 26. R. S. Clymer, on this slender foundation, has woven Lincoln into his imaginary Rosicrucian apostolic succession, fabricating a "Rosicrucian Club" in Washington, D.C., that centered on Randolph, Alexander Wilder, Lincoln, and the alchemist General E. A. Hitchcock. See his notes to Randolph's *Ravalette, the Rosicrucian's Story* (Quakertown: Philosophical Publishing Co., 1939), 64. It should be noted that Clymer also says that Randolph, at Lincoln's behest, interceded with the Russian government,

through the Russian Rosicrucians, to side with the Union during the Civil War. Clymer claimed actually to have seen the records of the "Secret Council" of the Russian fraternity on the contact, but the claim is most likely imaginary. See "Gen. E. A. Hitchcock, First American Alchemist and Rosicrucian," *The Initiates* 3 (May–June 1930–May–June 1931): 1–25, 6; and "Fraternitas Rosae Crucis . . . Historical Sketch," ibid., 5 (May–June 1932–May–June 1941): 110–31, 130.

23. See Randolph's letter, *New Orleans Tribune*, November 29, 1864, 2. In Boston at the end of September, Randolph spoke only of the possibility of visiting New Orleans and of his desire to aid the freedmen. "All Sorts of Paragraphs," *Banner of Light* 16, no. 2 (October 1, 1864): 5.

24. Ibid.

25. Quoted in Donald E. Everett, "Demands of the New Orleans Free Colored Population for Political Equality, 1862–1865," *Louisiana Historical Quarterly* 38, no. 2 (April 1955): 43–64, 55.

26. See generally, Everett, "Demands of the New Orleans Free Colored Population for Political Equality, 1862–1865."

27. Butler, like General Frémont, freed the slaves in his area, declaring them "contraband of war" and forcing Lincoln to rescind the order. He was a reformer through and through and later came to the defense of Victoria Woodhull (as did Randolph himself) when she was accused of free love. See Johanna Johnston, *Mrs. Satan: The Incredible Saga of Victoria C. Woodhull* (New York: Popular, 1967), 128, 165.

28. Practically everyone who even entertained the idea of extending the franchise to blacks, including Abraham Lincoln, believed in severely limiting the right to "qualified" blacks only. See Eric L. McKitrick, *Andrew Johnson and Reconstruction* (Chicago: University of Chicago Press, 1960), 56ff.

29. Letter, *New Orleans Tribune* (November 29, 1864). The nephew's full name is supplied by "All Sorts of Paragraphs," *Banner of Light* 16, no. 2 (October 1, 1864): 5, which states that Randolph's goal was the "secular education of freedmen."

30. Advertisement, "Dr. P. B. Randolph Examines and Prescribes in Special Cases Only," *Religio-Philosophical Journal* 1, no. 4 (October 21, 1865): 8.

31. Advertisement, "Interesting Lecture, " *New Orleans Tribune*, December 11, 1864, 3.

32. "Religious Notices," *New Orleans Daily Independent*, January 22, 1865, 3 ("spiritualists welcome").

33. *Seership!* 16–17; *Casca Llanna*, 73; *Soul!* 256ff. Randolph thought that since blacks were on the lowest rung of development, they naturally attracted

to themselves corresponding entities, whose "delight it is to deal in the black art or black magic." "Randolph's Letters—No. 3," *Religio-Philosophical Journal* 1, no. 3 (October 14, 1865): 3. As we shall see (chapter 8) Randolph later both condemned Voodoo and touted his sexual science as a synthesis of its best elements.

34. See *Anglo-African* (February 25, 1865), and "Lettre du Docteur P. B. Randolph, à l'Anglo-African," *New Orleans Tribune*, French ed., March 11, 1865, 2, in which Randolph says that he was the correspondent for the *Anglo-African* and other northern journals. On the *Anglo-African*, see Penelope L. Bullock, *The Afro-American Periodical Press, 1838–1909* (Baton Rouge: Louisiana State University Press, 1981), 55–63.

35. *New Orleans Tribune*, December 4, 1864, 2.

36. "A Word to the Anglo-African," *New Orleans Tribune*, March 10, 1865, 2.

37. See *New Orleans Tribune*, December 26, 1864. The Grand Mass Meeting that Randolph had addressed in New Orleans on December 2, 1864, had adopted a resolution endorsing the proceedings of the National Convention of Colored Men in Syracuse, especially the declaration of wrongs and rights. *New Orleans Tribune*, December 4, 1864. See generally Everett, "Demands of the New Orleans Free Colored Population for Political Equality, 1862–1865," 58–60.

38. *New Orleans Tribune*, January 10, 1865; Foner and Walker, *Proceedings of the Black State Conventions*, 1:247. The opposition was probably engendered by the fact that Randolph was from the North.

39. "The Meeting at Economy Hall," *New Orleans Tribune*, February 5, 1865, 2. The preceding day's paper carried brief (and favorable) comments on an earlier speech by Randolph. See also Everett, "Demands of the New Orleans Free Colored Population for Political Equality, 1862–1865," 60.

40. *Anglo-African* (February 25, 1865); *New Orleans Tribune*, English ed., March 10, 1865, and French ed., March 11, 1865.

41. "A Word to the Anglo-African," *New Orleans Tribune*, March 10, 1865, 2.

42. "Meeting at Economy Hall," *New Orleans Tribune*, March 11, 1865, 2. The *Anglo-African* leapt to Randolph's defense, attributing his problems to the haughtiness of the Creoles: "Randolph made the mistake of publicly criticizing the colored Creole leaders.'" Quoted in David C. Rankin, "The origins of black Leadership in New Orleans During Reconstruction," *Journal of Southern History* 40 (1974): 417–46, 426. On the controversy, see also Everett, "Demands of the New Orleans Free Colored Population for Political Equality, 1862–1865," 60.

43. See generally Englesman, "The Freedmen's Bureau of Louisiana," 145–224; Morris, *Reading, 'Riting, and Reconstruction*; John W. Blassingame, *black New Orleans 1860–1866* (Chicago: University of Chicago Press, 1973), 109; Peyton McCrary, *Abraham Lincoln and Reconstruction: The Louisiana Experiment* (Princeton: Princeton University Press, 1978), 157ff., 325ff. The military government of Louisiana that set up the schools was described by the *New York Times* as a "hermaphrodite government, half military and half republican, representing the alligators and frogs of Louisiana." Quoted in James M. McPherson, *Battle Cry of Freedom: The Civil War Era* (Oxford: Oxford University Press, 1988), 709.

44. In a letter to the *Religio-Philosophical Journal* on November 18, 1865, Randolph speaks of a year spent educating blacks, but he is probably referring to his lectures before the School of Liberty rather than to any employment as a teacher. "Randolph's Letters—No. 4, A Latter Day Sermon, "*Religio-Philosophical Journal* 1, no. 8 (November 18, 1865): 2. See also "A Present Day Sermon," ibid. 2, no. 19 (August 4, 1866): 2 (two years).

45. See appendix C.

46. Principal teachers in the Freedmen's Bureau schools were paid approximately $1,300 per year, a substantial amount. If it was actually paid it probably was the first steady income that Randolph had ever had.

47. Randolph to W. L. Garrison, October 14, 1865. The letter is in the Garrison Papers in the Boston Public Library.

48. "Randolph's Letters—No. 1," *Religio-Philosophical Journal* 1, no. 1 (August 26, 1865): 2.

49. Randolph to W. L. Garrison, October 14, 1865.

50. "Negroes Hold Mass Meeting at Abraham Lincoln School," *New Orleans Tribune*, October 27, 1865, 1. For a picture of the new school and the ceremonies marking its beginning, see Morris, *Reading, 'Riting and Reconstruction*, plate 5, after p. 167.

51. "Lecture by Dr. P. B. Randolph," *New Orleans Tribune*, January 14, 1866, 1; "Public Lectures," ibid., January 16, 1866, 2. The *Tribune* gave the lectures a gracious review while noting its earlier disagreements with Randolph, but quibbled over the details of Randolph's version of world history and the march of progress.

52. "A Present-Day Sermon," *Religio-Philosophical Journal* 2, no. 19 (August 4, 1866): 2.

53. *After Death* (1886), 10.

54. "A Present-Day Sermon," *Religio-Philosophical Journal* 2, no. 19 (August 4, 1866): 2.

55. *New Orleans Tribune*, April 18, 1866, 2. See also "Union Men Reportedly Flee to New Orleans from Country Parishes," ibid., April 19, 1866, 2.

56. *Curious Life*, 12.

57. See McKitrick, *Andrew Johnson and Reconstruction*, 274ff. The Civil Rights Act of 1866 is codified at 42 United States Code 1981 and 1982. For its history, see *Saint Francis College v. Al–Khazraji*, 107 S. Ct. 2022 (1987); *Shaare Tefila Congregation v. Cobb*, 107 S. Ct. 2019 (1987).

58. See "A Note From Brother Randolph," *Religio-Philosophical Journal* 2, no. 28 (July 28, 1866): 4; "A Present-Day Sermon," ibid. 2, no. 19 (August 4, 1866): 2.

59. *A Sad Case*, 4.

60. *Curious Life*, 19. Several of his endorsements are given in ibid., 42, 46ff. and in "Dr. P. B. Randolph and his Work," *Religio-Philosophical Journal* 2, no. 22 (August 25, 1866): 4. "The only grateful Republican," Randolph later said, was Grant, who actually paid his two-hundred dollar pledge. *Curious Life*, 51.

61. Randolph's reminder note to President Johnson, dated August 4, 1866, is in the Andrew Johnson Papers at the Library of Congress.

62. *Curious Life*, 51. The reference to Randolph's contribution to the civil rights bill of 1866 is exciting, but his name does not appear anywhere in the histories of the legislation.

63. *New York Herald*, September 4, 1866, 4.

64. Ibid., September 2, 3, 4, 1866. See also McKitrick, *Andrew Johnson and Reconstruction*, 441ff.

65. *New York Times*, September 5, 8, 1866, 1; *New York Herald*, September 5, 1855, 3; *New Orleans Tribune*, September 9, 1866. Randolph was "snubbed" by the chairman of the convention. *New York Herald*, September 7, 1866, 7.

66. *Chicago Tribune*, quoted in *Curious Life*, 16. For the speech, see *New York Herald*, September 8, 1866; *New Orleans Tribune*, September 27, 1866. The *Religio-Philosophical Journal* was exultant: "The world moves! A colored man, and he a leading spiritualist, is admitted into a great loyalist convention of the nation, and his voice, bold and eloquent, is listened to with marked attention by the First Statesmen of America." "Dr. P. B. Randolph and the Convention of the Southern Loyalists," *Religio-Philosophical Journal* 2, no. 26 (September 22, 1866): 5.

67. *New York Independent*, quoted in *Curious Life*, 39.

68. *Curious Life*, 32.

69. Quoted in *Curious Life*, 15–16. Various other reviews of his oratory on the pilgrimage are given in ibid., 37ff. His oratory was so compelling that one newspaper even reported that a Johnson sympathizer offered him three-hundred dollars *not* to speak. Ibid., 39. Randolph frequently commenced his orations by auctioning off President Johnson's dishonored pledge to his school:

"He began by saying that he came as an auctioneer. Andy Johnson had put down his name for $200 for a freedmen's school in Louisiana, but although often dunned, he would not pay it. 'Who bids 50 cents?' Nobody did." *New Orleans Tribune*, September 19, 1866. The general press was as scathing of the pilgrimage as it had been of the convention, referring to its participants as the "Wandering Miscegens." *New York Herald*, September 22 and 27, 1866. See also McKitrick, *Andrew Johnson and Reconstruction*, 441ff.

70. *Curious Life*, 19 (sixteen dollars he had received for his speeches); 37–38 (report to the *Religio-Philosophical Journal* on the trip and Branscombe); 37 (Syracuse); 42 (Norton of Texas accused him of stealing money raised for his school); "Randolph and his Friends," *Religio-Philosophical Journal* 3, no. 2 (October 6, 1866): 4 (Randolph hated "because I had several drops of African blood in my veins "). In undertaking his fundraising for the proposed school in Louisiana, Randolph had made it clear that all funds raised were for the school but that he would give lectures and speeches to support himself. *A Sad Case*, 8.

71. "Suicide," *Religio-Philosophical Journal* 18, no. 22 (August 14, 1875): 172.

72. *Curious Life*, 12ff.

73. "P. B. Randolph," *Religio-Philosophical Journal* 3, no. 11 (December 8, 1866): 4.

74. *Curious Life*, 19.

75. *Casca Llanna*, 243–44. Randolph also relates another old Southern myth, the story of the faithful former slave who, finding his master's beautiful daughter in need after the war, proceeds (in appropriate dialect) to offer help: "Old Ben hab got plenty land, and some money, an you'se welcome to bofe." Ibid., 245. See also *It Isn't all Right* (1861), 16 (true philanthropists are not those who "go into holy hysterics once a year, and from gaily-thronged platforms proclaim the negro a man and a brother, and next day 'damn his *black* picture' because he offers love to their daughters, or attempts to sit down at the same table—merely by way of testing their honesty, and perpetrating a 'black joke' at the same time.").

Chapter 8

1. The fault must have been at least partly Randolph's own, because initially he had enthusiastically offered his services to W. F. Jamieson in launching that worthy's new *Spiritual Reporter*, a journal that was to publish transcriptions of trance lectures by the leading mediums. See Randolph, "Spiritual Reporter," *Religio-Philosophical Journal* 3, no. 14 (December 29, 1866): 3. Jamieson was a minor trance speaker of the period, originally from Paw Paw, Michigan. See his advertisement in *Banner of Light* 12, no. 21 (February 14, 1863): 8, and

his reply to a letter from Moses Hull to the same journal, "Correspondence," *Banner of Light* 12, no. 26 (March 21, 1863): 3. He mixed his spiritualism with the usual populist/reform ideas, and was the author of such works as *Was Jesus Christ A Democrat?* (Boston: W. F. Jamieson, 1874). Joscelyn Godwin has pointed out to me the obituary ("Pioneer Dies at 108") of a Mrs. Paschal B. Randolph in the *Los Angeles Sentinel*, May 28, 1981, A1. The certificate of her marriage on July 20, 1893, lists her husband, Paschal Beverly Randolph, as twenty-six and a native of Illinois. The birth and marriage records for Chicago were destroyed in the great Chicago fire of October 1871, but Mrs. Florine F. Love of California, Randolph's great-granddaughter, has informed me that her grandfather was born in Chicago on January 27, 1867, and died on December 31, 1931. His mother was Martha McMaster of Louisiana. There was at least one other child of the union, a daughter named Parthenia. Their pictures, of which Mrs. Love kindly gave me copies, bear a resemblance to Randolph. Mrs. Love has told me that the story in the family is that Martha ran off with another man and left her children behind to be raised by her mother.

2. *Casca Llanna*, 21. He compares Mr. Jamieson's ideas to those of "a traveling philosopher of Hell's blackest school, named H——l"—obviously Moses Hull. On radicalism debauching his home, see ibid., 383. On Hull, see Sears, *The Sex Radicals*, 88.

3. *Curious Life*, 19–20.

4. Randolph continued to put in an appearance at spiritualist gatherings, but he seems to have taken no leading part. He attended, for example, the Fifth Annual Session of the National Association of Spiritualists in Rochester, New York, in September 1868, but did not speak. *Religio-Philosophical Journal* 4, no. 25 (September 12, 1868): 1–2.

5. *Curious Life*, 12.

6. *The Guide to Clairvoyance, and Clairvoyant's Guide: A Practical Manual for those who Aim at Perfect Clear Seeing and Psychometry; also, a Special Paper concerning Hashish, its Uses, abuses, and Dangers, its Extasia, Fantasia, and Illuminati. Printed for People of Common Sense Only* (Boston: Rockwell & Rollins, Printers, 122 Washington Street, 1867).

7. See her preface to *Guide to Clairvoyance*, 20. See also "Ancient Kaldi Oracle, or Rosicrucian Predictive Symph, translated from the Original Rosicrucian Tablets by P. B. R. in 1867." Another lightweight effort of Randolph about this time was "The Riddle of Hermes," a broadside conundrum for the solution of which Randolph (safely) offered five-thousand dollars. See appendix C.

8. *Guide to Clairvoyance* (1867), 42–44. When this passage was reworked in *Soul!* (1872), 161ff., the "associates" have disappeared and the claims for their powers have been transferred to "true Clairvoyants"—a consequence of

the failure of Randolph's attempts to refound his order in Boston. See below. Item no. 68 of Randolph's exhaustive list of questions (in *Guide to Clairvoyance*) to be considered before consulting him asks: "Can I become a Rosicrucian adept?"

9. *Guide to Clairvoyance*, 52.

10. Ibid.

11. The pamphlet mentions as members Douglas, Ross (senior), Taylor, Day, Annie Wood, Meredith, Luke, Rod Backus, Drake and Al Lewis, none of whom is otherwise known and none of whom reappears in Randolph's later groups.

12. *Casca Llanna*, 14 ff.

13. On "La Blondette" and Miss La Hue, see below.

14. *Love and its Hidden History* (1870 ed.), 139.

15. See, e.g., *Master Passion*, 79.

16. *Casca Llanna*, 75; *Seership!* 53–55.

17. In *Love and its Hidden History* (1869), 6, he says that the earlier editions of the book had sold nine thousand copies, a considerable feat for those days.

18. *Master Passion*, 61–67, quotes from what is either a book by him or one to which he contributed, entitled *Prostitution; Its Causes and Cure*. The cure, of course, was his elixirs. The theme of the "good-hearted prostitute" constantly reappears in Randolph's writings. Her true worth was to be recognized in the afterlife while her critics were condemned to lower status. See, e.g., *After Death*, 59–60 (which also gives Randolph story of being cared for by a prostitute in New Orleans when abandoned by everyone else). Franklin Rosemont has kindly called to my attention the recollection of an old progressive of Randolph being ministered to by a Magdalen who "under the genial influence of Randolph . . . afterwards reformed, and cultivated the angel in her nature." John R. Francis, *The Home Circle Fraternity, Evolution of a New Religion* (Chicago: Progressive Thinker Publishing House, 1910), 160.

19. Boston: Author, corrected and enlarged, 1868. For the printing history, see appendix C. The citations are to the edition of 1886, which differs in only minor ways from earlier editions.

20. *After Death*, 10 (masterpiece); 62ff. ("I was in the spirit; my soul was free"); 181 (vision of July 4, 1864, of his mother, dead thirty-three years).

21. *After Death*, 51.

22. Randolph specifies that the center was not Alcyone, but lay in that direction. *After Death*, 91. He intended to write a work on the mystery of this "lost Pleiad" to be called "Planes Beyond." See *After Death*, 194. On the

cosmology, see ibid., 18ff., 90ff. The myth of the central, pivotal sun and its usual identification with Alcyone is examined by S. C. Gould in his *Alcyone (in the Pleiades). The Grand Central Sun* (Manchester, NH, 1893). On Gould, see chapter 11. The idea of Alcyone as the pivot of the universe had its pseudo-scientific basis in the 1840s work of Maedler on the Central Sun. See W. E. Coleman, "Pseudo-Zodiacal Mysticism. The Star Alcyone.—Dr. Kenealy's 'Enoch.' The Zodiac of Denderah," *Religio-Philosophical Journal* 43, no. 16 (December 10, 1887): 1.

23. *After Death*, 18.

24. Ibid., 89 (God as one focus of ellipse), 90–92. The refinements to this visionary cosmology are given in *Ghostly Land* (1874).

25. *After Death*, 74ff. (poets, freebooters, Christians).

26. Ibid., 112 (round out character); 172 (vastation). This progressive loss of the characteristics and vices of earth on re-ascent through the spheres is a commonplace in late classical antiquity and figures prominently in the Hermetic *Asclepius*, for example.

27. *After Death*, 134.

28. Ibid., 71 ("Once, when *en rapport* with a vast brotherhood of learned Buddhists, in the better land, they taught, and I believed, that there would come a period when man would be so pure and perfect as to lose his identity, and be swallowed up in God."); 107 (sects in heaven); 174; 197 (narwana and absorption), ch. 3, 41ff. (Foli, Neridii, Pythagoreans, Christians). Randolph died two months before the founding of the Theosophical Society, but these passages on the Buddhists who maintained their deluded beliefs after death perhaps give some indication of what his reaction to the later teachings of the Theosophical Society might have been. Thomas Lake Harris (and his disciple Laurence Oliphant) advanced precisely this criticism and believed that the esoteric Buddhism of Theosophy was merely propaganda advanced by unprogressed Buddhists in the afterlife. See Harris, *The Wisdom of the Adepts. Esoteric Science in Human History* (Fountain Grove: privately printed, 1884). See also Margaret W. Oliphant, *Memoirs of the Life of Laurence Oliphant and of Alice Oliphant, His Wife*, 2 vols. (New York: Harper & Brothers, 1891), 2:268, on Laurence Oliphant's humorous skit, "Sisters of Thibet."

29. *After Death*, 203.

30. Ibid., 51ff., 54.

31. When Randolph republished *Dealings with the Dead* as *Soul! The Soul World* in 1872, he was careful to note this change in his ideas on the abode of spirits. *Soul!* 106. *After Death* also marks for Randolph a reaffirmation of his belief in Jesus Christ, though Jesus has become for him more of a cosmic figure, "the Christ of my soul," than the Jesus of history. *After Death*, 12–13.

32. *After Death*, 181 (he was working on the book on July 4, 1864, while living in an attic at no. 68 Sixth Avenue in New York).

33. Randolph's 1868 edition of *After Death*, but not the preceding articles published in late 1866, carries (66–67) his condemnation of the Davenport brothers. He says that he had been convinced of their fraud by M. B. Dyott. On Dyott's opinion of the Davenports, see *Religio-Philosophical Journal* (October 20, 1866), and the rejoinder in the issue of December 8, 1866. In *Seership!* (36), Randolph says that he wrote the book from materials given him by the brothers but later came to see them as "dead beats."

34. *Casca Llanna*, advertisement facing page 404.

35. *The Rosicrucian Dream Book: Containing Solutions of Over Three Thousand Different Dreams, etc. Collected and Translated from the Old English* (Boston: Randolph Publishing Co., 1871). The book is probably a reworking by Randolph of the *Celebrated Rodrey Dream Book* referred to in the *Rosicrucian's Story* (1863). F. Leigh Gardner states of the book that the "author . . . was a Pseudo Rosicrucian, his works are unimportant and of but feeble interest to the student." See *A Catalogue Raisonné of Works on the Occult Sciences*, 3 vols. (1923; reprint First Impressions, 1992): 1:78.

36. *Hermes Trismegistus: His Divine Pymander. Also, the Asiatic Mystery, The Smaragdine Tablet, and the Song of Brahm* (Boston: Rosicrucian Publishing Co., 89 Court St., 1871). For unknown reasons, the imprint on this was the Rosicrucian Publishing Co., but this was merely an alter ego of the Randolph Publishing Co.

37. See appendix C, for the knotty publishing history of these works.

38. Randolph was but one of a myriad of such, and is distinguished not so much by his medical/exoteric ideas as by his fully developed sexual magic. On these reformers, see Sears, *The Sex Radicals*, and Kern, *An Ordered Love*. For an example of the type, see O. S. Fowler, *Creative and Sexual Science: or, Manhood, Womanhood, and their Mutual Interrelations; Love, its Laws, Power, etc.; Selection, or Mutual Adaptation; Courtship, Married Life, and Perfect Children; Their Generation, Endowment, Paternity, Maternity, Bearing, Nursing, Rearing; Together with Puberty, Boyhood, Girlhood, etc.; Sexual Impairments Restored, Male Vigor and Female Health and Beauty Perpetuated and Augmented, etc., as Taught by Phrenology and Physiology* (Philadelphia: National Publishing Co., 1870; reprint, Chicago: Follett, 1971).

39. *Love! At Last!* 17; *Eulis!* 107 ("I truly believe, that if my rules were followed, the social millennium would be close at hand."); *New Mola!* 4 ("On my soul, I, the writer believe, that if ASGILL's Rules were followed, the social millennium would be close at hand.").

40. *Love! At Last!* 29.

41. *Love! At Last!* 5–6; *Golden Secret* (1872) ("I believe I understand sexism better than any other human being now on the globe. I have studied it,

not alone in books, but through thousands of living subjects, in half the lands beneath the sun."). See also *After Death*, 130, on his discovery in 1854 of the horrible consequences of onanism and his resolve to make sex his special study.

42. *Love! At Last!* 7–8. In desperate cases, in addition to his elixirs, Randolph recommended the wearing of an "electric disk" on various parts of the body to replenish the vital fluid of the onanist. Ibid., 8. Similar "electromagnetic" metal disks to be worn on the head or about the body at night were recommended for variety of other complaints and could be supplied for five dollars. *Love! At Last!*, 15. See also *Eulis!* 150 (onanism a disease); *After Death*, 58 (the worst suffering in the afterlife is reserved for masturbators and onanists).

43. *Love! At Last!* 41. On blending, see *Golden Secret*; *Eulis!* 90. See also chapter 10. Randolph's constant harping on the fatal attractiveness of such people would appear to reflect his own experience with women—such as "La Blondette" and the other sirens he mentions.

44. *Eulis!* 67; *Love! At Last!* 7, 39, and passim.

45. *Love! At Last!* 25. See also *Golden Secret*, part 14, "Theory of personal orbits": "She is love incarnate, but she only manifests certain physical phases of it at regular and stated periods; emotional phases at stated terms; devotional, and affectional, in varied phases, occur with the regularity of clock work." "The love orbits of women vary from five to seven days." Brunettes have shorter term, blondes longer ones. Randolph believed that he had discovered this law.

46. *Love! At Last!* 32. In the contemporary debate on women's issues Randolph typically had his own position. He thought that women were superior—not because of their intelligence or accomplishments but simply because they had the womb, the pathway to the aerial spaces. *Eulis!* 86. Socially, he thought that men and women were equal, but different, and he advised women not to unsex themselves by worrying about the ballot box. He rejected "Woman's Rightsism," but the term for him meant simply free love, harlotage, abortion, vampirism, and the abrogation of marriage. *Casca Llanna*, 28, 58, 77. Randolph's advertisements for *Curious Life* in the *Religio-Philosophical Journal* explicitly touted the book as the secret whereby women could control men—and this secret was also one of the charges leveled at him in the "Great Free Love Trial" (chapter 9).

47. *Love! At Last!* 30.

48. Ibid., 23–24.

49. Ibid., 32, 40.

50. Ibid., 31–32.

51. Gustav Meyrink, introduction to *Dhoula Bel*.

52. *Love! At Last!*, 6 (twin rings, each with a bit of the hair of the beloved).

53. *Love! At Last!* 11–12; 45.

54. Ibid., 7, 13.

55. Ibid., 13–14.

56. See chapter 5, and *After Death*, 49–50, 166.

57. *Love! At Last!* 40, 44; *Eulis!* 102, 159; *Casca Llanna*, 146 ("The human being probably comes originally from God as a MONAD, down to the male (speaking of the mystery—SOUL), passes to the brain centre, clothes itself from the substance of *his* spirit; passes thence to the prostate; there remains until it finds another garment—the minute head of a zoosperm, in the ultimate rite of incarnation. Up to *this* instant its life is nascent, and though it be now *wasted*, it can never be *destroyed*; but, escaping its thrall, again becomes a free monad, floating about in open space, until it again becomes incarnate, and finally achieves the end for which Eternal God designed it. Up to a certain point, then, its life is negative; but at the very instant it—the monad—comes in contact with the divine, immortal point concealed in every female ovum, its life becomes positive, and whosoever then destroys it, after the mother-force has once fairly closed upon it, is a MURDERER!").

58. *Love! At Last!* 39–40. The details of this method were apparently taught by correspondence in (lost) manuscripts entitled the "True Oriental Secret, or, the Laws of Human Love Revealed" and "Love and its Mystery." See appendix C.

59. See *Love! At Last!* 26, 34; *Curious Life*, 55–56; *Grand Secret* (1861), 36–40, 54, 67. See appendix C.

60. *Love! At Last!* 25. Still on the exoteric level, Randolph sounds surprisingly modern in emphasizing the importance of prenatal nurturing and education—avoiding stress and concentrating one's thoughts on the unborn child, wishing it well, and singing and reading to it in the womb. *Love! At Last!* 21–22; *Eulis!* (1874), 68, 84, 94; *After Death*, 81 (superior children are produced by the mother's exercising her mind upon the foetus and by unspecified magnetic operations on it).

61. *Love and its Hidden History*, 44–45; *Eulis!* 96–98, 127, 141 (accumulation of nerve aura; necessity of sleeping apart to avoid injuring magnetic spheres; avoiding too frequent sex).

62. *Eulis!* 69, 76. In Randolph's final works, loveless children, in fact, might not even be immortal. *Eulis!* part 2.

63. *Eulis!* 77; *Asiatic Mystery*.

64. *Eulis!* 74, 83.

65. Ibid., 78, 81.

66. *Asiatic Mystery*. This repeated emphasis on "strong-loving" mothers producing superior children, together with its corollary that bastards because of the strong magnetism that accompanied their generation were generally superior, undoubtedly reflects Randolph's idea of his own conception. See *Eulis!* 24 ("We are all *accidents!*—not a few of us unhappy ones,—I for instance."); 73; 81–82; *Ansairetic Mystery* (Bastards are usually but not necessarily better). See also chapter 1.

67. *Ansairetic Mystery; Eulis!* 111.

68. *Eulis!* 86, 102 (love is not sentiment, but magnetic interplay); *Love! At Last!* 38; *After Death*, 135 (love is triple: generative, equilibrative, expressive).

69. *Eulis!* 103, 137–38 ("The purpose it serves is a mystic one for beyond all doubt the ultimate of the human is deific—a fusion, mingling, interblending—at-one-ment with the Omnipotent God; what came from, must return to, the centre; and he who would be nearer God is he who loves the purest."); 141 (triplicate; intermingling of magnetisms).

70. *After Death*, 49–50 (the body when it breaths in the monad for the first time can use the nerve aura, and when the nerve aura, and the ether coalesce they create the immortal, individualized soul); 89 (monads are human seeds from the great vortex); 166 (monads cluster around head and quicken sperm and receive the individual man's tendencies).

71. *Eulis!* 79. See also *Casca Llanna*, 146.

72. *Eulis!* 127. See below, and also *Magia Sexualis*.

73. *Grand Secret* (1861), 7–8, 21.

74. *Eulis!* 219–20.

75. *After Death*, 166–68; *Asiatic Mystery*. Randolph also thought that "[r]ipe semen produces ripe children"—that is, that too frequent intercourse (the life of a "debauchee or human goat") led to puny, lifeless children.

76. *Triplicate Order*, 25; *Ravalette*, 249.

77. *Eulis!* 72.

78. Ibid., 126. There is a progression of this mutual exchange, beginning with the simple handshake and the kiss and culminating in the "fusion of the male and female spheres [which] constitutes the supremest joy of existence." *After Death*, 140.

79. *Eulis!* 88. In one of his rare allusions to the formal Western alchemical tradition, he equates his discovery to that alluded to in the strange *jeu d'ésprit* of Johann Heinrich Cohausen, *Hermippus Redivivus: or, The Sage's Triumph over Old Age and the Grave. Wherein a method is laid down for Prolonging*

the *Life and Vigour of Man. Including a Commentary upon an Antient Inscription, in which this Secret is Revealed; Supported by numerous Authorities. The Whole Interspersed with a great Variety of Memorable and well Attested Relations*, trans. John Campbell, 3d ed. (London: J. Nourse, 1771). Cohausen had uncovered an ancient inscription that attributed a Roman's longevity to "*puellarum anhelitus*," the breath and "aura" of young girls, and had advocated close companionship with them (but without sensual gratification) as the means of extending life. The secret, he thought, was that of the "Society of Rosicrucians," (158ff.) and of Artephius and the mysterious Oriental brotherhood mentioned by Paul Lucas in his *Voyage du Sieur Paul Lucas, fait par ordre du roy dans la Grèce, l'Asie Mineure, la Macedoine et l'Afrique* (Paris, 1712)—a passage that later became a commonplace of occult history. Cohausen also alludes to a mysterious preparation or wine (the "White Dove") said to achieve the same result. Ibid., 221. Isaac Disraeli maintains that the entire work was a jest by Campbell, but so successful a jest that at least one reader "took lodgings at a female boarding-school that he might never be without a constant supply of the breath of young ladies." Isaac Disraeli, *Curiosities of Literature*, 3 vols. (London: Routledge, Warnes, and Routledge, 1859), 1: 320–21. Randolph equated his protozone elixirs with this wine and with the potions mentioned by Hargrave Jennings and Bulwer-Lytton. *New Mola!* 5, 36. Artephius, whom Randolph cites, had basically the same idea: a magnet for extracting and accumulating the aura or spirit of youth from young men. See Hargrave Jennings, *The Rosicrucians, Their Rites and Mysteries* (Mokelumne Hill: Health Research, 1966), 24–37, who takes all of this seriously and quotes *Hermippus* in support. On the historical Artephius, see Raphael Patai, *The Jewish Alchemists: A History and Source Book* (Princeton: Princeton University Press, 1994), 140–43; 558. *The Secret Book of Artephius* has been reprinted by Alchemical Press: Edmunds, Washington, 1984. As we shall see, however, Randolph was strictly opposed to the precise method advanced in *Hermippus Redivivus*, which he thought of as a sexual vampirism of the energy of young girls (see chapter 9). See also *After Death*, 104. For Randolph, long life and energy were the product of a mutual magnetic exchange rather than of vampirism on the energies of passive virgins.

80. *Triplicate Order* (1875), 19 (on the 1874 foundation); *Soul!* (1872), 276; *Asiatic Mystery*, 107 (on 1871 foundation).

81. Freeman B. Dowd, *The Double Man*, 38.

82. Randolph is described in the letter as living at 29 Boylston Street in Boston at the time, but he began his Rosicrucian Rooms there only in early 1867. *Guide to Clairvoyance* (1867). In spring 1868 he was living at 19 Church Street, and in 1869 moved to Court Street. See Randolph's advertisement, *Religio-Philosophical Journal* (April 4, 1868) (Church Street), and "Notice," ibid. 6, no. 9 (November 20, 1869): 5 (the "renowned clairvoyant and seer" has moved his office to 89 Court Street in Boston). The preface to the first edition of *After Death*, published in March 1868, carries a dedication to Dowd and the otherwise unknown S. B. Watrous, of Fort Union, New Mexico, as "friends in

need." The problem is compounded by the fact that Randolph in his dedication to the 1871 republication of *The Rosicrucian's Story* to "Freeman" says (anachronistically) that since they last parted he has traveled over Egypt, Syria and Araby—that is, the 1861–62 trip. This cannot be true, and in fact "Freeman" simply replaced "Charles T" (Charles Trinius), to whom the original edition of 1863 had been dedicated. The deception must have been part of an effort to establish Dowd's long-standing connection with Randolph and the Rosicrucians.

83. See Clymer, *Book of Rosicruciae*, 1:144ff. (photographer); Dowd, *The Temple of the Rosy Cross. The Soul: Its Powers, Migrations and Transmigrations*, 2d ed. (San Francisco: Rosy Cross Publishing Co., 1888), 233 (Dowd a lecturer and phrenologist). Dowd's other travels are deduced from the places of publication of his books or the locations given in his copyright applications on them and from his rambling contributions in the 1860s and 1870s to the *Religio-Philosophical Journal*. In the late 1880s Dowd contributed to *The Gnostic*, a journal published in San Francisco by George Chainey, W. J. Colville, and Anna Kimball and "Devoted to Theosophy, Spiritualism, Occult Phenomena and the Cultivation of the Higher Life." The dates and place of publication coincide with those of the second, revised edition of *Temple of the Rosy Cross* and the establishing of a Rosicrucian group there. Kimball and Chainey were sexual and occult mavericks and deserve a book of their own. They were expelled from the Theosophical Society (and refused admission to the H. B. of L.) in the mid-1880s for their sexual ideas. Dowd joined the H. B. of L. in September 1885, under Peter Davidson. Despite his publications by that time and his direct relationship with Randolph, he appears to have joined simply as a neophyte. Dowd's wife, whose name is unknown but who was known in his Rosicrucian circles at the end of the century as "Sorona," may possibly be the one referred to in Davidson's dedication of *The Mistletoe and Its Philosophy* (Loudsville, 1892) to the sister-wife of [Hebrew] "abu ben Dud." The reading could be "David," but "Dowd" appears more likely. Sorona is possibly the Lucy L. Stout Dowd who published her poetry in Paul Tyner's *The Temple* in the late 1890s.

84. See "Letter from Davenport, Iowa," *Religio-Philosophical Journal* 3, no. 11 (December 8, 1866): 4.

85. Dr. Paschal B. Randolph ("Count de St. Leon"), *Love and its Hidden History: Also, The Master Passion, or the Curtain Raised on Woman, Love, and Marriage. Female Beauty; its Attainment, Culture and Retention, with Hints for the Increase of Woman's Power. A Book for Woman, Man, Wives, Husbands, and Lovers, for the Loving, the Unloved, and the Yearning Ones of the World*, 5th ed., rewritten and enlarged (Boston: Randolph & Co., 1870).

86. *Master Passion*, 166.

87. *Tom Clark and his Wife: Their Double Dreams and the Curious Things that Befel Them Therein; or, The Rosicrucian's Story* (1871).

88. *After Death*, 205–6 ("I suggested these ideas of F. B. Dowd, Esq., who has put such before the public.").

89. See, for example, the advertisements by Dowd "the eminent Rosicrucian" in the *Religio-Philosophical Journal* for June 15 through September 16, 1871, and in *Woodhull & Claflin's Weekly*, April 19, 1873. This lost work must have been among Dowd's books on "physiology" that Randolph says were seized by the police when they raided his office in February 1872. See chapter 9.

90. One of the themes of Dowd's *Double Man* (1895) is the sexual exhaustion of men through indiscriminate sexual intercourse during sleep with their departed loved ones. The reviewer of the second edition of his *Temple of the Rosy Cross* in *Lucifer* 3 (February 1889): 522, quite correctly equated these ideas with those of Randolph and the old disciple of Thomas Lake Harris, Laurence Oliphant, in his *Synpneumata, or Evolutionary Forms Now Creative in Man* (Edinburgh and London: Wm. Blackwood & Sons, 1885). *The Double Man* (210ff.) describes obliquely a systematic course of bodily treatment for immortalization and the development of the soul: "I ascertained that a spiritual body may be formed in these bodies of ours, which, when fully formed, may be detached from the physical form, projected, and therefore man may be double, first in his imagination, secondly, perceived and felt in his own consciousness, and thirdly an object being exactly like this body." Beyond this is the development of the "spiritual body" and the ability to appear and function on all levels (physical, astral and spiritual) at will. The ultimate goal of existence for Dowd was to progress as a triple being into the brama loka, the abode of the Gods—but not too far. Nirvana, for Dowd, was a reality but a dead-end creation of our own minds in which we could lose ourselves and cease to progress. Like the H. B. of L., Dowd was strongly opposed to later Theosophy, which he thought advocated nirvana rather than progress. See ibid., 292. Love (and sex) for Dowd were the real means of progress; celibacy (as advocated by the Theosophists) led only to the selfish delusion of nirvana. On the triple secret of sex (electronic, magnetic, and ethereal), see Try [F. B. Dowd], *Regeneration, Being Part II of the Temple of the Rosy Cross* (Salem: Eulian Publishing Co., n.d. but ca. 1898; New York: The Temple Publishing Co., 1900), 78ff. A. E. Waite considered Dowd's writings "moony vapourings" and commented that Dowd "had evidently sincere interest in his subject, but he seems to have known nothing about it." *Brotherhood of the Rosy Cross*, 613–15.

91. *Double Man*, 232ff.

92. See, e.g., *Seership!* (1870), 22 (Dowd "the selected grand master of the magnificent order"), and the advertising synopsis of the double volume *Love and its Hidden History* and *Master Passion* printed at the end of *Seership!* The book advertised, however (*Master Passion*, 166), merely refers to "Hargrave Jennings, for instance, from whom I have elsewhere quoted before, or Freeman Dowd, of Davenport, Iowa, who quotes from God himself." It is perhaps also to Dowd's activities in the West that Randolph is referring in *Seership!*

(1870 edition only), when he advises members of the *Fraternité de la Rosecroix*, to procure their mirrors "at head-quarters, as I have no time to spend for those who know the *true points of the compass; and all such must travel straight towards the setting sun*, and at the *end of the journey the* LIGHT *will be seen!*" This, however, could also be a reference to Dr. Pilkington, who lived on the West Coast.

93. Citations to *The Asiatic Mystery* are to the version printed by R. S. Clymer in his journal *The Initiates, A Magazine Issued by Authority of the Rosicrucian Fraternity and Devoted to Mysticism, Occultism and the Well-Being of Man* 3 (May–June 1930–May–June 1931): 107–3. The title of the manifesto is a misnomer, since the first Rosicrucian manifesto was published in connection with the San Francisco foundation in 1861 and published in *Ravalette* (1863).

94. *Asiatic Mystery*, 118.

95. Ibid., 114.

96. Ibid., 114–15.

97. Ibid., 115. Randolph says that "at his initiation" he chose the second, third, and fourth of these powers.

98. *Asiatic Mystery*, 110.

99. *Soul!* (1872), 276. The manifesto mentions among the false brethren "Baron" Fischer, who had been involved with Randolph in the original Rosicrucian foundation in San Francisco in 1861, and "the Cambridge gentleman" who accused Randolph of being a "Urimist." The new recruits probably included Flora S. Russel of Boston, who reproduced the "Asiatic Mystery" in her introduction to Randolph's *Divine Pymander* (1871), and Alfred E. Giles, who provided a historical introduction to the same work. Giles was an early spiritualist who lived in Hyde Park, Massachusetts. See *Spiritual Scientist* 2, no. 8 (April 29, 1875): 94. He was also the author of several undistinguished books and was later associated in various radical causes with A. L. Rawson and D. M. Bennett.

100. "Testimonial to F. B. Dowd, The Rosicrucian," *Religio-Philosophical Journal* 10, no. 2 (April 1, 1871): 3, gives Randolph's address in Boston for correspondence with Dowd, and Dowd's "physiological" papers feature in the Great Free Love Trial in February 1872, but these are the last mention of him in connection with Randolph. He is also omitted from the extensive dedication to Randolph's *Eulis!* (1874) and ignored in the list of officers given in *Triplicate Order* (1875). Later reprintings of the 1871 edition of *The Rosicrucian's Story* continue to carry the dedication to "Freeman," and his preface to *After Death* (1870) continued to be used after Randolph died in 1875, but this appears to be the result of reprinting from old plates rather than evidence of a reconciliation or of a continuing relationship. A further indication of a break with Dowd can be found in *Seership!* While the original printing (22) called

Dowd "the selected grand master" of the order, the Clymer edition reprinted by Health Research (26) omits Dowd totally. Given Clymer's belief in Dowd's role in the succession from Randolph, the omission must reflect a change in Randolph's later printings of the pamphlet.

101. E.g., *Religio-Philosophical Journal*, June 14, 1873 ("Rosicrucian Musings"); July 26, 1873 ("The Old Man of the Mountains"). In the latter, Dowd is described as a phrenologist and out-of-work teacher. If Dowd is the "Mr. D." who escorted Emma Hardinge Britten in Davenport in 1870, there is some indication of a connection between the two. See Britten, "Spiritualism in the West," *Banner of Light* 27, no. 26 (September 10, 1870): 1.

102. Philadelphia: J. R. Rue, Jr., Printer, 1882; 2d ed., San Francisco: Rosy Cross Publishing Co., 1888; 3d ed., Chicago: Rosy Cross Publishing House, 1897 and distributed through Paul Tyner's Temple Publishing Co. in Denver; 4th ed., Salem: Eulian Publishing Co., 1901.

103. *Curious Life*, 56, 59. He says that three of the only four men ever initiated in Boston proved unfit. The third reject may have been Isaac B. Rich of Boston, a machinist and instrument maker and one of the publishers of the *Banner of Light*, who had been Randolph's financial salvation after his arrest in 1872. The loyal initiate was probably John Kapp, of Sunsbury, Pennsylvania, of whom Randolph always spoke highly and who figured in his final revival of the order in 1874. See *Casca Llanna*, 273; *Curious Life*, 96 (Rich helping to buy back books); 35 (Kapp).

104. *Curious Life*, 56. This was an undistinguished effort, notable only for its unusual lack of Masonic influence and its paranoid insistence that the initiate be loyal to Randolph and not betray him.

105. *Curious Life*, 59 (ceremony). Randolph says that he went to Ohio "with the essentials requisite to put Bay on probation," which may imply some ritual paraphernalia. Ibid., 59.

106. *Curious Life*, 60. Randolph's reference for the rolling back of the "iron door" is to the "Lara" episode which he says is in *Ravalette*. The reference actually is to chapter 1 of *The Rosicrucian's Story*, in which the Rosicrucian has a vision and is barred from progress until he can truthfully say that he is an honest man. "Knights Builders" are members of one of Randolph's degrees in his final foundation in 1874.

107. *Love! At Last!* 11–12, 45.

108. *Eulis!* 166–67.

109. *Love! At Last!* 36.

110. *Casca Llanna*, 372.

111. F. B. Dowd, *Double Man*, 34–37. R. S. Clymer, for obvious reasons, claimed that this passage was interpolated by an enemy. The decline in Randolph, a "Son of Temperance" in the 1850s, is apparent.

Chapter 9

1. *Curious Life*, 7.

2. Ibid., 83. Randolph had had high hopes of patronage from James Fisk, an impressario and robber baron (he was a friend of Jay Gould), who thought highly of Randolph's sketch of his character, but the hopes were shattered when Fisk was murdered in January 1872. For the sketch appendix C.

3. The whole tale is given in part 2 of *Curious Life*, 54ff.

4. The Rosicrucian's oath is given in *Curious Life*, 56.

5. Ibid., 58.

6. Ibid., 57. In later years, Randolph found something worthwhile in Bay and was thankful that the man had fed him for several months. At the same time he raged at the eighty-six-year old-man ("one-third human, two-thirds goat") for his desire to marry a girl of fifteen. Bay's goal was to drain the vitality of the girl by sexual contact, a practice which Randolph says was common among a vast ring of wealthy men at the time. He says that there were sex rings all across America (he chose Boston and San Francisco for special mention) where the systematic rape of drugged young girls was practiced by an "atrocious gang, with its head-quarters in New York City, and having its laws, rules, countersigns, and pass-words, with branches here and there all over the vast country, and members in nearly every considerable city, town, and village of the land. There are papers which advertise their regular meetings; albeit in a blind way, so that none but the initiate can understand. The principal idea that forms the soul of this infamous band is this: Young girls are by them supposed, while pure, and preceding, and just subsequent to puberty, or their natural advance into womanhood, to be endowed with the power of prolonging the life of him who shall first, by means foul or fair, . . . succeed in debauching her. It is supposed that two-fifths of her allotted term of life will, by the deed, be transferred from her to him; and that the life-stock thus obtained, can be, and is, shared by all others of the band, on the principle of magneto-vital transfusion, not of blood, but of Nerve-aura." Randolph says that the conspiracy had been revealed by a man on the scaffold in the West a few years before. *Eulis!* 74, 99, 116–17, 132–33. He calls the group "Dentonites," a reference to William Denton, the co-author with his wife Elizabeth, of *The Soul of Things; or Psychometric Researches and Discoveries*, 3 vols. (1863; 6th ed., Boston: Authors, 1873–75), who had once been a favorite of Randolph. Compare *Guide to Clairvoyance* (1867), 23, and *Soul!* (1872), 151. This sex ring, if it is not a figment of Randolph's imagination, was obviously of interest to Randolph because its views on the beneficial, life-restoring results of sexual and magnetic union approached his own—except that, in his scheme of things, the results were mutual and life extending for both. The prolonging of life by intimacy with young girls was (without sexual intercourse) the doctrine expounded by Johann Heinrich Cohausen in his *Hermippus Redivivus* (1771). See chapter 8. The idea has a biblical precedent in the warming of the

aged King David by Abihag the Shulamite, who lay on his bosom. 1 Kings 1.1. The practice has not been uncommon in human history, witness Louis XIV and even Gandhi, and has parallels in Chinese popular medicine and alchemy. Randolph's final judgment on the practice is that it is wrong, simply because a young girl cannot love an old man. *Eulis!* 22.

7. *Curious Life*, 58–59.

8. Ibid., 59.

9. Ibid., 6.

10. Ibid., 63ff.

11. Ibid., 67. The letter had been printed by F. Smith, M.D., who had bought Randolph's general medical practice the preceding year.

12. *Curious Life*, 67–68. The proposal ignores the fact that it is unlikely that a private party's agreement to drop obscenity charges would have had any effect. Randolph admitted that it was only speculation on his part that French had any direct role in his arrest.

13. *Curious Life*, 59, 68.

14. Ibid., 61. Apparently Isaac B. Rich, whom Randolph praises in other places, advanced the money, or perhaps he advanced the money to buy back the attached books themselves. *Curious Life*, 96.

15. *Curious Life*, 65–66 (various notices).

16. Ibid., 64, quoting the *Boston Herald* (on *Master Passion*).

17. Boston: Randolph Publishing Co., 89 Court St., 1872.

18. *Curious Life*, 67–68.

19. Ibid., 75, 80.

20. See Blatt, *Free Love and Anarchism*, 126ff. (National Defense League to combat Comstock). Randolph attended the "Ultra Radical" convention in Chicago (the National Convention of Spiritualists) in September 1873 and defended Woodhull from the platform, as he had done the previous year when Woodhull was nominated for president of the United States and Randolph's old acquaintance Frederick Douglass was nominated for vice president. See *Eulis!* 134–37. See also *Proceedings of the Tenth Annual Convention of the American Association of Spiritualists*, 33, 66–73, 219–227 (which gives Randolph's speeches); "Tenth National Convention of Spiritualists," *Banner of Light* 34, no. 1 (October 1, 1873): 8. He not only defended Woodhull's right to speak but came close to advocating the idea that love justified any sexual union, including Andrew Jackson Davis's "transient marriages." Probably to keep up the appearance of representing a wide cross-section of the country, Randolph had been admitted to the convention as the "Representative of Utah."

"Tenth National Convention of Spiritualists," *Religio-Philosophical Journal*, 34, no. 1 (October 4, 1873): 8. Randolph was pilloried for his support of Woodhull. See, e.g., "Old Rats Instinctively Flee from Old Rotten Sinking Ships," *Religio-Philosophical Journal* 15, no. 25 (March 7, 1874): 4. On Comstock, see David Loth, *The Erotic in Literature. A Historical Survey of Pornography, as Delightful as it is Indelicate* (New York: Julien Messner, 1961), 142 ff. On Woodhull's arrest and candidacy, see Johnston, *Mrs. Satan*, 125ff., 144ff.; Blatt, *Free Love and Anarchism*, 73ff.

21. *Curious Life*, part 3, 69ff.

22. E.g., Angela M. Fogliato, "P. B. Randolph e la sua magia sessuale," in *La Nuova Italia 4, Il superuomo e i suoi simboli nella letteratura moderna* (1986): 183–209. Randolph said that he culled the arguments from correspondence he received on *Casca Llanna*.

23. *Curious Life*, 70, 71.

24. Ibid., 89.

25. Ibid., 78, 92; *Grand Secret*, 7; *Casca Llanna*, 78. There were hordes of these preachers at the time, ranging from the Saint Simonian missionary, "Père" Enfantin, to the German Archdeacon Ebel, and Reverend Jarvis Rider, Hiram Sheldon, and Sydney Rigdon. See McCormick, *The Temple of Love*, ch. 1; Dixon, *Spiritual Wives*, passim.

26. *Curious Life*, 89–90.

27. Ibid., 90.

28. Ibid., 88.

29. See *Ghostly Land* (1874). Randolph said that good grounds for divorce would in the future include "vicious habits; undue anger; . . . violent language; infidelity; chronic stupidity; uncleanly speech, conduct, habit; . . . barrenness; incurable disease engendered through vice and bad habit; insanity; cerebral unsoundness; pre-marital diseases; obtaining wife or husband under false pretenses; mercenary motives; . . . slovenly habits; incessant snoring; incurable eccentricity; vampirism; siding with mothers-in-law and relations against the mate; wasting the husband's resources in supporting outside parties; habitual lying; . . . refusal to supply needed food, raiment, shelter and comfort; extravagance; . . . unfounded jealousy; not loving the mate; . . . idiocy subsequent to marriage; . . . gossiping; . . . constitutional or acquired laziness; . . . chronic stupidity; vampirism; any skeleton in the closet; offensive odors, from breath, etc." *Ghostly Land*, 32–33. The list is too detailed not to reflect Randolph's own experiences.

30. See chapter 1. See also *After Death*, 157–61.

31. *Love and its Hidden History*, 69. The name of the manuscript is given in *Love! At Last!* 34.

32. See appendix C, for the publishing history.

33. Britten, *Nineteenth Century Miracles*, 430. Among the papers destroyed by the fire was the first of Robert H. Fryar's pamphlets on magic mirrors, presumably submitted to her for publication.

34. *Eulis!* 161. This may have been the English writing medium John Lowe who lived in Massilon and received cards written directly by spirits. See Britten, *Nineteenth Century Miracles*, 515–19.

35. Ibid., 115.

36. *New Mola!* endpiece, following page 63.

37. *Eulis!* 92; *New Mola!* 18 and introduction. One beneficial result of the fall, apparently, was that he lost the glasses he always used and took the occasion to try his system of ophthalmologic cures on himself. Ophthalmology thereafter became a medical subspecialty. *New Mola!* 42–43.

38. *Eulis!* 92.

39. *New Mola!* 1 (Kate Corson's introduction).

40. *The New Mola! The Secret of Mediumship! A Hand Book of White Magic, Magnetism, and Clairvoyance. The New Doctrine of Mixed Identities. Rules for obtaining the phenomena, and the celebrated Rules of Asgill, a Physician's Legacy, and the Ansairetic Mystery* (Toledo: P. B. Randolph, Publisher, 1873), 1–2, 9–10.

41. *New Mola!* 11.

42. Her death certificate shows that she was born in Indiana on April 10, 1854, and died in Toledo on March 12, 1938.

43. *New Mola!* 24, 63. She is perhaps the mirror seer mentioned in *Eulis!* 200. Gustav Meyrink, who acquired various of Randolph's manuscripts from her after his death, describes her as a "*Negrin*," but her picture does not bear this out. See plate 2. The *Religio-Philosophical Journal* (October 11, 1873), in an advertisement for *New Mola!* describes it as her discovery, without mentioning Randolph at all. The *Toledo City Directory* for 1876–77 lists her as the widow of Paschal Randolph, with an address at 105 Missouri Street.

44. There must have been some disagreement on the name, and the child's birth certificate omits a name entirely. In later life, the son, who became a successful surgeon in Toledo, called himself "Osiris William Randolph." He died on July 20, 1929. See his obituary in the *Journal of the American Medical Association* (August 24, 1929): 632, and the sketch of his life in John M. Killits, *Toledo & Lucas County, Ohio, 1623–1923* (Chicago and Toledo: S. J. Clarke Publishing Co., 1923), 495ff. (where his father is said to have been a native of Virginia).

45. *New Mola!* 61.

46. From a purely biographical point of view, Randolph appears to have come to the idea out of despair at his continual ill treatment during life. Surely his attackers could not be human, and surely they would not go on to eternal progress in the soul world! He reiterated these ideas in *Ghostly Land* and *Eulis!* in 1874. The idea of conditional immortality later was one of the core ideas of Madame Blavatsky in *Isis Unveiled* (1877). Although Randolph does not discuss the problem, the doctrine of conditional immortality obviously must have confirmed Randolph's ideas on reincarnation. By hypothesis, the unindividualized, unconscious monad that failed to become an individualized soul during life was immortal and went on to repeat the process of incarnation, always seeking individualization. Under the theory of conditional immortality, it must have been man's "spirit" (in Randolph's terms) that decayed into annihilation, perhaps again freeing up the monad for rebirth. This process, however, if it in fact reflects Randolph's ideas on the subject, can only be called "reincarnation" by distorting the term, since by definition the entity that underwent the process of rebirth was not individualized. For Madame Blavatsky's efforts at reconciling the idea of conditional immortality with a general denial of reincarnation, see chapter 12.

47. *New Mola!* 14–15. Randolph attributes this teaching to the authority of one of the loftiest spirits ever to visit the earth.

48. Randolph had also found an unnamed European to supply the funds to print *Dealings with the Dead* in 1861. See introduction by "The Son of Flora." A John Perceval of Notting Hill Square, London, appears in the pages of the *Spiritual Magazine*, with whose contributors, as we have seen, Randolph felt a considerable kinship, but all that can be learned about him is that he was a spiritualist and a "philanthropist." He was notable only because his father was assassinated in the lobby of the House of Commons. *Spiritual Magazine* 1, no. 7 (July 1860): 328; ibid. 4, no. 11 (November 1863): 527–28 (letter on his premonition of an earthquake). He may be the same as the "Mr. Percival" who appeared before the London Dialectical Society in 1869 and testified about the visions he had had in 1829–30 which caused him to be committed to an asylum. *Report on Spiritualism, of the Committee of the London Dialectical Society, Together with the Evidence, Oral and Written, and a Selection from the Correspondence* (London: Longman, Green, Reader and Dyer, 1871), 222.

49. Randolph says that he and Perceval conversed after Randolph had printed "the book called 'Eulis.'" The only edition of *Eulis!* surviving is that labeled the second edition, published in the summer of 1874. If the reference is to this edition, which is the only one known, the European visit took place later in 1874. The problem with this sequence is that, in the normal course, the patron whose generosity allows a "book to see the light" would have supplied the money before printing. Perhaps Randolph's contact with Perceval occurred before the printing but by correspondence, or perhaps the reference is to an earlier (perhaps private) edition of *Eulis!* in which case the visit to Europe could have been earlier, possibly before Randolph's accident in May 1873.

50. "Origin and Object of the H. B. of L.," in Godwin, Chanel, and Deveney, *The Hermetic Brotherhood of Luxor*, 95. The usual interpretation of this has been that the adept was the mysterious "Max Theon" and the neophyte Peter Davidson, but Theon himself appears to have claimed that he was the neophyte.

51. *The Occult Magazine* 1, no. 6 (July 1885): 41 (Davidson a member of the H. B. of L. for upwards of fourteen years); ibid. 2, no. 12 (January 1886): 7 (claim, probably imitative, by T. H. Burgoyne that he had known of the "objective, physical existence" of the adepts for fourteen years).

52. Ayton to unnamed "Dear Sir and Brother," May 14, 1886 (private collection). The reference to other persons initiated by Randolph in Britain is probably meant to include Walter Moseley, on whom see chapter 11.

53. See also chapters 2 and 11.

54. *New Mola!* 18.

55. Ibid., 62–63. He excepted from this the right to manufacture and sell the old form of his Protozone, "already bargained for in Europe."

56. *New Mola!* 17–18. Randolph's mention of Spence Hardy and his death at the hands of Ansaireh assassins is simply wrong. Robert Spence Hardy (1803–1868) was a noted student of Pali Buddhism, on which he wrote several works. He had no connection with the Nusa'iri at all, and appears to have died peacefully in bed in Yorkshire. See bio-bibliographical note in BCW, 10, 417–18. Randolph lists several of Hardy's books on Buddhism among his authorities for *Pre-Adamite Man*.

57. See appendix C.

58. *New Mola!* 17–18. The text of the rules is printed at pp. 56–62. On Asgill, see ibid., 5 (spirit); *Eulis!* (physician). R. Swinburne Clymer, in *The Divine Alchemy of Imperial Eulis, Esoteric, yet Practical, Instructions for the Transmutation of the Baser Metals (Man's Gross Passions) into the Pure and Shining Gold (the Illuminated Soul) of the Alchemists. The Randolphian Physician's Legacy to Mankind, and Asgill's Rules. Instructions in the Single and Double Breast Drill of the Initiates. For Students Only* (Quakertown: Printed but not Published by Philosophical Publishing Co., n.d., but the preface to the 5th ed. is dated August 7, 1945), paraphrases rules 1 through 7 as "Asgill's Rules, A Physician's Legacy to Mankind" (15–31); and he gives rules 8 through 14 (35–53) as "The Ansaireth Mystery," omitting the references to hashish and changing the "Giours" to "ghouls." Lest there be any doubt about Randolph's continuing interest in hashish during this period, rule 17 of *New Mola!* (60) recommends that, if Randolph's elixirs are not to hand, "granules made of one-fifteenth grain 'red' oxide of phosphor, and two grains solid extract of cannabin" may be used to restore general health and depleted sexual energy.

59. *New Mola!* 58.

60. Ibid., 60.

Chapter 10

1. Lately under the name *Alawis*, the Nusa'iri have risen to political prominence in Syria.

2. C. F. Volney, *Voyage en Egypte et en Syrie* (1787; reprint Paris: J. Gaulmier, 1959), 216, 279. Carsten Niebuhr, *Reisen durch Syrien und Palästina*, 2 vols. (Copenhagen, 1778), 2:357ff. The Nusa'iri had already been mentioned in the great *Bibliotheca Orientalis Clementino-Vaticana* (Rome: 1719–1728) of J. S. Assemani, but they received scant notice. The Maronite author attributed the origin of the Nusa'iri to the vision of an old man in 891 A.D., who had seen Christ and realized that he was the word of God and also Mohammed, 'Ali, and the angel Gabriel.

3. The pornographer Sellon, citing Buckingham, gives a different location. E. Sellon, *Annotations on the Sacred Writings of the Hindus, Being an Epitome of Some of the most Remarkable and Leading Tenets in the Faith of that People, Illustrating their Priapic Rites and Phallic Principles* (1865; reprint, London: privately printed, 1905), 46. On the unfortunate Sellon, who was the first to introduce the Tantra to the West, see his autobiography, *The Ups and Downs of Life* (London: Dugdale, 1867; reprint, Miami Beach: McMillan, 1987), which includes a useful introduction on his career. Francis King has shown Hargrave Jennings's borrowings from Sellon. King, *Sexuality, Magic and Perversion* (Secaucus: Citadel, 1974), 9. J. A. D[ulaure], *Des Divinités Génératrices, ou du culte du Phallus chez les Anciens et Modernes; Des cultes du dieu de Lampsaque, de Pan, de Vénus, etc.; Origine, motifs, conformités, raretés, progrès, altérations et abus de ces cultes chez différens peuples de la terre; de leur continuation chez les Indiens et les Chrétiens d'Europe; des moeurs des nations et des tems où ces cultes ont existé* (Paris: Dentu, 1805), 361–62, gives the same story of an unnamed Syrian sect near Aleppo offering their wives and daughters indiscriminately.

4. This is one of the most common accusations against sects. It appears in Clement of Alexandria (*Stromateis*) and Minucius Felix (*Octavius* 9) against the Gnostics, the opponents of Christianity against the Christians (Origen, *Contra Celsum* 6.27), and in various early travelers against other groups. See, e.g., Thomas Hyde, *Historia Religionis Veterum Persarum Eorumque Magorum* (Oxford, 1700), 497 (apparently against the Yezidis: "luminibus omnibus extinctis, in illicitam venerem promiscuerebant omnes"). On these sorts of accusations, see generally Carlo Ginzburg, *Ecstacies: Deciphering the Witches' Sabbath* (New York: Pantheon, 1991), 74–77. Edwards and Masters in their *Cradle of Erotica*, 122, state (without citation) that the "Nusairiyeh" as well as the Druses and Isma'ilis of Pakistan and India practice a sacred form of

nymphophilia, which seems unlikely, although such things are not unknown in the Middle East. See Peter Lamborn Wilson, *Scandal*.

5. Baron Antoine-Sylvestre de Sacy, *Exposé de la Religion des Druses*, 2 vols. (1838; reprint, Paris, 1964), 2:574, 691–92. The Druses had earlier appeared in Gibbon's *Decline and Fall of the Roman Empire*, where they were accused of secret nocturnal orgies. See also Philip K. Hitti, *The Origins of the Druze People and Religion*, Columbia University Oriental Studies, vol. 28 (New York: Columbia University Press, 1928), 52ff. (on charges against Druses and Nusa'iri and the involvement of the early Druses in sex worship); [Austin] Henry Layard, *Early Adventures in Persia, Susiana, and Babylon*, 2 vols. (London, 1887), 2:217, 318; M. G. S. Hodgson, *The Order of Assassins* (Se'Gravenhage, 1955), 91, 191, 207; Louis Massignon, "Doctrines Gnostiques in Islam," *Eranos-Jahrbuch* (1937).

6. As might be expected, justifications and explanations existed on various levels. "Woe to the faithful woman who refuses her favors to her brother, because the natural parts of the woman are the emblem of the imams of impiety. The member of the man as it enters the nature of the woman is the emblem of the spiritual doctrine and the action is thus the symbol of the defeat of the external law of the imams of impiety. The prohibition of illicit intercourse is only for those who speak contrary to the truth: theirs is fornication. But those who know the inner doctrine are no longer submitted to the yoke of the external law." De Sacy, *Exposé*, 573–74. This really expresses only "consequent" libertinism (the attitude that, since the libertine is saved or pure, he is above the law), not "practical" libertinism, the use of what is otherwise forbidden in order to promote spiritual growth. The former type of libertine is very common. An example is the Adamites, on whom see Frank E. Manuel and Fritzie P. Manuel, *Utopian Thought in the Western World* (Cambridge: Harvard University Press, 1979), 182–83. See also below.

7. According to more recent scholarship, the idea may have to be abandoned. See Farhad Daftary, *The Isma'ilis: Their History and Doctrines* (Cambridge: Cambridge University Press, 1990), 17–18.

8. See Nerval, *Les Illuminés* (Paris: Gallimard, 1976), 361–62 (Druses and Nusa'iri were the remains of the Eastern occultism that had begun to permeate the West with the Templars); Peter Partner, *The Knights Templar and Their Myth* (Rochester, Vt.: Destiny Books, 1990), 151.

9. Gérard de Nerval, *Voyage en Orient* (Paris, 1848–5), *Oeuvres*, vols. 10–11 (Paris, n.d.), 10:414ff.

10. Nerval then related (but discounted) the Frenchman's "drôle" story of how, in order to identify her later, he had snipped off a bit of the clothing of the woman he slept with—only to discover on matching the cloth that she was an ancient crone with grandchildren.

11. See René Basset, "Nusairis," *Encyclopedia of Religion and Ethics*, ed. James Hastings (New York: Charles Scribner's Sons, n.d.) 9:417–19.

12. Joseph von Hammer, *Die Geschichte der Assassinen aus Morgenländischen Quellen* (Stuttgart and Tübingen, 1818); C. W. King, *The Gnostics and Their Remains, Ancient and Medieval* (San Diego: Wizard, 1982), 410–14 (following von Hammer). On von Hammer, see Partner, *Knights Templar and Their Myth*, 138–44. For a critique of the supposed influence of the Druses and Nusa'iri on Freemasonry, see Arthur Edward Waite, *A New Encyclopædia of Freemasonry (Ars Magna Latomorum) and of Cognate Instituted Mysteries: Their Rites, Literature and History*, 2 vols. in 1 (New York: Weathervane, n.d.), 1:46–53.

13. Godfrey Higgins, *The Celtic Druids* (London: Rowland Hunter, 1829), 264–65; Higgins, *Anacalypsis, An Attempt to Draw Aside the Veil of Saitic Isis; or, An Inquiry into the Origins of Languages, Nations, and Religions*, 2 vols. (London: Longman, Rees, Orme, Brown, Green, and Longman, 1833–1836), 1:688–723. Hargrave Jennings followed Higgins in equating the Druses with the British Culdees.

14. F. Walpole, *The Ansayrii, and the Assassins, with Travels in the Further East, in 1850–51. Including a Visit to Nineveh*, 3 vols. (London: Richard Bentley, 1851).

15. Brown, *The Darvishes or Oriental Spiritualism*.

16. E. G. Browne, *A Literary History of Persia*, 2 vols. (Cambridge University Press: 1928), 1:171, 203; René Dussaud, *Histoire et Religion des Nosairis* (Paris: Emile Bouillon, 1900), 14, 106–19. Dussaud also emphasizes (43ff.) the great similarities between the Isma'ilis and the Nusa'iris.

17. F. W. Hasluck, *Christianity and Islam Under the Sultans*, 2 vols. (1929; new ed., New York: Octagon Books, 1973), 1:139–65.

18. Laurence Oliphant, *The Land of Gilead* (New York: D. Appleton & Co., 1881).

19. Britten, *Art Magic*, 205ff. (power of Nusa'iri, according to de Gobineau, to throw themselves from high peaks and to sit in the midst of fire without being injured). John Yarker, quoting Lyde, concluded that the Druses and the Ansairee were the heirs of the Jewish-Magian House of Wisdom in eleventh-century Cairo. John Yarker, Jr., *Notes on the Scientific and Religious Mysteries of Antiquity; The Gnosis and Secret Schools of the Middle Ages; Modern Rosicrucianism; and the Varied Rites and Degrees of Free and Accepted Masonry* (London, 1872), 32.

20. W. N. Birks and R. A. Gilbert, *The Treasure of Montsegur: A Study of the Cathar Heresy and the Nature of the Cathar Secret* (Wellingborough: Crucible, 1987), 141, 151ff. Mr. Birks's personal familiarity with the oral teachings of the Nusa'iri leads him to advance the thesis that their doctrines are identical with those of the Cathars and that, accordingly, the origins of the Cathars may be sought in the Near East. James Webb in *The Harmonious Circle: The Lives and Works of G. I Gurdjieff, P. D. Ouspensky and Their Followers* (Boston: Shambhala, 1987), 532, concludes that Randolph's ideas on sexual magic (which he thought

had to do with the creation of superior children and the production of a substance to coat the higher parts of the being) were the same as those taught by Gurdjieff in his early days in Moscow, and he seems to equate the Ansaireh with Gurdjieff's famous "Aissors." The Nusa'iris also make their appearance in Robert Allen Campbell, *Phallic Worship: An Outline of the Worship of the Generative Organs, As Being, or as Representing, the Divine Creator, with Suggestions as to the Influence of the Phallic Idea on Religious Creeds, Ceremonies, Customs and Symbolism — Past and Present* (St. Louis, R.A. Campbell & Co., 1887), 195, who calls them the "Worshippers of the Womb" and repeats the story of orgies with the lights out. Campbell, who was later involved in the origins of the H. B. of L., curiously does not mention Randolph. René Guénon's judgment on the Nusa'iris was that they were merely a sect, and not an authentic initiatic "path." See A. W. Y. [Abdel Wahed Yahia, Guénon], "Les trois montagnes sacrées: Sinaï, Moriah, Tabor," *The Speculative Mason* (January 1937). Hargrave Jennings, in his *Phallicism, Celestial and Terrestrial, Heathen and Christian. Its Connexion with the Rosicrucians and the Gnostics and its Foundation in Buddhism* (London: Redway, 1884), 265, gave a nice survey of his predecessors among the phallic mythologists and deemed the Nusa'iri to be Gnostics, identical with the Nazarains. He repeats the story of the extinguishing of the lights, and he alone adds the charge that the Nusa'iri had a plurality of wives— a curious accusation to level at a group that is at least ostensibly Muslim.

21. See, e.g., Richard Payne Knight, *A Discourse on the Worship of Priapus and its Connection with the Mystic Theology of the Ancients* (1786), and Thomas Wright, *The Worship of the Generative Powers during the Middle Ages of Western Europe* (1865/66), published together as *Sexual Symbolism: A History of Phallic Worship* (New York: Julien Press, 1957); Dulaure, *Des Divinités Génératrices*; "Sha Rocco," *The Masculine Cross and Ancient Sex Worship* (New York: Asa K. Butts, 1874), which was frequently reprinted throughout the century: *The Masculine Cross, or a History of Ancient and Modern Crosses and their Connection with the Mysteries of Sex Worship. Also an Account of Kindred Phases of Phallic Faiths and Practices* (London: 1891; a volume in the privately printed "Nature Worship and Mystical Series" that included several of Hargrave Jennings's minor works); *Sex Mythology, Including an Account of the Masculine Cross* (London Privately Printed, 1898); H. M. Westropp and C. S. Wake, *Ancient Symbol Worship. Influence of the Phallic Idea in the Religions of Antiquity*, 2d ed., with introduction and notes by Alexander Wilder (New York: Bouton, 1875); Thomas Inman, *Ancient Pagan and Modern Christian Symbolism*, 4th ed., revised and expanded (n.p., 1922).

22. Proper study of this practical side of the pullulating sects of late classical antiquity has been long in coming and has been hampered enormously by the fact that not a single practical ritual text from the period has survived as such. The closest approximations are the Greek Magical Papyri (especially the so-called "Mithras Liturgy"), the theurgical texts preserved in the Chaldean Oracles, and scattered bits of the Hermetica and the Egyptian

Gnostic texts, and all of these concentrate on the results of the ritual (primarily the heavenly ascent) rather than on the preparatory means to achieve the results. In recent years, nonetheless, there has been an increased recognition of the reality (at least the "imaginary reality") of the experiences of these sects and of the practical means employed to make them possible. A primary example of this is the re-evaluation as techniques rather than as symbolic curiosities of the practice of the Phibionites (described by Epiphanius in his *Panarion*) in which couples ritually engaged in 365 acts of intercourse with *coitus reservatus* in order to ascend through the spheres and the same number to re-descend. See I. P. Couliano, *Expérience de l'Extase. Extase, Ascension et Récit Visionnaire de l'Hellénisme au Moyen Age* (Paris: Payot, 1984), esp. 124–29; Couliano, *Out of This World: Otherworldly Journeys from Gilgamesh to Albert Einstein* (Boston and London: Shambhala, 1991), esp. ch. 9. On these cults, see Jean Doresse, *Les Livres Secrets des Gnostiques d'Egypte*, 2 vols. (Paris: Plon, 1958); S. Benko, "The Libertine Gnostic Sect of the Phibionites according to Epiphanius," *Vigiliae Christianae* 21 (1967), 130ff.; Benko, *Pagan Rome and the Early Christians* (Bloomington: Indiana University Press, 1984), 54–78. The same is true in more recent works on Jewish "Merkabah" mysticism. See, e.g., C. R. A. Morray-Jones, "Paradise Revisited (2 Cor 12:1–12): The Jewish Mystical Background of Paul's Apostolate," *Harvard Theological Review* 86, no. 2 (1993): 177–217, and 86, no. 3 (1993): 265ff., which takes seriously (181) the hekalot writings as "detailed instructions about the ascetic, liturgical and theurgic techniques that make the visionary journey possible." See also R. Zwi Werblowski, "Mystical and Magical Contemplation," *History of Religions* 1, no. 1 (Summer 1961): 9–36 (on "yihudim," the divine names used as techniques for causing dreams and revelations), and Moshe Idel, *Studies in Ecstatic Kabbalah* (Albany: State University of New York Press, 1988), 103–69; Idel, *The Mystical Experience in Abraham Abulafia* (Albany: State University of New York Press, 1988), 18–54. See also Idel's *Hasidism: Between Ecstasy and Magic* (Albany: State University of New York Press, 1995), 133ff., on "The Erotic Implications of the Mystico-Magical Model" and on "erotic Theurgy."

23. Madame Blavatsky, who, as we shall see, in the early days advised those seeking practical progress to travel in Asia Minor where the brothers were ready to impart their wisdom, was fascinated with the Druses but, in a curious omission, never mentions the Nusa'iri by name. For her, the Druses were the direct heirs of the Gnostic Ophites and of "the Ebionites, Nazarites, Hemerobaptists, Lampseans [and] Sabians," and were part of the universal secret brotherhood, the "mysterious school" that underlay all religions, cults, and creeds. In *Isis Unveiled* she quotes a long letter on the Druses from A. L. Rawson, who claimed to have been initiated by the Druses, and clearly intended her readers to believe that she too had been so initiated. To bolster her claims for this universal brotherhood of which the Druses were but a part, she quoted K. R. H. Mackenzie's *Royal Masonic Cyclopædia* (1877) on the Brotherhood of Luxor—the group that she (initially) insisted had directed the foundation of the Theosophical Society, and which the H. B. of L. later claimed as

its own ancestor. *Isis Unveiled*, 2:306–15. Hargrave Jennings, likewise, was fascinated as we have seen (chapter 6) with the notion that isolated sects and groups still maintained the living tradition of the ancient doctrines.

24. See Daftary, *The Isma'ilis: Their History and Doctrines*, 63–68 (Ghulat); 87–136 (Gnosticism; earliest Gnostic speculations in Ja'far al-Sadiq); 100–102 (Nusa'iri); 139–40 (cyclical history; cosmic intermediaries); 109 (Bardesanes); 195–98 (Druzes); 200–201 (Hamza and Nusa'iri); 357 (origin of Druses and Nusa'iri); 400 (Isma'ilis and Nusa'iri doctrine of metempsychosis); 532–33 (early nineteenth-century battles between Isma'ilis and Nusa'iri); 600 (bibliography). See also C. Cahen, "Note sur les origines de la communauté syrienne des Nusayris," *Revue des Etudes Islamiques* 38 (1970): 243–49. Louis Massignon, "Les Nusayris," in *Elaboration de l'Islam* (Paris, 1969), 109–14; *Mélanges Louis Massignon*, 2 vols. (Damascus: Institut Français, 1957); R. Strothmann, "Seelenwanderung bei der Nusairi," *Oriens* 12 (1959): 89–114; Henri Corbin, *Trilogie ismaelienne* (Tehran/Paris, 1961), 171 (on relationship of Persian "archetypes" and Nusa'iri theories of days and names); H. A. R. Gibb and J. H. Kramers, eds., *Shorter Encyclopaedia of Islam* (Ithica: 1953), s.v. "Nusairi"; Rudolf Strothmann, "Esoterische Sonderthemen bei den Nusa'iri," *Abhandlungen der deutsche Akadamie der Wissenschaften zu Berlin* 4 (1956; reprinted Berlin, 1958). Heinz Halm, *Die islamische Gnosis: Die extreme Schia und die 'Alawiten* (Zurich: Artemis, 1982) strongly defended the idea of the connection of the Nusairi with the Gnostics, but his conclusions were questioned by Couliano, who was an expert on Gnosticism. I. P. Couliano, *The Tree of Gnosis: Gnostic Mythology from Early Christianity to Modern Nihilism* (San Francisco: Harper, 1992), 36–38.

25. Edward E. Salisbury, "The Book of Sulaiman's First Ripe Fruit, Disclosing the Mysteries of the Nusairian Religion, by Sulaiman Effendi of 'Adhamah, with Copious Extracts," *Journal of the American Oriental Society* 8 (1866): 227–308. Salisbury notes (228), "[S]ome parts have been omitted for the sake of decency."

26. *Pre-Adamite Man*, 34.

27. *Casca Llanna*, 73. "Guebre" was the common nineteenth-century term for the remnants of the old Zoroastrian "fire worshippers" scattered in the Near East and around Baku in the Caucasus. Madame Blavatsky claimed to have participated in their rites at Baku. *Isis Unveiled*, 2: 632.

28. *Eulis!* 47. The reference to "Lydde" is to the Reverend Samuel Lyde, another missionary, who wrote two uninspired books on the Nusairi that are notable only for their charitable defense of the Nusa'iri from the charges of "licentiousness, obscenity and incest." See Rev. Samuel Lyde, *The Anseyreeh and Ismaeleh: A Visit to the Secret Sects of Northern Syria with a View to the Establishment of Schools* (London: Hurst & Blackett, 1853), 97–105 (Lyde does concede Burkhardt's charge that the Nusairi worhsipped the "pudendum muliebre"); *The Asian Mystery, Illustrated in the History, Religion, and Present State of the Ansaireeh or Nusairis of Syria* (London: Longman, Green, Longman,

and Roberts, 1860), 102ff. In *Ravalette* (72–73) and *Triplicate Order* (4–9), Randolph uses Lyde to buttress his claims on the antiquity of his antecedents.

29. Randolph's various phonetic spellings of "Marek el Gebel," which clearly indicate that he was trying to write what he had heard, are one instance of this. Another may be found in Randolph's use of the mock Arabic exclamation, "By Allah and the ten Imauns." *Love! At Last!* 18. The Nusa'iri are technically "Twelvers," believers in twelve imams, beginning with 'Ali and descending through Musa al-Khazim, the younger son of Ja'far al-Sadiq, while the Isma'ili proper trace the descent of their imams through Isma'il, Musa's elder brother who predeceased Ja'far. See Dafteri, *The Isma'ilis: Their History and Doctrines,* 94–95; Lyde (1860), 29; Dussaud, *Histoire et religion des Nusayris,* 44ff. Despite this, the tenth imam of the Twelvers, 'Ali al-Hadi, "the Director," assumed special importance for the Nusa'iris. Mohammed b. Nusayr (d. 883), the eponymous founder of the Nusa'iri, had initially proclaimed himself the Bab of the tenth imam. See Dafteri, *The Isma'ilis: Their History and Doctrines,* 101.

30. For an enlightening view of the inner workings of these milieus, including the use of drugs and sex, see Wilson, *Scandal.*

31. *Eulis!* 48. Robert Orme has called to my attention a fascinating and important book translated and published in the 1890s by Paul de Régla [P. A. Desjardin]: El Khôdja Omer Haleby Abou Othman's, *El Ktab des Lois Secrètes de l'Amour d'après El Khôdja Omer Haleby, Abou Othmân* (Paris: Librairie Nilsson, 1893). The book, which Desjardin claimed to have received from Haleby (d. 1886), in Turkey, is the translation of one part of a manuscript on the practical and theoretical occultism of sex. According to the text, sex is the key to nature and the mysteries, and its real secrets are communicated "mouth to mouth after long tests and ceremonies" (155) in secret societies. Through sexual intercourse "man in his turn becomes a god, creator of beings like to himself" (33), a "being like to God" (159–60). The book also inculcates the evil of onanism and gives common sense rules on avoiding hasty sex and a method of creating superior children—all ideas familiar from Randolph. Finally, like Randolph, the author taught the magic of the moment of orgasm: "When the supreme instant comes when the heaven opens to inundate you with its divine flame, give an energetic blow, make your Dkeur penetrate as much as possible, and project your sperm while pronouncing the sacred and magical formula 'In the name of God . . . the clement and merciful.'" Ibid., 260. While the existence of the document gives some form to the milieux in which Randolph must have moved and shows the existence of secret teachings on magical sexuality in the Near East that were accessible to the traveler, there is insufficient evidence to link Randolph directly with its teachings.

32. *The Ansairetic Mystery* is printed as appendix A and "The Mysteries of Eulis" as appendix B.

33. "The Mysteries of Eulis" survives in only one known manuscript (twenty-two pages of forty lines each) which bears John Yarker's colophon

and notation that he had bought it from Randolph's widow. See appendix C. The *Ansairetic Mystery* survives as a sheet, "printed but not published" by the *Toledo Sun* in 1873 or early 1874. The earliest reference to the work is an advertisement for "The Choice," a manuscript or printed sheet that listed "the 122 new derivative powers of the Human Will." "P. B. Randolph," *Banner of Light* 28, no. 25 (March 4, 1871): 5. The *Sun*, despite its staid-sounding name, was a radical free-thought journal edited by John A. Lant—a sexual radical and convert to Islam who, like many others, fell afoul of Anthony Comstock and spent five months in prison. On Lant, see Blatt, *Free Love and Anarchism* 110; Heywood, *Cupid's Yokes*, 12; "The Case of John A. Lant," *Banner of Light* 28, no. 20 (February 12, 1876): 5. Like Randolph, Lant was a delegate to the spiritualist convention in 1873. See *Proceedings of the Tenth Annual Convention of the American Association of Spiritualists*, 32, 33, 247. In the *Ansairetic Mystery* Randolph announced that he was preparing "an Especial Work on Sex matters," *Sexagyma*, which would be printed but not published. It is possible that this or some version of this is "The Mysteries of Eulis."

34. *Eulis!* 74–75; *After Death*, 258 ("I know that men and women fail and die through feebleness of Will; that LOVE lieth at the foundation.").

35. Paschal Beverly Randolph, M.D., *Eulis! The History of Love: Its Wondrous Magic, Chemistry, Rules, Laws, Modes, Moods and Rationale; Being the Third Revelation of Soul and Sex. Also, Reply to "Why is Man Immortal?" The Solution to the Darwin Problem. An Entirely New Theory*, 2d ed. (Toledo: Randolph Publishing Co., 1874).

36. Ibid., 100. This is from Randolph's earlier *Asiatic Mystery* (1871).

37. The terms appear together for the first time in *Golden Secret* (1872) where Randolph says that, though ancient and found in all Oriental lands and in the Vedas, they are new to the United States: "They are the grand secret of the sages, and, surviving all earthly and intellectual revolutions, come to the surface once more to save mankind." See also *Eulis!* 90.

38. For its antecedents, see *Dealings with the Dead*, 206; *Guide to Clairvoyance*, 52 ("If you want to be able to read the life-scroll of others, you must *first* learn to fix the attention on a single point, wholly void of other thought. *Second, think* the thing closely, and *third, will* steadily, firmly, to know the solution, and the vision thereof will pass before you like a vivid dream."); *Seership!* 71–72 ("Persistence of purpose to a given end, aim and purpose; Attention; Calmness; Will; Intensity; Polarity—sexual; and Repulsion—by magnetic currents").

39. A practice later advocated by, among others, Julius Evola.

40. Randolph earlier had used the term *Tirau-clairism* to denote the science of reading appearances by assuming the mental attitude, posture and facial expression of others, an ability he said he had learned from Machiavelli, whose ability to read the "body language" of others made him appear to be

a mind reader. See chapter 5 and *Dealings with the Dead*, 7. Randolph taught that in the sixth grand division of earth's spiritual girdle a form of tirau-clairism was imparted that enabled a person to look at another or at a portrait (or a picture of another's left hand) and decide to "what sphere, grade, division, section, order or fraternity, such persons may belong." See *After Death* (1868 ed. only), 191; *After Death* (later editions), 111. The reference makes it clear that the magical powers taught during this life by Randolph were part and parcel of the development of the soul after death.

41. *Eulis!* 90.

42. See above. Randolph had been teaching the two functions of breathing since *Grand Secret* (1861). The idea of a special, spiritual breathing is Randolph's version of the common Swedenborgian notion of 'Internal Respiration,' the process by which humans, moved by love, re-attain their original ability to breathe as the angels do. This, of course, also restores their ability to commune with the angels. The matter is exhaustively treated in a long series in the London *Spiritual Magazine* in 1862–1863 by the appropriately named "Respiro." See especially the conclusion, "Internal Respiration—Judgments," *Spiritual Magazine* 3, no. 10 (October 1863): 460ff. This inner breathing also formed the centerpiece of the magic of Randolph's old acquaintance Thomas Lake Harris and of his disciple Laurence Oliphant.

43. The *Ansairetic Mystery* advertises Randolph's mirrors for sale, and both it and "The Mysteries of Eulis" make it clear that mirror magic, either alone or in conjunction with sexual magic, was the road to true clairvoyance or "Psycho-vision." See also *Eulis!* 125, 201, 215–17.

44. *Ansairetic Mystery.* "The Mysteries of Eulis" gives the same secret in more veiled fashion: "At the moment his seminal glands open his nostrils expand, and while the seed is going from his soul to her womb he breathes one of two atmospheres, either fetid damnation from the border-spaces or Divine energy from the far heavens."

45. *Eulis!* 101.

46. See Godwin, Chanel, and Deveney, *The Hermetic Brotherhood of Luxor*, 246.

47. E.g., *Dealings with the Dead*, 108 (good spirits do not break the sphere, but approach "the crown of the head and infuse thoughts, else blend themselves with the subject, but never by destroying either consciousness or will"); 138 ("Sex really means more than people even remotely suspect. In the Soul-world . . . Sex is of mind—on earth it is of the body mainly. . . . Now let two such meet in the Soul-world, and if they are adapted to each other, their spheres—nay, their very lives—blend together; the result of which is mutual improvement, purification, gratification.").

48. *Ghostly Land*, 9–10.

49. "Randolph's Letters—No. 7," *Religio-Philosophical Journal* 1, no. 18 (January 27, 1866): 3. See also F. B. Dowd, *Double Man* (1895), where the theme is the reunion of soul affinities on both sides of the grave, and where there is a lengthy discussion of the problems of a man given over to unrestrained sexual intercourse with his disembodied wives. The notion of elevating sexual intercourse across the chasm of the grave with one's twin soul is explicitly advocated by Peter Davidson, the provincial grand master of the H. B. of L., in his touching letters to Arthur Arnould, whose dead wife haunted his sleep. See Godwin, Chanel, and Deveney, *The Hermetic Brotherhood of Luxor*, 381–87.

50. See *Ravalette*. This is a variant of the fairy tale of the Little Mermaid told by Hans Christian Andersen.

51. See generally Ida C., *Heavenly Bridegrooms. An Unintentional Contribution to the Erotic Interpretation of Religion*, introduction by Theodore Schroeder (New York, 1918); Emile Laurent and Paul Nagour, *L'Occultisme et l'Amour* (Paris: Vigot Frères, 1902), 65–71, 81–91; Brad Steiger, *Demon Lovers* (New Brunswick: Inner Lights, 1968), 106ff. Robert F. Fryar of Bath devoted a considerable part of his output to this theme, stressing its "Rosicrucian" elements. See, e.g., *Supernatural Generation* (n.p., privately Printed for the Editor, 1896) in which Fryar collects a nosegay of material on sex with the gods from the works of Thomas Inman. See also R. Merkelbach, *Roman und Mysterium in der Antike* (Munich/Berlin: Bech, 1962), 17ff. (sexual union with the god/goddess). Merkelbach's thesis on the origins of Greek novels has been discredited, but the material he collected is still valuable. Richard Reitzenstein, *Hellenistic Mystery Religions* (Pittsburgh: Pickwick Press, 1978): 118–31, 310–19 (on "love unions" with God), 308ff. A. Dietrich, *Eine Mithrasliturgie*, 4th ed. (Stuttgart, 1923), 121–27 (begetting of divine in man; love union with the god); A.-J. Festugière, *Révélation d'Hermès Trismégiste*, 4 vols. (Paris, 1950–54), 2:549, 2:220–24 (sacred marriage). The reality of the belief in antiquity is shown by the Roman matron gulled by a lecherous young man into believing she was chosen to sleep with Anubis (actually the young man himself in a darkened room). Josephus, *Antiquities* 18.3.4.

52. Maria de Naglowska adds to *Magia Sexualis* a warning on the dangers of "incubi and succubi, which reflect your vices and your hidden desires," but the warning, if it reflects Randolph's thoughts at all (it is supposedly from "your Brother Charsah"), is still consistent with the advocacy of sexual intercourse with appropriate spiritual entities. *Magia Sexualis*, 210.

53. See, e.g., H. P. Blavatsky, "Lodges of Magic," *Lucifer* 3, no. 14 (October 15, 1888): 89–93, reprinted in *BCW*, 10:124–33, and now in Godwin, Chanel, and Deveney, *The Hermetic Brotherhood of Luxor*, 370–72.

54. J. Bricaud, *L'Abbé Boullan, Sa Vie, Sa Doctrine et ses Pratiques Magiques* (Paris, Chacornac Frères, 1927), 51ff. This doctrine explains the fascination of Robert H. Fryar of Bath with "incubi and succubi." R. H. Fryar, ed., *Sub-Mundanes or the Elementaries of the Cabala. Unabridged. An esoteric work. Physio-*

Astro-Mystic. Annotated from the suppressed work of Father Sinistrari on "Incubi and Succubi" (Bath: Robert H. Fryar, 1886).

55. *Eulis!* 89 ("When we are in perfect magnetic rapport with an individual, that person can be made to imitate our action, think our thoughts, do as we do, and be for the time our exact counterparts.").

56. There is no indication that this lymph was eaten, as the Phibionites are accused of doing and Aleister Crowley actually did.

57. Clymer, *Divine Alchemy*, 131, 222, 236.

58. Dr. Massimo Introvigne has pointed out to me Mario Praz's conclusion in *The Romantic Agony* that one of the major ritual sections of *Magia Sexualis* that can not be found in Randolph's works is derived from Joséphin Péladan's novel *A coeur perdu*. See his *Il Cappello del Mago. I Nuovi Movimenti Magici, Dallo Spiritismo al Satanismo* (Milan: SugarCo Ed., 1990), 199. There was at least a belief in astrological circles that Randolph was an astrologer. Roger Parris has told me that Alexandre Volguine, the editor of the *Cahiers Astrologiques*, in his autobiography bemoaned the fact that Randolph's astrological writings had been lost. It seems more probable that they never existed. Another aspect of *Magia Sexualis* that appears to have been derived from the magical tradition rather than from Randolph is de Naglowska's material on the procedure for animating statues. The notion has a long history in classical and medieval magic and Hermeticism, but nowhere appears in Randolph's surviving works. On this magical animation, see Dodds, *The Greeks and the Irrational*, 292–95.

59. *Magia Sexualis*, 176.

60. See, e.g., the discussion in Massimo Introvigne, "Arcana Arcanorum: Cagliostro's Legacy in Contemporary Magical Movements," *Syzygy. Journal of Alternative Religion and Culture* 1, nos. 2–3 (1992): 117–35, of the "wet way" of immortalization (the use and eating of semen, the *materia prima*) in Cagliostro's Egyptian Rite and in the workings of that rite by Francesco Brunelli. On this aspect of the Rosicrucians generally, see Christopher McIntosh, *The Rosicrucians: The History and Mythology of an Occult Order* (Wellingborough: Crucible, 1987), 78–81 (prime matter and semen; sexual practice); 129–32 (Randolph).

61. The same approach has continued in our day. See, e.g., Karl R. H. Frick, *Die Erleuchteten. Gnostische-theosophische und alchemistisch-rosenkreuzerische Geheimgesellschaften bis zum Ende des 18. Jahrhunderts—ein Beitrag zur Geistesgeschichte der Neuzeit* (Graz: Akademische Druck, 1973); *Licht und Finsternis. Gnostiche-theosophische und freimaurerisch-okkulte Geheimgesellschaften bis an die Wende zum 20. Jahrhundert*, 2 vols. (Graz: Akademische Druck, 1975–78), 1:240ff. and passim. Frick's discussion of Randolph, which relies on Clymer's myths, is in *Licht und Finsternis*, 1: 429–37. A. E. Waite's considered judgment is very telling. He speaks of "a great experiment which—'once in time and somewhere in this world'—may have been practiced in hidden sanctuaries

that were homes of men and women. The doctrine of sex in the Zohar is that *desideratum* which I mentioned at the beginning, a Key general to the House of Doctrine: all other teachings in the great Theosophical miscellany may be said to encompass it. . . . It is the central root which I have mentioned, and from this root the Tree of Knowledge grows. As the Zohar intimates, it becomes the Tree of Life." *The Holy Kabbalah* (New York, n.d.), 599ff. On the more occult-conspiratorial side, see "Inquire Within" (Miss Stoddard), *Light-Bearers of Darkness* (London: Boswell, 1930).

62. From his edition of the *Divine Pymander* (1872), Randolph was familiar with the formal Hermetic tradition with its emphasis on the originally androgynous nature of man, the all-pervasive power of Eros and the rebirth of man. His edition, however, is a reprint of the first English edition of 1650 and lacks the Latin *Asclepius*, whose explicit discussion of the "mystery of procreation unto eternity" and the "divinity that arises in both natures from the sexual coupling" has given rise to enormous speculation over the centuries. The quotations are from the most recent translation, that by Brian P. Copenhaver, *Hermetica: The Greek Corpus Hermeticum and the Latin Asclepius in a New English Translation, with Notes and Introduction* (Cambridge: Cambridge University Press, 1992), 79. See also Reitzenstein, *Hellenistic Mystery Religions*, 310ff.; A. D. Nock and A.-J. Festugière, *Corpus Hermeticum*, 2d ed., 4 vols. (Paris: Belles Lettres, 1946–54), 2:376; A. E. Waite, "Woman and the Hermetic Mystery," *Occult Review* 15 (June 1912): 325ff. On the sexual side of alchemy, see S. Redgrove, *Bygone Beliefs* (London, 1920), especially chapter 10, "Phallic Element in Alchemical Doctrine." His conclusion (182) is that it "is by no means a fantastic hypothesis that the innermost mystery of what a certain school of mystics calls 'the secret Tradition' was a sexual one." See also Maurice Aniane, "Notes sur l'Alchemie, 'Yoga' cosmologique de la Chrétienté médiévale," in Jacques Masui, ed., *Yoga, Science de l'Homme Intégral* (Paris: Les Cahiers du Sud, 1953): 243–73.

63. See, e.g., Davidson's "Symbolical Notes to the First Degree," in Godwin, Chanel and Deveney, *The Hermetic Brotherhood of Luxor*, 126–27, which rehearses the mythology of the fall symbolized in the "Wheel of Ezechiel" that is featured by Hargrave Jennings, Emma Hardinge Britten, and Madame Blavatsky. For a considered occult judgment on the value of Randolph's sexual magic from a traditional point of view, see Julius Evola, *The Metaphysics of Sex* (New York: Inner Traditions International, 1983), 268ff. Evola had been a friend of Maria de Naglowska since their involvement with Dadaism around World War I and later translated *Magia Sexualis* into Italian. *Magia Sexualis. Forme e Riti* (Roma: Edizioni Mediterranee, n.d., c. 1977). The Fondazione "Julius Evola" has kindly sent me a copy of de Naglowska's *Malgré les Tempêtes . . . Chants d'amour* (Rome: Maglione and Strini, 1921) with her inscription to Evola. From his traditional viewpoint, Evola thought that Randolph's insistence on male ejaculation in the magic rite was erroneous, but he avoided the difficulty by proposing that perhaps what Randolph really intended was the separation of the "magical force" from the physical semen at the moment of orgasm.

64. *New Mola!* (1873), 36 ("I also, the last of the glorious Order . . . ").

65. See Britten, *Art Magic*, 79ff.; J. G. R. Forlong, *Rivers of Life, or Sources and Streams of the Faiths of Man in all Lands; Showing the Evolution of Faiths from the Rudest Symbolisms to the Latest Spiritual Developments*, 2 vols. (London: Quaritch, 1883), 2:579–80 (Druse cells in Palestine are the true prototypes of the Eleusinian cells and mysteries); R. P. Knight, *An Enquiry into the Symbolical Language of Ancient Art and Mythology* (London: Black & Armstrong, 1836), 7; Dulaure, *Des Divinités Génératrices*, 112–14. See also *"Aureus": The Golden Tractate of Hermes Trismegistus. Concerning the Physical Secret of the Philosopher's Stone. In Seven Sections* (Bath: Robert H. Fryar, 1886), with an introduction by John Yarker. The translation is that given in the famous *A Suggestive Inquiry into the Hermetic Mystery, with a dissertation on the more celebrated of the Alchemical Philosophers* (London, 1850), by Mary Anne South Atwood. The work carries as an appendix *A Key Explanatory of the Principal Plates Illustrating the Taro, and the Bath Occult Reprint Edition of the Works of "Hermes Trismegistus"* with the symbol of the H. B. of L. as frontispiece. The *Key* makes it clear that "[t]hose who consider the Eleusinian Mysteries to have been phallic will find a confirmation of their theory in this Key which relates the means taken by Baubo to gladden the mournful Demeter."

66. *Triplicate Order*, 17.

67. "Eolist" was an early term among spiritualists to identify their movement. Randolph used the word frequently to describe the more radical sort of spiritualist reformers.

68. *Eulis!* 112 (praise of "Furguson"); 168–69 (March 1874 foundation); Lehman, *Life of John Murray Spear*, 440 (in England in March 1865 Spear again met Ferguson who was traveling as "chaplain" with the Davenport brothers). See *Curious Life*, 48 (Ferguson's recommendation of Randolph's scheme to found a normal school); *Davenport Brothers*, 326 (praise for him); "A Sad Case" (recommendation). Like almost everyone else, Ferguson was a correspondent of Emma Hardinge Britten. See *Nineteenth Century Miracles*, 157.

69. In *Ghostly Land*, 11, 23, Randolph also mentions (and criticizes), Mickey Free, an Irish medium who apparently lived in Tennessee at the time and who may have played some role in the group.

70. See *Triplicate Order*, 17, 23, which makes it clear that both his Rosicrucian and his Ansairetic ideas were to be absorbed into the mysteries of the "Templars of Eulis"—the final expression of his ideas, embodying the primordial wisdom of Hermes and Melchizedek.

71. *Eulis!* 169.

72. Ibid., dedication. He speaks mysteriously of "the Superlative Order of Men and Women who constitute the E.W.A.S." Excluding Orientals, the book is dedicated to John F. Kapp, L. H. McLaughlin, Albert Burpee, John Temple, Gustav Shrader, Lewis and Jonathan Kirk.

73. See "Movements of Lecturers and Mediums," *Banner of Light* 36, no. 9 (November 28, 1874): 5. Randolph listed his address for the trip as "care of" Herman Snow, a Harvard-educated theologian turned reformer, who ran a radical bookshop on Kearney Street in San Francisco. Randolph's lectures in the West were regularly chronicled in *Common Sense*, a San Francisco spiritualist journal to which Luna Hutchinson was a regular contributor.

74. See "Suicide," *Religio-Philosophical Journal* 18, no. 22 (August 14, 1875): 172, which reprints Randolph's letter of July 20, 1875 ("I returned recently from gold and silver hunting in the Pacific Desert. I found lots of it, but don't propose to take any more in mines as I object to being murdered because I am a liberalist."). The exploitation of these mines, even with the aid of Randolph's spirit, proved impossible. See Luna Hutchinson, "P. B. Randolph," *Religio-Philosophical Journal* 22, no. 1 (March 17, 1877): 6.

75. Paschal Beverly Randolph, "Refounder, Organizer and Supreme Hierarch," *The Book of the Triplicate Order, Rosicrucia, Eulis, Pythianae* (San Francisco: Women's Publishing Co., Printed for the Brotherhood, Candidates, and Truth-seekers, 1875).

76. *Triplicate Order*, 4–16, quoting *Ravalette*, 73–87.

77. Randolph for unknown reasons claimed to have become hierarch on September 5, 1846, near his twenty-first birthday. *Triplicate Order*, 21.

78. *Triplicate Order*, 27. At the end he appends a wonderful list of those *prisci theologi* who had expounded the ideas of the Triplicate Order throughout history. The list includes Hermes, Jung-Stilling, Thomas Vaughn, and a hodge-podge of medieval alchemists, including Penette Flamel. Its most curious addition is the name of an unknown "Donna Olivia of Granada." Ibid., 29–30.

79. *Triplicate Order*, 19.

80. It is possible that each of these new degrees in turn was subdivided into three. See appendix to *Magia Sexualis* (although most of this is Maria de Naglowska's elaboration) and *Ansairetic Mystery*, where Randolph speaks of the mysteries to be revealed in "the third and higher degrees."

81. *Triplicate Order*, 16.

82. *Rosicrucian's Story* (1863), 14–15.

83. *Curious Life*, 55, 59ff. In the description of the degrees of the Brotherhood of Eulis appended to Maria de Naglowska's *Magia Sexualis* (1931), the first degree is given over to teachings on orders and fraternities, astrology and "occult chemistry." The second degree consists of teachings on sexual magic and on "mediumité occulte," and the third is devoted to the philosopher's stone. Ibid., 214–15. Because of the prominence given to astrology and to traditional alchemy, this list is probably de Naglowska's own version of the degrees rather than Randolph's.

84. *Curious Life*, 59ff. These rituals, or some version of them, probably circulated separately. R. S. Clymer in one of his pamphlets noted that he had worked Randolph's Rosicrucian rituals in 1910. *The August Fraternity, Order of the Rose Cross in America and H. Spencer Lewis, the Baron Munchausen of the Occult, of Special Interest to all Masons, Rosicrucians, Students of the Occult and Fraternal Organizations* (Quakertown: Philosophical Publishing Co., n.d., c. 1933), 21. A picture of the performance survives in one of H. Spencer Lewis's pamphlets attacking Clymer and shows a small group of men and women garbed in suitably romanticized Egyptian paraphernalia. Maria de Naglowska, in a frontispiece to *Magia Sexualis* (1931) also lists Randolph's "Le Rituel du premier degré" as a work soon to appear. This was only one of the five parts of the first degree of the Brotherhood of Eulis, as *Magia Sexualis* itself was the second part of the second degree.

85. *Triplicate Order*, 31.

86. Ibid., 18. The meaning of "W.H." and "A.H." is unknown. The constitution of the order was to be supplemented in each lodge by more practical by-laws, and the "Rules and Regulations of an Outer Circle adopted by the Supreme Grand Lodge at San Francisco, California," on February 13, 1875, are given by R. S. Clymer in *The Initiates* (July 1908): 119ff. and (April 1909): 20ff. These are noteworthy only because of the repeated ban of drunkards and men who have seduced, impregnated, and abandoned women. The rules provide that all applicants must first be members of the Rosicrucian fraternity, which confirms that the Rosicrucians were a "pool" for Eulis and were supposed to continue in some form. The rules also provide that the brethren shall wear a black Prince Albert coat and white tie at meetings.

87. *Triplicate Order*, 10–11, 23 (third degree).

88. The Supreme Grand Council was supposed to consist of the officers of the Supreme Grand Lodge, the chief officers of all Grand Lodges and the masters of guilds. Since only the Supreme Grand Lodge existed when this was written, the men named were probably its officers. David Board has pointed out to me that Thomas Docking must be the same as the man who was later active in the Theosophical Society. See, e.g., *The Path* 3, no. 1 (April 1888) (organization of the Point Loma Lodge of the Theosophical Society under Docking). He was a recent emigrant from New Zealand and was the person chosen by Randolph to announce the formation of a lodge of Eulis in California. See "Dr. Thomas Docking," *Common Sense* 1, no. 15 (August 22, 1874): 175; "The Order of Eulis," ibid. 1, no. 20 (September 26, 1874): 233.

89. Ibid., 31.

90. *Triplicate Order*, 9.

91. Ibid., 11 (initiation fee and monthly fees); 14 (bounty); 20 (money to Supreme Grand Corner Stone Lodge); 26 (fees). The same promises of health and disability insurance and death benefits were made in the Triplicate Order

as had been made in 1863, but Randolph was honest enough to admit that these were still to be arranged. Ibid., 11.

92. *Triplicate Order*, 4, 25. Randolph's concern for his infant son (and probably his distrust of Kate Corson) is obvious from a notice appended to the back cover of some copies of *Ghostly Land*: "From this July 25, 1874, Osiris B. Randolph has an equal interest in our business of Book-Publishing, and manufacture of our Remedials. The firm-name is K. Corson and Co."

93. *Triplicate Order*, 21.

94. Ibid., 18.

95. Ibid., 24.

96. *Beyond the Veil*, preface; "Letter from Luna Hutchinson," *Religio-Philosophical Journal* 18, no. 17 (July 10, 1875): 131; "Bishop Creek, Cal.," ibid. 18, no. 12 (July 17, 1875): 142.

97. Jesse Hutchinson had been the original owner of High Rock Cottage in Lynn, Massachusetts, where John Murray Spear began building his perpetual motion machine, and then had moved to California. See Andrew Jackson Davis, *Present Age and Inner Life* (New York, 1853). He continued active in spiritualism in California and died in the late 1850s. See Emma Hardinge Britten, *Modern American Spiritualism*, 106.

98. *Beyond the Veil: Posthumous Work of Paschal Beverly Randolph, Aided by Emanuel Swedenborg and Others, Through the Minds of Frances H. McDougall and Luna Hutchinson* (New York: D. M. Bennett, 1878; reprint, Mokelumne Hill, Calif.: Health Research, 1972). Luna Hutchinson had been involved with spiritualism for years and was the author of frequent letters to the *Religio-Philosophical Journal* and *Woodhull and Clafin's Weekly* on God, prayer, Steven Pearl Andrews, and the dawn of the women's era in American history. It is intriguing to conjecture that she is the "L. Hutchinson" who had been a student of Eliphas Lévi's in 1869–70 and who contributed to *L'Initiation* in the 1890s, though the identification is unlikely. See "Causerie sur l'au-dela," *L'Initiation* 5, vol. 17 (1892): 244ff.; "Notice sur le Mage Eliphas Lévi," ibid. 5, vol. 16 (1892): 127ff. Beginning in 1894 she is listed as a collaborator in the noninitiatory work of the review. Christopher McIntosh in his book on Eliphas Lévi, however, states that this L. Hutchinson was British.

99. See Michael Gomes, *The Dawning of the Theosophical Movement* (Wheaton: Quest Books, 1987), 81–82.

100. "Suicide," *Religio-Philosophical Journal* 18, no. 22 (August 14, 1875): 172. Jones asked whether the reference to the "fatal 29th day of March, 1875" was a premonition by Randolph of his own death, which it was. Randolph had had a vision that he would take his own life on that date and was joyful when it passed. See Luna Hutchinson, "Bishopscreek, Cal.—L. Hutchinson Writes," *Religio-Philosophical Journal* 19, no. 2 (September 2, 1875): 221.

101. The letter has been unearthed by Michael Gomes in a copy of the 1876 edition of *Ravalette and The Rosicrucian's Story* among Olcott's books at the Theosophical Library at Adyar, India. Mr. Gomes tells me that Olcott had many of Randolph's works. He apparently gave them to his father and then, after his father's death, got them back and gave them to the library at Adyar. The "Mrs. R. of B." is unknown, though she may be a Mrs. Blake whom Olcott was testing at the time. See chapter 13. She is undoubtedly the "lady in Brooklyn, N.Y., to whom impecuniosity had compelled" Randolph to sell his third-class "trinue" magic mirror. *Eulis!* 8. Her experiences with the magic mirror were detailed in "A Magic Mirror," reprinted by the *New York Sun* on June 30, 1875, 2, one of a series of such articles from the *Spiritual Scientist*—a journal then largely under the influence of Madame Blavatsky—which was probably the source of Randolph's information. Olcott had not mentioned the revelations in his *People from the Other World* (Hartford, 1875) which had originally appeared late the preceding fall as articles in the *Daily Graphic*.

102. *Davenport Brothers*, 304.

103. *Eulis!* 118, 119, 121–23.

104. *Toledo Blade*, July 29, 1875, 3, col. 3. His death certificate, as usual in such cases, listed the cause of death as "accident."

Chapter 11

1. See, e.g., Dr. Woldrich, "The Suicide," *Religio-Philosophical Journal* 22, no. 18 (July 14, 1877): 1 (gladly return); "Dr. P. B. Randolph," ibid. 28, no. 26 (September 11, 1875): 204 ("Today Randolph is the same uneasy character in the Spirit-World, as when here. . . . Brilliant in intellect, deeply logical in his writings, and eloquent as a speaker, yet he was eccentric. . . . [He] felt that he was not appreciated by the world, and that his color was a stigma on his character as a man."); Cyrus Lord, "P. B. Randolph Controls Mediums," ibid. 28, no. 25 (September 4, 1875): 195 (Randolph still felt no one loved him, and he was still erratic); "Paschal Beverly Randolph," *Banner of Light* 37, no. 22 (August 28, 1875): 4 (a gifted medium with a "strangely organized mind"). A. E. Waite said that in the late 1880s Randolph was still "occasionally 'communicating' with quite the average veracity of other 'controls' performed by the 'choir invisible.'" *The Real History of the Rosicrucians, Founded on their own Manifestoes, and on Facts and Documents Collected from the Writings of Initiated Brethren* (London: George Redway, 1887), 430.

2. *The Truth Seeker* (March 30, 1878): 206. I am indebted to Michael Gomes for calling this to my attention. *The Truth Seeker* was D. M. Bennett's freethought journal, begun in 1873, and Bennett was also the publisher of *Beyond the Veil*.

3. On the opposition of spiritualists to the introduction of "occultism" (by which they meant the old unscientific superstition of magic) into spiritualism, see R. Laurence Moore, "The Occult Connection? Mormonism, Christian Science, and Spiritualism," in *The Occult in America: New Historical Perspectives*, Howard Kerr and Charles L. Crow, eds. (Urbana: University of Illinois Press, 1986), 135–161; Stephen Richard Prothero, *Henry Steele Olcott (1832–1907) and the Construction of "Protestant Buddhism"* (Ann Arbor: University Microfilms, 1990), 76–79 (the "paradigm shift" from spiritualism to Theosophy and the consequent outrage of the spiritualists over the return to the "darkness of Egypt and the Middle Ages"); Gomes, *Dawning of the Theosophical Movement*, 82ff., 148ff. (Coleman's blasts at the Theosophists for their desire to return to the "demonological arts and incantations of the ancients for the purpose of working and controlling spirits, both human and inhuman"). See also H. P. Blavatsky, "The Claims of Occultism," *The Theosophist* 2, no. 12 (September 1881), reprinted in *BCW* 3: 271–75, who quotes M. A. Oxon's review of *Isis Unveiled*: "Those who mastered [*Isis*] bear away a vague impression that Spiritualism had been freely handled not altogether to its advantage and that a portentous claim had been more or less darkly set up for what was called occultism." For Davis's views, see "Andrew Jackson Davis' Column," *Religio-Philosophical Journal* 26, no. 2 (March 15, 1879): 1. For Coleman's extended condemnation of occultism and of Randolph, Blavatsky, Olcott and Britten as its principal originators, see Coleman, "Are the Truths of Modern Spiritualism Reliable?" *Religio-Philosophical Journal*, 4 parts, from 21, no. 18 (January 13, 1877): 1, 8 through 21, no. 21 (February 3, 1877): 1.

4. S. C. Gould, "Resumé of Arcane Fraternities in the United States," *Notes and Queries* (1900): 129. The same notice was published by Gould as "Rosicrucian Societies in the United States" in his *Historic Magazine and Notes and Queries* (1907): 323. Both notices distinguish Randolph's own "Brotherhood of Rosicrucians" that "existed in New England during the '60s and down into the '70s" from Dowd's "Temple of the Rosy Cross." Gould also separately mentions Eulis, which he thought had "its embryo . . . in Philadelphia, in the sixties" and then was organized in Boston. "It flourished for some ten years, calling itself a Rosicrucian Society, but had scarcely any fundamentals pertaining to those of the sixteenth and seventeenth centuries, nor even the Rosicrucians of modern times." Gould, "Order of Eulis," *Historic Magazine and Notes and Queries* (1905): 98.

5. "Mysteries of Eulis," appendix B. These minor Rosicrucians included W. J. Atkinson of Tipton, Missouri (who taught magic and urged his followers to Try!); G. H. Binkley, of Springfield, Ohio (who styled himself "G.M.∴A.E.M.R." and touted Eleusinian healing and the virtues of the sleep of Sialam); Colonel R. D. Goodwin, of St. Louis, Missouri (who founded a Continental League of 1876 to foster separation of church and state and taught astral travel, Rosicrucianism, and clairvoyance); and "John the Rosicrucian" (who may well be John Pilkington and who praised Randolph as "Supreme Grand Master of

Rosicrucia on the Globe"). See W. J. Atkinson, "Magic," *Religio-Philosophical Journal* 17, no. 16 (January 2, 1875): 6; G. H. Binkley, "Occult Sciences," ibid. 17, no. 20 (February 20, 1875): 2; Binkley, "Occultism vs. Spiritualism," ibid. 19, no. 21 (February 5, 1876): 376; M. J. Burr, "Ohlographs from George H. Binkley, M.D., G.M.," ibid. 20, no. 10 (May 20, 1876): 74; R. D. Goodwin, "The Rosicrucians," ibid. 34, no. 10 (May 19, 1883): 6; John the Rosicrucian, "P. B. Randolph," ibid. 20, no. 7 (April 29, 1876): 54. In the early 1880s, Randolph's spirit, which had since his death entered the "vestibule of the great Temple of Light . . . and become initiated into certain secrets of the great working Order," began to send veiled messages through a medium to his "associates" in the West, promising them passwords and further revelations. Albert Morton of San Francisco responded that his wife (who may be the H. R. Morton who was "Supreme Grand Guard" of Eulis—see chapter 10) had been controlled by Randolph's spirit for years and understood the messages. See "P. B. Randolph," *Banner of Light* 49, no. 3 (April 9, 1881): 6; Albert Morton, "P. B. Randolph," ibid. 49, no. 9 (May 21, 1881): 3; "Interesting Letter from Mr. Albert Morton, of San Francisco," ibid. 49, no. 11 (June 4, 1881): 2.

6. *The Temple of the Rosy Cross. The Soul: Its Powers, Migrations and Transmigrations*, 2d ed., revised (San Francisco: Rosy Cross Publishing Co., 1888). Through this meager reference, in turn, Heaney has passed into innumerable secondhand histories of the modern Rosicrucians.

7. The most notable of his associates in the transmission of his Rosicrucian ideas was Paul Tyner, a peripatetic social worker and indefatigable editor of and contributor to "New Thought" journals. How he came to know Dowd is unknown, but when he came to put out his journal *The Temple* (Denver: Temple Publishing Co., May 1897–November 1898), he gave prominent space in its pages to Dowd's ramblings and taught that "in the supreme development of sex in humanity must be found, I think, the Key to immortality" and that regeneration occurred "through recognition and development of the higher nature and potencies of sex—through its elevation and spiritualization." *The Temple* 1 (1897): 74. See also ibid. 2 (1898): 119–20. The journal functioned as an advertisement for what was called the "Western Cult of the Rosy Cross," whose representative in the current era was Dowd and which could be addressed in care of its Bureau of Instruction (Tyner). Ibid. 1 (1897): 65. The journal was a mixture of optimistic "New Thought," women's liberation, and translations of Zola and Karl Marx. See Charles S. Braden, *Spirits in Rebellion: The Rise and Development of New Thought* (Dallas: Southern Methodist University Press, 1963), 330. See also ibid., 182, which mentions Tyner's association with W. J. Colville, one of the editors of *The Gnostic*, the California journal that had published Dowd's articles in the late 1880s and which may be the connection between Dowd and Tyner. Tyner also taught, as did Dowd, that the immortality to be obtained was of the physical body, as well as of the soul. See Paul Tyner, *The Living Christ: An Exposition of the Immortality of Man in Soul and Body* (Denver: Temple Publishing Co. 1897). On Tyner generally and on his

seemingly quite genuine mystical experiences, see Richard Maurice Bucke, *Cosmic Consciousness. A Study in the Evolution of the Human Mind* (1901; New York: E.P. Dutton & Co., 1945), 351ff.

8. In his introduction to his edition of Randolph's *Soul!* Clymer says he first read one of Randolph's works in 1893, when he was fifteen. *Soul! The Soul World*, R. S. Clymer, ed. (Quakertown: Philosophical Publishing Co., 1932). He was then accepted as a neophyte in the fraternity in the late 1890s. See Clymer, *The Rosicrucian Fraternity in America*, 1:243; *Soul! The Soul World*, introduction; *The Rosicrucians—Their Teachings. The Fraternitas Rosae Crucis. American Section. The Manifestoes Issued by the Brotherhood, Order, Temple and Fraternity of the Rosicrucians since its Foundation in America have been Edited and the Teachings Made Applicable to Modern Conditions and the needs of the New Age*, revised ed. (Quakertown: Philosophical Publishing Co., n.d., copyright 1941), 23 ("My personal Occult life, study and training commenced under Dr. Phelps in 1895 and was concluded six years later under his direction."). Dr. James R. Phelps (1837–1902) was a dentist, astrologer, and old follower of J. C. Street and was said to have been the co-instructor of neophytes with "Sorona," the wife of F. B. Dowd. On Street, see chapter 6. Phelps claimed that his "authority . . . [went] back for years and was conferred by honored brothers" Randolph, Dowd and "John Healy" (that is, John Heaney, the dedicatee of Dowd's *Temple of the Rosy Cross*). R. S. Clymer, *The Sons of God. The Mystical Interpretation of the Teachings of the Masters. A Foreshadowing of the Coming Work of the Messenger of the New Age* (Quakertown: Philosophical Publishing Co., n.d., copyright 1925), foreword.

9. On Clymer's connection with the Phelons and their H. B. of A., L. and E., see *Rosicrucian Fraternity in America*, 1:244, and the introduction to the reprint of W. P. and Mira Phelon, *Three Sevens: A Story of Initiation* (Quakertown: Philosophical Publishing Co., 1938); *The Initiates* 3 (1909) (which has as a regular section the semi-official notes of the Hermetic Brotherhood). W. P. Phelon and his wife had been admitted to the H. B. of L. in 1887, and Clymer used the seal of the H. B. of L. as a frontispiece to one of his early pot-boilers, *The Divine Mystery. The Gods, Known in Early Ages as the Incubi and Succubi, Now Known as the Elementals. Solving the Mystery of the Immaculate Conception and How it Was, and Is, Possible. Giving Full Instructions for Development, and How to Come into Touch with Elementals. Also, The Human Soul Before and After Death. Constitution of Man and the Universe. Key of Gospel. Gospel Initiation. According to Pistis Sophia. The Inner Mystery* (Allentown: Philosophical Publishing Co., n.d., c. 1910). Clymer must also have received the H. B. of L. stream of occultism through his membership in Edouard Blitz's *Ordre Martiniste*. See his introduction to Randolph's *The Rosicrucian's Story* (Quakertown: Philosophical Publishing Co., 1939), which reproduces his certificate. On Papus's revived Martinists as a pool or source of candidates for his Rose Croix (and ultimately for the H. B. of L. strain of occultism), see the manuscript by Paul Vulliaud, "Histoires et portraits des Rose Croix," ch. 8, preserved in the archives of the

Alliance Israélite Universelle in Paris. See also Papus [Gérard Encausse], "L'Occultisme contemporain en France," in *Les Sciences Maudites*, F. Jolivet-Castelot, ed. (Paris: Maison d'Art, 1900) 3ff.; V.-E. Michelet, *Les Compagnons de la Hiérophanie. Souvenirs du Mouvement Hermétiste à la Fin du XIX siècle* (Paris: Dorbon-Ainé, n.d., c. 1938); René Guénon, "F.-Ch. Barlet et les Sociétés Initiatiques," *Voile d'Isis* 64 (April 1925): 217ff., reprinted now in Godwin, Chanel, and Deveney, *The Hermetic Brotherhood of Luxor*, 428–30.

10. See *Book of Rosicruciae*, 1:7ff.

11. See "The American Progressive Medical Association: Another Attempt to Organize the Twilight Zone of Professionalism," *Journal of the American Medical Association* (December 14, 1923): 2050–54, and Clymer's reply, *Dr. R. Swinburne Clymer Replies to "Dr." H. Spencer Lewis, The Mystic Swindler and the A.M.A. Article. Being an Exposé of His attempted Misuse of that Article as a Shield of and in Perpetuation of His Own Insidious Fraud* (Quakertown: R. Swinburne Clymer, n.d., c. 1935). See also R. S. Clymer, *The Fraternitatis Rosae Crucis. An Attempt to Harmonize the Spirit of the Writings of Those who are Known to have been Rosicrucians* (Quakertown: Philosophical Publishing Co., 1929) 80ff.; *The Rosicrucian Fraternity in America*, 1:86ff.

12. See Clymer, *Book of Rosicruciae*, 3:176, where Clymer relates the story of his encounter in 1902 with a mysterious stranger who approached him in a restaurant while he was reading a book on occultism. The stranger, who was supposedly the "Compte M. de St. Vincent," the successor to Guinotti, revealed great truths to Clymer and then prophesied that they would meet again. The story echoes, perhaps consciously, the initial approach of Max Theon to the young T. H. Burgoyne "in a park where Burgoyne sat reading a book on occultism." Godwin, Chanel, and Deveney, *The Hermetic Brotherhood of Luxor*, 361. A close reading of Clymer's various stories about Guinotti shows that he believed him to be the linguist, poet, song writer, and journalist Charles Mackay (1814–1889), remembered today as the author of *Memoirs of Extraordinary Popular Delusions and the Madness of Crowds*, 2d ed. (London: Office of the National Illustrated Library, 1852), an attack on the silliness of various superstitions and delusions (including the Rosicrucians)—an unlikely work for a secret master to have authored. More appropriately, he also published a long poem, *The Salamandrine, or, Love and Immortality* (London: How & Parsons, 1842), on the immortalization of the lovely "fire-spirit" (elemental) by her love for a man, which included a history of the antecedents of the idea in the *Comte de Gabalis*, *The Rape of the Lock* and Baron de la Motte Fouqué's *Undine*. He also adopted (and perhaps fathered) a young Italian girl who, as Marie Corelli, dallied with the Prince of Wales and authored *The Romance of Two Worlds*, *Ardath* and The *Soul of Lilith*, all of which abound in powerful secret masters who direct the course of world events. Randolph knew of Mackay and classed him among the "paper stainer" Rosicrucians. *Ravalette*, 72–73.

13. See appendix C.

14. R. S. Clymer was always very careful to say that the rights to Randolph's "system" had been granted to his organizations in 1895—a claim obviously intended to imply some formal agreement between Mrs. Randolph and the Dowd Rosicrucians. Clymer also continued, even though he had been distributing Randolph's manuscript works on sexual magic for years, to recognize Mrs. Randolph's rights to Randolph's published books. See R. S. Clymer, *The Rose Cross Order. A Short Sketch of the History of the Rose Cross Order in America, together with a Sketch of the Life of Dr. P. B. Randolph, the Founder of the Order. Also a Short History of the Persecutions and Prosecutions, which Resulted in Giving Him Greater Freedom than he had Before, and which Trial Proved that the Things of which he had been Accused were False* (Allentown: Philosophical Publishing Co., 1916), 20 (he would be glad to publish Randolph's works, but Mrs. Randolph controlled the rights); *The Initiates* (1908): 1–2 ("This Prospectus is from the writings of Dr. Randolph, permission and full authority was given to us in 1895 to follow this work and use this matter and all rules and regulations made by him."). Mrs. Randolph also stayed in touch with the offshoots of her husband's work at least to the extent of contributing a short biographical sketch of his life ("Pioneer Rosicrucian Workers in America, Number One: Pascal Beverly Randolph") to *Mercury* 2, no. 4 (February 19, 1917), the organ of the Societas Rosicruciana in America, a group founded by G. Winslow Plummer and S. C. Gould that emphasized the sexual side of occult development and still continues today. I am grateful to David Board and Joscelyn Godwin for bringing this to my attention.

15. Gustav Meyrink, trans. and ed., *Dhoula Bel: Ein Rosenkreuzer-Roman von P. B. Randolph, Aus dem Englischen Manuskript übersetzt und herausgegeben von Gustav Meyrink* (Vienna, Berlin, Leipzig, and Munich: Rikola Verlag, 1922), 6. Meyrink (1868–1932) was an Austrian occultist and novelist with a wide interest in various forms of sexual magic and psychic control of others. He was a member of the Theosophical Society and of its Esoteric Section and was involved with the T. S. Blue Star Lodge of Prague. See Horst Miers, *Lexikon des Geheimwissens*, 2d ed. (Munich: 1976), 283–84. The avidity of the members of the Blue Star Lodge for practical occult training was characteristic of the time. As soon as a book was published or they heard of a magician or mystic, they contacted the author or magician, seeking instruction. Once, they apparently contacted an eighty-year-old magician in the north of England who published a journal, *The Magic Mirror*, and practiced a system of ceremonial evocations that enabled him to "evoke the different forces dwelling in old trees." He taught a system of concentration that centered on the Pole Star and was "combined with the evocation of a certain spiritual Brotherhood, of which the Pole Star was both the symbol and the force-giving centre." All the members of the lodge attained identical visions that confirmed they were on to something, but they stopped the practice when their Viennese colleagues warned that the practice was dangerous. See Karel Weinfurter, *Man's Highest Purpose (The Lost Word Regained)* (1930; reprint, Kessinger, n.d.), 45–46. On Meyrink's interest in the sexual side of occultism, see the introduction to Richard Schmidt, *Fakire*

und Fakirtum im alten und modernen Indian Yoga-Lehre und Yoga-Praxis nach den Indischen Originalquellen (Berlin: Barsdorf, 1908), and the articles cited. Meyrink was a friend of Henri Clemens Birven, yet another sexual occultist. See Birven, *Lebenskunst in Yoga und Praxis* (Zurich: Origo, 1953).

16. See appendix B. I am grateful to Robert Orme for making a copy of the "Mysteries of Eulis" available to me. Meyrink's connection with Randolph may well have been through his contact with John Yarker's Antient and Primitive Rite in 1893. "Meyrink corresponded with the head of the rite, John Yarker, who made him acquainted with the writings of Paschal Beverly Randolph. He was the founder of the 'Eulis Brotherhood,' a sexual-magical Circle in the 'Hermetic Brotherhood of Luxor,' from which the O.T.O. took its inheritance." Josef Dvorak, "Abstürze beim aufsteig zum feuropfer," *Tantra* (Zurich) (July 1994): 11–16, 12.

17. Kate C. Randolph to R. Swinburne Clymer, June 10, 1907. I wish to thank Dr. Gerald E. Poesnecker, the present supreme grand master of the Fraternity of Rosicrucians at Quakertown, Pennsylvania, for giving me a copy of this important letter. The reference to the "Eulians" at Salem is to the organization run by Dr. Edward Holmes Brown of Salem, Massachusetts, who succeeded F. B. Dowd as supreme grand master of the Temple of the Rosy Cross and hierarch of Imperial Eulis in 1907 and whose organization passed into Clymer's hands on his death in 1922. See Clymer, *The Rosicrucian Fraternity in America*, 1:195ff. As "Eulis," Brown was the author of *The Word. Issued from the Temple of the Rosy Cross*, a book of undistinguished poems issued by the Eulian Publishing Company of Salem (n.d., c. 1917), and he also contributed occasional pieces to *Mercury*, the organ of the Societas Rosicruciana in America with which his Rosicrucians were allied.

18. See *The Divine Pymander of Hermes Mercurius Trismegistus*, Bath Occult Reprint Series, introduction by Hargrave Jennings (Bath: R. H. Fryar, 1884); *The Virgin of the World of Hermes Mercurius Trismegistus. Now First Rendered into English, with Essay, Introduction, and Notes, by Dr. Anna Kingsford and Edward Maitland*, author of "The Perfect Way," Bath Occult Reprint Series (London: George Redway, 1885); *Sepher Yetzirah: The Book of Formation, and the 32 Paths of Wisdom*, trans. and ed. W. Wynn Westcott (Bath: Robert H. Fryar, 1887); W. Wynn Westcott, *Tabula Bembina, sive Mensa Isiaca. The Isiac Tablet of Cardinal Bembo. Its History and Occult Significance* (Bath: Robert H. Fryar, 1887); *The Book of Nicholas Flamel (1650)*, ed. W. Wynn Westcott (Bath: Robert H. Fryar, 1889); *"Aureus": The Golden Tractate of Hermes Trismegistus. Concerning the Physical Secret of the Philosopher's Stone. In Seven Sections*, introduction by John Yarker (Bath: Robert H. Fryar, 1886); *The Letters of Hargrave Jennings, Author of "The Rosicrucians," "Phallicism," &c., &c. Forming the Unabridged Correspondence with the Editor of the Bath Occult Reprints, between 1879 and 1887, with Frontispiece*, introduction by John Yarker (Bath: Robert H. Fryar, 1895); *Continuation of the Comte de Gabalis, or New Discourses upon the Secret Sciences; Touching upon the New Philosophy. Posthumous Work*, trans. and introduction by John Yarker (Bath: Robert H. Fryar, 1897); *The Assistant Génies, and Irreconcileable Gnomes, or*

Continuation to the Comte de Gabalis, trans. and Introduction by John Yarker (Bath: Robert H. Fryar, 1897).

19. Joscelyn Godwin, Christian Chanel, and John Patrick Deveney, *The Hermetic Brotherhood of Luxor. Initiatic and Historical Documents of an Order of Practical Occultism* (New York: Samuel Weiser, 1995). On the extension of the work of the H. B. of L. into the *Mouvement Cosmique* of Max Theon, see the superb and enlightening thesis of Christian Chanel, "De la 'Fraternité Hermetique de Louxor' au 'Mouvement Cosmique': L'Oeuvre de Max Théon (contribution à l'étude des courants ésotériques en Europe à la fin du XIXème siècle et au début du XXème siècle," (Doctorat d'Etat, E.P.H.E., Section Ve, Paris, 1994).

20. "The Mysteries of Eros," reprinted in Godwin, Chanel, and Deveney, *The Hermetic Brotherhood of Luxor*, 213–78. The H.B. of L. teaching manuscript, "A Brief Key to the Eulian Mysteries," which is preserved in the archives of the Theosophical Society in Adyar, India, and a version of which is included in "The Mysteries of Eros," is even stronger in its language condemning Randolph: "The 'Mysteries of Eulis' as taught by the unfortunate P. B. Randolph, who fell a miserable victim to the fallacies of 'Eulis' by Committing Suicide— constitute the 2nd Degree of Grade I in our Noble Order, and exhibit in the Case of Poor Randolph the calamitous consequences of imperfect Initiation."

21. However, Osiris Randolph's granddaughter, an Italian contessa, has apparently come to glory in the mysteries of her great-grandfather. See Anna Maria Turi, "Randolph, un personaggio dai misteri insolubili," *Il Tempo* (Rome), July 10, 1978, which was kindly sent to me by the Fondazione Julius Evola. As Randolph feared, his daughter Cora Virginia Randolph, who was 15 or 16 at his death, was left penniless in Utica. In 1876 she wrote in despair to a spiritualist journal: "I have suffered the pangs of want, have often wished for something higher and nobler, but every wish and hope has withered before my gaze, till I have many times wished death would relieve me from the hard and toilsome life to which fate has consigned me." "Vermont," *Religio-Philosophical Journal* 40, no. 5 (October 28, 1876): 3. With the help of spiritualists who remembered her father and of Luna Hutchinson who gave her the profits from *Beyond the Veil*, Cora eventually found a home in Vermont. See "A Daughter of Dr. P. B. Randolph," *Banner of Light* 29, no. 21 (August 19, 1876): 8; William Magoon, "Cora V. Randolph," ibid. 29, no. 23 (September 12, 1876): 3; "The Appeal Will Not Be Made in Vain," *Religio-Philosophical Journal* 21, no. 2 (September 23, 1876): 14; "Correction," ibid. 21, no. 7 (October 28, 1876): 54; advertisement, "Beyond the Veil," *Banner of Light* 43, no. 16 (July 13, 1878): 7 (all copies to be sold for the benefit of Randolph's daughter).

22. "Resumé of Arcane Fraternities in the United States," *Notes and Queries* (October 1896): 271.

23. The claim of the Order's demise was not strictly true, since the branch of the H. B. of L. presided over by T. H. Burgoyne and, after his death, by Belle and Henry Wagner, was still active in the western United States.

24. "Resumé of Arcane Fraternities in the United States," *Notes and Queries* (April 1905): 90.

25. "Resumé of Arcane Fraternities in the United States," *The Rosicrucian Brotherhood* (1908): 161. I want to thank David Board for giving me a copy of this page and of the notice on the Hermetic Brotherhood of Light from *La France Antimaçonnique,* cited below, which were missing from the sets I examined.

26. A. C. de la Rive and others, "Francmaçonnerie et Sociétés Secrètes," 15 Parts, *La France Antimaçonnique,* from 26, no. 23 (June 6, 1912) through 28, no. 30 (July 23, 1914), some anonymous and most published as "Notice sur les diverses Sociétés Secrètes américaines que ne sont officiellement rattachés à la Maçonnerie." The notice on the "Fraternité Hermétique de Lumière" is in *La France Antimaçonnique* 28, no. 30 (July 23, 1914): 358. See also Arthur Preuss, *A Dictionary of Secret and Other Societies* (St. Louis: Herder: 1924), 171.

27. The essential parts of the 1912 "Jubilee Edition" of the OTO's journal, *Oriflamme,* from which the quotations are taken, are given in Clymer, *The Rosicrucian Fraternity in America,* 2:602ff. Various other theories of transmission from Randolph to the OTO have been proposed in addition to the claim for Kellner and the Hermetic Brotherhood of Light. The most obvious is the central role of the H. B. of L. in the revival of occultism in France in the 1890s, but it has also been suggested that the German Lutheran pastor E. C. M. Peithmann (1865–1943), who spent many years in the United States, was one of the paths through which Randolph's work was continued in Europe. See Massimo Introvigne, *Il Ritorno dello Gnosticismo* (Milan: SugarCo Ed., 1993), 160ff., and his *Il Capello del Mago. I Nuovi Movimenti Magici. Dallo Spiritismo al Satanismo* (Milan: SugarCo Ed., 1990), 252. On the OTO generally see H. Möller and Ellic Howe, *Merlinus Peregrinus. Vom Untergrund des Abendlandes* (Würzburg: Königshausen & Neumann, 1986); Ellic Howe and Helmut Möller, "Theodor Reuss: Irregular Freemasonry in Germany, 1900–1923," *Ars Quatuor Coronatorum* 91 (1978): 28–46. See also Peter-Robert König, "The OTO Phenomenon," *Theosophical History* 4, no. 3 (July 1992): 92–98; "Theodor Reuss as Founder of Esoteric Orders," ibid. 4, nos. 6–7 (April–July 1993): 187–93; "Veritas Mystica Maxima," ibid. 5, no. 1 (January 1994): 23–29; "Stranded Bishops," ibid. 5, no. 5 (January 1995): 169–75.

28. See A. E. Waite, *The Brotherhood of the Rosy Cross* (New York, n.d.), 569, who says that he was told that Moseley was a practical student of magic who used scryers and crystals and even more dangerous paths and ruined his health by the use of drugs for occult purposes under the guidance of Randolph. Moseley also stands in the chain of succession of Frederick Hockley's scrying manuscripts: Moseley bought them at Hockley's death, and Moseley's collection, in turn, was bought by F. G. Irwin. Geraldine Breskin and Robert Gilbert, at the Theosophical History conference in London in 1989 outlined the tenets of yet another mysterious group, "The Hermetic Society of 8," devoted to "conquering generation," of which Moseley, Frederick Holland, Kenneth Mackenzie, John Yarker, Irwin, W. W. Westcott, Benjamin Cox, Oxley, and "MacGregor" Mathers were members.

29. See Francis King, *Ritual Magic in England, 1887 to the Present Day* (London: Spearman, 1970), 120: Karl Kellner claimed to have derived his methods from an Arab and two Hindus, "but a more immediate source seems to have been a group of the European followers of the American occultist P. B. Randolph. Randolph suffered from an acute persecution complex—possibly not unreasonably in view of his partial negro ancestry—and took care to conceal his unusual sexual doctrines beneath a cloak of heavily-veiled symbolism. . . . Nevertheless, Randolph did pass on his teachings to a trusted and tiny group of his French followers who subsequently called themselves the H. B. of the Light, a name used by more than one group of nineteenth-century occultists. It was possibly from one or more members of this group that Kellner derived the techniques used in the O.T.O. although, of course, he certainly met Tantricks in the course of his oriental wanderings. It is interesting to note that a group ultimately deriving from Randolph has survived in France to this day and that the sexual teachings are identical with those of the O.T.O." See also King, *Sexuality, Magic and Perversion* (Secaucus: Citadel, 1974); Frater U∴D∴, *Secrets of the German Sex Magicians. A Practical Handbook for Men and Women* (St. Paul: Llewellan Publishing Co., 1991), 3ff. (the sexual magic of the higher degrees of the OTO are derived from "Czech and Austrian occultists involved in the sex magical practices of the black American magician, Paschal Beverly Randolph.").

30. *Sub-Mundanes or the Elementaries of the Cabala. Unabridged. An esoteric work. Physio-Astro-Mystic. Annotated from the suppressed work of Father Sinistrari on "Incubi and Succubi,"* R. H. Fryar, ed. (Bath, 1886). For an excellent bibliographical discussion of this obscure subject, see Montague Summers's introduction to Sinistrari's work, published as *Demoniality* (1927; reprint, New York: Benjamin Blom, 1972).

31. See the review by Madame Blavatsky, "Thoughts on the Elementals," *Lucifer* 6 (May 1890): 177ff., reprinted in *BCW*, 11:187ff. See also J. M. Peebles, *Spirit Mates, Their Origin and Destiny*, passim.

32. See H. P. Blavatsky, "Crows in Peacock Feathers," *Boston Daily Globe*, Friday Morning, March 8, 1889, 4, reprinted with an introduction and notes by Michael Gomes, *Canadian Theosophist* 66, no. 5 (November–December, 1985): 114–17. See also *H. P. Blavatsky to the American Conventions, 1888–1891* (Pasadena: Theosophical University Press, 1979), 15–22 ("The Theosophical Society has never been and never will be a school of promiscuous Theurgic rites."). Butler was the founder of "Solar Biology," which continues after a fashion today, and his group had direct connections with the H. B. of L. Michael Gomes has informed me that he had been admitted to the Theosophical Society in the branch at Rochester run by Mrs. Josephine Cables, one of the leaders of the H. B. of L. in America. Charles H. Mackay, whose insipid rules on "Esoteric Development" were appended to the Harvard manuscript of the H. B. of L.'s "Mysteries of Eros," was the managing editor of Butler's *The Esoteric* which offered for sale Randolph's *Pre-Adamite Man* (which probably

indicates some connection with Randolph's widow) and favorably reviewed the book. *The Esoteric* (December 1889): 261–62. I am indebted to Franklin Rosemont for bringing these passages in *The Esoteric* to my attention. On Butler, see also "Occultism for Barter. Esoteric Colleges and False Prophets," *The Path* 3 (March 1889): 381–83 (which demonstrates Butler's plagiarism from Thomas Lake Harris). On Mackay's later "Order of the West Gate," see Gould, "Resumé of Arcane Fraternities in the United States," *Historic Magazine and Notes and Queries* (1896): 276. One really curious offshoot of Butler's work was the "Ordo Roris et Lucis" (the Order of the Dew and the Light) or the "Ros. Crux Fratres," a fortune-telling and Rosicrucian endeavor that published *Lamp of Thoth* in Yorkshire in 1888. They advocated free love, food reform, and spiritualism and had as guides a variety of entities calling themselves by such names as *Francisco the Monk* and *Abdallah ben Yusuf*. They were accused, at least, of trying to beget children "on the astral plane," but the accusation may simply have been more of Madame Blavatsky's somewhat biased view of what Butler was up to. The announcement of the order in the pages of *Lucifer* in 1889 called forth the violent denunciations of S. L. Mathers and the first public announcement of the Order of the Golden Dawn. See *Lucifer* (June 15, 1889); King, *Ritual Magic in England*, 40ff.; René Guénon, *L'Erreur Spirite* (1923; Paris: Editions Traditionnelles, 1952), 132ff.

33. See Ida C[raddock], *Heavenly Bridegrooms. An Unintentional Contribution to the Erotic Interpretation of Religion*, introduction by Theodore Schroeder (New York, 1918). The orally transmitted third degree of Craddock's "Alphaism" included "Borderland Wedlock" in which the sense perceptions were so heightened that the true spirit partner was perceived. Craddock's reference to Paul Tyner in this regard establishes the underlying influence of Randolph. On Craddock's problems with Anthony Comstock, see Sears, *The Sex Radicals*, 262ff.

34. On de Naglowska, see the excellent study by Sarane Alexandrian, "Maria de Naglowska et le satanisme fémininé" in his *Les Libérateurs de l'Amour* (Paris: Editions du Seuil, 1977). There is also a very interesting unpublished memoir of her work by Marc Pluquet, "La Sophiale. Maria de Naglowska, sa Vie, son Oeuvre." I thank Massimo Introvigne for making this available to me. For rather sensationalistic views of her work and the occult sexual milieu of Paris before World War II, see Pierre Geyraud, *L'Occultisme à Paris* (Paris: Editions Emile-Paul Frères, 1953), 107ff.; *Les Sociétés Secrètes de Paris* (Paris: Ed. Emile-Paul Frères, 1938); M. Monestier, *Les Sociétés Secrètes Féminines* (Paris: Productions de Paris, 1963), 19–21; René Thimmy, *La magie à Paris* (Paris: Editions de France, 1934), 62–81; Henri Meslin, *Théorie et Pratique de la Magie Sexuelle; L'Amour et l'Occultisme* (Paris: Astra, n.d., c. 1938), 38ff.

35. D. Jean Collins, "Divining the Beloved Community," *Gnosis Magazine* 25 (Fall 1992): 36–40. The group is derived from the Brotherhood (or Church) of Light of Elbert Benjamin ("C. C. Zain"). I am grateful to Richard Bruce Pickrell for bringing this article to my attention.

Chapter 12

1. Gustav Meyrink, *Dhoula Bel*. Actually the book is not the missing *Dhoula Bel* but rather a verbatim translation of the published version of *Ravalette*. Meyrink's final judgment on Randolph was that he was "ein Schwärmer katexochen und ein Cagliostro im kleinem." On the incubation-induced vision of the *katechoi*, see H. Idris Bell, *Cults and Creeds in Graeco-Roman Egypt* (1953; reprint, Chicago: Ares Publishers, 1985), 21–22, 61–62.

2. *Dhoula Bel*, 7–11. On Madame Blavatsky's belief in and ideas on the deflecting of a sorcerer's malefic "current of Akas," see "Footnotes to 'The Life of Sankaracharya, Philosopher and Mystic,'" *The Theosophist* 1, no. 4 (January 1880): 89, reprinted in *BCW*, 2:217–19. She thought that, unless directed with sufficient will to break down obstacles and overpower the will of the victim, the current rebounds on the sender and adds that this "reversal of a maleficent current upon the sender may be greatly facilitated by the friendly interference of another person who knows the secret of controlling the Akasic currents." See also *Isis Unveiled*, 1:500. See generally, John Patrick Deveney, "A Note on Psychic Attacks," *Theosophical History* 5, no. 6 (April 1995): 194–97. Randolph's ideas on the sending of such lethal or harmful forces are set out in the *Ansairetic Mystery*.

3. References to Ayton abound in every book on the occult in England during the period. However, the only book devoted to him is Howe's edition of his letters, *The Alchemist of the Golden Dawn: The Letters of the Revd W. A. Ayton to F. L. Gardner and Others 1886–1905*, ed. Ellic Howe (Wellingborough: Aquarian, 1985). For a firsthand description of Gardner's own use of a magic mirror ("consecrated according to a Rosicrucian rite"), see F. Leigh Gardner, "The Magic Mirror," *Historic Magazine and Notes and Queries* (1905): 260–62. Ayton's own works were limited to his translation of a short life of John Dee and an anonymous article on the "Chinese Taro" that appeared in Thomas Moore Johnson's *The Platonist*. He also translated what he described as the "Prophecies" of the Abbot Trithemius (a key work for the teachings of the H. B. of L., which he sent to Madame Blavatsky, but the translation was never published. See "The Diaries of H. P. Blavatsky," *BCW*, 1:421.

4. Letter from Ayton to an unnamed applicant to the H. B. of L., dated August 6, 1884 (private collection).

5. H. B. of L. teaching manuscript. The language of the warning is quoted in chapter 11. The "Key" was incorporated in the comprehensive "Mysteries of Eros." See Godwin, Chanel, and Deveney, *The Hermetic Brotherhood of Luxor*, 213–78.

6. Letter from Ayton to an unnamed neophyte to the H. B. of L., dated May 18, 1885 (private collection). A version of Ayton's story is also presented in "Caution. Pseudo-Occultist Societies," *The Theosophist* 7 (January 1887): 255–56, which speaks of the manuscripts copied by the H. B. of L. from "the obscene works of the late P. B. Randolph, the Black Magician who made a stir in America

some 20 years ago, and appropriately terminated his career by suicide, and, as it is said, getting up suddenly from an Incantation directed against the Theosophical Society and performing the 'Happy Dispatch' with one of the instruments he had set before him as a symbol of his bitter hatred of the Theosophical Society." The author of the piece is either Thomas Wainman Holmes or Thomas H. Pattinson, both of whom were "chelas" of Ayton and the latter of whom was later active in the Order of the Golden Dawn. The article is reprinted in Godwin, Chanel, and Deveney, *The Hermetic Brotherhood of Luxor*, 365–69.

7. Maria de Naglowska, *Magia Sexualis*, introduction, 7–11. See also Frick, *Die Erleuchteten*, 2, vol. 1, 431. Madame Blavatsky's work scarcely seems designed to teach the masses.

8. London, 1894; republished Hudson, NY: Lindisfarne Press, 1993, with an excellent historical introduction by Christopher Bamford. See my review in *Theosophical History* 5, no. 2 (April 1994): 40–41. The essential readings on this subject are by Joscelyn Godwin ("The Hidden Hand," *Theosophical History* 3, nos. 2–5 [April 1990–January 1991]:35–43, 66–76, 107–17, 137–48), David Board ("The Brotherhood of Luxor and the Brotherhood of Light," ibid. 2, no. 5 [January 1988]:149–57), and H. J. Spierenburg ("Dr. Rudolf Steiner on Helena Petrovna Blavatsky," ibid. 1, no. 7 [July 1986]:159–74; and "Dr Rudolf Steiner on the Mahatmas," ibid. 1, no. 8, and 2, no. 1 [October 1986–January 1987]: 211–23, 23–31). Spierenburg's articles collect from the writings of Rudolf Steiner his various comments on the forces operating through Madame Blavatsky. The classic statement of the theory is given by Swami Narad Mani, the Chef de l'Observatoire secret européen de la "True Truth Samaj" d'Adyar, in "Baptême de Lumière, Notes pour servir à l'Histoire de la Société dite Théosophique," *La France Antimaçonnique*, various numbers beginning with 25, no. 43 (October 26, 1911) and running through 26, no. 9 (February 29, 1912). This was the source of many of the ideas René Guénon expressed in *Le Théosophisme*. The earliest proponent outside the H. B. of L. of the theory that Madame Blavatsky was the cat's paw of competing brotherhoods and that the later Theosophical Society was the work of "Adepts of the esoteric Buddhist cult" was Randolph's old associate, the sexual mage T. L. Harris. See his *Wisdom of the Adepts. Esoteric Science in Human History* (Fountain Grove: Privately Printed, 1884). For the classic statement (inspired by the H. B. of L.) of the occult mission to the United States in 1850 to combat materialism, see Papus, "L'Occultisme contemporain en France," in F. Jolivet-Castelot, ed., *Sciences Maudits* (Paris, Maison d'Art 1900), 3ff.

9. See generally his *L'Erreur Spirite* (Paris: Editions Traditionnelles, 1974), *Le Théosophisme*, and his two articles on F.-Ch. Barlet, now republished in Godwin, Chanel, and Deveney, *The Hermetic Brotherhood of Luxor*, 428–37.

10. *L'Erreur Spirite*, 20–21. Despite the hypothetical phrasing of his theories, Guénon had no real doubt about the involvement of the H. B. of L. in the origins of spiritualism. See ibid., 401–5.

11. Information on the books in Olcott's collection is from Michael Gomes who reviewed the holdings of the library of the Theosophical Society at Adyar, India. Olcott also includes one of Randolph's books in a list of recommended readings appended to his *People from the Other World* (Hartford: American Publishing Co., 1875). Olcott's use of *Ravalette* is in his "A Tap at Mrs. Tappan," *Banner of Light* 29, no. 26 (September 23, 1876): 2.

12. Both Randolph and Madame Blavatsky use Bulwer-Lytton's term *Scin-Laeca* to describe the projection of the double. H. P. Blavatsky, "A Story of the Mystical, Told by a Member of the Theosophical Society. A Dread Scene in Eastern Necromancy—Vengeance Marvelously Wrought by Occult Methods—Mysteries—the Scîn-Lâc," *New York Sun* (December 26, 1875), reprinted in *BCW*, 1:163–73 and in *A Modern Panarion*, 597. See also *Isis Unveiled*, 2:587–88 (point 9 of Madame Blavatsky's "fundamental propositions of the Oriental Philosophy" is the "voluntary and conscious withdrawal of the inner man (astral form) from the outer man (physical body)."); ibid., 2:620 (projection of the double). Randolph himself said that he had spent many years studying the mysteries of the scin lecca.

13. See Joscelyn Godwin, *The Beginnings of Theosophy in France* (London: Theosophical History Center, 1989), 4–7. See also J. N. Maskelyne, *The Fraud of Modern "Theosophy" Exposed. A Brief History of the Greatest Imposture Ever Perpetuated under the Cloak of Religion* (London: George Routledge & Sons, n.d., c. 1912), 18–19, on Madame Blavatsky's "experiments in hypnotism with a 'famous old mesmerist' who 'discovered her psychic gifts and was anxious to retain her as a sensitive, but she fled from Paris to escape his influence." Maskelyn, however, dates the experiments to 1849, which is almost certainly wrong. A poem by Michal, "Le Chanvre," extolling the virtues of hashish appeared in *L'Initiation* 1, vol. 3 (1889): 175–77.

14. Jean Overton Fuller, in her *Blavatsky and Her Teachers* (London and the Hague: East-West Publications, 1988), ch. 25, 54ff., discusses the evidence, including the fact that Home himself was only intermittently in Paris in 1858, and gives a chronology that leaves no time for Madame Blavatsky even to be in Europe between 1851 and 1858. This is clearly wrong. See D. D. Home, "From Moscow," *Religio-Philosophical Journal* 36, no. 4 (March 22, 1884): 8, who says her name was well known to him in Paris in the spring of 1858. Madame Blavatsky told the *New York Graphic* in an interview, "In 1858 I returned to Paris and made the acquaintance of Daniel Home. . . . Home converted me to Spiritualism." This was reprinted as "More about Materializations," *Spiritual Scientist* 1, no. 11 (November 19, 1874): 121–22. In her marginal comment on the *Graphic* article, she says: "The biggest lie of all. *I never saw in my whole life* either D. D. Home or his wife. I never was in the same city with him for a half an hour in my life." She adds that from 1851 to 1859 she was in California, Egypt, and India, and in 1856–58 she was in Kashmir and elsewhere. On all of this, see Michael Gomes, *Theosophy in the Nineteenth Century: An Annotated Bibliography* (New York: Garland Publishing, 1994), 202. See also Gomes, *Dawn-*

ing of the Theosophical Movement, 217 n. 92, who establishes that Home and Madame Blavatsky in fact never met. Despite this, she was clearly in Paris and London at various times in the 1850s, and her presence there may well have coincided with Randolph's.

15. *Seership!* 81. In the *Guide to Clairvoyance,* 22, he again speaks, apparently knowingly, of the use of an emerald as a scrying device, a familiarity which again may show some knowledge of Dalip Singh's emerald.

16. See K. Paul Johnson, *In Search of the Masters: Behind the Occult Myth* (South Boston, VA: Author, 1990). The revised and augmented version of this has now been published as *The Masters Revealed: Madame Blavatsky and the Myth of the Great White Lodge* (Albany: State University of New York Press, 1994).

17. *The Mahatma Letters to A. P. Sinnett from The Mahatmas M. & K. H.,* 209–10.

18. Madame Blavatsky's respect for and use of Bulwer-Lytton's novels are apparent from her writings, and an attempt has even been made, unsuccessfully, to show that her master was really a romanticized portrait of Lytton and that the Egyptian elements of her occultism especially were taken from his novels. S. B. Liljegren, *Bulwer-Lytton's Novels and Isis Unveiled* (Upsala, Copenhagen, and Cambridge: Harvard University Press, 1957). Madame Blavatsky did, nonetheless, regard Lytton as an "adept." See Joscelyn Godwin, "From the Archives. H. P. Blavatsky Writes to 'M. A. Oxon.': An Unpublished Letter," *Theosophical History* 4, nos. 6–7 (April 1993): 172–77, 173.

19. See *Isis Unveiled,* 1:129, 131ff., 142ff., 166, 178, 279, 333.

20. "Madame Blavatsky on the 'Himalayan Brothers,'" *The Spiritualist* (August 12, 1881), reprinted in *BCW,* 3:262–68

21. An example may be found in her reference to J. M. Ragon as "very learned for a non-initiate." "The Last of the Mysteries in Europe," *BCW,* 14:296n. See also *Isis Unveiled,* 1:306 (Swedenborg was a natural magician and seer, not an adept). An example of a person called an "initiate" is A. L. Rawson who is described as an initiate of the "Brotherhood of Lebanon" and of the Druses, into which latter organization it is strongly hinted Madame Blavatsky herself had been initiated. See *Isis Unveiled,* 2:312ff.; A. L. Rawson, "Two Madame Blavatskys.—The Acquaintance of Madame H. P. Blavatsky with Eastern Countries," *The Spiritualist* (April 5, 1878), reprinted in *Theosophical History* 3, no. 1 (January 1989): 27–30. See also H. S. Olcott, *Old Diary Leaves. The History of the Theosophical Society as Written by the President-Founder Himself,* 3d ed., 6 vols. (Adyar: Theosophical Publishing House, 1974–75): 1:23 (Rawson as an "adept"). Randolph himself had at least some passing familiarity in the Near East with the Druses. See *Casca Llanna,* 73, where he also mentions the mysterious Guebres—another of Madame Blavatsky's favorite mysteries. Rawson, of course, is a central pivot in all of these matters, since he traveled with

Madame Blavatsky in Egypt in the 1850s and studied the mysteries of hashish with her, and in the 1870s was associated with John Murray Spear (whose message Randolph bore to the World Convention in 1855) and D. M. Bennett (the publisher of Randolph's posthumous *Beyond the Veil*) in opposing Anthony Comstock's "obscenity" crusade. See chapter 9 and K. Paul Johnson, "Albert Leighton Rawson," *Theosophical History* 2, no. 7 (July 1988): 229–51. Rawson also was, as Michael Gomes informs me, the Theosophical Society member sent to Rochester, New York, in 1882 to initiate Mrs. Josephine Cables into the Theosophical Society—the same Mrs. Cables who next appeared as one of the heads of the H. B. of L. in America. See *The Occult Magazine* 1, no. 6 (July 1885): 48; A. L. Rawson, "The Rochester (U.S.A.) Theosophical Society," *The Theosophist* 4 (November 1882, Supplement): 2. Madame Blavatsky's judgment on Randolph as an initiate is confirmed by an interview she gave in 1877. After listing Plato, Pythagoras, and Simon Magus as adepts (and Cagliostro as a failed adept), she added: "Perhaps there are half a dozen Adepts in Europe. I have met none in this country. . . . P. B. Randolph, who committed suicide, was a real Adept." "Catechizing a Buddhist," New York *Sun*, May 6, 1877, 6.

22. Blavatsky, "Elementaries," *Religio-Philosophical Journal*, 23 (November 17, 1877), reprinted in *BCW*, 1:265–71. See also Michael Gomes, "Studies in Early American Theosophical History. IV. Colonel Olcott and the American Press," *Canadian Theosophist* 70, no. 6 (January–February 1990): 124ff.

23. *The Mahatma Letters to A. P. Sinnett*, 276–77 (letter 48). "M. A. (Oxon.)" (Stainton Moses) was given as an example of a mere medium.

24. Sinnett, *Incidents in the Life of Madame Blavatsky*, 191.

25. W. Q. Judge [Harij], "Lo Here! And Lo There!" *The Path* 4, no. 1 (April 1889):1–6, 2.

26. The *New York Mercury*, January 18, 1875, reprinted in *BCW*, 1:53–54, has an interview with Madame Blavatsky under the caption "Heroic Women," in which she is said to be "a member of the Order of Rosicrucians." See also "Important Note," *BCW*, 1:73 ("M ∴ brings orders to form a Society—a secret society like the Rosicrucian Lodge."); *BCW*, 1:100 (on the "HIRAF Club": "The Madame claimed to be a Rosicrucian."); James H. Wiggin, "Rosicrucianism in New York," *The Liberal Christian*, September 4, 1875, reprinted in Michael Gomes, "Studies in Early American Theosophical History. III. The Ante- and Post-Natal History of the Theosophical Society," 70, no. 3 (July–August 1989): 51–57, and in part in *The Occult World of Madame Blavatsky*, compiled and ed. Daniel H. Caldwell (Tucson: Impossible Dreams Publications, 1991), 64–65. The original letter to Colonel Olcott from the Brotherhood of Luxor was addressed to him "aux bons soins de Madame H. Blavatsky, F.G.S. ∴ R+". On Madame Blavatsky's mysterious "Rosicrucian jewel" that she hinted may have been Cagliostro's, see *BCW*, 1:425, 439; Olcott, *Old Diary Leaves*, 1:41; C. Jinarajadasa, ed., *Letters from the Masters of Wisdom, Second Series*, (Adyar: Theosophical Publishing House, 1977) letter no. 22.

27. "A Few Questions to 'HIRAF,'" *Spiritual Scientist* 3, nos. 19 and 20 (July 15 and 22, 1875): 202, 217–218, 224, 236–37, reprinted in *BCW*, 1:101–19.

28. "[T]hose who are willing to learn the Great Truth will find *the chance* if they only 'try' to meet someone to lead them to the door of one 'who knows *when* and *how*." "When the High Priests of the Temple of Osiris, of Serapis, and others, brought the neophyte before the dreaded Goddess Isis, the word 'Try' was pronounced for the last time; and then, if the neophyte could withstand that final mystery . . . he became an initiate." "A Few Questions to 'HIRAF,'" *BCW*, 1:103, 115.

29. *Letters from the Masters of Wisdom, Second Series*, 23 (Serapis alive); "Letters of H. P. B. to Dr. Hartmann. 1885 to 1886," *The Path* 10 (February 1896): 366ff. ("You have come to the conviction that the 'Masters' are 'planetary spirits'—that's good; remain in that conviction. . . . I wish I could hallucinate myself to the same degree."). Colonel Olcott speaks of one of the masters of the early days as "gone from men's sight, yet not dead," and mentions that when he and Madame Blavatsky were near the Suez Canal, "the venerable T∴ B∴ passing near the canal sends me his greetings." Olcott, *Old Diary Leaves*, 1:19, 52. See also M. K. Neff, *Personal Memoirs of H. P. Blavatsky* (Wheaton: Theosophical Publishing House, 1937), 219ff.; Gomes, *Dawning of the Theosophical Movement*, 8 n.12.

30. "Madame Blavatsky on the Views of the Theosophists," *The Spiritualist* (February 8, 1878): 68–69, reprinted in *BCW*, 1:290 ff. See also *BCW*, 1:295–96: "Let it not be inferred, though, from all this, that I, or any other real Theosophist, undervalue true Spiritual phenomena or philosophy, or that we do not believe in the communication between pure mortals and pure spirits, any less than we do in communication between bad men and bad spirits, or even of good men with bad spirits under bad conditions. Occultism is the essence of Spiritualism, while modern or popular Spiritualism I cannot better characterize than as adulterated, unconscious magic. We go so far as to say that all the great and noble characters, all the grand geniuses— the poets, painters, sculptors, musicians—all who have worked at any time for the realization of their highest ideal, irrespective of selfish ends—have been Spiritually inspired; not mediums, as many Spiritualists call them— passive tools in the hands of controlling guides—but incarnate, illuminated souls, working consciously in collaboration with the pure disembodied human and newly-embodied high Planetary Spirits, for the elevation and spiritualization of mankind. We believe that everything in material life is most intimately associated with Spiritual agencies. As regards psychical phenomena and mediumship, we believe that it is only when the passive medium has given place, or rather grown into, the conscious mediator, that he can discern between spirits good and bad."

31. *Old Diary Leaves*, 1:322. See also ibid., 1:12–13; 1:43–44. Randolph's familiarity with the unusual multiple spirit who called himself "John King"

went back at least to 1855 when he was first investigating the Davenport brothers. See chapter 8. It is interesting that it was in connection with the Davenports that he came to meet Colonel Olcott. For Madame Blavatsky, as well, King was a generic name. *H. P. B. Speaks*, 1: 237.

32. *Old Diary Leaves*, 1:17. In his diary for June 21, 1878, Olcott recorded that Madame Blavatsky had revealed that Luxor was a "section of the Grand Lodge of which she is a member." See Michael Gomes, "Studies in Early American Theosophical History. II. Initial Spiritualist Response to H. P. B.," *Canadian Theosophist* 70, no. 2 (May–June 1989): 30.

33. *Old Diary Leaves*, 1:75–76.

34. A photograph of the letter is given in C. Jinarajadasa, *The Golden Book of the Theosophical Society, A Brief History of the Society's Growth from 1875–1925* (Adyar: Theosophical Publishing House, 1925), figures 10 and 11, pp. 13–15. The frequent references in the early days to "Golden Gate of Truth" should be investigated and may mask the name of some group to which Madame Blavatsky gave her allegiance or to some degree of occult progress. See "From Madame H. P. Blavatsky to her Correspondents, An Open Letter Such as Few Can Write," *Spiritual Scientist* 3, no. 3 (September 23, 1875): 25–27, reprinted in BCW, 1:126–33, 130 ("Let it be understood, then, that I address myself but to the truly courageous and persevering. Besides the danger expressed above, the difficulties to becoming a practical Occultist in this country, are next to insurmountable. Barrier upon barrier, obstacles in every form and shape will present themselves to the student; for the Keys of the Golden Gate leading to the Infinite Truth, lie buried deep."); "Spiritualism and Spiritualists," letter to the *Spiritual Scientist* 3, no. 18 (January 6, 1876): 208–9, reprinted in *A Modern Panarion*, 72–77; "The Search after Occultism," letter to the *Spiritual Scientist*, reprinted in BCW, 1:186–87; 1:3 (letter to Olcott, advising him not to "poke your nose on the forbidden path of the Golden Gate without some one to pilot you."). Randolph, probably merely metaphorically, uses "Golden Gate" to refer to the entrance to the world of the spirits. *After Death*, 63.

35. *Old Diary Leaves*, 1:19.

36. Ibid.

37. See, e.g., *Old Diary Leaves*, 1:326–27 (Stainton Moses sees "glowing points of coloured light arranged in a triangle so as to form the mystic symbol of the Eastern Lodge of our Mahatmas."); [W. Stainton-Moses], "The Early Story of the Theosophical Society. A Chapter of History. No. II," *Light: A Journal of Psychical, Occult, and Mystical Research* 12 (July 23, 1892): 356 ("The ∴ is the mark of the lodge (of which John [King] is a member; having taken one degree before his death)." See also the facsimile of the June 11, 1875, Brothers of Luxor letter in G. A. Barborka, *H. P. Blavatsky: Tibet and Tulku* (Adyar: Theosophical Publishing House, 1966), facing page 246, which shows the delta with a superimposed S (presumably for Serapis) and what looks like a Greek

beta. Also, "Eastern Magic and Western Spiritualism," a lecture given by H. S. Olcott in early 1876, in H. S. Olcott, *Applied Theosophy and Other Essays* (Adyar: Theosophical Publishing House, 1975), 206, 237 (gold ring materialized in a moss rose for Olcott, bearing inside the inscription "To our Brother—followed by a triangle, a well-known kabbalistic symbol.").

38. As was the emblem of the winged globe, which Randolph used as the image of the soul and Madame Blavatsky later adopted for her Eastern or Esoteric Section.

39. See *Letters from Masters of Wisdom, Second Series*, 8–13: "It is characteristic of the letters written to Colonel Olcott by the Master Serapis (and by Tuitit Bey) that often he gives the exhortation 'Try.'" The term appears in letters 3 (four times), 4, 5, 7, 10 (five times) and 25. The original of the Brothers of Luxor letter, reproduced in Jinarajadasa, *The Golden Book of the Theosophical Society*, fig. 10, shows that the letter ends with "Try" followed by a delta with a line through it horizontally and dots in upper angles above the line and an inverted "three points" below. See also *H. P. B. Speaks*, 2:41 (Blavatsky letter to Olcott: "I have been entrusted with an arduous and dangerous task, Henry, to 'try' and teach you."); "Demolishing the Mahatmas," *O. E. Library Critic* 24, no. 3 (June–July 1936). On Randolph's use of Try! as a motto, see *After Death*, 22. See also *Dealings with the Dead*, 220: "You aspire to comprehend the mighty secret of the TRINE. You seek to become an acolyte of the imperial order of the Rosy Cross, and to re-establish it upon the earth; and no TRUE ROSICRUCIAN dares shrink from attempting the solution of the mysteries and problems that human minds in heaven or on earth may conceive or propound. Our motto—the motto of the great order of which I was a brother on earth,—an order which has, under a variety of names, existed since the very dawn of civilization on the earth—is 'Try.' " The last echo of Randolph's motto is in the H. B. of L. See T. H. Burgoyne, "The Kabbalah," *The Platonist* 3, no. 2 (February 1887): 106–12.

40. *Letters from Masters of Wisdom, Second Series*, 34, 36: Letter 13 states that Madame Blavatsky is "an Ellorian," and letter 12 repeats the claim: she is "an Ellorian—eternal and immortal is her Augoeides." Emma Hardinge Britten's *Ghost Land* had appeared in installments in her journal *The Western Star* from June through December 1872. See also Olcott, "Eastern Magic and Western Spiritualism," 232 (paraphrases the fourth-century traveler Fah-Hian as describing adepts flying through the air to a temple, "apparently Ellora"); *Isis Unveiled*, 1:567 (excavations at Ellora) and 1:590 (There were many races of men before ours and Ellora is a remnant of them. It is connected by subterranean passages to the ante-diluvial island on which the earlier race lived.). Serapis Bey, of course, belongs to the Ellora section of the Brotherhood of Luxor.

41. See H. P. Blavatsky, *The Key to Theosophy, being A Clear Exposition, in the Form of Question and Answer, of the Ethics, Science, and Philosophy for the*

Study of Which the Theosophical Society has been Founded (1889; Pasadena: Theosophical University Press, 1946), 303: In response to the question, "Do you reject 'Louis' as an Adept?" Madame Blavatsky proceeded to point out the telling ignorance of Louis in matters of science. For her earlier views on Emma Hardinge Britten as an authority, see *Isis Unveiled*, 1:367 Britten quoted in support of the connection of Akasa with the phenomena produced by fakirs).

42. The circular was first published in the *Spiritual Scientist* for April 29, 1875, and ran continuously through August. It is reprinted in *BCW*, 1:85–88 (which adds a facsimile of the circular). The editor's comments to the notice reveal the frustrations present and the hopes aroused: "Can it be that shades of the departed Magi, banded together into a Council, meet there to rule the spiritual destinies of mankind? . . . It is time that some Power, terrestrial or supernal, came to our aid, for after twenty-seven years of spiritual manifestations, we know next to nothing concerning mediumship, its causes, its perils, its advantages." "A Message from Luxor," *Spiritual Scientist* 2, no. 17 (June 24, 1875): 191.

43. H. P. Blavatsky, "The Science of Magic, Proof of its Existence—Mediums in Ancient Times, etc., etc.," *Spiritual Scientist* 3, no. 6 (October 14, 1875): 64–65, reprinted in *BCW*, 1:142–43.

44. *Royal Masonic Cyclopædia*, 461. The root of most of this confusion lies with Kenneth Mackenzie, whom we have already considered in connection with the London *Spiritual Magazine* and with the Fratres Lucis, and his insatiable desire to manufacture mysterious brotherhoods. In the *Rosicrucian Magazine* for April 1874, Mackenzie had mentioned a mysterious Hermetic Order of Egypt, an order "of a very exclusive character. I have only met with six individuals who possessed it, and of these two were Germans, two Frenchmen, and two of other nations. . . . They claim the privilege of possessing much knowledge, but they do not seem, so far as I have seen, to desire to impart it to others." In his *Royal Masonic Cyclopædia* (London, 1877, but published in sections 1875–77), 309, the Hermetic Brothers of Egypt reappeared as an occult fraternity that had endured from most ancient times, with officers, signs, passwords, "and a peculiar method of instruction in science, moral philosophy, and religion." Its members have never been numerous, Mackenzie added, and "if we may believe those who at the present time profess to belong to it," they possess "philosopher's stone, elixir of life, invisibility, and power to communicate with the ultramundane life directly." To demonstrate the superior level of his knowledge, Mackenzie concluded by saying that he had only met three persons who maintained the existence of the body and hinted they were members, men whose youthful appearance was belied by their direct knowledge of long-passed events—a claim reminiscent of Madame Blavatsky's master's tale of Vic de Lassa. See chapter 2.

45. The other two Americans have been forgotten.

46. H. P. Blavatsky, "Lodges of Magic," *Lucifer* 3, no. 14 (October 15, 1888): 89–93, reprinted in *BCW*, 10:124–33. See also H. P. Blavatsky, *Theosophi-*

cal Glossary (1892; Los Angeles: Theosophy Co., 1973), 193, which defines "Brotherhood of Luxor" as a "certain Brotherhood of mystics—better never divulged—as it led a great number of well-meaning people into being deceived and relieved of their money by a certain bogus mystic Society of Speculators, born in Europe, only to be exposed and fly to America." The real brotherhood, she adds, disdains the H. B. of L. and commercial mystics of Glasgow or Boston. This last is a reference to Hiram E. Butler. Even in the early days, Madame Blavatsky was insistent that the name given to the brotherhood was for convenience only. See Joscelyn Godwin, "From the Archives. H. P. Blavatsky Writes to 'M. A. Oxon.': An Unpublished Letter," *Theosophical History* 4, nos. 6–7 (April 1993), 172–77, 177: "[P]erhaps you may see some of the Brotherhood—I mean the one I belong to—not of Luxor—for Luxor is but an adopted name for the Committee."

47. In his *Old Diary Leaves*, published in 1895, Olcott says: "This title, Brotherhood of Luxor, was pilfered by the schemers who started, several years later, the gudgeon-trap called 'The H.B. of L.' The existence of the real lodge is mentioned in Kenneth Mackenzie's Royal Masonic Cyclopaedia (p. 461)."

48. One of the most acute observers of things Theosophical, Beatrice Hastings, noted her impression of the change from Luxor to India in the margin of a book: "This looks as if the previous efforts had been John King & Co., apparition shows, & now the *Indian company* had finally got control. No one ever saw T. B. & Serapis & J. K. any more, although Olcott clings on to Serapis as a name. Perhaps he never could be told the truth." Quoted in Gomes, "Studies in Early American Theosophical History," *Canadian Theosophist* 70, no. 2 (May–June, 1989): 30.

49. *The Key to Theosophy*, 301–2: "Behold, only fourteen years ago, before the Theosophical Society was founded, all the talk was of 'Spirits.' They were everywhere, in everyone's mouth; and no one by any chance even dreamt of talking about living 'Adepts,' 'Mahatmas,' or 'Masters.' One hardly heard even the name of the Rosicrucians, while the existence of such a thing as 'Occultism' was suspected even but by very few. Now all that is changed. We Theosophists were, unfortunately, the first to talk of these things, to make the fact of the existence in the East of 'Adepts' and 'Masters' and Occult knowledge known; and now the name has become common property." The statement is made explicitly in reference to the H. B. of L. and the Chevalier Louis. W. Q. Judge, as noted, at least recognized the preparatory role of Randolph and Emma Hardinge Britten.

50. "Important Note," BCW, 1:73. Jinarajadasa, *Golden Book of the Theosophical Society*, fig. 5, pp. 5–9, reproduces the note from Madame Blavatsky's scrapbook. See also *Old Diary Leaves*, 1:13 (to show the "fallacy of the spiritualistic theory of spirits"), 1:20–21; "Letters of H. P. B. to Dr. Hartmann, 1885 to 1886," *The Path* 10 (April 3, 1886): 366–73, 369: "I was sent to America on purpose and sent to the Eddies. There I found Olcott in love with spirits, as

he became in love with the Masters later on. I was ordered to let him know that spiritual phenomena without the philosophy of Occultism were dangerous and misleading. I proved to him that all that the mediums could do through spirits others could do at will without any spirits at all; that bells and thought-reading, raps and physical phenomena, could be achieved by anyone who had a faculty of acting in his physical body through the organs of his astral body; and I had that faculty ever since I was four years old. . . . Well, I told him the whole truth. I said to him that I had known Adepts, the 'Brothers,' not only in India and beyond Ladakh, but in Egypt and Syria,—for there are 'Brothers' there to this day. The names of the 'Mahatmas' were not even known at the time, since they are called so only in India. That, whether they were called Rosicrucians, Kabalists, or Yogis—Adepts were everywhere Adepts. . . . All I was allowed to say was—the truth: There is beyond the Himalayas a nucleus of Adepts, of various nationalities . . . and they are all in communication with Adepts in Egypt and Syria, and even Europe."

51. "A Few Questions to 'HIRAF,' " *BCW*, 1:116–17. See also "The Cycle Moveth," *Lucifer* 6 (March 1890): 1–10, reprinted in *BCW*, 12:120–32 (cyclical attempts to combat materialism); Alice Leighton Cleather, *H. P. Blavatsky: Her Life and Work for Humanity* (Calcutta: Thacker, Spink & Co., 1922), 15–16. At the end of his *People from the Other World* (453–54) Olcott makes the point explicitly: "This outbreak of spiritualistic phenomena is under the control of an Order, which while depending for its results upon unseen agents, has its existence upon Earth among men."

52. "Important Note," *BCW*, 1:73 (elementals); "A Few Questions to 'HIRAF,'" *BCW*, 1:112 ("spirits of the fifth sphere"); *Isis Unveiled*, 1:xxxvii (defining "Pagan Gods" as occasionally referring to "either divine planetary entities (angels), or disembodied spirits of pure men" but usually as signifying to the mystic "the idea of a visible or cognized manifestation of an invisible potency in nature." These are "simply Powers of the 'Unseen Universe'" personified for the moment for some purpose.).

53. *Unveiling*, 8–9, 12–17, 35–37, 40–46; *Dealings with the Dead*, 59, 84, 100–101, 106, 143, 215, 263–67; *After Death*, 102–3. See chapter 5.

54. See *Isis Unveiled*, 1:xxix (Elementals are creatures evolved in the earth, air, water, and fire. They "may be employed by the disembodied spirits— whether pure or impure—and by living adepts of magic and sorcery, to produce desired phenomenal results. Such beings never become men." In other words, there are spirits active at seances other than those of disembodied men); 1:xxx; 1:310–11 (Classes of other beings: "Elementary" creatures. The highest are the larvae or shadows of those who lived on earth, refused the spiritual light, and thus lost their immortality. Second are the invisible antitypes of men to be born. Third are the Elementals properly so called. These never become human beings and have no immortal spirit, no body, only astral forms. Proclus, Madame Blavatsky says, holds that from the zenith of the world to

the moon is the realm of "planetary spirits" in their hierarchies and classes, highest among them the "supercelestial" gods, then the "intercosmic" gods—the personified forces of nature who preside over elements and elementals.).

55. *Isis Unveiled*, 1:xxx.

56. Ibid., 1:319: "If during life the ultimate and desperate effort of the inner-self to reunite itself with the faintly-glimmering ray of its divine parent is neglected; if this ray is allowed to be more and more shut out by the thickening crust of matter, the soul, once freed from the body, follows its earthly attractions, and is magnetically drawn into and held within the dense fogs of the material atmosphere." There it gradually dissolves. These beings are "terrestrial" or "earthly" elementaries and "vampires," and in the East they are known as the "Brothers of the Shadow." These seek to retaliate for their sufferings on humanity, and use elementals for their purposes. See also ibid., 1:310 (highest class of "elementary" beings is the larvae or shadows of those who lived on earth, refused the spiritual light, and thus lost their immortality); 1:xxx (Elementary spirits, properly the disembodied *souls* of the depraved; "these souls have at some time prior to death separated from themselves their divine spirits, and so lost their chance for immortality." "Once divorced from their bodies, these souls (also called 'astral bodies') of purely materialistic persons, are irresistibly attracted to the earth, where they live a temporary and finite life amid the elements congenial to their gross natures. . . . [T]hey are now unfitted for the lofty career of the pure, disembodied being, for whom the atmosphere of earth is stifling and mephitic, and whose attractions are all away from it." They disintegrate atom by atom and are Larvae and mere detritus). See also "A Few Questions to 'HIRAF,'" *BCW*, 1:111–12, which denies that these evil spirits are eternal: there is no "endless, macrocosmal evil." For Randolph's views, see *Ravalette*, 68 (larvae between the rolling globes) and chapter 5.

57. *Isis Unveiled*, 1:xlv (Spiritualism must be completed by looking to the philosophy of the Brahmans and Lamaists of the Far East); 1:73 ("We believe that few of those physical phenomena which are genuine are caused by disembodied spirits." Magic is the fulfillment of spiritualism.).

58. See Madame Blavatsky, "Is it Idle to Argue Further?" *The Theosophist* 3 (January 1882), reprinted in *BCW*, 3:391–95 (reply to M. A. [Oxon.]); editor's notes on William Oxley's "Hierosophy and Theosophy," *The Theosophist* 4 (July 1883), reprinted in *BCW*, 4:557–60, and to M. A. (Oxon.)'s "Spirit Identity and Recent Speculations," *The Theosophist* 4 (July 1883), reprinted in *BCW*, 4:583–98; Emma Hardinge Britten, *Nineteenth Century Miracles*, 297–305 (departure of the Theosophical Society from its "original lines," beginning with the publication of the famous "Fragments of Occult Truth" that began to appear in *The Theosophist* in October 1881. "Fragments" for the first time presented the curious idea of impersonal or unindividualized reincarnation that became the hallmark of later Theosophy. "Fragments of Occult Truth," *The Theosophist* 3,

no. 1 (October 1881): 17–22; ibid. 3, no. 6 (February 1882): 157–60; ibid. 3, no. 12 (September 1882): 307–14; ibid. 4, no. 1 (October 1882): 2–5; ibid. 4, no. 2 (November 1882): 46–48; ibid. 4, no. 5 (March 1883): 131–37; ibid. 4, no. 6 (April 1883): 161–64; ibid. 4, no. 7 (May 1883): 194–95. A further supplement, "Karma (An Appendix to Fragments of Occult Truth)" appeared in ibid. 4 (July 1883): 252–53. Parts 4, 6, 7 and 8 of the series appear over the name "A Lay Chela," but it appears that parts 1–3 were the work of A. O. Hume and the rest were written by A. P. Sinnett, both working at the instance of Master Koot Hoomi. Undoubtedly Madame Blavatsky had a hand in the result as well. The articles are a watershed in Theosophical history and mark the separation of Theosophy from the Western occultism that had been developing. In France "Fragments" managed to affront both camps (the reincarnationists and the antireincarnationists) of French Theosophists. See Godwin, *The Beginnings of Theosophy in France* (London: Theosophical History Centre, 1989), 7ff.

59. *Isis Unveiled*, 1:73 ("We believe that few of those physical phenomena which are genuine are caused by disembodied spirits."); 1:320–21 ("For fear of being misunderstood, we would remark that while, as a rule, physical phenomena are produced by the nature-spirits, of their own motion and to please their own fancy, still good disembodied human spirits, under *exceptional* circumstances, such as the aspiration of a pure heart or the occurrence of some favoring emergency, can manifest their presence by any of the phenomena *except personal materialization*. But it must be a mighty attraction indeed to draw a pure, disembodied spirit from its radiant home into the foul atmosphere from which it escaped upon leaving its earthly body." Only the black magician compels the presence, by incantations of necromancy, of the tainted souls of those who have lived bad lives.); 1:xxxvi; 1:70 (the Eddy materializations: the figures were not the forms of the persons they appeared to be. "They were simply their portrait statues, constructed, animated and operated by the elementaries."); 1:492 (The ancients taught that no soul from the abode of blessed will return, unless "indeed, upon rare occasions its apparition might be required to accomplish some great object in view, and so bring benefit upon humanity." In this case, there was no need to "evoke" the "soul." It sent its messages either by simulacrum of itself or through messengers who appear in material form. What can be evoked are the larvae from sheol, the eighth sphere); 1:324–25 (Who presides at spiritualist circles? Subjective manifestations proceed from "good" demons. "Sometimes, but rarely, the planetary spirits—beings of a race other than our own—produce them; sometimes the spirits of our translated and beloved friends; sometimes nature-spirits of one or more of the countless tribes; but most frequently of all are terrestrial elementary spirits, disembodied evil men, the Diakka of A. Jackson Davis.").

60. *Isis Unveiled*, 1:67–69. See also "Madame Blavatsky on the Views of the Theosophists," *The Spiritualist* (February 8, 1878): 68–69, reprinted in BCW, 1:290 ff., 295–96. The differences between Theosophy and spiritualism, as those differences were conceived by Madame Blavatsky in her earlier period, are clear from an anonymous editorial comment that appeared in the first issue of

The Theosophist under the title "The Drift of Western Spiritualism," which lists the primary issues as the Theosophists' belief that more entities than simply the "spirits of the dead" were involved in creating the phenomena of spiritualism; that immortality was only conditional; and that "good spirits" did not physically manifest themselves. *The Theosophist* 1, no. 1 (October 1879): 7–8. See also Olcott's letter, "What Colonel Olcott Believes," *Spiritual Scientist* 3, no. 21 (January 27, 1876): 258.

61. The competing views struggled for supremacy even in the pages of Madame Blavatsky's chosen journal, the *Spiritual Scientist*. See, e.g., "An Important Question," *Spiritual Scientist* 3, no. 4 (September 30, 1875): 42–43 (it is an open question whether there exists a science, not of passive mediumship, but of active control of spirits by Will); H. S. Olcott, "Colonel Olcott Answers the Banner, a Reply the Reverse of Equivocal," *Spiritual Scientist* 3, no. 5 (October 7, 1875): 55; Hudson Tuttle, "Are Occultists to Capture Spiritualism?" *Spiritual Scientist* 3, no. 21 (January 27, 1876): 259 (the only value of "dust-covered occultism" lies in spiritualism); "The Truths of Spiritualism Against the Claims of Occultism," *Spiritual Scientist* 3, no. 16 (December 23, 1875): 186.

62. See *Isis Unveiled*, 1:xxv; 1:302 ("in the shoreless ocean of space radiates the central, spiritual, and *Invisible* sun." The Rosicrucians sought reality in "the astral ocean of invisible fire which encompasses the world." This is the "astral light."); 1:xxvii (Akasa is the source of life and energy; latent, "it tallies exactly with our idea of the universal ether," active, it is the omnipotent god. It is the means of every occult or magical operation); 1:125ff. (on the sacred central fire, astral light, æther); 1:129 ("mystic, primordial substance" which is the "Æther" This is Eliphas Lévi's astral fire); 1:270 (on myths of the sun: this "shows that the sun is meant allegorically here, and refers to the *central*, invisible sun, GOD . . . Light, in short."); 1:514 ("the central, spiritual SUN.").

63. *Isis Unveiled*, 1:315, 327–28.

64. Ibid., 1:302–3.

65. Ibid., 1:351–52, 368.

66. Ibid., 1:327–28.

67. Ibid., 1:327–28 (The ancients taught that man is a trinity of body, astral spirit, and immortal soul. "That which survives as an *individuality* after the death of the body is the *astral soul*, which Plato . . . calls the *mortal* soul, for, according to the Hermetic doctrine, it throws off its more material particles at every progressive change into a higher sphere. . . . The astral spirit is a faithful duplicate of the body, both in a physical and spiritual sense. The Divine, the highest and *immortal* spirit, can be neither punished nor rewarded. To maintain such a doctrine would be at the same time absurd and blasphemous, for it is not merely a flame lit at the central and inexhaustible fountain of light, but actually a portion of it, and of identical essence. It assures immortality to the individual astral being in proportion to the willingness of the latter to

receive it. So long as the *double* man, i.e., the man of flesh and spirit, keeps within the limits of the law of spiritual continuity; so long as the divine spark lingers in him, however faintly, he is on the road to an immortality in the future state."). See also the letter of Madame Blavatsky to W. H. Barr, November 19, 1877, published in Michael Gomes, "Studies in Early American Theosophical History. VII. H.P.B.'s American Correspondence," *Canadian Theosophist* 71, no. 4 (September–October 1990): 80.

68. *Isis Unveiled*, 2:588. This is the third of Madame Blavatsky's ten "fundamental principles of Oriental philosophy." See also ibid., 1:432 ("No astral soul, even that of a pure, good, and virtuous man is immortal in the strictest sense; 'from elements it was formed—to elements it must return.' Only, while the soul of the wicked vanishes, and is absorbed without redemption, that of every other person, even moderately pure, simply changes its ethereal particles for still more ethereal ones; and, while there remains in it a spark of the *Divine*, the individual man, or rather, his personal *ego*, cannot die. 'After death,' says Proclus, 'the soul (the spirit) continueth to linger in the aerial body (astral form), till it is entirely purified from all angry and voluptuous passions . . . then doth it put off by a *second dying* the aerial body as it did the earthly one. Whereupon, the ancients say that there is a celestial body always joined with *the soul*, and which is *immortal, luminous*, and *star-like.*' ").

69. *Isis Unveiled*, 1:315; 1:317 ("This doctrine of the possibility of losing one's soul and, hence, individuality, militates with the ideal theories and progressive ideas of some spiritualists, though Swedenborg fully adopts it. They will never accept the kabbalistic doctrine which teaches that it is only through observing the law of harmony that individual life hereafter can be obtained; and that the farther the inner and outer man deviate from this fount of harmony, whose source lies in our divine spirit, the more difficult it is to regain the ground." Swedenborg's followers, in other words, fail to recognize "the fact of the possible death and obliteration of the human personality by the separation of the immortal part from the perishable."). See also ibid., 1:319: "If during life the ultimate and desperate effort of the inner-self to reunite itself with the faintly-glimmering ray of its divine parent is neglected; if this ray is allowed to be more and more shut out by the thickening crust of matter, the soul, once freed from the body, follows its earthly attractions, and is magnetically drawn into and held within the dense fogs of the material atmosphere." These souls gradually dissolve and are "terrestrial" or "earthly" elementaries. In the East they are known as the "Brothers of the Shadow." They are "vampires," who seek to inflict their sufferings on humanity, and who use elementals. The doctrine of conditional immortality is also common to the teachings of the H. B. of L. A marginal note to "The Laws of Magic Mirrors," one of the order's teaching manuscripts, states it clearly. At death, the soul of the irreligious occultist "falls into the infrahuman spheres of existence; his chance of immortality is lost forever, and in the midst of the Elementaries whom he thinks to have made his slaves, he leads a malicious existence of uncertain duration, until, his vitality being entirely spent, he falls gradually into unconsciousness,

a phantom which vanishes, and disintegrates atom by atom into the elements which surround it. Then he disappears finally, leaving not even a shadow after him." Godwin, Chanel, and Deveney, *The Hermetic Brotherhood of Luxor*, 204.

70. *Isis Unveiled*, 1:xvii, 289ff., 327–28, 626.

71. Ibid., 1:303.

72. See ibid., 1:xvii, 315ff., 502; "Madame Blavatsky on the Views of the Theosophists," *The Spiritualist* (February 8, 1878): 68–69, reprinted in *BCW*, 1:290–300 and in *A Modern Panarion*, 138; Blavatsky, "Erroneous Ideas Concerning the Doctrines of the Theosophists," *La Revue Spirite* (January 1879), reprinted in *BCW*, 2: 14–25, 18–19 ("Does that mean that the individuality is lost in that absorption? Not at all. . . . It is only by identifying itself with that divine intelligence that the *Ego*, soiled with earthly impurities, can win its immortality."). One of the clearest statements of this earlier cosmology and anthropology can be found in Allan O. Hume's "A Buddhist Catechism," *The Theosophist* 2 (September 1881): 270–71, that appeared the month before the appearance of the series of articles that most clearly marked the transformation of Theosophy. After establishing that the "Ego, the conscious personal entity" is possibly but not necessarily immortal, Hume repeats that this Ego, if it has "attached itself mainly to the desires of the flesh" is separated from the immortal spirit and disintegrates. "If, on the other hand, this *Ego* has been perserveringly struggling to free itself from earthly desires and passions and acquire virtue and holiness; in other words, to unite itself with the immaterial element and hold the material one as much at arms length as possible, then after death a closer union is effected between the *nirvana* affinity, or as it may, for want of a better name, be termed the spirit and the spiritual form, and they pass together to a higher stage of existence, and so on step by step the spiritual body growing less and less material at every stage, until finally when the last trace of its materiality disappears, the *Ego* or spiritual consciousness has become interfused into the spirit, and this passing to *nirvana*, although then merged in the universal, still retains the personal, consciousness, and thus the *Ego* secures immortality, no longer conditioned, but absolutely, no longer isolated, but an integral part of the whole."

73. See chapter 5.

74. *Isis Unveiled*, 1:xxxvi–xxxvii, 12, 179, 292, 345, 348–49, 351–52, 480. See also "A Few Questions to 'HIRAF,'" *BCW*, 1:112; "Madame Blavatsky on the Views of the Theosophists," *The Spiritualist* (February 8, 1878): 68–69, reprinted in *BCW*, 1:290–96 (the only examples of reincarnation are failures of nature: dead children and congenital idiots). The meaning of these fairly clear statements and the conflict of these views with Madame Blavatsky's later ideas on reincarnation have been the subject of interminable debate among Theosophists since the early 1880s—so much so that the editor of the Theosophical University Press reprint of *Isis Unveiled* has thought it necessary to

include with the volumes several of Madame Blavatsky's subsequent attempts at exegesis of the passage cited. For a further indication of Madame Blavatsky's early rejection of reincarnation, see her letter of March 1875 to Professor Corson. *Unpublished Letters of H. P. Blavatsky*, compiled and with introduction by Eugene Rollin Corson (London: Rider & Co., 1929), 138

75. As it was later to be the doctrine of the H. B. of L. See the introduction to Godwin, Chanel, and Deveney, *The Hermetic Brotherhood of Luxor*, 186–88.

76. In the years before she wrote *Isis Unveiled*, Madame Blavatsky also advocated a variant on this theme according to which it was not the monad's reaching human status that marked its decision point between immortality and annihilation. Rather, in becoming a human we have already transmigrated through four "spheres." Hereafter we progress through seven more stages or "regions" (much like those described by Randolph in *After Death*) in an effort to shed our evil ways, and only in the last of these (which she loosely calls the "Seventh Sphere") are we faced with the choice between immortality and annihilation. Even in this schema, however, what is at issue is transmigration, not reincarnation, though the impersonal immortal "Spirit" of the failed immortal may, after refreshing itself in the eternal Spirit, again re-enter the cycle of transmigration. See her letter to Olcott, dated May 21, 1875, in *H. P. B. Speaks*, 1:37ff., which discusses an article the "Lodge" would soon send to him on man's postmortem progress through the "spheres." See also "A Few Questions to 'HIRAF,'" *BCW*, 1:142

77. *Isis Unveiled*, 1:352–57. Colenel Olcott, in an article in which he cites *Ravalette* to demonstrate a living adept's power to control spirits, also begins to discuss the same mystery, and then draws back, unwilling to "trench upon the rights of others who have taught me." Olcott, "A Tap at Mrs. Tappan," *Banner of Light* 29, no. 26 (September 23, 1876): 2.

78. Ibid., 1:357. The same idea is set forth in "Madame Blavatsky on the Views of the Theosophists," *The Spiritualist* (February 8, 1878): 68–69, reprinted in *BCW*, 1:290ff., 295–98.

79. *Isis Unveiled*, 1:357–58.

80. There really cannot be any debate on the novelty of Madame Blavatsky's later views and their change from earlier teachings. Colonel Olcott was completely frank: "She and I believed, and taught orally as well as wrote, that man is a trinity of physical body, astral body (soul—the Greek *psyché*) and divine spirit. This will be found set forth in the first official communication made by us to the European reading public. It was an article entitled 'the Views of the Theosophists,' and appeared in the *Spiritualist* for December 7, 1877. In it, speaking for our whole party, I say: 'We believe that the man of flesh dies, decays, and goes to the crucible of evolution, to be worked over and over again; that the astral man (or *double*, or soul), freed from physical imprisonment, is followed by the consequences of his earthly deeds, thoughts and desires. He either becomes purged of the last traces of earthly grossness,

and, finally, after an incalculable lapse of time, is joined to his divine spirit, and lives forever as an entity, or, having been completely debased on earth, he sinks deeper into matter and is annihilated.'" Olcott, *Old Diary Leaves*, 1:286. Olcott dated the change in doctrine to the middle of the publication of "Fragments of Occult Truth." See also his comments on reincarnation occurring only in the case of failures of nature, ibid., 1:280–83, and on the fact that the brothers in the early days denied reincarnation with those exceptions and taught that "human souls, after death, passed on by a course of purificatory evolution to other and more spiritualized planets. I have notes of a conversation between a Mahatma and myself in which this same theory is affirmed." Ibid., 1:278. See also Olcott's letter of May 20, 1876, to M. A. Oxon. on the Baroness von Vay's wanting to join the Theosophical Society: "If she wants to come in with us she can (but she must scrape off her Re-incarnation shoes at the door; there's no room for *that* in our Philosophy." [W. Stainton Moses], "The Early Story of the Theosophical Society. A Chapter of History. No. II," *Light: A Journal of Psychical, Occult, and Mystical Research* 12 (July 23, 1892): 354–57. The conclusion is buttressed by a note in Madame Blavatsky's scrapbook, probably from late 1876: "Mind is the quintessence of the Soul—and having joined its divine Spirit *Nous*—can return no more to earth. IMPOSSIBLE." *BCW*, 1:233. Master Koot Hoomi had to remind the puzzled A. P. Sinnett that it was only in July 1881 that he had begun to teach Sinnett the doctrine of the rebirth of the impersonal "Spiritual Monad." *Mahatma Letters to A. P. Sinnett*, 329 (letter 57). For the chronology, see Margaret Conger, *Combined Chronology for Use with The Mahatma Letters to A. P. Sinnett and The Letters of H. P. Blavatsky to A. P. Sinnett* (Pasadena: Theosophical University Press, 1973), 13. The mahatma letters have now been reprinted in a more easily used edition in chronological sequence. *The Mahatma Letters to A. P. Sinnett from The Mahatmas M. & K.H., Transcribed and Compiled by A.T. Barker, In Chronological Sequence*, arranged and edited by Vincente Hao Chin, Jr. (Quezon City, Philippines: Theosophical Publishing House, 1993). Citations in the notes here are to the standard original edition by Barker. A. P. Sinnett, to whom the mahatmas made various attempts to explain the change in ideas, had the forthrightness to tell his mahatma that he thought the master was "exercising his ingenuity" in coming up with the labored explanations and that the Theosophists had "'an inclination to tolerate *subtler* and *more tricksey* ways of pursuing an end' than generally admitted as honourable by the *truth-loving, straight-forward* European." *Mahatma Letters to A. P. Sinnett*, 288ff. (letter 52) and 182ff. (letter 24). The italics are the mahatma's and are meant to be ironical. See also A. W. Trethewy, *The "Controls" of Stainton Moses ("M. A. Oxon.")* (London: Hurst & Blackett Ltd., c. 1925), 188–89, who discusses Madame Blavatsky's early teachings on reincarnation and its exceptions and the agreement of those ideas with the doctrines propounded by Moses's control, "Imperator," and the disagreement of those early doctrines with those of the later Theosophical Society. It is perhaps significant that at the very time that Madame Blavatsky's influence was greatest on the *Spiritual Scientist* the journal published Emma Hardinge Britten's explicit attack on the doctrine and ran

Alexander Aksakov's disquisition on the origins of the doctrine with Allan Kardec. See Emma Hardinge Britten, "The Doctrine of Reincarnation," *Spiritual Scientist* 2, no. 11 (May 20, 1875): 128–29, and Alexander Aksakov, "Researches on the Historical Origins of the Reincarnation Speculations of French Spiritualists," *Spiritual Scientist* 3, no. 1 (September 9, 1875): 1. Britten believed that the idea of reincarnation was coming to the fore because of the control of mediums by certain "Hindu Spirits." Aksakov's piece also ran in the *Banner of Light* 37, no. 25 (September 18, 1875): 3.

81. Without belaboring the point, commencing with the famous eight-part series, "Fragments of Occult Truth," that began to appear in the October 1881 issue of *The Theosophist*, the masters behind the Theosophical Society began to teach that after death, in the case of a person with some spirituality, the sixth and seventh immortal and nonindividualized principles of man, together with "some of the more abstract and pure of the mortal attributes of the 5th principle or animal Soul, its manas (mind) and memory" passed into "Devachan"—a sort of "sweet dream" where the "eternal imperishable, but also *unconscious*" "Monad" of the higher principles rests, self-absorbed in the pure delights of the few remaining elements of personality taken over from the fifth principle. Finally, after the Devachanic time-out, even the remnants of the fifth (personal) principle are burned away, and only the immortal and absolutely nonpersonal sixth and seventh principles go on, not to progress through the celestial spheres, but to rebirth again on earth. The crucial change was that this reincarnating entity, even though called the "true Ego" was impersonal or nonindividual. The true ego, even though it may once have enlivened John Smith, was in reincarnating free of that taint, and John Smith was no more. The doctrine was spelled out at length in "Fragments of Occult Truth" and began to appear in the same issue of *The Theosophist* that carried the beginning of that series. See Madame Blavatsky's notes to Eliphas Lévi, "Death," *The Theosophist* 3, no. 1 (October 1881): 12–15, reprinted in *BCW*, 3:287–91. "Fragments" and "Death" in turn called forth a vast literature from Madame Blavatsky and others and extended annotation from Master Koot Hoomi in his letters to A. P. Sinnett. See Blavatsky, "Death and Immortality," *The Theosophist* 4, no. 2 (November 1882): 28–30, reprinted in *BCW*, 4:250–56; *Mahatma Letters to A. P. Sinnett*, 103 (letter 14); T. Subbha Row, "The Aryan-Arhat Esoteric Tenets on the Sevenfold Principle in Man," *The Theosophist* 3 (January 1882): 93–99, reprinted with Madame Blavatsky's notes in *BCW*, 3:400–24; Madame Blavatsky, "Seeming Discrepancies," *The Theosophist* 3 (June 1882): 225–26, reprinted in *BCW*, 4:119ff.

Chapter 13

1. See H. P. Blavatsky, "The Science of Magic, Proofs of its Existence—Mediums in Ancient Times, etc., etc.," *Spiritual Scientist* 3, no. 6 (October 14, 1875): 64–65, reprinted in *BCW*, 1:134–38; *Isis Unveiled*, 1:360–67, 487–88, 490 (mediums are passive agents of others while the magician uses his will and commands spirits). Point 6 of Madame Blavatsky's "fundamental proposi-

tions" (*Isis Unveiled*, 2:587–88) is this distinction between the medium and the adept. See also Olcott, "Eastern Magic and Western Spiritualism," in *Applied Theosophy and Other Essays*, 206, 217–18, 243.

2. On will as the essence of magical action, see *Isis Unveiled*, 1:55–61, 144, 434, 500, 616; 2:592, 596. Point 10 of Madame Blavatsky's fundamental propositions (*Isis Unveiled*, 2:589) is the equation of practical magic with mesmerism. See also Blavatsky, "The Science of Magic," *BCW*, 1:134–38.

3. See "From Madame H. P. Blavatsky to her Correspondents, An Open Letter Such as Few Can Write," *Spiritual Scientist* 3, no. 3 (September 23, 1875): 25–27, reprinted in *BCW* 1:126ff: "[W]ould-be aspirants must not lure themselves with the idea of any possibility of their becoming practical Occultists by mere book-knowledge." The whole point of Madame Blavatsky's first serious literary effort, "A Few Questions to 'HIRAF,' " *Spiritual Scientist* 3, nos. 19 and 20 (July 15 and 22, 1875): 202, 217–18, 224, 236–37, reprinted in *BCW* 1:101–19, was that the "Oriental Rosicrucians" were "ever ready to help the earnest student struggling 'to become' with practical knowledge.

4. "From Madame H. P. Blavatsky to her Correspondents," *BCW*, 1:132.

5. For the Theosophical position in the 1880s (that is, after Madame Blavatsky and Colonel Olcott had left New York) on practical occultism, see W. Q. Judge, *Practical Occultism: From the Private Letters of W. Q. Judge* (Pasadena: Theosophical University Press, 1980), 115 ("our third object is *not* the *development* of psychic power, it is the *investigation* of it."); 135. See also Pythagoras [pseud.], "Considerations of Magic," *The Path* 1, no. 12 (March 1887): 377–80 (the practice of magic builds up the ego and leads to "second death); *The Path* 1, no. 1 (April 1886): 2 ("The study of what is now called 'practical occultism' has some interest for us, and will receive some attention, but is not *the* object of this journal. We regard it as incidental to the journey along the path. . . . Astral body formation, clairvoyance, looking into the astral light, and controlling elementals is all possible, but not at all profitable"); "Theosophy in the Press," *The Path* 1, no. 5 (July 1886): 156–58 ("In fact, we make bold to assert, from our own knowledge and from written documents, that the Mahatmas, who started the Society, and stand behind it now, are distinctly opposed to making prominent these phenomenal leanings, this hunting after clairvoyance and astral bodies."). See also Blavatsky, "Practical Occultism. Important to Students," *Lucifer* 2, no. 8 (April 1888), reprinted in *BCW*, 9, 155–62 (the distinction between theoretical and practical occultism is the same as that between Theosophy and the occult sciences); Blavatsky, "Occultism Versus the Occult Sciences," *Lucifer* 2, no. 9 (May 1888): 173–81, reprinted in *BCW*, 9, 249–61. The idea of a fundamental change in Madame Blavatsky's approach to practical occultism was a staple of H. B. of L. propaganda. She herself recognized a change coinciding with her departure for India in late 1878: "Arrived at Bombay, we had to drop Western and take to Eastern Rosicrucianism." See "Letters of H. P. B. to Dr. Hartmann, 1885 to 1886," *The Path* 10 (March 1896): 366–73, 366. Though the change is clear, the

judgment on the reasons for it varies widely and depends on the reader's views on the possibility of a progressive revelation of the secret doctrines over time, one that reveals the deeper and complementary aspects of earlier, apparently contradictory, statements. Colonel Olcott, faced with the changes in the masters' teachings, adopted just such an approach in the face of his problems in reconciling revelations. See *Old Diary Leaves* 1:33, 286.

6. Preamble and By-Laws of the Theosophical Society, quoted in Jinarajadasa, *The Golden Book of the Theosophical Society*, 23.

7. The usual explanation is that Sotheran and Madame Blavatsky had a falling out over the former's violent socialism. See Boris de Zirkoff's bio-bibliography appended to *BCW*, 1, s.v. Sotheran; Johnson, *The Masters Revealed: Madame Blavatsky and the Myth of the Great White Lodge*, 81. This was certainly true, but Sotheran's political views (which grated on Madame Blavatsky's aristocratic sensibilities) were really only an excuse for instituting secrecy. The secrecy was necessary because Sotheran, as Madame Blavatsky noted in her scrapbooks, began to "revile our experiments & denounce us to Spiritualists & impede the Society's progress." *BCW*, 1:194.

8. On Sotheran, see Godwin, *The Theosophical Enlightenment*, 283–84; Johnson, *The Masters Revealed: Madame Blavatsky and the Myth of the Great White Lodge*, 80–89. On his later work with A. L. Rawson in the Order of Ishmael, see John Yarker, "The Order of Ishmael or B'nai Ismael," *Historic Magazine and Notes and Queries* (1907): 262–64.

9. Charles Sotheran, "Alessandro di Cagliostro: Imposter or Martyr?" *Spiritual Scientist* 2, no. 14 (June 10, 1875), 163ff. Under the influence of Madame Blavatsky and Charles Sotheran, the *Spiritual Scientist* also published articles by Kenneth Mackenzie (December 30, 1875) and other members of the Soc. Ros. See Michael Gomes, "Studies in Early American Theosophical History. I. Elbridge Gerry Brown and the Boston 'Spiritual Scientist,' " *Canadian Theosophist* 70, no. 1 (March–April 1989): 14. From January through August 1876 it ran as a regular feature a translation of Agrippa's *De occulta philosophia* and also featured (June 15, 1876) an excerpt from Randolph's old friend W. G. Palgrave on the identification of the Nabatheans and the Sabaeans.

10. Editor's note to George Corbyn, "Rosicrucianism," *Spiritual Scientist* 2, no. 22 (August 5, 1875): 257.

11. Charles Sotheran, "Ex Nihilo Nihil Fit," *Spiritual Scientist* 2, no. 25 (August 26, 1875): 299.

12. See the interview with Sotheran by "A," "Is He Koot Hoomi, Blavatsky's 'Mahatma?' One of the Great Mysteries of Modern Theosophy Thought to Have been at Last Unveiled. The Mystic 'Brothers.' Charles Sotheran Picked Out to be the Man, But he Refuses to Publicly Acknowledge it," *New York Herald*, Sunday, November 16, 1891, sec. 1, 10. See also Sotheran, "Honors to Madame Blavatsky," *Banner of Light* 42, no. 19 (February 2, 1878): 3

(Madame Blavatsky "claims on good grounds to have been received into the ancient branch of the 'Rosie Cross' in the far East.").

13. The oath signed by Thomas A. Edison in April 1878 is reproduced as figure 30 in Jinarajadasa, *The Golden Book of the Theosophical Society*, 29. On the secrecy observed in the early days of the society, see also Michael Gomes, "Abner Doubleday and Theosophy in America: 1879–1884," *Sunrise* (April/May 1991): 151ff.

14. Eventually, this ritualistic, secret element of the Theosophical Society was abandoned—or, perhaps more exactly, pushed underground, to emerge in 1888 in the Esoteric Section, Madame Blavatsky's belated and ambivalent re-acknowledgment of the fundamental human desire for personal occult progress. Even in the years when degree work within the society had publicly fallen into disuse, however, it is clear that some sort of practical training connected with progress through a degree structure continued secretly. See W. Q. Judge, *Practical Occultism*, 88–90 (letter of June 8, 1888, to Olcott complaining that Elliott Coues's branch was allowing members to label themselves "F.T.S. 2°" when the rule had always been that "those who are in that degree are bound not to reveal it"); ibid., 299 ("altho the E.S. was begun in 1875 it consisted for years of but 7 or 8 members in the U.S."); Anonymous [Judge], "To Aspirants for Chelaship," *The Path* 3 (July 1888): 105–9. Judge made it clear that "[i]n the first establishment of the T.S. other degrees than that of a mere diplomaed member were recognized, but no one save H. P. Blavatsky has had the authority to confer those degrees. She has now fully announced the first of those [in the Esoteric Section], although during all these 14 years they have existed and included certain members who were also members of the T.S." Apparently this early work was organized along Masonic lines from the first, because Judge mentions that Madame Blavatsky had appointed "a certain fellow" (Judge?) to attend to the "entered apprentices" of the society. He referred in support of this claim to a letter from Madame Blavatsky, dated 1875, in which the "Esoteric Section" work was discussed. See "Answers to Questioners," *The Path* 4, no. 3 (June 1889): 87–88. This all could be self-aggrandizement, but it is consistent with the story told by G. H. Felt, discussed below. The idea of practical occult work in the society kept reappearing in the 1880s, despite efforts to suppress it. Boris de Zirkoff, the editor of Madame Blavatsky's *Collected Writings* says (*BCW*, 12:479) that the "first attempt to establish a group of students for the specific purpose of deeper esoteric studies and training" was the petition of the London Lodge in mid-1884, but there is no doubt that the work went on secretly from the beginning, as is hinted at in "Chelaship and Lay Theosophists," *The Theosophist* 4, no. 10 (July 1883, Supplement): 10–11. The Esoteric/Eastern Section, when it was finally formed in 1888 in response to the insistent demands of students for practical occultism, was advertised as a "body of Esoteric students to be organized on the ORIGINAL LINES" of the society. See "The Esoteric Section and the Theosophical Society," *The Path* 3, no. 8 (November 1888): 263.

15. *Old Diary Leaves*, 1:468–69. In retrospect, Olcott said that he realized that the idea was simply a repetition of Cagliostro's efforts to found the Egyptian Lodge in the eighteenth century. The model was to be John Yarker's ritual of the Sât B'hai, which he had sent Madame Blavatsky in November 1877. See Gomes, *Dawning of the Theosophical Movement*, 169. Yarker later said that order's "*raison d'être* ceased to be necessary when the *Theosophical Society* was established by the late H. P. Blavatsky, which at one time at least had its secret signs of Recognition." John Yarker, *The Arcane Schools; A Review of Their Origins and Antiquity; with a General History of Freemasonry, and its Relation to the Theosophic, Scientific, and Philosophic Mysteries* (Belfast: William Tate, 1909), 492–93. Sotheran also made the connection between Madame Blavatsky and Cagliostro's Egyptian Rite (which, he thought, centered on communication with pure spirits through young children). See Sotheran, "Honors to Madame Blavatsky," *Banner of Light* 42, no. 19 (February 2, 1878): 3. Endreinck Agardi, the disciple of one of Blavatsky's masters, also hinted that it was likely Cagliostro would be seen in America in 1876. "An Unsolved Mystery," *BCW* 1: 161.

16. Jinarajadasa, *The Golden Book of the Theosophical Society*, 26, gives a photograph of the circular describing the degrees and sections, and the text ("The Theosophical Society, Its Origin, Plan and Aims") is reprinted in *BCW*, 1:375ff.

17. Jinarajadasa, *The Golden Book of the Theosophical Society*, 26.

18. *Old Diary Leaves* 1:399–400.

19. Ibid., 1:402.

20. *The Theosophist*, 1, no. 7 (April 1880): 179.

21. *Isis Unveiled*, 1:xii. See also the letter of Madame Blavatsky written immediately after the founding of the new society: "Olcott is now organizing the Theosophical Society in New York. It will be composed of learned occultists and kabbalists, of *Philosophes Hermetiques* of the nineteenth century, and of passionate antiquaries and Egyptologists generally. We want to make an experimental comparison between spiritualism and the magic of the ancients by following literally the instructions of the old Cabbalas, both Jewish and Egyptian." Quoted in V. S. Solovyoff, *A Modern Priestess of Isis* (London: Longmans, Green, and Co., 1895), 256-57, and in Narad Mani, "Baptême de Lumière," *La France Antimaçonnique*, 25, no. 49 (December 7, 1911), 538.

22. *Isis Unveiled*, 1:634.

23. Ibid., 2:635.

24. Ibid., 2:636.

25. Blavatsky, "A Few Questions to 'HIRAF,' " *BCW*, 1:114.

26. Olcott speaks longingly of the early days "when real adepts taught eager pupils and genuine phenomena happened." *Old Diary Leaves*, 1:50. Madame Blavatsky, as we have seen in discussing the Brothers of Luxor, made it

clear that even before the founding of the society certain individuals had been accepted as neophytes ("chelas") of the order. See also "The Original Programme of the Theosophical Society," *BCW* 7:145–75 (Madame Blavatsky was "sent to America in 1873 for the purpose of organizing a group of workers on a psychic plane, [and] two years later the writer received orders from her Master and Teacher to form the nucleus of a regular Society."); Blavatsky, letter of April 12, 1875, to V. S. Solovyoff, in Solovyoff, *Modern Priestess of Isis,* 248 ("I am only now beginning to collect adepts; I have collected half a dozen, . . . the best and brightest minds in America.").

27. An echo of this can be found in the work of Alice Leighton Cleather, who was a careful observer of trends within the movement. In her *H. P. Blavatsky, Her Life and Work for Humanity* (Calcutta: Thacker, Spink & Co., 1922), 10, 14, 22–26, she argues persuasively for the chelaship theory of the society's sections, but she appears in error in blaming Olcott's rejection of "esotericism" for the perversion of the original scheme.

28. See "To the Public," *Spiritual Scientist* 6, no. 6 (April 12, 1877): 63, and *Banner of Light* 41, no. 4 (April 21, 1877): 8, reprinted in *BCW* 1:245 (the Theosophical Society "has been from the first a secret organization").

29. Sotheran set out the reasons for his disagreement with the society and Madame Blavatsky in a letter printed in the *Banner of Light,* January 15, 1876, 5. "I am confident the pretensions of the Society are fallacious; further, that the position taken by the President in his inaugural address, and the expressions of other members, are of such a character as to only render the body ridiculous in the estimation of all thinking persons." The reference to Olcott's inaugural address is to his touting of the work of G. H. Felt. See below. However, Sotheran's doubts as to Felt's methods should not be read as a rejection by him of practical occultism of all sorts. His opposition, rather, appears to have been to "the prominence given occult phenomena on the ground that it could but add to the burdens imposed by the ignorant upon those who demonstrated laws they could not master." [Laura C. Langford-Holloway], "Helena Petrovna Blavatsky: a Reminiscence," *The Word,* 22 (December 1915): 136–53. W. Q. Judge makes it clear that the oath of secrecy was instituted because of Felt's experiments. See "General Pertinent Observations," *The Path* 10 (January 1896): 319ff. Judge comments on Henry Newton's revelations to a New York newspaper on the early days: "He was a spiritualist and left us quite soon, and retained a paper he had no official right to. This was a pledge of secrecy, given because another person was then promising to show wonderful occult performances that never came off. The paper is signed by H. P. B. among others. All this being spread out at length in a great New York daily, attention was once more turned to the Theosophical movement." The reference is to the interview with Newton in the *New York Herald,* November 10, 1895.

30. *Le Théosophisme,* 24, 31, 23–24. In making Felt a member of the Brotherhood of Luxor, Guénon is following Narad Mani, "Baptême de Lumière," *La France Antimaçonnique* 26, no. 2 (January 11, 1912): 19.

31. *Le Théosophisme*, 29–31.

32. Ibid., 28. Guénon's version of events follows two articles by "Quaestor Vitae," published in *Light* in November 1895, which purport to give the views of Henry J. Newton, a New York spiritualist and first treasurer of the Theosophical Society. The articles are reprinted as "The Real Origin of the Theosophical Society" in *Theosophical History* 1, no. 7 (July 1986): 176ff. Quaestor Vitae and Henry J. Newton both were strong adherents of the theory that Madame Blavatsky's "departure for the East was accompanied by her departure from Western Occultism." Ibid., 181. On the purposes of the original society, Newton quoted the preamble to the first by-laws, which stressed that the members "seek to obtain knowledge of the nature and attributes of the Supreme Power and of the higher spirits, by the aid of physical processes." Ibid., 182. Quaestor Vitae, whoever he may have been, is also the one who ferreted out and publicized the story of Madame Blavatsky's acting as a subject for mesmerist Victor Michal in France in the 1850s. See below. If this Quaestor Vitae is the same as the person of that name who wrote *The Process of Man's Becoming, Based on Communications by Thought-transference from Selves in Inner States of Being* (London: Duckworth & Co., 1921), he was a believer in mental communications from living adepts and deceased individuals who had been born in an earlier incarnation of our solar system. Guénon thought that the unspecified papers supposedly left by Felt with Madame Blavatsky were one of the principal bases of *Isis Unveiled*, but this is mere slander. *Le Théosophisme*, 95–96.

33. *Old Diary Leaves*, 1:114ff.

34. Guénon thought that Felt had been deliberately introduced to the company by "a journalist named Stevens," a story that comes from Quaestor Vitae and Henry J. Newton. See Michael Gomes, "Studies in Early American Theosophical History, pt. VI, Rev. Wiggin's Review of George Henry Felt's 1875 Lecture on the Cabala," *Canadian Theosophist* 71, no. 3 (July–August 1990): 63–69.

35. James Santucci has graciously allowed me to see his unpublished article, "Forgotten Magi," which gives all that there is to know about Felt's biography.

36. See Gomes, *Dawning of the Theosophical Movement*, 85. Two versions of a prospectus for his proposed 1,100-page book exist, one issued by J. W. Bouton after the publication of *Isis Unveiled*. These list enthusiastic reviews of his ideas by various Masonic periodicals, presumably from the period in which, as we shall see, Felt was trying to make the practical working of his ideas into a higher grade within Masonry.

37. *Old Diary Leaves*, 1:116. It is difficult to conceive what this must have looked like. All versions of Felt's talks follow the same description, which indicates that very few people actually understood what the Star of Perfection was supposed to have been.

38. See Michael Gomes, "Studies in Early American Theosophical History, Pt. VI, Rev. Wiggin's Review of George Henry Felt's 1875 Lecture on the Cabala," *Canadian Theosophist* 71, no. 3 (July–August 1990): 65. There is some confusion over exactly what Felt said he was going to produce. While elementals or elementaries figure prominently in all accounts as the object of his work, there were also reports at the time and afterward (always by the spiritualists who had been present) that Felt had also taught "communion of mortals with the dead, and the reciprocal intervention of each in the affairs of the other." See Emma Hardinge Britten, *Nineteenth Century Miracles*, 296; "The Existence of Elementaries to be Demonstrated," *Spiritual Scientist* 3, no. 18 (January 6, 1876): 214. See also Quaestor Vitae, "The Real Origin of the Theosophical Society," *Theosophical History* 1, no. 7 (July 1986), 176ff., who says that Felt could "invoke the phantoms of the dead."

39. *Old Diary Leaves*, 1:117.

40. See Michael Gomes, "Studies in Early American Theosophical History, Pt. VI, Rev. Wiggin's Review of George Henry Felt's 1875 Lecture on the Cabala," *Canadian Theosophist* 71, no. 3 (July–August 1990): 68 (Henry J. Newton quotes Felt as saying that the Egyptians and Indians "produce the phenomena of so-called materialization by a combination of aromatic gum and herbs, instead of a seance of persons to draw the necessary power from. I have produced these phenomena in that way, and can do it again."). See also Quaestor Vitae, "The Real Origin of the Theosophical Society" in *Theosophical History* 1, no. 7 (July 1986): 176 (Felt "claimed he could invoke the phantoms of the dead, by using certain magical formula, combined with the burning of aromatic herbs, &c., and without the presence of a Spiritualistic medium."). The subject of magic crystals also came up in the discussions following Felt's initial lecture (see note 68, below), and it is possible that Felt's herbal recipes had some connection with the manufacture or consecration of magic mirrors. See Godwin, *The Theosophical Enlightenment*, 287: "[The] most likely possibility is that Felt was referring to some form of scrying, perhaps with chemically treated mirrors such as the French magnetists had been experimenting with, and Randolph described in *Seership!*"

41. See Randolph, *Seership!* 60–61: "There are hundreds who visited the 'Rosicrucian Rooms' in Boylston St., Boston, who marveled greatly at hearing no raps, or ticks, and seeing no clouds pass over the splendid mirror there owned and used, until perfumes were scattered and incense burned—whereupon, thousands of patterings rained upon the silver tripod, and glory-clouds, in presence of and seen by scores, floated over the black-sea face of the peerless mirror." In *The Occult Magazine* 1, no. 1 (February 1885): 6ff., the editor (Peter Davidson) quotes Eckartshausen on the narcotic properties of such fumigations and adds: "There are certain powerful substances which will exalt the nervous susceptibility, as well as assist in clarifying the veil of atmospheric density, inducing trance, etc., and increasing the power of representation, and consequently of the Astral Visions." On the use of such

"magische-nekromantischen Räucherungen," see Karl Kieswetter, *Geschichte des Neuren Occultismus*, 2 vols. (1891–95; reprinted New York: Arno 1976), 2:726ff.; Kieswetter, "Magische Räucherungen," *Der Sphinx. Monatschrift für die geschichtliche und experimentale Begründung übersinnlichen Weltanschauung auf monisticher Grundlage* 1 (1886): 219ff. Kieswetter tried these fumigants himself but only got a strong headache. See E. Howe, *Astrology: A Recent History, Including the Untold Story of its Role in World War II* (New York: Walker & Co.), 78. He is reported to have died of the use of drugs to develop clairvoyance.

42. Olcott, *Old Diary Leaves*, 1:138.

43. Ibid.

44. Ibid., 1:140. They also investigated frail, piano-moving mediums. See "Spiritualism and Theosophy," in Olcott, *Applied Theosophy and Other Essays*, 153, 169, 231.

45. Gomes, *Dawning of the Theosophical Movement*, 99, quoting Olcott's letter to E. S. Spaulding in August 1876. Similarly, the primary reason for the enthusiasm for the alliance of the Theosophical Society with Swami Dayananda's Arya Samaj was Madame Blavatsky's claim that in the swami the society could find an adept, "a Yogi himself and an Initiate into the mysteries of the *Yoga-Vidya* (or secret sciences)," to instruct its members in practical occultism. See, e.g., *The Path* 9 (July 1894): 130 (Madame Blavatsky had told Olcott that "the Swami's body was inhabited by an Adept of the Himalayan Brotherhood"); Blavatsky, "Echoes from India: What is Hindu Spiritualism?" *Banner of Light* (October 18, 1879), reprinted in *BCW*, 2:68–80, 207; Blavatsky, "Letter of Madame Blavatsky, Dr. Rotura's Discovery," *La Revue Spirite* (December 1879), reprinted in *BCW*, 2:205–8. See also *The Autobiography of Alfred Percy Sinnett* (London: Theosophical History Centre, 1988), 17. It was the final disillusionment with these claims of practical instruction that prompted a revolt within the British Theosophical Society and the hasty institution by Olcott of a sort of lodge within a lodge that appears to have degenerated quickly into mere mediumship. As usual in these intra-society conflicts, Madame Blavatsky (and not her masters) received the blame for exciting "many . . . to vague expectations of a training and experience for which necessarily very few are fitted." "C. C. M." [C. C. Massey], "Theosophy and Spiritualism," *The Theosophist* 2, no. 12 (August 1881): 260.

46. Emma Hardinge Britten, "Another Book on 'Art Magic,'" *Spiritual Scientist* 6, no. 1 (September 6, 1876): 8–9. The letter was written in July 1876. The same guarded response, necessitated no doubt by the oath of secrecy, is given in the society's notice, "To the Public," published in the *Spiritual Scientist* and in the *Banner of Light* in April 1876.

47. *Old Diary Leaves*, 1:126.

48. "Inaugural Address of the President of the Theosophical Society," in Olcott, *Applied Theosophy and Other Essays*, 24, 43–44. Olcott's confidence in the future of Felt's experiments was clear: "As a believer in Theosophy, theoretical

and practical, I personally am confident that this Society will be the means of furnishing such unanswerable proofs of the immortality of the soul, that none but fools will doubt." Ibid., 27. See also Olcott, "Occultism and Spiritualism," *Spiritual Scientist* 3, no. 25 (February 24, 1876): 295.

49. The spiritualist press found Olcott's conditional praise of Felt "droll." See Hiram Corson's letter, "The Theosophical Society and its President," *Banner of Light* 28, no. 15 (January 8, 1876): 2. Olcott responded with a "confession of faith." See Olcott, "The Theosophical Society and its President. Colonel Olcott's Reply to Professor Corson—a Confession of Faith," *Banner of Light* 28, no. 17 (January 22, 1876): 2.

50. *Old Diary Leaves*, 1:138. Felt's last appearance in Theosophical history is his rejoinder, "Mr. Felt's Disclaimer," published in the *New York Herald*, December 1, 1895, sec. 6, 8, to an account of the early days of the society. See Michael Gomes, "Studies in Early American Theosophical History. III. The Ante- and Post-Natal History of the Theosophical Society," *Canadian Theosophist* 70, no. 3 (July–August 1989): 52. The best factual account of Felt's role in the society in late 1875 and early 1876 and of the institution of the obligation of secrecy is given in Gomes, "Studies in Early American Theosophical History. III. The Ante- and Post-Natal History of the Theosophical Society," *Canadian Theosophist* 70, no. 4 (September–October 1989): 76ff.

51. *Old Diary Leaves*, 1:138–39.

52. *BCW*, 1:192–93.

53. *Old Diary Leaves*, 1:126–31.

54. From the text of the letter and the fact that it was found by Olcott in his own papers when writing *Old Diary Leaves* in the early 1890s, it appears that Felt had felt constrained by his oath of secrecy and had asked the council of the society for permission to write. The immediate cause of the retort was probably the letter of John Storer Cobb, the treasurer of the Theosophical Society, printed in the *Spiritualist*, February 22, 1878, which said Felt's experiments produced nothing. I am grateful to James Santucci for this reference.

55. See "A Reminiscence," *The Path* 7 (February 1893): 343–44. If this was not actually written by Judge himself, it clearly reflects his recollections. The piece, while confirming the practical experiments, only confuses matters in attempting to add to Olcott's recollections on the Felt letter published in *Old Diary Leaves*: "The letter was drafted by William Q. Judge and copied out by Felt, and the person he speaks of in the letter as experimenting with is Brother Judge. These things I state advisedly and with permission. It was intended for use at a meeting of the T.S. in 1876, but instead of using that a paper was read by Brother Judge embodying the facts and including many other results of different experiments." It is hard to see how Judge could have drafted the Felt letter, and the assignment of the letter to 1876 is contradicted by the letter itself. The reference to permission for revealing these facts is interesting because it indicates that even in 1893 concern for preserving the

secrecy of the early work was still strong. The article is reprinted in volume 1 of *Echoes of the Orient: The Writings of William Quan Judge*, Dara Eklund, ed., 3 vols. (San Diego: Point Loma Publications, 1975). The results of Judge's experiments are confirmed by a letter of Madame Blavatsky, dated June 15, 1877: "There is Judge, who has become simply a holy Arhat. He sees visions and flies; and he asserts that he passes out of the body every night and roams in infinite space." Quoted in Solovyoff, *Modern Priestess of Isis*, 276, and in Narad Mani, "Baptême de Lumière," *La France Antimaçonnique* 25, no. 50 (December 14, 1911): 540.

56. *Old Diary Leaves*, 1:131.

57. The change in emphasis may have been the result of the disastrous results obtained. One of the masters in the early 1880s commented that of the five "lay chelas" chosen by the society, three had become criminals and two went insane. *Letters from the Masters of Wisdom, First Series*, ed. C. Jinarajadasa (1919; Adyar: Theosophical Publishing House, 1988), 31.

58. Point 9 of Madame Blavatsky's fundamental axioms of occultism was the separation of the "astral body." *Isis Unveiled*, 2:587–88. Colonel Olcott bragged in his first annual address to the Theosophical Society that four neophytes of the society had in fact developed this power. See Gomes, *Dawning of the Theosophical Movement*, 98. Olcott also says that he had some considerable success in this regard as well. See *Old Diary Leaves*, 1:385, 390–91. It was precisely at this time (1875–76), moreover, that Madame Blavatsky, as she revealed to her sister, ceased being plagued by her "ancient 'spooks' " and began developing this same power herself. See "Letters of H. P. Blavatsky," *The Path* 9, no. 9 (December 1894): 269–70, and ibid., 9, no. 10 (January 1895): 299. Of course, in typical fashion, she also claimed to have had this power since the age of fourteen. See C. Jinarajadasa, ed., *H. P. B. Speaks*, 2:61. This astral travel was also one of the powers sought to be developed by the H. B. of L. See the *Occult Magazine* 1, no. 5 (June 1885): 40, in which Peter Davidson replied to the question "Are any of our *young* Members capable of projecting their Astral Double?" "We reply, Yes, undoubtedly so. Amidst a mass of correspondence upon this subject, we quote the following extract from a letter we have just received from a Continental Lady Member:— ' ... I looked and saw through the shell that covered me, the light of my lamp shining, whilst I also saw the shadow of a moving form.... *I felt free from my body*, and was flying through the rooms. ... This was the first time I was able to soar with ease and comfort, and by degrees it became a pleasure.... I went on until I came to an arched window, and looking through it, the atmosphere became intensely clear.... At last *I returned to my wearied body*.... I well know this is the result of my *mirror-training*,' etc. An English member also recently developed this faculty."

59. See W. Q. Judge's comments to Madame Blavatsky's early letters to her sister: "About this time H. P. B. appears to have been greatly troubled, for though some members of the nascent Theosophical Society were able to get 'visions of pure Planetary Spirits,' she could only see 'earthly exhalations,

elementary spirits' of the same category, which she said played the chief parts in materializing seances." "Letters of H. P. Blavatsky," *The Path* 9, no. 9 (December 1894): 268. See also "Madame Blavatsky on the Views of the Theosophists," *The Spiritualist* (February 8, 1878): 68–69, reprinted in *BCW*, 1:290ff., 295–96.

60. "A Magic Mirror," *Spiritual Scientist* 2, no. 13 (June 3, 1875): 150. The piece is reprinted in the *New York Sun*, June 30, 1875, 2, which frequently gave space in its columns to contributions about Colonel Olcott and Madame Blavatsky and their doings.

61. "The Napoleon Mirror," *Spiritual Scientist* 2, no. 16 (June 24, 1875): 186; "The Revelations of a Mirror. Embracing a Series of Prophecies, Allegories, Scenes, and Adventures," ibid., 188; "Revelations of a Mirror, No. II," ibid. 2, no. 17 (July 1, 1875): 195. The visions were mainly of a political nature, predictions of the overthrow of the French republic by a descendant of Napoleon, reminiscent of Randolph's visions in the sleep of Sialam in *Ravalette*. The seer was said to be illiterate, and her visions were taken down by another. The earliest is dated May 1874, a fact which doesn't necessarily imply Olcott's involvement at the time. Despite Randolph's identification of the Brooklyn lady as "Mrs. R," the owner of the mirror may have been Mrs. C. E. Blake (or Jane C. Blake) of Brooklyn whom Olcott was "testing" in May 1875. See "Remarkable Phenomena," *Spiritual Scientist* 2, no. 23 (August 12, 1875): 274. At least as late as 1882, Colonel Olcott, then in India, was still in the habit of exhibiting a crystal (received from his friend Adelma von Vay) in his lectures and, in at least one instance, gave a magic mirror to a friend to experiment with. Madame Blavatsky, in commenting on these facts and quoting the friend's letter describing his experiences ("beautiful phantasmagoria!"), warned of the danger of the practice for those of a mediumistic nature, but stated: "If a person, naturally endowed with a certain amount of clairvoyant power, gazes for a while into the crystal, he will see a succession of visions coming into its heart—landscapes, scenes by sea and land, faces of living and dead persons, and sometimes messages written on scrolls which unwind of themselves, or printed in books, that appear and then fade away." "Visions in the Crystal," *The Theosophist* 3, no. 11 (August 1882): 287–88, reprinted in *BCW*, 4:180–82.

62. Quoted in *Letters from the Masters of Wisdom, Second Series*, 15; facsimile in *BCW*, 1:95.

63. "Echoes from India," *Banner of Light* 46 (October 18, 1879), reprinted in *BCW*, 2:68–80.

64. *Isis Unveiled*, 1:596 (The last queen of the Incas consulted "the consecrated 'black mirror'," which shows the universality of the tradition; these magic mirrors, usually black, were consecrated near Agra and also fabricated in Thibet and China and in Mexico.). See also her notes to "An Excellent Magic Mirror," *The Theosophist* 4 (March 1883): 142–43, reprinted in *BCW*, 4:356–57, in which she says that the mirror proposed (a carafe filled with black ink)

was almost as good for promoting "conscious clairvoyance" as "the ancient concave black mirror of the East" and assures her readers that, if they were appropriately moral, they could expect assistance in their mirror work from chelas and even higher entities. See also Blavatsky, "A Bewitched Life (As Narrated by a Quill-Pen)," *Nightmare Tales* (London: Theosophical Publishing Society, 1892), 7–67, reprinted in *BCW*, 6:355–406 (wonderful vision-inducing steel mirror); "The 'Doctrine of the Eye' & The 'Doctrine of the Heart,' or the 'Heart's Seal,'" *BCW*, 4: 443–53, 451 ("the 'mirror' was a part of . . . the Eleusinian Mysteries.").

65. *Isis Unveiled*, 1:467–68. She says that at this time she was part of a group of nine persons, seven men and two women, who were involved in such experiments and who held "spiritual *seances*" with some "holy mendicants" and with a "Syrian, half-heathen and half-Christian, from Kunankulam (Cochin State), a reputed sorcerer." Ibid., 4:468. She also was familiar with what she calls "Persian mirrors" (crystals to detect thieves) and their use among the Kurds (*Isis Unveiled*, 2:630–31) and described her experiences with what appears to have been a Bektashi mirror magician in Constantinople. "The Luminous Circle. Wonderful Powers of the Divining Girl of Damascus. A Theosophical Tale told by an Old Traveler in the Far East.—A Magic Moon.—What was Seen Therein.—The Dervishes of Constantinople.—A Dwarf's Transformation," *New York Sun*, January 2, 1876, reprinted in *BCW* 1:177–86. In her letters to Prince Dondoukoff-Korsakoff, she says that in her pursuit of the "Red Virgin," she learned "necromancy and astrology, crystal-gazing and spiritualism." See below.

66. "An Unsolved Mystery," *Spiritual Scientist* 3, no. 25 (November 25, 1875): 133–35, reprinted in *BCW*, 1:151–59.

67. The letter is printed in Joscelyn Godwin, "Colonel Olcott Meets the Brothers: An Unpublished Letter," *Theosophical History* 4, no. 1 (January 1994): 5–9. The letter was written to C. C. Massey and W. S. Moses in the first half of 1876.

68. Another indication of crystal use occurs in the Reverend Wiggin's account of the events of the night of Felt's lecture on the "Lost Canon of Proportions of the Egyptians." One of those present, probably Dr. Pancoast, who had an interest in the subject (he later was one of the subscribers to R. H. Fryar's *Magnetic Magic*, as his name on the flyleaf of my copy shows), showed Felt a crystal he either had brought with him or had picked up in Madame Blavatsky's rooms and apparently asked him how it related to his theories. Felt could not (or would not) enlighten the inquirer at the time. See Wiggin, "The Cabala," *The Liberal Christian*, September 28, 1875, reprinted with an introduction by Michael Gomes, "Studies in Early American Theosophical History. VI. Rev. Wiggin's Review of George Henry Felt's 1875 Lecture on the Cabala." *Canadian Theosophist* 71, no. 3 (July–August 1990): 63–69.

69. See A. L. Rawson, "Mme. Blavatsky, A Theosophical Occult Apology," *Frank Leslie's American Magazine* 33 (February 1892), reprinted in *Theosophical History* 2, no. 6 (April 1988): 209–20. On Madame Blavatsky's encounters with Metamon in the 1850s and later, in 1871, at the time she founded her *Société Spirite* in Cairo, see Olcott, *Old Diary Leaves*, 1:23; Sinnett, *Incidents in the Life of Madame Blavatsky*, 59–60, 160; "Fragments from H. P. B.'s 'Mystical History,' " transcribed and with notes by Michael Gomes, *The Theosophist* (September 1991): 552–60 (part 5 of a seven-part series). On Metamon and the H. B. of L., see Guénon, *Le Théosophisme*, 14, 301, 313–14; Godwin, Chanel, and Deveney, *The Hermetic Brotherhood of Luxor*, introduction. It was as a consequence of Madame Blavatsky's stories of her earlier *Société Spirite* that Olcott in the fall of 1875 proposed founding a "Miracle Club"—the forerunner of the Theosophical Society. See *The Theosophical Movement, 1875–1950* (Los Angeles: The Cunningham Press, 1951), 39. Rawson mentions that Madame Blavatsky had the idea of such a club or society in Cairo even in the 1850s but that Metamon had advised delay in starting it.

70. See Hannah M. Wolff, "Madame Blavatsky," a letter to the editor of *The Better Way* that was later reprinted in the *Religio-Philosophical Journal* (January 2, 1892): 501–2; A. L. Rawson, "Mme. Blavatsky, A Theosophical Occult Apology." Wolff says Madame Blavatsky was "addicted" to hashish which she thought far surpassed opium.

71. A. L. Rawson quotes her as telling him: "Hasheesh multiplies one's life a thousand fold. My experiences are as real as if they were ordinary events of actual life. Ah! I have the explanation. It is a recollection of my former existences, my previous incarnations. It is a wonderful drug, and clears up a profound mystery." "Mme. Blavatsky, A Theosophical Occult Apology," *Theosophical History* 2, no. 6 (April 1988): 211. On Madame Blavatsky's rejection of these recollections of past lives as proof of reincarnation, see *Isis Unveiled*, 1:179. Hashish is not found in the index volume to her collected writings, but she does quote (*BCW*, 7:58) Théophile Gautier's description of the hashish experience. The attitude of some of the early Theosophists to drugs as means of liberating the soul from the body may also be seen in a review in *The Theosophist* of a book by Dr. George Wyld, in which the reviewer stresses that it was at precisely this point that Wyld's ideas (on the use of nitrous oxide) coincided with "the brightest and noblest of Aryan psychologists." M. A. (Cantab.) [pseud.], "Dr. Wyld's New Book," *The Theosophist* 2, no. 5 (February 1881): 107–10. Wyld had been an early enthusiast for spiritualism in the late 1850s, when he may have met Randolph, and was a founding member of the British Theosophical Society. By the 1880s at least he had become associated with R. H. Fryar, who solicited subscriptions for an edition of the works of Cahagnet with a preface by Wyld. See S. C. Gould's *Notes and Queries*, 2 (December 1885): 676.

72. See, e.g., *Isis Unveiled*, 1:xxv; 2: 589; Blavatsky, "Erroneous Ideas Concerning the Doctrines of the Theosophists," *La Revue Spirite* (January 1879), reprinted in *BCW*, 2: 14–25, 21.

73. See also *Isis Unveiled*, 1:357–58; Blavatsky, "The Esoteric Character of the Gospels," *Lucifer* (November 1887), reprinted in *BCW*, 8:204n.; Blavatsky, *The Secret Doctrine*, 2:558. There is a curious verbal coincidence (at least) in connection with the use by Randolph and Madame Blavatsky of the term *Sleep of Sialam*. In the "Mysteries of Eulis," circulated first in 1873–74, Randolph has an inquirer ask: "'But how do you know that such [powers, potencies, vast intelligences] exist?' Because 1st. In the sleep of Sialam I and others have seen them; and we know they were not of this or similar earths, because they are organically different, and look no more like a human apparition than a negro does like a Kalmuc Tartar." Ultimately the comparison goes back to Bulwer-Lytton, who, in *Zanoni*, had described the myriads of entities in the universes and commented that "these races and tribes differ more widely each from the other, than the Calmuch from the Greek." This unlikely comparison of Kalmucks and negroes, however, coupled with the sleep of Sialam, may be a playful echo of Madame Blavatsky's constant, self-deprecating references to her "Kalmucko-Buddhisto-Tartaric features." See Blavatsky, "The Knout," *Religio-Philosophical Journal* 24, no. 2 (March 16, 1878): 8, reprinted in *BCW* 1:319–25. See also *Old Diary Leaves*, 1:4–5.

74. John Yarker, "The Society of the Rosy Cross," *The Rosicrucian Brotherhood* 1, no. 3 (July 1907): 113–24. Gould also published this in his *Historic Magazine and Notes and Queries* 25, no. 10 (October 1907): 225–36.

75. Yarker, "The Society of the Rosy Cross," 119.

76. Ibid., 121.

77. P. B. Randolph, *The "Learned Pundit," and "Man with Two Souls," His Curious Life, Works and Career. The Great Free-Love Trial* (Boston: Randolph Publishing Co., 1873).

78. See Zanoni [T. H. Burgoyne], *The Light of Egypt*, vol. 2 (Denver: Astro-Philosophical Publishing Co., 1900), xi, 105.

79. Belle M. Wagner, *Within the Temple of Isis*, 2d ed. (Denver: Astro-Philosophical Publishing House, 1899). A very good illustration of the transmutations to which blending was subject can be found in the work of Edouard Blitz, the Martinist delegate of Papus to the United States and (at times) a co-worker with Papus, Gould, Clymer, etc. In his edition of Dom Antoine-Joseph Pernety's *Treatise on the Great Art, A System of Physics According to Hermetic Philosophy and Theory and Practice of the Magisterium* (Boston: Occult Publishing House, 1898), he describes in great detail what he calls "evocation," the only method whereby one may succeed in reconstituting the lost science without a master. This is a permanent transmutation in which the celestial "mentor" "will *incarnate* himself in his disciple whose mind, now a plastic clay, will acquire in its highest degree the faculty of *receptivity*, and will become susceptible of receiving the least impressions from the outer world. The Influence of the being thus evoked, thus brought back into the world by an irresistible

magnetism, will then unite with the Operator and continue, through the latter's instrumentality, the work which death interrupted."

80. "Letters of H. P. Blavatsky," *The Path* 9, no. 9 (December 1894): 266–70. See also *H. P. B. Speaks, 1: 224–25* ("At first it seemed to me that he pushed me out of my body, but soon I seemed to become accustomed to it, and now during the moments of his presence *in* me, it only seems (to me) that I am *living* a *double* life.").

81. *Dealings with the Dead,* 11–12.

82. "Letters of H. P. Blavatsky," *The Path* 9, no. 10 (January 1895): 297–98. In *Isis Unveiled* (1:333), Madame Blavatsky quotes a passage from Dupotet on this same phenomenon that could have been written by Randolph himself: "I am preparing to shock every opinion, and provoke laughter in our most illustrious scientists . . . for I am convinced that *agents of an immense potency* exist *outside of us;* that they can *enter in us;* move our limbs and organs; and use us as they please. . . . Every religion admitted the reality of *spiritual agents."*

83. Madame Blavatsky's fickleness consequent upon her changing controls was often commented upon. See, e.g., *Old Diary Leaves,* 1:27ff.; 1:269–70; A. L. Rawson, "Mme. Blavatsky, A Theosophical Occult Apology," *Theosophical History* 2, no. 6 (April 1988): 209 (Madame Blavatsky was "always very social and companionable when not 'possessed.' "); Leslie Price, *Madame Blavatsky Unveiled? A New Discussion of the Most Famous Investigations of the Society for Psychical Research* (London: Theosophical History Centre, 1986), 20–21. Olcott stresses that in the early New York days the "erudition of *Isis Unveiled* had not yet overshadowed her" and that "she was a totally different personage then from what she became later on." *Old Diary Leaves,* 1:33. Olcott explicitly uses the term "blend" to describe the interpenetration of Madame Blavatsky's personality by those of her masters. Ibid., 1: 408–09.

84. "Crows in Peacock Feathers," *Boston Daily Globe* (March 8, 1889), 4, reprinted by Michael Gomes, *Canadian Theosophist* 66, no. 5 (November–December, 1985): 114–17.

85. Madame Blavatsky did write to Alexander Aksakov that the society was closed to free lovers, and Colonel Olcott stirred up a hornet's nest by denouncing the free-love and "individual sovereignty" elements within spiritualism. See Solovyoff, *A Modern Priestess of Isis,* 265, and Olcott's letters to the *New York Tribune,* August 30 and September 17, 1875. See also Michael Gomes, "Studies in Early American Theosophical History. IV. Colonel Olcott and the American Press," *Canadian Theosophist* 71, no. 1 (March–April 1990), 3, on Olcott's other attacks on free love; "Free Love and Moral Degeneration," *Spiritual Scientist* 2, no. 26 (September 2, 1875): 306–7.

86. "Spiritualistic Morals in London," *The Theosophist* 4 (July 1882): 142, reprinted in *BCW,* 4:143. This was part of a heated exchange of charges about the prevalence in materializing spiritualist circles of spiritual "husbands" and

"wives" who obsessed immoral mediums. Randolph (with his "Spirit Mother") is singled out as an example of the evil. See "A Sad Look Out," *The Theosophist* 3 (April 1882): 174; "A Storm in A Tea Cup," ibid. 3 (July 1882): 249–50; "Spiritualistic Black Magic," ibid. 4 (January 1883): 92–93. Harris's boasts about his spirit child are in his poem *The Lord: The Two-in-One*.

87. See *Isis Unveiled*, 2:461ff. On the myth of man's sexual differentiation and fall, see ibid., 1:297, 303, 428; 2:264ff. The wheel and its explanation later formed the central thesis of the H. B. of L.'s teaching manuscript on "Symbolical Notes to the First Degree" and also feature prominently in the works of Emma Hardinge Britten. See Godwin, Chanel, and Deveney, *The Hermetic Brotherhood of Luxor*, 127–28. See also Hargrave Jennings, *The Rosicrucians, Their Rites and Mysteries*, 4th ed., rev. (London, 1888), 58, 71–72, 338–53; Emma Hardinge Britten, *Art Magic*, 43ff. Madame Blavatsky was also familiar with the usual nineteenth-century phallic mythographers, such as Payne Knight, and as we have already discussed, she was comfortable with the role of sexual excitement in certain magical operations—as witness her knowledge of the ritual consecration of "Bhattah mirrors" described by Colonel Fraser. The choice of Alexander Wilder as her editor and Bouton as her publisher for *Isis Unveiled* is itself significant in this regard, since Wilder was thoroughly convinced of the central role of phallicism in mythology and of the importance of sex in occultism in general. See his discussion of the normality of sex in *Woodhull & Claflin's Weekly* (October 15, 1870) and also his article "The Primeval Race Double-Sexed," *The Theosophist* 4 (February 1883): 112. The 1880 cataloge of J. W. Bouton, the publisher of *Isis Unveiled*, included all of the standard mythological phallicists: Hargrave Jennings, *Rosicrucians*; K. R. H. Mackenzie, *Royal Masonic Cyclopædia*; Higgins, *Anacalypsis*; Inman, *Ancient Faiths* and *Ancient Faiths and Modern*; Yarker, *Scientific and Religious Mysteries of Antiquity*. Bouton also sold Wake and Clark's *Serpent and Siva Worship* and Payne Knight's *Ancient Art and Mythology*—both of which carried learned introductions by Wilder. The cataloge is attached to John A. Weisse, *The Obelisk and Freemasonry* (New York: J. W. Bouton, 1880). Weisse was a vice president of the Theosophical Society and a co-worker with A. L. Rawson in his fringe Masonic endeavors. Madame Blavatsky's final word on the truths of universal phallicism and the dangers of "the most *shameful practices*" to which their misunderstanding led is in her *Secret Instructions to Probationers of an Esoteric Occult School* (Mokelumne Hill: Health Research, 1969), 5.

88. Explicit accusations of sexual goings-on in the early days of the Theosophical Society in New York are not lacking, but they appear baseless. In 1878, C. C. Blake, a member of the British Theosophical Society, spread the word that the New York Theosophists and the Arya Samaj were "practicing Siva worship—performing the Linga and Sakti Puja!!!" See "The Diaries of H. P. Blavatsky," *BCW*, 1:409–16. *The Pall Mall Gazette* on October 9, 1878, carried Blake's attack on the Arya Samaj as a revival of the old religion "associated with some of the mysterious rites of which the trustees of the British Museum

prudently keep the memorials in a cellar." See Deveney, "A Note on Psychic Attacks," *Theosophical History* 5, no. 6 (April 1995): 194–97. Blake was no stranger to the sexual mysteries of "Sakti Puja," since he had appreciatively attended a lecture on the subject by Edward Sellon, the pornographer who introduced Tantra to the West. See Pisanus Fraxi [pseud.], *Index Librorum Prohibitorum: Being Notes Bio- Biblio- Econo-graphical and Critical, on Curious and Uncommon Books* (1877; reprint, *The Encyclopedia of Erotic Literature*, vol. 3 [New York: Documentary Books, n.d., c. 1962]), 378ff. A perceptive reviewer of *Isis Unveiled* noted that the closest analogy to the book was the Sellon's papers on the "Pujas of the East." "Isis Unveiled," *Religio-Philosophical Journal* 23, no. 16 (March 2, 1878): 3.

89. *Letters from Masters of Wisdom, Second Series*, 41–42 (letter 19). For Madame Blavatsky's thoughts on the reality of sexual intercourse with "pisachas" and with "elementals" guising themselves as the "spirits of the dead" and the prevalence of the practice in spiritualism, see above, note 86, and her review of Robert H. Fryar's edition of *Le Comte de Gabalis*, "Thoughts on Elementals," *Lucifer* 6 (May 1890): 177–88, reprinted in BCW, 12:187–205. See also her comment, "Miscellaneous Notes," in *Lucifer* 3, no. 14 (October 1888): 131–32, reprinted in BCW, 10:155–56, on the difference between the allegories of celestial brides and the "astral Ninons de l'Enclos" who descend to hysterical epileptics. John Yarker obliquely contended for the reality of such intercourse in an article he published in Madame Blavatsky's *Theosophist*. See John Yarker, "The Bene Elohim and the Book of Enoch," *The Theosophist* 3 (April 1882): 71–72 ("I need only say that the writer asserts that the Rosicrucians believed in the reality of such commerce as that alleged against the Beni Elohim, and that married women might have progeny of the spirits. . . . These sexual angels, both male and female, might live a thousand years, but only become immortal by such earthly attachments.").

90. *H. P. B. Speaks*, 2:13ff. Their authenticity has been questioned by, among others, Jean Overton Fuller, but the doubts expressed appear to rest more on a priori assumptions about Madame Blavatsky herself and her teachers than on the evidence. See Jean Overton Fuller, *Blavatsky and Her Teachers* (London and the Hague: East-West Publications, 1988), 235–38. The sexual connotations of the Red Virgin and the salt were taken as a matter of course in Madame Blavatsky's time. See, e.g., Albert G. Mackey, "The Origin of the Rosicrucians," *The Rosicrucian Brotherhood* 1, no. 1 (January 1907), 3ff. ("The seed of the Red Dragon is the crude, material light, but is also connected with the 'dewey' question [which] cannot be discussed in public."). On the connection between "dew" (the Latin *ros*) with its sexual connotations and the Rosicrucians, see K. R. H. Mackenzie, *Royal Masonic Cyclopaedia*, s.v. "Rosicrucians," 616, which also says that the "'dewey' question cannot be discussed in public." The rather recondite search for the Red Virgin implies a familiarity with the by-ways of alchemy and the occult by Madame Blavatsky, which has been plausibly explained by Marion Meade, *Madame Blavatsky: The*

Woman Behind the Myth (New York: G.P. Putnam's Sons, 1980), 47ff. Madame Blavatsky was also very familiar with at least the nineteenth-century Masonic versions of Cagliostro's "Egyptian Rite." This, in its original working, had a strong sexual element phrased in alchemical terms. See Massimo Introvigne, "Arcana Arcanorum: Cagliostro's Legacy in Contemporary Magical Movements," *Syzygy: Journal of Alternative Religion and Culture* 1, nos. 2–3 (1992): 117–35. A version of the rite (from a text published in the *Cahiers Astrologiques* in 1948) has recently been published. *Cagliostro's Secret Ritual of Egyptian Rite Freemasonry* (Kila, MT: Kessinger Publishing Co., n.d.). Colonel Olcott came to see the efforts to found the Theosophical Society as a continuation of those of Cagliostro in the eighteenth century. See note 15, above.

91. *H. P. B. Speaks*, 2:62–67.

92. Quoted in Gomes, *Dawning of the Theosophical Movement*, 148.

93. W. E. Coleman in his well-known charge of plagiarism leveled at Madame Blavatsky lists Randolph's *Pre-Adamite Man* as one of the principal sources of *Isis Unveiled*. See W. E. Coleman, "The Sources of Madame Blavatsky's Writing," in Solovyoff, *Modern Priestess of Isis*, appendix C, 357ff. The charge in this instance, however, is certainly overstated. Madame Blavatsky does cover much of the same ground as Randolph had and she discusses "Pre-Adamite" spirits and the like and cites ("for what is worth") a statement from Randolph's book (*Isis Unveiled*, 1:127), but it is difficult to discern any extensive pattern of plagiarism of Randolph's work generally. Gertrude Marvin Williams, one of Madame Blavatsky's hostile biographers, similarly says that she took the occasion of *Isis Unveiled* to "toss bouquets to men who might be useful" to her, including "P. B. Randolph, leading American Rosicrucian." *Priestess of the Occult, Madame Blavatsky* (New York: Knopf, 1946), 114. If she did, the bouquets are carefully disguised, and Randolph, who had been dead for more than two years when *Isis* was published, can scarcely have been considered useful to her.

Works Cited

A. [pseud.]. "Is He Koot Hoomi, Blavatsky's 'Mahatma?' One of the Great Mysteries of Modern Theosophy Thought to Have been at Last Unveiled. The Mystic 'Brothers.' Charles Sotheran Picked Out to be the Man, But he Refuses to Publicly Acknowledge it." *New York Herald*, November 16, 1891, sec. 1, 10.

Aksakov, Alexander. "Researches on the Historical Origins of the Reincarnation Speculations of French Spiritualists." *Spiritual Scientist* 3, no. 1 (September 9, 1875): 1–2. Published also in *Banner of Light* 27, no. 25 (September 18, 1875): 3.

Alexandrian, Sarane. "Maria de Naglowska et le satanisme féminin." In *Les Libérateurs de l'Amour*. Paris: Editions du Seuil, 1977.

Allibone, S. Austin. *A Critical Dictionary of English Literature and British and American Authors Living and Deceased, From the Earliest Accounts to the Latter Half of the Nineteenth Century*. 3 vols. Philadelphia: J. B. Lippincott & Co., 1870.

"All Sorts of Paragraphs." *Banner of Light* 7, no. 18 (July 28, 1860): 5; ibid. 16, no. 2 (October 1, 1864): 5.

"American Medium, An." *The Yorkshire Spiritual Telegraph* 3 (January 1857): 125.

"American Progressive Medical Association, The: Another Attempt to Organize the Twilight Zone of Professionalism." *Journal of the American Medical Association* (December 14, 1923): 2050–54.

Andrews, Stephen Pearl. *The Basic Outline of Universology. An Introduction to the Newly Discovered Science of the Universe; Its Elementary Principles; and the First Stages of their Development in the Special Sciences*. New York: Dion Thomas, 1872.

———. "Universology." *Tiffany's Monthly*, parts 4–7, from March 7, 1857.

Aniane, Maurice. "Notes sur l'Alchemie, 'Yoga' cosmologique de la Chrétienté médiévale." In *Yoga, Science de l'Homme Intégral*. Edited by Jacques Masui. Paris: Les Cahiers du Sud, 1953.

"Answers to Questioners." *The Path* 4, no. 3 (June 1889): 87–88.

"Appeal Will Not Be Made in Vain." *Religio-Philosophical Journal* 21, no. 2 (September 23, 1876): 14.

Artephius. *The Secret Book of Artephius*. Edmunds, WA: Alchemical Press, 1984.

Ashburner, John. "Can Force Create Matter." *Spiritual Magazine* 1, no. 5 (May 1860): 223ff.; 1, no. 11 (November 1860): 486ff.

———. "Letter of Dr. Ashburner to Mr. G. J. Holyoake." *The Yorkshire Spiritual Telegraph* 3, no. 11 (February 8, 1857): 150–52, 162–65.

Assemani, J. S. *Bibliotheca Orientalis Clementino-Vaticana*. Rome: 1719–1728.

Atkinson, W. J. "Magic." *Religio-Philosophical Journal* 17, no. 16 (January 2, 1875): 6.

Ayton, William Alexander. *The Alchemist of the Golden Dawn. The Letters of the Reverend W. A. Ayton to F. L. Gardner and Others 1886–1905*. Edited by Ellic Howe. Wellingborough: Aquarian, 1985.

Azcuy, Eduardo A. *El Occultismo y la Creacion Poetica*. Buenos Aires: Ed. Sudamerica, 1966.

Balzac, Honoré. *Séraphita*. 1835.

Banner of Light, The. A Weekly Journal of Romance, Literature, and General Intelligence. Edited by Luther Colby and others. Boston. 1857 through 1887.

Barborka, G. A. *H. P. Blavatsky, Tibet and Tulku*. Adyar: Theosophical Publishing House, 1966.

Barrett, Francis. *The Magus, or Celestial Intelligencer*. 1801. Reprint, New York: Samuel Weiser, n.d.

Basset, René. "Nusairis." *Encyclopedia of Religion and Ethics*. Edited by James Hastings. New York: Charles Scribner's Sons, n.d.

Bays, Gwendolyn. *The Orphic Vision. Seer Poets from Novalis to Rimbaud*. Lincoln: University of Nebraska Press, 1964.

Bednarowski, M. F. *Nineteenth Century American Spiritualism: An Attempt at a Scientific Religion*. Ann Arbor: University Microfilms, 1973.

Bell, H. Idris. *Cults and Creeds in Graeco-Roman Egypt*. 1953. Reprint, Chicago: Ares Publishers, 1985.

Bell, Howard Holman, ed. *Minutes of the Proceedings of the National Negro Conventions*. New York: Arno Press, 1969.

Benko, S. "The Libertine Gnostic Sect of the Phibionites according to Epiphanius." *Vigiliae Christianae* 21 (1967): 130ff.

———. *Pagan Rome and the Early Christians*. Bloomington: Indiana University Press, 1984.

Best, St. George. "The Magic Mirror. A Faithful Record of a Strange Experience." *The Path* 9, no. 8 (November 1894): 239–44, and ibid. 9, no. 9 (December 1894): 270–75.

Besterman, Theodore. *Crystal-Gazing: A Study in the History, Distribution, Theory and Practice of Scrying*. N.p., n.d.

Bibliotheca Esoterica, Catalogue Annoté et illustré de 6707 ouvrages anciens et modernes qui traitent des sciences occultes . . . en vente à la Librairie Dorbon-Ainé. Paris, n.d.

Binkley, G. H. "Occultism vs. Spiritualism." *Religio-Philosophical Journal* 19, no. 21 (February 5, 1876): 376.

———. "Occult Sciences." *Religio-Philosophical Journal* 17, no. 20 (February 20, 1875): 2.

Birks, W. N., and R. A. Gilbert. *The Treasure of Montsegur. A Study of the Cathar Heresy and the Nature of the Cathar Secret.* Wellingborough: Crucible, 1987.

Birven, Henri Clemens. *Lebenskunst in Yoga und Praxis.* Zurich: Origo, 1953.

Blassingame, John W. *Black New Orleans 1860–1866.* Chicago: University of Chicago Press, 1973.

Blatt, Martin Henry. *Free Love and Anarchism. The Biography of Ezra Heywood.* Urbana: University of Illinois Press, 1989.

Blavatsky, Helena Petrovna. "A Bewitched Life As Narrated by a Quill-Pen." In *Nightmare Tales.* London: Theosophical Publishing Society, 1892. Reprinted in *BCW*, 6:355–406.

———. "Catechizing a Buddhist." *New York Sun*, May 6, 1877, 6.

———. "The Claims of Occultism." *The Theosophist* 2, no. 12 (September 1881): 258–60. Reprinted in *BCW*, 3: 271–75.

———. "Crows in Peacock Feathers." *Boston Daily Globe*, March 8, 1889, 4. Reprinted with an Introduction and Notes by Michael Gomes, *Canadian Theosophist* 66, no. 5 (November–December 1985): 114–17.

———. "The Cycle Moveth." *Lucifer* 6 (March 1890): 1–10. Reprinted in *BCW*, 12:120–32.

———. "Death and Immortality." *The Theosophist* 4, no. 2 (November 1882): 28–30. Reprinted in *BCW*, 4:250–56.

———. "The Diaries of H. P. Blavatsky." *BCW*, 1:406–440.

———. "The 'Doctrine of the Eye' & The 'Doctrine of the Heart,' or the 'Heart's Seal.'" *BCW*, 4:443–453.

———. "Echoes from India: What is Hindu Spiritualism?" *Banner of Light* 46, no. 4 (October 18, 1879): 7, reprinted in *BCW*, 2:68–80.

———. "Elementaries." *Religio-Philosophical Journal* 23 (November 17, 1877). Reprinted in *BCW*, 1:265–71.

———. "Erroneous Ideas Concerning the Doctrines of the Theosophists." *La Revue Spirite* (January 1879). Reprinted in *BCW*, 2: 14–25.

———. "The Esoteric Character of the Gospels." *Lucifer* (November 1887). Reprinted in *BCW*, 8:204.

———. "An Excellent Magic Mirror." *The Theosophist* 4 (March 1883): 142–43. Reprinted in *BCW*, 4:356–57.

———. "A Few Questions to 'HIRAF.'" *Spiritual Scientist* 3, nos. 19 and 20 (July 15 and 22, 1875): 202, 217–18, 224, 236–37. Reprinted in *BCW*, 1:101–19.

———. "Footnotes to 'The Life of Sankaracharya, Philosopher and Mystic.'" *The Theosophist* 1, no. 4 (January 1880): 89, and 1, no. 8 (May 1880): 203. Reprinted in *BCW*, 2:217–19.

———. "Fragments from H. P. B.'s 'Mystical History.'" Transcribed and with notes by Michael Gomes. *The Theosophist* (September 1991): 552–60.

———. "From Madame H. P. Blavatsky to her Correspondents, An Open Letter Such as Few Can Write." *Spiritual Scientist* 3, no. 3 (September 23, 1875): 25–27. Reprinted in *BCW*, 1:126–33.

———. *H. P. Blavatsky: Collected Works.* Compiled by Boris de Zirkoff. 15 vols. Wheaton: Theosophical Publishing House, 1966–1991. Cited as *BCW*.

————. *H. P. Blavatsky to the American Conventions, 1888–1891*. Pasadena: Theosophical University Press, 1979.

————. "Important Note." *BCW*, 1:73.

————. *Isis Unveiled: A Master-Key to the Mysteries of Ancient and Modern Science and Theology*. 2 vols. New York: Bouton, 1877. Reprint, Pasadena: Theosophical University Press, 1976.

————. "Is it Idle to Argue Further?" *The Theosophist* 3 (January 1882). Reprinted in *BCW*, 3:391–95.

————. *The Key to Theosophy, being A Clear Exposition, in the Form of Question and Answer, of the Ethics, Science, and Philosophy for the Study of Which the Theosophical Society has been Founded*. 1889. Reprint, Pasadena: Theosophical University Press, 1946.

————. "The Knout." *Religio-Philosophical Journal* 24, no. 2 (March 16, 1878): 8. Reprinted in BCW, 1:319–25.

————. "The Last of the Mysteries in Europe." *BCW*, 14:296.

————. "Letter of Madame Blavatsky, Dr. Rotura's Discovery." *La Revue Spirite* (December 1879). Reprinted in *BCW*, 2:205–8.

————. "Letters of H. P. Blavatsky." 13 parts. *The Path* 9, no. 9 (December 1894): 265–70, through 10, no. 9 (December 1895): 267–70.

————. "Letters of H. P. B. to Dr. Hartmann, 1885 to 1886." 3 parts. *The Path* 10, no. 10 (January 1896): 297–300, through 10, no. 12 (March 1896): 366–73.

————. "Lodges of Magic." *Lucifer* 3, no. 14 (October 15, 1888): 89–93. Reprinted in *BCW*, 10:124–33.

————. "The Luminous Circle. Wonderful Powers of the Divining Girl of Damascus. A Theosophical Tale told by an Old Traveler in the Far East.—A Magic Moon.—What was Seen Therein.—The Dervishes of Constantinople.—A Dwarf's Transformation." *New York Sun*, January 2, 1876. Reprinted in *BCW* 1:177–86.

————. "Madame Blavatsky on the 'Himalayan Brothers.'" *The Spiritualist* (August 12, 1881). Reprinted in *BCW*, 3:262–68.

————. "Madame Blavatsky on the Views of the Theosophists." *The Spiritualist* (February 8, 1878): 68–69. Reprinted in *BCW*, 1:290–300.

————. "Miscellaneous Notes." *Lucifer* 3, no. 14 (October 1888): 131–32. Reprinted in *BCW*, 10:155–56.

————. "Mme. Blavatsky on Fakirs." *Banner of Light* 41, no. 4 (April 21, 1877): 8. Reprinted in *BCW*, 1:241–43.

————. *A Modern Panarion: A Collection of Fugitive Fragments from the Pen of H. P. Blavatsky*. 1895. Reprint, Los Angeles: Theosophy Co., 1981.

————. "More about Materializations." *Spiritual Scientist* 1, 11 (November 19, 1874): 121–22.

————. Notes on Eliphas Lévi, "Death." *The Theosophist* 3, no. 1 (October 1881): 12–15. Reprinted in *BCW*, 3:287–91.

————. Notes on "The Bhattah Mirrors." *The Theosophist* 4, no. 3 (December 1883): 72–74. Reprinted in *BCW*, 6:6–8.

————. "Occultism Versus the Occult Sciences." *Lucifer* 2, no. 9 (May 1888): 173–81. Reprinted in *BCW*, 9; 249–61.

————. "The Original Programme of the Theosophical Society." *BCW*, 7:145–75.

————. "Practical Occultism. Important to Students." *Lucifer* 2, no. 8 (April 1888). Reprinted in *BCW*, 9:155–62.

————. "The Science of Magic, Proof of its Existence—Mediums in Ancient Times, etc., etc." *Spiritual Scientist* 3, no. 6 (October 14, 1875): 64–65. Reprinted in *BCW*, 1:134–43.

————. *The Secret Doctrine.* 2 vols. London: Theosophical Publishing House, 1888.

————. *Secret Instructions to Probationers of an Esoteric Occult School.* Mokelumne Hill: Health Research, 1969.

————. "Seeming Discrepancies." *The Theosophist* 3 (June 1882): 225–26. Reprinted in *BCW*, 4:119–22.

————. "Spiritualism and Spiritualists." *Spiritual Scientist* 3, no. 18 (January 6, 1876): 208–9. Reprinted in *BCW*, 1: 186–87.

————. "Spiritualistic Morals in London." *The Theosophist* 4 (July 1882): 142. Reprinted in *BCW*, 4:143.

————. "A Story of the Mystical, Told by a Member of the Theosophical Society. A Dread Scene in Eastern Necromancy—Vengeance Marvelously Wrought by Occult Methods—Mysteries—the Scîn-Lâc." *New York Sun* December 26, 1875. Reprinted in *BCW*, 1:163–173.

————. *Theosophical Glossary.* 1892. Reprint, Los Angeles: Theosophy Co., 1973.

————. "The Theosophical Society, Its Origin, Plan and Aims." *BCW*, 1:375ff.

————. "Thoughts on Elementals." *Lucifer*, 6 May 1890: 177–88. Reprinted in *BCW*, 12:187–205.

————. *Unpublished Letters of H. P. Blavatsky.* Compiled and with Introduction by Eugene Rollin Corson. London: Rider & Co., 1929.

————. "An Unsolved Mystery." *Spiritual Scientist* 3, no. 25 (November 25, 1875): 133–35. Reprinted in *BCW*, 1:151–59.

"Blending State, The." *Spiritual Magazine* 3, no. 6 (June 1862): 278ff.

Blitz, Edouard, ed. Dom Antoine-Joseph Pernety, *Treatise on the Great Art, A System of Physics According to Hermetic Philosophy and Theory and Practice of the Magisterium.* Boston: Occult Publishing House, 1898.

Blood, Benjamin Paul. *Pluriverse, an Essay in the Philosophy of Pluralism.* Boston: Marshall Jones & Co., 1920.

Board, David. "The Brotherhood of Luxor and the Brotherhood of Light." *Theosophical History* 2, no. 5 January (1988): 149–57.

Bois, Jules. *Le Monde Invisible.* Paris: Flammarion, 1902.

"Boston Reform Conference." *Banner of Light* 4, no. 14 (January 1, 1859): 4; ibid. 7, no. 18 (July 28, 1860): 4; ibid. 7, no. 19 (August 4, 1860): 5; ibid. 7, no. 20 (August 25, 1860): 8; ibid. 8, no. 7 (November 10, 1860): 5; ibid. 8, no. 11 (December 9, 1860): 8; ibid. 8, no. 13 (December 22, 1860): 8.

Braden, Charles S. *Spirits in Rebellion: The Rise and Development of New Thought.* Dallas: Southern Methodist University Press, 1963.

Braude, Ann. "News from the Spirit World: A Checklist of American Spiritualist Periodicals." *Proceedings of the American Antiquarian Society* 99, no. 2 (1989): 399–462.

———. *Radical Spirits; Spiritualism and Women's Rights in Nineteenth-Century America*. Boston: Beacon Press, 1989.

Bricaud, J. *L'Abbé Boullan, Sa Vie, Sa Doctrine et ses Pratiques Magiques*. Paris, Chacornac Frères, 1927.

Brittan, S. B. "The Bible and Inspiration." *The Telegraph Papers* 2 (1853): 454–60.

Britten, Emma Hardinge. "Another Book on 'Art Magic.' " *Spiritual Scientist* 6, no. 1 (September 6, 1876): 8–9.

———, ed. *Art Magic; or, Mundane, Sub-Mundane and Super-Mundane Spiritism. A Treatise in Three Parts and Twenty-Three Sections: Descriptive of Art Magic, Spiritism, the Different Orders of Spirits in the Universe Known to be Related to, or in Communication with Man; Together with Directions for Invoking, Controlling, and Discharging Spirits, and the Uses and Abuses, Dangers and Possibilities of Magical Art*. New York: Author, 1876.

———. *Autobiography of Emma Hardinge Britten*. Manchester and London: John Heywood, 1900.

———. "The Doctrine of Reincarnation." *Spiritual Scientist* 2, no. 11 (May 20, 1875): 128–29.

———, trans. and ed. *Ghost Land, or, Researches into the Mysteries of Occultism, Illustrated in a Series of Autobiographical Sketches, in Two Parts*. 1876. Reprint, Progressive Thinker Publishing House: Chicago, 1897. Reprint, Mokelumne Hill: Health Research, 1970. Partial French translation: *Au pays des Esprits, ou roman veçu des Mystères de l'Occultisme*. Paris: Edition de l'Initiation, 1903.

———. *Modern American Spiritualism: Twenty Years' Record of the Communion between Earth and the World of Spirits*. New York: Author, 1870. Reprint, New York: University Books, 1970.

———. "On Living Spirits and Dying Spiritualism." *Banner of Light* 7, no. 18 (July 28, 1860): 2.

———. *The Place and Mission of Woman*. Boston: Hubbard W. Swett, 1859.

———. "Spiritualism in the West." *Banner of Light* 27, no. 26 (September 10, 1870): 1.

———. "Valedictory. Emma Hardinge's Farewell to her American Friends." *Banner of Light* 17, no. 17 (July 15, 1865): 4, and ibid. 17, no. 18 (July 22, 1865): 8.

Brown, Jr., Burton Gates. *Spiritualism in Nineteenth Century America*. Ann Arbor: University Microfilms, 1972.

Brown, Edward Holmes [Eulis]. *The Word. Issued from the Temple of the Rosy Cross*. Eulian Publishing Company of Salem n.d. [c. 1917].

Brown, John P. *The Darvishes or Oriental Spiritualism*. 1868. Reprint, Birmingham: Frank Cass & Co. Ltd., 1968.

Brown, Peter. *The Body and Society. Men, Women and Sexual Renunciation in Early Christianity*. New York: Columbia University Press, 1988.

Brown, W. T. "The Mystic's Soul Flight. The Chevalier de B." *Religio-Philosophical Journal* 42, no. 2 (March 5, 1887): 6.

Browne, E. G. *A Literary History of Persia*. 2 vols. Cambridge University Press, 1928.

Brownson, Orestes. *The Spirit-Rapper: An Autobiography*. Boston: Little, Brown & Co., 1854.

Buchanan, J. R. "Hindoo Philosophy." *The Telegraph Papers* 2 (1853): 48–51.

Bucke, Richard Maurice. *Cosmic Consciousness. A Study in the Evolution of the Human Mind*. 1901. Reprint, New York: E.P. Dutton & Co., 1945.

Bullock, Penelope L. *The Afro-American Periodical Press, 1838–1909*. Baton Rouge: Louisiana State University Press, 1981.

Burgoyne, T. H. [Zanoni]. *The Light of Egypt*. Vol. 1, Chicago, Religio-Philosophical Publishing House, 1889. Vol. 2, Denver: Astro-Philosophical Publishing Co., 1900.

———. "The Kabbalah." *The Platonist* 3, no. 2 (February 1887): 106–12.

Burnside, G. L. "French vs. American Spirits," *Banner of Light* 14, no. 15 (January 1, 1864): 1.

Burr, M. J. "Ohlographs from George H. Binkley." *Religio-Philosophical Journal* 20, no. 10 (May 20, 1876): 74.

Burton, Jean. *Heyday of a Wizard: D. D. Home, The Medium*. New York: Knopf, 1944.

Cagliostro's Secret Ritual of Egyptian Rite Freemasonry. Kila, MT: Kessinger Publishing Co., n.d.

Cahagnet, L.-A. *The Celestial Telegraph; or, Secrets of the Life to Come Revealed Through magnetism: Wherein the Existence, the Form, the Occupations, of the Soul after its Separation from the Body are Proved by Many Years' Experiments, by the Means of Eight Ecstatic Somnambulists, who had Eighty Perceptions of Thirty-Six Deceased Persons of Various Conditions. A Description of Them, their Conversations, etc., with Proofs of their Existence in the Spiritual World*. 1850. Reprint, 2 vols. in 1. New York: Arno, 1976.

———. *Magnétisme: Encyclopédie Magnétique Spiritualiste Traitant Spécialement des Faits Psychologiques, Magie Magnétique, Swedenborgianisme, Nécromancie, Magie Céleste, etc.* 7 vols. Paris: Author and Germer Ballière, 1854/55–1862.

Cahen, C. "Note sur les origines de la communauté syrienne des Nusayris." *Revue des Etudes Islamiques* 38 (1970): 243–49.

Caldwell. "Re-Incarnation." *Banner of Light* 33, no. 16 (July 19, 1873): 3.

Campbell, Robert. *Phallic Worship: An Outline of the Worship of the Generative Organs, As Being, or as Representing, the Divine Creator, with Suggestions as to the Influence of the Phallic Idea on Religious Creeds, Ceremonies, Customs and Symbolism — Past and Present*. St. Louis, R. A. Campbell & Co., 1887.

Capron, E. W. *Modern Spiritualism: Its Facts and Fanaticisms, its Consistencies and Contradictions*. Boston: Bela Marsh, New York: Partridge & Brittan, 1854.

"Carried Off by Spiritualism." *Banner of Light* 4, no. 3 (October 16, 1858): 4.

"Case of John A. Lant, The." *Banner of Light* 28, no. 20 (February 12, 1876): 5.

"Caution. Pseudo-Occultist Societies." *The Theosophist* 7 (January 1887): 255–56.

Chacornac, Paul. *Eliphas Lévi, Rénovateur de l'occultisme*. Paris: Chacornac, 1926.

Chanel, Christian. "De la 'Fraternité Hermétique de Louxor' au 'Mouvement Cosmique': L'Oeuvre de Max Théon contribution à l'étude des courants ésotériques en Europe à la fin du XIXème siècle et au début du XXème siècle." Doctorat d'Etat, E.P.H.E., Section Ve, Paris, 1994.

Chase, Warren. "B. F. Hatch and the Mediums." *Banner of Light* 4, no. 1 (October 2, 1858): 4.

"Chelaship and Lay Theosophists." *The Theosophist* 4, no. 10 (July 1883, Supplement): 10–11.

Child, A. B. "Hashish." *Banner of Light* 4, no. 6 (January 22, 1859): 3.

———. "History of Mediums. No. 5. Miss Emma Hardinge." *Banner of Light* 3, no. 18 (July 31, 1858): 7–8.

———. "History of Mediums, No. 10: Dr. Charles Main." *Banner of Light* 4, no. 6 (November 6, 1858): 8, and 4, no. 7 November 13, 1858: 2.

———. *Whatever Is, Is Right*. Boston: Berry, Colby, and Co., 1861.

Christian Spiritualist, The. Edited by J. H. Toohey and Horace Day. Published by the Society for the Diffusion of Spiritual Knowledge. New York. Weekly, May 13, 1854, to May 2, 1857.

"Clairvoyance and Psychometry." *The Telegraph Papers* 6 (1855): 54.

Clark, U., ed. *The Spiritual Register for 1859, Facts, Philosophy, Statistics for Spiritualism*. Auburn and Boston, n.d.

Cleather, Alice Leighton. *H. P. Blavatsky: Her Life and Work for Humanity*. Calcutta: Thacker, Spink & Co., 1922.

Clement of Alexandria. *Stromateis*.

Clymer, R. Swinburne. *The August Fraternity. Order of the Rose Cross in America, and H. Spencer Lewis, The Baron Munchausen of the Occult*. Quakertown: Philosophical Publishing Co., n.d. [c. 1933].

———. *Book of Rosicruciae. A Correct History of the Fraternitas Rosae Crucis or Rosy Cross, the Men Who Made the Order Possible, and Those who Maintained the Fraternity throughout the Centuries. Together with the Fundamental Teachings of These Men according to the Actual Research in the Archives of the Fraternity*. 3 vols. Quakertown: Philosophical Publishing Co., 1946.

———. *The Divine Alchemy of Imperial Eulis, Esoteric, yet Practical, Instructions for the Transmutation of the Baser Metals Man's Gross Passions into the Pure and Shining Gold the Illuminated Soul of the Alchemists. The Randolphian Physician's Legacy to Mankind, and Asgill's Rules. Instructions in the Single and Double Breast Drill of the Initiates. For Students Only*. 5th Ed. Quakertown: Printed but not Published by Philosophical Publishing Co., n.d. [c. 1945].

———. *The Divine Mystery. The Gods, Known in Early Ages as the Incubi and Succubi, Now Known as the Elementals. Solving the Mystery of the*

Immaculate Conception and How it Was, and Is, Possible. Giving Full Instructions for Development, and How to Come into Touch with Elementals. Also, The Human Soul Before and After Death. Constitution of Man and the Universe. Key of Gospel. Gospel Initiation. According to Pistis Sophia. The Inner Mystery. Allentown: Philosophical Publishing Co., n.d. [c. 1910].

————. *Dr. R. Swinburne Clymer Replies to "Dr." H. Spencer Lewis, The Mystic Swindler and the A. M. A. Article. Being an Exposé of His attempted Misuse of that Article as a Shield of and in Perpetuation of His Own Insidious Fraud.* Quakertown: R. Swinburne Clymer, n.d. [c. 1935].

————. *The Fraternitatis Rosae Crucis. An Attempt to Harmonize the Spirit of the Writings of Those who are Known to have been Rosicrucians.* Quakertown: Philosophical Publishing Co., 1929.

————. "Fraternitas Rosae Crucis. An Outline History of the Men and Events Leading up to the Foundation of the Fraternity, Its Teachings and Activities to the Present Time." *The Initiates* 5 (May–June 1932–May–June 1941): 110–31.

————. "Gen. E. A. Hitchcock, First American Alchemist and Rosicrucian." *The Initiates* 3 (May–June 1930–May–June 1931): 1–25, 6.

————. *The Rose Cross Order. A Short Sketch of the History of the Rose Cross Order in America, together with a Sketch of the Life of Dr. P. B. Randolph, the Founder of the Order. Also a Short History of the Persecutions and Prosecutions, which Resulted in Giving Him Greater Freedom than he had Before, and which Trial Proved that the Things of which he had been Accused were False.* Allentown: Philosophical Publishing Co., 1916.

————. *The Rosicrucian Fraternity in America.* 2 vols. Quakertown, Rosicrucian Foundation, 1935.

————. *The Rosicrucians—Their Teachings. The Fraternitas Rosae Crucis. American Section. The Manifestoes Issued by the Brotherhood, Order, Temple and Fraternity of the Rosicrucians since its Foundation in America have been Edited and the Teachings Made Applicable to Modern Conditions and the needs of the New Age.* Revised ed. Quakertown: Philosophical Publishing Co., n.d. [1941].

————. *The Sons of God. The Mystical Interpretation of the Teachings of the Masters. A Foreshadowing of the Coming Work of the Messenger of the New Age.* Quakertown: Philosophical Publishing Co., n.d. [c. 1925].

————, ed. *Ravalette, the Rosicrucian's Story,* by Paschal Beverly Randolph. Quakertown: Philosophical Publishing Co., 1939.

————, ed. *Seership, Guide to Soul Sight. A Practical Guide for those who Aspire to Develop the Vision of the Soul. The Magic Mirror and How to Use It.* Quakertown: Confederation of Initiates, n.d. [c. 1930].

————, ed. *Soul! The Soul World,* by Paschal Beverly Randolph. Quakertown: Philosophical Publishing Co., 1932.

Cohausen, Johann Heinrich. *Hermippus Redivivus: or, The Sage's Triumph over Old Age and the Grave. Wherein a method is laid down for Prolonging* the *Life and Vigour of Man. Including a Commentary upon an Antient Inscription, in which this Secret is Revealed; Supported by numerous Authorities. The Whole Interspersed with a great Variety of Memorable and well Attested Relations.* Translated by John Campbell. 3d ed. London: J. Nourse, 1771.

Cohen, I. Bernard. "Ethan Allan Hitchcock." *Proceedings of the American Antiquarian Society* 61 (1951): 29–129.

Coleman, Benjamin. "Spiritualism in America." *Spiritual Magazine* 2, no. 9 (September 1861): 385ff.

Coleman, W.E. "Are the Truths of Modern Spiritualism Reliable?" 4 parts. *Religio-Philosophical Journal* 21, no. 17 (January 13, 1877): 1 and 8, through 21, no. 21 (February 3, 1877): 1.

———. "The Law of Immortality versus Re-Incarnation." *Banner of Light* 33, no. 17 (July 26, 1873): 8.

———. "Pseudo-Zodiacal Mysticism. The Star Alcyone.—Dr. Kenealy's 'Enoch.' The Zodiac of Denderah." *Religio-Philosophical Journal* 43, no. 16 (December 10, 1887): 1.

———. Review of *Beyond the Veil. The Truth Seeker* (March 30, 1878): 206.

Collins, D. Jean. "Divining the Beloved Community." *Gnosis Magazine* 25 (Fall 1992): 36–40.

"Conference of Aug. 8." *The Telegraph Papers* 6 (1855): 95–96.

Conger, Margaret. *Combined Chronology for Use with The Mahatma Letters to A. P. Sinnett and The Letters of H. P. Blavatsky to A. P. Sinnett.* Pasadena: Theosophical University Press, 1973.

"Convention of Colored Citizens." *Syracuse Daily Journal*, October 6, 1864, 2, and October 7, 1864, 2.

Cooke, C. *Curiosities of Occult Literature.* London: Arthur Hall, Smart, and Allen, n.d. [c. 1863].

Copenhaver, Brian P. *Hermetica. The Greek Corpus Hermeticum and the Latin Asclepius in a New English Translation, with Notes and Introduction.* Cambridge: Cambridge University Press, 1992.

Corbin, Henri. *Trilogie ismaelienne.* Tehran/Paris: 1961.

Corbyn, George. "Rosicrucianism." *Spiritual Scientist* 2, no. 22 (August 5, 1875): 257.

Corelli, Marie [Mary Mackay]. *Ardath, The Story of a Dead Self.* London: R. Bentley & Son, 1890.

———. *A Romance of Two Worlds.* London: R. Bentley & Son, 1887.

———. *The Soul of Lilith.* New York: F. M. Buckles & Co., 1892.

Cornish, D. T. *The Sable Arm: Negro Troops in the Union Army 1861–1865.* New York: Longman, 1956.

"Correction." *Religio-Philosophical Journal* 21, no. 7 (October 28, 1876): 54.

"Correction—Reincarnation, A." *Banner of Light* 33, no. 11 (July 5, 1873): 2.

Corson, Hiram. "The Theosophical Society and its President." *Banner of Light* 28, no. 15 (January 8, 1876): 2.

Couliano, I. P. *Expérience de l'Extase. Extase, Ascension et Récit Visionnaire de l'Hellénisme au Moyen Age.* Paris: Payot, 1984.

————. *Out of This World. Otherworldly Journeys from Gilgamesh to Albert Einstein.* Boston and London: Shambhala, 1991.

————. *The Tree of Gnosis: Gnostic Mythology from Early Christianity to Modern Nihilism.* San Francisco: Harper, 1992.

Courtney, W. S. "Individual Sovereignty." *The Telegraph Papers* 2 (1853): 296–308.

C[raddock], Ida. *Heavenly Bridegrooms. An Unintentional Contribution to the Erotic Interpretation of Religion.* Introduction by Theodore Schroeder. New York, 1918.

Craven, Avery. *The Coming of the Civil War.* Chicago: University of Chicago Press, 1957.

Crosland, Newton. *Apparitions: A New Theory.* 2d ed. London: E. Wilson, 1856.

"Crystal-Seeing in Lancashire." *Spiritual Magazine,* n.s., 1 (1866): 516–22.

Curry, Leonard P. *The Free Black in Urban America, 1800–1850: The Shadow of the Dream.* Chicago: University of Chicago Press, 1981.

Daftary, Farhad. *The Isma'ilis: Their History and Doctrines.* Cambridge: Cambridge University Press, 1990.

Daniel H. Caldwell, ed. *The Occult World of Madame Blavatsky.* Tucson: Impossible Dreams Publications, 1991.

D'Arch Smith, Timothy. *The Books of the Beast.* Wellingborough: Crucible, 1987.

Darnton, Robert. *Mesmerism and the End of the Enlightenment in France.* New York: Schocken, 1970.

"Daughter of P. B. Randolph, A." *Banner of Light* 29, no. 21 (August 19, 1876): 8.

Daumal, René. *Mount Analogue.* London: Vincent Stuart, 1959.

Davidson, Peter. "The Mysterious Brothers—An Old Tale Retold." *The Theosophist* 3, no. 5 (February 1882): 120–21, and 3, no. 6 (March 1882): 153–54.

Davies, John D. *Phrenology: Fad and Science. A 19th Century American Crusade.* N.p.: Archon Books, 1971.

Davis, Andrew Jackson. "Andrew Jackson Davis' Column." *Religio-Philosophical Journal* 26, no. 2 (March 15, 1879): 1.

————. *The Diakka, and their Earthly Victims; being an Explanation of Much that is False and Repulsive in Spiritualism.* 1873; Boston: Colby & Rich, 1886.

————. *Lectures on Clairmativeness. All the Mysteries of Human Magnetism and Clairvoyance explained by the celebrated Jackson Davis, of Poughkeepsie, New York.* New York, 1845.

————. "Old Testament Inconsistencies." *The Telegraph Papers* 2 (1853): 142–58.

————. "The Origin of the Devil." *The Spirit Messenger* 1, no. 6 (1853).

————. *Present Age and Inner Life: A Sequel to Spiritual Intercourse.* N.p.: C. Partridge, 1853.

————. *The Principles of Nature, Her Divine Revelations, and a Voice to Mankind.* New York: S. S. Lyon & W. Fishbough, 1847.

————. "Spiritual Perception of Nature in Clairvoyance." *Spiritual Magazine* 2, no. 9 (September 1861): 417ff.

"Declaration of Wrongs and Rights, Made by the Colored Men of the United States of America, in Convention Assembled, in Syracuse, N.Y., Oct. 4th, 1864." *Syracuse Daily Journal,* October 7, 1864, 2.

Delaage, Henri. *Perfectionnement physique de la Race Humaine*. Paris, 1850.

de la Rive, A. C. "Francmaçonnerie et Sociétés Secrètes." 15 Parts. *La France Antimaçonnique*, from 26, no. 23 (June 6, 1912) through 28, no. 30 (July 23, 1914) (some anonymous, and most published as "Notice sur les diverses Sociétés Secrètes américaines que ne sont officiellement rattachés à la Maçonnerie").

"Demolishing the Mahatmas." *O.E. Library Critic* 24, no. 3 (June–July 1936).

Denton, William and Elizabeth. *The Soul of Things; or Psychometric Researches and Discoveries*. 3 vols. 6th ed. Boston: Authors, 1873–75.

"Departed." *Banner of Light* 14, no. 24 (March 5, 1864): 3.

"Des Manifestations spirituelles des Etats-Unis d'Amérique." *La Table Parlante, Journal des Faits Marveilleux* 1 (1854): 78–87

"Destiny of Nations: A Prophetic Declaration." *Banner of Light* 28, no. 25 (August 27, 1870): 2.

Deveney, John Patrick. "A Note on Psychic Attacks." *Theosophical History* 5, no. 6 (April 1995): 194–97.

———. Review of C. G. Harrison, *The Transcendental Universe*. *Theosophical History* 5, no. 2 (April 1994): 40–41.

Dietrich, A. *Eine Mithrasliturgie*. 4th ed. Stuttgart, 1923.

Disraeli, Isaac. *Curiosities of Literature*. 3 vols. London: Routledge, Warnes, and Routledge, 1859.

Dixon, Jacob. "Clairvoyance as a Means of Cure." *Spiritual Magazine* 1, no. 11 (November 1860): 506–19.

———. "The Experiences of a Medium." *Spiritual Magazine* 2, no. 8 (August 1863): 360–69.

———. *Hygienic Clairvoyance*. London: W. Horsell, 1859.

———. Letter. *Spiritual Magazine* 2, no. 4 (April 1861): 191–92.

———. Letter. *Spiritual Magazine* 2, no. 12 (December 1861): 559.

———. "Robert Owen and the Spirits." *The Telegraph Papers* 2 (1853): 490–92.

———. "The Westminster Review and Spiritualism." *The Herald of Progress. Devoted to the Discovery and Application of Truth* (December 15, 1860): 2.

Dixon, William Hepworth. *Spiritual Wives*. 2d ed. Philadelphia: J. B. Lippincott & Co., 1868.

"Dr. P. B. Randolph." *Religio-Philosophical Journal* 28, no. 26 (September 11, 1875): 204.

"Dr. Thomas Docking." *Common Sense* 1, no. 15 (August 22, 1874): 175.

Dodds, E. R. *The Ancient Concept of Progress and other Essays in Greek Literature and Belief*. Oxford: Oxford University Press, 1975.

———. *The Greeks and the Irrational*. Berkeley and Los Angeles: University of California Press, 1951.

Doresse, Jean. *Les Livres Secrets des Gnostiques d'Egypte*. 2 vols. Paris: Plon, 1958.

Doten, Lizzie. "Poe's Poem." *Banner of Light* 8, no. 12 (December 15, 1860): 4.

Dowd, Freeman B. Advertisement. *Religio-Philosophical Journal* (June 15 through September 16, 1871).

———. Advertisement. *Woodhull & Claflin's Weekly* (April 19, 1873).

————. *The Double Man.* Boston, Arena Publishing Co., 1895.

————. "Letter from Davenport, Iowa." *Religio-Philosophical Journal* 3, no. 11 (December 8, 1966): 4.

———— [Try]. *Regeneration, Being Part II of the Temple of the Rosy Cross.* Salem: Eulian Publishing Co., n.d. [c. 1898]. Reprint, New York: The Temple Publishing Co., 1900.

————. *The Temple of the Rosy Cross.* Philadelphia: J. R. Rue, Jr., Printer, 1882; 2d ed. San Francisco: Rosy Cross Publishing Co., 1888. 3d ed. Chicago: Rosy Cross Publishing House, 1897. 4th ed. Salem: Eulian Publishing Co., 1901.

Doyle, A. C. *The History of Spiritualism.* 2 vols. New York, l926.

"Dr. Gully on the Late Lord Lytton's Relation to Spiritualism." *Spiritual Magazine,* n.s., 8 (1873): 235.

"Drift of Western Spiritualism, The." *The Theosophist* 1, no. 1 (October 1879): 7–8.

"Dr. P. B. Randolph." *Banner of Light* 6, no. 24 (March 10, 1860): 4.

"Dr. P. B. Randolph and his Work." *Religio-Philosophical Journal* 2, no. 22 (August 25, 1866): 4.

"Dr. P. B. Randolph and the Convention of the Southern Loyalists." *Religio-Philosophical Journal* 2, no. 26 (September 22, 1866): 5.

"Dr. Randolph Again." *Banner of Light* 4, no. 11 (December 11, 1858): 8.

"Dr. Randolph at Allston Hall." *Banner of Light* 8, no. 16 (January 19, 1861): 8.

"Dr. Randolph at the Melodeon." *Banner of Light* 4, no. 13 (December 25, 1858): 8.

"Dr. Randolph in Boston." *Banner of Light* 4, no. 11 (December 11, 1858): 4.

D[ulaure], J. A. *Des Divinités Génératrices, ou du culte du Phallus chez les Anciens et Modernes; Des cultes du dieu de Lampsaque, de Pan, de Vénus, etc.; Origine, motifs, conformités, raretés, progrès, altérations et abus de ces cultes chez différens peuples de la terre; de leur continuation chez les Indiens et les Chrétiens d'Europe; des moeurs des nations et des tems où ces cultes ont existé.* Paris: Dentu, 1805.

Dupotet, J. *La Magie Dévoilée, ou Principes de Science Occulte.* Paris: Editions Pygmalion, 1977.

Dussaud, René. *Histoire et Religion des Nosairis.* Paris: Emile Bouillon, 1900.

Dvorak, Josef. "Abstürze beim aufsteig zum feuropfer." *Tantra* (Zurich) (July 1994): 11–16.

Eckenrode, J. *The Randolphs: The Story of a Virginia Family.* Indianapolis: Bobbs-Merrill, 1946.

Edwardes, Allan, and R. E. L. Masters. *The Cradle of Erotica: A Study of Afro-Asian Sexual Expression and an Analysis of Erotic Freedom in Social Relationships.* New York: Bantam, 1977.

Egypt and the Holy Land in Historic Photograph: 77 Views by Francis Frith. Introduction by Julia Van Haaften, Commentary by Jon E. Manchip. White. New York: Dover, 1980.

Eliade, Mircea. "Significations de la 'Lumière Intérieure.'" *Eranos-Jahrbuch* 25 (1957): 189–242.

——. "Spirit, Light and Seed." *History of Religions* 11 (August 1971): 1–30. Reprinted in *Occultism, Witchcraft and Cultural Fashions: Essays in Comparative Religions*. Chicago and London: University of Chicago Press, 1976, 93–119.

Ellis, J. B. *Free Love and its Votaries; or, American Socialism Unmasked: Being an Historical and Descriptive Account of the Rise and Progress of the Various Free Love Associations in the U.S. and of the Effects of their Various Teachings upon American Spiritualism*. New York: U.S. Publishing Co., 1870.

Encausse Gérard [Papus]. "L'Occultisme contemporain en France." In *Sciences Maudits*. Edited by F. Jolivet-Castelot. Paris, Maison d'Art 1900.

Encausse, Philippe. *Sciences Occultes, ou 25 anneés d'occultisme occidental; Papus, sa vie, son oeuvre*. Paris: OCIA, 1949.

Englesman, John Cornelius. "The Freedmen's Bureau of Louisiana." *The Louisiana Historical Quarterly* 32, no. 1 (January 1949): 145–224.

"Esoteric Section and the Theosophical Society, The." *The Path* 3, no. 8 (November 1888): 263.

Everett, Donald E. "Demands of the New Orleans Free Colored Population for Political Equality, 1862–1865." *Louisiana Historical Quarterly* 38, no. 2 (April 1955): 43–64, 55.

Evola, J. *Magia Sexualis. Forme e Riti*. Roma: Edizioni Mediterranee, n.d. [c. 1977].

——. *The Metaphysics of Sex*. New York: Inner Traditions International, 1983.

"Existence of Elementaries to be Demonstrated, The." *Spiritual Scientist* 3, no. 18 (January 6, 1876): 214.

Fairchild, J. H. *Oberlin: The Colony and the College*. Oberlin, Ohio: E. J. Goodrich, 1883.

Falk, Maryla. *I 'Misteri' di Novalis*. Naples, 1939.

Fenno, A. W. "The Rosicrucians." *Banner of Light* 12, no. 24 (March 7, 1863): 8.

Festugière, A.-J. *La Révélation d'Hermès Trismégiste*. 4 vols. 2d ed. Paris: J. Gabalda, 1954.

"Final Correction, A." *The Liberator* 28, no. 53 (December 31, 1858): 211.

Fogliato, Angela M. "P. B. Randolph e la sua magia sessuale." In *La Nuova Italia 4, Il superuomo e i suoi simboli nella letteratura moderna* (1986):183–209.

Foner, Philip S., and George E. Walker, *Proceedings of the Black State Conventions, 1840–1865*. 2 vols. Philadelphia: Temple University Press, 1980.

Forlong, J. G. R. *Rivers of Life, or Sources and Streams of the Faiths of Man in all Lands; Showing the Evolution of Faiths from the Rudest Symbolisms to the Latest Spiritual Developments*. 2 vols. London: Quaritch, 1883.

Foster, W. Z. *The Negro People in American History*. New York: International Publishers, 1954.

Fowler, O. S. *Creative and Sexual Science: or, Manhood, Womanhood, and their Mutual Interrelations; Love, its Laws, Power, etc.; Selection, or Mutual Adaptation; Courtship, Married Life, and Perfect Children; Their Generation, Endowment, Paternity, Maternity, Bearing, Nursing, Rearing;*

Together with Puberty, Boyhood, Girlhood, etc.; Sexual Impairments Restored, Male Vigor and Female Health and Beauty Perpetuated and Augmented, etc., as Taught by Phrenology and Physiology. 1870. Reprint, Philadelphia and Chicago: Follett, 1971.

Francis, John R. *The Home Circle Fraternity, Evolution of a New Religion.* Chicago: Progressive Thinker Publishing House, 1910.

Franklin, John Hope, and Alfred A. Moss, Jr. *From Slavery to Freedom.* New York: Knopf, 1988.

Frater U∴D∴ *Secrets of the German Sex Magicians. A Practical Handbook for Men and Women.* St. Paul: Llewellan Publishing Co., 1991.

Fraxi, Pisanus [pseud.]. *Index Librorum Prohibitorum: Being Notes Bio- Biblio-Econo-graphical and Critical, on Curious and Uncommon Books.* 1877. Reprint, vol. 3. *The Encyclopedia of Erotic Literature.* New York: Documentary Books, n.d. [c. 1962].

"Free Love and Moral Degeneration." *Spiritual Scientist* 2, no. 26 (September 2, 1875): 306–7.

Frick, Karl R. H. Frick. *Die Erleuchteten. Gnostische-theosophische und alchemistisch-rosenkreuzerische Geheimgesellschaften bis zum Ende des 18. Jahrhunderts—ein Beitrag zur Geistesgeschichte der Neuzeit.* Graz: Akademische Druck, 1973.

———. *Licht und Finsternis. Gnostich-theosophische und freimaurerisch-okkulte Geheimgesellschaften bis an die Wende zum 20. Jahrhundert* 2 vols. Graz: Akademische Druck, 1975–78.

Frothingham, O. B. *Gerrit Smith. A Biography.* New York: G. P. Putnam's Sons, 1909.

Fryar, Robert H. "Crystal Gazing." *The Rosicrucian Brotherhood* 1, no. 4 (October 1907): 145ff. Also published in *Historic Magazine and Notes and Queries* 25, no. 10 (October 1907): 241–43.

———, ed. *The Assistant Génies, and Irreconcileable Gnomes, or Continuation to the Comte de Gabalis.* Translated and Introduction by John Yarker. Bath: Robert H. Fryar, 1897.

———, ed. *"Aureus": The Golden Tractate of Hermes Trismegistus. Concerning the Physical Secret of the Philosopher's Stone. In Seven Sections.* Introduction by John Yarker. Bath: Robert H. Fryar, 1886.

———, ed. *Continuation of the Comte de Gabalis, or New Discourses upon the Secret Sciences; Touching upon the New Philosophy. Posthumous Work.* Translated and Introduction by John Yarker. Bath: Robert H. Fryar, 1897.

———, ed. *The Divine Pymander of Hermes Mercurius Trismegistus.* Bath Occult Reprint Series. Introduction by Hargrave Jennings. Bath: R. H. Fryar, 1884.

———, ed. *Magnetic Magic, A Digest of the Practical Parts of the Masterpieces of L. A. Cahagnet, H.F.T.S., "Arcanes de la future dévoilés," and "Magie Magnétique."* Now translated for the first time from the French by the Editor, with the portrait of the Author. N.p.: Privately Printed for Subscribers, 1898.

————, ed. *Sexagyma, A Digest of the Works of John Davenport—"Curiositates Eroticae Physiologiae" and "Aphrodisiacs and Anti-Aphrodisiacs," with a Bio-Bibliographical Memoir of the Author.* Privately Printed for Subscribers, 1888.

————, ed. *Sub-Mundanes or the Elementaries of the Cabala. Unabridged. An esoteric work. Physio-Astro-Mystic. Annotated from the suppressed work of Father Sinistrari on "Incubi and Succubi."* Bath, 1886.

————, ed. *Supernatural Generation.* N.p.: Privately Printed for the Editor, 1896.

————. "Visions in Mirrors and Crystals." *Religio-Philosophical Journal* 25, no. 1 (September 7, 1878): 6.

Fuller, Jean Overton. *Blavatsky and Her Teachers.* London and the Hague: East-West Publications, 1988.

Fuller, Robert C. *Mesmerism and the American Cure of Souls.* Philadelphia: University of Pennsylvania Press, 1982.

Funk, D. M. "Cahagnet's 'Celestial Telegraph.' " *Banner of Light* 34, no. 2 (November 11, 1873): 3.

Gardner, F. Leigh. "The Magic Mirror." *Historic Magazine and Notes and Queries* (1905): 260–62.

————. *A Catalogue Raisonné of Works on the Occult Sciences.* 3 vols. 1923. Reprint, First Impressions, 1992.

Gardner, H. F. "P. B. Randolph in Boston." *Banner of Light* 6, no. 7 (November 12, 1859): 4.

Garver, Will. *Brother of the Third Degree.* 1894. Reprint, Chicago: Metaphysical Library, 1946.

Geyraud, Pierre. *Les Sociétés Secrètes de Paris.* Paris: Editions Emile Paul Frères, 1938.

————. *L'Occultisme à Paris.* Paris: Editions Emile-Paul Frères, 1953.

"Ghost Land." *Spiritual Scientist* 5, no. 14 (December 7, 1875): 145, 147.

Gibb, H. A. R., and J. H. Kramers, eds. *Shorter Encyclopaedia of Islam.* Ithica: 1953, s.v. "Nusairi."

Gilbert, R. A. *The Golden Dawn and the Esoteric Section.* London: Theosophical History Centre, 1987.

Ginzburg, Carlo. *Ecstacies: Deciphering the Witches' Sabbath.* New York: Pantheon, 1991.

Giraud, Jules. "Testament d'un Haschischéen." *L'Initiation* 1, no. 2 (1889): 59–70.

Gnostic, The, Devoted to Theosophy, Spiritualism, Occult Phenomena and the Cultivation of the Higher Life." Edited by George Chainey, W. J. Colville, and Anna Kimball. Vol. 1, no. 11 (July 1888). San Francisco.

Gobineau, Joseph-Arthur de. *Essai sur l'inégalité des races humaines.* 4 vols. Paris, 1853–1855.

Godwin, *Arktos, The Polar Myth in Science, Symbolism and Nazi Survival.* Grand Rapids: Phanes Press, 1993.

————. *The Beginnings of Theosophy in France.* London: Theosophical History Centre, 1989.

———. "Colonel Olcott Meets the Brothers: An Unpublished Letter." *Theosophical History* 4, no. 1 (January 1994):5–9.

———. "From the Archives. H. P. Blavatsky Writes to 'M. A. Oxon.': An Unpublished Letter." *Theosophical History* 4, nos. 6–7 (April 1993): 172–77.

———. "Hargrave Jennings." *Hermetic Journal* (1991): 49–77.

———. "The Hidden Hand." *Theosophical History* 3, nos. 2–5 (April 1990–January 1991): 35–43, 66–76, 107–17, 137–48.

———. *The Theosophical Enlightenment*. Albany: State University of New York Press, 1994.

Godwin, Joscelyn, Christian Chanel, and John Patrick Deveney. *The Hermetic Brotherhood of Luxor. Initiatic and Historical Documents of an Order of Practical Occultism*. New York: Samuel Weiser, 1995.

Goldfarb, R. M. and C. R. *Spiritualism and Nineteenth Century Letters*. New Jersey, 1978.

Gomes, Michael. "Abner Doubleday and Theosophy in America: 1879–1884." *Sunrise* (April/May 1991): 151ff.

———. *Dawning of the Theosophical Movement*. Wheaton: Quest Books, 1987.

———. "The History of a Humbug, The Letters of H. P. Blavatsky to Elliott Coues." *Canadian Theosophist*, 9 parts, from 65, no. 4 (September–October 1984): 73–76, through (January–February 1986): 127–37.

———. Introduction and notes to H. P. Blavatsky, "Crows in Peacock Feathers." *Canadian Theosophist* 66, no. 5 (November–December, 1985): 114–17.

———. "Studies in Early American Theosophical History. *Canadian Theosophist*, 7 parts, from 69, no. 6 (January–February 1989): 121–29, through 71, no. 4 (September–October 1990): 80.

———. *Theosophy in the Nineteenth Century: An Annotated Bibliography*. New York: Garland Publishing, 1994.

———. Transcriber, and introduction to "Fragments from H. P. B.'s 'Mystical History.'" *The Theosophist* (September 1991): 552–60. Part 5 of a seven-part series.

Goodwin, R. D. "The Rosicrucians." *Religio-Philosophical Journal* 34, no. 10 (May 19, 1883): 6.

Gougenot des Mousseaux, Henri-Roger. *La Magie au dix-neuvième siècle, ses Agents, ses Vérités, ses Mensonges*. Paris: E. Dentu, 1860.

Gould, Sylvester Clark. *Alcyone in the Pleiades. The Grand Central Sun*. Manchester, NH, 1893.

———. "Order of Eulis." *Historic Magazine and Notes and Queries* (April 1905): 98.

———. Resumé of Arcane Fraternities in the United States." *Historic Magazine and Notes and Queries*, various numbers, including (1896): 272, (1900): 129, and (1905): 90, and *The Rosicrucian Brotherhood* (1907): 323, and (1908): 161.

Grandin, D. S. "John Randolph." *The Liberator* 28, no. 45 (November 5, 1858): 177.

——. "Randolph Again." *The Liberator* 28, no. 47 (November 19, 1858): 187.

——. "The Wrong Man Impeached." *The Liberator* 28, no. 49 (December 3, 1858): 195.

"Grand Mass Meeting at Economy Hall." *New Orleans Tribune*, December 3, 1864, 2.

"Great Meeting of the Colored People at Economy Hall, . . . The Oration of Dr. P. B. Randolph, of New York." *New Orleans Era*, December 3, 1864, 2.

Guénon, René [A. W. Y., Abdel Wahed Yahia]. "Les trois montagnes sacrées: Sinaï, Moriah, Tabor," *The Speculative Mason* (January 1937).

——. "F.-Ch. Barlet et les Sociétés Initiatiques." *Voile d'Isis* 64 (April 1925): 217ff. Reprinted in Godwin, Chanel and Deveney, *The Hermetic Brotherhood of Luxor*.

——. *L'Erreur Spirite*. 1923. Reprint, Paris: Editions Traditionnelles, 1952.

——. "Rose-Croix et Rosicruciens." *Le Voile d'Isis* (May 1931): 275ff.

——. *Le Théosophisme, Histoire d'une Pseudo-Religion*. Augmented edition. Paris: Editions Traditionnelles, 1969.

Hall, Lesly A. "Forbidden by God, Despised by Men: Masturbation, Medical Warnings, Moral Panic and Manhood in Great Britain, 1850–1900." In J. D. Font, ed., *Forbidden History. The State, Society, and the Regulation of Sexuality in Modern Europe*. University of Chicago Press, 1992.

Halm, Heinz. *Die islamische Gnosis: Die extreme Schia und die 'Alawiten*. Zurich: Artemis, 1982

Hamill, John, ed. *The Rosicrucian Seer: The Magical Work of Frederick Hockley*. With a bibliographical note by R. A. Gilbert. Wellingborough: Aquarian Press, 1986.

Hammer, Joseph von. *Die Geschichte der Assassinen aus Morgenländischen Quellen*. Stuttgart and Tübingen, 1818.

Harris, Thomas Lake. *The Lord: The Two-in-One*. Salem-on-Erie, NY: Brotherhood of the New Life, 1876.

——. *The Wisdom of the Adepts. Esoteric Science in Human History*. Fountain Grove: Privately Printed, 1884.

Harrison, C. G. *The Transcendental Universe. Six Lectures on Occult Science, Theosophy, and the Catholic Faith, Delivered before the Berean Society*. 1894. Reprint, Edited with an Introduction by Christopher Bamford. Hudson, New York: Lindisfarne Press, 1993.

Hasluck, F. W. *Christianity and Islam Under the Sultans*. 2 vols. 1929. Reprint, New York: Octagon Books, 1973.

Hatch, Benjamin Franklin. "Obsession of Evil Spirits." *Banner of Light* 3, no. 26 (September 25, 1858): 7.

——. *Spiritualists' Iniquities Unmasked and the Hatch Divorce Case*. New York: Author, 1859.

Hayden, William. "Letter from England." *The Telegraph Papers* 2 (1853): 403–5.

——. "Seven Years with the Spirits in the Old and New World; Being a Narrative of the Visit of Mrs. W. R. Hayden to England, France and Ireland; with a Brief Account of her Early Experience as a

Medium for Spirit Manifestations in America." *Banner of Light,* various numbers from 1, no. 7 (May 21, 1857): 6–7, through 2, no. 10 (December 5, 1857): 6.

"Heroic Women." *New York Mercury,* January 18, 1875. Reprinted in *BCW,* 1:53–54.

Heywood, E. H. *Cupit's Yokes: or, The Binding Forces of Conjugal Life, An Essay to Consider Some Moral and Physiological Phases of Love and Marriage, Wherein is Asserted the Natural Right and Necessity of Sexual Self-Government.* Princeton, MA: Co-Operative Publishing Co., 1878.

Higgins, Godfrey. *Anacalypsis, An Attempt to Draw Aside the Veil of Saitic Isis; or, An Inquiry into the Origins of Languages, Nations, and Religions.* 2 vols. London: Longman, Rees, Orme, Brown, Green, and Longman, 1833–1836.

———. *The Celtic Druids.* London: Rowland Hunter, 1829.

Hitchcock, E. A. *Remarks on Alchemy and the Alchemists.* Boston: Crosby, Nichols & Co., 1857.

Hitti, Philip K. *The Origins of the Druze People and Religion.* Columbia University Oriental Studies, vol. 28. New York, 1928.

Hockley, F. "On the Ancient Magic Crystal, and its Connexion with Mesmerism." *The Zoist* 8 (1849): 251–66.

Hodgson, M. G. S. *The Order of Assassins.* Se'Gravenhage, 1955.

Home, D[aniel] D[unglas]. "From Moscow." *Religio-Philosophical Journal* 36, no. 4 (March 22, 1884): 8.

———. *Incidents in My Life.* London: Longman, Green, Longman, Roberts & Green, 1863.

Hopfner, Th. *Griechische-ägyptischer Offenbarungszauber,* Studien zum Paläographie und Papyruskunde, nos. 21, 23. 2 vols. Leipzig: H. Haessel-Verlag 1921–24.

Howe, Ellic. *Astrology: A Recent History, Including the Untold Story of its Role in World War II.* New York: Walker & Co., 1967.

———. "Fringe Masonry in England, 1870–85." *Ars Quatuor Coronatorum* 85 (1972): 242–95.

———, and Helmut Möller. "Theodor Reuss: Irregular Freemasonry in Germany, 1900–1923." *Ars Quattor Coronatorum* 91 (1978): 28–46.

Howitt, William. *The History of the Supernatural in All Ages and Nations, and in All Churches, Christian and Pagan: Demonstrating a Universal Faith.* 2 vols. London: Longman, Green, Longman, Roberts & Green, 1863.

———. "Spirites, Fusionists, and Re-Incarnationists in France." *Spiritual Magazine,* n.s., 1 (1866): 17–27.

Hume, A. O. "A Buddhist Catechism." *The Theosophist* 2 (September 1881): 270–71.

Humphreys, Hugh C. "'Agitate! Agitate! Agitate!' The Great Fugitive Slave Law Convention and its Rare Daguerreotype." *Madison County Heritage* 19 (1994): 1–64.

Hutchinson, L. "Causerie sur l'au-dela." *L'Initiation* 5, vol. 17 (1892): 244ff.

————. "Notice sur le Mage Eliphas Lévi." *L'Initiation* 5, vol. 16 (1892): 127ff.

Hutchinson, Luna. "Bishop Creek, Cal." *Religio-Philosophical Journal* 18, no. 20 (July 17, 1875): 142.

————. "Letter from Luna Hutchinson." *Religio-Philosophical Journal* 18, no. 17 (July 10. 1875): 131.

————. "Bishop Creek, Cal.—L. Hutchinson Writes." *Religio-Philosophical Journal* 19, no. 2 (September 2, 1875): 221.

————. "P. B. Randolph." *Religio-Philosophical Journal* 22, no. 1 (March 17, 1877): 6.

Hutchinson, Luna, and Fanny Green, eds. *Beyond the Veil: Posthumous Work of P.B. Randolph, Aided by Emanuel Swedenborg and Others, Through the Minds of Frances H. McDougall and Luna Hutchinson.* New York: D. M. Bennett, 1878.

Hyde, Thomas. *Historia Religionis Veterum Persarum Eorumque Magorum.* Oxford, 1700.

Idel, Moshe. *Hasidism: Between Ecstasy and Magic.* Albany: State University of New York Press, 1995.

————. *The Mystical Experience in Abraham Abulafia.* Albany: State University of New York Press, 1988.

————. *Studies in Ecstatic Kabbalah.* Albany: State University of New York Press, 1988.

"Important Note." *BCW,* 1:73

"Important Question, An." *Spiritual Scientist* 3, no. 4 (September 30, 1875): 42–43.

Initiates, The. A Rosicrucian Magazine. Edited by R. Swinburne Clymer. Allentown, April 1908–September 1910.

————. *The Initiates. A Magazine Issued by Authority of the Rosicrucian Fraternity and Devoted to Mysticism, Occultism and the Well-Being of Man.* Edited by R. Swinburne Clymer. Quakertown, 5 Vols. May-June 1928-May-June 1941.

————. *The Initiates and the People. A Magazine Teaching Religious and Philosophic Truths in Harmony with the Divine Law and the Mystical Interpretation, as taught by the Temple of Illuminati and the Church of Illumination. Try.* Edited by R. Swinburne Clymer. Allentown. September 1912–September 1912.

Inman, Thomas. *Ancient Pagan and Modern Christian Symbolism.* 4th ed. Revised and Expanded. N.p., 1922.

"Interesting Lecture." *New Orleans Tribune,* December 11, 1864, 3.

Introvigne, "Arcana Arcanorum: Cagliostro's Legacy in Contemporary Magical Movements." *Syzygy: Journal of Alternative Religion and Culture* 1, nos. 2–3 (1992): 117–35.

————. *Il Cappello del Mago: I Nuovi Movimenti Magici, Dallo Spiritismo al Satanismo.* Milan: SugarCo Ed., 1990.

————. *Il Ritorno dello Gnosticismo.* Milan: SugarCo Ed., 1993.

Isaacs, E. J. *A History of Nineteenth-Century American Spiritualism as a Religious and Social Movement.* Ann Arbor: University Microfilms, 1975.

"Isis Unveiled." *Religio-Philosophical Journal* 23, no. 16 (March 2, 1878): 2.

Jacquart, Danielle, and Claude Thomasset. *Sexuality and Medicine in the Middle Ages.* Princeton: Princeton University Press, 1988.

Jamieson, W. F. Advertisement. *Banner of Light* 12, no. 21 (February 14, 1863): 8.

———. "Correspondence." *Banner of Light* 12, no. 26 (March 21, 1863): 3.

———. *Was Jesus Christ A Democrat?* Boston: W. F. Jamieson, 1874.

Jennings, Hargrave. *The Childishness and Brutality of the Times. Some Plain Truths in Plain Language.* London: Vizetelly & Co., 1883. Reprint, Kessinger Publishing Co., n.d.

——— ["F.R.C. Rosicrucian"]. *Curious Things of the Outside World. Last Fire.* 2 vols. London: T. & W. Boone, 1861; *Curious Things of the Outside World; The Rosicrucians, Their Rites and Mysteries.* London: Hotten, 1870.

——— ["An Indian Missionary"]. *The Indian Religions, or, Results of the Mysterious Buddhism.* London: T. C. Newby, 1858. 2d ed., Revised and Enlarged. London: Redway, 1890.

———. *The Letters of Hargrave Jennings, Author of "The Rosicrucians," "Phallicism," &c., &c. Forming the Unabridged Correspondence with the Editor of the Bath Occult Reprints, between 1879 and 1887, with Frontispiece.* Preface by "Invictus" and Introduction by John Yarker. Bath: Robert H. Fryar, 1895.

———. *Live Lights or Dead Lights: Altar or Table?* London: John Hodges, 1873.

———. *One of the Thirty: A Strange History, Now for the First Time Told.* London: J. C. Hotten, n.d. [c. 1873].

———. *Phallicism, Celestial and Terrestrial, Heathen and Christian. Its Connexion with the Rosicrucians and the Gnostics and its Foundation in Buddhism.* London: Redway, 1884.

———. *The Rosicrucians, Their Rites and Mysteries.* Mokelumne Hill: Health Research, 1966.

Jinarajadasa, C. *The Golden Book of the Theosophical Society, A Brief History of the Society's Growth from 1875—1925.* Adyar: Theosophical Publishing House, 1925.

———, ed. *H. P. B. Speaks.* 2 vols. Adyar: Theosophical Publishing House, 1950–51.

———, ed. *Letters from the Masters of Wisdom, First Series.* 1919. Reprint, Adyar: Theosophical Publishing House, 1988.

———, ed. *Letters from the Masters of Wisdom, Second Series.* 1925. Reprint, Adyar: Theosophical Publishing House, 1977.

"John Murray Spear." *Banner of Light* 33, no. 17 (July 26, 1873): 4.

John the Rosicrucian. "P. B. Randolph." *Religio-Philosophical Journal* 20, no. 7 (April 29, 1876): 54.

Johnson, G. W. "Shall Mediums Come to California." *Banner of Light* 10, no. 10 (November 30, 1861): 4.

Johnson, K. Paul. "Albert Leighton Rawson." *Theosophical History* 2, no. 7 (July 1988): 229–51.

———. *In Search of the Masters: Behind the Occult Myth.* South Boston, VA: Author, 1990.

————. *The Masters Revealed: Madame Blavatsky and the Myth of the Great White Lodge*. Albany: State University of New York Press, 1994.

Johnston, Johanna. *Mrs. Satan: The Incredible Saga of Victoria C. Woodhull*. New York: Popular, 1967.

Jonsson, Inge. "New Jerusalem in the World." In *Emanuel Swedenborg: A Continuing Vision*. Edited by R. Larsen et al. New York: Swedenborg Foundation, 1988.

"Joseph Barker in America." *Spiritual Magazine* 3, no. 5 (May 1862): 219–28.

Josephus. *Antiquities of the Jews*.

Judge, William Quan. *Echoes of the Orient: The Writings of William Quan Judge*. Edited by Dara Eklund. 3 vols. San Diego: Point Loma Publications, 1975–1987.

————. "Lo Here! And Lo There." *The Path* 4, no. 1 (April 1889): 1–6.

————. "Mesmerism." *Lucifer* 10 (May 1892): 197–205.

————. *Practical Occultism: From the Private Letters of W. Q. Judge*. Edited by Arthur L. Conger. Pasadena: Theosophical University Press, 1980.

Jung-Stilling, Johann Heinrich. *The Life of John Henry Stilling*. Gettysburg: Press of the Theological Seminary, 1831.

Kaplen, Fred. *Dickens and Mesmerism: The Hidden Springs of Fiction*. Princeton: Princeton University Press, 1975.

Kern, Louis J. *An Ordered Love: Sex Roles and Sexuality in Victorian Utopias—the Shakers, the Mormons, and Oneida Community*. Chapel Hill: University of North Carolina Press, 1981.

Kerr, Howard. *Mediums, and Spirit-Rappers, and Roaring Radicals. Spiritualism in American Literature, 1850–1900*. Urbana: University of Illinois Press, 1972.

Kerr, Howard, and Charles L. Crow, eds. *The Occult in America: New Historical Perspectives*. Urbana: University of Illinois Press, 1983.

Kieckhefer, Richard. *Magic in the Middle Ages*. Cambridge: Cambridge University Press, 1989.

Kieswetter, Karl. *Geschichte des Neuren Occultismus*. 2 vols. 1891–95. Reprint, New York: Arno 1976.

————. "Magische Räucherungen." *Der Sphinx. Monatschrift für die geschichtliche und experimentale Begründung übersinnlichen Weltanschauung auf monistischer Grundlage* 1 (1886): 219ff.

Killits, John M. *Toledo & Lucas County, Ohio, 1623–1923*. Chicago and Toledo: S. J. Clarke Publishing Co., 1923.

Kimball, Anna. Advertisement. "Electric and Magnetic Treatment." *Religio-Philosophical Journal* 11, no. 11 (December 2, 1871): 7.

King, C. W. *The Gnostics and Their Remains, Ancient and Medieval*. San Diego: Wizard, 1982.

King, Francis. *Ritual Magic in England, 1887 to the Present Day*. London: Spearman, 1970.

————. *Sexuality, Magic and Perversion*. Secaucus: Citadel, 1974.

King, Francis X. *The Flying Sorcerer, Being the Magical and Aeronautical Adventures of Francis Barrett, Author of the Magus*. London: Mandrake, 1992.

Klaw, Spencer. *Without Sin*. New York: Allen Lane Press, 1993.

Knight, Richard Payne. *A Discourse on the Worship of Priapus and its Connection with the Mystic Theology of the Ancients*. 1786. Reprint [with Thomas Wright], *Sexual Symbolism: A History of Phallic Worship*. New York: Julien Press, 1957.

————. *An Enquiry into the Symbolical Language of Ancient Art and Mythology*. London: Black & Armstrong, 1836.

König, Peter-Robert. "The OTO Phenomenon." *Theosophical History* 4, no. 3 (July 1992): 92–98.

————. "Theodor Reuss as Founder of Esoteric Orders." *Theosophical History* 4, nos. 6–7 (April–July 1993): 187–93.

————. "Stranded Bishops." *Theosophical History* 5, no. 5 (January 1995): 169–75.

————. "Veritas Mystica Maxima." *Theosophical History* 5, no. 1 (January 1994): 23–29.

Lane, E. W. *An Account of the Manners and Customs of the Modern Egyptians*. 5th ed. London: John Murray, 1860.

[Langford-Holloway, Laura C.] "Helena Petrovna Blavatsky: a Reminiscence." *The Word* (December 22, 1915): 136–53.

"Last Leaf from Our Journal, The." *The Yorkshire Spiritual Telegraph* 3, no. 11 (February 8, 1857): 148–50.

Laurent, Émile, and Paul Nagour. *L'Occultisme et l'Amour*. Paris: Vigot Frères, 1902.

"Law of Immortality versus Re-Incarnation, a Lecture by William Emmette Coleman, Criticized and Reviewed." *Banner of Light* 33, no. 25 (September 20, 1873): 8.

Lay Chela, A [pseud.]. "Fragments of Occult Truth." *The Theosophist*, 8 parts and a supplement from 3, no. 1 (October 1881): 17–22, through 4, no. 9 (July 1883): 252–53.

Layard, [Austin] Henry. *Early Adventures in Persia, Susiana, and Babylon*. 2 vols. London, 1887.

"Lecture by Dr. P. B. Randolph." *New Orleans Tribune*, January 14, 1866, 1.

"Lectures on Spiritualism, &c." *New England Spiritualist* 1, no. 37 (December 15, 1855).

Lefébure, E. "Le miroir d'encre dans la magie Arabe." *Revue Africaine* 49 (1905): 205–27.

Le Forestier, René. *La Franc-Maçonnerie Templière et occultiste aux XVIIIe et XIXe siècles*. Paris: Aubier, Eds. Montaigne, 1970.

Le Loup, Yvon [Paul Sédir]. *Histoire et doctrines des Rose-Croix*. Lyon, 1932.

————. *Les miroirs magiques*. Paris: Chamuel, 1895.

"Le Spiritualisme en Amérique." *Journal du Magnétisme* 15 (1856): 43–44, 364–76.

Lehman, Neil B. *The Life of John Murray Spear: Spiritualism and Reform in Antebellum America*. Ann Arbor: University Microfilms, 1973.

Lepinte, Christian. *Goethe et l'occultisme*. Paris: Les Belles Lettres, 1957.

Lesky, Erna. *Die Zeugungs- und Vererbungslehren der Antiken und ihre Nachwirken*. Wiesbaden, 1956.

Letter. *The Yorkshire Spiritual Telegraph* 3, no. 11 (February 8, 1857): 153–54.

"Letter from New York." *Banner of Light* 3, no. 3 (April 17, 1858): 5.

Lévi, Eliphas. *The History of Magic, Including a Clear and Precise Exposition of its Procedure, Its Rites and Its Mysteries.* Translated by A. E. Waite. New York: Weiser, 1973.

———. *Transcendental Magic: Its Doctrine and Ritual.* Translated by A. E. Waite. Chicago: Occult Publishing House, 1910.

Lewis, H. S. *Rosicrucian Questions and Answers.* 2d ed. San Jose: AMORC, 1932.

Liljegren, S. B. *Bulwer-Lytton's Novels and Isis Unveiled.* Upsala, Copenhagen, and Cambridge: Harvard University Press, 1957.

Lloyd, J. W. *The Karezza Method, or Magnetation. The Art of Connubial Love.* Roscoe, CA: Author, 1931.

Lord, Cyrus. "Dr. P. B. Randolph Controls Mediums." *Religio-Philosophical Journal* 28, no. 25 (September 4, 1875): 195.

"Lord Lytton." *Spiritual Magazine*, n.s., 8 (1873): 130.

Loth, David. *The Erotic in Literature: A Historical Survey of Pornography, as Delightful as It Is Indelicate.* New York: Julien Messner, 1961.

Lucas, Paul. *Voyage du sieur Paul Lucas, fait par l'ordre du Roy dans la Grèce, l'Asie Mineure la Maçedoine et l'Afrique.* 2 vols. Paris: Nicholas Simant, 1712).

Ludlow, Fitz Hugh. *The Hasheesh Eater: Being Passages from the Life of a Pythagorean.* 1857. Reprint, San Francisco: City Lights, 1979.

Lyde, Samuel. *The Anseyreeh and Ismaeleh: A Visit to the Secret Sects of Northern Syria with a View to the Establishment of Schools.* London: Hurst & Blackett, 1853.

———. *The Asian Mystery, Illustrated in the History, Religion, and Present State of the Ansaireeh or Nusairis of Syria.* London: Longman, Green, Longman, and Roberts, 1860.

Lytton, Earl. *The Life of Edward Bulwer.* 2 vols. London: Macmillan, 1913.

Lytton, Edward Bulwer-. *Zanoni.* Philadelphia, n.d.

"M. Regazzoni et le Magnétisme à Francfort." *Journal du Magnétisme* 14 (1855): 8–19.

M. A. Cantab. [pseud.]. "Dr. Wyld's New Book." *The Theosophist* 2, no. 5 (February 1881): 107–10.

Mackay, Charles. *Memoirs of Extraordinary Popular Delusions and the Madness of Crowds.* 2d ed. London: Office of the National Illustrated Library, 1852.

———. *The Salamandrine, or, Love and Immortality.* London: How & Parsons, 1842.

Mackay, Earnest A. *The Civil War and New York City.* Syracuse: Syracuse University Press, 1990.

Mackenzie, Kenneth R. H. "Leaves from a Spirit Diary, Leaf the First." *Spiritual Magazine* 1, no. 6 (June 1860): 281–85.

———. "A Retrospect of Spiritual Appearances and Manifestations." *Spiritual Magazine* 2, no. 6 (June 1861): 257–60.

———. *The Royal Masonic Cyclopædia.* 1877. Reprint, introduction by John Hamill and R. A. Gilbert. Wellingborough: Aquarian Press, 1987.

———. "Spiritualism in Paris." *Spiritual Magazine* 3, no. 2 (February 1862): 94–95.

———. "Spirituo-Magnetic Attraction." *Spiritual Magazine* 1, no. 4 (April 1860):174ff.

Mackey, Albert G. "The Origin of the Rosicrucians." *The Rosicrucian Brotherhood* 1, no. 1 (January 1907): 3ff.

"Magia Sexualis." *La Flèche*, March 15, 1933.

"Magic Mirror, A." *Spiritual Scientist* 2, no. 13 (June 3, 1875):150. Reprinted in the *New York Sun*, June 30, 1875, 2.

Magoon, William. "Cora V. Randolph." *Banner of Light* 29, no. 23 (September 12, 1876): 3.

Mahatma Letters to A. P. Sinnett from The Mahatmas M. & K. H., The. Transcribed and compiled by A. T. Barker, In Chronological Sequence. Arranged and edited by Vincente Hao Chin, Jr. Quezon City, Philippines: Theosophical Publishing House, 1993.

Mahatma Letters to A. P. Sinnett from The Mahatmas M. & K. H., The. Transcribed and compiled by A. Trevor Barker. 1923. Reprint, Pasadena: Theosophical University Press, 1975.

Main, Charles. Advertisement. *The New England Spiritualist* (January 26, 1856).

———. "Hygienic Institute for the Treatment of Every Known Disease." *Banner of Light* 11, no. 13 (June 21, 1862): 7.

Mani, Swami Narad. Chef de l'Observatoire secret européen de la "True Truth Samaj" d'Adyar [pseud.]. "Baptême de Lumière, Notes pour servir à l'Histoire de la Société dite Théosophique." *La France Antimaçonnique*, from 25, no. 43 (October 26, 1911), through 26, no. 9 (February 29, 1912).

Mann, W. Edward. *Orgone, Reich and Eros. Wilhelm Reich's Theory of Life Energy*. New York: Simon and Schuster, 1973.

Manuel, Frank E., and Fritzie P. Manuel. *Utopian Thought in the Western World*. Cambridge: Harvard University Press, 1979.

Marcus, Steven. *The Other Victorians. A Study of Sexuality and Pornography in Mid-Nineteenth-Century England*. New York: Basic Books, 1966.

Maskelyne, J. N. *The Fraud of Modern "Theosophy" Exposed. A Brief History of the Greatest Imposture Ever Perpetuated under the Cloak of Religion*. London: George Routledge & Sons, n.d. [c. 1912].

———. *Modern Spiritualism. A Short Account of its Rise and Progress, with Some Exposures of So-Called Spirit Media*. London: Frederick Warne, n.d. [c. 1876].

Massey, C. C. [C. C. M.]. "Theosophy and Spiritualism." *The Theosophist* 2, no. 12 (August 1881): 260.

Massignon, Louis. "Doctrines Gnostiques in Islam." *Eranos-Jahrbuch* 1937.

———. *Mélanges Louis Massignon*. 2 vols. Damascus, Institut Français, 1957.

———. "Les Nusayris." In *Elaboration de l'Islam*. Paris, 1969.

Maxey, Alicia. "Peterboro has Place in Black History." *Syracuse Herald American*, February 19, 1995, C1–C2.

McCormick, Donald. *The Temples of Love*. New York: Citadel, 1965.

McCrary, Peyton. *Abraham Lincoln and Reconstruction: The Louisiana Experiment*. Princeton: Princeton University Press, 1978.

McDougall, Frances H., and Luna Hutchinson, eds. *Beyond the Veil: Posthumous Work of Paschal Beverly Randolph. Aided by Emanuel Swedenborg and Others, Through the Minds of Frances H. McDougall and Luna Hutchinson*. New York: D.M. Bennett, 1878.

McDougall, Frances H. Green. "Letter from Fanny Green." *The Spiritual Telegraph* (February 26, 1859): 435.

McIntosh, Christopher. *Eliphas Lévi and the French Occult Revival*. London: Rider, 1972.

———. *The Rose Cross and the Age of Reason. Eighteenth-Century Rosicrucianism in Central Europe and its Relationship to the Enlightenment*. Leiden: E. J. Brill, 1992.

———. *The Rosicrucians: The History and Mythology of an Occult Order*. Wellingborough: Crucible, 1987.

McKitrick, Eric L. *Andrew Johnson and Reconstruction*. Chicago: University of Chicago Press, 1960.

McLean, Adam, ed. *A Treatise on Angel Magic: Being a Complete Transcription of Ms. Harley 6482 in the British Library*. Grand Rapids: Phanes Press, 1990.

McPherson, James M. *Battle Cry of Freedom: The Civil War Era*. Oxford: Oxford University Press, 1988.

———. *The Negro's Civil War. How American Negroes Felt and Acted During the War for the Union*. New York: Vintage, 1965.

Meade, Marion. *Madame Blavatsky: The Woman Behind the Myth*. New York: G. P. Putnam's Sons, 1980.

"Mediums for India." *Banner of Light* 8, no. 12 (December 15, 1860): 5.

"Meeting at Chapman Hall Last Sunday." *The Spiritual Telegraph* (January 12, 1856).

"Meeting at Economy Hall, The." *New Orleans Tribune*, February 5, 1865, 2, and March 11, 1865, 2.

Melville, John. *Crystal-Gazing and the Wonders of Clairvoyance, Embracing Practical Instructions in the Art, History, and Philosophy of the Ancient Science*. London: Nichols & Co., 1910.

Mercier, Alain. *Eliphas Lévi et la pensée magique au XIXe siècle*. Paris: Seghers, 1974.

Merkelbach, R. *Roman und Mysterium in der Antike*. Munich and Berlin: Bech, 1962.

Merrill, Walter M., ed. *The Letters of William Lloyd Garrison*. Vol. 5. *Let the Oppressed Go Free, 1861–1867*. Cambridge and London: Belknap Press, 1979.

Meslin, Henri. *Théorie et Pratique de la Magie Sexuelle; L'Amour et l'Occultisme*. Paris: Astra, n.d. [c. 1938].

"Message from Luxor, A." *Spiritual Scientist* 2, no. 17 (June 24, 1875): 191.

Meyrink, Gustav, trans. and ed. *Dhoula Bel: Ein Rosenkreuzer-Roman von P. B. Randolph, Aus dem Englischen Manuskript übersetz und herausgegeben von Gustav Meyrink.* Vienna, Berlin, Leipzig, and Munich: Rikola Verlag, 1922.

Michal, Victor. "Le Chanvre." *L'Initiation* 1, vol. 3 (1889): 175–77.

Michelet, V.-E. *Les Compagnons de la Hiérophanie. Souvenirs du Mouvement Hermétiste à la Fin du XIX siècle.* Paris: Dorbon-Aîné, n.d., [c. 1938].

Michell, John. *Eccentric Lives and Peculiar Notions.* London: Thames and Hudson, 1984.

Miers, Horst. *Lexikon des Geheimwissens.* 2d ed. Munich: 1976.

Miller, George N. *The Strike of a Sex.* Stockham Publishing Co., n.d. [c. 1900].

Minucius Felix. *Octavius.*

"Miss Doten's Renunciation of Spiritualism." *Banner of Light* 3, no. 11 (June 12, 1858): 4.

Möller, Helmut, and Ellic Howe. *Merlinus Peregrinus: Vom Untergrund des Abendlandes.* Würzburg: Königshausen & Neumann, 1986.

Monestier, M. *Les Sociétés Secrètes Féminines.* Paris: Productions de Paris, 1963.

Moore, R. Laurence. *In Search of White Crows: Spiritualism, Parapsychology, and American Culture.* New York: Oxford University Press, 1977.

———. "The Occult Connection? Mormonism, Christian Science, and Spiritualism." In *The Occult in America: New Historical Perspectives.* Edited by Howard Kerr and Charles L. Crow. Urbana: University of Illinois Press, 1986.

Moreau, Jacques-Joseph. *Hashish and Mental Illness.* New York: Raven Press, 1973.

Morray-Jones, C. R. A. "Paradise Revisited 2 Cor 12:1–12: The Jewish Mystical Background of Paul's Apostolate." *Harvard Theological Review* 86, no. 2 (1993): 177–217, and 86, no. 3 (1993): 265ff.

Morris, Robert C. *Reading, 'Riting, and Reconstruction: The Education of Freedmen in the South, 1861–1870.* Chicago: University of Chicago Press, 1976.

Morton, Albert. "Interesting Letter from Mr. Albert Morton, of San Francisco." *Banner of Light* 49, no. 11 (June 4, 1881): 2.

———. "P. B. Randolph." *Banner of Light* 49, no. 9 (May 21, 1881): 3.

Moses, W. Stainton [M. A. (Oxon.)]. "Early History of the Theosophical Society, The. A Chapter of History. No. II." *Light* 12 (July 23, 1892): 354–57.

———. "Spirit Identity and Recent Speculations." *The Theosophist* 4 (July 1883). Reprinted in *BCW*, 4:583–98.

Moss, Jr., Alfred A. *From Slavery to Freedom.* New York: Knopf, 1988.

"Movements of Lecturers and Mediums." *Banner of Light* 36, no. 9 (November 28, 1874): 5.

"Mr. Davis' Late Pamphlet." *The Spiritual Telegraph* (January 15, 1859): 376.

"Mr. Felt's Disclaimer." *New York Herald*, December 1, 1895, sec. 6, 8.

"Mr. Randolph in England." *The New England Spiritualist* 1, no. 35 (December 1, 1855).

"Mr. Randolph's First Lectures." *The New England Spiritualist* 1, no. 38 (December 22, 1855).

"Mr. Randolph's Lectures." *The New England Spiritualist* 1, no. 37 (December 15, 1855), and 1, no. 39 (December 29, 1855).

Muncy, Raymond Lee. *Sex and Marriage in Utopian Communities in Nineteenth Century America*. Bloomington: Indiana University Press, 1973.

Mystic, A [pseud.]. "Andrew Jackson Davis, The Great American Seer." *The Shekinah* 3 (1853) 1–18.

Naglowska, Maria de. *Malgré les Tempêtes . . . Chants d'amour*. Rome: Maglione and Strini, 1921.

———, trans. *Magia Sexualis*. Paris: Robert Télin, au Lys Rouge, 1931.

"Napoleon Mirror, The" *Spiritual Scientist* 2, no. 16 (June 24, 1875): 186.

"National Convention." *New Orleans Tribune*, October 25, 1864, and October 27, 1864, 2.

Neff, M. K. *Personal Memoirs of H. P. Blavatsky*. Wheaton: Theosophical Publishing House, 1937.

"Negroes Hold Mass Meeting at Abraham Lincoln School." *New Orleans Tribune*, October 27, 1865, 1.

Nerval, Gérard de. *Les Illuminés*. Paris: Gallimard, 1976.

———. *Voyage en Orient*. 1848–51. Reprint, vols. 10–11. *Oeuvres*. Paris, n.d.

"New England Anti-Slavery Convention." *The Liberator* 30, no. 23 (June 8, 1860): 190.

New England Spiritualist, The. Edited by A. E. Newton. Boston, 1855–1857.

Newman, William R. *Gehennical Fire: The Lives of George Starkey, an American Alchemist in the Scientific Revolution*. Cambridge, MA.: Harvard University Press, 1994.

"New Paper in New York, A." *The Telegraph Papers* 4 (1854): 289–91.

"New York Correspondence." *Banner of Light* 4, no. 13 (December 25, 1858): 8.

"New York Correspondence, Dr. Randolph Again." *Banner of Light* 4, no. 8 (September 12, 1858): 8.

"New York Correspondence: P. B. Randolph's Definition of Spiritualism." *Banner of Light* 4, no. 10 (December 4, 1858): 5.

Nichols, T. L. *Supramundane Facts in the Life of Rev. Jesse Babcock Ferguson, A.M., LL.D., including Twenty Years' Observation of Preternatural Phenomena*. London: F. Pitman, 1865.

Niebuhr, Carsten. *Reisen durch Syrien und Palästina*. 2 vols. Copenhagen, 1778.

Nock, A. D., and A.-J. Festugière. *Corpus Hermeticum*. 4 vols. 2d ed. Paris: Editions Belles Lettres, 1946–54.

"Note From Brother Randolph, A." *Religio-Philosophical Journal* 2, no. 28 (July 28, 1866): 4.

"Notice." *Yorkshire Spiritual Telegraph and British Harmonial Advocate* 2, no. 17 (August 1856): 208–9.

Noyes, John Humphrey. *History of American Socialisms*. New York: Hillary House Publishers, 1961.

———. *Male Continence*. Oneida: Office of the American Socialist, 1866.

Numa Pandorac. "Testament d'un Haschischéen." *L'Initiation* 1, vol. 2 (1889): 59–70.

Obituary [Güldenstubbé]. *Spiritual Magazine*, n.s., 8 (1873): 329–32.

"Occultism for Barter. Esoteric Colleges and False Prophets." *The Path* 3 (March 1889): 381–83.

O'Conor, E. "Letter from London—P. B. Randolph." *Banner of Light* 12, no. 8 (November 15, 1862): 3.

Olcott, H. S. *Applied Theosophy and Other Essays.* Adyar: Theosophical Publishing House, 1975.

———. "Colonel Olcott Answers the Banner, a Reply the Reverse of Equivocal." *Spiritual Scientist* 3, no. 5 (October 7, 1875): 55.

———. "Occultism and Spiritualism." *Spiritual Scientist* 3, no. 25 (February 24, 1876), 295.

———. *Old Diary Leaves. The History of the Theosophical Society as Written by the President-Founder Himself.* 3d ed., 6 vols. Adyar: Theosophical Publishing House, 1974–75.

———. *People from the Other World.* Hartford, 1875.

———. "A Tap at Mrs. Tappan. Col. Olcott Reviews her History of Occultism." *Banner of Light* 29, no. 26 (September 26, 1876): 2.

———. "The Theosophical Society and its President. Colonel Olcott's Reply to Professor Corson—a Confession of Faith." *Banner of Light* 28, no. 17 (January 22, 1876): 2.

———. "What Colonel Olcott Believes." *Spiritual Scientist* 3, no. 21 (January 27, 1876): 258.

"Old Rats Instinctively Flee from Old Rotten Sinking Ships." *Religio-Philosophical Journal* 15, no. 25 (March 7, 1874): 4.

Oliphant, Laurence. *The Land of Gilead.* New York: D. Appleton & Co., 1881.

———. *Synpneumata, or Evolutionary Forms Now Creative in Man.* Edinburgh and London: Wm. Blackwood & Sons, 1885.

Oliphant, Margaret W. *Memoirs of the Life of Laurence Oliphant and of Alice Oliphant, His Wife.* 2 vols. New York: Harper & Brothers, 1891.

Onians, R. B. *The Origins of European Thought about the Body, the Mind, the Soul, the World, Time and Fate.* Cambridge: Cambridge University Press, 1951.

Oppenheim, Janet. *The Other World: Spiritualism and Psychical Research in England, 1850–1914.* Cambridge: Cambridge University Press, 1985.

"The Order of Eulis." *Common Sense* 1, no. 20 (September 26, 1874): 233.

Origen. *Contra Celsum.*

Orton, J. R. Letter. *Spiritual Telegraph* (December 4, 1858): 318.

———. "Mr. Davis and the Old Testament." *The Telegraph Papers* 2 (1853): 430–43.

"Osiris B. Randolph." *Journal of the American Medical Association* (August 24, 1929): 632.

Owen, Alex. *The Darkened Room: Women, Power and Spiritualism in Late Victorian England.* Philadelphia: University of Pennsylvania Press, 1990.

Owen, Robert. "Expériences de Table Parlante Faites au Londres." *La Table Parlante, Journal des Faits Marveilleux* 1 (1854): 220–22.

———. "Letter from England." *The Telegraph Papers* 2 (1853): 240–41.

———. *New Existence of Man on Earth, Part VII.* London, 1855.

Oxley, William. "Hierosophy and Theosophy." *The Theosophist* 4 (July 1883). Reprinted in *BCW*, 4:557–60.

"Paschal Beverly Randolph." *Banner of Light* 37, no. 22 (August 28, 1875): 4.

Pasteur, Claude. "Monsieur Philippe, un juste parmi les hommes." *Nouveau Planète* (May–June 1971): 53–65.

Patai, Raphael. *The Jewish Alchemists: A History and Source Book.* Princeton: Princeton University Press, 1994.

Path, The. A Magazine Devoted to The Brotherhood of Humanity, Theosophy in America, and the Study of Occult Science, Philosophy, and Aryan Literature. Edited by William Quan Judge. 10 vols. New York, 1886–1896.

"P. B. Randolph." *Religio-Philosophical Journal* 3, no. 11 (December 8, 1866): 4.

"P. B. Randolph." *Banner of Light* 6, no. 17 (January 21, 1860): 4.

"P. B. Randolph." *Banner of Light* 28, no. 25 (March 4, 1871): 4.

"P. B. Randolph." *Banner of Light* 49, no. 3 (April 9, 1881): 3.

"P. B. Randolph and J. V. Mansfield." *Banner of Light* 6, no. 3 (October 15, 1859): 3–4.

"P. B. Randolph at the Melodeon." *Banner of Light* 4, no. 14 (January 1, 1859): 5, 8.

"P. B. Randolph at Washington Hall, Charlston." *Banner of Light* 6, no. 10 (December 3, 1859): 5.

"P. B. Randolph in the 'Ministry.'" *The Spiritual Telegraph* (November 13, 1858): 284.

"P. B. Randolph Lecture." *The Spiritual Telegraph* (December 11, 1858): 323.

"P. B. Randolph's Lectures." *The Spiritual Telegraph* (November 27, 1858): 207.

"P. B. Randolph's Reply and Position." *The Spiritual Telegraph* (November 20, 1858): 296.

Peebles, J.M. *Seers of the Ages: Embracing Spiritualism, Past and Present. Doctrines Stated and Moral Tendencies Defined.* 4th ed. London: J. Burns, Progressive Library, Boston: Wm. White & Co., 1870.

———. *Spirit Mates, Their Origin and Destiny. Sex-Life, Marriage, Divorce. Also a Symposium by Four Noted Writers. Spirit Mates—Their Pre-Existence, Earth Pilgrimages, Reunions in Spirit Life.* Edited by Robert Peebles Sudall. Battle Creek: Peebles' Publishing Co., 1909.

Perceval, John. Letter. *Spiritual Magazine* 1, no. 7 (July 1860): 328.

———. Letter. *Spiritual Magazine* 4, no. 11 (November 1863): 527–28.

"Permanent Happy Existence of the Human Race, or the Commencement of the Millenium in 1855." *The Spiritual Telegraph* 7 (December 20, 1854): 260.

"Personal." *The Telegraph Papers* 2 (1853): 514.

"Petition des Quinze Mille Citoyens des Etats-Unis au Congrès." *La Table Parlante, Journal des Faits Marveilleux* 1 (1854): 212–15.

Phelon, W. P., and Mira. *Three Sevens: A Story of Initiation.* Quakertown: Philosophical Publishing Co., 1938.

"Philanthropic Convention, Held in Utica on the 10th, 11th and 12th Sept., 1858, to Consider 'The Cause and Cure of Evil.'" *The Spiritual Telegraph* (October 9, 1858): 234.

Pilkington, John B. *Religion And Science: Or, Christianity, Religion, And The Bible Versus Philosophy And Science* (San Francisco: Woman's Pub. Co., 1875).

Pillsbury, Parker. "The Utica Convention." *The Liberator* 28, no. 40 (October 1, 1858): 158.

"Pioneer Dies at 108." *Los Angeles Sentinel*, May 28, 1981, A1.

"Pioneer Rosicrucian Workers in America, No. 3: Freeman B. Dowd." *Mercury* 2, no. 13 (September 10, 1917): 1.

Pluquet, Marc. "La Sophiale. Maria de Naglowska, sa Vie, son Oeuvre." Unpublished manuscript.

Podmore, Frank. *From Mesmer to Christian Science: A Short History of Mental Healing.* New Hyde Park: University Books, 1963.

———. *Mediums of the Nineteenth Century.* 2 vols. New Hyde Park: University Books, 1963.

———. *Robert Owen, A Biography.* New York: D. Appleton and Co., 1924.

Poe, Edgar Allan. *Great Tales and Poems of Edgar Allan Poe.* New York: Washington Square Press, 1951.

"Poem by Poe, Through Lizzie Doten, A." *Banner of Light* 8, no. 22 (February 23, 1863): 4.

Poliakov, Leon. *Il mito ariano.* Milan: Rizzoli, 1976.

Poole, C. O. "A Review of Clairvoyance, the Superior Condition and Nirvana." *Banner of Light* 42, no. 24 (March 9, 1878): 2.

Porphyry. *Vita Plotini.*

"Present-Day Sermon, A." *Religio-Philosophical Journal* (August 4, 1866): 2.

Preuss, Arthur. *A Dictionary of Secret and Other Societies.* St. Louis: Herder: 1924.

Price, Leslie. *Madame Blavatsky Unveiled? A New Discussion of the Most Famous Investigations of the Society for Psychical Research.* London: Theosophical History Centre, 1986.

Proceedings of the National Convention of Colored Men, Held in The City of Syracuse, N.Y., October 4, 5, 6, and 7, 1864; with the Bill of Wrongs and Rights, and the Address to the American People. Boston: Geo. C. Rand & Avery, 1864.

Proceedings of the Tenth Annual Convention of the American Association of Spiritualists, Held at Grow's Opera Hall, Chicago, on Tuesday, September 16. N.p., n.d. [Chicago, 1873].

Progressive Annual for 1863, The; Comprising an Almanac, a Spiritual Register and a General Calendar of Reform. New York: Andrew Jackson Davis and Co., 1863.

Prothero, Stephen Richard. *Henry Steele Olcott 1832–1907 and the Construction of "Protestant Buddhism."* Ann Arbor: University Microfilms, 1990.

"Public Lectures." *New Orleans Tribune*, January 16, 1866, 2.

Putnam, Allen. "John M. Spear." *Banner of Light* 33, no. 21 (August 23, 1873): 3.

Putney, Martha S. *Black Sailors: Afro-American Merchant Seamen and Whalemen Prior to the Civil War.* New York, Westport and London: Greenwood Press, 1987.

Pythagoras [pseud.]. "Considerations of Magic." *The Path* 1, no. 12 (March 1887): 377–80.

Quaestor Vitae [pseud.]. *The Process of Man's Becoming, Based on Communications by Thought-transference from Selves in Inner States of Being.* London: Duckworth & Co., 1921.

———. "The Real Origin of the Theosophical Society." *Theosophical History* 1, no. 7 (July 1986): 176ff.

Quarles, Benjamin. *The Negro in the Civil War.* Boston: Russell and Russell, 1953.

"Quarterly Convention." *Banner of Light* 35, no. 12 (July 4, 1874): 3.

Randolph, Cora V. "Vermont." *Religio-Philosophical Journal* 40, no. 5 (October 28, 1876): 3.

Randolph, K[ate] C[orson]. "Pioneer Rosicrucian Workers in America, Number One: Pascal Beverly Randolph." *Mercury* 2, no. 4 (February 19, 1917).

Randolph, Robert Isham. *The Randolphs of Virginia: A compilation of the Descendants of William Randolph of Turkey Island and his Wife Mary Isham of Bermuda Hundred.* N.p., n.d. [Chicago, 1936?].

"Randolph and his Friends." *Religio-Philosophical Journal* 3, no. 2 (October 6, 1866): 4.

"Randolph's Lectures." *Banner of Light* 6, no. 10 (December 3, 1859): 5.

Rankin, David C. "The Origins of Black Leadership in New Orleans during Reconstruction." *Journal of Southern History* 40 (1974): 417–46.

Rawson, A. L. "Mme. Blavatsky, A Theosophical Occult Apology." *Frank Leslie's American Magazine* 33 (February 1892). Reprinted in *Theosophical History* 2, no. 6 (April 1988): 209–20.

———. "Rochester U.S.A. Theosophical Society, The." *The Theosophist* 4 (November 1882, supplement): 2.

———. "Two Madame Blavatskys.—The Acquaintance of Madame H. P. Blavatsky with Eastern Countries." *The Spiritualist* (April 5, 1878). Reprinted in *Theosophical History* 3, no. 1 (January 1989): 27–30.

Record of the Action, The, of the Convention Held at Poughkeepsie, New York on July 15 and 16, 1873 for the Purpose of Facilitating the Introduction of Colored Troops into the Service of the United States. New York, 1863.

Redgrove, S. *Bygone Beliefs.* London, 1920.

Régla, Paul de [P. A. Desjardin], ed. *El Ktab des Lois Secrètes de l'Amour d'après El Khôdja Omer Haleby, Abou Othmân,* by El Khôdja Omer Haleby Abou Othman. Paris: Librairie Nilsson, 1893.

Reichenbach, Karl von. *Researches of Magnetism, Electricity, Heat, Light, Crystallization, and Chemical Attraction, in their Relations to the Vital Force.* London: Taylor, Walton and Maberly, 1850.

"Reincarnation." *Banner of Light* 33, no. 3 (April 19, 1873): 4.

Reitzenstein, Richard. *Hellenistic Mystery Religions.* Pittsburgh: Pickwick Press, 1978.

Religio-Philosophical Journal, Devoted to Spiritual Philosophy. The Arts and Sciences, Literature, Romance and General-Reform. Edited by S. S. Jones, John C. Bundy, and others. Chicago, 1865–1905.

"Religious Notices." *New Orleans Daily Independent,* January 22, 1865, 3.

"Remarkable Phenomena." *Spiritual Scientist* 2, no. 23 (August 12, 1875): 274.

"Reminiscence, A." *The Path* 7 (February 1893): 343–44.

Report on Spiritualism, of the Committee of the London Dialectical Society, Together with the Evidence, Oral and Written, and a Selection from the Correspondence. London: Longman, Green, Reader, and Dyer, 1871.

Respiro [pseud.]. "Internal Respiration—Judgments." *Spiritual Magazine* 3, no. 10 (October 1863): 460ff.

"Revelations of a Mirror, The. Embracing a Series of Prophecies, Allegories, Scenes, and Adventures." *Spiritual Scientist* 2, no. 16 (June 24, 1875): 188.

"Revelations of a Mirror, No. II." *Spiritual Scientist* 2, no. 17 (July 1, 1875): 195.

Review of *Pre-Adamite Man*, by Paschal Beverly Randolph. *The Esoteric* (December 1889): 261–262.

Review of *The Hashish Eater*, by Fitz Hugh Ludlow. *Spiritual Magazine* 1, no. 11 (November 1860): 519.

Richer, Jean. *Gérard de Nerval et les doctrines ésotériques.* Paris: Editions du Griffon d'Or, 1947.

"Robert Owen's Movements in England." *The New England Spiritualist* 1, no. 33 (November 17, 1855).

Roberts, J. M. *The Mythology of the Secret Societies.* London: Secker & Warburg, 1972.

Robertson, James. *A Noble Pioneer, The Life Story of Mrs. Emma Hardinge Britten.* Manchester, n.d.

Rosemont, Franklin. Introduction to Benjamin Paul Blood, *The Poetical Alphabet.* Chicago: Black Swan Press, 1978.

"Rosicrucians, The." *Banner of Light* 11, no. 9 (May 24, 1862): 4.

Row, T. Subbha. "The Aryan-Arhat Esoteric Tenets on the Sevenfold Principle in Man." *The Theosophist* 3 (January 1882): 93–99. Reprinted with Madame Blavatsky's notes in *BCW*, 3: 400–424.

Sacy, Antoine-Sylvestre de. *Exposé de la Religion des Druses.* 2 vols. 1838. Reprint, Paris, 1964.

"Sad Look Out, A." *The Theosophist* 3 (April 1882): 174.

Salisbury, Edward E. "The Book of Sulaiman's First Ripe Fruit, Disclosing the Mysteries of the Nusairian Religion, by Sulaiman Effendi of 'Adhamah, with Copious Extracts." *Journal of the American Oriental Society* 8 (1866): 227–308.

Sandburg, Carl. *Abraham Lincoln: The War Years.* 4 vols. New York: Harcourt, Brace and Co., 1939.

Schele de Vere, M. *Modern Magic.* New York: Putnam, 1873.

Schmidt, Richard. *Fakire und Fakirtum im alten und modernen Indian Yoga-Lehre und Yoga-Praxis nach den Indischen Originalquellen.* Berlin: Barsdorf, 1908.

Schneider, Herbert W., and George Lawton, *A Prophet and a Pilgrim, Being the Incredible History of Thomas Lake Harris and Laurence Oliphant; Their Sexual Mysticism and Utopian Communities Amply Documented to Confound the Skeptic.* New York: Columbia University Press, 1942.

Schrödter, Willy. *A Rosicrucian Notebook: The Secret Sciences Used by Members of the Order.* New York: Weiser, 1992.

Schuchard, Marsha Keith. "Swedenborg, Jacobitism, and Freemasonry." In *Swedenborg and His Influence.* Edited by E. J. Brock et al. Bryn Athyn: Academy of the New Church, 1988.

Sears, Hal D. *The Sex Radicals: Free Love in High Victorian America.* Lawrence: University Press of Kansas, 1977.

Sellon, E. *Annotations on the Sacred Writings of the Hindus, Being an Epitome of Some of the most Remarkable and Leading Tenets in the Faith of that People, Illustrating their Priapic Rites and Phallic Principles.* London: Privately Printed, 1905.

———. *The Ups and Downs of Life.* 1867. Reprint, Miami Beach: McMillan, 1987.

Sex Mythology, Including an Account of the Masculine Cross. London, Privately Printed, 1898.

Sha Rocco [pseud.]. *The Masculine Cross and Ancient Sex Worship.* New York: Asa K. Butts, 1874. Reprint, *The Masculine Cross, or a History of Ancient and Modern Crosses and their Connection with the Mysteries of Sex Worship. Also an Account of Kindred Phases of Phallic Faiths and Practices.* London, 1891.

Shekinah, The. Edited by Samuel B. Brittan. Quarterly. 3 vols. New York, 1852–1854.

Shorter, Thomas. "Glimpses of Spiritualism in the East." *Spiritual Magazine* 2, no. 3 (March 1861): 107.

———. "Spiritualism in Biography—J. Heinrich Jung Stilling." *Spiritual Magazine* 3, no. 7 (July 1862): 289–309.

——— [Thomas Brevior]. *The Two Worlds, the Natural and the Spiritual: Their Intimate Connexion and Relation Illustrated by Examples and Testimonies, Ancient and Modern.* London: F. Pitman, 1864.

"Siamese Sorcery." *Banner of Light* 16, no. 2 (April 11, 1874): 2.

Sinnett, A. P. *The Autobiography of Alfred Percy Sinnett.* London: Theosophical History Centre, 1988.

———, ed. *Incidents in the Life of Madame Blavatsky Compiled from Information Supplied by her Relatives and Friends.* London: Redway, 1886.

Smith, Gerrit. Letter. *The Liberator* 28, no. 43 (December 31, 1858): 211.

Solovyoff, Vsevolod S. *A Modern Priestess of Isis.* London: Longmans, Green, and Co., 1895.

Sotheran, Charles. "Alessandro di Cagliostro: Imposter or Martyr?" *Spiritual Scientist* 2, no. 14 (June 10, 1875), 163ff.

———. "Ex Nihilo Nihil Fit." *Spiritual Scientist* 2, no. 25 (August 26, 1875): 299.

———. "Honors to Madame Blavatsky." *Banner of Light* 42, no. 19 (February 2, 1878): 3.

———. Letter. *Banner of Light* 28, no. 16 (January 15, 1876): 5.

Spear, John Murray. "The Destruction of the New Mola." *The Telegraph Papers* 5 (1855): 396–99.

———. *Twenty Years on the Wing. Brief Narrative of my Travels and Labors as a Missionary Sent forth and Sustained by the Association of Beneficents in Spirit Land.* Boston: W. White & Co., 1873.

Spierenburg, H. J. "Dr. Rudolf Steiner on Helena Petrovna Blavatsky." *Theosophical History* 1, no. 7 (July 1986):159–74.

———. "Dr. Rudolf Steiner on the Mahatmas." *Theosophical History* 1, no. 8, and 2, no. 1 (October 1986–January 1987): 211–23, 23–31.

Spirit Messenger, The. Edited by Apollos Munn, Frances H. Green, and R. P. Ambler. Springfield and New York, 1850–1852.

"Spirit-Power Circle, Charing Cross, London." *The Yorkshire Spiritual Telegraph* 3, no. 10 (January 31, 1857): 131–33.

"Spirits in Syria, The." *The Telegraph Papers* 2 (1853): 75.

"Spirits of Sleeping Mortals, The." *Spiritual Scientist* 2, no. 2 (March 18, 1875): 21.

"Spiritual Annexation." *The Telegraph Papers* 7 (1855): 80–84.

"Spiritualism and Reform." *Religio-Philosophical Journal* 2 (July 16, 1866): 4.

"Spiritualism in France." *The Telegraph Papers* 2 (1853): 426–28.

"Spiritualistic Black Magic." *The Theosophist* 4 January 1883: 92–93.

"Spiritualist Societies of London, The." *Banner of Light* 35, no. 7 (May 16, 1874): 2.

"Spiritual La Mountain—Individual Predictions vs. Eternal Truths, A." *Banner of Light* 33, no. 26 (September 27, 1873): 8.

Spiritual Magazine, The. Edited by Thomas Shorter and William Wilkinson. London, 1860–1875.

"Spiritual Meetings." *Religio-Philosophical Journal* 17, no. 2 (September 26, 1874): 4–5.

"Spiritual Mountebanks." *The Spiritual Telegraph* (November 6, 1858): 277. Reprinted in *Tiffany's Monthly* 4 (1858): 312ff.

Spiritual Philosopher. Edited by La Roy Sunderland. Boston, 1850.

Spiritual Telegraph, The. Devoted to the Illustration of Spiritual Intercourse. Edited by Samuel B. Brittan and Charles Partridge. Weekly. New York, 1852–1857.

Spurlock, John Calvin. *Free Love, Marriage and Middle-Class Radicalism in America, 1825–1860.* Ann Arbor: University Microfilms, 1987.

"S.S.S.5." *The Occult Magazine* 1, no. 6 (July 1885): 47–48.

Stanhope, [Fourth] Earl. Introduction to *An Introduction to the Study of Animal Magnetism*, by Baron Dupotet de Sennevoy. London: Saunders & Otley, 1828.

Stearns, Madelaine. *The Pantarch: A Biography of Stephen Pearl Andrews.* Austin: University of Texas Press, 1968.

Steiger, Brad. *Demon Lovers.* New Brunswick: Inner Lights, 1968.

Steward, James Brewer. *Holy Warriors: The Abolitionists and American Slavery.* New York: Hill and Wang, 1976.

Stockham, A. B., and L. H. Talbot. *Koradine. A Prophetic Story.* 1893. Reprint, Chicago: Alice B. Stockham Publishing Co., 1897.

Stockham, Alice Bunker. *Karezza. Ethics of Marriage.* 1896. Reprint, Chicago: Stockham Publishing Co., n.d. [c. 1900].

———. *Tokology. A Book for Every Woman.* Chicago: Alice B. Stockham & Co., 1895.

Stocking, G. W. "French Anthropology in 1800." *Isis* 55 (1964): 134–50.

Stoddard, Miss. *Light-Bearers of Darkness.* London: Boswell, 1930.

"Storm in A Tea Cup, A." *The Theosophist* 3 (July 1882): 249–50.

Strachan, Francoise, ed. *The Aquarian Guide to Occult: Mystical, Religious, Magical London and Around.* London: Aquarian Press, 1970.

Street, John C. *The Hidden Way Across the Threshold.* London: G. Redway, 1889.

Strothmann, Rudolf. "Esoterische Sonderthemen bei den Nusairi." *Abhandlungen der deutsche Akadamie der Wissenschaften zu Berlin* 4 (1956). Reprint, Berlin, 1958.

———. "Seelenwanderung bei der Nusairi." *Oriens* 12 (1959): 89–114.

"Suicide." *Religio-Philosophical Journal* 8, no. 22 (August 14, 1875): 172.

Summers, Montague. Introduction to *Demoniality*, by L. Sinistrari. 1927. Reprint, New York: Benjamin Blom, 1972.

Sunderland, La Roy. "The Case of A. J. Davis." *The Spiritual Telegraph* (February 26, 1859): 434ff.

Sutton, E. A. *Living Thoughts of Swedenborg.* London: Cassell, 1947.

Swedenborg, Emanuel. *The Delights of Wisdom Pertaining to Conjugial Love, After Which Follow the Pleasures of Insanity Pertaining to Scortatory Love.* New York: Swedenborg Foundation, 1954.

Telegraph Papers, The [excerpts from *The Spiritual Telegraph*]. Edited by S. B. Brittan. 9 vols. New York: Partridge & Brittan, 1853–1857.

Temple, The. A Monthly Magazine Devoted to the Fuller Unfoldment of the Divinity of Humanity. Edited by Paul Tyner. Denver: Temple Publishing Co., May 1897–November 1898.

"Tenth National Convention of Spiritualists." *Banner of Light* 34, no. 1 (October 1, 1873): 8.

"Test Mediums Wanted in California." *Banner of Light* 10, no. 5 (October 26, 1861): 3.

"Testimonial to F. B. Dowd, The Rosicrucian." *Religio-Philosophical Journal* 10, no. 2 (April 1, 1871): 3.

Theosophical Movement, 1875–1950, The. Los Angeles: The Cunningham Press, 1951.

Theosophist, The. A Monthly Journal Devoted to Oriental Philosophy, Art, Literature and Occultism. Conducted by H. P. Blavatsky under the auspices of the Theosophical Society. Bombay/Adyar: The Theosophical Society, 1879–.

"Theosophy in America." *The Theosophist* 3 (April 1882): 186.

"Theosophy in the Press." *The Path* 1, no. 5 (July 1886): 156–58.

Thimmy, René [pseud.]. *La magie à Paris.* Paris: Editions de France, 1934.

Thomas, J. L. *The Liberator: William Lloyd Garrison.* Boston, Little Brown, 1963.

Thomas, Northcote. *Crystal Gazing, its History and Practice, with a Discussion of the Evidence for Telepathic Scrying.* New York: Dodge Publishing Co., 1905.

Tiffany's Monthly. Edited by Joel Tiffany. New York, 1856–1859.

"To Aspirants for Chelaship." *The Path* 3 (July 1888): 105–9.

Tomlinson, Gary. *Music in Renaissance Magic: Toward a Historiography of Others.* Chicago and London: University of Chicago Press, 1993.

Toohey, J. H. W. "The Need of Science in Spiritualism." *Spiritual Scientist* 1, no. 1 (September 10, 1874): 1–2.

"To the Public." *Spiritual Scientist* 6, no. 6 (April 12, 1877): 63, and *Banner of Light* 41, no. 4 (April 21, 1877): 8. Reprinted in *BCW* 1: 245.

Townsend, Chauncey Hare. *Mesmerism Proved True, and the Quarterly Reviewer Reviewed.* London: T. Bosworth, 1854.

Townsend, Tappen. "Harmonial Convention." *The Telegraph Papers* 4 (1854): 49–58.

Transfiguration Church: A Church of Immigrants, 1827–1977. New York, n.d.

Trethewy, A. W. *The "Controls" of Stainton Moses "M. A. Oxon."* London: Hurst & Blackett Ltd., n.d. [c. 1925].

"Truths of Spiritualism Against the Claims of Occultism, The." *Spiritual Scientist* 3, no. 16 (December 23, 1875): 186.

"Turgescence Mammaire." *Journal du Magnétisme,* 14 (1855): 159.

Tuttle, Hudson. "Are Occultists to Capture Spiritualism?" *Spiritual Scientist* 3, no. 21 (January 27, 1876): 259.

———. "Hashish." *Banner of Light* 10, no. 19 (February 1, 1862): 3.

Two Worlds, The. Edited by Emma Hardinge Britten. Manchester, 1887–1892.

Tyner, Paul. *The Living Christ: An Exposition of the Immortality of Man in Soul and Body.* Denver: Temple Publishing Co. 1897.

"Union Men Reportedly Flee to New Orleans from Country Parishes." *New Orleans Tribune,* April 19, 1866, 2.

Univercoelum and Spiritual Philosopher. Edited by Samuel B. Brittan. New York, 1847–1849.

Ursus. "Sham Teachers of Occultism." *The Occult Magazine* 1, no. 8 (September 1885): 63.

Utica City Directory 1861–62 and 1863–64.

"Utica Convention, The." *The New England Spiritualist* (October 9, 1858).

Viatte, Auguste. *Les sources occultes du Romantisme. Illuminisme—Théosophie, 1770–1820.* 2 vols. Paris: H. Champion 1927.

Virgin of the World of Hermes Mercurius Trismegistus, The. Now First Rendered into English, with Essay, Introduction, and Notes, by Dr. Anna Kingsford and Edward Maitland, author of *"The Perfect Way."* Bath Occult Reprint Series. London: George Redway, 1885.

"Visions in the Crystal." *The Theosophist* 3, no. 11 (August 1882): 287–88. Reprinted in *BCW,* 4:180–82.

Volney, C. F. *The Ruins, or, Meditations on the Revolutions of Empires: and the Law of Nature.* Baltimore: Black Classics Press, 1991.

———. *Voyage en Egypte et en Syrie.* 1787. Reprint, Paris: J. Gaulmier, 1959.

Vulliaud, Paul. "Histoires et portraits des Rose Croix." Manuscript in the Alliance Israélite Universelle, Paris.

Wagner, Belle M. *Within the Temple of Isis.* 2d ed. Denver: Astro-Philosophical Publishing House, 1899.

Waite, A. E. *The Brotherhood of the Rosy Cross.* New York, n.d.

———— [Doctor of Hermetic Philosophy]. *The Harmonial Philosophy. A Compendium and Digest of the Works of Andrew Jackson Davis, the Seer of Poughkeepsie.* Chicago: Advanced Thought Publishing, Co., n.d. [c. 1930].

————. *The Holy Kabbalah.* New York, n.d.

————. *Mysteries of Magic.* London, 1897.

————. *A New Encyclopædia of Freemasonry, Ars Magna Latomorum and of Cognate Instituted Mysteries: Their Rites, Literature and History.* 2 vols. in 1. New York: Weathervane, n.d.

————. *The Occult Sciences: A Compendium of Transcendental Doctrine and Experiment, Embracing an Account of Magical Practices; of Secret Sciences in Connection with Magic; of the Professors of Magical Arts; and of Modern Spiritualism, Mesmerism and Theosophy.* London: Kegan Paul, Trench, Trübner & Co., 1891.

————. *The Real History of the Rosicrucians, Founded on their own Manifestoes, and on Facts and Documents Collected from the Writings of Initiated Brethren.* London: George Redway, 1887.

————. *Shadows of Life and Thought.* London: Selwyn & Blount, 1938.

————. "Woman and the Hermetic Mystery." *Occult Review* (15 June 1912): 325ff.

Walpole, F. *The Ansayrii, and the Assassins, with Travels in the Further East, in 1850–51. Including a Visit to Nineveh.* 3 vols. London: Richard Bentley, 1851.

Webb, James. *The Harmonious Circle. The Lives and Works of G. I. Gurdjieff, P. D. Ouspensky and Their Followers.* Boston: Shambhala, 1987.

————. *The Occult Underground.* LaSalle: Open Court, 1974.

Weinfurter, Karel. *Man's Highest Purpose The Lost Word Regained.* 1930. Reprint, Kessinger, n.d.

Weisse, John A. *The Obelisk and Freemasonry.* New York: J. W. Bouton, 1880.

Welton, Sarah. Letter. *Spiritual Magazine* 2, no. 2 (January 1861): 46–47.

Welton, Thomas. *Mental Magic. A Rationale of Thought Reading, and its attendant Phenomena, and their application to the Discovery of New Medicines, Obscure Diseases, Correct Delineations of Character, Lost Persons and Property, Mines and Springs of Water, and All Hidden And Secret Things.* Edited by Robert H. Fryar. London: George Redway, 1884.

Werblowsky, R. J. Zwi. "Mystical and Magical Contemplation: The Kabbalists in Sixteenth–Century Safed." *History of Religions* 1, no. 1 (Summer 1961): 9–36.

Westcott, W. Wynn. *The Rosicrucians, Past and Present, at Home and Abroad.* 1900. Reprint, Mokelumne Hill, CA: Health Research, 1966.

————. *Tabula Bembina, sive Mensa Isiaca. The Isiac Tablet of Cardinal Bembo. Its History and Occult Significance.* Bath: Robert H. Fryar, 1887.

————, ed. *The Book of Nicholas Flamel 1650.* Bath: Robert H. Fryar, 1889.

————, trans. and ed. *Sepher Yetzirah: The Book of Formation, and the 32 Paths of Wisdom.* Bath: Robert H. Fryar, 1887.

Western Star, The. A Magazine Devoted to a Record of the Facts, Philosophy, and History of the Communion Between Spirits and Mortals. Edited by Emma Hardinge Britten. 6 nos. Boston, July–December 1872.

Westropp, H. M., and C. S. Wake, *Ancient Symbol Worship. Influence of the Phallic Idea in the Religions of Antiquity.* 2d ed. Introduction and Notes by Alexander Wilder. New York: Bouton, 1875.

"What the Thing Is." *Banner of Light* 4, no. 7 (November 13, 1858): 4.

White, Howard A. *The Freedmen's Bureau in Louisiana.* Baton Rouge: Louisiana State University Press, 1970.

Wiggin, James H. "The Cabala." *The Liberal Christian,* September 28, 1875. Reprinted in Michael Gomes, "Studies in Early American Theosophical History. VI. Rev. Wiggin's Review of George Henry Felt's 1875 Lecture on the Cabala." *Canadian Theosophist* 71, no. 3 (July–August 1990): 63–69.

———. "Rosicrucianism in New York." *The Liberal Christian,* September 4, 1875. Reprinted in Michael Gomes, "Studies in Early American Theosophical History. III. The Ante- and Post-Natal History of the Theosophical Society." *Canadian Theosophist* 70, no. 3 (July–August 1989): 51–57.

Wilder, Alexander. Letter. "The Primeval Race Double-Sexed." *The Theosophist* 4 (February 1883): 112.

———. Letter. *Woodhull & Claflin's Weekly* October 15, 1870.

———. *The Rosicrucian Brotherhood.* Edmonds, WA: Sure Fire Press, 1990.

———. "The Rosicrucians." *The Rosicrucian Brotherhood* 1, no. 3, 81, 83.

Williams, Gertrude Marvin. *Priestess of the Occult, Madame Blavatsky.* New York: Knopf, 1946.

[Williams, J. Shoebridge?]. *The Patriarchal Order, or True Brotherhood.* N.p., n.d. [Cincinnati, 1855?].

Wilson, Peter Lamborn. *Scandal: Essays in Islamic Heresy.* Brooklyn: Autonomedia, Inc., 1988.

Woldrich, Dr. "The Suicide." *Religio-Philosophical Journal* 22, no. 18 (July 14, 1877): 1.

Wolff, Hannah M. "Madame Blavatsky." *Religio-Philosophical Journal* (January 2, 1892): 501–2.

Woodhull and Clafin's Weekly. Edited by Victoria Woodhull and Tennessee Claflin. 6 vols. New York, 1870–1876.

"Word on Stimulants, A." *Banner of Light* 8, no. 14 (December 29, 1860): 4.

"Word to the Anglo-African, A." *New Orleans Tribune,* March 10, 1865, 2.

Wright, Thomas. *The Worship of the Generative Powers during the Middle Ages of Western Europe* 1865/66. Reprint [with Richard Payne Knight], *Sexual Symbolism, A History of Phallic Worship.* New York: Julien Press, 1957.

Yarker, John. *The Arcane Schools; A Review of Their Origins and Antiquity; with a General History of Freemasonry, and its Relation to the Theosophic, Scientific, and Philosophic Mysteries.* Belfast: William Tate, 1909.

———. "The Bene Elohim and the Book of Enoch," *The Theosophist* 3 (April 1882): 71–72.

———. *Notes on the Scientific and Religious Mysteries of Antiquity; The Gnosis and Secret Schools of the Middle Ages; Modern Rosicrucianism; and the Varied Rites and Degrees of Free and Accepted Masonry.* London, 1872.

———. "The Order of Ishmael or B'nai Ismael." *Historic Magazine and Notes and Queries* (1907): 262–64.

———. "The Society of the Rosy Cross." *The Rosicrucian Brotherhood* (1907): 113–124, and *Historic Magazine and Notes and Queries* 25, no. 10 (October 1907): 225–36.

Yates, Frances. *The Rosicrucian Enlightenment.* London: Routledge and Kegan Paul, 1972.

Yorkshire Spiritual Telegraph. Keighley, 1855–1857.

Index

Printed in the United States
216368BV00001B/7/A

9 780791 431207